WBGU

German Advisory Council on Global Change

World in Transition

A Social Contract for Sustainability

The Council Members

Prof Dr Hans Joachim Schellnhuber CBE (chair)
Director of the Potsdam Institute for Climate Impact Research, external professor at the Santa Fe Institute and chair of the Governing Board of the Climate-KIC of the European Institute of Innovation and Technology

Prof Dr Dirk Messner (vice chair)
Director of the German Development Institute, Bonn

Prof Dr Claus Leggewie
Director of the Institute for Advanced Study in the Humanities, Essen, Institute for Advanced Study of the University Alliance Metropolis Ruhr

Prof Dr Reinhold Leinfelder
Geologist and palaeontologist, focus on geobiology, integrative biodiversity and science communication; Professor at the Institute of Biology, Humboldt-University, Berlin

Prof Dr Nebojsa Nakicenovic
Vienna University of Technology and Deputy Director, International Institute for Applied Systems Analysis (IIASA), Laxenburg, Austria

Prof Dr Stefan Rahmstorf
Professor of Physics of the Oceans, Potsdam University and head of the Climate System department at the Potsdam Institute for Climate Impact Research

Prof Dr Sabine Schlacke
Professor of Public Law, specializing German, European and International Environmental and Administrative Law, Bremen University

Prof Dr Jürgen Schmid
Director of the Fraunhofer Institute for Wind Energy and Energy System Technology, IWES

Prof Dr Renate Schubert
Professor for Economics at the Swiss Federal Institute for Technology and director of the Institute for Environmental Decisions, ETH Zurich (Switzerland)

WBGU is an independent, scientific advisory body to the German Federal Government set up in 1992 in the run-up to the Rio Earth Summit. The Council has nine members, appointed for a term of four years by the federal cabinet. The Council is supported by an interministerial committee of the federal government comprising representatives of all ministries and of the federal chancellery. The Council's principal task is to provide scientifically-based policy advice on global change issues to the German Federal Government.
The Council

- analyses global environment and development problems and reports on these,
- reviews and evaluates national and international research in the field of global change,
- provides early warning of new issue areas,
- identifies gaps in research and initiates new research,
- monitors and assesses national and international policies for sustainable development,
- elaborates recommendations for action,
- raises public awareness and heightens the media profile of global change issues.

WBGU publishes flagship reports every two years, making its own choice of focal themes. In addition, the German government can commission the Council to prepare special reports and policy papers. For more information please visit www.wbgu.de.

WBGU

German Advisory Council on Global Change

World in Transition

A Social Contract for Sustainability

With 62 Figures

German Advisory Council on Global Change (WBGU)

WBGU Secretariat
Luisenstraße 46
D-10117 Berlin
Germany

Phone.: +49 30 263948 0
Fax: +49 30 263948 50
Email: wbgu@wbgu.de
Web: http://www.wbgu.de

Copy deadline: 17.03.2011

Bibliographic information published by the Deutsche Nationalbibliothek
The Deutsche Nationalbibliothek lists this publication in the Deutsche Nationalbibliografie; detailed bibliographic data are available in the Internet at http://dnb.d-nb.de.

ISBN 978-3-936191-37-0

WBGU Berlin 2011

Translation: KERN AG, Global Language Services, Berlin (www.e-kern.com)

The R&D project that generated this report was conducted on behalf of the German Federal Ministry of Education and Research and the Federal Ministry for the Environment, Nature Conservation and Nuclear Safety under grant number 01RI0708AA. Responsibility for the content of this publication rests with the author.

Design: WERNERWERKE GbR, Berlin
Cover photo: © Erhard Dauber, Photographer Bochum

Production: WBGU
Typesetting: WBGU
Printing and binding: AZ Druck und Datentechnik GmbH

FSC www.fsc.org MIX Paper from responsible sources FSC® C008457

WBGU used certified eco-friendly paper for this publication.

Council Staff and Acknowledgments

This Report builds upon the expert and committed work performed by the WBGU Secretariat staff and the assistants of the WBGU members.

Scientific Staff at the Secretariat

Dr Inge Paulini
(Secretary-General)

Dr Carsten Loose
(Deputy Secretary-General)

Dr Karin Boschert

Dr Rüdiger Haum

Dr Benno Pilardeaux
(Media and Public Relations)

Dr Astrid Schulz

Dr Birgit Soete

Administration, Editorial Work and Secretariat

Vesna Karic-Fazlic (Accountant)

Mario Rinn, BSc (System Administration and Graphics)

Martina Schneider-Kremer, MA (Editorial Work and Typesetting)

Margot Weiß (Secretariat)

Scientific Staff to the Council Members

Dr Steffen Bauer
(German Development Institute, DIE, Bonn)

Dipl-Phys Christoph Bertram
(Potsdam Institute for Climate Impact Research, PIK)

Dipl-Volksw Julia E. Blasch (Institute for Environmental Decisions, ETH Zurich, Switzerland)

Daniel Klingenfeld, MSc, MPP
(Potsdam Institute for Climate Impact Research, PIK)

Dr Susanna Much (University Bremen, Research Centre for European Environmental Law)

Olivia Serdeczny, MA
(Potsdam Institute for Climate Impact Research, PIK)

Alexander Schülke, MSc, MPP
(Department of Biology at the Humboldt University Berlin)

Dr Niels B. Schulz (International Institute for Applied Systems Analysis, IIASA, Laxenburg, Austria)

Dr Bernd Sommer (Institute for Advanced Study in the Humanities, KWI, Essen)

Dr Michael Sterner (Fraunhofer Institute for Wind Energy and Energy System Technology, IWES, Kassel)

Dipl-Phys Amany von Oehsen
(Fraunhofer Institute for Wind Energy and Energy System Technology, IWES, Kassel)

WBGU owes a debt of gratitude to the important contributions and support provided by the authors of commissioned expert studies. This report builds on the following individual expert studies, available on the WBGU website:

- Prof Dr Rolf Peter Sieferle (University of St. Gallen, Switzerland): 'Lehren aus der Vergangenheit für die Transformation zu einer klimafreundlichen Gesellschaft', 2010.
- Prof Dr Stephan Leibfried, Prof Dr Frank Nullmeier and Prof Dr Gerd Winter (University of Bremen) in collaboration with Matthias Dietz, MA, Dr iur Olaf Dilling and Dr phil Alexandra Lindenthal: 'Möglichkeiten der globalen Steuerung und globalen beschleunigten Umgestaltung hin zu einer klimaverträglichen Gesellschaft', 2010.
- Dr Nils Meyer-Ohlendorf, Michael Mehling, Katharina Umpfenbach (Ecologic Institute, Berlin): 'Analyse der Konjunkturprogramme zur Bewältigung der Finanz- und Wirtschaftskrise aus Umweltsicht', 2009.

The Council particularly enjoyed the valuable input of numerous distinguished experts provided through hearings at its regular meetings:

Prof Dr Hans-Christoph Binswanger (Institute for Economy and Ecology at the University of St. Gallen); Dipl.-Geogr. Dieter Gerten (Potsdam Institute for Climate Impact Research); Prof Dr Arnulf Grübler (IIASA Laxenburg); Prof Dr Andreas Irmen (Faculty of Law, Economics and Finance, University of Luxembourg); Prof Dr Helmut Jungermann (Faculty for Mechanical Engineering and Transport Systems, Technische Universität Berlin); Dr Andreas Kraemer and Dr Nils Meyer-Ohlendorf (Ecologic Berlin); Prof Dr Stephan Leibfried and Prof Dr Frank Nullmeier (Centre for Social Policy Research, ZeS, University of Bremen); Dr Alexandra Lindenthal (Collaborative Research Centre 'Transformations of the State' at the University of Bremen); Dr Malte Meinshausen (Potsdam Institute for Climate Impact Research); Prof Dr Rolf Peter Sieferle (DOK Faculty, University of St. Gallen); Prof Dr ir. Jan Rotmans (Faculty of Social Sciences, Erasmus University Rotterdam); Prof Peter J. G. Pearson (Imperial College London) and Prof Dr Christian Welzel (Leuphana University of Lüneburg).

The WBGU also wishes to thank all those who promoted the progress of this report through discussion, comments, contributions, advice and research, or by reviewing parts of the report:

Dipl Umweltwiss Tim Beringer (Potsdam Institute for Climate Impact Research, PIK e.V.); Prof Dr Hubertus Buchstein (Professor for Political Science at the University of Greifswald and Chairman of the Deutsche Vereinigung für Politische Wissenschaft, (DVPW, German Political Science Association); Dr Erika Claupein (Max Rubner-Institut, Karlsruhe); Dr Fritz Reusswig (Potsdam Institute for Climate Impact Research, PIK e.V.); Prof Keywan Riahi (IIASA International Institute for Applied Systems Analysis, Laxenburg); Prof Dr Gary Schaal (Helmut Schmidt University Hamburg); Imke Schmidt (Institute for Advanced Study in the Humanities Essen, KWI); Dr Imme Scholz (German Development Institute, DIE, Bonn).

The WBGU would also like to thank the distinguished visitors of the WBGU Workshop 'Land use Emissions' on 12 April 2010: Dr Astrid Agostini PRo(FAO, Rom), Dr Annette Freibauer (VTI, Braunschweig) and Prof Wolfgang Lucht (PIK, Potsdam) and the participants of the informal scenario workshop on 7 May 2010: Dr Brigitte Knopf (PIK, Potsdam) and Dr Antonio Pflüger (BMWI).

The WBGU Secretariat is indebted to the team at WERNERWERKE GbR, Berlin, Ann-Christine Cordes and Maximilian Werner, for developing the new flagship report layout and for their tireless support in its inaugural implementation.

Contents

Boxes

Tables

Figures

Acronyms and Abbreviations

ACER	European Agency for the Cooperation of Energy Regulators
ADAM	Adaptation and Mitigation Strategies (EU Project)
ADFC	Allgemeiner Deutscher Fahrrad-Club [German Cycling Federation]
ARPA	Advanced Research Project Agency (US Ministry of Defense)
ASEM	Asia-Europe Meeting
BAT	Best available technology
BAU	Business as usual
BBSR	Bundesinstitut für Bau-, Stadt- und Raumforschung (BMVBS) [The Federal Institute for Research on Building, Urban Affairs and Spatial Development, Germany]
BDA	Bund deutscher Architekten [Association of German Architects]
BMBF	Bundesministerium für Bildung und Forschung [Federal Ministry of Education and Research, Germany]
BMU	Bundesministerium für Umwelt, Naturschutz und Reaktorsicherheit [Federal Ministry for the Environment, Nature Conservation and Nuclear Safety, Germany]
BMVBS	Bundesministerium für Verkehr, Bau und Stadtentwicklung [Federal Ministry of Transport, Building and Urban Development, Germany]
BMZ	Bundesministerium für wirtschaftliche Zusammenarbeit und Entwicklung [Federal Ministry for Economic Cooperation and Development, Germany]
BNE	Bildung für nachhaltige Entwicklung
BSE	Bovine spongiform encephalopathy
BTA	Border Tax Adjustment
C	Carbon
CBD	Convention on Biological Diversity
CCPI	Climate Change Performance Index
CCS	Carbon Dioxide Capture and Storage
CDIA	Cities Development Initiative for Asia (BMZ)
CDM	Clean Development Mechanism (Kyoto Protocol, UNFCCC)
CERN	Conseil Européen pour la Recherche Nucléaire [European Organization for Nuclear Research]
CFL	Compact Fluorescent Lights
CGIAR	Consultative Group on International Agricultural Research
CH_4	Methane
CHP	Combined Heat and Power
CIAT	International Center for Tropical Agriculture, Columbia
CIMMYT	Centro Internacional de Maiz y Trigo (CGIAR) [International Maize and Wheat Improvement Center, Mexico]
CIP	Centro Internacional de la Papa (CGIAR) [International Potato Center, Peru]
CFCs	Chlorofluorocarbons

COP	Conference of the Parties
CO_2	Carbon dioxide
CSP	Concentrated Solar Power
CSR	Corporate Social Responsibility
C40	Cities Climate Leadership Group
DAI	Verband Deutscher Architekten- und Ingenieurvereine e.V. [Association of German Architects and Engineers]
DDT	Dichlorodiphenyltrichloroethane (Insecticide)
DFI	Development Finance Institutions
DII	DESERTEC Industrial Initiative
DLR	Deutsches Zentrum für Luft- und Raumfahrt [German Aerospace Center]
ECJ	European Court of Justice
ECSC	European Coal and Steel Community
EEC	European Economic Community
EEG	Erneuerbare-Energien-Gesetz [Renewable Energy Sources Act, Germany]
EIA	Energy Information Administration (USA)
EIB	European Investment Bank
EIT	European Institute of Innovation and Technology (EU)
EnEG	German Energy Saving Act
EnEV	Energy Saving Building Regulation
ENTSO-E	European Network of Transmission System Operators for Electricity
ENTSO-G	European Network of Transmission System Operators for Gas
ESCO	Energy Service Companies
ESSP	Earth System Science Partnership
EU	European Union
EU EDIT	European Distributed Institute of Taxonomy (EU)
EU ETS	European Union Emissions Trading System
EVS	European Values Survey
EWS	Power company of the city of Schönau,Germany
EWZ	Power company of the city of Zurich, Switzerland
ExWoSt	Experimenteller Wohnungs- und Städtebau (BBSR) [Experimental Housing and Urban Development, Germany]
FAO	Food and Agriculture Organization of the United Nations
FiT	Feed-in-tariffs
FMStG	Finanzmarktstabilisierungsgesetz [Financial Markets Stabilization Act, Germany]
FONA	Rahmenprogramm Forschung für nachhaltige Entwicklung (BMBF) [Research for Sustainable Development, Germany]
FSC	Forest Stewardship Council
GATT	General Agreement on Tariffs and Trade
GBEP	Global Bioenergy Partnership (G8-Initiative)
GCCA	Global Climate Change Alliance (EU)
GDP	Gross Domestic Product
GEA	Global Energy Assessment
GEF	Global Environment Facility (UNDP, UNEP, World Bank)
GET FiT	Global Energy Transfer Feed-in Tariffs
GLASOD	The Global Assessment of Human Induced Soil Degradation (ISRIC)
GPI	Genuine Progress Indicator
GHG	Greenhouse Gas
Gt	Gigatons
GuD	Gas-steam Power Plant
GW_e	Gigawatt of electricity

HANPP	Human Appropriation of Net Primary Production
HDI	Human Development Index
HFC	Hydrofluorocarbons
HIV	Human Immunodeficiency Virus
IASS	Institute für Advanced Sustainability Studies
IAASTD	International Assessment of Agricultural Knowledge, Science and Technology for Development
IATA	International Air Transport Association
ICA	International Co-operative Alliance
ICR	InnovationsCity Ruhr (Germany)
IIASA	International Institute for Applied Systems Analysis
ICLEI	International Council for Local Environmental Initiatives
IEA	International Energy Agency (OECD)
IEWB	Index of Economic Well Being
IFAD	International Fund for Agricultural Development (UN)
IFC	Internationale Finanzkorporation (World Bank)
IFIC	International Feed-in Cooperation
IMAGE	Integrated Model to Assess the Global Environment
IMF	International Monetary Fund
IPBES	Intergovernmental Science-Policy Platform on Biodiversity and Ecosystem Services
IPCC	Intergovernmental Panel on Climate Change (WMO, UNEP)
IPEEC	International Partnership for Energy Efficiency Cooperation (IEA)
IRENA	International Renewable Energy Agency
IRRI	International Rice Research Institute, Philippines
ISRIC	International Soil Reference and Information Centre
KfW	KfW Bank Group (Germany)
KIC	Knowledge and Innovation Communities (EIT)
LADA	Land Degradation Assessment
LDC	Least Developed Countries
LED	Light Emitting Diode
LEED	Leadership in Energy and Environmental Design (USA)
LIFDC	Low-Income Food-Deficit Countries (FAO, WFP)
LOHAS	Lifestyle of Health and Sustainability
LULUCF	Land Use, Land-Use Change and Forestry (Kyoto Protocol, UNFCCC)
MDG	Millennium Development Goals (UN)
MERGE ETL	An Optimisation Equilibrium Model With Two Different Endogenous Technological Learning Formulations (EU)
MESSAGE	Model for Energy Supply Systems and their General Environmental Impact (IIASA)
MESAP	Modell Modulare Energie System Analyse & Planung (DLR)
MOF	Mixed-Oxide Fuel
N	Nitrogen
N_2O	Nitrous Oxide
NEPE	National Development Plan for Electric Mobility (BMU, Germany)
NAMAs	Nationally Appropriate Mitigation Actions
NGO	Non-Governmental Organisation
NIMBY	Not In My Backyard
NLM	Sustainable Land Management (BMBF)
OECD	Organisation for Economic Co-operation and Development
P	Phosphorus
PCBs	Polychlorinated Biphenyls
PIK	Potsdam Institute for Climate Impact Research (Germany)
POPs	Persistent Organic Pollutants
PPA	Power Purchasing Agreements

PPP	Public-Private-Partnership
PRSP	Poverty Reduction Strategy Papers (Governments, IWF, World Bank)
PUR	Public Understanding of Research
PUSH	Public Understanding of Science and Humanities
PV	Photovoltaics
RCP	Representative Concentration Pathways (IPCC)
R&D	Research and Development
RECIPE	Report on Energy and Climate Policy in Europe (WWF, Allianz)
REDD	Reducing Emissions from Deforestation and Forest Degradation in Developing Countries (UNFCCC)
REN21	Renewable Energy Policy Network for the 21st Century
RES	Directive on Electricity Production from Renewable Energy Sources (EU)
RNE	Rat für Nachhaltige Entwicklung [German Council for Sustainable Development]
SAW	Senatsausschuss Wettbewerb [Senate Competition Committee, Germany]
SÖF	Sozial-ökologische Forschung [Social-ecological Research]
SRU	Sachverständigenrat für Umweltfragen [German Advisory Council on the Environment]
TEU	Treaty on European Union
TFEU	Treaty on the Functioning of the European Union
UBA	Umweltbundesamt [Federal Environment Agency, Germany]
UN	United Nations
UNCCD	United Nations Convention to Combat Desertification in Countries Experiencing Serious Drought and/or Desertification, Particularly in Africa
UNCSD 2012	United Nations Conference on Sustainable Development 2012
UNDP	United Nations Development Programme
UN DESA	United Nations Department of Economic and Social Affairs
UNECE	United Nations Economic Commission for Europe
UNEP	United Nations Environment Programme
UNESCO	United Nations Educational, Scientific and Cultural Organization
UNFCCC	United Nations Framework Convention on Climate Change
UNIDO	United Nations Industrial Development Organisation
WBGU	Wissenschaftlicher Beirat der Bundesregierung Globale Umweltveränderungen [German Advisory Council on Global Change]
WEA	World Energy Assessment (UNDP, UNDESA, WEC)
WEC	World Energy Council
WRI	World Resources Institute
WTO	World Trade Organization
WWF	World Wide Fund for Nature
WVS	World Values Survey

Summary for Policy-Makers

A new Social Contract

In recent history, the ongoing pro-democracy movements in a number of Arab states and the fall of the Berlin Wall have served as proof of the power and dynamics of transformative processes. There are several lessons to be learned from these upheavals for the transition to sustainability: firstly, unsustainable situations can lead to dramatic collapse. Moreover, transformative forces often remain hidden below the surface for quite some time. This is evident today not least in the quantifiable global change in values to embrace sustainability. After all, the downfall of dictatorships whose mainstay has been the extraction of crude oil and natural gas (Soviet Union, Libya) also reveals the formerly hidden costs of a 'fossil' industrial metabolism.

Normatively, the carbon-based economic model is also an unsustainable situation, as it endangers the climate system's stability, and therefore the natural life-support system for future generations. The transformation towards a low-carbon society is therefore as much an ethical imperative as the abolition of slavery and the condemnation of child labour.

For quite some time now, the fossil economic system has been changing all over the world. The WBGU views this structural transition as the start of a 'Great Transformation' into a sustainable society, which must inevitably proceed within the planetary guard rails of sustainability. Long-term studies show clearly that worldwide, an ever-increasing number of people desire this move towards sustainability and a long-term approach. Moreover, the nuclear disaster in Japan makes it clear that we must choose the fast lane towards a low-carbon future without nuclear energy.

Now, it is first and foremost a political task to overcome the barriers of such a transformation, and to accelerate the change. In the WBGU's view, a long-term oriented regulatory framework must be developed for this to ensure that prosperity, democracy and security are achieved with the natural boundaries of the Earth system in mind. Above all, development paths must be pursued which are compatible with the 2 °C climate protection guard rail agreed upon by the global community at Cancún in 2010. This drastic change in direction must be accomplished before the end of the current decade in order to reduce global greenhouse gas emissions to a minimum by 2050, and thereby to maintain the possibility of avoiding dangerous climate change. Hence, time is of the essence here.

In its flagship report, the WBGU elaborates explicitly on the fact that the technological potential for comprehensive decarbonisation is available, outlines business and financing models for the transition, and points out that the political instruments needed for a climate-friendly transformation are widely known. The council also describes how the requisite transformation encompasses profound changes to infrastructures, production processes, regulation systems and lifestyles, and extends to a new kind of interaction between politics, society, science and the economy. Various multilevel path dependencies and obstacles must be overcome. Furthermore, the transformation can only succeed if nation states put global cooperation mechanisms before their own short-term oriented interests, in order to make a trend reversal, particularly as far as the global economy is concerned, towards climate-friendliness and sustainability possible. And not least, from a global perspective, this is also about issues of fairness – issues that need resolving.

This 'Great Transformation', then, is by no means an automatism. It very much depends on 'organising the unplannable' if it is to succeed within the available tight timeframe. This is unique in history, as the 'world's great transformations' (Jürgen Osterhammel) of the past were the result of gradual evolutionary change.

Adding together all of these challenges involved in the transformation to come, it becomes clear that the upcoming changes go far beyond technological and technocratic reforms: the business of society must be founded on a new 'business basis'. *This is, in fact, all about a new global social contract for a low-carbon and sustainable global economic system.* It is based on the central concept that individuals and civil societies, states and the global community of states, as well as the economy and science, carry the joint responsibility for the avoidance of dangerous climate change, and the aversion of other threats to humankind as part of the Earth system. The social contract consolidates a culture of attentiveness (born of a sense of ecological responsibility), a culture of participation (as a democratic responsibility), and a culture of obligation towards future generations (future responsibility).

One key element of such a social contract is the 'proactive state', a state that actively sets priorities for the transformation, at the same time increasing the number of ways in which its citizens can participate, and offering the economy choices when it comes to acting with sustainability in mind. The social contract also encompasses new forms of global political will formation and cooperation. The establishment of a 'UN Council for Sustainable Development', on par with the UN Security Council, and the forming of international alliances of climate pioneers between states, international organisations, cities, corporations, science and civic organisations, would be examples of this.

The WBGU has developed the concept of a new social contract for the transformation towards sustainability – not so much on paper, but rather in people's consciousness – as an analogy to the emergence of the industrialised societies during the course of the 19th century. Karl Polanyi (1944) referred to this process, too, as a 'Great Transformation', and showed that stabilisation and acceptance of the 'modern industrialised societies' were only successful through the embedding of uncontrolled market dynamics and innovation processes into a constitutional state, democracy and the creation of the welfare state – i.e. through the emergence of a new social contract.

The WBGU, by highlighting the technical and economic feasibility of the transformation, by describing the change agents, by identifying barriers, and by developing political and institutional approaches to overcome these, illustrates the transition to climate-friendliness and sustainability's 'conditions of possibility' (Immanuel Kant). In doing so, the WBGU wants to encourage policy-makers, but also the economy and the social protagonists, to dare to make the change.

Low-Carbon Challenge

Climate protection plays a particularly important part in the transformation towards sustainability, as it is a *conditio sine qua non* for sustainable development: although climate protection alone cannot guarantee the conservation of the natural life-support systems on which humanity depends, it is nevertheless foreseeable that without effective climate protection, mankind will soon have to do without some essential development opportunities.

During the past few years, anthropogenic climate change has become a central topic of social discourse. There is a global political consensus that rapid global warming by more than 2 °C would overtax our societies' ability to adapt. The consequences would be environmental crises with major social, economic and security-political risks. The avoidance of dangerous climate change has therefore become one of the biggest challenges facing humankind.

If restricting global warming to a mean temperature change of 2 °C is to succeed with a probability of at least two-thirds, then, by the middle of this century, no more than around 750 Gt of CO_2 from fossil sources may still be released into the atmosphere (WBGU, 2009). This global CO_2 budget would already be exhausted in around 25 years' time if emissions were to be frozen at current levels. We therefore need fast, transformative counteraction. By the middle of the century, the global energy systems must largely be decarbonised.

Search processes going in this direction can be observed in many countries worldwide. Europe, South Korea, China, Indonesia, India and some of the USA's states, amongst others, are endeavouring to decouple prosperity growth from greenhouse gas emissions. Many companies realise that in an increasingly prosperous world with soon-to-be 9 billion people, the next global innovation cycle must be low-carbon and resource friendly. Long-term investments, particularly in renewable energy sources as well as in energy and resource efficiency, not only serve atmosphere protection, but also reduce the numerous dependencies on the import of fossil fuels, at the same time determining future innovation centres and the reordering of global economic hierarchies. The remodelling process will open up new prospects, including for European societies whose strength lies in innovation.

A Future without Nuclear Energy

The WBGU's analyses in this report show that ambitious global climate protection is possible even without using nuclear energy. At the centre of any decarbonisation strategy must be the massive extension of the renewable energies, and the infrastructure they need. However, the move towards sustainable energy systems can only succeed if, concurrently, the huge potentials for efficiency increase are fully tapped, and changing our wasteful lifestyles is no longer a taboo subject, particularly in the industrialised and industrialising countries.

Several countries are currently planning to increase their use of nuclear energy. The WBGU urgently advises against this, above all because of the not negligible risk of serious damages, the still unresolved issues concerning final storage, and the danger of uncontrolled proliferation. Existing plants should be replaced by sustainable energy technologies as soon as possible, and, in the case of evident safety deficiencies, be closed down immediately. However, the phase-out of nuclear energy must not be compensated by renewed or intensified brown or black coal based energy generation.

Climate Protection in Three Key Transformation Fields

The transition to climate-friendliness within the scope of sustainable development mainly concerns the following three key supporting pillars of contemporary global society. These pillars should be the starting point for any political agenda: *firstly*, the energy systems, including the transport sector, which the entire economy depends on, and which are currently facing a new wave of growth due to the fast-paced dynamics of the development of the industrialising countries. The energy sector causes around two-thirds of today's long-lived greenhouse gas emissions. *Secondly*, the urban areas, currently responsible for three-quarters of global final energy demand, and whose population will double to 6 billion by 2050. *Thirdly*, the land-use systems (agriculture and forestry, including deforestation), which are currently responsible for almost a quarter of global greenhouse gas emissions. Land-use does not just have to provide enough food for a world population that continues to grow, and becomes more demanding, but also has to deal with a growth in demand due to the increasing use of bioenergy and bio-based raw materials.

In all three of the fields described, the world is still far away from setting a clear course towards sustainability. The mitigation actions announced by the majority of governments within the scope of the international climate negotiations so far will certainly not be enough to comply with the 2 °C guard rail. Nevertheless, the dynamics of a transformation that is already in progress should not be underestimated. The debate on the limits to growth, ongoing since the 1970s, and the quest for low-carbon development paths have now taken central stage in our societies. This opens up opportunities for extending the low-carbon experiments, industries, niches and efficiency islands that already exist in many countries, and gives us the chance to speed up the change in economic strategy, from dependence on the use of fossil energy carriers to a low-carbon way of doing business. Measures which, taken on their own, appear not to be particularly ambitious can, in such a dynamic situation of change, develop significant impact as a whole, and trigger the tipping points of development. Nevertheless, the transition to climate-friendliness in all three fields is a great challenge.

- The *transformation field 'energy'* is so significant because the world is still continuing down a 'high-carbon growth path' with rapidly increasing CO_2 emissions. If the 2 °C guard rail is to be observed, though, the global emissions trend must be reversed by 2020 at the latest, as the drastic reduction rates which would otherwise be necessary later would overtax societies. A global energy turnaround that also takes global development dynamics into account is what is required. More than 80% of the worldwide energy supply is still based on environment and climate damaging fossil energy carriers, whilst around 3 billion people still do not have access to essential modern energy services. The challenge lies in giving these people access to modern energy services as soon as possible, whilst at the same time significantly reducing global CO_2 emissions from the use of fossil energy carriers. This can only succeed if energy efficiency is drastically increased and lifestyle changes are triggered, leading to a limitation of the overall energy demand. The requisite decarbonisation of energy systems means that the pressure is on to act, not just in the industrialised countries, but also in the dynamically growing newly industrialising and developing countries. Even the poorer developing countries must veer towards a low-emission development path in the medium-term. The era of fossil energy carrier reliant economic growth must be brought to an end.
- The *transformation field 'urbanisation'* is so significant because the urbanisation process is the major driving force behind energy demand. Urban expansion creates new, long-lived infrastructures that are going to impact on the energy demand for a long time to come. Currently, already around half of the world's population lives in cities. In Asia, the urban population will double to 3 billion people within the next couple of decades. It is likely that by 2050, as many people will be living in cities as there are on Earth today. The current urbanisation wave must therefore be redirected towards low-carbon urban development very quickly indeed – and that in a situation where we do not have one single, functioning, low-carbon model city that we might learn from. The modification of existing urban structures is also very important; it needs a lot of time, and therefore a determined approach.

- In the *transformation field 'land-use'*, the conversion of natural ecosystems (forests, grasslands, wetlands) into agricultural land is one of the major sources of greenhouse gas emissions. The main focus must therefore be on stopping deforestation and forest degradation as quickly as possible. Worldwide, forest areas are currently being reduced at a rate of about 13 million hectares per year. According to projections by the Food and Agriculture Organisation of the United Nations (FAO), in order to secure the food supply for a growing world population, global food output must increase by up to 70% by 2050. Agriculture's challenge is covering the strong growth in demand for agricultural produce in a sustainable way, including biodiversity protection, and, at the same time, to mitigate emissions along the whole life cycle, from field to consumer. One particular challenge here is the change in eating habits in favour of animal products in many regions of the world.

Conducive and Impeding Factors

One positive aspect is that many of the alternatives for putting sustainable progress in the three transformation fields as described into action are already available. The respective technologies are already in use or under development. Thanks to modern communication technologies and worldwide knowledge networks, climate-friendly innovation and learning processes can be shared fast, even with countries where this is not politically wanted. The policy and economic steering instruments are also well-known and could, assuming a corresponding public willingness to create the framework conditions, soon be adapted to decarbonisation.

The financial challenges of the transformation are significant, but controllable. Globally, the additional investment required for transformation into a low-carbon society, compared with the cost of 'just carrying on as we are', probably lies somewhere in the region of at least US$ 200 to up to 1,000 billion per year by 2030, and would significantly exceed this amount between 2030 and 2050. These investments will be offset by later savings of a similar size, and the avoidance of the immense costs of dangerous climate change. Through innovative business models and financing concepts, we can resolve these issues.

Not least, a positive fact in the WBGU's view is that an ever-growing part of the world population is developing value systems that include focusing on the protection of the natural environment, or that this aspect is at least gaining in significance. Policy-making should acknowledge this trend, and show much more courage when it comes to making pro-climate protection decisions.

However, this positive development is hindered by factors that impede a transformation.

Political, institutional and economic path dependencies, interest structures and veto players make the change into a sustainable society more difficult. Annual consumption subsidies for fossil-based energies are estimated to range between US$ 300 to over 500 billion worldwide. However, this is not just about a lot of money and the corresponding interests of the established high-carbon sectors of the economy. The economic model of the past 250 years, with its rules and regulations, research environments, training and qualification systems and social role models, and its foreign, security, development, transport, economic and innovation policies, was almost without exception geared towards the use of fossil energy carriers. This complex system must now be fundamentally modified with a view to the decarbonisation of energy systems and radical increases in energy efficiency. John Maynard Keynes put it in a nutshell when describing one of the key challenges of this kind of profound system change: 'The difficulty lies not so much in developing new ideas as in escaping from old ones.'

Moreover, the transformation must be achieved within a very tight timeframe, which, for complex societies, particularly in the context of international negotiation systems, poses a significant challenge. At the same time, our societies must be willing to act in an anticipatory manner, on the basis of scientific findings. For this to happen, politics, economy and society must wholeheartedly embrace long-term orientation.

The urbanisation waves in the developing regions, a significant proportion of which are caused by high-carbon growth in many parts of the world, are a further huge challenge for the transformation process, but also a great opportunity. Particularly in the rapidly growing economies of the newly industrialising countries, the change into low-carbon cities has to be effected within a very short period of time. On the one hand, this is asking a lot in terms of the transformation and learning capacities of those countries. On the other hand, in most of those countries, the prevailing tenet is that climate change has primarily been caused, and continues to be caused, by the OECD countries, and that therefore, the presumably costly investments into climate protection measures must, for the most part, be made in the established industrialised countries. This issue has so far not been resolved by a global burden sharing agreement. The situation is made more difficult by the availability of cheap coal in many of the newly industrialising countries.

The WBGU analysis also shows that current global governance institutions are not very well prepared for the transformation. This applies in particular to the three key transformation fields energy, urbanisation and land-use. Furthermore, no truly assertive climate pioneer alliances exist to accelerate the establishment of post-fossil, transnational structures.

Overall, though, the WBGU's central message is that the transformation into a low-carbon global society is essential, and achievable. In some sectors, regions and countries, it has already begun. Above all, we must now refrain from preventing the transformation, and instead forge ahead with initiatives that serve its acceleration.

Transformation Concept and Implementation Strategy

Characteristics of Great Transformations

The WBGU views this worldwide remodelling of economy and society towards sustainability as a 'Great Transformation'. Production, consumption patterns and lifestyles in all of the three key transformation fields must be changed in such a way that global greenhouse gas emissions are reduced to an absolute minimum over the coming decades, and low-carbon societies can develop. The extent of the transformation ahead of us can barely be overestimated. In terms of profound impact, it is comparable to the two fundamental transformations in the world's history: the Neolithic Revolution, i.e. the invention and spreading of farming and animal husbandry, and the Industrial Revolution, which Karl Polanyi (1944) called the 'Great Transformation', meaning the transition from agricultural to industrialised society.

The WBGU's Transformation Strategy

The great transformations the human race has so far experienced were, for the most part, the uncontrolled results of evolutionary change. The challenge, unique in history, with regard to the upcoming transformation into a climate-friendly society is advancing *a comprehensive change for reasons of understanding, prudence and providence*. The transformation must be anticipated, based on scientific insights regarding the risks of continuing on high-carbon development paths, in order to avoid the 'standard historic reaction', a change of direction in response to crises and disasters. The quest for suitable strategies has gained hugely in importance for corporations, in politics, in science and for society as a whole.

Figure 1 illustrates a possible course the transformation could take. To achieve decarbonisation, misguided incentives must be abolished, and the number of obstacles must be diminished. Figure 2 illustrates the temporal dynamics of the transformation into a low-carbon society, possible paths leading to failure to achieve the transformation, and the different levels of action.

Europe and the whole world currently stand at a crossroads. By now, there are change agents in all areas of society; in many countries, they even hold positions that can claim acceptance by the majority. The German federal government, the EU, the governments of the People's Republic of China, India, the USA, South Korea, Japan and Indonesia are all pro sustainable development, and have presented corresponding strategies, 'green growth' models or energy sector remodelling plans. In addition, all over the world, a number of low-emission technologies have seen dynamic development over the past few years. Renewable energies have become an important economic and employment factor. Globally, many cities have already implemented climate-friendly future concepts, in some major corporations, formerly small departments for corporate social responsibility have grown into 'innovation centres for sustainable markets', and in science, research alliances dealing with the transformation into a climate-friendly society have been formed.

So there is a lot of movement, and in the right direction. Nevertheless, there is a very real danger that the dynamics between change and dogged insistence on the established will lead into a lock-in (fig. 2); the transformation into a low-carbon society could also fail. For example, the increasing energy efficiency of vehicles could be overcompensated by a rebound effect, e.g. the more rapid growth in their number. Or states could agree on mitigating their greenhouse gas emissions, but these could nevertheless be far below the required ambition level. Renewable energies could gain in significance, but they might only be an addition to the still dominating fossil energy carriers, rather than replacing them. If the transformation were to be implemented in this kind of half-hearted and slow manner, it could lead to a '3-4°C world' with the respective, almost uncontrollable consequences for nature and society. The important thing now is to set the course in such a way that a result like this becomes improbable.

Historical analyses show that a 'concurrence of multiple change' (Osterhammel, 2009) can trigger historic waves and comprehensive transformations. The social dynamics for a change in the direction of climate protection must therefore be created through a combination of measures at different levels:

- It is knowledge-based, based on a joint vision, and guided by the precautionary principle.

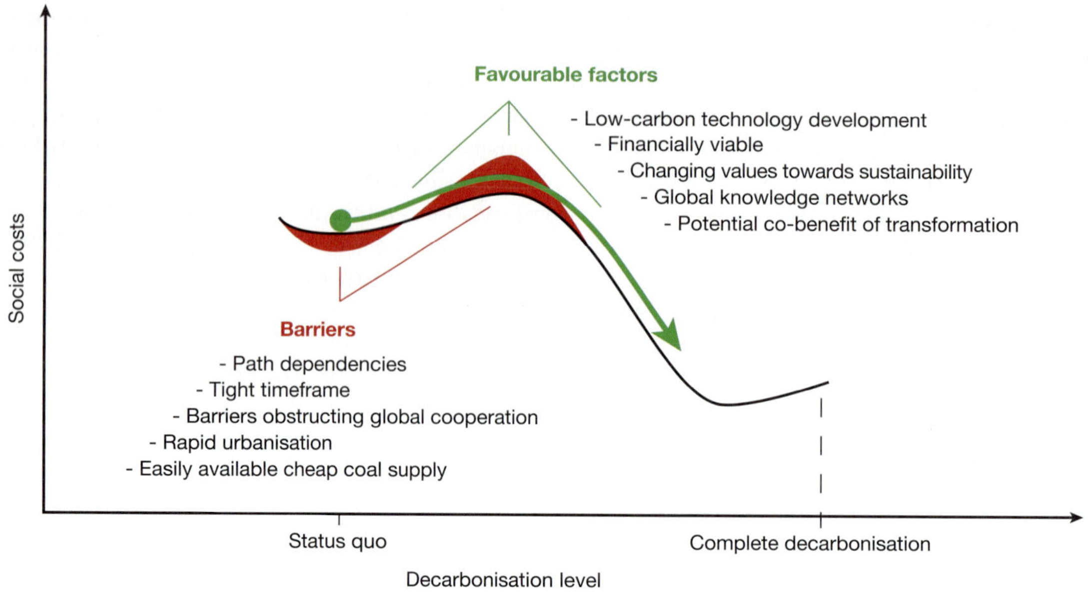

Figure 1
Topography of the transformation: the first step towards turning the global society's status quo into low-carbon (complete decarbonisation) is the overcoming of obstacles, shown here as an increase in social costs. This increase is currently intensified through barriers (red): the social costs of the status quo appear to be lower than appropriate, due to, for example, misguided incentives such as subsidies for fossil energy carriers, or environmental costs that are not internalised. At the same time, the barriers to be overcome appear to be higher than they actually are: although overcoming various barriers requires a high degree of effort, for example, the costly overcoming of path dependencies, this is compensated by favourable factors: many low-carbon technologies are already available, and their deployment is financially viable. Aided by the favourable factors, barriers can be diminished to pave the way for the transformation. Once the decisive barriers have been overcome, the move towards low-carbon can be expected to develop its own dynamics.
Source: WBGU

- It relies heavily on the change agents, who can test and advance the options for leaving behind an economy reliant on the use of fossil resources, thus helping to develop new leitmotifs, or new visions, to serve as guiding principles for social transition. Initially, the change agents are involved as marginalised protagonists; they could, however, develop into an effective force, greatly advancing the transformation (fig. 2).
- It needs a proactive state to allow the transformation process to develop into a certain direction by providing the relevant framework, by setting the course for structural change, and by guaranteeing the implementation of climate-friendly innovations. The proactive state gives the change agents leeway, and supports them actively.
- It also counts on the cooperation of the international community and the establishment of global governance structures as the indispensable driving force for the intended transformation momentum.

The Decarbonisation of Energy Systems is Achievable

The most important starting point for the transformation towards sustainability is the reduction of CO_2 emissions from the use of fossil energy carriers. Apart from decarbonisation, a second major goal of a remodelling of the energy systems is overcoming global energy poverty.

The WBGU shows explicitly that the decarbonisation of energy systems on a global level is feasible, both from a technical and an economic point of view. The long-term economic costs of such a transformation amount to just a few percent of the global GDP. For the transformation to succeed, it is imperative that the reduction of the carbon dioxide intensity of the global GDP is greatly accelerated. Assuming an economic growth of 2–3%, if a development path were to be followed that would lead to not more than 750 Gt CO_2 emissions from fossil sources by 2050, then, over the next few years, the speed at which the CO_2 intensity of the global economic output is reduced would have to be at least twice as fast as it has been in the past.

However, there is more than one way to transform energy systems in the direction of climate protection.

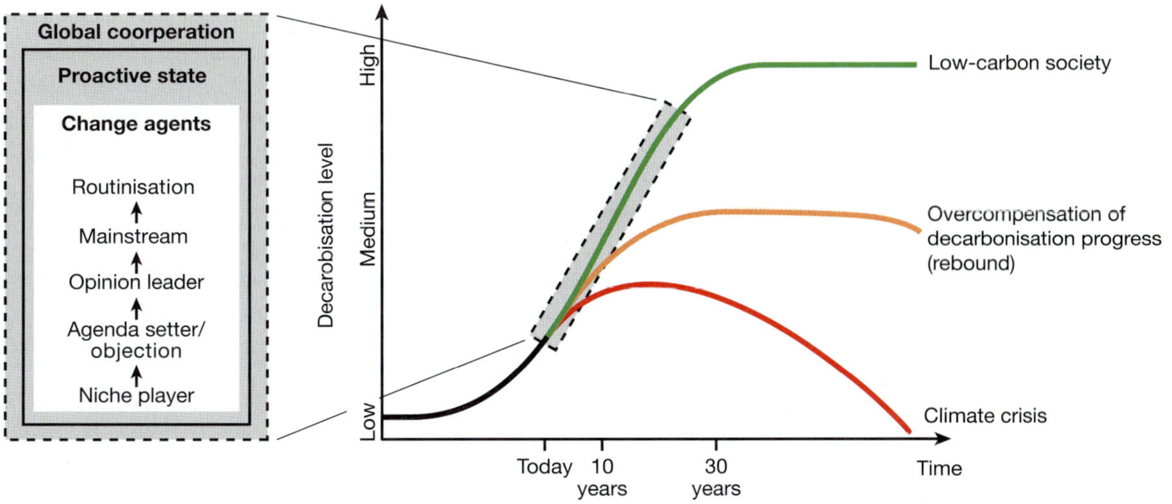

Figure 2
The transformation's temporal dynamics and action levels. The goal of the transformation is a low-carbon society. Central to the transformation is the decarbonisation of energy systems. Left: The proactive state and the change agents are the key players. As far as the change agents are concerned, they must move away from a marginalised existence and increase their impact through widespread inclusion in social routines. Right: Decisive action for a change of course towards transformation must be taken within the next decade if the conversion is to succeed within the next 30 years. The sustainable path (green) manages the transition from high-carbon to low-carbon society in time. Overcompensation for decarbonisation advances (for example through rebound effects) could lead to rendering climate protection measures ineffective, so that the transformation fails (yellow). Moderate endeavours only carry the risk of path dependencies that will lead to a global climate crisis (red).
Source: WBGU, modified acc. to Grin et al., 2010

The actual energy paths followed will differ between states and regions, depending on political, technological and cultural circumstances and preferences, and individual geographical features. The use of nuclear power and the relevance of carbon capture and storage (CCS) in particular could develop in very different directions, both regionally and nationally – especially through policy decisions. The WBGU advises against the use of nuclear power. CCS, on the other hand, is a necessary climate protection measure for countries that continue to use fossil energies. In combination with the use of bioenergy, CCS could also turn out to be an important option for actively withdrawing CO_2 from the atmosphere during the second half of the 21st century. In its recommendations, however, the WBGU focuses on development paths where these two technologies play only a marginal role. Rather, the WBGU recommends a strategy that relies primarily on an accelerated use of renewable energies, with a medium-term prospect of covering 100% of demand. This goal requires a simultaneous pursuit of drastic improvements in energy efficiency.

In the WBGU's opinion, a look at the various transformative scenarios suggests that the global final energy demand should not rise to more than 400–500 EJ per year by 2050; it currently amounts to approx. 350 EJ per year. Without a change in political direction, though, the final energy demand could more than double. Hence, downsizing this demand in the industrialised and the economically fast growing newly industrialising countries is a crucial task.

Utilise Changing Values

Creating the relevant attitudes and preferences is an indispensable premise for a successful transformation to a low-carbon society. Politicians must make the intended transition agreeable to the vast majority (acceptance), obtain their consent (legitimation), and invite cooperation (participation). There is ample evidence, such as the results of the international World Values Survey, which has been conducted since 1981, or the debate on alternatives to GDP as a prosperity indicator, to suggest that the core values of a large part of the world population include the protection of the natural environment. There is a relatively broad, cross-cultural consensus to transform the predominant economic strategy so that it becomes embedded in sustainable environmental management. Political options that pick up on post-materialistic values and sustainability-oriented attitudes are therefore not antitheses to the majority view in industrialised societies. They are also popular amongst opinion leaders in the newly industrialising countries, seeking to catch-up in terms of economic development. For all of the reasons mentioned, it is clear that policy-makers can certainly be more courageous when it comes to making pro climate protection decisions. People are far more willing to tackle this issue than generally thought.

A New Global Social Contract

The idea of a new social contract refers to the necessity of humankind taking collective responsibility for the avoidance of dangerous climate change and other dangers to the planet. For one thing, this needs a voluntary capping of the usual options for economic growth in favour of giving the people in those parts of the world already suffering the consequences of our irresponsible behaviour, and particularly future generations, room to manoeuvre. For another, the transformation needs a powerful state, counterbalanced by extended participation on the part of its citizens.

The idea of a social contract takes the original concept found in the natural law theories of early modern history one step further, and today's revised edition must address four major challenges:

1. Because of progressive economic and cultural globalisation, the nation state can no longer be considered the sole basis for the contractual relationship. Its inhabitants must responsibly take transnational risks and natural dangers, and the legitimate interests of 'third parties', i.e. other members of the world community, into account.
2. Traditional contract philosophy presupposed the fictitious belief that all members of a society are equal. Considering the disproportionate distribution of resources and capabilities in today's international community, we must have effective, fair global compensation mechanisms in place.
3. The natural environment should be given increased consideration when revising the social contract.
4. The contract has to bring two important new protagonists into the equation: the self-organised civil society and the community of scientific experts.

The new social contract is an agreement to change: the global citizenship consents to expecting innovations that have a normative link to the sustainability postulate, and, in exchange, agrees to surrender the instinct to hang on to the established. The guarantor in this virtual contract is a proactive state that involves its citizens in future decisions requisite to the agreement of sustainability targets. This in turn is linked to a culture of attentiveness (born of a sense of ecological responsibility), a culture of participation (as a democratic responsibility), and a culture of obligation towards future generations (future responsibility). It is by no means the case that the contract calls for a merely superficial or even resigned acceptance on the part of civil society: rather, the civil society is acknowledged as an active partner with shared responsibility for the success of the transformation process, and mobilised, thereby legitimising the process. The concept of a proactive state is therefore indelibly intertwined with the acknowledgment of civil society, and the innovative forces in the economy, in science and in administration.

Ten Measure Bundles with Major Strategic Leverage: Recommendations for Action

Strategic Perspectives

The transformation into a low-carbon society means nothing less than a paradigm shift from fossil to post-fossil society that must take place in the form of a societal search process. Although specific sustainability objectives can be defined (like restricting anthropogenic global warming to a temperature rise of 2 °C, or stopping deforestation globally), it is not possible to provide an exact description of the ultimate desired state of economy and society. However, the objectives and direction of global economic development can take their lead from globally established and, for the most part, universally accepted standards (Human Rights, UN Conventions, Rio Declaration, Millennium Development Goals, etc.). Widely accepted, above all, is also the imperative, voiced by Hans Jonas, amongst others, that current actions should not result in irreparable damages for coming generations to deal with, i.e. that we should not leave them worse basic conditions for survival, but rather improved conditions for survival, if at all possible.

The global perspective also dictates that despite all our differences and unique cultural characteristics, the global societies' development opportunities should not diverge too much. The principle of common but differentiated responsibilities set down in the Rio Declaration and the UN Framework Convention on Climate Change (UNFCCC) means that for the time being, the developing countries shall be given more leeway with regards to the transformation than the newly industrialising or industrialised countries. The agreed parameters allow plenty of room for a range of different strategies. In accordance with each country's specific conditions, every sector and society should develop and follow its own individual transformation path. The WBGU sees two ideal, typical transformation options for this:

1. *Polycentric strategy:* The current climate protection endeavours in the different sectors and at different levels are bundled and considerably stepped up. The WBGU is convinced that this strategy can be implemented soon, and with the existing means, and is reasonably realistic. Measures which, taken

on their own, have little transformative impact can, through clever mixing and skilful combination, have a far greater impact and generate unexpected movement, far more than a simple addition might lead us to believe. Taken in total, a societal tipping point can be reached, beyond which resistance to the transformation significantly decreases, the requisite political willingness grows, and the acceleration gains considerable momentum.

2. *Focused strategy:* Here, the focus is on concentrating on just a few major course changes that can have high transformative impact – but which a great number of the protagonists currently view as unrealistic, because they would need to be pushed through in the face of powerful forces insistent on preserving the status quo. Some of these major course changes are however necessary to achieve the scale and speed the transformation into a low-carbon society needs to reach.

Both polycentric and focused transformation strategy are aiming for a 'Great Transformation', though, hence both differ from the incremental politics of short-term crisis management and the ever-procrastinating negotiation of compromises.

In this report, the WBGU advocates an intelligent combination of both strategies. There are concrete recommendations for the intensification of current climate protection endeavours with regards to the three transformation fields of energy, urbanisation and land-use. The more small-scale measures show results, and the more change agents become actively involved, start networking, and start to initiate changes on different levels, all working towards a transformation, the sooner decision-makers will be encouraged to tackle the major, supposedly unpopular course changes. In a societal environment as dynamic as this, measures which are still viewed as unrealistic today could certainly become realisable tomorrow. The WBGU has therefore ranked its recommendations according to ambition level, i.e. according to their transformative impact *and* political achievability. This provides for explicitly including major course changes in our recommendations which may still seem unrealistic from today's point of view, but which may well turn out to be inevitable in the long term.

Practical Recommendations for Action: Ten Transformative Measure Bundles

The scale and speed of the current transformation endeavours are by far not enough to avoid a dangerous climate change, and the risk of an irreversibly unsustainable global development. We are still a long way away from reaching the tipping point with regards to sustainable global resource conservation and value generation. In the following, the WBGU therefore outlines ten measure bundles with major transformative impact to accelerate and spread the transformation to sustainability.

Bundle 1: Improve the Proactive State with Extended Participation Opportunities

A central element in a social contract for transformation is the proactive state with extended participation in a multilevel system of global cooperation. It entails two aspects, frequently thought of as separate or contradicting: on the one hand empowering the state, which actively determines priorities and underlines them with clear signals (for example with bonus/malus solutions), and on the other hand, giving citizens more extensive opportunities to have a voice, to get involved in decision-making and to take a more active role in politics. A powerful (eco-)state is often thought of as restricting the autonomy of the 'man in the street', whilst at the same time, any meddling on the part of the citizen is viewed with misgivings as a disturbance factor to political-administrative rationality and routines. A precondition for a successful transformation policy, though, is the simultaneous empowerment of state and citizens with regard to the common goal of sustainable policy objectives.

The proactive state is firmly anchored in the tradition of a liberal and constitutional democracy, but it develops this democracy further with a view towards the future sustainability of democratic communities and liberal civil societies, and takes into account the boundaries imposed on economic and social development by a finite planet. Whereas climate protection is often regarded as a restriction and unreasonable deprivation, a proactive and enabling form of government has the explicit task of preserving available choices and the current room to manoeuvre for future generations and even, if possible, to extend these.

The WBGU recommends the approach of these goals on four interconnected levels: substantive through provision of climate protection targets in climate protection legislation; constitutionally, through the setting of a respective national objective regarding climate protection; procedurally, through extending the opportunities for citizens and civil society organisations for public participation in decision-making, access to information and legal protection; and institutionally through mainstreaming the climate policies of government institutions (for example, by way of the establishment of a joint ministry for environment, climate and energy).

The level of ambition, and therefore the transformative impact of these elements, increases through combination, and a corresponding definition of content with regard to the following elements: as a central measure, the WBGU suggests climate protection legislation with ambitious mitigation targets, to be reached by 2050 (bundle 9), along the lines of the WBGU's budget approach. Another important legislative measure would be the introduction of a comprehensive, obligatory climate impact assessment scheme for any legislative proposal. Contrary to the existing planning and approval procedures, the public should be informed at the earliest opportunity about projects that have a major impact on climate protection and the transition to sustainable energy systems, and be given the chance to become actively involved in the planning and approval process. Further avenues for legal redress in the form of supra-individual collective actions should be opened up, in addition to the existing legal remedies, to allow judicial examination of planning and approval decisions. The use of ombudsmen and ombudswomen with a 'right to remonstrance' and a 'right to monitor', as well as prompt, iterative deliberation proceedings with the corresponding inclusion of scientific expert knowledge and non-professional expertise would, in the WBGU's view, complete the procedural system for climate protection relevant decisions by administrative and legislative authorities.

The German federal administrative bodies should undergo a climate mainstreaming at federal, state and local level. All of the measures described above that are of a material, legal, procedural-legislative and institutional nature (extended participation, climate mainstreaming, climate protection legislation, climate impact assessment, extended legal remedies) stand for, and concretise, the national goal of climate protection. Legislative, executive and judiciary bodies are legally bound to act.

National policies have reached their limits, both in terms of time and scope. We must therefore discuss how the (supposed) interests of future generations can be taken into account in contemporary elections and polls, and how people beyond national borders can be included, in accordance with transnational democracy. The WBGU proposes an extension to parliamentary legislative procedure in the form of a deliberative 'future chamber' to provide an institutional anchor for future-oriented interests. To avoid interest and party political interference, chamber membership could, for example, be decided by drawing lots.

Statehood transcends national borders and sovereignties, particularly as far as climate, energy and the environment are concerned; this aspect also requires new supra- and transnational institutions. One prime example for such improvement, in the opinion of the WBGU, is the European Union's network of institutions, as the EU, after all, will also benefit from impulses for a deepening of its integration through joint, citizen-friendly climate, environment and energy policies (bundle 3). Although it does not have a central legal act on climate protection, it has set material targets as far as renewable energies, energy efficiency and climate protection are concerned. Further harmonisation is required with respect to energy policy. The EU obliges its member states to give its citizens access to information on environmental issues, to give them the chance to participate, and to make legal remedies available to them. The recently established Directorate General for Energy could be a first step towards future climate mainstreaming, although so far, this directorate has not been sufficiently committed to a transformative energy policy. Constitutionally, climate protection is anchored in the Treaty on the Functioning of the European Union; it could, however, certainly be codified as an explicit goal.

On an international level, central arenas for global governance of energy, urbanisation and land-use would have to be established for the transformation (bundle 10). Exemplary for mobilisation of the global community is the Aarhus Convention, so far limited to Europe, which obliges its member states to advise their citizens of environment-relevant projects, and provides them with ways in which to participate, obtain information, and legal recourse.

Bundle 2: Advance Carbon Pricing Globally

The WBGU believes that carbon pricing is the most important political measure for decarbonisation, and a necessary element of any regulatory framework for the transformation into a climate-friendly society. However, the price of carbon has to be at a level that is high enough to achieve the transformative impact called for, i.e. it must be substantially higher than the current European emissions trading price level. Price is a signal which can be given either through taxation, or through the introduction of a cap and trade system. Assuming that the institutional capacities are given, and that stringency can be guaranteed, the WBGU considers cap and trade to be the more effective instrument.

The WBGU proposes the following steps, with progressive ambition levels:

- *Refine the European Emissions Trading System (EU ETS) and reach a G20 agreement on carbon pricing (low ambition level):* The EU ETS should be continued, simplified in terms of administration, and supported by ambitious caps on emissions. The EU-wide goal for emissions reduction should be increased to at least 30% below 1990 levels by 2020, not least to regain EU credibility in international climate politics. A carbon price should also be introduced for sources of diffuse emissions, such as transport, which so far have not been included. At the same time, the EU should lobby for the introduction of carbon pricing policies in all G20 states.

- *Pursue the linking of emissions trading systems (medium ambition level):* Parallel to this, linking of current emissions trading systems should be encouraged. The more countries join a linked system, the higher the chances that other countries will follow their example. For countries that have not introduced national emissions restrictions, sectoral approaches should be considered. In countries that are currently unable to introduce emissions trading systems due to a lack of institutional capacity, the introduction of a CO_2 tax would be a reasonable measure.
- *Establish an emissions trading scheme that is as global as possible, with joint emissions restrictions (high ambition level):* The speedy and comprehensive integration of the major high-emission countries in a global emissions trading scheme would ensure that significant global emissions reductions can be achieved. To send a price signal both for investments and consumption, emissions trading should take place at corporate level. Such an emissions trading scheme requires a high level of international cooperation and must therefore be based on principles of fair distribution, as, for example, suggested in the WBGU's budget approach (2009).

Bundle 3: Promote a Common European Energy Policy

Goal of a common European energy policy should be the decarbonisation of the energy systems by the middle of the century. To achieve this, the WBGU recommends consistent and strong support for renewable energies, a coordinated, speedy extension of grid infrastructures, grid access, as well as storage facilities, and strong foreign and development EU policies on energy to promote the integration of neighbouring states, such as Norway or the North African countries. Such a common European energy policy would have a great symbolic effect, and would underscore Europe's commitment to joint action in key future-oriented fields, strengthen the Union's competitiveness, and serve as an inspiration to the global economy. The WBGU proposes the following three steps, with progressive ambition levels:

- *Strengthening of the objective 'climate protection', and elaborating existing energy political measures (low ambition level):* To guarantee all-encompassing consideration of decarbonisation in all areas influenced by EU policies, climate protection should be given symbolic and constitutional support by being explicitly defined as an EU goal. Ambitious goals that go further than the EU renewable energy directive, which defines the targets to be reached by 2020, should be set, to be reached by 2050: climate protection objectives must be elaborated, and binding energy efficiency targets must be agreed. The financial support given to renewable energy carriers should be better coordinated on an EU-wide level, and, in the long-term, harmonised (bundle 4). These material provisions should be procedurally accompanied by extending monitoring scope, such as, for example, the introduction of collective European legal action.
- *Realisation of a single European energy market (medium ambition level):* To ensure a continent-wide sustainable energy supply, the WBGU strongly recommends pushing ahead with the realisation of a single European energy market to provide better support for renewable energies. Independent network operators would guarantee unrestricted grid access. Unrestricted grid access and cross-border networks are indispensable for the efficient integration of renewable energies into the existing grid, and for a guaranteed reliable supply. This is the only way that allows the development of a single European market for energy and gas with uniform prices.
- *Europe-wide energy strategy on union basis (high ambition level):* The EU should pool its continent-wide renewable energy potentials and, taking the differing geographical and economic conditions for the production and storage of renewable energies into account, drive ahead their cost-efficient extension. Apart from the harmonisation of existing promotion schemes, this requires joint planning of grid expansion, including the securing of the requisite funds. The WBGU advises the German federal government to support augmentation of EU legislative authority to allow for the definition and implementation of a European energy strategy, including the determination of the respective energy carriers, and the extension and rebuilding of cross-border infrastructures, to achieve a decarbonised, EU-wide energy system by 2050 based on the largest possible share of renewables.

Procedurally, we recommend a division of labour between the EU and its member states: the EU provides the legal framework for the energy mix and the extension and rebuilding of infrastructural projects. The actual legal form and the implementation of planning and application procedures for infrastructure-related projects should be the member states' tasks.

Bundle 4: Accelerate Promotion of Renewable Energies on a Global Level through Feed-In Tariffs

The transformation speed that needs to be reached to protect the climate and avoid the imminent risk of path dependencies on fossil energy technologies can only be achieved by accelerating and increasing the use of renewable energies. The WBGU therefore advises the German federal government to strongly support, both at EU and global level, the widespread use of feed-in tariffs as a useful instrument. The most important accompanying measure, as it creates the one vital precondition an accelerated expansion of renewable energies depends on, is extension of the infrastructure, above all the construction of high-capacity transmission grids and storage facilities. Simultaneously, subsidies for fossil energy carriers should gradually be phased-out, as they are currently several times higher than the subsidies for renewable energy carriers. This ratio must be reversed as soon as possible.

- *Harmonise EU feed-in tariffs step by step:* Initially, the EU should strive for a binding EU-internal agreement for the introduction of feed-in tariffs in all member states, and for gradual harmonisation of the various national feed-in tariffs. However, complete harmonisation cannot be implemented immediately, as the transport capacities of Europe's electric power grids are as yet far away from being capable of allowing a limiting of the extension of renewable energies to ideally suited locations only. A harmonised, EU-wide feed-in tariff would be a sensible option once the grids are in place, and should already be prepared in advance. Renewable energies should also enjoy a Europe-wide feed-in priority status. The tariff should degress gradually to take into account changing market conditions, in line with the cumulative performance of each technology used. At an early stage, the potential integration of North Africa into this Europe-wide feed-in tariff system should be explored.
- *Drive ahead worldwide acceptance of feed-in tariffs:* Germany should, both as a pioneer of the feed-in tariff system and on the basis of having already gained practical experience, step up the knowledge transfer with regards to a system implementation. The International Feed-in Cooperation (IFIC) should receive more support, both financially and in terms of staffing, to allow further development into a centre of excellence that attracts international interest. In addition, the German federal government should suggest the founding of an initiative to encourage global adoption of the feed-in tariff system. The UN Conference for Sustainable Development (Rio+20 Conference) in 2012 would be a suitable occasion for the launch. The UN General Assembly has declared 2012 the 'International Year for Sustainable Energy for All'. Within the scope of this initiative, bilateral partnerships between industrialised and developing countries could be proposed, including support in terms of capacity and financing. An international financing mechanism should also be established to provide the (co-)funding needed for financing feed-in tariff systems in developing countries. The funding required for the extension of the necessary infrastructure, like grids and storage facilities, should also be taken into consideration here. The International Renewable Energy Agency (IRENA) could function as a platform for initiative administration and coordination. The initiatives and systems supporting feed-in tariffs should gradually be phased out towards the middle of the century, as in all probability, renewable energy carriers will be competitive by then, even without subsidies.

Bundle 5: Promote Sustainable Energy Supply Services in Developing and Newly Industrialising Countries

If the 2 °C guard rail is to be complied with, there is very little room for manoeuvre left for greenhouse gas emissions intensive development paths in developing and newly industrialising countries. These countries need support with guaranteeing all of their people access to the basic essentials of a modern energy supply by 2030. They need support that allows them to establish a sustainable energy infrastructure (AGECC, 2010). If they do not succeed, there is a risk of path dependencies on high-carbon energy systems that would be very difficult and costly to overcome, and it would take decades to do so. The WBGU proposes the following steps, with progressive ambition levels:

- *Adapt concepts and strategies (low ambition level):* The goal of overcoming energy poverty should be anchored more firmly in all developmental policy planning processes. The WBGU also proposes that the World Bank should develop a measurable, sophisticated strategy for low-carbon transformation, with the requirements of the 2 °C guard rail as the benchmark. During the implementation of a global decarbonisation strategy, and in supporting the establishment of a low-carbon infrastructure, the regional development banks should also play a more prominent role. Development cooperation should set concrete energy political targets on this basis.

- *Extend the use of modern energy in rural areas (medium ambition level):* Stepping up the use of existing technologies is one way to quickly and inexpensively improve the quality of life for many hundreds of millions of people. Efficiency optimisation in bioenergy use and switching to electricity and gas are crucial for overcoming energy poverty. Beyond poverty reduction, the European Development Cooperation should be guided systematically by the goal of low-carbon growth. Particularly in sub-Saharan least developed countries and in southern Asia, it should contribute to the establishment of low-carbon infrastructures, thereby supporting climate-friendly growth in these countries, too.
- *Commence large-scale implementation soon, and accelerate it (high ambition level):* The EU should offer strategic 'decarbonisation partnerships' to developing and newly industrialising countries for low-carbon energy system establishment that go far beyond the scope of current EU climate-related cooperative partnerships. The WBGU recommends rapid large-scale expansion of existing model projects, and improvement of the preconditions for expansion, acceleration and multiplication of further pilot projects. One concrete measure is the major extension of the Africa-Europe Energy Partnership, and the potential expansion of Desertec further south. The G20 should use the Rio+20 Conference to set a clear signal for this.

Bundle 6: Steering the World's Rapid Urbanisation towards Sustainability

Cities have a key function in the transformation process, not least because around three-quarters of global primary energy is used in urban areas – a rising trend. For currently rapidly growing urban structures, for example in Asia, high-carbon path dependencies must be prevented, as they would hinder low-carbon development for many decades. The issue of low-carbon urbanisation should therefore be as high up as possible on the international political agenda. The following recommendations are important steps, but hardly enough to overcome this challenge. The WBGU proposes the following measures, with progressive ambition levels:

- *Improve global communication and information (low ambition level):* Initially, scientific and methodical foundations should be laid through the generation of regular progress reports on global urbanisation trends. Verifiable methods and standardised illustrations of greenhouse gas intensity in cities, including all of the relevant protagonists and sectors, as well as direct and indirect emissions, should be developed. On the strength of these, UN Habitat should be upgraded, its current role with regard to the setting of standards should be expanded, and its staff significantly increased, ultimately leading to further development into a central organisation for issues concerning sustainable urban development.
- *Develop and implement technologies and planning for low-carbon cities (medium ambition level):* Technologies and different ways of using renewable energies that are particularly suitable for use in urban areas should enjoy strong support in the form of special programmes (for example UN, World Bank or bilateral governmental cooperation), within the scope of an 'emergency plan for sustainable urbanisation'. Germany should become increasingly involved in international technology cooperation. In addition, the network of existing initiatives, cooperating cities, town twinning and protagonist associations should be improved. The adaptation to the unavoidable aspects of climate change should be one of the priorities here. Sustainable urban and regional planning are key issues that have so far been neglected in transformation management; they should play a bigger role in development cooperation and development bank programmes (global training initiative, capacity increase). Moreover, the World Commission on Dams might be a role model for establishing a 'World Commission on Low-Carbon Urban Planning'. At this ambition level, the WBGU proposes the creation of a UN Specialised Agency for sustainable urbanisation, with a strong mandate, which UN Habitat would then become part of (bundle 10).
- *Large-scale launch of beacon projects and initiatives (high ambition level):* The World Bank should support the implementation of particularly ambitious mitigation strategies that address the goal of 'climate-neutral mega-cities' to make investment sums in the region of two-digit billions possible. The WBGU also believes that Germany should call for a bundled European initiative for the development of actions with signal effect to promote low-carbon urbanisation in Asia. In Europe and in Germany, too, model regions and niches for change agents should be created to test ambitious concepts for low-carbon mobility and urban development. A model region could be the Berlin metropolitan area, in particular the area within the Berlin urban rail system (S-Bahn) circle line or within the scope of the International Building Exhibition 2020 (IBA).

Bundle 7: Advance Climate-Friendly Land-Use

Priority of any globally sustainable land-use policy must be securing the food supply for just under a billion mal- and undernourished people. Furthermore, demand for agricultural produce is going to rise because of the growing share of animal products and the increase in biomass production for energy and industry. At the same time, competition for arable land, by now a rare commodity, will become even fiercer due to soil degradation, water shortages and increasing climate impacts. The necessary mitigation of greenhouse gas emissions from land-use is an additional challenge. For these reasons, the transformation of global land-use is one of the central tasks for the future.

- *Establish a 'Global Commission for Sustainable Land-Use' (medium ambition level):* Land-use must be given a significantly higher priority on the international political agenda, and given a firmer institutional footing. The WBGU reaffirms its previous recommendation of establishing a new 'Global Commission for Sustainable Land-Use' for this purpose, with extensive authority regarding integrated land-use, that would have to go far beyond issues concerning agriculture or food security (WBGU, 2010a). Amongst others, it should have the following responsibilities: determination of the current state of scientific knowledge regarding global land-use, setting objectives and launching initiatives to encourage climate-friendly eating habits, developing a minimum sustainability standard for all biomass products, and exploring options for global land management.

Around a quarter of world-wide greenhouse gas emissions can be attributed directly to agriculture and land-use change. These emissions can be mitigated, but land-use systems cannot become completely emissions-free, not least because of the nitrous oxide resulting from the use of nitrogen fertilisers. Without a significant contribution from land-use, climate stabilisation cannot succeed. Mitigation of greenhouse gas emissions should therefore become another core element of new strategies for global, integrated land-use management. The most important starting points for this are forest management, agricultural production, and eating habits. In each of these three categories, the respective ambition level of the recommendations are noted:

- *Stop deforestation and transition towards sustainable forest management:* A central goal of climate-friendly land-use is stopping deforestation and destructive forest-use. As an important platform for international dialogue, the REDD-plus Interim Partnership should be used for advancing the application of ecological and social minimum standards (low ambition level). In addition, the WBGU reaffirms its previous recommendation to extend the cooperation in the field of forest management with the major 'forest countries' with a view to forming strategic alliances (WBGU, 2010b) for joint development and testing of the technical and administrative framework conditions for sustainable forest management, and for REDD-plus-projects (medium ambition level). Particular attention should be paid to the protection and renaturation of (frequently forested) peatlands. The multilateral negotiations on a REDD-plus regime within the scope of the UNFCCC should be intensified to create the global framework for a legally binding mechanism, and to provide the required long-term planning security (medium ambition level).
- *Support climate-friendly agriculture:* Global agriculture must cover the expected rapid growth in demand for food, bioenergy and biomass as an industrial feedstock in a sustainable manner, and at the same time significantly reduce greenhouse gas emissions. Development policy should address this challenge, and encourage investment and incentive structures aiming for a sustainable, climate-friendly intensification of agriculture. One goal should also be the halving of agricultural post-harvest losses by the middle of the century. Equally, an international consensus on a minimum standard for sustainable bioenergy production should soon be reached (medium ambition level; WBGU, 2010a). The WBGU again emphasises not least the major significance of a rapid and more extensive liberalisation of global agricultural trade under the World Trade Organisation (WTO). The agricultural subsidies in the EU and the other OECD countries should soon be reduced further, and market access for developing countries should be improved. Negative impacts of liberalisation on poorer developing countries should be offset by international financial support (high ambition level).
- *Promote climate-friendly eating habits:* One priority that demands critical attention, apart from food wasted in households, are the changing eating habits in favour of animal products. In total, around three-quarters of agricultural land is already dedicated to livestock production, seen as the most dynamic factor in land-use alongside population growth. Successfully steering demand away from this would have a major transformative impact, and is therefore considered 'high ambition level'. The WBGU recommends stepping up education, together with food labelling identifying the environmental impact, as measures to be speedily implemented. Canteens run by public authorities should schedule one or two

meat-free days a week by way of setting an example. EU subsidies supporting livestock production should be phased out as quickly as possible. Due to the substantial leverage of these impacts, the option of including the emissions intensity of foodstuffs as a criterion in the taxation of agricultural products within the scope of a tax reform should be examined.

Bundle 8: Encourage and Accelerate Investments into a Low-Carbon Future

The transformation into a climate-friendly society needs substantial additional investments in sustainable energy and land-use systems (several hundred billion US$ per year). State policies must therefore aim to make investment into low-carbon technologies more attractive, and to abolish current misguided incentives and investment barriers. The ambition levels of the recommendations in the following four areas depend on the level of development of the respective countries (industrialised, newly industrialising, or developing), and on the stringency of their political implementation, so ambition levels are not explicitly identified:

- *Provide stable framework conditions for climate-friendly investments:* The most important precondition for investments into low-carbon technologies and infrastructures are long-term, stable climate and energy policy framework conditions with ambitious targets, for example within the scope of climate protection legislation or a decarbonisation strategy. Apart from carbon pricing and phasing out of subsidies for fossil energy carriers (bundle 2), technology-specific funding should be granted, and binding efficiency standards for buildings, vehicles and energy consuming products should be introduced, or become more stringent. In the interim, tax incentives, for example for investments in sustainability and sustainable assets, should be an additional measure for a certain period of time.
- *Open up new financing sources at state level:* Ambitious carbon pricing and the phasing out of subsidies are important financing sources for the transformation. Of further relevance for developing and newly industrialising countries are financial transfers within the scope of the UN Framework Convention on Climate Change (UNFCCC). To make these available, the Green Climate Fund should immediately be turned into a binding mechanism, which offers grants without repayment. The fund should finance mitigation measures in developing and newly industrialising countries which are strategically integrated into decarbonisation road maps. Grants for mitigation projects in developing countries funded by existing multilateral funds should also be increased. The funds for mitigation, adaptation, technology transfer and capacity-building that have already been agreed by the industrialised countries as available from 2020 onwards should be in addition to Official Development Assistance, and exceed US$ 100 billion per year. Levies on international shipping and aviation and the introduction of a tax on international financial transactions could generate further funds. Potentially, a global emissions trading system (bundle 2) could become an international financing instrument for the transformation.
- *Strengthen mechanisms to encourage private investment:* A large part of the investments will have to come from non-governmental sources. For many countries, we can assume that, due to historically low net investments but high private profits, considerable private capital exists; for Germany, empirically sound data is available to prove this. The release of these funds should be stimulated through suitable framework conditions and government measures to raise the rate of return for investments (for example low-interest loans), and to minimise the risks (for example credit guarantees). At national or EU level, the WBGU advocates the establishment of national Green Investment Banks to consolidate existing grants. For institutional investors with a long-term investment horizon (for example pension funds and insurance companies) the Green Investment Banks should offer attractive terms. To strengthen venture and equity capital markets, favourable taxation could be introduced, or the Green Investment Banks could establish new Venture Capital Funds. The development banks should extend their regular lending in the field of renewable energies and energy efficiency, and expand it through the jointly financed climate investment fund, not least in order to encourage additional, private investment through leverage. Existing microfinancing approaches in German development cooperation to promote decentralised energy generation from renewable sources should be increased. Concerning the Clean Development Mechanism (CDM), the WBGU recommends the future limiting of this mechanism to the Least Developed Countries, enhancing the development aspect, and the inclusion of programme-based and sectoral measures.
- *Encourage new business models:* The high initial investment burden for individual investors could be shared if traditional seller-buyer business models were turned into business models with new financing and ownership structures. These would allow businesses to offer their customers combined packages in certain areas (for example mobility, housing,

production and consumption) that include services as well as real assets, instead of just tangible goods. Car sharing and energy contracting provided by energy service companies are examples of this. Cooperative societies are also suitable for financing larger investments. To have a major transformative impact, new business models such as these must become more widely accepted, and more widely established.

Bundle 9: International Climate and Energy Policy

As infrastructures for energy generation, transport and production have a long lifetime, any current conversion and extension projects must already be geared towards climate protection. As most of the additional energy infrastructures are expected to be built in developing and newly industrialising countries, a climate protection scheme that is limited to the more prosperous countries cannot solve the problem. Global cooperation is therefore necessary to ensure that the requisite funds for climate-friendly development are also available to poorer countries, and that all countries have access to climate protection technologies and the respective expert knowledge. International climate and energy policy is the forum for achieving a global consensus on transformation targets and ambitions. There is also no better alternative for negotiations on balancing global equity than the UN level. Although some operative goals like the sharing of climate protection related knowledge and technologies can be advanced on a subglobal level, the strengthening and institutionalisation of the fragmented international energy policy, and a convergence of climate policies, should nevertheless be systematically pursued to accelerate the technological shift.

International Climate Policy

The gap between the claims and the reality of international climate policy is widening. In the agreements of the Cancún Climate Conference, a restriction of global warming to less than 2 °C above the pre-industrial level is recognized as the long-term goal, the urgent need for action is identified, and a review process is initiated. An effective regime with internationally binding obligations on emissions targets, on the other hand, seems to have been put on the back-burner. Currently, climate protection depends on the voluntary pledges for limiting emissions on the part of the states. These pledges altogether are currently not enough to achieve compliance with the 2 °C guard rail. The WBGU proposes the following steps for an international climate policy, each with progressive ambition levels:

- *Ambitious unilateral targets within a pledge and review system (low ambition level):* An absolute minimum should be higher mitigation target ambitions on the part of the states within the scope of a pledge and review system (voluntary, internationally verified climate protection measures and payments) to a level that is compatible with observing the 2 °C guard rail. The WBGU recommends that German and EU mitigation levels should be more or less in line with the budget approach proposed by the WBGU (2009). Compliance with the 2 °C guard rail requires global greenhouse gas emissions of no more than 44 Gt CO_2 eq per year by 2020. By 2020, in accordance with its share of the global population figures, Germany would have to reduce its emissions by 56% compared to 1990. It could meet this demand through a reduction of its own emissions, stocked up with transferred funds. For example, domestic emissions could be reduced by around 40%, offsets or CDM could also play a small part in this, the remainder would be covered by finance and technology transfers amounting to at least € 4–8 billion annually, which would allow an additional mitigation of 0.2 Gt CO_2eq annually in other countries. The level of reduction the whole of the EU is responsible for would be around 40%, around 30% of which could be realised within the region, plus annual financing and technology transfers worth around € 11–22 billion for mitigation measures in other countries. These amounts do not include finance and technology transfers for adaptation to climate change or compensation for climate damages. On the other hand, to allow the global climate protection goal to be met, countries where emissions are still low, but which are currently on a dynamic growth path, would have to aim for development paths with emissions levels significantly lower than they would be if the global budget were to be applied equally per-capita, by as early as 2020. They should be supported in this in the form of the above mentioned finance and technology transfers from high emission countries. During this process, the physically achieved emission reductions should always be in line with the respective countries' mitigation potentials. The development of appropriate decarbonisation road maps should be a precondition for access to the Green Climate Fund. The technology mechanism agreed in Cancún offers a very good starting point for a global offensive to promote the spread of climate-friendly technologies, and should be put into operation as soon as possible. All of the described aspects of international technology transfers should be taken into account here. Parallel to this, Germany and the EU should become actively involved in determining the vital long-term global emissions target.

- *Pioneer coalitions for mandatory climate protection (medium ambition level):* Many states are prepared to go beyond pledge and review. Through coalitions, both within the framework of the UN negotiation process and independent of it, the EU should contribute to reaching ambitious partial agreements on climate protection. These kinds of sub-global alliances could, for example, play an important role in forest protection, the establishment of climate-friendly infrastructures, or help to establish acceptance of emissions trading systems. Beyond these alliances, however, the EU should also increasingly seek coalitions for a binding treaty within the scope of the UNFCCC. Apart from unconditionally and stringently raising its own mitigation targets, the EU should also show a clear commitment to continuation and further development of the Kyoto Protocol.
- *Comprehensive mandatory global climate protection regime (high ambition level):* The ultimate goal of international climate policy should be a comprehensive, binding agreement for global emissions restriction. In its budget approach, the WBGU (2009) outlined the basic elements of such a treaty: a 2 °C guard rail compatible maximum global budget for CO_2 emissions from fossil sources would be allocated across all countries on an equal per-capita basis. All countries should agree to present internationally verifiable decarbonisation road maps that clearly state the planned national emissions path up to 2050. In the WBGU's view, CO_2 from non-fossil sources and other greenhouse gases should be governed by separate regulations to achieve a more direct impact. The WBGU has repeatedly proposed an independent international agreement for the protection of terrestrial carbon stocks (WBGU, 2004). Priority should here be given to the stopping of deforestation in the developing countries (bundle 7). Mitigation of fluorinated greenhouse gases could be accelerated and simplified through a special agreement along the lines of the Montreal Protocol (WBGU, 2009). As far as the as yet unregulated, short-lived radiative forcing substances such as soot particles and ozone-forming gases are concerned, there could be separate agreements directly related to national air pollution control.

International Energy Policy

The most important objectives of the transformation of global energy use towards climate-friendliness are (1) limiting final energy demand whilst at the same time ensuring access to modern, sustainable energy services for all people, (2) the decarbonisation of the energy supply, and (3) the introduction of new, low-carbon technologies in the transport sector, in buildings technology, and in industry. One important starting point for the relevant international energy and technology policies is the agreement of norms and the setting of standards. Beyond this, international cooperation can also accelerate the development of key technologies for the transformation. Ultimately, cooperation plays an important role in breaking down the barriers obstructing a global diffusion of technologies for a low-carbon development. Currently, there is a lack of legal and institutional foundations for an effective international energy policy for the transformation. The WBGU recommends building upon existing organisations to gradually establish global sustainable energy governance, and proposes the following steps, with progressive ambition levels:

- *Open up IEA, consolidate and strengthen IRENA (low ambition level):* The International Energy Agency (IEA) is an influential, international energy institution. However, membership, role and energy political objectives regarding a sustainable energy policy have so far been restricted. The IEA's policies should focus more on sustainable energy use and sustainable energy systems, methods should be made more transparent, and access for non-OECD countries should be accelerated. The International Renewable Energy Agency (IRENA), established in 2009, can take on the important task of acting as the global voice for the diffusion of renewable energies and the requisite industries in all country groups in future. The WBGU recommends continuing to actively support the establishment of IRENA. In future, IRENA should play a major role worldwide with regards to energy issues to advance the increased use of renewable energies, on par and in cooperation with existing organisations in the field and the civil society.
- *Upgrade UN-Energy and strengthen sustainable energy policies within the UN system (medium ambition level):* The link between energy policies and development assistance policies on a global level has long been neglected. The WBGU therefore recommends to upgrade UN-Energy to the level of official UN programme. The UN general assembly has declared 2012 the 'International Year for Sustainable Energy for All'. This should be utilised to agree access to modern energy services by 2030 for all people as an additional Millennium Development Goal.
- *Make IRENA the central organisation for global sustainable energy policies (high ambition level):* IRENA's mandate should be extended to encompass all energy systems and low-carbon energy options,

including issues regarding system integration and energy efficiency on the demand side. Step by step, IRENA could then be developed further into an International Sustainable Energy Agency (WBGU, 2004). The federal government should actively support turning IRENA into one of the central organisations for energy policy in the long-term, that can effectively advance the global transformation of energy systems.

- *Use the G20 as the driving force for a sustainable global energy and climate policy (high ambition level):* Considering the urgency of the global energy shift, political willingness to act must significantly increase, and political leaders must be mobilised. As an alliance of the economically and politically leading industrialised and newly industrialising countries, which together cause approx. 80% of global greenhouse gas emissions, the G20 occupies a prominent position. The German federal government should encourage the G20 in their determined pursuit of a sustainable energy political agenda, and the creation of the institutional foundations required for effective global cooperation.

Bundle 10: Pursue a Revolution in International Cooperation

The world desperately needs a higher level of international cooperation if climate- and environmentally-friendly global development is to be achieved in the long-term. Considering this aspect, the WBGU recommends:

1. Using the Rio+20 Conference as a chance for setting the course of international environmental and developmental policy towards improved cooperation and climate-friendliness.
2. The conference should therefore pave the way for a comprehensive cooperative global governance architecture, without which a worldwide transformation to sustainability cannot succeed.

International Environmental and Developmental Policy in Context with the Rio+20 Conference

The UN Conference on Sustainable Development (Rio+20 Conference) scheduled for 2012 provides an excellent opportunity for elaborating international environmental and developmental policies. In view of the background provided by the two key issues defined for the conference, 'Green Economy in the Context of Sustainable Development and Poverty Eradication', and 'Institutional Framework for Sustainable Development', the least the WBGU would expect is the adoption of a global 'Green Economy Roadmap', and profound institutional reforms within the scope of the UN.

- *Green Economy Roadmap and institutional reforms (low ambition level):* With the 'Green Economy Report' presented by UNEP in 2011, the international community gathering in Rio has been provided with a suitable and timely basis for discussion and decision-making with regards to binding agreements. The WBGU believes that a binding 'UN Green Economy Roadmap' with specific targets in terms of both content and timing should be decided in Rio, to be implemented within the framework of national Green Economy Strategies that include verifiable indicators by 2030. The focus should be on low-carbon oriented, quantifiable targets and secondary targets, as these have proven successful in the context of the Millennium Development Goals for the conversion of energy systems, and on issues of urban development and sustainable land-use. Concurrently, poverty eradication strategies and especially the further implementation of the MDGs should be integrated into the higher-ranking Green Economy Roadmap in a way that explicitly allows direct focusing on the demands of the transformation. Key starting points for this are the securing of access to modern forms of energy for all people, and an improved food supply through the sustainable intensification of agriculture. As of now, the multilateral institutions involved in developmental policy-making should be coherently guided in their operative strategies by the target systems serving poverty reduction and low-carbon development.
The implementation of the UN Green Economy Roadmap should also be supported by long overdue institutional reforms. The WBGU reaffirms its recommendation that UNEP should be politically upgraded and expanded to a UN Specialised Agency under particular consideration of the developmental dimension of international environmental policy. The Rio+20 Conference is also an opportunity to lay the groundwork for more fundamental reforms of the UN's development assistance political architecture.
- *Fundamental reform of multilateral environmental and developmental policy (medium ambition level):* An ambitious summit result would be a comprehensive modification of the multilateral environmental and developmental architecture in line with the transformation. In the context of the Rio+20 Conference, both the German federal government and the EU should initiate a process aimed at prompt transformation of the major operative international development agencies (such as the World Bank, regional banks, UNDP, UNIDO) into change agents for low-carbon transformation. The WBGU takes its

inspiration here from the 2006 reform proposals presented by the High-Level Panel on System-wide Coherence, and also recommends that these are geared explicitly towards an environment- and climate-friendly developmental policy.

In addition, system-wide coherence, taking the transformation into account, demands closure of the huge governance gaps in the key transformation fields of energy, urbanisation and land-use on an international level (bundles 6, 7 and 9), and the gradual abolition of transformation impeding and expensive parallel structures. The Rio+20 Conference should task the standard multilateral organisations with the drafting of concrete restructuring plans, to be presented to the member states by 2014 for decision-making. The benchmark guiding all these actions should be compliance with the international climate policy's 2 °C guard rail. New organisations would only be established if the demand for global regulation in the three transformation fields could not be satisfied within the foreseeable future through the reorganisation of already existing structures.

- *United Nations 2.0 (high ambition level):* Considering the scale of the described challenges of the transformation, the WBGU believes that there are plenty of arguments for an even more radical approach that would go beyond the existing UN architecture, a fundamental restructuring of the organisation. Currently, this does not seem feasible in political terms, as it would need a political leadership that is guided by a profound realisation of vital global necessities, for example, in the UN Security Council as well as other industrialised and newly industrialising countries. If this were the case, a reform should start with a review of the UN Charter, and aim for a completely restructured United Nations organisation. Its purpose would be to take the planetary guard rails into account as a guiding principle that governs UN actions, and the pursuit of which would guarantee protection of climate and environment as much as peace, security and development.

  The Rio+20 Conference should at least admit to this kind of vision, and initiate an intergovernmental consultation process aimed at substantially extending the UN Charter. The drawing up of a 'Charter for Sustainable Development' that codifies the joint responsibilities and duties of all states and their (global) citizens regarding the protection of the Earth system would be a significant step towards a global social contract. This could form the basis for a contemporary review of the UN – for example the establishment of a 'Council for Sustainable Development', on par with the Security Council, reflecting a 21st century world of states – which would be a formal expression of the normative need for a global we-identity.

Extensive Global Governance Architecture for the Transformation

A generally high level of international cooperation, global coordination and political pro-activeness are central conditions for the success of the transformation. The global development dynamics trend reversal that is needed will therefore not be achievable without comprehensive, long-term oriented international regulatory policies with an equitable world order as its goal. In the following, the WBGU outlines three steps with progressive ambition levels on the path towards the necessary 'revolution in global cooperation'.

- *Revitalised multilateralism (low ambition level):* Inevitably, non-cooperation regarding central issues of global environmental and climate change leads to an escalation of conflicting interests and distributional conflicts. To prevent this, the key actors of world politics must find a new mode of international diplomacy as soon as possible. In the view of the WBGU, the G20 are generally suitable for handling this task, as they not only carry a high level of climate political responsibility, but also have correspondingly high potentials for transformation. The WBGU therefore recommends working towards the goal of a global transformation road map within the scope of the G20, or a comparable sub-global constellation. The benchmark for the practical decisions this kind of plan might include should at the very least be a G20 crisis management in the context of the global financial crisis. The interests of smaller and poorer developing countries would have to be taken into account in a plausible way to allow for a gradual pro-transformation mobilisation across the international community as a whole. The German federal government and the European Union should, through credible leadership, also aim for a high level of ambition as far as this joint cause is concerned, and meet the other states with a committed and mediating attitude. The G20 could then even become the driving force behind modernising the entire UN system.
- *Transformative global infrastructure development (medium ambition level):* The transformation focuses on three fundamental national and global economy 'infrastructures': the energy systems, urban areas, and land-use systems. Compliance with the 2 °C guard rail is only possible if we have changed our course towards low-carbon in all three of these transformation fields by 2020. However, all three fields lack problem-adequate global governance mechanisms to coordinate global and national trans-

formation goals, develop the corresponding indicators and routes for transformation, and define suitable incentive systems.
Accordingly, the WBGU recommends that suitably capable international organisations are either authorised to act, or newly established and provided with adequate resources. One important point of reference is provided by the UNFCCC, particularly in view of the emissions restrictions that have been negotiated there. The mechanisms that were additionally agreed upon, for example on the transfer of technology or forest protection, should be developed and implemented quickly (bundles 7 and 9). In the transformation field of energy, the German federal government should actively support a shift in the objectives of the IEA towards sustainable energy policies, the improvement of organisation accessibility for developing countries, the strengthening of IRENA as the driving force behind the international diffusion of regenerative energies, and the upgrading of the status of UN-Energy (bundle 9). Regarding urbanisation (bundle 6) and global land-use (bundle 7), the WBGU initially recommends the establishment of a 'World Commission for Low-Carbon Urban Development' and a 'Global Commission for Sustainable Land-Use'. On the strength of the findings of the latter commission, the FAO should then develop a suitable range of instruments to ensure the climate friendliness of national and global land-use paths. Due to the impact of the rapid urbanisation on climate protection, and the fact that the UN-Habitat programme is not adequately equipped to deal with this aspect, the WBGU also recommends the establishment of a UN Specialised Agency for sustainable urbanisation with a strong mandate (bundle 6).

> *Equitable new global system (high ambition level):* In accordance with the global social contract for sustainability, the ultimate goal of a revised global governance architecture must be the creation of a new, equitable global system. Its institutions must put the international community in a position that leaves them capable of appreciating the complex interdependencies of the global society within the scope determined by the limits imposed by our planet, as soon as within the first half of the 21st century, to allow for timely and adequate response. This demanding process is comparable with the embedding of market dynamics in constitutional states, democracies and welfare states during the last great transformation into an industrialised society, which led to the stabilisation and acceptance of this new form of society in the first place.
Politically, this requires a historically unprecedented transcending of established sovereignty concepts and purely power-driven global politics in favour of ensuring the long-term availability of global commons. Sustainable strategies and concepts must be developed for this in order to embed sustainable global development in transnational democratic structures, to formulate answers to the 21st century questions regarding global equity and distribution of resources, and, not least, to be able to claim worldwide legitimacy.
This means concrete academic search processes, for example by global governance theoreticians, international law experts, cosmopolitans, transnationalists and philosophers of justice to formulate legitimate and realisable norms, rules and procedures which, all together, could form the basis of an ideal global social contract. This would be something of a quantum leap for civilisation, on par for example with the transition of the feudal systems to constitutional states and democracy. Comparably to the Universal Declaration of Human Rights, however, it should in principle also be possible to reach a universal consensus regarding human civilisation's ability to survive within the natural boundaries imposed by planet Earth. This necessarily presupposes an extensive 'Global Enlightenment', which must be aimed towards promoting cooperative behaviour and accelerating the formation of relevant global social standards and debate. The WBGU strongly advises the use of the coming Rio+20 Conference as a historic chance for such an enlightenment process. A corresponding summit declaration could serve as a future reference framework and point of reference for global enlightenment, and help to initiate an effective, long-term paradigm shift.

Synthesis of Measures

In the face of the imminent challenge, policy-making should pave the way for several of the steps with a high level of ambition, even if these currently still appear to be of a rather visionary nature. For example, a climate policy that focuses primarily on measures with the lowest level of ambition is hardly likely to comply with the 2 °C guard rail. Ultimately, a great number of demanding measures will be required to make it possible for the transformation to succeed.

The bundles of measures must also be put together wisely. The combination possibilities describe a continuum across different operating levels: at one end, there are polycentric transformation approaches at different levels of ambition, with an initially limited geographical or sectoral extent, that rely on a 'concurrence of multiple change' to create an irreversible general momentum. At the other end are strategies aimed at the highest level of ambition, and ultimately at the establishment of a comprehensive global architecture for the transition into a low-carbon society. In particular, the global approach is aimed at the enforcement of a legally binding world climate agreement to establish an upper limit for global emissions and instruments for global emissions trading, and at multilateral mechanisms for the climate-friendly transformation of urbanisation, land-use, and the energy systems. Along this continuum, there is a wide range of choices. Particularly ambitious, polycentric transformation policies can work in different ways:

- *Geopolitics – forming sub-global alliances*: To accelerate the transformation, the forging of intergovernmental alliances between climate pioneers should be increased. For Germany and the EU, the major newly industrialising countries China, India and Brazil are particularly important in this respect. Suitable topics would be the promotion of renewable energies or emissions trading, areas in which pioneer partnerships could set standards and establish structures that should gradually be 'globalised'. These alliances should also serve the discussion on a fair burden-sharing of decarbonisation measures.
- *Establish incentive systems for dynamic protagonists in the transformation fields*: In the transformation fields, positive incentive systems for dynamic protagonists could speed up the low-carbon transformation. Thus, generously funded programmes for low-carbon investment projects by the World Bank and by regional development banks could provide considerable incentives for leaving the established fossil development path. Substantial loan programmes for a competition to identify and support the 10 or 20 most visionary models for the building of low-carbon cities in developing or industrialising countries could initiate or accelerate search processes in that direction. This path could be followed independent of the progress of geopolitical alliances.
- *Focus on transformation barriers:* One particularly difficult obstacle the transformation must overcome is presented by the global annual subsidies for fossil energy carriers in the region of three-digit billion figure amounts. A politically supported international alliance of change agents in economy, civil society and science could contribute to breaking down this barrier impeding progress towards sustainability.

This outline of polycentric transformation strategies clearly shows the extensive scope of options for innovative paths. The ten bundles of measures presented by the WBGU are representative of the wide spectrum of strategies available to us. The 2 °C guard rail is the most important benchmark any measures have to consider. To stay credible, the European Union should, as far as emissions reductions are concerned, agree on the raising of its own reduction target to at least 30% for the year 2020, complemented by substantial, legally binding international climate protection financing commitments.

The Role of the Knowledge Society in the Transformation Process: Recommendations for Research and Education

Social Renewal by Comprehension

Research and education are going to play a central role during the requisite transformation process, as the realisation of the necessity for restructuring the world economy has been triggered mainly by scientific knowledge. Society should therefore decide on actions that are not a direct response to recently experienced events, but motivated by foresight and precaution. For this purpose, the debate between science, politics and society should be far more structured, more obligatory, and livelier, to ensure a constructive discourse about the best ways to achieve sustainability. Research and education that assume participation can make a decisive contribution to this.

The transformation is a societal search process that should be supported by experts. In collaboration with politics, the economy, and society, research and education are tasked with developing visions for a low-carbon society, exploring different development paths, and developing sustainable technological and social innovations. Concurrently, the social framework for a culture of participation should be strengthened. To this end, education should enable people to develop an awareness of current problems, to learn systemic thinking, and to act responsibly. Promoting research and education is therefore a key task for the modern, proactive state, which should provide targeted support for the integration of the scientific expert community into the social contract.

The Four Transformative Pillars of the Knowledge Society

To clarify the different roles research and education play in the transformation process, the WBGU suggests differentiation between 'transformation research' and 'transformation education' on the one hand, and 'transformative research' and 'transformative education' on the other hand. The subject of transformation research or transformation education is the transformation as such, and the conditions needed for realising it. Transformative research or transformative education is tasked with advancing the transformation process with the aid of specific information, methods and technologies (fig. 3).

Transformation Research

The WBGU proposes the establishment of a new scientific discipline, 'transformation research' (Tr), which specifically addresses the future challenge of transformation realisation. This discipline explores transitory processes in order to come to conclusions on the factors and causal relations of transformation processes. Examples from history could provide the basis for analysing observed transformative moments. One such example would be the integration of the steam engine into the mechanisation of cotton processing around 1785. This one, seemingly innocuous step led to a rapid rise in textile production efficiency, which in turn led to a rise in the demand for raw materials, thus (co-)triggering the Industrial Revolution. It was, though, embedded in a complex causal network of further factors and historically evolved framework conditions. This equally applies to transformations at another level, for example the normatively motivated abolition of slavery. Transformation research should draw conclusions for the transformation to sustainability based on an understanding of the decisive dynamics of such processes, their conditions and interdependencies. It is important here to learn how to anticipate acceleration moments in order to create the relevant favourable framework conditions. One particular challenge for transformation research is the creation of a network of social, natural and engineering sciences in order to understand the interaction between society, the Earth system, and technological development.

Transformative Research

The WBGU uses the expression transformative research (tR) to describe research that actively advances the transformation. Transformative research supports transformation processes with specific innovations in the relevant sectors. It encompasses, for example, consumer research, which is needed for the development of new business models such as the shared use of resource-intensive infrastructures, and research for technological innovations like efficiency technologies. Transformative research can have a wider transformative impact if, as of a certain development stage, development activities for low-carbon innovations are embedded into a systemic context, their impact on climate and sustainability is verified, and they reflect

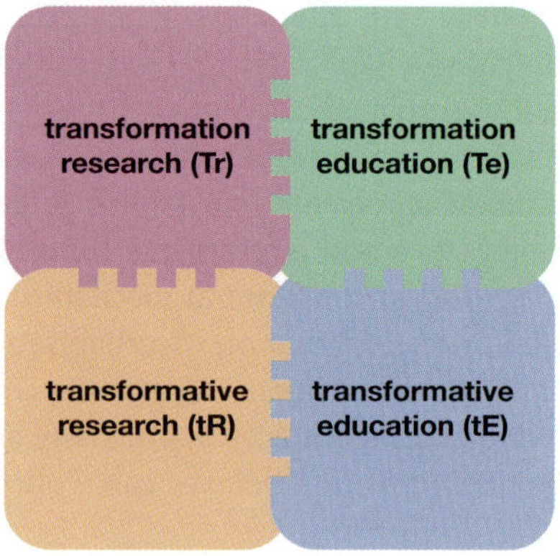

Figure 3
Typification of transformation research and education.
Source: WBGU

the conditions required for transformative impact. So although achieving higher degrees of efficiency in photovoltaics – for example through development of new, different material combinations – is necessary, the aspect of global usability should also be taken into account at the earliest possible stage. This also applies to the development of new investment models for energy efficient technologies. Their intercultural transferability should also be considered at an early stage, yet equally, attention should be paid to measures against rebound effects and potential path dependencies. Transformative research therefore encompasses a spectrum that reaches from purely discipline-based to system-based research. This means that the application-oriented exploration of highly-efficient storage technologies can have as much of a transformative impact as an interdisciplinary project for the development and implementation of SuperSmart Grids.

The ongoing exchange of information between both types of research leads to 'cross-fertilisation', and in turn with society, the economy, and politics, thus offering the best possible support to the transformation. Absolutely crucial for this is a higher level of science communication, including the targeted utilisation of the new media. This provides a wide range of opportunities for interactive, participative shaping of the social dialogue.

In this context, the education sector must also take on more responsibility. As an important channel of knowledge communication, education provides the foundations for each individual's knowledge-based self-concept, thereby creating the social preconditions needed for the transformation. Transformation research should be linked closely to transformation education. Categories and interaction are described in the following.

Transformation Education

Transformation education (Te) makes the scientific findings of transformation research available to society. As 'education for participation', it critically reflects on the requisite basic requirements – like a thorough understanding of the pressure to act, and a global sense of responsibility – and generates a systemic awareness of the different action paths. It is especially about communication of knowledge at the interface of engineering, social and Earth system sciences. Suitable narratives of change should be developed, so that these can be fed into everyday discourse through creative forms of knowledge communication, and develop further scope there. Through a focus on change agents, an awareness of the preconditions for the transformation can be firmly ensconced in education. Change can only be imagined through a dynamic view of the world. In view of this, educational institutes should increasingly teach sustainability-oriented knowledge, and the skills necessary for lifelong learning and systemic thinking. This also includes a better understanding of the scientific research process, its possibilities, and its limits.

Transformative Education

Transformative education (tE) generates an understanding of action paths and possible solutions. Related educational content would, for example, be innovations that are likely to have transformative impact, or that have already had a transformative impact. The current stage of research should be made understandable, and should be actively shared with society. To facilitate this, education should, if possible, attempt to establish a relation to the key factors of the transformation. For example, renewable energies could be a topic in physics lessons, whilst concurrently, international energy partnerships are discussed in the social science subjects. Geography lessons might be about, for example, low-carbon cities. Transformative education should also be responsible for creating a basic general problem awareness, which is also reflected in theme-specific educational opportunities. In accordance with this, the boundaries between the different disciplines should be less strict, and comprehension of the broader, interdisciplinary and global contexts should be strived for. In economics, for example, global material flows, from resources to waste products such as CO_2, could be analysed. So the lesson would be about embedding the economy into the planetary boundaries.

Both types of education should regard society as a stakeholder in the transformation process, with the aim of also allowing participation in the education process itself in the future. People can only comprehend the transformative power of their actions if they see themselves as an active factor. Respective educational structures are an essential precondition for this.

Current Research Programmes

Currently, a number of programmes with implicit transformation relevance are running both at German federal republic and EU level. The WBGU analyses relevant programmes in its report. Certain criteria are applied, such as, for example, 'international scope' and 'interdisciplinarity', to show the positive trends apparent in the different research programmes, but also to identify their weaknesses. On the basis of this analysis, the WBGU concludes that research policy in the individual areas, like urbanisation and land-use, is already addressing the challenges posed by the transformation through innovative research agendas and programmes, frequently in a low-carbon context, even though funding is inadequate. In many cases, interdisciplinarity, too, has already been admitted into research programmes, although overall, incentive structures to encourage interdisciplinarity are as yet insufficient. As far as the factors that are needed for transformation acceleration are concerned, many research grants are already focusing on innovation, which is a very welcome sign. Nevertheless, the emphasis is too much on the purely technical side, in comparison with social conditions and the corresponding systemic approaches, which is also why too much attention is paid to supply rather than demand.

Recommendations

Considering the identified challenges for research and education and the analyses carried out, the WBGU has reached the following conclusions in terms of recommendations.

Research

- Science and research should dedicate themselves even more to the low-carbon transformation within the context of sustainability. Research should focus more on transformation-relevant issues and subjects and the new field of transformation research. At the same time, it should increasingly meet a number of structural demands, such as, for example, a systemic, long-term, cross- and transdisciplinary direction. It should develop technological and social low-carbon innovations, evaluate these, and assess the required conditions for their global diffusion. This also includes the development, evaluation, and public discussion of strategies and policy options. Accordingly, research programmes should reflect these demands.

- The WBGU calls for the establishment of a new field of studies, 'transformation research', which examines transformation processes and the social preconditions within the scope of planetary boundaries. To develop this new field of inquiry, the WBGU proposes a joint societal search and discussion process. This process could be overseen by The Alliance of Scientific Organizations in Germany.
- Overall, in order to face the current challenges successfully and accelerate the transformation, substantial additional research and development funding is required. Concurrently, research should be consolidated both at EU and international level, as no country can develop all the solutions required on its own.
- Funding for the central transformation field energy should be substantially increased. The WBGU emphasises its 2003 recommendation to increase direct public spending in the industrialised countries on research and development in the energy field tenfold, largely through reallocation. Grants for energy generation through nuclear fusion could be stretched across a longer term to release funds for higher priority tasks.
- The current funds for the German Federal Ministry of Education and Research (BMBF) sustainability research, particularly the framework programme 'Research for Sustainable Development', and 'Socio-Ecological Research' (SÖF) should be significantly increased, and SÖF's global perspectives should be considerably extended.
- Interdisciplinary research should be supported by concrete measures. This requires changing the existing incentive systems, and introducing new ones. The WBGU proposes that the German Rectors' Conference, the Joint Science Conference, the German Research Foundation and the Academies of Sciences meet to consult on recommendations and directives for the implementation and rating of interdisciplinary transformation research.
- In the course of drawing up the 8th EU Framework Programme for Research, the German federal government should lobby for a stronger focus on the transformation; environment and energy research should be given particular weight.
- Internationally, Germany and the EU should forge stronger research alliances with research centres in emerging economies. In the scope of its development cooperation, Germany should step up the promotion and support of education, science and research capacities in the less developed countries.
- The WBGU suggests that a coming Initiative for Excellence should focus thematically wholly on the subject of research in the context of the transformation for a resource friendly, sustainable and liveable society.
- The current evaluation of the Consultative Group on International Agricultural Research (CGIAR) is an opportunity to direct their activities towards climate friendliness and sustainability.

Education

- Transformation education should be given a higher priority in the German sustainability strategy. It should also be integrated into school and university curricula, vocational qualification, and further studies. This encompasses exchange programmes, new combinations of bachelor and masters courses, teacher training modules for transformation-relevant systemic education, and degree programmes for transformation sciences.
- Through coherent policies, subject-relevant education and vocational qualification systems should be redesigned in such a way that they can dedicate themselves to the demands of sustainable development. At the same time, opportunities for life-long on-the-job learning should be extended through publicly funded further education courses and post-graduate qualifications, for example in the form of a 'sabbatical' with regard to transformation for employees.
- The WBGU also suggests the establishment of low-carbon business schools and interdisciplinary faculties for low-carbon land-use, energy science, urbanisation and transformation-specific management in order to support the transformation process.
- During the UN 'Decade of Education for Sustainable Development', institutional mechanisms should be developed to ensure that sustainable development education continues once the decade has passed. The UNESCO could initiate a process that could be designed similar to the continuation of the International Decade for Natural Disaster Reduction (IDNDR). That way, successful activities could be continued through local and national institutions.

Field of Interaction Education–Research

- In view of the overriding importance of the issue, the WBGU further suggests the establishment of a German federal university with a research and education profile that focuses on the transformation towards sustainability. Research and teaching should be inter- and transdisciplinary.

- The WBGU proposes an extensive education and research programme 'Participation in the Science for Transformation', aimed at education and knowledge for the benefit of the environment and sustainability, achieved through participation of non-scientists.
- Science policy and science should initiate interdisciplinary and society-wide dialogues on subjects such as visions for a 'decarbonised society', requirements for transformation research, stepping up inter- and transdisciplinary research, or priority research issues. The dialogue could also be stimulated in a cultural and artistic form, for example in museums, at future exhibitions or music and film festivals.
- To increase the involvement of social actors, the establishment of participative formats should be promoted. Appropriate would be, for example, networked biodiversity, environmental and climate 'stations', or participation in model participation projects on subjects such as electromobility, alternative agriculture, or new forms of housing.
- The WBGU suggests the introduction of a voluntary social year in 'education and research'.

A reform of research and education towards sustainability not only paves the way to a knowledge-based social contract for this 'Great Transformation', but also opens up specific future opportunities for those who participate. In accordance with the social contract, educative opportunities that encompass the communication of a sense of responsibility, a sense of justice and the skills needed for proactiveness should be encouraged. School education should also not just endeavour to instigate cross- and transdisciplinary approaches, but also an understanding of the scientific process as a whole.

Science and research policy can serve as a role model on an international level if it continues to expand in the direction it is in part already heading, towards systemic, transformation-relevant research.

Therefore, the social contract addresses future generations in two ways, as it is they who will participate in bringing about the change in future. Above all, however, it is also in our young citizens' interest to rapidly accelerate the transformation and to stop impeding it – now.

Conclusion

The 'fossil-nuclear metabolism' of the industrialised society has no future. The longer we cling to it, the higher the price will be for future generations. However, there are alternatives which would at least give all people access to the chance of a good life within the boundaries of the natural environment. Without a global agreement to actually dare to experiment with these alternatives, we will not manage to find our way out of the crisis of late modernity. So nothing less than a new social contract must be agreed to. Science will play a decisive, although subservient, role here. Ultimately, sustainability is a question of imagination.

'Imagination is everything. It is the preview of life's coming attractions.' (Albert Einstein)

Preamble

It's not because things are difficult that we dare not venture. It's because we dare not venture that they are difficult.
Seneca (1 BC–AD 65)

Action for a Low-Carbon and Equitable Future

In 2009, sixty Nobel Laureates published a memorandum appealing to the global public to take 'Action for a Low Carbon and Equitable Future', highlighting the fierce urgency with which we must transform our high-carbon economies into sustainable and equitable systems (The St. James's Palace Memorandum, 2009). This states that 'decarbonising our economy offers a multitude of benefits, from addressing energy security to stimulating unprecedented technological innovation. A zero carbon economy is an ultimate necessity and must be seriously explored now.' In view of everything we know, the Nobel Laureates are absolutely right, and what they are describing is a challenge of a dimension never before experienced by humanity. In order to avoid dangerous climate change, the great transformation into a low-carbon society must start – or rather, must be accelerated – as soon as possible. This means: in the coming decade, we must trigger serious production process, infrastructure and lifestyle changes to be able to reduce global greenhouse gas emissions to a minimum by 2050. In addition, the disconcerting events in Fukushima make it absolutely clear that the path towards a low-carbon future must be nuclear energy free. The avoidance of dangerous climate change is a key element in the transformation towards sustainability: climate protection alone cannot guarantee the conservation of humanity's natural life-support systems; however, without climate protection, the essential development opportunities that mankind needs will soon be erased.

There have been plenty of 'great transformations' in the history of mankind. The two most significant, and also the two best-known, are the Neolithic Revolution, i.e. the transition from hunter-gatherer society to agricultural society, and the Industrial Revolution. Whilst the historical transformations were on the whole evolutionary and occurred gradually, developing in stages, humanity must now, for the first time ever, actively bring about and accelerate a great transformation, as otherwise the 2 °C guard rail will soon be broken.

The WBGU has taken this as its starting point, and examines what form a societal search process for the transformation could take, and how the transformative development 'corridor' may be widened. On the one hand, it must be shown how existing measures can have a transformative effect through intensification and bundling. On the other hand, the WBGU also identifies innovative instruments with immediate transformative effect. Overall, conclusions are reached as to what the German federal government, as an important player on the international stage, can do. Equally, the public and society as a whole are also addressed – on a national, European, and even global level; all citizens can make important contributions to the achievement of this Herculean task.

Contribution to the 2012 UN Conference on Sustainable Development in Rio de Janeiro

The WBGU examines the options for a low-carbon transformation from a global perspective, differentiating between developing, newly industrialising, and industrialised countries, and considers the challenges in terms of international cooperation. The forthcoming 2012 UN Conference on Sustainable Development in Rio de Janeiro offers the next opportunity of focusing appropriately, at a UN level, on this issue of the challenges humankind faces. This report is intended as a contribution to this: policy-makers and society shall be supported in the debate on the transformation, and in its accomplishment. The report aims to reassure economic, political and social decision-makers and (future) change agents that the transformation can be successfully realised.

Core Questions

In the following report, the arguments and viewpoints held by the WBGU are laid out on the basis of the core questions cited below. Attempts are made to find answers to these core questions, and to highlight paths for overcoming conflicting aims.

- Is the transformation technologically feasible?
- Are the costs of the transformation financially feasible?
- What are the measures, processes and instruments that are necessary for the transformation into a low-carbon society?
- Which concrete political measures should be introduced immediately?
- What are the roles played by nation state and EU in shaping the searching and transformation process? Do nation states, particularly the democracies, have the strength for huge fundamental changes? Are we seeing the beginnings of cross-border governance and trans- or supranational democracy?
- What is the significance of the social actors in the transformation process?
- What are the opportunities that should be used for bi- and multilateral cooperation?
- What should be achieved at the 2012 UN Conference on Sustainable Development in Rio de Janeiro?
- What are the current knowledge gaps? How can science accompany this process of searching; how would the scientific community have to adapt to the existing challenges?

The recommendations developed by the WBGU, with their different levels of ambition, are intended to be options for policy-makers. The recommended measures are designed to indicate a fundamental pattern for the reversal, in full awareness of the fact that long-running processes such as these are hardly predictable and are therefore inherently searching processes. These searching processes should be initiated and shaped by the state, and accompanied by research. Some of the recommended measures are of a very high level of ambition, so that, from a current point of view, they may still seem unrealistic in political terms; they could, however, become realisable only a few years from now. One example for the 'unthinkable' is the moratorium on Germany's seven oldest nuclear power plants as a consequence of the nuclear catastrophe in Fukushima in March 2011. The temporary shutdown of these nuclear reactors for three months, ordered by the CDU/FDP coalition government, and their vote for an accelerated nuclear phase-out in Germany would have been unimaginable prior to Fukushima. And who would have been able to predict the success of Eastern Europe's 'Velvet Revolution' in 1984; who could have foreseen the 2010/11 revolutions in the Arab world?

Increasing Knowledge

In the past few years, there have been numerous publications on 'low-carbon transformation' or the 'green economy'; however, these studies have frequently focused only on specific elements of the issue (for example technical measures, financial, or governance aspects), and many examined them primarily from a national point of view. In several respects, this report has followed a completely new approach:

1. The transformation into a low-carbon society is examined in its entirety. The technical, social, economical, and legal feasibility is investigated, including currently existing obstacles and barriers.
2. The transformation into a low-carbon society is examined from a global point of view, differentiating between developing, newly industrialising and industrialised countries.
3. Apart from the lessons to be learnt from historical experiences, the findings of transition research are also taken into account.
4. The role of social actors in transformation processes is examined to reveal that they can fulfil a whole range of important functions, for example as catalysts, and that ultimately, the transformation is supported by them.
5. Apart from energy systems, a field which has already enjoyed frequent examination, further central transformation fields such as land use and urbanisation are investigated.
6. All of these recommendations have been developed under consideration of the fact that there is enormous pressure in terms of time: global greenhouse gas emissions must exceed their maximum within the next decade if the avoidance of dangerous climate change is to stand a chance.
7. These elements are the inspiration for the WBGU's guiding principle, and its understanding of the transformation when considering the design of the requisite searching process. This guiding principle is also intended as a foundation for further social debate.

The transformation is feasible!

In terms of dimension, the transformation into a low-carbon society is on par with a new Industrial Revolution in fast motion. Particularly in view of this, it represents an unprecedented challenge in the history of humankind, as it must be based on scientific research and knowledge, and must be accomplished under great time pressure. It should be mentioned here that the WBGU, in the face of this epochal task, faced a dilemma: on the one hand, concrete and implementable, manageable, science-based recommendations for policy-makers and society to facilitate urgently required changes were to be developed; on the other hand, the issue seemed far too complex at times, difficult to grasp, hardly limitable, and teeming with social obstacles and path dependencies that are difficult to overcome. In short: the problem seemed almost unsolvable. Subsequent to some very difficult and controversial – particularly with regard to numerous conflicting aims – as well as constructive debates and (also) interdisciplinary learning processes, the WBGU has reached the ultimate conviction that the great transformation into a low-carbon society is not just necessary, but really feasible. Not least because the required transformation already conforms to the population's predominant value systems in many countries, and can therefore justly, and positively, be regarded as an addition to the subjective life satisfaction of large parts of the population. It is desired by opinion leaders and large parts of the population – and not just in rich countries, either. Because the great transformation offers the chance, as many governments have already recognised, to transform the energy and economic systems whilst at the same time accelerating the catch-up development of the developing and newly industrialising countries, thus advancing global equality. Concurrently, because of the shared responsibility of states and societies, and the responsible interaction of all social actors in this process, the transformation can contribute not only to overcoming the legitimation crisis in democracies, but even also to a strengthening and a revitalisation of democracy.

World in Transition

1

A New Age – The Anthropocene

The extent of environmental changes caused by humankind has altogether reached another dimension since the industrialisation. The population has grown from just under 1 billion then to almost 7 billion today. Energy use, around 600 W per person in agricultural societies, rose to 4,750 W per person in the highly industrialised nations of the north. One important driving factor of this expansion has been the use of fossil energy carriers, which has made possible both intensive agriculture and the huge increase in material flow, amounting to around 10–30 t per person per year in industrial societies (Box 1-2).

Humankind has also reengineered around half of the world's land surface. Humans already use almost a quarter of the biomass produced globally each year on all land (IPCC, 2007a), and over 40% of the renewable, accessible water resources (MA, 2005b). Collectively, various anthropogenic global material and energy fluxes by now far exceed any natural flows. As a consequence, developments in many of the vital environmental dimensions are reaching a crisis stage: water resources, soils, forests and oceans have been overexploited or are being destroyed, biodiversity is undergoing a drastic reduction, and important biochemical flow patterns have been radically changed by humankind, for example the carbon and nitrogen cycles. The Board of the Millennium Ecosystem Assessment has reached the following conclusion: 'Human activity is putting such strain on the natural functions of the Earth that the ability of the planet's ecosystems to sustain future generations can no longer be taken for granted.' (MA, 2005d). Without a doubt, humankind has become the Earth ecosystem's dominating force (Vitousek et al., 1997b).

A great number of scientists therefore support Nobel prize winner Paul Crutzen's proposal of viewing the current industrial age as a new geological epoch (Crutzen and Stoermer, 2000; Crutzen, 2002; Steffen et al., 2007). This geological epoch, called the 'anthropocene' (also 'Menschenzeit' or 'The Age of Man', Schwägerl, 2010), not only refers to the effects humankind has had on the Earth system, but also to the cognitive changes undergone by a global civilisation with an increasing awareness of itself as a driving force. International research therefore initiated relevant, globally coordinated programmes as early as the 1950s (for example the International Geosphere-Biosphere Programme, Man and the Biosphere Programme, etc.) in order to better understand the interdependencies in the Earth system.

Sustainable Development

The beginning of the anthropocene also marks the beginning of a new era of responsibility, as in terms of technology, humankind has by now advanced so far that it could unbalance the Earth system to an extent that would have dire consequences for human societies and ecosystems. The megatrends of a dynamic, globalised economy, together with a population which will in all probability continue to increase up to the middle of the century, are on a collision course headed for the planetary guard rails (Box 1-1). We are currently risking the Earth system's capability of continuing to provide human civilisation with the stable life-support system which made its development over the last 10,000 years possible in the first place.

For the past few decades, international environmental policy has addressed these issues. The Rio de Janeiro Earth Summit in 1992 hailed an important turning point on this relatively new political stage. The concept of sustainable development, debated and further defined since then at environmental conventions and by civil society organisations, has been, at least rhetorically, recognised as the guiding principle that should govern all actions, even if not consistently implemented. Policies for combating global environmental problems are gaining in importance; nevertheless, apart from a few exceptions (for example with regard to stratospheric ozone; Section 1.1.5.3) they have so far failed: negative trends have not abated, on the contrary, in many cases, they have even intensified (Section 1.1.6).

This chapter relates to the agenda of the United Nations Conference on Environment and Develop-

Box 1-1

The WBGU's Concept of Planetary Guard Rails in the Context of Sustainable Development

Certain Earth system conditions must be avoided at all costs. The concept of the Earth system's planetary guard rails has been developed by the WBGU since 1994, with regard to climate change and other areas of global change (soils, biodiversity, etc.; WBGU, 1995a, 2005, 2006). Rockström et al. (2009a, b) adopted the concept, using the term 'planetary boundaries'. International environmental policy even accepted the '2°C climate protection guard rail' as a political target. The WBGU describes planetary guard rails as quantitatively definable damage thresholds, whose transgression either today or in future would have such intolerable consequences that even large-scale benefits in other areas could not compensate these (WBGU, 2006). Once the guard rails have been transgressed, global environmental change becomes a socially intolerable risk for human civilisation.

However, keeping within the limits of all guard rails by no means implies that all socio-economic deficits or ecological damages can be averted, as global guard rails can under no circumstances take all of the widely differing regional and sectoral impacts of global change into account. Furthermore, knowledge about global environmental change is limited and bears the potential for misjudgements. From this perspective, observance of the guard rails is a necessary, but not sufficient, premise for the sustainability of future development.

Guard rails do not demarcate exactly defined system limits, within which there is hardly any risk at all, and beyond which we can immediately expect serious damages or even disasters. The changes which occur are frequently creeping changes, which cumulatively, over decades or generations, will ultimately have extremely negative effects, but which are difficult to perceive and comprehend (the 'shifting baseline' phenomenon; Pauly, 1995). Particularly in view of this gradual systemic change, guard rails can serve as an orientation aid. Nevertheless, especially with regard to the 2°C guard rail, it should be emphasised that the avoidance of Earth system tipping points – for example the irreversible melting of Greenland's ice sheet, the collapse of tropical coral reefs due to global warming, and other non-linear processes – plays a central role in defining the scope. Against this background, scientists are advising policy-makers to establish certain guard rails on the basis of scientific reasoning. Determining the point at which these burdens become intolerable must then take place on the part of the politicians in the form of a democratic decision-making process.

Compliance with the guard rails ensures that the Earth system's resources and services, the precondition for securing humankind's natural life-support systems and sustainable development, can be preserved. In analytical terms, the term 'sustainable development' can be defined as a vector of the respective welfare dimensions (for example, meeting basic needs like food and medical care, criteria for individual qualifications such as education and collective qualifications like institutional legitimacy or benchmarks for a 'good life', such as access to experiencing nature), whose norm increases with time. Temporary increases in some dimensions, for example caused by the consumption of finite resources, must not hinder long-term development opportunities. Guard rails delimit the scope in which development can take place sustainably; transgression of these limits must therefore be avoided.

A timely gradual course adjustment avoids the drastic measures that would be necessary if we were to suddenly 'slam on the brakes' once we reach the guard rail, or rather, once a sudden severe change of course would be the only remaining option. An abrupt change such as this is usually not only associated with tremendous costs, it can also trigger social shifts and crises.

It is therefore paramount to pre-empt and avoid any transgression of the guard rails. Any path on collision course with a guard rail should be changed through suitable policies in such a way as to prevent transgression. The use of appropriate policy instruments, but also self-propelling social processes are major factors for gradually exerting influence over the development path. Anticipatory sustainability policies should aim at a timely achieving of changes, so that the social adaptation to the course change can be managed without excessive breaks and costs. Forward-looking implementation of a policy to prevent climate change is a sensible measure, and also makes far more economic sense than later costly, drastic emissions reductions and adaptation measures.

The setting of guard rails and the subsequent skilful implementation of suitable steering instruments can serve to accelerate a positive pace of development, rather than impeding it. Awareness of planetary guard rails and the appropriate action to be taken can drive humankind's progress. A major 'co-benefit' of the decarbonisation of the energy systems, for instance, is an energy supply that is clean and does not depend on finite fossil resources. Moreover, a fair burden-sharing in terms of decarbonisation efforts also opens up new development prospects, particularly for many poorer countries. Reduced conflict potential, and better conditions, for example with regard to education, diet, medical care, but also more scope for cultural and artistic development, could emerge to give human development a new impetus.

Guard rails and social progress are therefore by no means a contradiction in terms; on the contrary, they are mutually supportive. This certainly applies in the long run, as guard rail transgression endangers the basic requirements for sustainable development. However, even in the short-term, inevitable transformation processes bear the potential for impacting catalytically for advancing human development.

ment (Rio de Janeiro, 1992) and attempts to determine the current status quo of a 'world in transition', not only with reference to global environmental problems (Section 1.1), but also with regard to the dynamic global economic and social megatrends defining an increasingly globalised civilisation (Section 1.2). In this report, the WBGU focuses on the dynamics of the globalisation, reflected in the various megatrends, or the way these dynamics act as drivers. Contemporary crises such as, for example, food and crude oil price spikes, and, not least, the financial and economic crisis (Box 1.2-1) can be regarded as symptoms of an overtaxation of the world's institutional structures in a globalised world, in which cross-linking and critical interdependencies have dramatically increased. Viewed as an entity, these megatrends are a perfect illustration of the necessity of sustainable development, and the required framework conditions. They pose a considerable hindrance to reaching the development goals: not only is a large part of the global population still excluded from the dynamic wealth increase, but in fact, almost 1 billion people actually continue to live in life-threatening poverty (Section 1.2.1).

Some of the major environmental issues, for example climate change (Section 1.1.1), have by now become so urgent that they are generally referred to as a 'task for humankind'. Even if not all of the causes and consequences of the different global environmental change issues or development problems can be elaborated individually here, the final balance sheet not only clearly shows that despite some major successes, the actual challenge of sustainable development remains unsolved, but moreover, that the remaining timeframe for action is fast becoming shorter.

One single WBGU report can hardly provide the extensive analysis and solution search that comprehensive global sustainable development requires. The following chapters focus on climate and energy issues, as climate change mitigation is a central element of sustainability. Anthropogenic climate change is closely interlinked with other environmental issues, frequently creating feedback dynamics (Section 1.1.6). The more extensive the impacts of climate change become, the more difficult it will be to solve other global environmental changes, and to master the challenge of achieving sustainable development in the newly industrialising and developing countries. Moreover, climate change has a 'long braking distance', and must be restricted very quickly indeed if significant negative impacts are to be avoided. For these reasons, this report focuses primarily on the question of how to achieve the change into a low carbon society without undermining sustainability efforts in other essential areas, such as sustainable land use or the conservation of biodiversity.

To bear the context of a more comprehensive sustainability agenda in mind, this chapter briefly summarises the extensive correlation of the various issues. The message is clear: economy and society must urgently undergo a fundamental change to ensure the preservation of humankind's natural life-support systems and the future prospects of humankind. Climate change mitigation is a necessary element; however, alone, it is not sufficient.

1.1 Earth System Megatrends

1.1.1 Climate Change, Climate Impact

By now, there is a scientific consensus on the elemental issues in connection with anthropogenic climate change which has also found acceptance at all political levels. Both IPCC reports (most recently IPCC, 2007a, b, c), and the WBGU's policy advice reports (2003, 2008, 2009a) extensively illustrate and elaborate the scientific basis for anthropogenic greenhouse gas emissions, the consequences for the global mean temperature, the changes in the Earth system, and the effects on ecosystems and human societies.

Rapidly progressing, unabated climate change will constitute a crisis for humankind, as it means that the relatively stable climatic era since the last Ice Age in which human civilisations have developed will come to an end (Figure 1.1-1a). In the past 2,000 years, fluctuations in mean global temperature amounted to less than 1 °C. Neither our agriculture and forestry nor our culture, society, infrastructures, etc. are prepared for a rapid and significant climate change of several degrees Celsius.

Some aspects of climate change are impacting faster than anticipated by science. The deglaciation rate of sea ice, ice sheets and glaciers has been underestimated, for instance (Figure 1.1-1c). Current estimates (Allison et al., 2009) have revised the sea-level rise rate to at least double the rate stated by the IPCC (2007a). The 1m sea-level rise guard rail recommended by the WBGU (2006) could therefore already be broken before the end of the century (Figure 1.1-1b; Rahmstorf, 2007; Vermeer and Rahmstorf, 2009). CO_2 emissions are also responsible for another global environmental problem: ocean acidification (Box 1.1-2).

By now, avoiding global warming of more than 2 °C has not only become the generally declared aim of scientists, but also that of politicians. Global warming of more than 2 °C would probably have dangerous, irreversible and hardly controllable consequences for nature and human society (WBGU, 1995b, 2007a). As yet, it is still possible to comply with this limit, but the technical, economic and political challenges are considerable (UNEP, 2010a).

The 16th Conference of the Parties to the United Nations Framework Convention on Climate Change (UNFCCC) in Cancún not only made it perfectly clear that climate change is one of the greatest challenges of our time, but also that the climate change mitiga-

Box 1-2

The Concept of Industrial Metabolism

For consumers, household waste is an obvious result of modern life. Each inhabitant of an industrialised country with a typical lifestyle generates around 400–600 kg per year, largely due to consumer goods packaging, for example around food. The environmentally friendly disposal of this waste continues to inspire heated social debates. Less obvious for the consumer, on the other hand, is the prior environmental impact 'upstream' in a product's lifecycle (Figure 1-1).

In total, these often by far exceed the resource investment ultimately evident to consumers in the form of household waste. To manufacture an aluminium can containing fruit juice, for instance, bauxite must first be extracted, the electricity for the melting process must be generated, crude-oil based coatings and packaging also have to be produced, etc. Moreover, all upstream input and processes are connected by transport networks which themselves are resource-intensive. Fruit production, drinks manufacture, cold chains and distribution to retailer and, ultimately, consumer also contribute to the environmental impact. Process chain analysis methods ('lifecycle assessment') have been developed to illustrate the environmental impact of the entire lifecycle of a product 'cradle to grave'. This strategic approach to environmental reporting allows, for example, comparisons between a circular economy, which continues to recycle the same material resources, from 'cradle to cradle', and conventional 'linear' resource use. It also allows the linking of consumption patterns, production processes and resource consumption, and highlights alternative action choices (UNEP, 2010c).

At a higher aggregation level, it also serves to describe the cumulative social-industrial metabolism for individual industrial sectors, region and countries, and at global level (Ayres and Simonis, 1994; Figure 1-2). In this account, the social activity based anthroposphere is viewed as an integral element of the global biosphere. This perspective serves to describe environmental impact not only on the output side (as an overload of the sink capacities of environmental systems, for example through nutrient-rich waste waters, greenhouse gases, etc.), but also on the input side as resource scarcity or overuse of renewable or non-renewable sources.

From this perspective, a typical inhabitant of an industrialised country directly consumes around 10–20 t of material every year (excluding water and air, and indirect material consumption, for instance through induced soil erosion) to sustain themselves and their livestock, and support the technical infrastructure (assets, commodities, buildings, transport networks, etc.). In the industrialised countries, these material flows consist of around a third each of fossil energy carriers, biomass (food, feed, wood and fibres) and mineral resources (construction and industrial minerals). This entire process, just like the biological metabolism concept, can be represented as an energetic process, and also in the form of a material balance (input = output + net stock changes). Output can be differentiated according to target medium: into the atmosphere (such as greenhouse gases, dust or aerosols), into soils, or rather, the geosphere (for example landfills), or into the hydrosphere (as waste water). In industrialised countries, emissions are usually dominated by CO_2.

Figure 1-3 illustrates current material consumption trends and global freight traffic volume in the 20th century. Direct material extraction rose from around 7 to around 59 billion t annually (or from 4.5 to 9 t per person per year). At the same time, the transport of goods has increased since 1850 to about 10,000 t km per person per year. The global market integration is leading to ever longer distances between raw material extraction, production and consumption. Integrated methods for the analysis and illustration of the environmental impacts

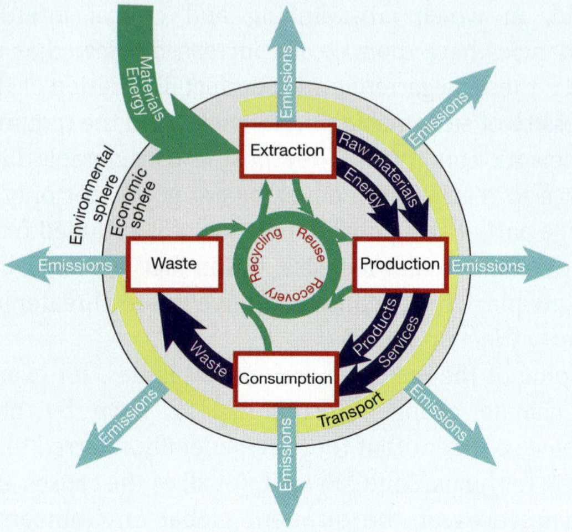

Figure 1-1
Industrial metabolism: schematic illustration of material use, production, consumption and emissions.
Source: based on EEA, 2010a

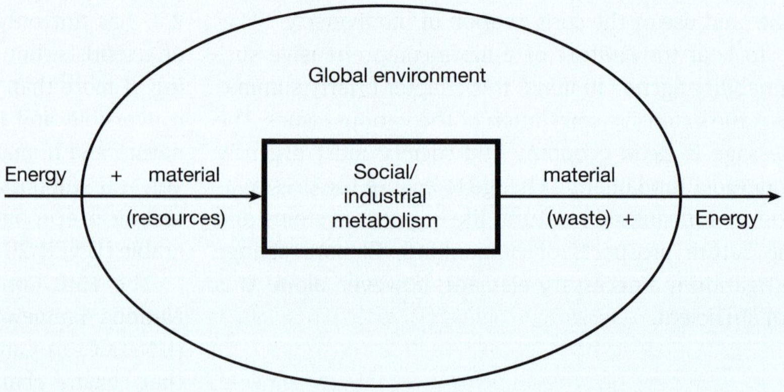

Figure 1-2
Socio-economic metabolism as a component part of the global environment.
Source: based on Odum, 1971

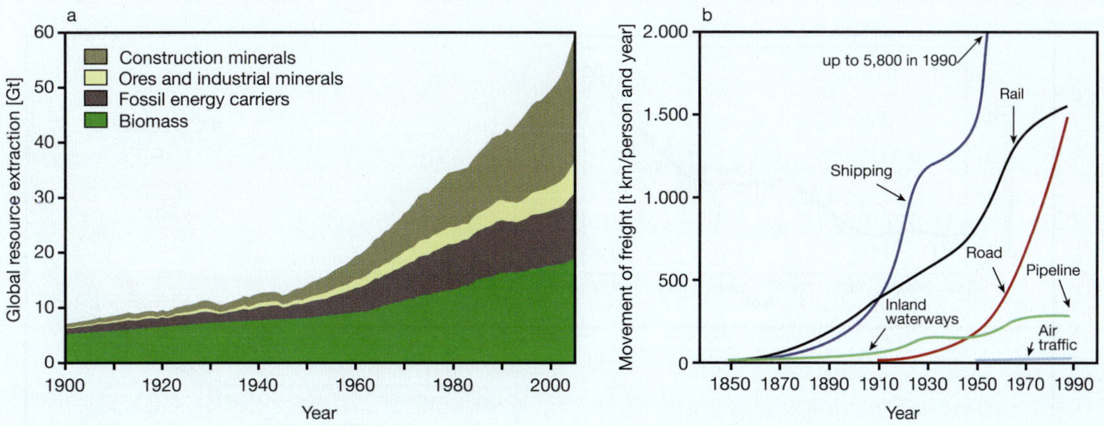

Figure 1-3
Direct resource extraction 1900–2005 (a) and development of global freight volume 1850–1990 (b).
Sources: Gilbert, 2001; Krausmann et al., 2009

of consumption are therefore called for. Such balances make it possible to connect environmental impact with the driving forces of social activity (OECD, 2008). They not only serve to illustrate how the environment is changing, but why, making strategic and preventative policy decisions easier.

Numerous industrialised countries and international organisations such as the OECD and the EU now record the national direct material consumption, and the resource intensity of their economic activities, as part of national environmental statistics. The Statistical Office of the European Communities has developed basic methodical principles for the generation of such an accounting system as part of the overall economic balance (Eurostat, 2001). Achieving sustainable consumption patterns through green growth strategies requires an increased decoupling of resource consumption and economic growth and, in the long term, a circular economy for material resources. Relevant programmes to encourage environmentally friendly production strategies with slogans such as the '3 R Principle: Reduce, Reuse, Recycle' are being supported by a number of UN organisations, for example UNIDO and UNEP, within the scope of the Marrakech Process. To improve the knowledge base and scientific policy consultation in this field, UNEP has established an International Panel for Sustainable Resource Management (for example UNEP, 2010d).

tion guard rail must not be transgressed, and that deep cuts in global greenhouse gas emissions are required (UNFCCC, 2010). In fact, there is some debate on whether this maximum damage threshold should be lowered only 1.5 °C.

CO_2 accumulates in the atmosphere due to its long life-span, so further global warming can only be prevented if the CO_2 emissions from fossil sources are stopped almost completely. The extent of anthropogenic climate change depends largely on how quickly global CO_2 emissions can be successfully reduced. Analyses of plausible emissions pathways show that a maximum of around 750 Gt CO_2 from fossil sources may be released into the atmosphere up to the middle of the century to allow a two-thirds probability of compliance with the 2 °C guard rail (Box 1.1-1). Post-2050, only a small, remaining amount of CO_2 may be emitted. The era of the fossil energy driven economy must therefore end as soon as in the first half of this century (WBGU, 2009). Global emissions should peak as soon as possible; at the latest, however, by 2020, as otherwise, the reduction rates that would be necessary by 2050 would be so drastic as to overburden the technical, economical and social capacities of our societies (Figure 1.1-2).

The world is still a long way away from this vital trend reversal. Despite 2008's financial and economic crisis, global CO_2 emissions from the use of fossil fuels only fell by 1.3% in consequence; 2009 was still the year with the second-highest emissions in the history of humankind, with 2008 in the lead. The preliminary results for 2010 show that this emissions decline has probably already been overcompensated and emissions are continuing on their pre-crisis growth path (Friedlingstein et al., 2010). The 2010 average concentration of CO_2 in the atmosphere already amounted to 389 ppm (Tans, 2011), compared to approx. 280 ppm before the Industrial Revolution (IPCC, 2007a). Limiting climate change requires the immediate decoupling of economic growth from greenhouse gas emissions. These do not only include CO_2, which is primarily released through the combustion of fossil energy carriers (Section 1.2.3), but also other climate-impacting gases (CH_4, N_2O, and industrial gases). Other sectors in which emissions must also fall drastically include land use and industry (WBGU, 2007a).

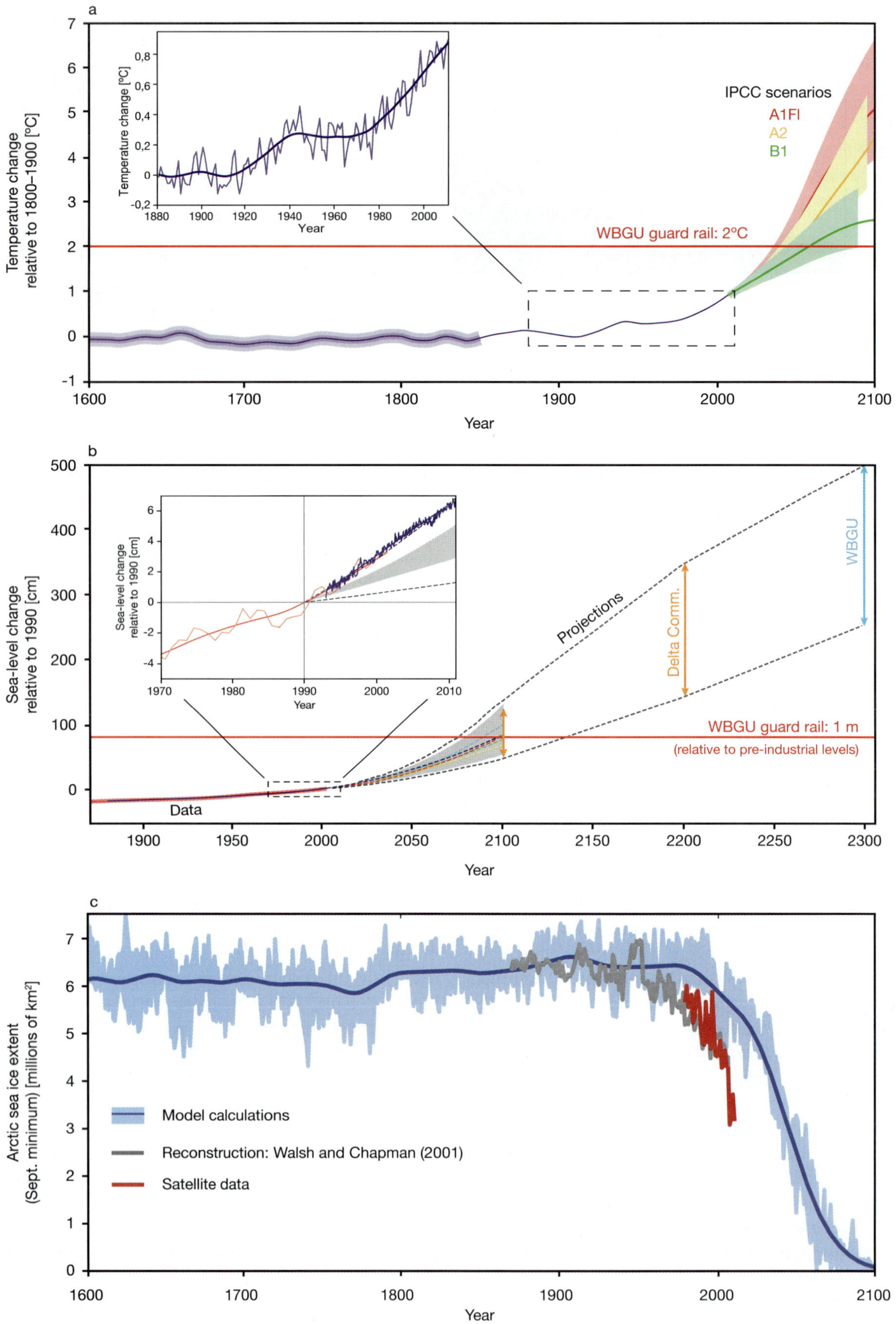
a
Temperature change relative to 1800–1900 [°C]
Temperature change [°C]
Year
IPCC scenarios
A1FI
A2
B1
WBGU guard rail: 2°C
Year
b
Sea-level change relative to 1990 [cm]
Sea-level change relative to 1990 [cm]
Year
Projections
Delta Comm.
WBGU
WBGU guard rail: 1 m
(relative to pre-industrial levels)
Data
Year
c
Arctic sea ice extent (Sept. minimum) [millions of km²]
Model calculations
Reconstruction: Walsh and Chapman (2001)
Satellite data
Year

Figure 1.1-1
Development over time of temperature, sea-level and Arctic sea ice extent.
a) Past (Mann et al., 2008) and future (IPCC, 2007a) global temperature curve. Three different emission scenarios are shown (B1, A2 and A1FI); the coloured areas are the associated climatological uncertainty spans. Without successful climate change mitigation measures, the 2°C guard rail would be transgressed even in the most optimistic scenario (B1; green). Inset: recorded temperatures to 2010 (NASA, 2011). The measured data shows annual values for global temperature relative to the 1880–1920 average, and an adjusted climate trend line.
b) Current projections of global sea-level rise up to 2300 (relative to 1990). Red: WBGU guard rail of 1m above the pre-industrial level (WBGU, 2006). As the sea level has risen by around 15 centimetres between the beginning of industrialisation and 1990, the line is here shown at less than 1 m. Data: Sea-level data based on Church and White (2006). Projections: grey area and dotted lines based on Rahmstorf (2007); orange bar based on Delta Committee (2008); light blue bar based on WBGU (2006). The differing assumptions underlying these projections are explained in the sources cited. Inset: orange: sea-level data based on Church and White (2006); blue: satellite data up to 2010, updated based on Cazenave et al. (2008); grey area and dotted lines: projections from the IPCC Third Assessment Report (IPCC, 2001).
c) Extent of Arctic sea ice at the summer minimum (September), according to observed data, reconstruction (Walsh and Chapman, 2001) and a series of model calculations by the Max Planck Institute for Meteorology, Hamburg (based on Jungclaus et al., 2010).
Source: based on WBGU, 2009, amended

The negotiations for a global climate treaty commenced in 1990, and led to the UNFCCC in 1992. Today, with 192 signatories, it enjoys almost universal membership. Its most important achievement is the formulation of a common climate change mitigation goal, to succeed in stabilising the greenhouse gas concentrations in the atmosphere at a level that would prevent dangerous anthropogenic interference with the climate system (UN, 1992). Its framework convention character, however, means that complementing decisions for implementation are needed. Since 1995, many such decisions have been agreed in 16 Conferences of the Parties (COP) to date, including the Kyoto Protocol in 1997. It contains binding emissions targets for industrialised countries for the period 2008–2012, and was designed to allow for subsequent commitment periods. However, the protocol was never ratified by the industrialised countries' largest emitter, the USA, and the negotiations on further commitment periods in Cancún in 2010 were also fraught with difficulties. Although only moderately ambitious (the industrialised countries committed to reducing their emissions by 5%, compared to 1990 levels, for the period 2008–2012), the Kyoto Protocol has frequently been viewed as a trial run for climate change mitigation instruments (such as the trading of allowed emissions between parties, and the Clean Development Mechanism), and has certainly contributed much to testing these. Negotiations on long-term international cooperation have been ongoing since COP 13 in 2007 on Bali. So far, however, the hope that these will ultimately lead to a comprehensive and legally binding agreement that can be operationalised has not been fulfilled. The negotiations do not only concern climate change mitigation, but also increasingly adaptation to climate change. Central unresolved issues are aspects of equity, particularly with regard to the industrialised countries' responsibility to support the developing countries' climate change mitigation and adaptation efforts both financially and with technology transfers. Progress has been made, however, with regard to a consensus on the overall ambition level of climate protection efforts; the view that the rise in temperature must be limited to 2 °C or even 1.5 °C has become prevalent in the debate (UNFCCC, 2010). However, the resultant consequences with regard to the required measures have so far been ignored. The 'Cancún Agreements' that have been passed at COP 16 could make the further negotiation process somewhat easier as some aspects have been preliminarily agreed; however, the important question of future emissions reductions is by and large excluded.

To summarise, it can be stated that although the UNFCCC and its decisions currently provide adequate goals in terms of the general aspiration level, these are not acted upon and remain abstract, nor are they supported by appropriate concrete measures. Currently, nothing would support the expectation that the sum total of the climate change mitigation measures and targets planned by the states themselves, and reported to the convention, will be enough to avoid global warming of more than 2 °C. A binding agreement which would oblige the states to develop and keep to adequate plans does not appear to be on the horizon.

1.1.2
Loss of Ecosystem Services and Biodiversity

Humankind has also had a dramatic impact on the biosphere. At a rapidly increasing speed, forests, savannahs and grasslands are being cleared to make way for agriculture. Globally, more than three-quarters of the ice-free landmass is showing signs of anthropogenic change, and around a third of this area is used for agriculture, this looks likely to increase (Ellis and Ramankutty, 2008; Ramankutty et al., 2008). A growing

Box 1.1-1

The Global CO_2 Emissions Budget

Recent studies have shown that in the long run, CO_2's already major impact in terms of climate change, compared to more short-lived greenhouse gases and aerosols, will become even more dominant due to its long life-time in the atmosphere (Allen et al., 2009; Meinshausen et al., 2009). The WBGU focused on this fact in its special report 'Solving the climate dilemma: The budget approach' (WBGU, 2009). As more recent emissions data has now become available, the following reviews the still permissible CO_2 budget. According to Meinshausen et al. (2009), the emission of 1,160 Gt CO_2 from anthropogenic sources between 2000 and 2050 leads to 2°C guard rail transgression with a probability of 33%. Based on data from CDIAC (2011), Le Quére et al. (2009) and GCP (2011), the WBGU estimates that for the period 2000–2010, CO_2 emissions from fossil sources and cement production amounted to 314 Gt CO_2, and emissions from land-use changes to 45 Gt CO_2; i.e. according to this estimate, anthropogenic CO_2 emissions for the period 2000–2010 amounted to approx. 360 Gt CO_2 in total. This would leave a permissible budget of approx. 800 Gt CO_2 for emissions from anthropogenic sources between 2011 and 2050 if compliance with the 2°C guard rail is to carry a probability of two-thirds. What does this mean in terms of emissions from fossil sources? Friedlingstein et al. (2010) cite an average 4.0 Gt annual CO_2 emissions from land-use changes for the period 2000–2009. The Parties to the Convention on Biological Diversity have set themselves the target of at least halving the natural ecosystem loss rate, including forests, by 2020 (CBD, 2010b). If therefore the respective emissions were successfully halved by 2020, and would subsequently continue to sink at the same rate down to zero, CO_2 emissions from land-use change between now and 2050 could be limited to 40 Gt. However, if these emissions were not halved until 2030, and not reduced to zero until 2050, it would mean emissions of 80 Gt CO_2. Therefore, depending on how successfully CO_2 emissions from land-use change are contained, i.e. above all by reducing deforestation in the tropics (Section 4.1.7), 720–760 Gt CO_2 from fossil sources could still be emitted by 2050. Raising the probability of limiting anthropogenic global warming to 2°C to 75% would reduce the permissible budget for CO_2 from fossil sources to 560–600 Gt CO_2. If deforestation is not successfully contained, this budget will shrink even further.

Particularly due to new, significantly lower estimates of land-use emissions since 2000 (Friedlingstein et al., 2010), the 750 Gt CO_2 estimate cited in the WBGU budget for 2010–2050 therefore still applies as a rough guideline for the permissible 2011–2050 budget. Figure 1.1-2 depicts three schematic pathways of global CO_2 emissions from fossil fuels that would be compatible with such a budget. It becomes clear that the evident consequence of a temporal shift in the global emissions peak is that the required reduction rates in order to comply with the budget are substantially higher in later years.

Although the dominant warming effect originates from CO_2 emissions, these calculations also include the impact of the other greenhouse gases regulated by the Kyoto Protocol. It is assumed that the cumulated emissions of these other greenhouse gases for the period 2010–2049 will amount to approx. 500 Gt CO_2eq (Meinshausen et al., 2009).

Figure 1.1-2
Examples of global emission pathways with emissions of 750 Gt CO_2 between 2010 and 2050.
Source: WBGU, 2009

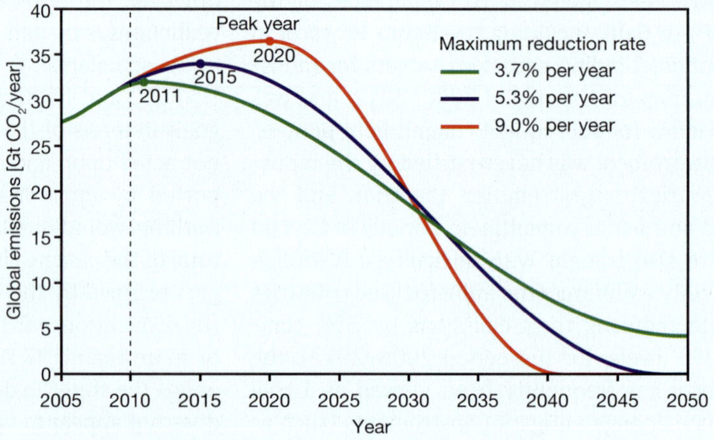

global population, which also becomes more demanding (for example concerning the consumption of animal products), increased bioenergy production and biomass use, and an expanding infrastructure are major reasons for growing land-use pressures (WBGU, 2010a; van Vuuren, 2009; PBL, 2010; Section 1.2.5). Moreover, coral reefs and mangrove forests are being destroyed, lakes over-fertilised, rivers dammed, and fish resources overexploited (WBGU, 2001b, 2006; MA, 2005b; CBD, 2010b). All this leads to a massive loss of biodiversity: compared to the natural background rate, the current rate of extinction of floral and faunal species has already increased by a factor of between a hundred and a thousand (MA, 2005b). In the extensively studied species groups, a large proportion is considered endangered or already extinct (22% of mammals, 14% of birds, 31% of amphibians, 28% of conifers and 52% of cycads; Vié et al., 2008), current conservation measures appear to be inadequate (for example Hoffmann et al., 2010).

Box 1.1-2

Ocean Acidification

CO_2 emissions not only lead to climate change, but also directly impact ocean chemistry. So far, around a third of anthropogenic CO_2 emissions have been absorbed by the oceans, and turned into carbonic acid in the ocean water, thus leading to a measurable acidification (The Royal Society, 2005). This has already led to an approx. 30% rise in the concentration of hydrogen ions, equalling a reduction of around 0.11 units of pH value compared to pre-industrial levels (WBGU, 2006). Acidification is progressing at least 100 times faster than ever before in the past 20 million years (Rockström et al., 2009b). The fact that the atmospheric CO_2 concentration has already been higher in earlier ages is not a counterargument, as the acidification is particularly caused by the pace of the CO_2 increase, which decouples it from natural chemical buffer processes (WBGU, 2006).

Unabated continuation of this trend would lead to acidification of the oceans that is unparalleled over the past millions of years, and irreversible for thousands of years. Acidification impedes the growth of calcifying organisms (for example corals, mussels, snails and certain groups of plankton), leads to biodiversity loss, can create anoxic death zones in oceans (Hofmann and Schellnhuber, 2009), changes the biogeochemical dynamics in sea water (for example of calcium carbonate, organic carbon, nitrogen and phosphorus; Doney et al., 2009), and generally endangers the existence of marine ecosystems (for example coral reefs; Hoegh-Guldberg et al., 2009). These fundamental changes can have far reaching consequences for the millions of people who, directly or indirectly, depend on the ocean (Doney et al., 2009).

The WBGU has proposed the following guard rail: the pH level of the near-surface ocean layer should not fall in any major ocean region by more than 0.2 units against pre-industrial levels (WBGU, 2006). Rockström et al. (2009a, b) have chosen a different indicator and suggest that the calcium carbonate saturation (of aragonite) should amount to at least 80% of the pre-industrial value $\Omega = 3.44$, so that the near-surface layers are not undersaturated, enabling most coral systems to survive. The acidification issue alone is reason enough to restrict CO_2 emissions. Climate policies should therefore ensure that anthropogenic CO_2 emissions are restricted independently of the reduction of other greenhouse gas emissions. So far, the special role of CO_2 has not been adequately taken into account in UNFCCC negotiations.

Human societies need resources which nature delivers: food, fibres, building materials and industrial raw materials are just some examples. We also depend on ecosystem services: coastal protection, freshwater supply, pollination, soil fertility, unpolluted air, etc. (MA, 2005c). Not least, we need floral and faunal species because their genetic and physiological blueprints are vital for the further development of useful crops to safeguard global food security, or for medical and technical research (WBGU, 2001a; Chivian and Bernstein, 2008).

As biodiversity and ecosystem services have the character of public goods which are not traded on markets, and which do not carry a specific price tag, the economic system hugely underestimates their importance (Sukhdev, 2008; TEEB, 2010). In consequence, the degradation and destruction of natural ecosystems and the diversity of their species and gene pools continues, so that considerable loss of biodiversity can be expected in this century (Pereira et al., 2010). The 6th extinction crisis of species in geological history is an imminent danger, irreversible and, this time round, caused by humankind (Leakey and Lewin, 1996; Chapin III et al., 2000). This new mass extinction can only be avoided through strict protection of the endangered species (Barnosky et al., 2011).

The disappearance of species and genes renders the remaining ecosystems more vulnerable to disturbances (Suding et al., 2008). In addition to the large-scale land-use changes mentioned above, climate change (Section 1.1.1), the considerable intensification of nutrient cycles (Section 1.1.5), and the global dispersal of invasive alien species through increasing intercontinental traffic (Figure 1-3b) constitute further global disturbances which have greatly increased since the industrialisation, straining the ecosystems even further. Unabated climate change alone means risking the irretrievable loss of 20–30% of floral and faunal species (IPCC, 2007b). This increases the risk of sudden, non-linear and unforeseeable changes in ecosystems (Scheffer et al., 2001; Hastings and Wysham, 2010), which can even affect ecosystem structures of continental dimensions and extensive oceanic regions (Scheffer, 2009; for example collapse of cod stocks off the shore of Newfoundland, Hutchings and Myers, 1994; Amazonas region: WBGU, 2008). The ability of the planet's ecosystems to provide the natural life-support systems needed to sustain future generations can therefore no longer be taken for granted (MA, 2005d).

In economic terms, as with climate change, the timely avoidance, or at least limiting, of the problem is considerably more viable than a later repair of the damages (TEEB, 2010; Table 1.1-1).

A planetary guard rail for the loss of biodiversity is particularly difficult to define, due to the diversity of species, their extremely varied importance for the functioning of the ecosystems, and the huge knowledge gaps. As nature reserves are one of the most important instruments for the conservation of biodiversity and ecosystem services, they are suitable as a rough indicator for biosphere protection. The WBGU proposed the following guard rail for biosphere conservation (2006):

Table 1.1-1
Estimates of cost and benefits of restoration projects in different biomes.
Source: Sukhdev, 2008

Biomes or ecosystems	Typical cost of restoration (high scenario) [US$/ha]	Estimated annual benefits from restoration (average scenario) [US$/ha]	Net present value of benefit over 40 years [US$/ha]	Internal rate of return [%]	Benefit/ cost ratio
Coral reefs	542,500	129,200	1,166,000	7	2.8
Coastal ecosystems	232,700	73,900	935,400	11	4.4
Mangroves	2,880	4,290	86,900	40	26.4
Inland wetlands	33,000	14,200	171,300	12	5.4
Lakes and rivers	4,000	3,800	69,700	27	15.5
Tropical forests	3,450	7,000	148,700	50	37.3
Other forests	2,390	1,620	26,300	20	10.3
Woodland and shrubland	990	1,571	32,180	42	28.4
Grasslands	260	1,010	22,600	79	75.1

10–20% of the global area of terrestrial ecosystems, and 20–30% of the area of marine ecosystems should be designated as parts of a global, ecologically representative and effectively managed system of protected areas. At the 10th Conference of the Parties in Nagoya, the Convention on Biological Diversity (CBD) defined its targets by 2020 as increasing protected areas on land to 17%, and marine areas to 10% (CBD, 2010a). Although officially, around 12% of global land areas are already under protection (BIP, 2010), the existing protected area systems are neither adequately representative, nor sufficiently well planned, financed or managed (CBD, 2004). Moreover, even a perfectly functioning system of protected areas cannot halt the loss of biological diversity alone. This needs sustainable land use of cultivated areas, the linking of protected areas with the surrounding countryside, and the restriction of climate change and ocean acidification. Rockström et al. (2009a, b) base their planetary boundary on the species extinction rate, and believe that a rate ten times that of the natural background rate of species extinction is a limit beyond which adverse large-scale system changes cannot be excluded. However, the current extinction rate of floral and faunal species is today already 100–1,000 times higher than the natural background rate, and this rate is set to increase further (MA, 2005b), so in essence, using this parameter, humankind has already broken this boundary and is deep within the danger zone (Rockström et al., 2009b).

The CBD is viewed as the most important international agreement on biodiversity. There are also further intergovernmental agreements, focusing on certain aspects of biodiversity. The CBD has endeavoured to improve implementation of the agreed targets in the Parties to the Convention since 1993, with the aid of work programmes, standard setting and finance transfers for developing countries. The international community's target of significantly reducing the biodiversity loss rate by 2010 has not been reached: since then, the loss rate has even gained momentum. Not one of the 21 sub-targets agreed has been achieved, and significant progress has been made in only four of these subtargets. Of the 15 indicators included, two are pointing upwards, three show no clear trend, and eleven indicate a worsening of the situation (CBD, 2010b). Models show that without a fresh political approach, the loss of biodiversity will continue (PBL, 2010). A new strategic plan was drafted at the Conference of the Parties in Nagoya. It intends to stop the loss of biodiversity and to establish the basis for this by 2020 (CBD, 2010a). However, despite some ambitious target setting on the part of the existing global institutions, a trend reversal in the area of biodiversity has not yet been achieved.

1.1.3 Land Degradation and Desertification

Land degradation is caused primarily by deforestation, overgrazing, the expansion of non-sustainable agricultural production, soil salinisation, soil sealing, and urban growth (IAASTD, 2009; UNEP, 2002, 2007). According to UNEP, around 20,000–50,000 km^2 of productive land are lost annually, mainly through soil erosion (UNEP, 2007). Assessments regarding the extent of land degradation vary, depending on the methodical approach used. However, the consensus in the scientific community is that unabatedly progressing land degradation and desertification represent global problems which will considerably limit the scope for action with regard to agricultural production, nature conservation, water catchment areas and forests, and not least climate change mitigation in the coming decades (Eswaran et al., 2001; MA, 2005e).

The first global assessment of land area degradation, based on expert opinions, was the Global Assessment of Human Induced Soil Degradation (GLASOD) presented by the International Soil Reference and Information Centre in 1990, which included changes over the past centuries (WBGU, 1995a). GLASOD estimates that globally, between 1940 and 1990, slightly less than 2 billion hectares of land (the equivalent of 15% of global land area) were subjected to anthropogenic degradation, with all countries being affected (Oldeman et al., 1990, 1991). Subsequently, 65% of agriculturally used land showed signs of degradation, of which 25% were moderate, and 40% strong, or very strong. Recent research also including satellite data concludes that globally, degradation has affected around a third of the arable land (IAASTD, 2009). Drylands are seen as particularly prone to soil degradation, especially desertification (MA, 2005e; Hutchinson and Herrmann, 2008).

Unlike GLASOD, the latest interim findings report by the Land Degradation Assessment in Drylands (LADA; Bai et al., 2008) shows that over a fifth of global arable land is affected by degradation. This report is based on satellite data on net primary production, and empirical in situ analyses between 1981 and 2003. According to LADA, improved soil canopy can also be observed in almost 16% of global terrestrial land areas: 18% on arable land, 23% in forests, and 43% on pastures. Two factors which have led to a partial improvement of the vegetation canopy, or biomass production, are additional irrigation, and large-scale reforestation projects.

However, from a global perspective, in comparison with soil improvement, land degradation is the dominating trend: in many developing countries, land degradation threatens food security and the development potential of rural areas (WBGU, 2010a).

A sensible measure to support the avoidance of further land degradation would be the agreement of a planetary guard rail for global soil protection. Rockström et al. (2009a) propose that a maximum of 15% of the total global terrestrial area should be used for agriculture. To date, slightly less than 12% has already been converted. The WBGU has suggested the stabilisation of the natural yield potential in 300–500 years as a planetary guard rail for anthropogenic soil degradation (WBGU, 2010a). Soil loss should not exceed soil reformation. Depending on soil properties, a tolerance limit could be set to achieve this. In the temperate zone, the WBGU envisages a tolerance limit of 1–10 t soil loss per hectare per year.

The United Nations Convention to Combat Desertification (UNCCD) addresses land degradation and desertification, important areas for development cooperation for many decades now. Effective climate change mitigation can hardly be achieved without sustainable land use. To date, desertification has caused the release of an estimated 18–28 Gt C (the equivalent of 66–103 Gt CO_2) of soil carbon (FAO, 2009d). Grasslands and pasture are major potential carbon sinks: through the sustainable management of grassland areas and the restoration of degraded grassland, 100–800 Mt CO_2 could be stored globally each year (FAO, 2009d).

Considering the importance of soil protection and sustainable land use, the global institutions dealing with these areas do not have a very high profile. Of the three 'Rio conventions', the desertification convention has always been somewhat neglected in international environmental policy-making. Whilst there is at least an international agreement on combating land degradation in drylands, there is still no sign of any comprehensive, global, legally binding regulation addressing this issue beyond drylands or forest protection.

1.1.4
Water Shortage and Water Pollution

Overall freshwater use has increased almost eight-fold over the last century (Shiklomanov, 2000), and is continuing to grow by about 10% each decade. A growing global population with rising demands will also lead to a considerably increased future water demand, particularly because of the continued growth in irrigation agriculture.

Humankind's impact on the global water balance increases every year (Shiklomanov and Rodda, 2003); currently, over 40% of renewable, accessible water resources are subject to anthropogenic use or control (MA, 2005b). Increasingly, the problem is not simply overuse, but also water pollution. Agriculture (salinisation, nutrient and sediment contamination), industry and households (nutrients and pollutants) pollute lakes, rivers and coastal waters, causing considerable ecological, health and development problems (IWMI, 2007). Groundwater tables are falling in many water catchment areas, many large rivers are overused, badly polluted and biologically depleted, a quarter of these do not reach the sea any more due to massive water use (for example the Yellow River in China; the Colorado in North America).

In some regions, water crises have already exacerbated serious social conflicts (WBGU, 2008). A third of the world population is affected by water scarcity; approximately 1.1 billion people do not have access to clean drinking water. Water pollution is an equally critical problem: 2.6 billion people do not have access to basic sanitation facilities, posing a serious threat to human health (UNDP, 2006). A lack of clean water causes diseases and is one of the most common causes of child mortality in developing countries. At 17%, gastrointestinal infections were the most common cause of death of children under 5 in developing countries, killing 1.8 million globally in 2000 (UNESCO, 2009). Climate change exacerbates these problems. It will negatively impact the water balance in many regions, affecting the amount of water available, or impair its seasonal distribution (IPCC, 2007b; WBGU, 2008).

This inspired the agreement of one of the Millennium Development Goals, to halve the number of people without access to water by 2015, compared to 1990 levels (Millennium Development Goal 7, Target 10; UN, 2010). This goal is achievable if the appropriate efforts are made, even though it is unlikely that the situation will improve in some regions, for instance in sub-Saharan Africa or Oceania (UNICEF and WHO, 2004; WBGU, 2005).

Rockström et al. (2009a) propose a planetary boundary for global freshwater use. Removing more than a total of around 4,000 km^3 of water from all rivers, lakes and ground water ('blue water') per year harbours a significant risk of non-linear system responses (major shifts in water balance, collapse of ecosystems), both on a regional and continental scale. Although current usage of around 2,600 km^3 per year, with a rapidly rising tendency, leaves some room to manoeuvre, this will in all probability not be the case anymore by 2050 due to the necessary agricultural expansion and intensification.

A globally agreed framework for a sustainable freshwater policy along the lines of the three Rio conventions has so far not been set by the international community. Other than climate, freshwater is an environmental good whose protection and sustainable use can often be achieved most efficiently locally, in the respective water catchment areas. In view of this, regional or national solutions appear more sensible. However, as water scarcity and pollution of freshwater resources are also a trend that can be observed on a global level, there is also a need for a global regulation or agreement. Contrary to the three Rio conventions, global water policy is a dialogue process, organised by a non-governmental organisation, the World Water Council. Every three years, a World Water Forum is held in which all stakeholders participate (UN, states, NGOs, private sector, science, etc.) to advance the dialogue on sustainable freshwater use.

1.1.5 Raw Materials, Nutrients, Pollutants

For around the past 150 years, mineral material flows have increased drastically. Coal and ores, crude oil, and natural gas are the best-known examples of the extraction of finite raw materials fuelling the global economy since the Industrial Revolution. Some of these resources are now becoming scarce (Section 4.1.2; Figure 1-3a).

However, artificially manufactured nitrogen fertilisers and the extraction of mineral phosphor deposits (Box 1.1-3) are also vital for providing the growing global population with food, and for agriculture in general. Effective climate change mitigation requires the conversion of large parts of the economic system, not least in terms of energy supply and mobility (Section 4). In this context, the focus is now on other mineral resources, which will be required in considerably large volumes in future, and which are relatively rare, or whose deposits are distributed extremely disproportionately; Section 1.1.5.1 cites some examples of these.

Anthropogenic pollutant emissions have led to numerous global environmental problems and adverse effects on people's health: greenhouse gases change the Earth atmosphere's radiation balance (Section 1.1.1); nutrients enter the biosphere and provoke changes in ecosystems on a large scale; stratospheric ozone layer depleting substances are still being released into the atmosphere (Section 1.1.5.3); regionally, aerosol particles sometimes have an extremely adverse effect on both people and ecosystems; toxic chemicals which are hazardous to health are released into the environment. Not least, in consequence, water pollution is becoming an increasingly critical development problem (Section 1.1.4).

The following is limited to outlining only a few of these problems by way of examples.

1.1.5.1 Increasing Scarcity of Strategic Mineral Resources: Examples

Lithium

Almost a third of the globally extracted lithium is used in modern batteries, found in, for example, mobile telephones and notebook computers. Even today, lithium batteries already exhibit an annual growth rate of around 20%. The massive expansion of electromobility would increase lithium battery demand even further (USGS, 2010a). There has been some controversy

Box 1.1-3

Peak phosphorus

Besides nitrogen and potassium, phosphorus is one of the three main components of artificial fertilisers. Whilst nitrogen can be obtained from the air in practically unlimited quantities using the energy-intensive Haber-Bosch process, phosphorus is a scarce finite resource which, unlike for example crude oil, is irreplaceable by other energy carriers or substances. Phosphorus is indispensable as a crop nutrient to ensure the required increase in productivity per crop area to maintain the food security of a growing world population, and to meet the rising demand for bioenergy and bio-based products from land use (Section 1.2.5). Almost 60% of phosphorus reserves of approx. 16 billion t are in Morocco and China (although China does not export); South Africa and the USA are next on the list (USGS, 2010c). Cordell et al. (2009) estimate that the extraction maximum (peak phosphorus) could already be reached in 2030; according to Déry and Anderson (2007), the peak has even already been exceeded in 1989. As with crude oil (peak oil), the quality of the remaining phosphate minerals subsequently declines, leading to rising production costs. Unlike oil, however, phosphates cannot be substituted, but they can be recycled. Important coping strategies are the more efficient use of phosphate fertiliser, the completion of nutrient cycles in agricultural production, particularly through the use of organic fertilisers, and the reclamation of nutrients from waste water. Despite the future major importance of this problem in terms of food security, it is still not on the international political agenda (Vaccari, 2009; Cordell, 2010; Craswell et al., 2010).

on whether lithium scarcity could actually prevent the large-scale use of electric cars (for example Tahil, 2007; Meridian International Research, 2008; Evans, 2008). According to US Geological Survey calculations (USGS, 2010b), current economically exploitable reserves amount to 9.9 million t, identified resources total around 25.5 million t, and global production in 2009 is estimated at 18,000 t; therefore, scarcity does not appear to be an issue in the medium-term, particularly if effective recycling measures are implemented (Angerer et al., 2009b). The latest research by the US Ministry of Defence has shown significant, as yet uncharted lithium reserves in Afghanistan.

Rare Earths, Rare Metals and Semimetals

Gallium and indium are used in the photovoltaic industry, neodymium is an important element used in the manufacture of permanent magnets, for example for electric engines and wind power stations, germanium is used in optoelectronics, scandium in fuel cells, tantalum in micro capacitors (for instance for mobile telephones), and platinum for fuel cells and various catalytic converters. These elements are at the top of a list of those relevant for future technologies, where in some cases, the expected demand in 2030 will considerably outstrip current production levels (Angerer et al., 2009a). Demand for all of these raw materials is expected to rise, for some significantly; the use of rare earths could triple between 2000 and 2014 (Service, 2010). Accordingly, rare earth prices have already shown significant increases. There is therefore some concern that raw material shortages could limit large-scale solar energy expansion, or the expected strong demand for electric engines and generators. Not least for reasons of cost-efficiency, over 90% of the currently available rare earths are extracted in China; however, in 2010, China's export volume fell by 29%, compared to 2008 levels (Schüler et al., 2011). Higher export duties for these strategic raw materials were introduced, so scarcity could become exacerbated (Service, 2010). In response, there are plans to open, or reopen, alternative extraction sites (for example Mountain Pass mine in California, Mount Weld mine in Australia; Schüler et al., 2011).

Conclusions

The EU has presented a raw material initiative (EU COM, 2008c), and also developed a list of the 14 raw materials critical for the EU (EU COM, 2010h). The German federal government introduced its raw material strategy in October 2010 (BMWi, 2010d), which focuses primarily on raw material supply security from the German perspective. The WBGU believes that this strategy is a step in the right direction. However, it is mainly concerned with securing the supply of strategic mineral raw materials in the short to medium term. There is not enough emphasis on the fact that in the long term, the course should be set towards a circular economy, particularly towards recycling and usage efficiency. The international long-range and secondary effects with regard to sustainable development in export countries play only a marginal role in the raw material strategy. Although environmental and development political aims are mentioned, it seems that these are superseded by the primary aim of securing the raw material supply.

A raw material strategy should integrate the avoidance of negative impacts on environment and development from the start, and should also be more expansive by combining the following elements for each respective raw material and application: securing and expanding the supply, usage efficiency, recycling, and substitution. Particularly the significant potential for efficiency optimisation and recycling of the listed strategic minerals has been examined only marginally (Schüler et al., 2011).

In the case of imminent, permanent price increases for certain raw materials, substitution seems the obvious choice. For example, neodymium scarcity, about which concerns are frequently voiced, could lead to an increase in the price of permanent magnets, which are also used in the construction of modern wind power stations. However, electric generators, such as those used in wind power stations or engines for electric vehicles, could also be realised without the use of permanent magnets. There are also sufficient alternatives available which could be used in photovoltaic technology to generate solar energy, rather than relying on materials with limited availability. Comparable alternatives also exist for the catalytic converters used in hydrogen electrolysis or fuel cells. In principle, the WBGU therefore does not consider the limited availability of rare materials to be a risk endangering the rapid conversion towards low-carbon energy systems.

1.1.5.2
Nutrient Cycles

Nitrogen (N) and phosphor (P) are – besides CO_2 and water – the two vital plant nutrients whose global cycles are relevant for the Earth system. Anthropogenic change and acceleration of both cycles has been significant in order to increase agricultural production through the use of mineral fertilisers (Vitousek et al., 1997a; Mackenzie et al., 2002; Section 1.2.5). Oversupply with these nutrients can change ecosystems to such an extent that threshold values are exceeded, triggering fundamental structural changes or collapse. This pattern can be observed at all dimensional scales, from small local ecosystems (meadows, lakes) to large-scale anoxic marine environments (for example dead zones in the Gulf of Mexico or the Baltic Sea; Diaz, 2001).

The anthropogenic production of reactive nitrogen (fertilisers, combustion processes and the cultivation of nitrogen-fixing legumes) has increased tenfold since industrialisation (from approx. 15 to approx. 156 Mt N per year), today exceeding natural flows. Over half of all synthetic nitrogen fertiliser ever produced has been applied post-1985 (MA, 2005a). Its use is expected to increase even further to approx. 267 Mt per year by 2050 (Galloway et al., 2004; Bouwman et al., 2009). As a planetary boundary, Rockström et al. (2009b) recommend limiting nitrogen input to around 35 Mt N per year, roughly the equivalent of a quarter of current amounts, to prevent the slow erosion of ecosystem resilience through eutrophication and acidification.

The use of phosphor as a fertiliser has tripled between 1960 and 1990 (MA, 2005a). Today, around 20 Mt P per year are extracted for use as mineral fertiliser; however, the easily accessible resources will soon become scarce (Box 1.1-3; Rockström et al., 2009a). Ultimately, around half of this ends up in the oceans (8.5–9.5 Mt P per year). For comparison: prehistorical input into the oceans amounted to merely approx. 0.2 Mt P per year (Mackenzie et al., 2002). Such a huge input increase of phosphor into the oceans could, in the long term, lead to expansive anoxic zones, or dead zones, in the oceanic deep seas, as has been the case before in the history of the Earth (Handoh and Lenton, 2003). Despite the massively increased anthropogenic phosphor flow, Rockström et al. (2009a) believe that a planetary boundary of 11 Mt P per year should be sufficient to prevent critical load limits from being reached. In view of the increasing demand for agricultural products (Section 1.2.5), this boundary has almost been reached.

1.1.5.3
Depletion of the Stratospheric Ozone Layer

Over the past few years, the annual seasonal stratospheric ozone hole over Antarctica has continued to reach record dimensions, fluctuating slightly from year to year. Recovery can not be expected as yet, despite the successes of the Montreal Protocol that led to the reduction of emissions of ozone-depleting substances, as the processes are still in saturation. This also applies more or less to the Arctic stratospheric ozone depletion in the spring; again there has been no measurable trend reversal. In the global mean, the ozone layer has also not yet recovered to pre-1980 levels, however, over the past few years, total column ozone has stabilised at around 3.5% (northern hemisphere), and 6% (southern hemisphere) below pre-1980 levels. Accordingly, clear-sky UV radiation levels in mid- and higher latitudes are still higher than they were pre-1980.

The atmospheric concentration of the ozone-depleting substances regulated by the Montreal Protocol (measured in terms of their stratospheric ozone depletion potential) is expected to fall to 1980 levels by the middle of the 21st century. Nevertheless, the ozone layer is not expected to fully return to its pre-1980 condition but to remain permanently altered due to the impact climate change has on atmospheric circulations. Total ozone columns in the tropics are expected to remain lower than they were in 1980, whilst outside the tropics, they are expected to increase (Li et al., 2009). Without the regulation of ozone-depleting substance emissions as stipulated by the Montreal Protocol, the globally-averaged column ozone could have been expected to decrease by 17% by 2020, and by 67% by 2065, which by then would have led to a doubling of skin damaging UV radiation levels during the summer months in the northern mid-latitudes (Newman et al., 2009).

The Montreal Protocol, in force since 1989 and continuously reviewed and tightened over the years, can therefore be seen as successful. Beyond protecting the ozone layer, it has also contributed to climate change mitigation, as many of the ozone-depleting substances regulated in the Montreal Protocol are also strong greenhouse gases. Velders et al. (2007) estimate that the global climate change mitigation effect of the Montreal Protocol through avoided emissions in the period 1990 to 2010 considerably exceeds that of the Kyoto Protocol.

However, particularly in Antarctica, an effect in the opposite direction is to be expected: the annual formation of the ozone hole influences the local climate via lower atmospheric flows. In the past decades, the warming in Antarctic summer which otherwise would have been expected due to anthropogenic climate change has been reduced in this way. In a future where the ozone hole does not develop anymore, a corresponding increase in warming can be expected in Antarctica (for example Son et al., 2009).

1.1.5.4
Pollutants: Examples

This report would like to mention only two groups of globally significant pollutants by way of example:

- *Persistent organic pollutants:* One group of toxins presenting a particular health hazard for people and the environment are the synthetically produced persistent organic pollutants (POPs), characterised by their great toxicity, strong mobility, and persistence (long life). Their number and volume has significantly increased, they are spreading globally, and, not least, they are particularly dangerous because they can accumulate in the food chain (UNEP, 2007). In her 1962 book 'Silent Spring', considered an important trigger for the environmental movement by many, Rachel Carson highlighted this issue (Carson, 1962; Kroll, 2006). Ten years later, the pesticide DDT was banned in the US, and as of 2004, the Stockholm Convention is effective, aimed at initially banning 'the dirty dozen' (nine pesticides, PCBs, dioxins, and furans). Some of these substances are intentionally produced synthesised products for a particular use, for example as a pesticide; others are unintentionally created pollutants, such as, for example, dioxins, which are the result of combustion processes. These are a major source of POPs in developing countries (UNEP, 2003).
- *Heavy metals:* Another important example is provided by toxic heavy metals that are released into the environment, such as lead and mercury. These substances also have a long life-span, disperse globally and accumulate: in the Arctic, for example, high concentrations of mercury and POPs can now be found in both people, and animals living in the wild (Hansen, 2000). Whilst the conversion to lead-free petrol has mitigated lead contamination, mercury continues to increase, and still remains inadequately regulated (UNEP, 2007).

1.1.6
Interaction of Global Environmental Changes

Global environmental changes are complexly interlinked (Table 1.1-2). In some instances, for example with regard to the avoidance of summer smog, goals run parallel, leading to win-win measures: mitigating toxic tropospheric ozone also mitigates the greenhouse effect (Section 1.1.5.3). Most of these interrelations, however, are intensifying effects; the overall impact of global environmental change is therefore likely to exceed the sum of the individual effects.

An example of this kind of pronounced positive feedback loop is the conversion of natural ecosystems (forest, grasslands, peatlands) for agricultural or forestry use. Deforestation and drainage release the major carbon reserves stored in biomass and soils into the atmosphere as CO_2 emissions (partly with a delayed effect). Moreover, sink efficiency also often decreases, if the secondary ecosystems have a lower CO_2 absorption capacity than the original vegetation. As climate change also contributes to biodiversity loss, and impedes ecosystems function, these two major environmental changes lead to mutual intensification (Section 1.1-2).

On the other hand, these interrelated impacts can be used for synergistic environmental policies. An effective policy for the protection of forests and peatlands would not only have a positive effect on climate change, but would also slow down biodiversity loss. Current forest protection efforts within the scope of the climate convention (Sections 4.1.7.1, 7.3.7.2) are therefore of outstanding strategic importance (WBGU, 2010b).

Climate change is characterised not only by the great number of intensifying feedback loops leading to other environmental problems, but also by the dimensions of these intensifying effects. The WBGU has analysed these links, and concluded that people and society may expect considerable effects (WBGU, 2008). Unabated climate change would, for instance, cause vegetation zones to shift, meaning not only that forestry and agriculture have to be expansively adapted, but also that 20–30% of floral and faunal species might become extinct (IPCC, 2007b). The global water balance would

Table 1.1-2
Interaction of Global Environmental Changes. Red: cumulative intensifying effect; green: cumulative alleviating effect; black: neutral or unknown effect, or impact to be analysed individually.
Source: WBGU

Impact of on	Climate change	Biodiversity loss	Freshwater scarcity and pollution	Soil degradation, desertification	Pollutants and nutrients
Climate change		CO_2 emissions through the loss of natural ecosystems (stocks and sinks); albedo change		Loss of CO_2 stock and sink function: albedo increase	Impact of aerosols: CFCs; ground-level ozone; stratospheric ozone
Biodiversity loss	Overtaxation of ecosystems' and species' ability to adapt (e.g. coral bleaching)		Degradation of limnic ecosystems; species loss	Ecosystem degradation; species loss	Accumulation of pollutants in natural ecosystems; eutrophication; species loss
Freshwater scarcity and pollution	Altered precipitation volumes and patterns	Altered local hydrological balances, e.g. through deforestation, increased sediment load in rivers		Increased pollutant and sediment burden	Contamination of water resources (e.g. through mercury, pesticides); sediment burden
Soil degradation, desertification	Desertification as a consequence of less precipitation in arid areas	Increased erosion through loss of plant cover	Salinisation		Soil burdening through heavy metals and organic substances
Pollutants and nutrients		Less air filtration; decelerated pollutant degradation	Decelerated pollutant degradation	More dust through wind erosion	

also be severely affected. A tendency towards less precipitation in drylands, and increased rainfall in the wet areas of the upper latitudes, can already be observed. At the same time, more extended dry periods and heavy rainfalls can be expected, increasing the risk of droughts and flooding, respectively. Without decisive climate change mitigation, these interrelated environmental impacts could overload many societies' ability to adapt over the next few decades, ultimately even leading to national and international security threats (WBGU, 2008).

One implication of this analysis is that international environmental policies should increasingly focus on integrative approaches which address several environmental problems concurrently, or concentrate on interactions and points where environmental problems meet. However, so far, these are the exception, and must be accorded a far higher degree of attention (Section 1.3).

1.2 Global Economic and Social Megatrends

In view of the Earth system megatrends, and the economic and social megatrends, it becomes clear that a transformation into a low-carbon, sustainable society is essential (Section 3). Without a change in direction, the natural life-support systems of humankind are in danger, drastically limiting future social development. The transformation is accompanied by the dynamic megatrends of a globalised economy and society, as evidenced by the global financial and economic crisis (Box 1.2-1).

The transformation is of key relevance particularly for the dynamics of the socio-economic development of the developing and newly industrialising countries (Section 1.2.1). If the required development advances are to be made in a sustainable way, they must be achieved without collision with the planetary guard rails. This is a major challenge, especially in view of the

Box 1.2-1

Impacts of the Global Financial and Economic Crisis

The 2007 to 2009 financial and economic crisis, which initially affected US finance markets, then spread on to European and, ultimately, global markets, directly impacted the real economy and led to the biggest global recession since the late 1920s. Unlike the 1997/98 Asia crisis, which was regionally restricted, it threatened the stability of the entire global financial system. An immediate breakdown was only averted through massive liquidity extension on the part of the central banks, coupled with coordinated key interest rate reductions and expansive state guarantees for defaulted loans. In addition, debt-financed economic stimulus packages helped to stabilise demand in the large national economies, and to prevent a negative spiral of diminishing economic performance and growing unemployment.

The immediate and determined response of the international community proves that under severe pressure to act, transformative turnarounds are possible. Despite the fact that the crisis has been temporarily contained, however, the world is faced with considerable structural challenges to set the course towards a sustainable and stable economic system.

The crisis should also be used as an opportunity to accelerate sustainable development. National economic stimulus packages provide an opportunity for a targeted redirecting of investment flow in the sense of a 'Green New Deal', to promote sustainable growth – or 'green growth' (Edenhofer and Stern, 2009). Key areas for investments into the future are, for example, the switch to energy systems based on low-carbon technologies, and the increase of energy efficiency on the demand side (Chapter 4). Nevertheless, active policy measures to support the business agenda cannot be maintained indefinitely. The spiralling national debt, particularly the USA's, but also of other OECD countries, limits the room for manoeuvre in terms of further public investments.Therefore, consumers and companies must become more involved in global climate financing. China, on the other hand, appears to have emerged from the crisis stronger, and has the financial resources to redirect growth specifically towards sustainability, and to leapfrog a large part of the established high-carbon development path. This opens up huge opportunities for a managed transformation; however, as yet, a fundamental change of course still remains to be set.

At a global level, the crisis-related slump in economic performance in 2009 merely meant a breather in terms of emissions growth: at 1.3%, global CO_2 emissions decreased less drastically than originally anticipated, and they are expected to rise again by 3% in 2010 (Friedlingstein et al., 2010). The room for manoeuvre gained by global climate protection through the temporary emissions decline is threatening to be lost again through two effects: on the one hand, the large newly industrialising countries are undergoing a rapid catch-up process, which currently still relies largely on fossil-based energy systems. CO_2 emissions attributed to China and India rose in 2009 despite the global economic crisis by about 8% and 6.2% respectively (Friedlingstein et al., 2010), and a trend reversal is not in sight. On the other hand, the current economical dynamics in many developing countries is based primarily on expanded resource extraction for export, particularly also to the emergent newly industrialising countries, increasing the pressure on the ecosystems even further. Therefore, in the sense of acceleration of sustainable development, the economic crisis was by no means a catalyst.

From a forward-thinking perspective, far reaching conclusions regarding the future structuring of global governance mechanisms can be drawn from the crisis. Globalisation consequences and dynamics at an economic level are clearly disproportionate to the current opportunities for institutional monitoring – and control – of the process at global level. Not least, the outbreak of the global financial and economic crisis has served to prove that the existing structures of national regulations constitute an inadequate global regulation framework for coping with systemic risks. The development of efficient global institutions is therefore of major importance to manage the globalisation process, and to reduces the vulnerability of the system to further crises (UN, 2009a).

Apart from the blatant failure of existing warning and control mechanisms to avoid global crises, the financial and economic crisis has above all revealed the degree of global integration and interdependencies. These have meant that a problem originally limited to the US real estate market was able to trigger sudden consternation on international finance markets through the global trade with inadequately collateralised, certificated mortgages, with the resultant shockwaves subsequently affecting the real economy. Newly industrialising and developing countries are also affected by the crisis, as it led to less demand for export goods, for instance, negatively impacting development and employment opportunities. Potential financing problems are also a consequence of the crisis; developed countries are blocking capital seekers from other regions through new issues of government securities (World Bank, 2009a). These added difficulties with regard to the financing situation, in conjunction with, at least temporarily, lower growth rates, hold huge challenges for developing countries and impede achievement of the Millennium Development Goals (World Bank, 2010a). Particularly for the poorest countries, which do not benefit from the economical dynamics in the newly industrialising countries, there are now fewer development opportunities. OECD countries' cutbacks of official development assistance could also have a particularly drastic effect in this regard. The risk remains that the global financial crisis means a setback for some parts of the world, particularly in terms of socio-economic development. The negation of recent economic progress is a serious threat, especially in Africa (Debiel et al., 2010).

The far-reaching feedback effects, which have merely been outlined here, illustrate that systemic thinking and acting under adoption of a long-term perspective are the fundamental premises for avoiding future economic, social and ecological crises.

dynamic growth of greenhouse gas emissions in these countries.

One positive factor is the apparent trend towards democratisation, which allows broad and liberal discourse, thereby promoting the establishment of a social consensus for the necessary transformation (Section 1.2.2).

Ultimately, the imminent radical changes to the industrial metabolism focus particularly on three main pillars of today's global society:

1. The energy systems, also including the transport sector, which the entire economy depends on. These are currently faced with a new surge of growth, due to the accelerated development dynamics in the newly industrialising countries (Section 1.2.3). The energy sector causes around two-thirds of today's long-lived greenhouse gas emissions.
2. The urban areas, currently responsible for three-quarters of global final energy demand. Their population will double to 6 billion by 2050 (Section 1.2.4).
3. The land-use systems (agriculture and forestry, including deforestation). They are currently responsible for almost a quarter of global greenhouse gas emissions (Section 1.2.5). Land use does not only have to provide enough food for a world population that continues to grow, and to become more demanding, but also has to deal with a growth in demand due to the increasing use of bioenergy and bio-based raw materials.

1.2.1 Development

Substantial Progress

Over the past 20 years, there has been substantial progress in many areas of human development. Today, most people live healthier and longer, are better educated, and have improved chances of covering their basic needs (UNDP, 2010). One indicator for this is the Human Development Index, which illustrates the three dimensions of health, education and standard of living through life expectation at birth, literacy and school entry rates, and a weighted per capita income. Countries with the most significant development progress not only include emerging economies such as China, Indonesia and South Korea, but also poor countries such as Nepal, Oman and Tunisia, where great progress has been achieved in the non-income related areas of human development (UNDP, 2010). However, the development progress made by these countries varies greatly. Whilst a quarter of the developing countries has achieved only moderate improvements over the past 40 years, a further quarter has managed great development progress (UNDP, 2010). The effects of improved health care, however, are currently counteracted mainly by the fact that in 19 countries (nine of these sub-Saharan African countries), the general state of health has again changed for the worse, and life expectation gone down, particularly due to HIV infections and a higher adult mortality in countries in transition. Simultaneously, the socio-economic disparities within and between states have frequently increased.

New Geography of Global Growth

The majority of people living below the poverty line no longer live in the poor developing countries. This initially surprising fact stands for the growing heterogeneity in the development dynamics of countries, such that the classical categorisation into industrialised, newly industrialising and developing countries cannot reflect this adequately. The OECD report on the 'shifting of wealth' reveals the global structural changes that have occurred in the past decade (OECD, 2010c). This new '4-speed world' (James Wolfensohn) therefore includes affluent, converging, struggling and poor countries (Figure 1.2-1; measure: income and per capita growth in comparison to the industrialised countries). Between the 1990s, still viewed as a lost decade in terms of development, and the 2000s, there has been significant global development progress, and shifts in geographical diffusion patterns. A 'new geography of global growth' (OECD, 2010c) has become apparent: whilst some countries continue to suffer from absolute poverty, and no development progress at all is on the horizon, there are developing countries which are on the path to the middle-income group of countries; this also includes some sub-Saharan states in Africa. Finally, there are countries that are catching up economically, coming close to the prosperity level of wealthy countries. Between the 1990s and the 2000s, the number of countries where per capita growth has doubled, compared to the OECD countries, has increased from 12 to 65 ('converging'). Over the same period, the number of poor countries has fallen from 55 to 25. However, a number of countries have not benefited from these growth dynamics ('poor').

Regional Shifts of Absolute Poverty

An analysis by the Institute for Development Studies, distinguishing between low- and middle-income countries and fragile or conflict-affected states, showed similar results (Sumner, 2010). Thus, the number of low-income countries (based on World Bank classification), following a rise in the 1990s, fell from 60 to 39 between 2000 and 2009. Correspondingly, the number of middle-income countries has greatly increased (Sum-

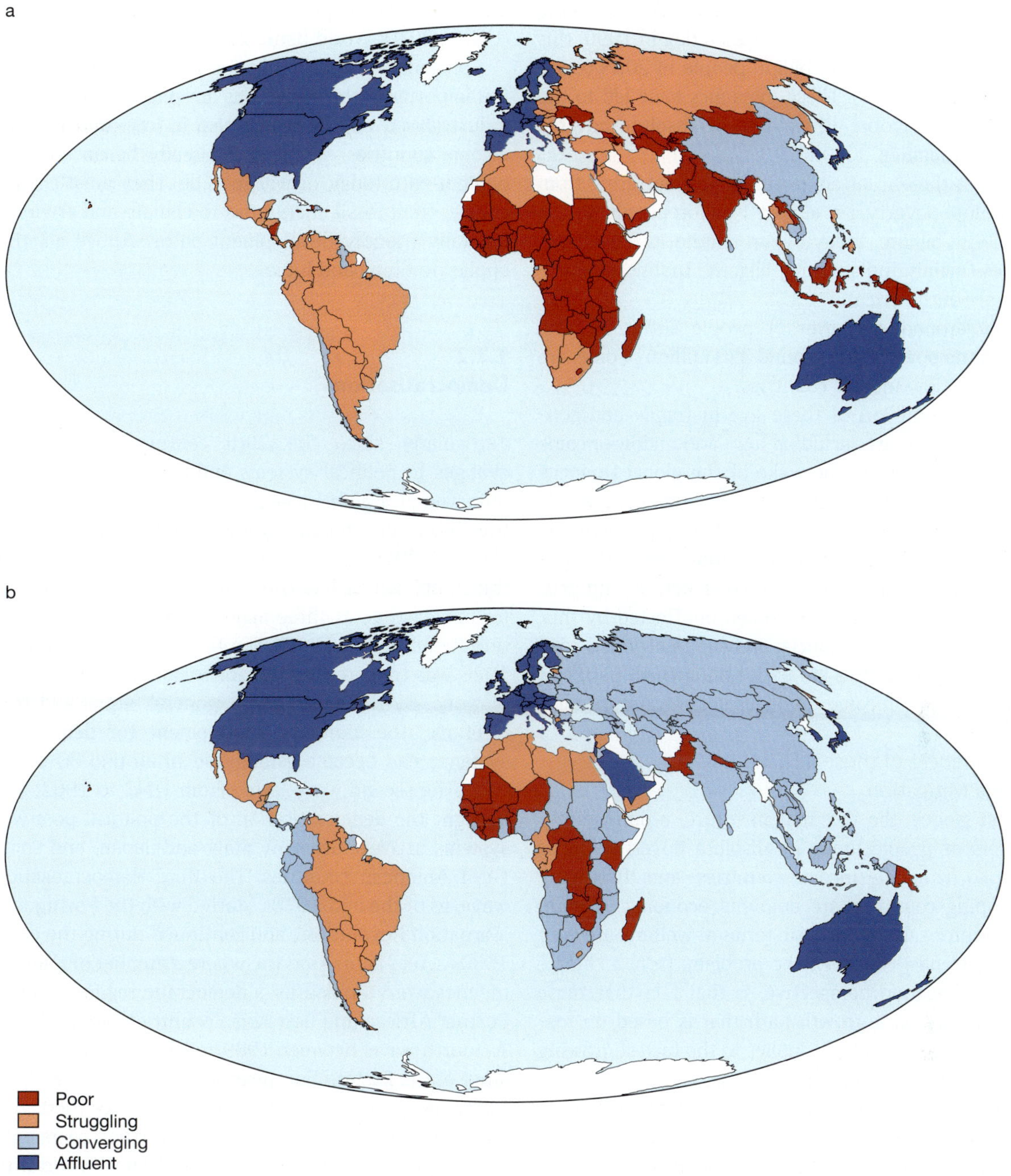

Figure 1.2-1
Dynamics of national wealth development: the '4-speed world'; a) 1990s; b) 2000s. Between the 1990s and the last decade, there has been considerable wealth progress, causing shifts in geographical patterns of countries with differing rates of growth and GDP per capita. Today, four distinct country groups can be differentiated according to their growth dynamics: poor, struggling, converging and affluent countries. Whilst some countries continue to suffer from absolute poverty (red), and no wealth progress at all is in sight, there are developing countries which are on the path to the middle-income and high-income group of countries, albeit struggling to keep up sustained growth rates (orange, this also includes some sub-Saharan states in Africa). And finally, there are countries that are catching up quickly due to sustaining high rates of growth; coming close to middle-income and high-income countries (light blue).
Source: OECD, 2010c

ner, 2010). Whilst 1.81 billion people were still living below the poverty line of US$ 1.25 a day in 1990, this went down to only 1.38 billion people in 2005 (Chen and Ravallion, 2008). These dynamics have led to the following new global distribution of absolute poverty structure (Sumner, 2010):

- Almost three-quarters of the people suffering from absolute poverty, i.e. almost 1 billion people, or the 'bottom billion', today live in middle-income countries (mainly India, China, Nigeria, Indonesia, Pakistan, South Africa).
- Only around a quarter of people suffering from absolute poverty, i.e. around 370 million people, are living in low-income countries.

Around 300 million of these live in fragile and conflict-affected states, including low- and middle-income countries. Even if, in the wake of the global financial and economic crisis (2009–2010), the number of people globally living in absolute poverty has again increased by 65 million people (Ravallion and Chen, 2010), it can be assumed that the observed structural and geographical shifts will largely remain unaffected by this. Although the global financial and economic crisis continues, many countries are back on a growth path (for example middle-income countries in Latin America).

Consequences of these Dynamics for Climate Change Mitigation

At first glance, the fact that in future, around three-quarters of people living in absolute poverty will be doing so in middle-income countries, and that many developing countries are enjoying economic growth, and therefore also progress in terms of welfare, are very positive trends. However, the problem, from a climate change mitigation perspective, is that fact that these countries are on a growth path that is based on fossil fuels. This particularly applies to the fastest growing countries (China, India, Brazil, etc.).

Many low-income countries (for example sub-Saharan African countries), and middle-income countries (for example in Latin America) are also pursuing a resource-based export model (mainly agricultural commodities), which usually exacerbates the degradation of the natural environment (for example deforestation, soil degradation, water scarcity).

These growth trends are not only unsustainable from an environmental and climate perspective, they are also going to impede or prevent the achievement of the Millennium Development Goals (MDG). Both Human Development Report 2010 and Global Development Report 2010 conclude that non-sustainable production and consumption patterns represent the biggest threat to development progress, and that a transition towards low-carbon development paths is therefore necessary (UNDP, 2010; World Bank, 2010b).

For climate change mitigation to succeed, it is of central importance that emissions are reduced not only in industrialised countries, but also in low- and middle-income countries, which may already be on a development path today, or will soon be. They must change course, from fossil energy use to climate and environmentally friendly development paths. Above all, this applies to China and India.

1.2.2
Democratisation

Particularly since the 20th century, fundamental changes to political systems and social orders can be observed at a global level; this is characterised by the transition from an authoritarian to a democratic system (Merkel, 2010). Samuel P. Huntington described this transition, which has continually also inspired counter movements, as three major waves of democratisation (Huntington, 1991). The first wave from 1828 to 1926 was triggered by the American and French revolutions. By the early 1920s, general, equal and free elections, the minimum requirement for democratic systems, had become established in around 30 countries. The second wave lasted from 1943 to 1962, and brought the democratisation of the political post-war systems in West Germany, Italy and Japan, and some Latin American countries. The third democratisation wave, as of the mid-1970s, started with the Portuguese 'Carnation Revolution', and continued during the early 1980s across Latin America, where a number of military regimes were toppled by a democratic regime change. Further African and East Asian countries followed suit. A 'fourth wave' between 1989 and 1991 led to the collapse of the Eastern European socialist systems and the former dominions of the Soviet Union. Since then, global democratisation has progressed further, seemingly also gaining a foothold in the Arabic-Islamic world with the 'Jasmine Revolution' in Tunisia in 2011 (Freedom House, 2010; Leggewie, 2011). The global democratisation trend has been confirmed by the quantitative Polity study, started by political scientist Ted Robert Gurr (Gurr and Eckstein, 1975; Figure 1.2-2). If it were to transpire that only the granting of liberties allows permanently stable societies, the current wave of democratisation (always with distinct politico-cultural differences) could also engulf further autocratic regimes such as that of the People's Republic of China. In that case, democracy would have established itself as a model for political order worldwide.

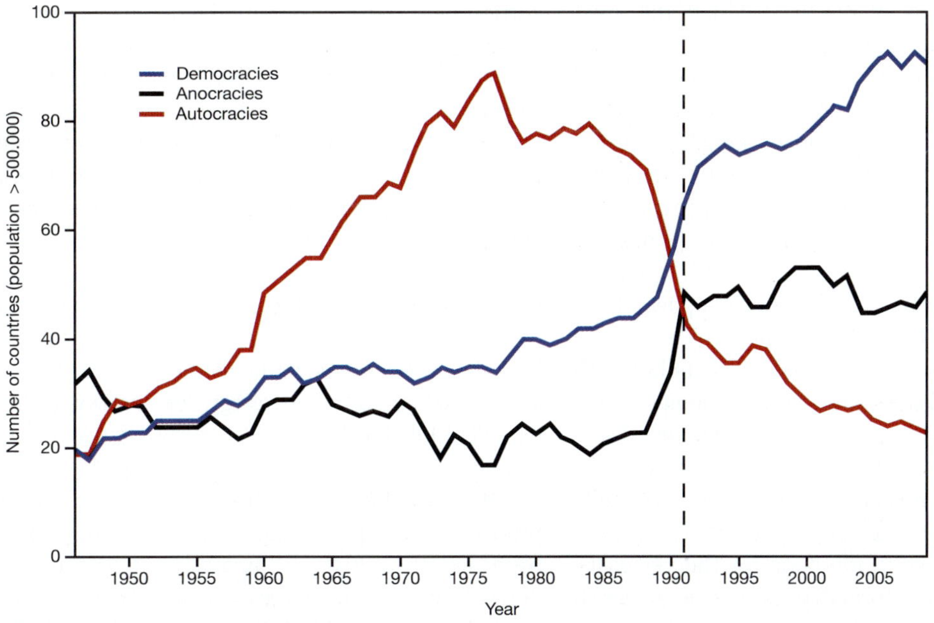

Figure 1.2-2
Changing global government types 1946–2009. Within the scope of the Polity IV project, a combined democracy-autocracy scale was developed, which records the institutional governance form of states and ranges from +10 (= fully institutionalised democracy) to -10 (= fully institutionalised autocracy). States reaching a value of +6 or above on the scale are recorded as democracies; states with -6 or less points are autocracies, all states in between (i.e. from -5 to +5) are mixed forms, and are referred to as anocracies. For the period of 1946 to 2009, the figure shows the number of states (with a total population figure of more than 500,000) with democratic, autocratic and anocratic forms of governance. The dotted line refers to the rapid democratisation wave during the early 1990s, when the number of democracies rose by more than 50%, from 48 in 1989 to 77 in 1994.
Source: Marshall and Cole, 2009

Principles of Democracy

Even if globally and historically, varying forms have emerged, the core element of democracy remains the congruence of rulers and ruled. Democracy, to quote Abraham Lincoln, is 'government of the people, by the people, for the people'. Its most important achievement is therefore the requirement of legitimation for all acts of governance, which in democratic systems is guaranteed by the political equality of all. Democracies put their trust in the (political) 'wisdom of crowds'; that is why it works with different variants of the majority rule, which, however, also allows minorities to have their say, effectively and fairly, and protects them. Democratic political systems are also embedded in legal orders and the rule of law, and are subject to a system of checks and balances. Effective decision-making advantages such as the reversibility of decisions and effective stakeholder participation on the part of the citizens, instigated through direct and indirect involvement in the decision-making process and through public multi-level communication, go hand in hand with these principles. Improved consolidation of preferences and interests, best-possible use of widespread knowledge, and the highest input legitimation of any political system therefore represent the rationality and comparative advantage of democracies. No democratic system has ever achieved the absolute optimum (Schmidt, 2006). There are also many 'defective democracies' (Merkel et al., 2003), that continue to show elements of autocratic forms of governance. Moreover, over the past few years, the established liberal democracies are exhibiting signs of a crisis, as described in the 'post-democracy' thesis, for example, which assumes an internal hollowing out of formal democratic institutions which continue to exist, through a decline in (election) participation and the increasing importance of democratically non-legitimised groups (Crouch, 2004; Section 5.3.2). Despite these by all means serious problems and developments, the outlined general democratisation trend continues worldwide, beyond the western core countries.

Democracy as an Important Premise for Transformation

In recent years, the climate change has given rise to the question of whether democratic political systems can actually overcome this and other planetary challenges, or whether autocratic systems are not better equipped to deal with the great transformation (Chapter 3) by simply ordering it. The WBGU is convinced (Sections 5.3.2, 6; Box 5.3-1) that the great transformation is about the finding of legitimate, fair, creative and permanent problem solutions for a sustainable life. In doing so, the citizens' inherent right to actively participate in shaping and working towards the vision of a climate-friendly society cannot be ceded. Increasingly, demands for the right to get involved in decision-making are also being made, as recent citizens' protest campaigns, for example with regard to the 'Stuttgart 21' railway station or nuclear power have shown (Sections 5.3.1.4, 5.4.1.3). The aims of a 'good life' must be discussed globally by citizens, in line with the changing values across all social environments, and with the inclusion of the scientific community (Sections 2, 8). In the WBGU's view, only a democratic public allows this kind of debate, to make the required self-restrictions and the chances of a better life for all people plausible, and to form the basis for the necessary political decisions. Transformation is a societal search process, and therefore requires more, rather than less, democracy (Sections 5.3.2 5.4.2).

Against the background of the current debate on democratic systems' ability to perform, this conclusion may not be the obvious one. It is certainly true that as yet, democracy has not proven its future capacity to deal with the described challenges and the imminent great transformation (Section 5.3.2). However, this does not imply that democracy as such should be questioned, but that further development in terms of its content, and its modernisation, should be pursued, including at a global governance level (Section 5.3.5.2). Not least, the great transformation is therefore a test of the future viability of democratic systems (Leggewie and Welzer, 2009).

1.2.3
Global Energy Trends: Demand and Production

Energy Demand

Energy is a basic premise for human development. It is essential for the socio-economic activities of all societies, in the form of light, heat, mechanical power or electricity. At the same time, energy use is responsible for the largest share of anthropogenic greenhouse gas emissions (Section 1.1.1). The distribution of energy use is currently distinctly uneven. Around half of global primary energy demand originates in OECD countries, which make up merely 20% of the population, but generate around three-quarters of global GDP (Figure 1.2-3). Concurrently, 2.8 billion people still primarily rely on traditional biomass as their primary energy source for cooking, and 1.4 billion people do not have access to electricity. In non-OECD countries, where the current per capita consumption is still low, the demand for energy is rising particularly fast. This is due to the rapid development progress since the 1990s described in Section 1.2.1, and their increasing market integration as a consequence of globalisation. OECD country demand, on the other hand, is satisfied. In 2009, China superseded the USA as the country with the highest energy demand, for example (IEA, 2009b).

If only existing and already planned government policies related to the energy sector were implemented (New Policies Scenario), the IEA estimates that the global primary energy demand would rise by 1.2% annually, so that by 2035, the energy demand would already exceed 2008 levels by 36%. 93% of this expected increase can be attributed to non-OECD countries, driven by the faster growth of the economy, industrial production, the population and urbanisation in these countries (IEA, 2010c). China alone is responsible for 36% of this expected increase in global energy demand by 2035, India for 18%. The OECD countries' energy demand increases only slowly in this scenario; however, in 2035, the USA is still the second-largest energy consumer after China (IEA, 2010c). A generally expected trend is the relative increase of electricity in the final energy demand mix.

In the Global Energy Assessment's baseline scenario (GEA, 2011), it is assumed that the global primary energy demand will more than double by 2050, from approx. 470 EJ in 2010 to around 1,100 EJ per year (Figure 1.2-4).

The global economy's energy intensity, i.e. the amount of energy used in relation to the gross domestic product, has steadily decreased over the past few decades. As responsible factors, the IEA cites improved energy efficiency, change of energy carriers, and structural changes in the global economy away from energy-intensive industries. Again there are marked differences between the OECD and non-OECD countries (Figure 1.2-3). Without the energy intensity improvements achieved between 1980 and 2008, today's global energy demand would be 32% higher (IEA, 2010c).

Energy Production

Today's global energy supply relies overwhelmingly on the use of fossil fuels (Figure 1.2-4). They steadily gained in importance, from the beginning of industrialisation up to the 1970s, when their share in the global primary energy supply peaked at 87% (Grübler, 2008a). Since then, it has varied between 84% and 86%. However, the relative significance of the respective individual fossil fuels has clearly changed. In 1925, coal dominated the fossil energy supply, contributing 45% to the global energy supply. Subsequently, its share dropped to around 25% by the 1970s. At the

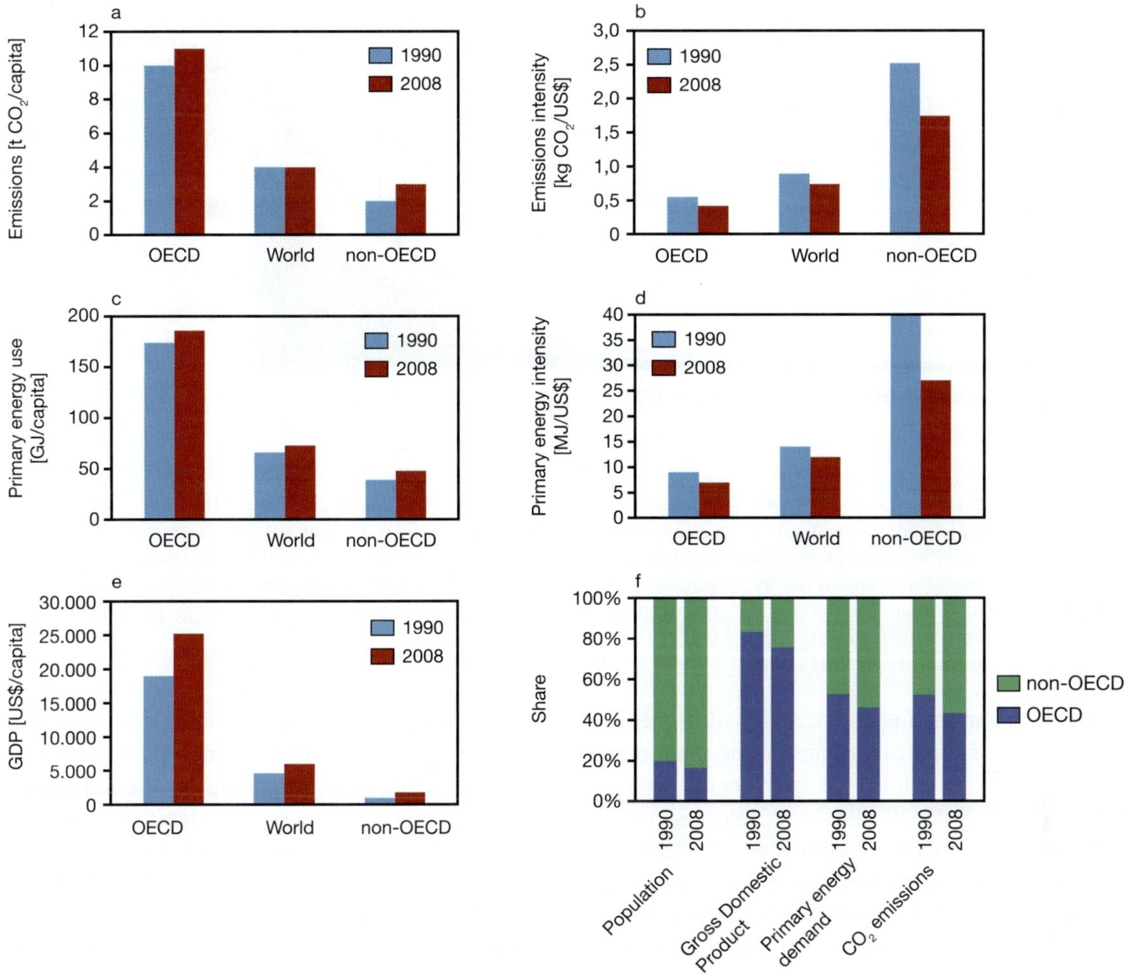

Figure 1.2-3
Trends in major drivers of anthropogenic climate change. Stated are the CO_2 emissions from the use of fossil fuels per capita (a) and in relation to economic output (b), the primary energy use per capita (c) and in relation to economic output (d), and the economic output per capita (e), respectively divided according to OECD and non-OECD countries, plus global values. In addition, the share OECD or non-OECD countries contribute to the global population, global GDP, global primary energy demand and global CO_2 emissions from the use of fossil fuels is shown (f).
Sources: WBGU, based on IEA (2010e, f) and World Bank (2011b) data)

same time, crude oil, the fossil fuel dominant since the mid-1960s, peaked at over 46% of primary energy. As a consequence of oil price fluctuations in the 1970s, the energy supply resource basis was intentionally diversified further; the proportion of natural gas in the primary energy mix, for example, has risen from less than 16% to over 22% since then. Since the early 2000s, the relative significance of coal has increased again, particularly through the rapid economic growth in China and India. Overall, this has led to a rise in the global significance of coal as primary energy, from around 24% in 2000 to 28% in 2008.

Nuclear energy has been commercially produced and expanded since the 1950s, although it did not start to make major contributions to the electricity supply until the 1970s. Most nuclear power plants were built between 1970 and 1990, a period during which the global capacity expanded from around 50 to around 350 GW_e. In 2008, 2,731 TWh electricity, or 13% of global electric power, were generated by nuclear power plants. In the early 1990s, nuclear power already contributed 19% to global electricity generation, it is therefore declining. As yet unpredictable is the extent to which the dispute regarding the risks of nuclear energy, reignited in many countries in the aftermath of the reactor accidents in Fukushima, will impact on its global use.

Renewable energy carriers have been used for a number of purposes since the beginning of civilisation, and were indeed the only source of energy until the advent of the Industrial Revolution. These included, for example, firewood for cooking, heating and light-

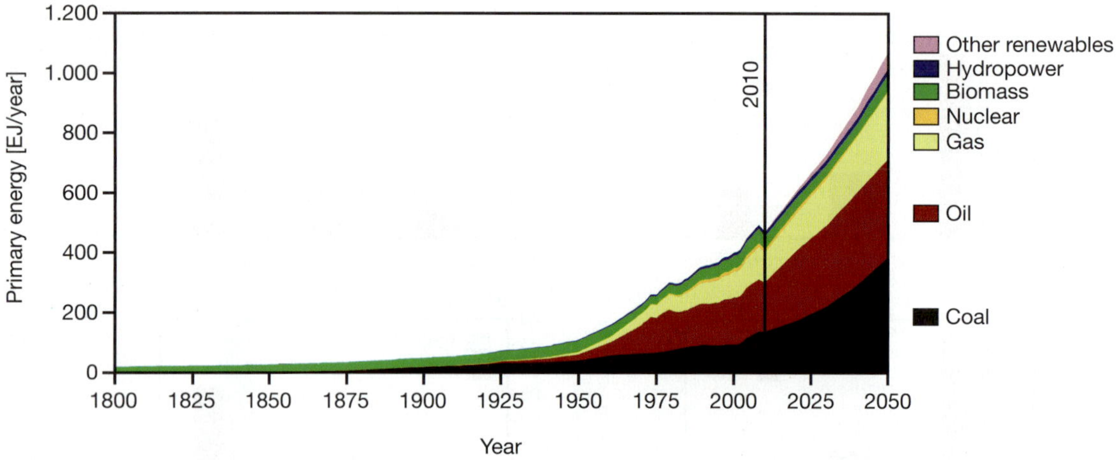

Figure 1.2-4
Development of global primary energy demand (business as usual) between 1800 and 2050. For the period 1800–2008, actual primary energy demand is shown, and from 2010, demand according to the GEA baseline scenario is presented. With a probability of around 99%, the emissions that would be associated with a scenario like this would lead to transgression of the 2 °C guard rail. Temperatures would rise by approx. 5 °C. The development illustrated here should therefore be avoided at all cost. Contrary to this scenario, the primary energy demand must be significantly restricted, and the energy mix must be changed in order to protect the climate (Section 4.6).
Source: WBGU, on the basis of GEA 2011 data

ing, solar energy for heating and drying, hydro-energy or wind power for pumping or irrigation. The traditional bioenergy carriers are still the primary energy source for a great number of people in many developing countries; however, their use can be associated with adverse effects on health and environment, and is by no means always sustainable (WBGU, 2010a). It is often predominantly the task of women and children to collect firewood, limiting their chances of taking part in education measures or other productive activities. They also frequently suffer disproportionately from respiratory problems through particle pollution from inefficient hearths.

Modern renewable energies today deliver 19% of the global electricity supply, and meet 10% of the heating needs of industry and buildings (IEA, 2010c). The expansion of renewable energies enjoys worldwide political support, leading the IEA to expect that their share in the energy mix will increase. In the IEA's 'New Policies' Scenario, they achieve a global share of a third of the electricity supply by 2035, and 16% of heat generation. Although this anticipated increase in the use of renewable energies leads to the relative decarbonisation of energy generation, it is by no means sufficient to reduce energy-related greenhouse gas emissions. On the contrary, in this scenario, emissions continue to rise up to 2035.

Energy-Related Emissions

95% of anthropogenic CO_2 emissions (excluding land-use emissions) can currently be attributed to the energy sector; the remaining 5% originate from industrial processes. Electricity and heat generation cause 45% of these emissions, 20% can be attributed to transport systems. A further 20% are generated through the use of fossil fuels in industry and construction (WRI-CAIT, 2011). Energy-related emissions are currently fundamentally developing in the wrong direction: between 1990 and 2000, global CO_2 emissions rose by 1.1% per year; in the subsequent seven years, this figure has already risen to 3% annually (IEA, 2010a). As the most important factors for this, the IEA cites the increasing energy demand in coal-based economies, as well as an increasing use of coal in response to rising oil and gas prices. Whilst emissions from the use of coal grew by 0.6% yearly between 1990 and 2000, this rate increased to 4.8% per year in the period between 2000 and 2007 (IEA, 2010a). Coal, whose deposits are far more evenly distributed around the world than those of crude oil, for example, is promoted in most countries (including Germany) for reasons of strategic supply security, and globally attracts subsidies amounting to billions.

Energy Infrastructure and Path Dependencies

A particular cause for concern is the fact that the long life-span of energy generation infrastructures means that current energy sector investments will impact upon the energy mix, and thereby one of the decisive factors in terms of emissions, for decades to come. The energy sector therefore relies on timely and future-oriented political course changes, as otherwise there is a risk of path dependencies that would make adequate climate change mitigation impossible. Even if the growth in final energy demand will primarily take place in non-OECD countries, and the overall energy demand in the OECD countries is not going to rise significantly, the OECD countries must still make considerable investments in the energy generation infrastructure, as the old infrastructure must be replaced. The IEA New Policies' Scenario assumes that 35% of the cumulative global energy investments between 2010 and 2035 will have to be made in OECD countries, even though their energy demand will only grow by 3% over this period in this scenario (IEA, 2010c). So in terms of climate change mitigation, the important aspect is steering investments all over the world in the right direction: the OECD countries' existing high-carbon energy infrastructure must be replaced by low-carbon energy generation capacities, whilst at the same time, the increasing energy demand from non-OECD countries must be met through the expansion of the capacities of climate-friendly energy forms.

1.2.4 Urbanisation

Trends

Even though urban settlements have existed for thousands of years, limited agricultural yields meant that for a very long time, the proportion of people living in cities was less than 5% of the total population. Historically, societies in China, India and the Middle East were at the top of the urbanisation charts; even in 1800, Peking was probably still the most populous city in the world (Chandler, 1987; McNeill, 2002). In just a few generations, since the early 20th century, the global urban population has grown from around 165 million people, or approx. 10–15% of the total population, by a factor of 20 to currently 3.5 billion. Around half of the global population now lives in urban areas, although these are not always distinctly separate from rural regions, with various local statistics applying different definitions. This dynamic urbanisation process continues at great speed, leading to a population growth in urban areas of more than 1 million people a week. The average global population growth in rural areas, on the other hand, is expected to stagnate even before 2020, and the remaining net population growth will mainly occur in cities. Migration is one major factor for this. By 2050, the urban population will almost double to approx. 6.4 billion people, or an expected 69% of the global population, which will by then exceed 9 billion (Box 1.2-2; UN DESA, 2009b).

Today, the majority of the overall global urban population lives in Asia. Their number will double over the next two decades; Asian cities therefore have a key role to play in the transformation. The highest relevant urban growth rates, however, can currently be observed in African countries, also due to the comparatively low initial basis. Africa is the least urbanised continent, not least because of the colonial past and its economic structures, which focus on the extraction sector (UN-Habitat, 2010a; Figures 1.2-6, 1.2-7).

Over the past few years, many regions of the world have rapidly become wealthier: in the past decade, the number of countries with a per capita income growth rate that is, in comparison, double the rate of growth in OECD countries has increased considerably. Over the same period, the number of poor countries has considerably fallen (Section 1.2.1).

Currently, five of the worldwide 21 megacities with more than 10 million inhabitants are located in 'developed' global regions. In 15 years' time, due to economic development progress, there will be 29 megacities with approx. 470 million inhabitants in total, of which 23 will be located in 'less developed' global regions. However, the highest proportion (>50%) of urban inhabitants, currently 1.8 billion people, in 2025 2.4 billion, lives in settlements with less than 500,000 inhabitants. The exact number of these settlements and their names or geographical locations are currently not included in official UN statistics; further research is needed in this respect. As these settlements are as yet less restricted in terms of infrastructure than the megacities, they could potentially play an important role in cost effective climate stabilisation.

The challenge in terms of climate change mitigation is that without a redirection into climate-friendly channels, this combination of rapid urbanisation and increasing wealth can have an extremely negative impact on climate change. The positive trend of increased wealth also means increased energy and resource consumption. For this reason it is vital that the urban densification process, particularly in the up-and-coming newly industrialising and developing countries, is made climate-friendly.

This rapid urbanisation is primarily taking place in countries with only insufficient capacities for orderly urban planning (UN-Habitat, 2009; Figure 1.2-6). One visible result takes the form of the rapidly expanding slums found particularly in the townships of developing countries. 62% of Africa's urban residents live in slums, 43% in southern Asia (UN-Habitat, 2009). Overall, almost 1 billion people, or almost a third of city dwellers, live in slums. These informal settlements frequently lack basic urban development standards, and their inhabitants enjoy no legal protection whatsoever. They often have no access to either electricity or clean water that is safe to drink, or hygienic waste and wastewater disposal facilities. Slums tend to be

Box 1.2-2
Global Population Growth up to 2050

The global population will grow from 6.8 billion (2009) to 9 billion people by the middle of the century (medium UN DESA scenario, 2009b; Figure 1.2-5). The increase will mainly occur in developing countries. The population will grow most in the 49 least developed countries (LDC). Half of the global population growth by 2050 takes place in nine countries: India, Pakistan, Nigeria, Ethiopia, USA, DR of the Congo, Tanzania, China and Bangladesh. In contrast, population growth will stagnate in the wealthier countries (in part also decline).

The global population is aging, as the birth rate will decrease by 2050, also in the developing countries, and life expectancy will increase. This process will be particularly rapid in the 49 LDC. There, the average number of children per woman is expected to fall from the current 4.39 to 2.42; globally, this will go down from 2.56 to 2.02. At the same time, according to UN projections, the proportion of over-60s will rise fastest globally (initially particularly in the industrialised countries; delayed, but subsequently also particularly rapidly, in the developing countries).

Present economic socio-economic disparities will remain the major driving force for international migration: UN projections for the period 2010–2050 predict net immigration into the following countries: USA (1.1 million), Canada (214,000), Great Britain (174,000), Spain (170,000), Italy (159,000), Germany (110,000), Australia (100,000) and France (100,000). The largest emigration movements are expected in Mexico (-334,000), China (-309,000), India (-253,000), the Philippines (-175,000), Pakistan (-161,000), Indonesia (-156,000) and Bangladesh (-148,000).

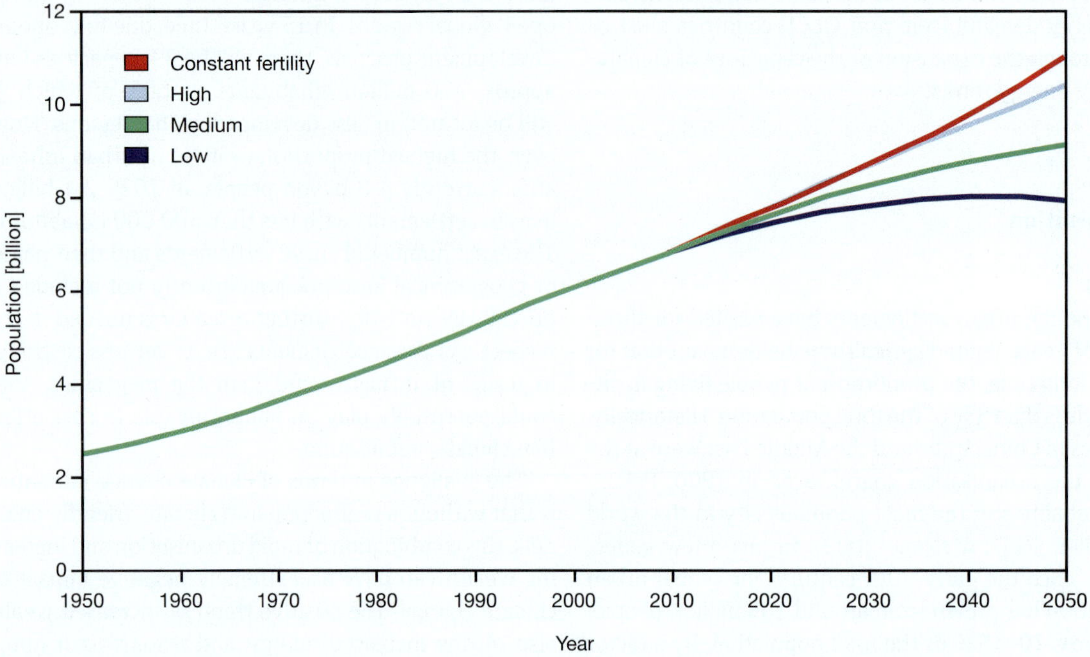

Figure 1.2-5
Global population 1950–2050. Various projections and variants.
Source: UN DESA, 2009b

located in areas that are prone to flooding, or on unsecured slopes, exposed to the risk of mudslides. In the event of a disaster, the lack of access roads in many places means no effective access for the fire brigade or emergency services. Nevertheless, these kinds of settlements remain attractive for their inhabitants, as they are often located in relative proximity to the markets and economic hubs of major cities, thereby allowing access to income generation.

In the least developed countries, sustainable urban development must therefore make considerable efforts to improve the urban residents' living conditions; however, it should also integrate the consideration of adaptation and mitigation targets with a view to climate change (for example, water supply, access to clean, environmentally friendly and safe energy sources for lighting and cooking, high-capacity public transport system connections, alternatives to corrugated iron roofs for better protection against the heat, flood protection).

Drivers and Victims of Climate Change

Cities are demand centres, and commercial production sites. Through the emissions this generates, they are

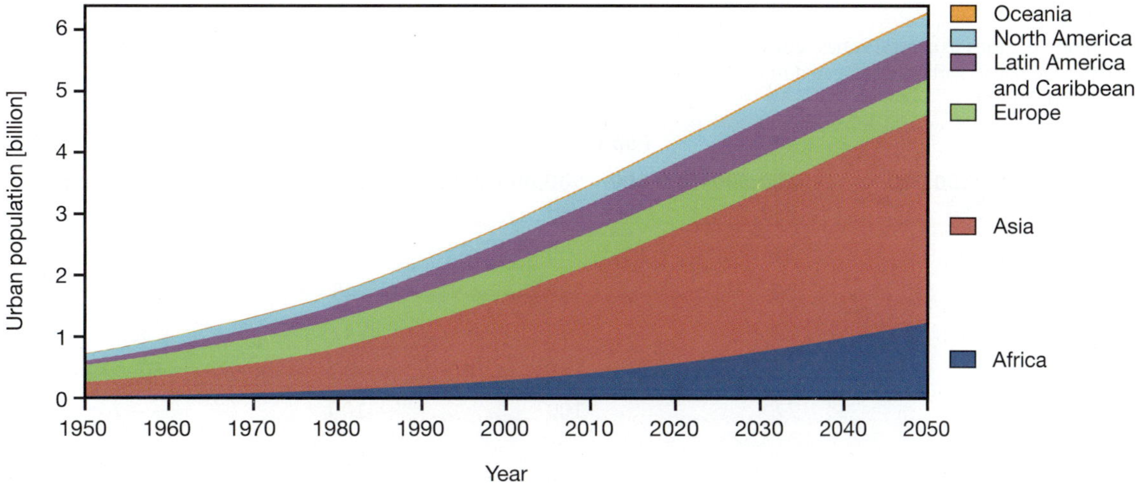

Figure 1.2-6
Number of city dwellers per continent: development up to 2050.
Source: UN DESA, 2010

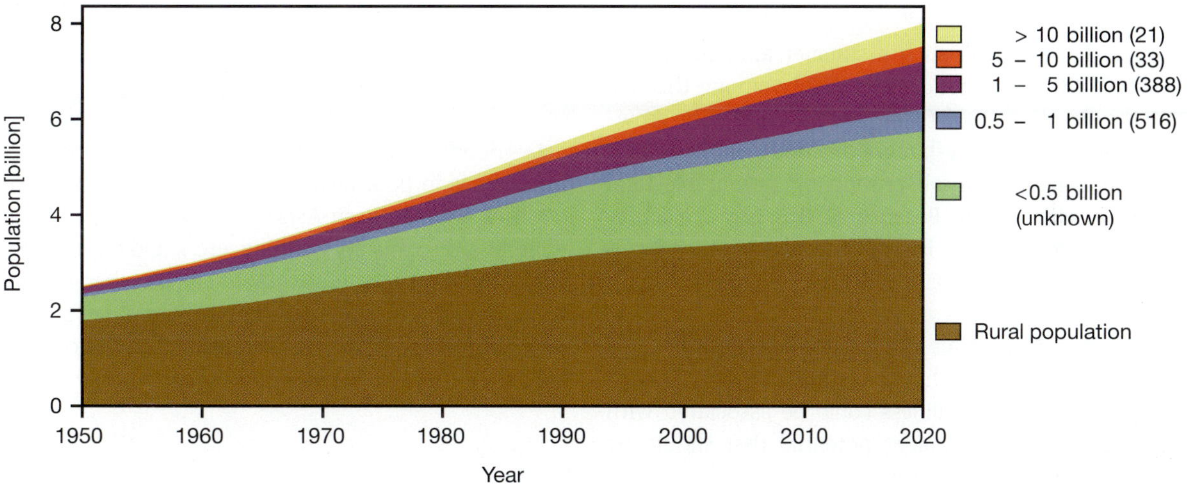

Figure 1.2-7
Population figure broken down according to urban settlement size and rural population. The number of settlements in 2009 is shown in brackets. The number of settlements with less than 500,000 inhabitants remains unknown.
Source: UN DESA, 2010

important accelerators of climate change. Cities already consume around three-quarters of global final energy (GEA, 2011), and possibly cause an even higher share of energy-related anthropogenic greenhouse gas emissions. Cities therefore play a key role in the transformation process, and are laboratories for innovative, climate-friendly development paths (OECD, 2010c).

Cities are not only climate change drivers, but are also victims of climate change: settlements tend to be concentrated particularly in coastal areas, and are therefore increasingly affected by the consequences of sea-level rise (Table 1.2-1; Figure 1.2-8; Corfee-Morlot et al., 2009). Although cities in developing countries suffer particularly from exposure to the risks of unabated climate change, the New Orleans flood disaster in 2005 shows that these risks are by no means restricted to developing countries. One OECD scenario reaches the conclusion that a 50 centimetre sea-level rise by 2070 would triple the coastal populations at risk from floods, whilst the volume of direct losses would rise tenfold. Some of this increased risk exposure (from 5% of GDP in 2008 to 9% of GDP in 2070), however, can actually also be attributed to the dynamics of rapid urbanisation. Increased flood risk through changes in glacial and precipitation patterns means that riverside cities frequently face similar challenges. At the same time, many cities also have to deal with pronounced water shortages during the dry season.

In the summer, heat islands form in many densely populated areas, exacerbating heat wave impacts. In

Table 1.2-1
Concentration of cities in coastal zones. For various population figures, the proportion of cities along the coast is shown. Major cities are particularly often located in coastal regions.
Source: OECD, 2010d

	Population figure				
Region	**<100,000 [%]**	**100,000–500,000 [%]**	**500,000–1 million [%]**	**1–5 million [%]**	**>5 million [%]**
Africa	9	23	39	50	40
Asia	12	24	37	45	70
Europe	17	22	37	41	58
Latin America	11	25	43	38	50
Australia and New Zealand	44	77	100	100	–
North America	9	19	29	25	80
Small island states	51	61	67	100	–
World	13	24	38	44	65

Europe, for instance, such a summer anomaly led to over 40,000 additional deaths, mainly among the sick and the elderly, in 2003 (Robine et al., 2008). The growing demand for energy-hungry air conditioning units is a prime example of a self-reinforcing, potentially fatal adaptive action loop. Because of this, peak electricity demand has now shifted to the summer months in many southern European countries.

Use Synergy Potentials and Economies of Scale

A rapid urbanisation that takes place under the primacy of climate-friendliness could be associated with a considerable development potential that should be used: improved access to education, health care, and income generation can be achieved far more efficiently in urban areas (World Bank, 2009b). The large number of urban households and their proximity to each other brings down the cost per unit of water and electricity supply. In terms of resource management, cities also provide unique opportunities for creating efficient and integrated urban systems. Systematic cross-sector urban and regional planning should therefore exploit the synergies between low-carbon urban development and other urban development goals (Corfee-Morlot et al., 2009).

Key Role in the Transformation Process

Cities have a key role to play in the low-carbon transformation, as they are major CO_2 emitters. At the same time, cities can function as laboratories for climate-friendly development. In view of the low-carbon transformation, the challenge is fourfold: *firstly*, existing inefficient urban infrastructures must be transformed (industrialised countries, South America, existing urban structures in Asia), *secondly*, the currently rapidly evolving new urban areas (in newly industrialising countries, particularly in Asia) must be made climate-friendly, *thirdly*, poverty in the densely populated urban areas in poor developing countries (particularly in Africa and southern Asia) must be overcome (slum rehabilitation, capacity building, etc.), and *fourthly*, the ability to adapt to the inevitable climate change must be improved. Particular attention should be paid to exploiting the synergies between climate-political aims and established urban development goals.

1.2.5
Increasing Land-Use Competition: Food Production, Bioenergy, Forests

Humankind already uses almost a quarter of global plant-based biomass net production, mainly for agricultural and forestry related products (Haberl et al., 2007; Figure 1.2-10). This proportion is expected to increase, as natural ecosystems continue to be converted into croplands or plantations (albeit at a declining speed), and production intensity will have to continue to increase. A brief analysis of current land-use trends shows that land-use related conflicts (including those about water; Section 1.1.2) will probably intensify significantly (Steinfeld et al., 2006; WBGU, 2010a; IAASTD, 2009).

Over the past few decades, increased agricultural production has overcompensated population growth (IAASTD, 2009). The area of agriculturally used land has hardly increased (from 1.4 to 1.5 million hectares, 1950–2005); rather, drastic productivity increases

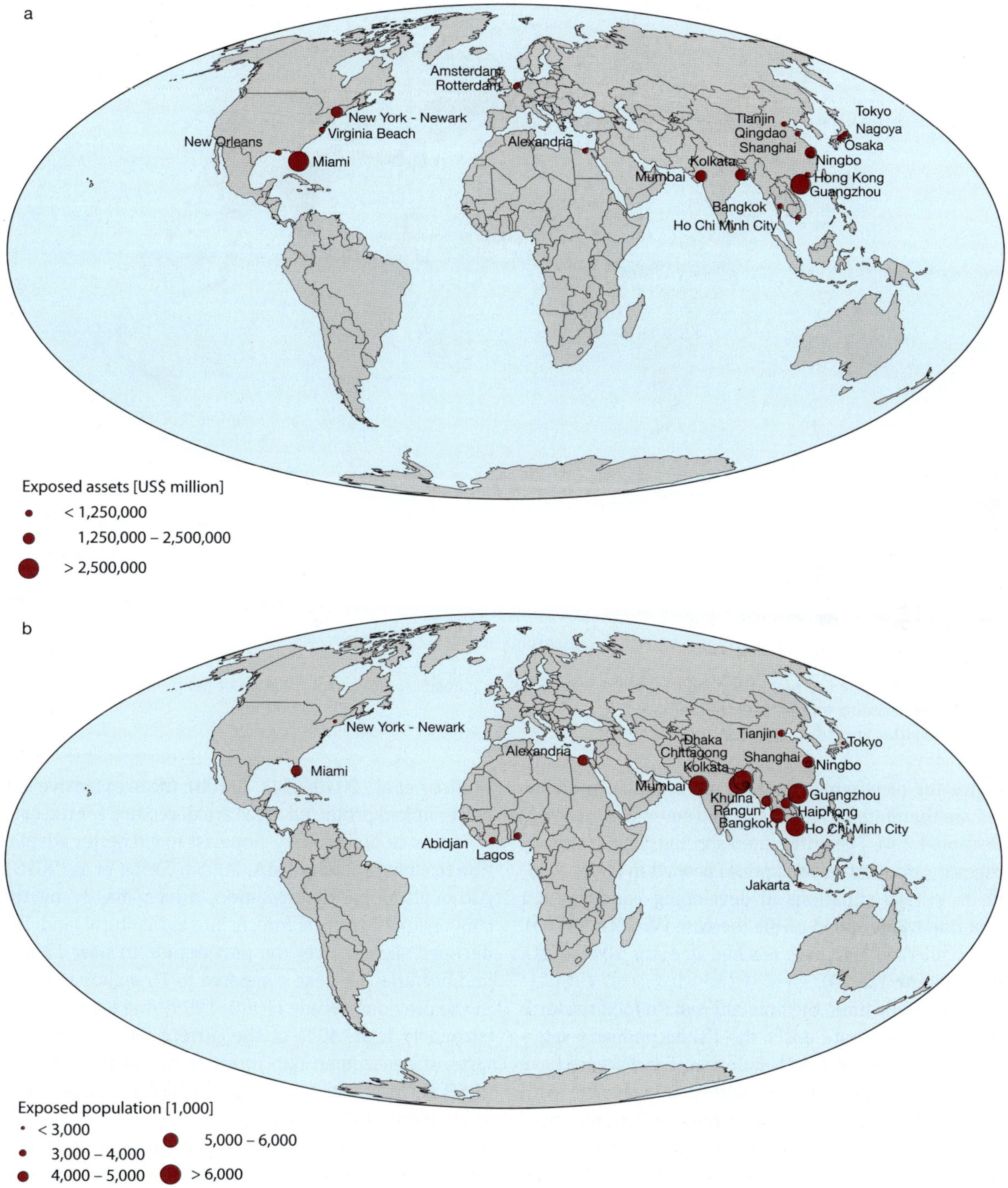

Figure 1.2-8
The 20 most important port cities: assets (a) and people (b) exposed to climate change risks.
Source: Nicholls et al., 2008

have been achieved, so that today, on average, considerably more is harvested per hectare of cropland. The intensification of agriculture through the use of artificial fertilisers, pesticides, new plant varieties, mechanisation and not least irrigation has made this productivity increase possible (Green Revolution; Section 3.5.2). Current food shortages are therefore above all a distribution problem. On average, sufficient food to feed the global population can be produced (WBGU, 2005; FAO and IFAD, 2008). This could change, for not only will there be another approx. 2.6 billion people by 2050 (FAO, 2009a; Box 1.2-2), but the growth of high-income urban social environments in newly industrialising and developing countries is accompanied by a pref-

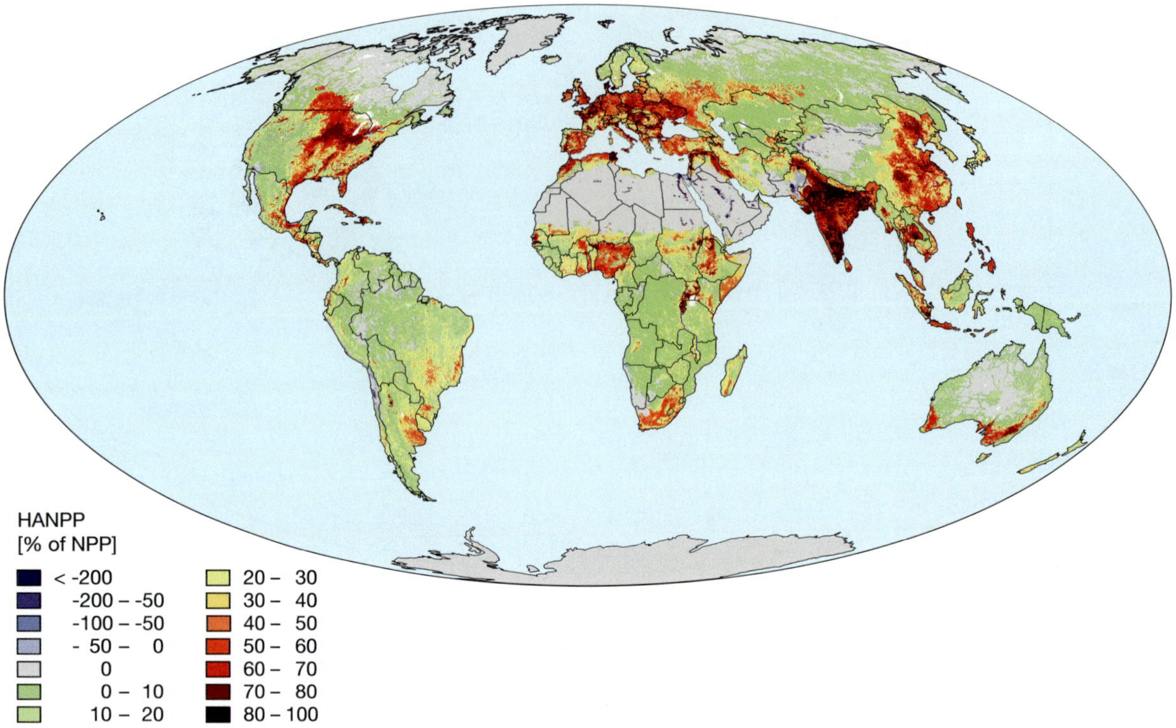

Figure 1.2-9
Map showing net primary production (NPP), used or influenced by humans (human appropriation of net primary production, HANPP), disregarding anthropogenic fires.
Source: Haberl et al., 2007

erence for diets which contain more animal products and are therefore far more land and emissions intensive (Section 4.3.4). The anticipated shortages have already affected prices. After food prices peaked in 2008, leading to critical situations in developing countries not least due to the speed of the increase (WBGU, 2010a), a new all-time high was reached in early 2011 (FAO, 2011; Figure 1.2-10).

At the same time, the only alternative food resource is facing a desperate crisis: the fishing industry regularly overexploits fish populations, catch volumes have stagnated for over ten years, and climate change, acidification and oceanic pollution are new environmental impacts adding to the strain (WBGU, 2006; FAO, 2009b; UNEP, 2010b). In future, the fishing industry will find it increasingly difficult to achieve current catch volumes, as there are hardly any unused marine regions left (Swartz et al., 2010).

Global food demand will rise considerably (IAASTD, 2009). Even more so than in the past, this rising demand will have to be met with production intensification on already cultivated land. For reasons of climate and biodiversity protection, the continued conversion of yet more natural ecosystems (particularly primary forests, wetlands, savannahs, etc.) is not a sustainable option (Section 4.1.7.1; van Vuuren, 2009; Godfrey et al., 2010; CBD, 2010b). More extensive and better linked protected areas are necessary for the conservation of biodiversity, not least to aid better adaptation to climate change (MA, 2005a; Turner et al., 2010). Although global deforestation, driven mainly by the conversion of tropical forests into agricultural land, has declined slightly over the past decade to now 13 million hectares per year, compared to 16 million per year in the previous decade (1990–1999), the level remains extremely high. 40% of the current 540 million hectares of Amazonian rain forest alone could be lost by 2050, releasing an estimated 117 Gt CO_2 (Soares-Filho et al., 2006; IPCC, 2007b).

Not least, the necessity of climate change mitigation and energy system decarbonisation exacerbates land-use competition. Bioenergy use plays a major role here, as production has tripled over the past 10 years, and is set to increase further (FAO, 2009a). The resultant new link between energy and food markets means that in future, political crises will affect food prices even more (WBGU, 2010a; Figure 1.2-10; Box 4.1-4). Rapidly increasing prices for agricultural products could be tolerated far more easily by those demanding bioenergy or bio-based raw materials than by the almost 1 billion people suffering from a lack of food security (FAO, 2008). Even a moderate bioenergy production

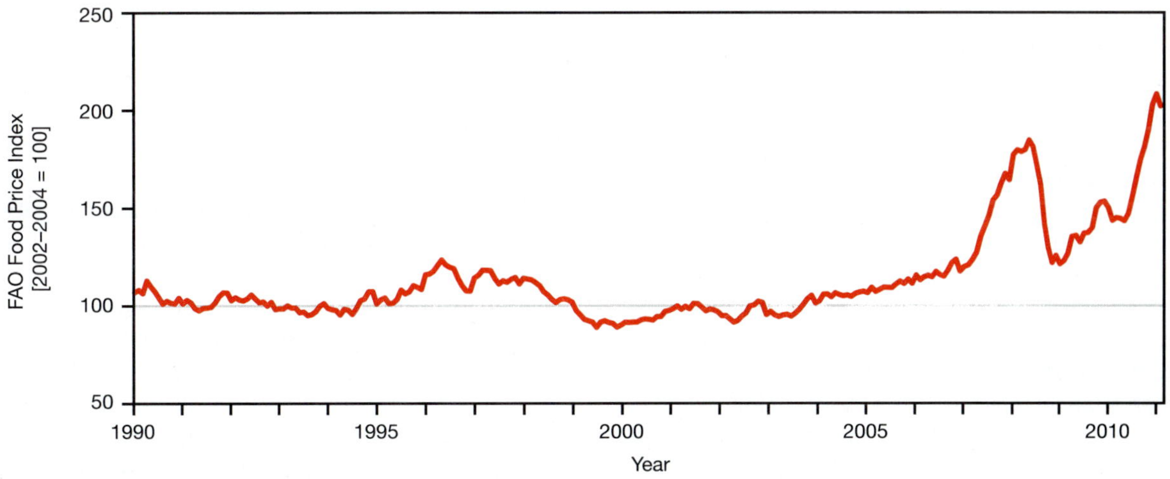

Figure 1.2-10
Food price development 1990–2011 (FAO Food Price Index, adjusted for inflation).
Source: FAO, 2011

expansion to 100 EJ per year as recommended by the WBGU (2009a) would imply that agricultural productivity would have to rise by 1.2–1.4% each year until 2055, particularly in sub-Saharan Africa and in the Middle East (Lotze-Campen et al., 2009). In addition, the demand for biomass for material use will grow to increasingly replace the crude oil based materials used in the chemical industry with biologically produced materials (BMBF, 2010b).

The competition for limited arable land is exacerbated by increasing production risks. Advancing soil degradation (Section 1.1.3) and increasing water shortages (Section 1.1.4; Rockström and Karlberg, 2010) can be observed at a global level. Moreover, depending on the characteristics of climate change, negative effects on agriculture and food security are expected in many regions, particularly those already frequently suffering from droughts, floods and poverty today, for example sub-Saharan Africa (Gregory et al., 2005; IPCC, 2007b). It seems that between 2000 and 2009, net primary production of land ecosystems already shows a slight climate-related decline (Zhao and Running, 2010). Climate change is expected to impact severely on global harvest yields in the second half of the century (Fischer, 2009). Taken together, these trends indicate that the transformation of global land use constitutes a key challenge (Godfrey et al., 2010).

Agricultural production will be required to increase considerably. Global agricultural production increase estimates anticipate the required increase to range from 50% to as much as 70% by 2050 (IAASTD, 2009; FAO, 2009a; Bruinsma, 2009). To achieve this, the current trend must first be reversed, as the global agricultural production growth rate has been in decline for roughly the past three decades (FAO, 2003). Accordingly, prices for agricultural goods are expected to continue to rise in the coming decades (IAASTD, 2009). One can only hope that this will serve as an incentive to channel more investments into this sector; currently, they are close to a historical low (Halweil and Nierenberg, 2011). Increased production must be augmented with improvements in the usage of agricultural products (Godfrey et al., 2010). Conversion to a healthier diet in the industrialised countries and the rapidly growing middle-income social environments in the newly industrialising and developing countries would equal a conversion to less consumption of animal products. The reduction in the associated land requirement would considerably reduce land-use pressure (Section 4.3.4; WBGU, 2010a).

Land-use competition is increasingly becoming a central sustainability issue, and is a potential future conflict area (GO Science, 2011; WBGU, 2009, 2010a). There is a consensus on the dimensions of the challenge and the considerable need for reform and development. In contrast, there is no broad scientific or political consensus on which strategies are best suited to ensure sustainable global land use. Primarily, this concerns the question of appropriate intensification techniques (for example the pros and cons of green genetic engineering, and of intensive use of agrochemicals), the issue of definition and importance of sustainability in agricultural production (for example consideration of soil protection or biodiversity, links to rural poverty, and equity), and suitable framework conditions and production structures that take the extremely different regional conditions into account (role of subsidies, industrial farming versus smallholdings).

In recent years, moneyed investors (for example from Saudi Arabia or China) have increasingly attempted to secure themselves access to sizeable areas of arable agricultural land (several million hectares in total), particularly in Africa, in order to cover their own national biomass production deficits, or to generate profit, from large-scale industrial food or bioenergy production and subsequent export. This can be classified as a symptom of increasing land-use competition (FAO et al., 2009; von Braun, 2010). In principle, any additional direct investments in agriculture in developing countries are to be welcomed; however, these large-scale projects, often tellingly referred to as 'land grabbing', could fuel land-use conflicts if they are carried out non-transparently and without participation of the local population, and do not take local conditions and rights into account. This could intensify the already precarious situation of many African smallholders (von Braun and Meinzen-Dick, 2009; BMZ, 2010).

1.3 Conclusions: The Transformation Towards Sustainability

Humankind currently lives in the Anthropocene, i.e. the geological age in which the detrimental effects of human actions on the environment have reached a dimension that is comparable to natural influences (Crutzen and Stoermer, 2000). The Earth system's megatrends (Section 1.1) are so dangerous because they significantly impact on humankind and society. If the planetary guard rails are not complied with (Box 1-1), resources or Earth system services that are extremely important for humankind are in danger. An unabated continuation of these trends could for example have serious consequences for global food security (Section 1.2.5). The guard rails define the limits within which development and progress can take place sustainably. Some of these megatrends have set humankind on a collision course with the planetary guard rails (for example climate change: Section 1.1.1), others have already led to transgression (e.g. biodiversity: Section 1.1.2; Rockström et al., 2009b).

At the same time, the positive development progress in many developing and newly industrialising countries is associated with an increase in resource-intensive lifestyles (Section 1.2). The idea that all people should be able to enjoy a lifestyle that equals today's predominant lifestyle in the industrialised countries, characterised by the use of fossil energy carriers, cannot be realised. To avoid non-sustainable development paths, the developing and newly industrialising countries would have to leapfrog technological development stages. The industrial countries should therefore lead the way off current development paths to demonstrate that it is also possible to follow sustainable paths. A lifestyle must be found that is consistent with the guiding principle of global sustainable development. It must also allow the catch-up development of poorer countries, equally guided by the criteria of global sustainability, and allow for inclusion of the so far excluded 'bottom billion'.

A change of course is therefore an urgent imperative. A transformation towards sustainability must take place, as otherwise, the natural life-support systems of a continuously growing global population are in danger, considerably restricting the development chances of future societies (Section 3; Raskin et al., 2010). In view of the dimensions, the dynamics and the close interaction of the Earth system's megatrends and global economic and social megatrends, it becomes clear that the transformation towards sustainability must be a Great Transformation. In terms of profound impact, it is comparable to the two fundamental transformations in world history: the Neolithic Revolution, i.e. the invention and diffusion of agriculture and animal husbandry, and the Industrial Revolution, a term used to describe the transition from agricultural to industrialised society. Furthermore, it must take place within the planetary guard rails, advance rapidly within a very tight timeframe, and given a high rank on the political agenda.

High Priority for Climate Change Mitigation as a Precondition for Sustainable Development

Analysis of megatrends shows that climate change plays a particularly important role. It exacerbates contemporary environmental crises; concurrently, some environmental problems affect climate change retroactively, triggering feedback dynamics (Section 1.1.6). Anthropogenic climate change is only just starting to become apparent, and its effects on economy and society will increase over the coming decades. The bottom line is that unabated climate change could have a disastrous negative impact on economy and society (Section 1.1.1; IPCC, 2007b). The global rise in mean temperature can endanger the livelihood of many people, particularly those in developing regions, increase the susceptibility to poverty and social immiseration, thereby not least threatening human security. Particularly in weak and fragile states with inefficient institutions and government systems, climate change would overtax the ability to adapt to changing environmental conditions, for instance dealing with the consequences of extreme events such as droughts, flooding or harvest loss. New security risks might evolve, triggering additional environmental migration (WBGU, 2008). For the following reasons, the WBGU has decided to focus on the transformation into a low-carbon society, albeit embedded into the context of sustainable development, in this flagship report.

- Compliance with the 2 °C guard rail is a conditio sine qua non for sustainable development. Once this guard rail is broken, it will become extremely difficult, or even impossible, to keep within the other planetary guard rails (Section 1.1.6). Unabated climate change will also prevent the achievement of other development goals, particularly combating poverty (WBGU, 2005; Section 1.2.1). Climate change mitigation therefore has a particularly important part to play in the transformation towards sustainability: although climate protection alone cannot guarantee the conservation of the natural life-support systems on which humankind depends, it is nevertheless foreseeable that without effective climate protection, mankind will soon lose essential development opportunities.
- Time is particularly of the essence where climate protection is concerned. The greenhouse gas emissions trend must be turned around within the next 10 years as otherwise, compliance with the 2 °C guard rail will be unachievable (Section 1.1.1; Box 1.1-1). First steps towards energy system decarbonisation, i. e. the avoidance of CO_2 emissions from fossil sources, have already been taken and must be significantly accelerated (Section 4).
- The extent of the required reorganisation is a particularly major challenge. Regarding the transformation towards a low-carbon society within the scope of sustainable development, policies should primarily address the following three main pillars of contemporary global society: *Firstly,* the energy systems, including the transport sector, which the whole economy depends on and which currently, due to the rapid development dynamics in the newly industrialising countries, are facing yet another wave of growth. The energy sector causes around two-thirds of today's long-lived greenhouse gas emissions (Section 1.2.3). *Secondly,* the urban areas, currently responsible for three-quarters of global final energy demand. Their population will double to 6 billion by 2050 (Section 1.2.4). *Thirdly,* the land-use systems (agriculture and forestry, including deforestation). They are currently responsible for almost a quarter of global greenhouse gas emissions (Section 1.2.5). Land use not only has to provide enough food for a world population that continues to grow, and to become more demanding, but also has to deal with a growth in demand due to the increasing use of bioenergy and bio-based raw materials. These sectors must be fundamentally restructured worldwide to avoid breaking the 2 °C guard rail, without endangering efficiency in the three transformation fields energy systems, urban areas and land-use systems.

Over the past few years, anthropogenic climate change has reached the centre stage in societal discourse. There is now a global political consensus that rapid global warming by more than 2 °C would overtax our societies' ability to adapt (Section 1.1.1; UNFCCC, 2010). Although the low-carbon transformation continues to be recognised as a huge challenge for humankind, it is approached with little ambition. It is not only absolute greenhouse gas emissions that have continued to rise in recent years. Contrary to the long-term trend, the CO_2 intensity of energy generation has also again increased. Without redirection, the remaining global carbon budget will soon be exhausted (Box 1.1-1). Climate change mitigation and the inferential necessity for energy system decarbonisation has therefore become an essential element for sustainable development. The 'transformation into a low-carbon society' is therefore the main focus of this flagship report.

Although climate protection is the most urgent step on the path towards sustainability, other environmental and developmental issues also require solution strategies, some of which have already been outlined and are now the subject of international discussion, or are seeing implementation. However, the measures of the various strategies must be consolidated and aligned, as they overlap extensively with other sustainability dimensions, and can have secondary effects on these (Section 1.1.6). In part, synergies emerge: the protection of primary forests from deforestation for climate change mitigation also favours the conservation of biodiversity, and impacts positively on the quality of life of local or indigenous communities (WBGU, 2001a). Other measures are accompanied by negative secondary effects, for example the use of bioenergy; although it can substitute fossil energy carriers, it can also, if not used carefully, have an extremely negative impact on food security, biodiversity conservation and even climate change mitigation (Box 4.1-4; WBGU, 2010a).

The associated risks and undesired secondary effects of climate protection strategies and measures on other sustainability dimensions and future tolerance should therefore be carefully examined prior to large-scale implementation. The pronounced interconnectedness of problematic issues and solution approaches requires this 'sustainability check'. The debate on the certification of bioenergy and timber products has corresponding solutions to offer. The sustainability check should be taken into account at the earliest possible stage of strategic solution approaches, and carried out initially in small-scale pilot projects. The WBGU planetary guard rails (Box 1-1) could serve as a first rough screener with regard to the environmental dimensions, and the Millennium Development Goals with regard to developmental dimensions. Apart from sustainability compatibility checks, long-term monitoring in the form of an early warning system should also be implemented to highlight critical environmental changes in time. Civil society participation should also play a role in the process at the earliest possible stage, to obtain a better assessment of specific local issues, which, ultimately, serves legitimation and acceptance. An obligatory sustainability check is certainly not unrealistic, but rather a requirement to avoid expensive and time-consuming technological dead ends.

Key Factors for the Transformation

The key factors impeding or promoting the low-carbon transformation process are identified during the course of this report. This chapter has already illustrated some of the factors listed below; others are elaborated in subsequent chapters. Impediments are:

- *Tight timeframes:* The analysis in Section 1 shows that the transformation must take place within a very tight timeframe if the planetary guard rails are to be upheld. This equals a major challenge for complex societies, particularly in the context of international negotiation systems (Chapter 5).
- *Rapid urbanisation:* The urbanisation waves in the developing regions, a significant proportion of which are founded on high-carbon based economic growth, are a further huge challenge for the transformation process, but also a great opportunity (Sections 1.2.4, 5.4.5.2).
- *Path dependencies:* The dimensions of global energy systems, coupled with the long life-span of the related infrastructure, account for the inertia with regard to adjustment processes (Sections 1.2.3, 4.2). Political, institutional and economic path dependencies, interest structures and veto players impede the transition into a sustainable society (Chapter 5). The worldwide subsidies in the three-digit billion range for fossil energy carriers are one example of this.
- *Availability of cheap coal*: The fact that the fuel coal is cheaply available in many currently dynamically growing newly industrialising countries reinforces path dependencies and impedes the transformation (Section 4.1.2).
- *Global cooperation blockades:* The analysis also shows that existing global governance instruments and the implementation of the strategies and recommendations thus developed do not suffice to solve complex global environmental problems (Sections 1.1, 5.4.4). Sample deficits include the partial fragmentation or lack of coherence between the various treaties and institutions; the main drawback, however, is the inadequate enforceability of the agreements. The global community is not well prepared for the transformation; this also applies to the three key transformation fields energy, urbanisation and land use. Developing international environmental law and global institutions further towards an integrated strategy for dealing with global environmental and development issues therefore remains an important future challenge (Sections 5.4.4, 7.3.9, 7.3.10).

During its course, this report elaborates how these impeding factors can be overcome, and how transformation-relevant promoting factors can be identified and reinforced. The following factors are of essential importance in terms of achievability of the transformation into a low-carbon society:

- *Value change towards sustainability:* The initial question is whether the population is actually willing to share the burden of such a fundamental reorganisation of the infrastructure. Do people's values accord a high enough priority to the protection of the natural environment? Is there a global cross-cultural consensus for the transformation of the current way of life towards sustainability and climate change mitigation? These questions are of paramount importance for policy-makers in order to be able to assess the level of legitimation and acceptance in terms of the transformation process. Chapter 2 poses these questions and shows that values are already changing at a global level. Chapter 6 focuses on the transformation's societal actors and examines how innovations can spread faster, aided by these changed values.
- *Technology:* The most important starting point for climate protection is the energy system. The crucial question is therefore whether the technical and sustainable potentials of climate-friendly energy carriers will be sufficient. However, the energy system decarbonisation strategy must not impede the overcoming of energy poverty. Moreover, it must be ascertained whether the technologies for setting the course towards climate protection are available in the area of land use, which is another major greenhouse gas emitter. The question of technical feasibility is analysed and answered in Chapter 4.
- *Financing:* Another issue in terms of implementing the transformation is whether it is economically achievable, and how substantial the transformation-relevant financial challenges are. This calculation should not only take the additional investment requirements into account, but also consider the long-term savings achieved through the use of renewable energies in terms of fuel cost avoidance, and the avoidance of the huge costs that would be the consequence of dangerous climate change. These

issues are examined in Section 4.5, 'Financing the Transformation into a Low-Carbon Society'.

- *Steering instruments:* Besides the technical and economical achievability, there is also the issue of societal implementation of the transformation to be considered. Are the political, economic and legal steering instruments available to structure the framework conditions in such a way as to promote the energy system decarbonisation? Could these instruments be used to also establish a central guideline in the other two transformation fields of urbanisation and land use? These issues are dealt with in Chapter 5, 'Structuring the Transformation'.

Based on the overall analysis, the WBGU's key conclusion is that the transformation into a low-carbon global society is not only vital, but also achievable. In some sectors, regions and countries, it has already begun.

Changing Values: The Global Transformation of Values has already begun

2

2.1 Values and Value Change

Transforming economy and society fundamentally, rapidly, and on a global scale - against people's wishes and prevalent values - is neither possible nor desirable. The reason for the latter: if you view dangerous climate change, for example, or the extinction of species, not just as adverse changes to the natural life-support systems, but above all as a possible huge curtailment of individual scope and global social development options, you cannot pursue solutions that authoritatively curtail precisely this scope and those options (Leggewie, 2010). *Firstly,* therefore, the adequate propagation of the appropriate attitudes and preferences is an indispensable premise for a successful transformation towards sustainability (Raskin et al., 2002; Leiserowitz et al., 2006). An environmental and climate policy that is both effective and democratically legitimate must 'make people go with the flow', i.e. it must make the intended transition agreeable to large majorities (acceptance), obtain general consent (legitimation), and invite their cooperation (participation). *Secondly,* the indispensable social and political mobilisation cannot (solely) rely on minimisation and relinquishment targets, which usually trigger anxiety about the future and loss aversion. It must match perceptions of what a good and successful life is, and these again must be widely shared and attractive. Transformation strategies for averting Earth system crises should (and can) put the realisation of goals on the daily agenda, goals which a great number of people all over the world strive for anyway, and support decisions which, after balancing all the pros and cons, can be made 'without regret' (no-regret strategies).

In the following, the WBGU brings forward a two-fold argument. *Firstly,* that the necessary transformation into a low-carbon society already corresponds to some of the prevalent attitudes and value systems in many of the world's countries (Box 2.1-1). *Secondly,* that the transformation can therefore be viewed as a positive factor in the sense of increasing subjective life satisfaction for large parts of the population.

Value systems are always linked to cultural and social context. In pluralistic societies, they are 'negotiated', i.e. hotly debated, against the background of practical problems and dilemmas. Value conflicts are just as normal as distribution conflicts, and – always assuming that they are carried out peacefully and solved amicably – promote social change and cultural innovation (Dahrendorf, 1957). Any kind of reflexion on the development progress and transformation chances of today's societies must start with empirically proven values and attitudes. This highlights many issues, such as: what are the value systems in the poor and in the wealthy regions of the world, and how do they differ? And, again region-specific, how is the relationship between the goal of (increasing) material wealth on the one hand, and postmaterialist ideals of self-expression and consideration of the natural environment on the other, developing? What rank is accorded to the growth of both national economies and the global economy in relation to environmental and climate protection?

Since the beginning of the modern era, attitudes and considerations inspired by personal benefit maximisation have established themselves. With the advent of industrial mass production, the 'good life' has increasingly become synonymous with material wealth. In the course of the 'Great Transformation' (Polanyi, 1944), the economy has been extensively disembedded from its relation to society and life worlds. This functional differentiation of the economic system has lent it an autonomy that has made possible a previously unimagined extent of productivity growth. However, it has also led to the whole social order being subjected to economic principles (Schimank, 2009). This is (only) the case once market principles affect all other subsystems (such as politics, culture, family, etc.) thereby turning rational cost-benefit analysis into the interpretation pattern that determines the actions of society as a whole. This focusing of individual and collective attitudes and preferences has had as much of a determining impact on the self-definition and self-observation

Box 2.1-1

Values, Attitudes and Opinions

The terms 'values', 'attitudes' and 'opinions' have different meanings in psychology, sociology and political sciences (see Häcker and Stapf, 1994). For the most part, it is assumed that attitudes are based on values, and that these attitudes influence people's behaviour, even if research (Eckes and Six, 1994) assumes that there is no particularly close connection between attitudes and behaviour. In this report, the WBGU uses these terms as follows:

1. Personal and cultural values: According to Kluckhohn (1951), values are a shared perception of something worth having or striving for. Cultural values therefore refer to something that has evolved socio-culturally, something that exists independent of individuals. Personal values, on the other hand, refer to the subjective concepts of desire and specific value orientation. Personal values or value orientation therefore describe the individuals' relatively stable preferences with regard to different values (Häcker and Stapf, 1994).
2. Attitudes: Contrary to the rather abstract 'values' and 'value systems', attitudes relate to certain objects, people (groups), ideas and ideologies, or specific situations (Häcker and Stapf, 1994). Attitudes represent evaluation and action tendencies with regard to attitude objects, and are usually stable in the medium-term. They are therefore neither long-term value systems, nor short-term intentions.
3. Opinions: Are generally considered to be the verbalisation of attitudes and values (Rokeach, 1968). Attitudes are usually measured by several items, i.e. asking carefully selected questions and statements which are indicators for certain attitudes to evaluate one attitude object, thereby ensuring that the results are reliable.

of developed industrialised societies as it has on the implementation of socio-economic modernisation in most of the developing societies in the south. This generalisation (or tunnel vision) means that the aspects of a 'good life' and sustainable development have become secondary.

Nevertheless, a rethinking process seems to be currently taking place in many parts of society in a great number of countries; just one example from Germany to highlight this, and prove the point: according to a survey published in the autumn of 2010, carried out by the Emnid Institute and commissioned by the Bertelsmann Foundation, a significant part of the German population views growth and capitalism with scepticism: a mere third of Germany's citizens believes that growth will automatically impact positively on their own personal quality of life. Immaterial values such as social justice or environmental protection are accorded so much importance that they influence the attitude Germans have towards the economic system; for example, 88 percent of respondents think that the current system is not suitable for taking environmental protection, resource conservation, and social redistribution, adequately into account. The majority would like a 'new economic system', and does not really believe in the resilience and crisis resistance of purely market-driven economic systems. Particularly younger Germans do not trust the market's self-restorative powers, and call for improved compatibility between economic growth and environmental protection. The survey substantiates that in Germany, postmaterialist thinking is by no means limited to the well-off and educated. For the majority of respondents, health, social relationships and environmental status were deemed to be far more important sources of personal quality of life than 'increasing money and wealth' (Figure 2.1-1). 75% of respondents with higher education entrance qualifications, and 69% of respondents with a mere school leaving certificate, agreed with the statement 'I consider wealth to be less important than environmental protection and debt reduction' (Bertelsmann Foundation, 2010).

The increasingly sceptical view of the current economic system's performance and its externalities rests not least on the realisation of the system's social costs that result from economic activities relying on short-term benefits and gains (Section 1.1), but also on the improvements of material wealth in low-income household settings, leaving space for alternative, postmaterialist value-orientations and lifestyles. These have emerged from the eco (or green) niche, and – as will be shown in the following – are now increasingly determining general perspectives; this also applies in economically less developed regions.

2.2 Changing Values and Environmental Consciousness

2.2.1 The Theory of Value Change: An Explanation of the Increasing Prevalence of Postmaterialist Values since the Second World War

This 'silent revolution' (Inglehart, 1977) – the gradual advance of values mindful of, amongst other aspects, the environment and sustainability – can be explained with a Theory of Value Change (Inglehart, 1977, 1998),

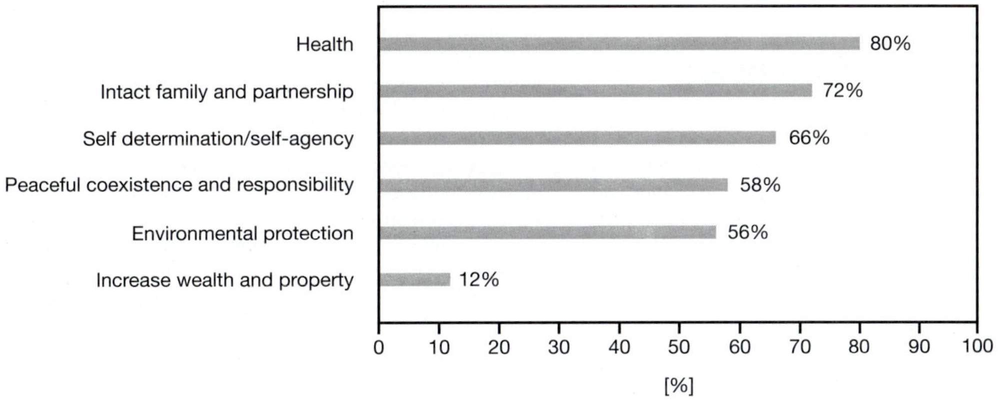

Figure 2.1-1
What citizens consider important in terms of quality of life; statements on quality of life (in %, multiple answers permitted) from the Emnid Institute's representative telephone survey (N=1001), conducted in Germany, commissioned by the Bertelsmann Foundation.
Source: Bertelsmann Foundation, 2010

which, if applied, reveals the intergenerational advance of postmaterialist values and attitudes, particularly since the Second World War. In the dichotomy assumed by Inglehart, material needs gratification also includes the pursuit of economic stability and growth, such as price stability, and both national and social 'peace and order', as well as physical needs – all in all, therefore, the striving for physical security (Inglehart, 1998). Postmaterialist needs, on the other hand, include elements such as self-expression, which are to be found in the gratification of spiritual, creative and aesthetic needs, and furthermore the desire to participate in state and society, as well as the valuing of freedom of opinions, and tolerance. These two value spheres are by no means mutually exclusive as the international debate on value change has shown (Klages, 2001). It is much rather a case of their being positioned on a continuum in the direction of a value synthesis as changing values actually do not develop independently. The change correlates to the postmaterialists' rising income and education level; due to the gratification of their material needs and their time budgets, they are able to spend leisure time with partners, family and friends, to dedicate themselves to a leisurely enjoyment of art and culture, and to feel personally accepted and appreciated in these contexts. Initially, this post-Second World War postmaterialist value change in the industrialised societies could only be expressed hypothetically. Inglehart et al., however, managed to prove the value change theory empirically, supported by World Values Survey (WVS) data (Inglehart, 2008; Box 2.2-1).

Inglehart et al. argue that, over the past 25 years, 'constraints' – i.e. the existence of, and emphasis on, normative axioms and/or practical constraints – have shifted on a global level, and particularly in affluent and 'secure' societies, to the extent of an effective widening of choices that promote the individual's autonomy to act, linked with the respective (postmaterialist) value systems (Inglehart, 2008; Inglehart et al., 2008). Interesting with regard to the global transformation process is the fact that, on the basis of the WVS data, this trend can not just be observed in the 'rich west' (of Europe and North America), but also – although at a different level – in five different cultural spheres (Confucian cultural sphere, Protestant and Catholic Europe, the Anglo-Saxon, and the Hispanic worlds; Inglehart et al., 2003; Welzel, 2006). This does not necessarily mean that certain material values are disappearing completely from people's value-consciousness, or that they have indeed already disappeared. Neither does it mean that they do not continue to determine the actual behaviour of individuals and groups; it simply shows that the shift moves on a continuum.

2.2.2 Attitudes to Environment and Sustainability in various Countries and World Religions

Inglehart views the emergence and increasing power of new social movements – like the conservation, peace or homosexual movements – as the expression of a wider cultural value change (Inglehart, 2008). Concern about the natural environment is, just like the valuing of tolerance, an element of a postmaterialist attitude pattern that corresponds to the diffusion of self-expression values. The history of the conservation movement in the western industrialised states has shown that above all, apart from a value change towards postmaterialist attitudes, being directly and perceptibly affected by environmental pollution and damage creates environmental consciousness (Hünenmörder, 2004).

Regardless of the exact reasons responsible for the relevant developments, the results of the WVS emphatically document the level of importance that public

Box 2.2-1

Ronald Inglehart and the World Values Survey

In terms of number of publications and citations, the US American political scientist Ronald Inglehart is seen as the most influential researcher in the field of value change (Rössel, 2006). Apart from his theoretical works, Inglehart has also had a major influence of value change research through the World Values Survey (WVS) in his capacity as WVS executive committee chairman. The WVS is one of the most comprehensive and empirically most valid set of data which makes it possible to draw conclusions on the attitudes and value orientations of people from all over the world. The WVS is an ongoing empirical study that is conducted by an international network of research institutions and researchers. In five waves of data collection since 1981, more than 330,000 people worldwide have been interviewed; the 6th wave is currently being carried out. The study started in 1981 in 20 mainly western European states. All in all, over the past almost 30 years, data from 97 countries, all cultural spheres, and all world regions has been collected. More than 88% of the world's population live in these countries (Figure 2.2-1). The spectrum of countries covered by the survey is correspondingly comprehensive: people living in long-established democracies were interviewed, but also people in the former Eastern Bloc, countries with more of an authoritarian tradition. The survey was run in some of the richest nations on earth, but also in countries where the average annual income per capita is less than US$ 300 (Inglehart, 2003). The WVS is therefore one of the few sets of data that covers the majority of the world population in the long-term, and permits the formulation of concrete statements regarding the world society's attitude and value system trends.

During the WVS, a sample, as representative as possible, of between 1,000 and 3,500 people aged 18 to 85 is interviewed face-to-face, using a standard questionnaire. In each of the respective countries, local leading social scientists are recruited on a cooperative partner basis to collect the data. It is hoped that this way, the national and cultural specifics of each of the countries surveyed are taken into account, and that the questionnaires are accordingly modified. The questionnaires are always translated into each of the respective country's languages, providing that it is spoken by at least 15% of the population. The WVS is one of the few studies that collects data multi-nationally, and over long time-spans. With the WVS, an empirical database that is generally considered to be unique has been created for the field of value change research (Rössel, 2006).

Apart from socio-demographic data, the WVS also collects information regarding attitudes and positions on a wide spectrum of issues. This includes, amongst other items, the areas of work, family, politics and society, or religion and ethics. For the most part, the WBGU analysis focuses on illustrating the results from the group of questions headed 'environment'.

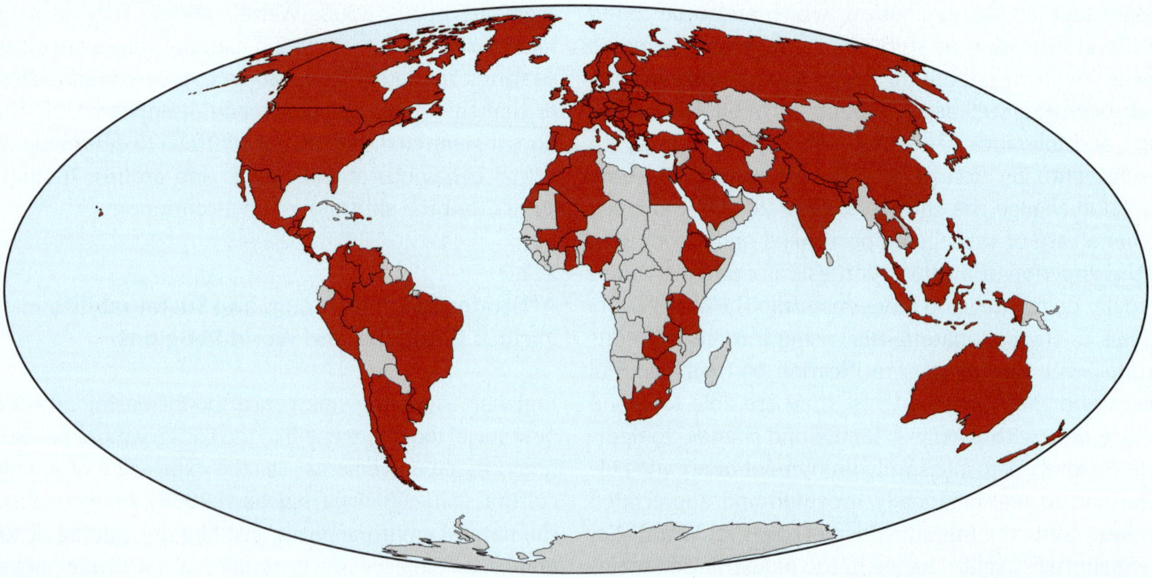

Figure 2.2-1
Countries covered by the World Values Survey, and sample sizes. Red: 97 countries where people have been interviewed for the WVS up to 2007.
Source: WVS, 2010

Wave	Years	Countries	Population	Sample
1	1981–1984	20	4.7 billion	25,000
2	1989–1993	42	5.3 billion	61,000
3	1994–1998	52	5.7 billion	75,000
4	1999–2004	67	6.1 billion	96,000
5	2005–2008	57	6.7 billion	> 77,000

opinion in many of the world's countries today accords to aspects of sustainability. Nowadays, the population views environmental problems, in particular climate change, as one of the important political issues – and this not just in the comparatively rich northern countries, but also in many of the developing and newly industrialising countries. The results of the 5th WVS wave (2005–2008) show that despite the continuing high-profile trivialisation through so-called climate sceptics, a total of 89.3% of respondents in 49 countries (n = 62,684) consider global warming to be a serious or very serious problem. This result and all of the following results quoted are based on WVS data (2009). Even in countries where the climate-sceptical public element is comparatively large – like the USA, South Africa or China – the vast majority of respondents views climate change as a serious or very serious problem (Figure 2.2-2).

Not only climate change, but also the loss of plant or animal species or biodiversity is considered as a serious, or very serious, issue by a similar number of respondents (90.9%; n = 64,573). Materialist value systems, i.e. the preference of physical and socio-economical security, continue to be important in a great number of countries and tend to dominate in the materially less prosperous and crisis-ridden societies, in accordance with the value change theory (Inglehart, 2008). However, different survey items designed to give insights into the ranking of environmental conservation resulted in high agreement levels in almost all of the countries that were included in the survey. For example, the majority of respondents (54.6%; n = 73,461) state that protecting the environment should be given priority, even if it causes slower economic growth and some loss of jobs.

Breaking down the data according to country reveals that although environmental protection is ranked above economic interests, particularly in the rich OECD states (like Norway, Canada, Australia, or Switzerland), this preference is, however, also marked in the population of a whole range of developing and newly industrialising countries in South America (such as Colombia, Argentina, or Chile) and Asia (such as China or Vietnam; Figure 2.2-3). Although the environmental consciousness of societies is partly subject to strong fluctuations, and must not be viewed outside the respective social and economic contexts (Hünenmörder, 2004), the approval rating over the entire period of the 3rd (1995–1998), 4th (1999–2002) and 5th (2005–2008) WVS waves show that the preference of environmental protection over economic growth and job creation is, overall, relatively stable in the surveyed countries. Furthermore, the results of the 5th wave (2005–2008) show that a majority of respondents (57.3%; n = 68,123) would be prepared to pay more taxes if the income thus

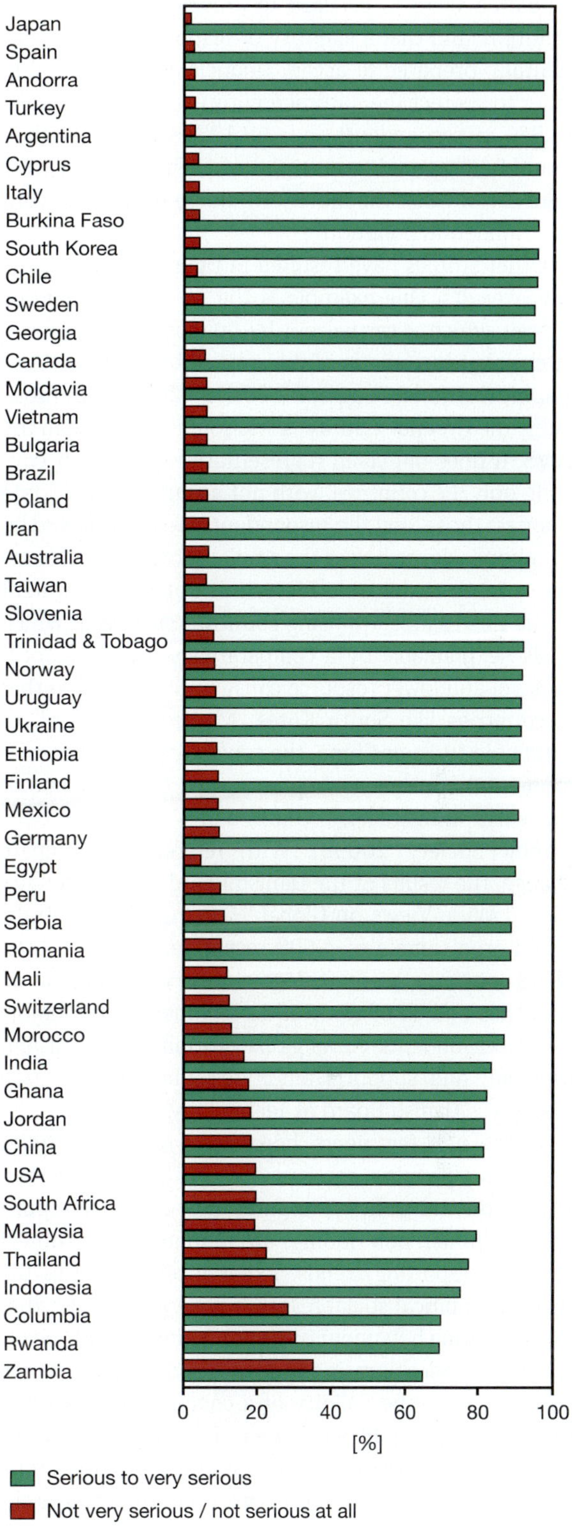

Figure 2.2-2
How serious an issue is global warming, or the greenhouse effect? Results of the 5th wave of the World Value Survey for 49 countries (N = 62,684). Respondents could choose to answer 'very serious', 'somewhat serious', 'not very serious', or 'not serious at all'.
Source: WVS, 2009 (own calculations)

generated were to be used to prevent environmental pollution, and that a majority of respondents is fundamentally prepared to accept financial losses as well in order to protect the natural environment: for example, 65.8% of respondents (n = 68,123) stated that they would be prepared to give part of their income if they were certain that the money would be used to prevent environmental pollution.

Other studies have resulted in figures similar to the WVS results. One example is the so-called Greendex Survey, which is carried out by opinion research institute GlobeScan, and is commissioned by National Geographic (National Geographic Society, 2009a). Methodically, the Greendex Study is less sophisticated than the WVS. It does not claim representativeness, so far covering only 17 countries, with not a single African state amongst those, and the respondents are interviewed by telephone. Nevertheless the results show that, on average, a more sustainable lifestyle is not only prevalent in the newly industrialising countries surveyed, which is also explainable by a comparatively lower prosperity level and lower resource consumption, but also that in countries like South Korea, Mexico and Brazil, or equally in India or China, the sensitivity towards environmental issues is more pronounced than in some of the early-industrialised OECD states (National Geographic Society, 2009b). With reference to climate change, the results of the Danish Board of Technology's 'World Wide Views on Global Warming' (2009) study, based on a sample of 4,000 respondents from a total of 38 countries, were analogous to WVS results: in all countries and all of the world's regions, a large majority of respondents views global warming as an urgent problem, and supports ambitious climate protection measures (Danish Board of Technology, 2009).

In the past few years, however, a range of studies measuring people's reservations against climate and environmental policy measures has also been published. Opinion poll findings are fundamentally subject to media reporting trends. Experiences gained in the field of empirical social research have also shown that the answering behaviour of respondents depends heavily on the exact phrasing used in the questions, which strongly limits the validity of a comparison of studies that operate with different items. In recent years, public debates refer to opinion polls in the USA and Europe which supposedly prove a rising scepticism towards climate research results with regard to the anthropogenic causes of global warming, and a gradual withdrawal of the support for climate protection measures on the side of the population (Eurobarometer, 2009; Pew Research Center, 2009; BBC, 2010; Gallup, 2010).

In terms of method, it should be noted, particularly with reference to the BBC and Gallup polls, that the

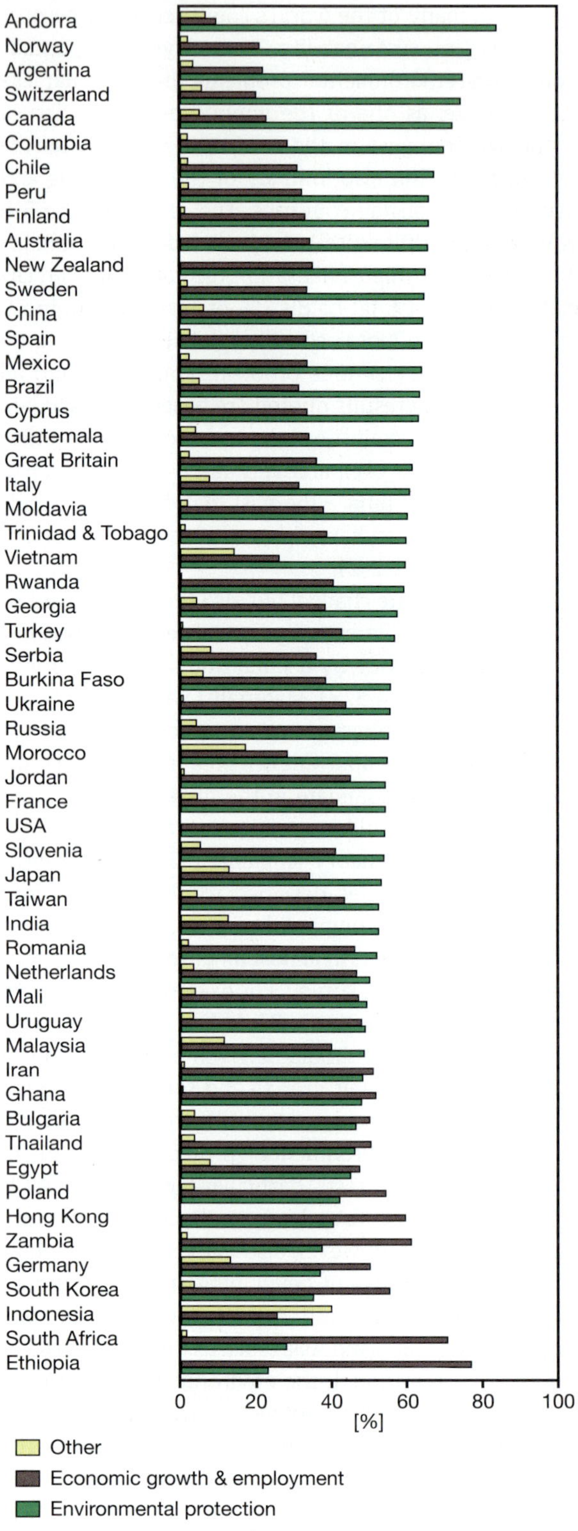

Figure 2.2-3
What is more important: protecting the environment, or economic growth and creating jobs? Results of the 5th wave of the World Value Survey for 56 countries (N = 73.461). For method see Box 2.2-1.
Source: WVS, 2009 (own calculations)

wording of the research questions is ambiguous, and tends to focus on respondents' perception of the public debates on the causes of climate change, rather than the survey participants' personal opinion (Krosnick, 2010). Furthermore, the reporting and public discussion of the surveys pays hardly any or no attention to the fact that despite a decline in the agreement levels regarding individual question items, a large majority of respondents to these polls also continues to view climate change as a serious or very serious problem, and/or supports political climate protection measures (Eurobarometer, 2009; Pew Research Center, 2009; BBC, 2010). Current representative surveys with question items that are unambiguously worded conclude that even in the USA, sample majorities of more than 70% believe global warming to be caused by humankind, and support political climate protection measures (Stanford University, 2010). There is hardly any other political field (such as migration, or economic and social policies) that shows these kind of approval ratings and trends (Krosnick, 2010). Even if the population of a great number of countries agrees with sustainability-oriented policies, there are still misgivings and conflicting aims to which environmental and climate policy must do justice (Section 2.4).

2.2.3 Openness for Innovations and Attitudes towards New Technologies, Science and Renewable Energies

Any kind of successful transformation into low-carbon and sustainable societies requires the development of new technologies, and the prompt and widespread diffusion of technical and social innovations. It is to be expected that extensive agreement with post-materialist values will be subject to pressure at the precise moment in time when climate and environmental protection are not just abstractly postulated views, but concrete political endeavours, such as the implementation of infrastructure projects. The widespread introduction of renewable energies, and the improvement of energy efficiency (Section 4.6), impacts on the everyday practices of a great number of people in key life areas, such as how and where they live, or their mobility (Sections 4.3.2, 4.3.3). A certain openness towards technological inventions and their application is therefore a precondition for the successful decarbonisation of the economy, and our society. The WVS contains a series of items designed to evaluate people's attitudes to technology and science. The results of the study suggest that in many countries, technological development and scientific progress are mainly seen as a good thing. During the 5th wave (2005–2008), for example, 69% of respondents (n = 77,460) stated that they would welcome the development of new technologies being accorded more importance in the near future. A total of 77.5% of respondents (n = 62,718) hope that science and technology will create more opportunities for the next generation.

Other studies furthermore show that large parts of the population in various countries and world religions particularly support the extension and more widespread use of renewable energies (comparable items have so far not been included in the WVS questionnaire). Renewable energies (in particular solar power and wind technology) are far more socially accepted than fossil and nuclear energy carriers. This is made exemplarily clear for the EU by the Eurobarometer data shown in Figure 2.2-4.

The studies for the EU region also show that 'only' or 'at least' – depending on the observer's perspective – 40% of Europeans would be prepared to pay more for energy from renewable sources, whilst 54% reject this (Eurobarometer, 2006). In principle, renewable energies also appeal greatly to the US population (Environics, 2007; Leiserowitz et al., 2010). Equally, a widespread social acceptance of renewable energy sources is documented in developing and newly industrialising countries like India (Iniyan et al., 2001).

Despite the high levels of support that renewable energies enjoy in general surveys, practical experiences have shown that at a local level, protest is also sometimes voiced – for example with regard to the installation of wind power plants (Woods, 2003; Wüstenhagen et al., 2007). Such objections are partially rooted in residents being bothered or stressed by the noises that wind energy plants make, or their signal lights (BMU, 2010a). Other surveys also report rejection tendencies within the population for aesthetic reasons (Faiers and Neame, 2006; Sidiras and Koukios, 2004), or refer to the so-called NIMBY ('Not In My Backyard') phenomenon, describing a social phenomenon that can be observed across a range of areas. It stands for a rejection of something that is generally supported, as soon as it encroaches on the own living environment and personal space.

Some studies (Jobert et al., 2007; Schweizer-Ries, 2010), however, also show that under consideration of various institutional and territorial factors, as well as the participation of local residents in planning processes, a high social acceptance level can be reached for wind energy projects, or for the construction of power lines. Denmark for example, where acceptance of wind technology (and generally all renewable energies) is particularly widespread, is exemplary, because its citizens, or citizen cooperatives own many of the installed

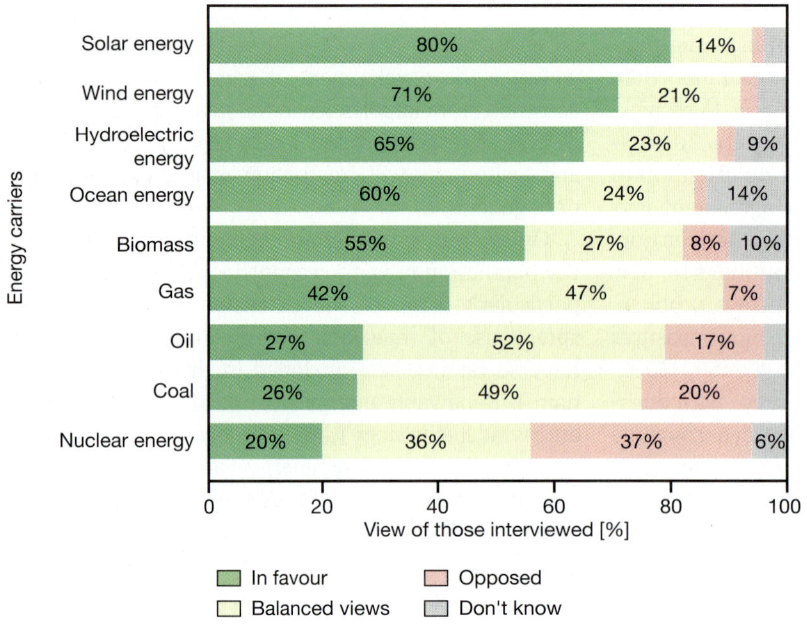

Figure 2.2-4
Acceptance of different energy sources within the European Union (EU 25, in %, respondents could choose on a scale from 1-7 (1= strongly opposed, 7= strongly in favour) to express their opinion. Codes 1-2 correspond to 'opposed', 3-5 'balanced views' and 6-7 'in favour'.
Source: Eurobarometer, 2007

wind energy plants, and therefore benefit financially directly from wind power generation (Tranaes, 2006). Case studies from England also prove that financial participation or cooperative ownership significantly increase the acceptance of renewable energy projects (Ison, 2010).

As a first conclusion, it should be kept in mind that there is considerable evidence that the protection of the natural environment and sustainability aspects ranks highly in the value systems of large parts of the population in different world regions. Despite its absolute strength and persistence, independent of changing trends, this value change in many of the OECD and newly industrialising countries went hand in hand with the formation of 'green' social movements and political parties. In many countries, departments for the environment have been introduced at state and supranational level, and sustainability issues have a firm place in the cross-functional activities of policy-making and administration. Politicians and civil society actors have been given a broader legitimation basis for ecological policies. Policies that are purely based on economic performance, on the other hand, clearly appear to have lost their attractiveness and plausibility.

2.3 The GDP Debate as an Expression of Changing Values

The debate on alternatives to gross domestic product (GDP) as a welfare indicator that has currently flared up again can also be seen as an expression of the described value change. A discussion which, initially, was led in society's 'ecological niches' has become a matter of concern for governments and the EU Commission: since 2007, various initiatives for measuring national welfare and social progress have been pioneered by the United Nations, the OECD (Istanbul World Forum 'Measuring and Fostering the Progress of Societies'), the European Community (Beyond GDP) and Eurostat, and, most recently, by the French President Sarkozy (Stiglitz-Sen-Fitoussi-Commission on the Measurement of Economic Performance and Social Progress). In November 2010, backed by joint application of all major German parties (CDU/CSU, SPD, FDP and Green Party), the German Bundestag also established an inquiry commission, 'Growth, Prosperity, Quality of Life – options for a sustainable economy and social progress in the social market economy', whose initiators voiced the opinion that the assessment of human development and subjective life satisfaction ought to be decoupled from growth indicators.

Both parliamentary and government initiatives agree that they consider the indicator GDP, or GDP per capita, as unsuitable for adequately reflecting national welfare, social progress and aspects of sustainable development (Box 2.3-1). The debate on alternatives to GDP as an indicator is hardly a recent one, however. Since the 1970s, and the Club of Rome's study on 'The Limits to Growth' (Meadows et al., 1972), there have been scientific and political discussions on how to adequately measure welfare, human development, social progress and natural environmental changes. These have been based on, amongst other aspects, the manifold debates on quality of life, humanisation of working environments, and social indicators as a basis for welfare-state related planning and development cooperation. Those who use GDP per capita as a welfare indicator were and are mostly aware of the fact that this indicator can only give, at best, a very rough estimate of the welfare situation in countries. GDP, or GDP per capita, after all exclusively measure economic market activities and monetary values. The calculation of GDP takes only flow values into account, and excludes the existing stocks, meaning that any conclusions regarding the sustainability aspect of these business transactions cannot be drawn. The cost of, for example, remedying environmental damages leads to a higher GDP per capita, even though it only serves the restoration of the status quo. Goods and services that do not have a market price, or are not actually traded, such as ecosystem services, housework, voluntary work or subsistence economic activities, are not included in the GDP. Equally, GDP per capita does not reflect education and health system quality; only the respective input costs are included. The GDP per capita also makes no statement regarding an economy's income distribution (Stiglitz et al., 2009b), although the equality or inequality of income distribution is considered to be welfare-relevant (Wilkinson and Willet, 2009).

So therefore, the GDP per capita is neither intended nor suitable for the measuring of welfare or sustainability (Nordhaus and Tobin, 1973; Stiglitz et al., 2009b). This applies to an even greater extent to the measuring of people's subjective wellbeing: an increase in an economy's performance ability does not necessarily automatically lead to an increase in subjective wellbeing. A rising GDP per capita does not inevitably lead to rises in individual income, and rising individual incomes – at least once a certain level of material gratification has been achieved – do not increase the subjective wellbeing further (Easterlin, 1974; Layard, 2005; Leiserowitz et al., 2006; Inglehart et al., 2008; Frey and Stutzer, 2009; Stiglitz et al., 2009a). In the long-term, too, there is apparently no clear correlation between rising incomes and subjective happiness (Stiglitz et al., 2009a). Individual studies, though, have shown that a significant positive correlation between real income and subjective wellbeing can exist, and that this equally applies to poorer and richer countries (Stevenson and Wolfers, 2008; Deaton, 2008; Eckersley, 2009). By trend, a higher GDP is also particularly promotive for areas that usually impact positively on individual wellbeing, such as education, health and security. An increasing GDP also tends to help to reduce unemployment levels. Not to be unemployed appears to have a strong positive impact on subjective wellbeing (Clark and Oswald, 1994; Oswald, 1997).

The current indicator debate shows the need for measurable welfare and sustainability dimensions that go beyond GDP per capita. These would be welcomed by many politicians and large parts of the civil society. A growing number of politicians and citizens question the dominance of economic growth (measured as GDP) as a basis for political decisions. In the face of urgent ecological, economic and social problems, a reorientation towards 'qualitative' growth (based on a more comprehensive welfare and/or sustainability concept) is long overdue, also as a political target value (Box 2.3-1).

Which indicators and indices should be used to replace or complement the GDP is ultimately a political issue. Because apart from aspects like data availability and quality, the question of which welfare indicators should be used as the measure for successful policies depends above all on which economic, ecological and social goals the respective policies should pursue. Only then can be decided which type of indicator (monetary or non-monetary, objective or subjective, i.e. personal assessment by individuals, individual indicator, compound indicators, or set of indicators) are best suited to collect this data to measure the respective target achievement. The Stiglitz-Sen-Fitoussi Commission used by President Sarkozy made a few suggestions for developing statistical reporting further (Box 2.3-2).

2.4 The Gap between Attitudes and Behaviour

What conclusions can be drawn from the 'GDP-scepticism', the approval ratings measured in surveys regarding the position of environment and sustainability, and the presently existing global value orientations? *Firstly,* it becomes clear that a transformation into a more sustainable society would evidently be welcomed by a significant part of the world society. There appears to be a relatively wide, cross-cultural consensus that the prevalent way of doing business should be embedded in higher-ranking goals of sustainability, environmental conservation, and climate protection, or generally in aspects of a more caring and careful resource management. To put it another way: anyone supporting sustainability is not, or no longer, swimming against the tide. This conclusion is not a marginal note in a report that deals with the preconditions and possibilities of a global transformation. *On the contrary,* it shows that a part of the population welcomes the goal of such a transformation. Political options that pick up on postmaterialist value orientations and sustainability-oriented attitudes are not complete antitheses to the majority view in rich and industrialising societies. They are also widespread amongst the opinion leading groups in the

Box 2.3-1

Alternative Concepts for Measuring Welfare and Sustainability

A number of alternative indicators for measuring welfare and sustainability have been developed and evaluated since the 1970s (Table 2.3-1). Some concepts, such as the Genuine Progress Indicator (GPI), still use the GDP as a basis, modifying it by monetising ecological and social factors that impact welfare (for example environmental degradation, voluntary work), then adding or subtracting these values.

Other approaches no longer use the GDP as a starting point, but instead add various monetary and non-monetary factors together to give one index (compound indices). Examples for this method are, amongst others, the United Nations Development Programme's Human Development Index (HDI), and the Index of Economic Wellbeing (IEWB). The HDI, for example, is made up of part-indicators for the areas of health, education, and material living standard. Beyond these, there are different approaches that explicitly not only measure the current level of welfare, but also the sustainability aspect of business activities. Of these, some focus only on ecological sustainability, whereas others also include additional sustainability dimensions.

Another approach is the 'Gross National Happiness' index conceived by the Himalayan state of Bhutan. This takes more than just the GDP-relevant values into account to measure the performance capability of a society. On the contrary, a range of other values, such as 'spiritual wellbeing', 'health', 'good government' or 'biodiversity' are included (Adler, 2009). In terms of sustainability measurement, there are also approaches like overall eco-balance, which could be considered a modification of the GDP approach. The various sustainability aspects are shown separately from the GDP here. The KfW Sustainability Indicator or the German federal government's sustainability indicators are also in this category. Their counterparts at European level are Eurostat's Sustainable Development Indicators.

The following table summarises some of the concepts that have been suggested, and categorises them according to sustainability dimensions included.

Table 2.3-1
Overview of concepts for measuring welfare and sustainability (*index includes subjective indicators).
Source: WBGU

Type of measuring concept	Name of index/indicator	Economic Dimension	Social Dimension	Ecological Dimension
Beyond GDP: monetised indicators/indices	Measure of Economic Welfare	x	x	x
	Index of Sustainable Economic Welfare (ISEW)	x	x	x
	Genuine Progress Indicator (GPI)	x	x	x
	Full Cost of Goods and Services (FCGS)	x		x
	National Welfare Index (NWI)	x	x	x
Beyond GDP: overall eco-balance/ satellite systems	Overall eco-balance/UN System of Environmental and Economic Accounting (SEEA)	x		x
Non-monetised indicators/indices	Ecological Footprint			x
	Living Planet Index			x
Compound indicators/indices (integration of monetised and non-monetised values)	Human Development Index (HDI)	x	x	
	Index of Economic Wellbeing	x	x	x
	Happy Planet Index*		x	x
	KfW Sustainability Indicator	x	x	x
	Sustainable Development Indicators (Eurostat)	x	x	x
	Index of Economic Freedom	x	x	
	Environmental Sustainability Index (ESI)/ Environmental Performance Index (EPI)	x		x
	Gross National Happiness* (Bhutan)	x	x	x
	Canadian Index of Wellbeing* (CIW)			
	Corruption Perception Index (CPI)		x	
	National Accounts of Well-being*		x	

newly industrialising countries, which are even more reliant on catching up, i.e. on the increase and diffusion of material prosperity.

The conclusion that many people all over the world show a marked sensitivity towards environmental issues, and have shown in surveys that they would be prepared to support a more sustainable economy and way of living, and accept technological innovations, however, does not mean that a widespread actual rejection of non-sustainable practices has already taken place, and that concrete environmental policy reforms such as, for example, the introduction or increase of eco-taxation, or the introduction of environmental standards, enjoy the unequivocal approval of all citizens. In the course of such reforms, significant political objections must regularly be overcome (OECD, 2001; Thalmann, 2004), and it is certainly not a rare phenomenon that on the one hand, people profess support for

Box 2.3-2

Stiglitz-Sen-Fitoussi Commission Recommendations for Measuring Economic Performance and Social Progress

The Stiglitz-Sen-Fitoussi Commission on the Measurement of Economic Performance and Social Progress identified eight dimensions that impact quality of life in its report: material wealth, health, education, personal activities/paid employment, political participation and governance, social relationships, environmental conditions and existential (physical and economic) insecurity. According to the Commission, these should be taken into account when measuring social progress. The most important of the Commission's other recommendations made in their September 2009 final report are (Braakmann, 2009; Michaelis, 2009; Stiglitz et al., 2009b):

- Net domestic product, net national income or disposable income should form the basis of longer-term and international comparisons instead of gross domestic product, as gross domestic product or gross national income still includes write-offs (value losses) and does not reflect householders' real incomes and actual consumption.
- In addition, the measurement should generally be expanded from aggregated to household level, as there can be considerable gaps between the aggregated national income and the average real income of households.
- Disposable income and consumption should be stated according to the so-called consumption concept, which includes individually attributable state services (education and healthcare provision, amongst others) that increase individual consumption.
- The assessment of economic activity should not only consider quantitative changes in economic performance, but also qualitative changes (amongst others improved services, better-quality products).
- Social groups' share in economic growth should be made visible by publishing data on income and wealth distribution according to household groups, and explicitly recording inequalities between different social groups, sexes and generations.
- Non-paid services like homemaking, subsistence economy and voluntary work should be included when measuring welfare, as should the value of leisure time.
- Sustainability should be measured separately from the current welfare level, as it is an independent concept; a multi-dimensional set of indicators (dashboard) should be defined for this.
- To evaluate sustainability, assets and liabilities should be compared, and natural, human, and social capital should be accounted for to reveal changes in the portfolio.
- Equally, (non-monetised) physical indicators should be included to illustrate ecological sustainability.
- Indicators of the subjective wellbeing of a country's citizens should also be surveyed, including indicators for material wealth, as well as immaterial aspects impacting quality of life.
- In this context, subjective indicators like happiness and life satisfaction should be included in the official statistics.
- The statistics agencies should allow the further development of compound indices by making the relevant data and methods available.

ambitious climate protection in surveys, yet at the same time, they also object to paying higher prices for electricity and fuel from fossil energy carriers (Leiserowitz et al., 2006). What leads to this gap between attitudes and actions?

One of the key reasons for why people don't (always) do that which – by their own admission – is important to them is that value systems are often abstract concepts that are perceived as a hypothetical area of life. The corresponding surveys are therefore not perceived under inclusion of all of the actually expectable consequences, and accordingly, questions are answered hypothetically. In general, sociological and socio-psychological research has shown that the perception of problems does not necessarily trigger 'right', i.e. for example environmentally friendly, actions (Diekmann and Preisendörfer, 1991; Kuckartz, 2010), or that there is little correlation between attitudes and behaviour (Eckes and Six, 1994).

There are 'barriers' (Leiserowitz et al., 2006) preventing value systems from impacting behaviour, at both individual and social or structural level. An actual change of behaviour requires a material and cognitive basis. The suitable socio-economic and legal framework must also be given. Frequently, for example, the intention to use environmentally friendly public transport for private journeys and commuting is hampered by a status quo bias, but also by a lack of basic information, (supposed) disadvantages in terms of cost (both monetary and non-monetary), and wrong fiscal incentives, and a lack of infrastructure. The relatively stable trends towards a rather high level of sensitivity towards environmental issues presented in Section 2.2 must therefore not hide the fact that other, sometimes completely contrasting values and framework conditions also partially influence actual decisions.

Election research proves that, apart from personality factors – which, for example, include the attitudes acquired in socialisation processes – structure-related determinants (like social hierarchy, social class, or the political system) and short-term situation-related influences (such as candidate sympathies, practical issues, or election campaign development) also significantly influence voting decisions (Schultze, 2003; Broschek and Schultze, 2006). Areas as diverse as diffusion research, ethnological studies and relevant development cooperation experiences show that – beyond any kind of rational benefit calculation – it is people's cultural practices that are particularly important when new ideas and technologies or behaviour patterns are actually introduced (Rogers, 2003). The introduction, for example, of simple, seemingly plausible practices can fail if these collide with existing cultural values or norms (Rogers, 2003). The applicable system of cultural norms does not just determine whether new everyday practices in society are adopted by a certain social group, but also how the adoption is carried out.

Differing norms and dispositions are not just found in different societies and cultural zones; they also differ according to social class within societies. Studies based on the Sinus Institute's (now called Sinus Sociovision) representative life world research show that people with certain lifestyles have (so far) shown hardly or no interest in sustainability issues. Conversely, however, the studies also clearly show that there is a significant potential for sustainable behaviour in social groups with an ecological affinity, a potential which, moreover, is still a long way from having been fully realised (Kleinhückelkotten, 2006). It is also remarkable in this context that the citizen segment with an ecological affinity has become much more extensive over the past few years (Wippermann, 2009). In addition, the main barriers which make it more difficult for certain individuals or social environments to make sustainable decisions are considered to be the lack of long-term orientation, loss aversion, and path dependencies in general.

2.4.1
Lack of Long-Term Orientation and Loss Aversion

The transformation of societies towards low-carbon economic activity can only succeed if the actors involved, particularly the consumers and voters, take their decisions in such a way that future generations' costs and benefits are also adequately taken into account. Frequently, such long-term oriented decisions are accompanied by higher costs in the short-term than exclusively short-term oriented decisions. For example, there is still relatively little demand for energy efficient household appliances as these tend to be quite expensive at the point of purchase. In the medium- and long-term, however, the higher purchasing price is offset by lower running costs. This equally applies to investments in buildings insulation and the conversion of heating systems, car purchases, and so on. With all of these decisions, the exact, tangible value of the future benefit is uncertain, and therefore difficult to grasp, unlike the relatively high cost at the point in time when the purchase is made. The fact that many individuals are characterised by loss aversion, particularly in uncertain decision situations (Kahneman and Tversky, 1979; Paech, 2005), contributes even more to this effect of an overriding awareness of the short-term effects. So in view of the described time architecture of cost and benefits, options which are more expensive in the short-term but cheaper in the long run often tend to be 'left by the wayside'.

There are many causes for the lack of long-term orientation and/or the loss aversion of individual decision-makers. A particularly important role is played by subjective factors like lack of knowledge and uncertainty regarding the pressure to act. The higher the uncertainty is, the more likely it becomes that those deciding will discount future gains, which is why long-term projects are more difficult to realise. Since losses typically have an extremely high level of negative influence on benefit perception, as opposed to the far smaller positive influence of the perceived benefit in the case of gains, consumers will attempt to refrain from actions that they perceive might lead to (substantial) losses (Kahneman and Tversky, 1979). The later the benefits of an action become apparent, and the earlier the costs – the typical distribution of cost and benefit of transformative actions over a period of time – the higher the loss risk is estimated to be, thereby reducing the likelihood that individual actors will welcome and support such action options. In any case, the lower the disposable income or the living standard of those deciding, the more widespread short-term oriented acting and the avoidance of losses are (Lorenzoni et al., 2007).

One method of overcoming those barriers to behaviour changes that are the result of a lack of long-term orientation and loss aversion is the employment of so-called 'nudges'. Nudges, i. e. triggers for desired behaviour changes, are currently the focus of an international discussion on so-called 'libertarian paternalism' strategies (Thaler and Sunstein, 2008). One of the prominent examples of such nudges are default options, which, from a paternalistic perspective, stipulate 'good' solutions as the standard, but always include the option of choosing an alternative (opt out). When there is a divergence in terms of time between the costs and benefits of an action, nudges can help individuals to make their decisions in such a way that the benefit is optimised in the long-term (for examples see Box 5.2-5).

2.4.2
Path Dependencies

For the transformation of economy and society towards sustainability, the political, economical and technological path dependency is also a significant barrier (Liebowitz and Marjolis, 1995; Pierson, 2004). An existing system of institutions (norms, contracts, negotiating and decision-making modi, etc.), but also of technologies and infrastructures, can hinder far-reaching social changes. Already existing technologies, infrastructures and socio-cultural patterns can produce these kind of lock-in effects, restricting the behaviour and the development potential over several investment cycles (Freeman, 1992).

In the 20th century, an extensive high-carbon infrastructure that rests on the massive and self-propagating application of fossil energy carriers was established in the OECD states. Various economic and social institutions have stipulated specific development paths, thereby excluding others (Urry, 2010). In politics and the economy, path dependent processes and developments frequently result in mistakes becoming the established norm, and the continued absence of learning effects. Individual and political decision-makers, as well as the public, are led by crisis management routines that were developed for past problem cases. Clinging to past thought and action patterns can lead to an 'objective' pressure to change, which merely results in modification, rather than transformation of the status quo, delaying the replacement of the fossil-nuclear energy system with a sustainable energy system even further.

2.5 On the Way to a Shared Global Transformation Vision?

The transformation outlined in this report depends on being widely acceptable (and this also in societies with a so far low material development level). On the basis of the global values surveys, the WBGU has been able to make clear that postmaterialist value systems have found a wide, and, in the past decades, growing consensus, not just in richer countries, although there is no discernible automatism for the realisation of such value preferences and the disposition to act accordingly. Usually, there is a wide gap between awareness and action. However, when people do not just, or do not primarily, base their agreement with political norms and goals on actual actions, but also on mind-sets and projections, then the presence of a potentially high approval rating with a stronger position on environmental conservation and climate protection is by no means trivial. The transformative measures and regulations outlined in this report, which could potentially have a far-reaching effect on habits and things taken for granted, are easier for political and economic decision-makers to justify if they are presented not only as a relinquishment, but also as agreeing at least in part with preferences and desires that are prevalent in the world population in any case.

The diffusion of environmental consciousness and postmaterialist values in numerous countries and world regions represents an important precondition for a transformation towards sustainability. Persons and institutions which act by and large in agreement with the prevalent values carry great strategic weight as so-called change agents, or pioneers of change (Section 6.2). They bear witness to the fact that a transformation towards sustainability is possible, and that the room to manoeuvre for reflecting the corresponding values and positions in concrete actions exists in society. In this way, people who share a predisposition towards sustainability, but for whom, with regard to their concrete behaviour, other, contrary criteria tend to be more significant, could be motivated to support sustainable economic activity, and change their own behaviour and consumption patterns in this direction.

Then the transformation would not only be down to 'planetary boundaries', but also backed by the 'open frontiers' of humankind's existence. New, alternative ways of living and entrepreneurial visions are constantly being developed and, for example, held up as role models for a 'good life'. These kinds of role models appear to have a solid basis in people's everyday preferences (Graham, 2010).

All cultures used to, and in fact still do, feature convincing aspects and dimensions of 'good life' and happiness designed for universalisation, and not as average values of subjective human preferences and conditions, but as evaluation criteria for certain life world contexts and choice situations. In the practical philosophy inspired by Aristotle's Nicomachean Ethics, 'good living' as such (eu zēn, 'to live well') is worth pursuing for its own sake – all other commodities or virtues are only worth striving for in relation to this 'goodness'. In today's practical philosophy, which refers only partially to the ethical theories of ancient Greece, a 'good life' is also not a condition, but an action, an acting that is guided by reason and emotion. It is not only, or not primarily, based on a great number of material possessions, pleasant experiences or plentiful enjoyment, but rather on humaneness in a comprehensive sense that benefits fellow men and women and the environment. This includes personal development, i.e. development of the opportunities a person has available to them, just as much as a sense of community, a taking over of responsibility for the general well-being, and various justness principles. A 'good life' is usually dependent on the fulfilment of certain basic requirements, also on the existence of scope for individual actions and options that must be secured by material standards. Beyond that, immaterial factors play a role in the 'pursuit of happiness' in all cultures, such as the recognition received from others, being embedded in different kinds of communities and networks, yet also the fulfilment of aesthetic and hedonistic pleasures. Any transformation strategy which can make it plausible that the suggested or stipulated changes are compatible with these immaterial goals, i.e. that they do not necessarily represent a negative impact on subjective life satisfaction, but that they can in fact improve it, promises far more success than a strategy which, by external force alone, stipulates mitigations, thereby triggering problem repression and loss aversion.

From a liberal point of view, any attempt to normatively pitch 'good living' (in Aristotle's sense) against respective individual needs bears the risk of authoritarian paternalism. Modern societies view themselves as 'multi-optional' (Gross, 2005), i.e. the gratification of individuals' needs takes the empirical and normative precedence. The individual pursuit of happiness is therefore hampered only by the avoidance of causally attributable damages to others. This argumentation allows the discounting of past environmental damages, as these are compensated by future welfare increases. However, against the background of the risks revealed in Chapter 1 – global climate change, the loss of biodiversity, and the multiple crises faced by the world society – it becomes increasingly doubtful whether such a focus actually still protects today's individual freedoms and those of coming generations. Subsequent to the emergence of liberal basic human rights (18th century), political participation rights (19th century) and social rights (20th century), there are many who feel that the progressive development of rights has reached the point where a new kind of right must be strived for: an ecological basic right (Marshall, 1992; Menke and Pollmann, 2007). A closer look at the awareness of the limits to growth should therefore not just focus on the natural restrictions imposed by limited resources, stresses, emissions and so on, but also on the possible consequences of unlimited growth for the individual freedom of future generations. Self-imposing restrictions today, for example with regard to the quantity and origin of consumer goods and services, guarantee future options for action which in all probability will, if we wait any longer, disappear. Taking a closer look, we must therefore conclude that restrictions which today are initially perceived as a relinquishment could actually result in taking some of the burden off the people and societies of the future without subjecting today's generation to unbearable restrictions and immeasurable costs.

Self-imposing restrictions to avoid dangerous climate change and other damages to the Earth system is not a new, revolutionary idea. People are, as currently proved by the smoking ban and balanced budget amendments, quite capable of reducing the degree of their own spontaneous first-tier desires (short-term preferences) in favour of second-tier desires, i.e. wish-related desires (Frankfurt, 2001; Schaal and Ritzi, 2008), and to commit to cooperation to achieve these (Tomasello, 2009). They thereby prove a precautionary attitude towards possible preference, or the future development of these preferences. This problematic issue is highlighted by historic transformations, whose structural patterns will be determined in the following chapter.

The Great Transformation: A Heuristic Concept

3

The WBGU understands imminent change in politics, economy and society that is required in order to master the challenges described in Chapter 1 as a 'Great Transformation'. The key requirements this comprehensive transformation must fulfil stem from the planetary boundaries, which make the conversion of national economies and the global economy under consideration of these boundaries compulsory, in order to avoid irreversible damages to global ecosystems and their consequences for humankind.

Production, consumption patterns and lifestyles must be altered in such a way as to reduce greenhouse gas emissions to a minimum in the coming decades (decarbonisation of the energy systems and establishment of low-carbon societies), to minimise the scarcity of essential resources (above all land, water, strategic mineral resources) through major resource efficiency increases, and to avoid abrupt changes within the Earth system (tipping points), through economic and development strategies which take the guard rails of the Earth system (planetary boundaries) into account.

Such a transformation cannot succeed without a hitherto unparalleled level of global cooperation, the further development of normative infrastructures in the international system, new welfare concepts, technology leaps, multifaceted institutional innovations and flexible reform alliances. The WBGU considers only two great transformations, waves of change or civilisation phases in the history of humankind to be comparable to the Great Transformation faced now: the Neolithic Revolution, i.e. the transition from hunter-gatherer to agricultural society (Winkler, 2009; Box 3-1), and the Industrial Revolution, already referred to as a 'Great Transformation' by the Hungarian economist Karl Polanyi (1944) (Box 3.2-1).

To date, no comprehensive theory adequately rendering the complexity of great transformations exist. However, a transformation concept is necessary in order for this profound change to be suitably elaborated and analysed in depth, and for the development of a systematic approach that facilitates the illustration of the Great Transformation's processes and dynamics, levels of action, change agents and actor constellations. Sustainable political, economic and social transformation strategies for the transition to a decarbonised and resource efficient (global) economy and society can be only developed this way.

How to describe a great transformation, and how to influence it? The first important aspect is that the Great Transformation goes beyond changes in the medium term (Section 3.5), which are analysed by various theories:

The theory on the 'long waves of economic change' describes Kondratiev waves, or economic cycles driven by basic innovations (Kondratiev, 1926; Mensch, 1975; Freeman and Louca, 2001; Perez, 2002). In this context, it is has been observed that key innovations leading to profound economic change and transformative investment waves occur every 40–60 years (1780–1850 steam engine, mechanical loom, coal, iron; 1840–1890 railway, steel production, agricultural methods; 1890–1940 electricity, chemistry, automobile, mass production; 1940–1990 electrical engineering, petrochemistry, computer, plane/rockets; 1990 to present, information and communication technologies). The Great Transformation leading to a global economy and society able to provide wealth, stability and democracy within the planetary boundaries evidently also depends on basic innovations to make low-carbon and resource efficient economic activities possible. However, it goes far beyond even the time frame of Kondratiev´s cycles, as its objective is bringing the current industrial age to a close. It also includes social, cultural and political processes of change that are not only of a technological nature, or determined by technology.

Evolutionary economics draws on the concept of fundamental innovations, differentiating between incremental and radical innovations and a change in techno-economic paradigms (Freeman, 1996). We can learn a great deal from these approaches for the Great Transformation, as the transition towards a low-carbon and resource-efficient economy must obviously go hand in hand with radical innovations that affect large parts of the economy, and of society, and will lead to

Box 3-1

The Neolithic Revolution

The Neolithic Revolution describes the emergence and expansion of sedentary societies during the New Stone Age. Between 10,000 and 5,000 BC, after previously living exclusively in nomadic hunter-gatherer communities, humankind developed agriculture, animal husbandry and how to store food in different regions around the globe at the same time, thus creating the preconditions for sedentariness (Sieferle, 2010; Figures 3.2-1, 3.2-2).

The fundamental characteristics of agricultural civilisations are very similar all over the world. This suggests convergent evolutionary processes in which goal-oriented steering cannot have played a major role. Rather, the systemic conditions of agricultural production methods, despite the socio-technical advances achieved since then, provide agricultural societies with only very limited scope for unique developments and differentiating characteristics (Sieferle, 2010). Once a society had assimilated the first steps on the path towards agriculture, for example the regular harvesting of wild plants, the next logical step, i.e. the intentional sowing of seed, was inevitable.

Although the Neolithic Revolution is an evolutionary change between one age and the next, it permanently changed humankind's basis for civilisation, and the world as a whole. From an economic perspective, sedentariness and agriculture brought previously unimagined material wealth and economic growth. This became particularly apparent in the evolution of advanced agricultural civilisations (Weisdorf, 2005).

Compared to the status quo ante, sedentariness, coupled with agriculture and food storage, allowed the evolution of considerably more complex and differentiated societies. Economic historians emphasise that an early adoption of agricultural production methods and the farming lifestyle led to such fundamental differences with regard to technological development and social organisation. These were so profound that, to a certain degree, they still determine the various countries' economic output today. Moreover, there are indications, for example in India, that it is less the historical length of time of agricultural production that is decisive in this regard, but rather the respective development stage of the agrarian tradition, and the technological and social skills adopted thereof (Putterman, 2008).

With the economic growth of agricultural societies, their energy demand and the degree of interference in natural environments also increases, as agricultural societies reengineer their environments far more intensively and systematically than hunters and gatherers (Haberl, 2006). Agrarian societies' main energy source is biomass, which is used more controlled and more intensive than previously (Figure 3.2-1). Furthermore, a substantially larger share of biomass net primary production is used as food and feedstock, firewood, and construction material. Although hunters and gatherers also withdraw biomass from their environment, they use this comparatively unsystematically, unmodified and in lower volumes.

There is some controversy as to why hunting and gathering was replaced by sedentariness and agriculture, as our knowledge about prehistory is incomplete and largely speculative. All attempts at explanation assume that the climatic changes towards the end of the Ice Age played a decisive role. However, it is unclear whether this impacted negatively on environmental conditions, leading to resource scarcity, or, precisely the opposite, whether this actually improved environmental conditions, leading to an overabundance of food.

To put it simply, in the first case, a lack of prey would have been the key driver for developing agriculture. In the second case, it would have been the overabundance of prey that would have made sedentariness, the domestication of animals and a more complex degree of organisation, such as the systematic cultivation of wild barley, possible in the first place. A third theory supposes that initially, global warming allowed hunting sedentariness, and a sudden climatic cold snap forced the sedentary hunters to turn to agriculture. A fourth approach looks for an explanation not in the relative improvement or deterioration of environmental conditions through climatic changes, but in the increasing constancy of environmental conditions after the climatically volatile Pleistocene. Whilst hunters and gatherers were flexible and able to adapt to climate fluctuations, the continued constancy of climatic conditions also allowed relatively inflexible, but in the long term more productive lifestyles such as agriculture.

Regardless of the specific causes, sedentariness and agriculture allowed a historically unprecedented acceleration of cultural, social, technological and economic development. The end of the imperative of always adapting to fluctuating climatic conditions brought other compulsory needs to adapt, and co-evolutionary processes in agriculture (for example the emergence of parasites) and settlement communities (for example competitive pressure through foes, and social disparities). The solution of a problem usually led to an unforeseen set of new problems, which again called for responsive action, thereby promoting innovation and development (Sieferle, 2010).

a change of the 'high-carbon paradigm'. However, just as in Kondratiev's long wave theory, innovation theories tend to look at changes in terms of medium-term time span.

Moreover, the complexity of the Great Transformation goes well beyond changes which are, at their core, technological, something that is addressed by parts of evolutionary economics also deals with. The most difficult changes which must be brought about in order to achieve the Great Transformation transcend technologies – changing lifestyles, for instance, or revolutionising global cooperation, overcoming policy-related barriers, and dealing responsibly with permanent, cross-generational changes (Chapters 5, 6). Technologies can help to simplify these challenges of comprehensive economic and social change. However, they are not the ultimate key, or even the only key, to the Great Transformation.

Along with the innovation theories and the theory of long waves, transformation theories dealing with the transition of socialist countries towards market economy and democracy also encompass some of the Great Transformation's important dimensions (Merkel, 2010). This is not surprising, as these approaches examine the profound remodelling of economies and society, attempting to develop transformation-relevant strategies. The essential difference between these transformations and the transition to a global economy within planetary boundaries is the fact that during their transition towards a market economy, the formerly socialist countries could refer to existing guiding principles and models in western countries for guidance.

In contrast, there are no established role models for the Great Transformation to sustainability. Achieving wealth, decarbonisation, radical resource efficiency and democracy at around the same time is a historic challenge all countries will have to face in equal measure. It is particularly the wealthy nations – in view of their greenhouse gas emissions and resource consumption – that are failing to do so. Currently, there is not a single low-carbon model country to serve as an orientation guide for reform processes in other countries. Moreover, the transformation theories dealing with the transition from socialist to westernised societies focus on national systems, whilst the 21st century's Great Transformation must encompass both national societal changes and, above all, processes of global change.

The present transformation theories can certainly contribute elements and structural characteristics to a heuristic concept for analysis of the Great Transformation; however, they are not construed to describe the epochal change that is required, in the view of the WBGU, to secure the stability of the planetary system, widespread prosperity and democracy in the long term.

3.1 Key Characteristics of the Great Transformation

With their works on long term transformative change to sustainability, Grin et al. (2010) are making important contributions to a better understanding of the transitional processes referred to by the WBGU as the Great Transformation. Grin et al.'s approach (2010) refers to the transformation concepts and theories outlined above, particularly from the areas of evolutionary economics and innovation research, but also from the historical sciences, and elaborates these in terms of a more comprehensive change towards sustainable development. Grin et al. (2010) refer to 'transition' when analysing comprehensive change processes, and to 'transformations' as phases within a transition. This distinction is not necessarily made in the German-speaking social scientific community to describe far reaching processes of social, economic, cultural and political change. In this report, the WBGU uses the term 'transformation', not least with reference to Karl Polanyi's 'Great Transformation' (1944) to describe an all-encompassing transition.

Historical phases of comprehensive economic, technological, cultural and political change affecting not only individual niches and sectors, but transforming whole societies, can, with reference to Giddens (1984), Bourdieu (1977) and Braudel (1958), be understood as processes during the course of which 'changing practices, structural change, and exogenous tendencies occur in parallel to each other and may sometimes interact so as to produce non-incremental changes in practices and structures' (Grin et al., 2010). The authors here adopt the view of economic historian Braudel (1958) that profound change is based on change processes which vary in pace and follow differing historical time scales. Geographical, geological, but also social and mental structures, change very slowly and gradually (structural history); economic structures, actor and power constellations and the availability of natural resources can change within a few years or decades (conjunctural history); certain moments and events in history (11 September 2001, beginning and end of the Second World War; global economic crises 1929/30 and 2007–2009) can lead to course changes, shocks, lasting crises or windows of opportunity for changes (eventful history). Great transformations are therefore not linear processes or the result of intentional actions by powerful actors, but the consequence of interlinked dynamics occurring at different time scales, which then, in their compounded form, create a certain direction of the transition (for example during the course of the fundamental change from agricultural to industrial societies, Box 3.2-1, Figures 3.2-1, 3.2-2).

Grin et al. (2010) refer to the concept of co-evolution for the analysis of interactions between different subsystems. 'Economic, cultural, technological, ecological, and institutional subsystems co-evolve in many ways and can reinforce each other to co-determine a transition (...) we speak of co-evolution if the interaction between societal subsystems influences the dynamics of the individual societal subsystem, leading to irreversible patterns of change'. On this basis, the authors develop a bundle of the general characteristics of major transformation processes to concentrate their complexity:

- Major change processes occur in a co-evolutionary manner, rely on a great number of changes in different socio-technical (sub)systems, and take place at local, national and global action levels.
- They include both the development of (niche) innovations as well as their selection on the part of the

users, and their social embedding through markets, regulations, infrastructures and new social guiding principles.
- They are influenced by a large number of political, scientific, economic and civil social actors and consumers.
- Ultimately, they are radical processes with regard to their impact and range; they may, however, sometimes take place very slowly over several decades.

If these characteristics are applied, then great transformations have no clearly defined epicentre from which they emanate, and are hardly manageable. It is true that neither of the historical civilisation leaps of humankind (Neolithic and Industrial Revolution, Boxes 3-1, 3.2-1) categorised by the WBGU as Great Transformations were steered processes; rather, they were the consequence of evolutionary transition. A central challenge, and historically without precedent, in the transformation towards a low-carbon, resource efficient global economy within the planetary boundaries is therefore the shaping of this complex process (Messner, 1997). The imminent transition must gain momentum on the basis of the scientific findings and knowledge regarding the risks of continuation along the resource intensive development path based on fossil fuels, and shaped by policy-making to avoid the historical norm of a change in direction in response to crises and shocks. In the event of a climate crisis, following the 'historical norm' could have irreversible and unpredictable consequences for humanity (WBGU, 2009). Climatologists and natural scientists have the knowledge and skills to project the future impact of global warming on water availability, land degradation or sea-level rise with the aid of projection models. Contemporary societies therefore not only have recourse to a 'past laboratory' (history), but also a 'future laboratory' to make their decisions. Society must learn to 'learn from the future' (Chapter 8).

Grin et al.'s transformation concept (2010), but also other social-science theories on social change (Braudel, 1958; Messner, 1997; Mayntz, 2009; Fischer, 2010; Ostrom, 2010), however, point out that even complex transformations do not occur simply as a uncontrolled self-propelling process on the strength of the complex internal dynamics of processes and structures in the sense of co-evolution; they can also be influenced by identifiable actor constellations. Actor constellations with sufficient power, resources and creativity, prepared to welcome innovations and reforms in order to overcome established barriers, can be effective drivers of change, or they can channel, consolidate and shape processes of change which develop their own dynamics. How much room for manoeuvre these actors have depends on the overall constellation in which they act. The following shows that the current imminent profound change towards a sustainable global society certainly offers ample openings for political shaping.

To achieve success, change agents must in any case (beyond their powers and willingness to reform) be able to plausibly call attention to the limits of the established social concept (in this case an economic structure that depends largely on the use of fossil energy carriers, i.e. a high-carbon economy, and have appealing guiding principles at their disposal (narratives) to serve as guidelines the social change. This study intends to contribute to such a narrative for the Great Transformation towards sustainability.

Recent research in the fields of behavioural economics (Akerlof and Shiller, 2009), evolutionary anthropology (Dunbar, 2010), political economy (Ostrom and Walker, 2003), or on 'Actor-oriented Institutionalism' (Mayntz, 2002) concur with regard to the importance of widely accepted narratives to guide the activities of actors. Narratives reduce complexity, create a basis for current and future-oriented action plans, are a foundation for the co-operation between actors, and support reliability of expectations. Over the past two hundred years, the prevailing narrative shared by all economic systems has been a model of prosperity based on the unlimited availability of fossil fuels and other resources. What is needed now is a new 'storyline' to further develop human civilisation as well as the terms 'modernisation' and 'development'. That is easier said than done. Because John Maynard Keynes (1883–1946) was probably quite correct when he surmised: 'The difficulty lies not so much in developing new ideas as in escaping from old ones.'

Without changed narratives, guiding principles or meta-narrations which will redefine the future of economy and society, there can be no shaping of the Great Transformation. In essence, this identifies two important elements for shaping the transition towards a low-carbon global economy (change agents and narratives) referred to in more detail later (Chapters 4, 5, 6).

3.2 The 'Global Metamorphoses in the 19th and 21st Century': Four Central Arenas for the Transformation

In his 1,500 page treatise 'Verwandlung der Welt – Eine Geschichte des 19. Jahrhunderts' ('Global Metamorphosis – a History of the 19th Century', 2009), the historian Osterhammel describes the great transformation which led to the industrial society. He analyses the period from 1770 to the 20th century. Instead of a transformation, he refers to the phase of intense change from agricultural to industrial societies he observes in 'the five or six decades around 1800', which he variously refers to as the 'Schwellenjahrzehnte' - the decades of emergence, the 'Epochenwandel' - a time of epochal transition, 'Sattelzeit' - a time of historical discontinuity - or 'Wendezeit', the turning point (Osterhammel, 2009). It is interesting that he describes the characteristics of epochal change much like Grin et al. (2010) do. Osterhammel also concludes that great epochal transitions leading to a 'global metamorphosis' last several decades. In these phases of 'Übergänge' and 'Zäsuren' (transitory and incisive change), economic, cultural and social, but also ecological processes progressing at different speeds (Braudel, 1958) become more concentrated to gel into transformative dynamics, influenced by a great number of actor groups which ultimately, albeit with potentially differing intentions, advance the change into a specific direction (Osterhammel, 2009).

History therefore knows no clearly definable temporal evolutionary tipping points heralding an epochal change. Historical waves and comprehensive transformations are actually the result of 'Häufigkeitsverdichtungen von Veränderungen', 'a concurrence of multiple changes, which can either be an ongoing progress, or take place with interruptions; they can occur either additively or cumulatively, either reversibly or irreversibly, either at a steady, or an unsteady pace' (Osterhammel, 2009, ad hoc translation by the WBGU). Only ex-post analysis reveals whether an epochal change, as in this event from the era of agricultural to the era of industrial societies (Box 3.2-1) has taken place.

The non-linearity of far reaching social transformations becomes particularly apparent in the non-parallelism between the history of ideas and the real political changes. A look at history shows that considerable time passes before radical ideas and new guiding principles permeate societies to ultimately lead to great changes. John Locke (1632–1704) argued for Enlightenment and Reason for the entire second half of the 17th century. French philosopher René Descartes (1596–1650) established French rationalism expanded later by Voltaire (1694–1778) and Rousseau (1712–1778). Kant's famous essay 'An Answer to the Question: What is Enlightenment?', in which he demanded 'man's emergence from his self-imposed immaturity', was published in 1784. Whilst the philosophers of the Age of Enlightenment advocated liberty, reason and the 'welfare of humanity', and 'preconceived' democratic societies, their own were still dominated by the counter-enlightenment philosophies propagated by either the Catholic or the Protestant Church, depending on locality. In either case, they were living a life still far removed from the new ideals of the Enlightenment. For a remarkably long time, the advocates of Enlightenment themselves adhered to some established concepts of restriction of liberties. Only a minority of the great European philosophers of the Age of Enlightenment, including Adam Smith and Rousseau, protested against the slavery practised primarily by the colonial powers, and the transatlantic slave trade which peaked in the second half of the 18th century. Initially, this 'humanity', whose liberty the Enlightenment philosophers advocated, did certainly not include all of humankind (Winkler, 2009; Section 3.5.1).

Moreover, Osterhammel's reconstruction of the global 'metamorphosis' during the 19th century underlines that there were four transformation arenas of paramount importance for the epochal change into an industrialised society. These transformation arenas of the most recent major epochal shifts also have a central bearing on the 21st century's Great Transformation. Civilisation's last great leap, into an industrial society, was based on an overlapping and the concentration of far reaching change processes with regard to

- the energy basis for economy and society,
- the significance of time for the economy, and in society,
- communication, knowledge and logistics infrastructures,
- power transformation and social change.

An outline illustrating Osterhammel's findings on the global transition in the 19th century aids better understanding of current transformation processes.

The Energy Transformation in the 19th Century – Basis for the Industrial Revolution

Any form of economic activity requires an energy supply. A lack of access to affordable energy is one of the most dangerous straits societies can experience. The process of industrialisation was above all an energy regime change (Sieferle et al., 2006; Figure 3.2-1). Until the late 18th century, pre-industrial societies were based on a limited range of energy sources other than manpower. Water, wind, firewood, peat and beasts of burden limited the economies' productive capacity and ability to expand (Figure 3.2-1). The worry that energy availability might not keep pace with population growth was ever-present. The 'Malthus Controversy', instigated by his 'Essay on the Principle of Population' (Malthus, 1798), testified to these worries, and became embedded in the historical memory of many generations (Figure 3.2-2).

Around 1780, all global societies depended on the use of energy from biomass. A good century later, at the beginning of the 20th century, the world was divided into a small group of industrialised countries, where the expansion of infrastructures for the use of fossil energy

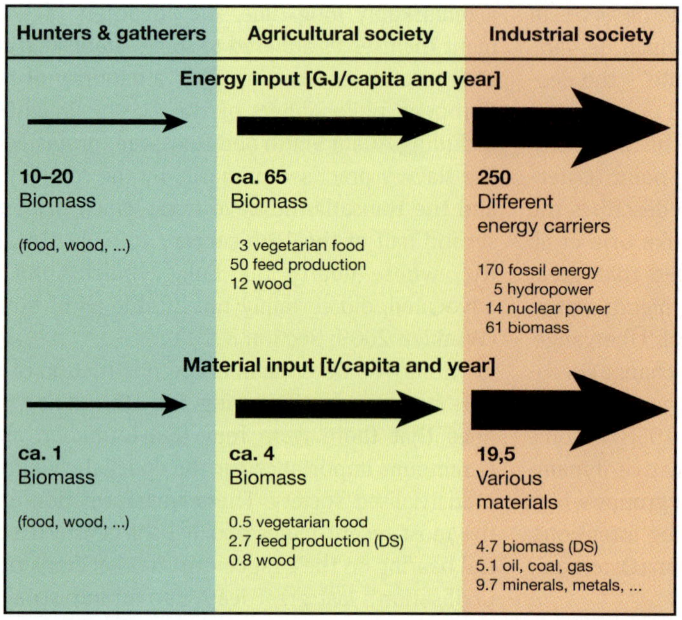

Figure 3.2-1
Growing energy input in gigajoule (GJ) per capita per year, and material input in t per capita per year in the wake of the Neolithic and Industrial Revolutions in industrialised countries (estimated). DS = tonnage stated as dry substance.
Source: based on Fischer-Kowalski and Haberl, 1998

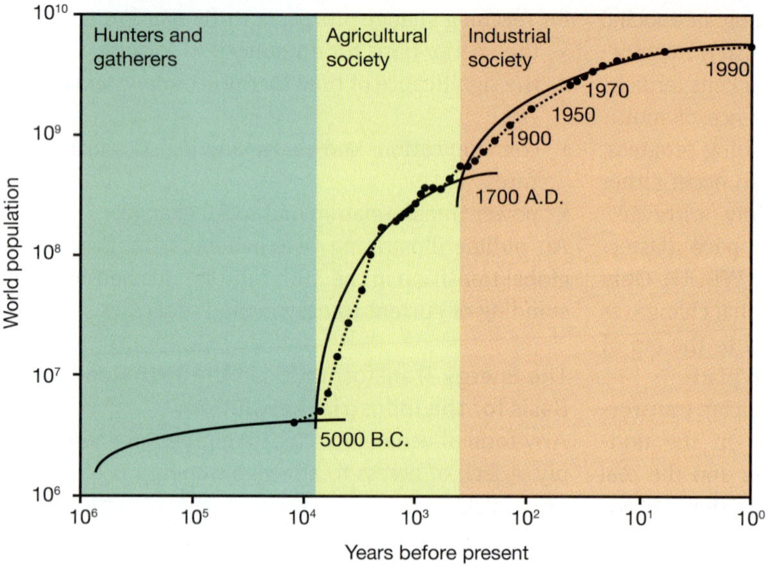

Figure 3.2-2
Global population growth in the wake of the transitions from hunter and gatherer to agricultural society, and from agricultural to industrialised society, from approx. 1 million people to several billion.
Source: Kates, 1996

carriers had succeeded, and a majority of nations which were forced to continue to rely on traditional energy sources. The energy regime changeover in these industrialised countries was by no means sudden. The 'era of fossil fuels' (Osterhammel, 2009) commenced around 1820. During this phase, the per capita income, previously stagnant over a long period, also grew. The substitution of animal and human muscle power and wood and peat with energy stored in a fossil fuel (coal) revolutionised the economy (Box 3.2-1).

Coal drove steam engines, ships and railways, and catapulted the industrialising societies into an era of interconnectedness, acceleration and national integration. As late as the middle of the 19th century, coal provided only a small, but steadily rising amount of the energy used, even in Europe. The history of crude oil began in Pennsylvania in 1859, when it was first extracted commercially. It took around seven decades for mineral fuels (coal and oil) to overtake biomass in global economic importance, even though the majority of the global population remained reliant on traditional energy carriers by the end of the 19th century. Japan represents an interesting case of catch-up, learning, copying and accelerated fossil development. In 1860, Japan still lagged many decades behind Great Britain in terms of energy technology. By 1900, however, it had completely caught up.

The predominance of a fossil energy regime (particularly in Great Britain, Germany and the USA) since the 1880s led to a second generation of industrial innova-

Box 3.2-1

The Industrial Revolution

The Industrial Revolution is a complex process of economic and social remodelling of pre-industrial societies which initially took place on the British mainland (Osterhammel, 2009). From England, the process of industrialisation spread to the European continent during the course of the 19th century (Belgium, Switzerland, France, Germany, Russia, Italy), and to North America and Japan. In China and India, and Argentina, Chile, Brazil and Mexico, the required preconditions for industrialisation were not developed for political reasons (Osterhammel, 2009). According to Sieferle's interpretation (2010), the Industrial Revolution started in Great Britain because, in comparison with Asia, Europe was not such an established agrarian society, and political competitiveness between the individual countries was high. In the wake of the Industrial Revolution and industrialisation, energy system and source were chosen according to the resources available in each respective country.

Energy became the central leitmotif of the 19th century. In all of the newly industrialising countries, biomass, manpower and animal power were gradually replaced by fossil energy carriers in combination with new technologies (steam engine, railway, car, tractor). Initially, coal was the primary source, later joined by oil and gas, hydropower and electricity (Osterhammel, 2009; Sieferle, 2010). Agricultural capacities were released through the increased cultivation of food, rather than feedstock, and the reduction in forestry. The conversion of the economy and the energy system was a long-term evolutionary process, accompanied by modifications to existing institutions and labour structures. Communication, technology transfer – including non-licensed imitation, industrial espionage and international trade all played a major role in diffusing industrialisation.

In contrast to the latecomers in the second half of the 18th century, conditions in Britain were particularly favourable for the Industrial Revolution: a unified country and coherent, centralised government, civil peace, short and cheap transport routes and, thanks to the colonies, an abundance of natural resources at its disposal, and an extended economic area. Precision engineering and tool making skills, an avid interest in innovations, a general spirit of free enterprise and a liberal economic structure were also conducive factors advancing the Industrial Revolution (Meyerhoff and Petschow, 1996; Berg, 2008; Holst and Fischer, 2008; Otto, 2008; Osterhammel, 2009; Sieferle, 2010).

Moreover, in the run up to the Industrial Revolution, there had been some changes in Britain which strengthened the concept of private property – for example the introduction of patent law – and lent support to innovative agricultural production methods, releasing manpower (Otto, 2008). Even in the 18th century, Britain's economic growth outstripped population growth, which contributed as much to the emergence of a middle class as to domestic demand for superior quality goods. Mass production – later automated – allowed these products to be cheaply manufactured and sold (Osterhammel, 2009; Sieferle, 2010). Furthermore, an intellectual elite started to emerge, and there was a high degree of willingness on the part of the wealthy to invest in new ideas and technologies (Sieferle, 2010). With the industrialisation, cities grew and developed, aiding the diffusion of socio-technical innovations and innovation processes. At the same time, there was a general awareness of living in a new epoch, promoting open-mindedness for innovations and experiments.

Continental Europe (particularly Belgium, Switzerland, France, Germany, Russia), North America and Japan did not enjoy Britain's favourable conditions, or only to a limited extent; however, these were gradually created during the course of the 19th century through a high level of intervention on the part of the emerging nation states. Each of these countries therefore followed its own development path. There were also individual actors in these nations, such as businessmen, scientists, advisors or politicians who, inspired by the developments in England, strived for a comparable industrialisation and economic system (Meyerhoff and Petschow, 1996; Bischoff, 2008; Osterhammel, 2009).

In Germany, for example, a government-steered, fast catch-up industrialisation process took place soon after the founding of the German Reich in 1871 (Box 3.2-2). This included the creation of new institutions, for example technical universities, and the abolition of others, for example the guild system. This allowed Germany to soon outperform England in the heavy industry, mechanical engineering and chemicals production sectors. At the dawn of the 20th century, countries such as the USA and Germany contributed significantly to the global diffusion of industrialisation with their inventions, the labour organisation structures they had devised, and their international trade activities (Osterhammel, 2009).

Not least, the Industrial Revolution and widespread industrialisation are also so significant because for the first time they allowed humankind emancipation from the energy basis and resource 'land', and to increase productivity (Sieferle, 2010). Necessary preconditions were a functioning system of law and order, land reforms, investment in human resources, skilled labour, access to natural resources, sufficient capital and a willingness to embrace progress, as reflected by the new intellectual elite's common world vision and the emerging spirit of enterprise (Osterhammel, 2009; Sieferle, 2010). For the first time ever, humankind succeeded in maintaining the momentum of a sudden wave of innovation.

The Industrial Revolution shows that pioneering processes require political framework conditions. Pioneering processes include investments, innovative actors and a common guiding principle or world view. Suitable framework conditions include a liberal economic structure and the institutionalised collaboration of government, commercial enterprise, and science. However, industrialisation is by no means the only path to economic growth. Countries such as, for example, the Netherlands, Canada, Australia or Argentina adopted new technologies and labour organisation structures and turned from agricultural societies into modern commercial and service economies without any particular industrialisation efforts (Osterhammel, 2009).

tions that were based on the new energy carriers: electricity (light bulb, electric engines, power plant technologies), chemicals and the automobile. The energy revolution therefore triggered a complex, self-contained innovation cycle. This was accompanied by other innovations, such as radio transmission (1895) and cinematography (1895).

The transition into the 'fossil energy century' was not only a process of economic-technical transformation. Energy became a 'cultural Leitmotiv' (Osterhammel, 2009). The links between science and industry became closer, and the age of large-scale industrial research began (Boxes 3.2-1, 3.6-1). The scientific organisations 'invented the method of invention' (Alfred North Whitehead, from Osterhammel, 2009). Commercially successful inventors such as Werner Siemens, who discovered the electrodynamic principle in 1866, and Thomas Alva Edison, who investigated electricity generation and distribution, helped to shape the founding years in Germany's Wilhelminian era. Fossil energy carriers completely altered the way humankind saw the world, as people were no longer forced to depend on elemental natural forces, particularly in the form of fire. By way of the steam engine, fossil fuels released previously unimaginable forces and application possibilities, increased the productivity of manpower in the emerging industry and in agriculture, and, thanks to the railway, allowed acceleration and geographical interconnectedness.

These changes also affected business sciences and economics. In the middle of the 19th century, Karl Marx referred to industrialism and capitalism as new social structures; in 1848, John Stuart Mill outlined the various approaches of traditional political economy in his comprehensive synthesis 'Principles of Political Economy', which became the analytical foundation for an economy in which industry was replacing agriculture as the leading sector. These changes also resonated in art and philosophy. Around 1830, the heyday of philosophical idealism and romanticism in European, in particular French, German and English literature, came to an end. European painting underwent a transition towards realism.

Over the first decades of the 19th century, the fossil transformation led to the epoch of industrialism, which dramatically changed the global power balance. Until well into the 17th century, various empires had co-existed and competed with each other without the emergence of any clear superiority structures. The European colonial powers (such as Spain, England, the Netherlands), China, the Ottoman Empire and India were all on a par in terms of society, economy and science. The fossil revolution defined the West as the centre of this newly emerging industrial global economy.

Industrialism's New Time Regime

Industrialism was accompanied by, and based on, a revolution of the meaning of 'time', and its uniformity. At the beginning of the 19th century, no country in the world knew the synchronisation of time signals beyond city limits. Towards the end of the century, at the International Meridian Conference in Washington in 1884, 25 nations agreed to adopt a standard world time. This 'time reform' (Osterhammel, 2009) made the alignment of railway and shipping, and later also air traffic, timetables possible, and served as the foundation for international commercial transactions and business. The fossil age therefore fundamentally changed people's rhythm of life, and the way time was perceived. Electrification meant that a day was no longer defined by sunrise and sunset. Technology allowed the synchronisation of clocks, heralding the age of timetables, timed intervals and the acceleration of operating procedures. It may sound trivial to highlight the acceleration of processes and mobility as one of the characteristics of the great industrial transformation; however, 'the impact this experience had on historical development cannot be overestimated, as it meant that, for the first time in human history, it was possible to move from place to place faster and more reliably than on horseback, and independently of favourable winds on sea.' (Osterhammel, 2009, ad hoc translation by the WBGU). Together with advancing enlightenment and the improvement of hygienic conditions, and the subsequent increase in life expectation, both present and future took on another meaning altogether for people – industrialism therefore opened up completely new horizons of time. Industrial modernity also hailed a departure into the future.

Creation of Networked Infrastructures

The linking of geographical spaces and the creation of the basic infrastructures of the industrial age took place during the first half of the 19th century. In 1883, Friedrich List drew up a railway network, a rather daring vision of the future at the time, as no country in the world had anything like a railway network before 1850. Since the 1870s, it has become possible to circumnavigate the world north of the equator solely with steam-powered modes of transport, without resorting to horses, camels, bearers or own muscle power – even though only very few people were in a position to explore these new possibilities, so vividly described by Jules Verne in his 'Around the World In Eighty Days' (1872).

The third quarter of the 19th century also marked the beginning of a world linked by cables, allowing communication over long distances for the first time in history. For a number of decades, the telegram was the cheapest 'long distance communication medium'. The

Box 3.2-2

Drivers accelerating the Transformation Example: Germany's Wilhelminian Period

The four major transformation arenas outlined in Section 3.2 – energy basis, temporal perception, infrastructures and social change – allow the systematic analysis of great transformations, as elaborated with regard to the Industrial Revolution. Fundamental change processes must be initiated in these areas to achieve sufficient acceleration and appropriate extent of the transformation process. Important transformation-accelerating drivers can be identified using the example of Germany's Wilhelminian period at the end of the 19th century; their interaction made the country's economy the most dynamic in the world at that point in time.

Key to this comprehensive transformation process were not least the close links between invention, innovation and diffusion processes to allow positive feedback loops and accelerate the dynamics of the transition process. Three interconnected factors were of major significance; together, they formed a 'golden triangle' for innovation processes: *firstly,* the building up of scientific-technical capacities in universities and scientific research institutions in conjunction with the qualification of skilled professionals; *secondly,* the emergence of the 'industries of tomorrow' (or an even longer-term perspective), for example first uses for the then new energy carrier electricity, or a rapidly growing traffic and transport sector, and their commercial exploitation by companies such as, for instance, AEG and Borsig; *thirdly,* high net investment quotas, allowing a rapid diffusion of innovations. The net investment quota in Germany rose from almost 10% in 1850 to over 15% at the peak of the Wilhelminian period (Hoffmann, 1965), i.e. three times greater than today's (Section 4.5). The state played a central role (Figure 3.2-3), above all by supporting capacity building efforts through the establishment of scientific research institutions; it also created favourable framework conditions for private entrepreneurs, which allowed rapid expansion into new business sectors (Box 3.2-1).

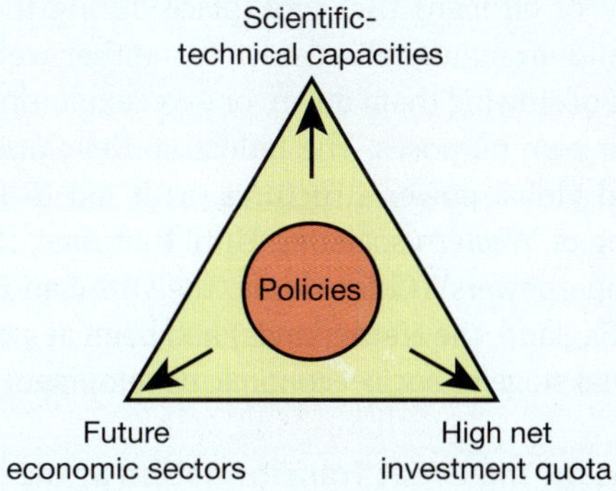

Figure 3.2-3
Elements of the transformative surge of innovations during the Wilhelminian period in Germany.
Source: WBGU

However, the transformation process progressed not just exclusively in the area of new technical solutions, but in line with the four transformation arenas also in social terms. Particularly the emergence and increased prosperity of the middle classes had a great impact, as it advanced the transformation process and also inspired new cultural ideas. To understand the demands of the transformation today, the elements of this 'golden triangle' of favourable conditions for innovation processes continue to provide important points of reference for government action. However, the changed framework conditions, and some additional factors, must be taken into account – above all the international dimension and the legitimisation of decision-making. Chapter 7 gathers these elements and extends the 'golden triangle' for innovation processes to the 'transformation rhombus' (Figure 7.1-3).

telephone's triumphant progress began in 1877/1879 with the establishment of communal exchanges in New York and Paris. However, for several decades, the telephone initially allowed only local communication. Gradually, private households and companies were connected to the new networked infrastructures for water, gas and electricity – the birth of utility grids. It was only these infrastructures which allowed the gradual emergence of the modern forms of economy through interconnected cities, trade routes and knowledge systems. As comparatively recently as the early 20th century, only a small minority of the global population had access to these technical systems.

During the course of the development of technical infrastructures and the linking of people, companies, cities and economic regions which, alongside the new perception of time, also led to an altered perception of geographical distances, there also emerged regulatory systems, legal dimensions and bureaucracies to stabilise these interactions. The epoch of nation states is closely bound to the transformations in the course of the transition to industrialism.

Power Shifts and Social Change

The upheaval of industrialisation also altered the social and political structures of societies. These dimensions of the transformation have been described by authors as varied as Adam Smith, Karl Marx, Karl Polanyi and Max Weber. The downfall of the centuries-old institution of aristocracy, still the mainstay of all societies in the 18th century, coincided with the rise of industrial societies. These social minorities in whose hands the means of all economic and social power lay, who viewed their privileges as a god-given right, who owned all economic resources of the pre-industrial societies (manpower and land) whilst despising any kind of physical and menial work themselves, were not capable of stopping the technical, institutional and normative innovations (for example the French Revolution's basic concept of the equality of all men) that took place during the transition into an industrialised society, neither were they capable of slowing them down, or even exploiting them for their own purposes. The Industrial Revolution also changed global power structures, as it led to the triumphing of Western societies. Until that time, the various 'superpowers' (China, India, the Ottoman Empire, Spain, England, the Netherlands) had been at a more or less equal stage of socio-economic development.

Lessons for the Great Transformation at the Beginning of the 21st Century

The outlined blurring of boundaries and profound incisions in and between the four fields of action during the course of the global 'metamorphosis' in the 19th century represents an interesting backdrop for the description of the dynamics of the current transformation. The four action fields described are again central to the upheaval. They differ fundamentally only in terms of direction and quality of the transition:

1. *Energy basis:* a central element of the low-carbon transformation is the expansion of a largely renewable energy infrastructure, and a leaving behind of the 'fossil age' (Chapter 4). Like the transition into an industrial society, this process will lead to a radically changed economic structure.
2. *Changed 'time regime':* on the one hand, economic, political and institutional change processes must be vastly accelerated during the transition into a climate-friendly society, in order to still manage to avoid irreversible damages to the Earth system, and dangerous climate change (Chapters 1, 4, 5). However, accelerated change in complex societies, which are interconnected to a high degree and distinguished by the division of powers and control, with difficult to grasp, interlinked interests ('checks and balances') is no mere triviality. The same applies to the international negotiation system. On the other hand, people, companies and political organisations will have to learn to apply a long-term perspective to their actions, to take on responsibilities and practise preventative instead of reactive problem solving, because the decisions which are taken today (for example continuing along a fossil development path) will show their effects for many decades (for instance sub-regional water shortages), centuries (for example the melting of large-scale ice sheets) or even thousands of years to come (such as the sea-level rise). Our societies' social, economic and political institutions, and possibly also people's cognitive and normative capabilities, have as yet not adapted to these challenges. Just as during the transition to the industrial society, profound cultural changes are also imminent today (Chapters 2, 6).
3. *New basic infrastructures as a foundation for the low-carbon society:* just as central to the low-carbon transformation as it was to the Industrial Revolution is the energy supply. However, analysis of the central action fields for the transformation into a low-carbon society makes it clear that the three main infrastructures of national economies and societies, and the global economy as such, must be redirected towards the goal of decarbonisation (Chapter 4). Apart from the energy system, this also applies to urban spaces on a global level, as these contribute significantly to greenhouse gas emissions, and will continue to grow over the coming decades, as the number of city dwellers will roughly double by 2050, from 3 to 6 billion (Chapter 1). On the other hand, the Great Transformation can only succeed if concurrently, emissions from traditional forms of land use (deforestation; agricultural greenhouse gas emissions) are also radically reduced. Whether we can successfully create a climate-friendly society therefore stands and falls within three transformation fields: energy systems trend reversal; climate-friendly shaping of the currently accelerating urbanisation, and climate-compatible land use (Chapters 4, 5, 6, 8).
4. *Social change and power shifts:* just as during the transition into an industrial society, the break with the old-established required by the low-carbon transformation is blocked by impeding actors defending their traditional privileges and roles; there are those with something to lose from the transformation, and those with something to gain. Industries based on the use of fossil energy carriers will lose their competitive advantages, low-carbon and resource compatible innovations will create new industries, the established hierarchies between universities and research institutions will change, new social guiding principles and narratives will gain the upper hand. The transformation is accompanied by a comprehensive social change marked by conflicts between the old and the new development paradigm, and their respective diverging interests (Chapters 2, 6). Furthermore, global power constellations will change. China, India, Brazil and other rising economies will be the new global economic centres. The western industrialised societies cannot manage the transformation towards a low-carbon global economy by themselves, even if they attempted to do so with all their might. The creation of a low-carbon global economy is conceivable only if the new powers share this development path, or, even better, if they turn into forces driving the transformation. After all, global social changes

will affect the normative armamentarium of all societies. Just as the Enlightenment paved the way for, and had a huge influence on, industrialisation and democracy, this contemporary issue is about reaching an unparalleled level of global cooperation, and international fairness, because the transformation must take place within such a tight timeframe. Ultimately, it is also about reviewing the relationship between humankind and nature. The low-carbon transformation is therefore not only an economic and technological process; on the contrary, it also necessitates a normative reorientation and cultural learning processes.

In comparison with the 'global metamorphosis' in the 19th century, the Great Transformation is distinguished by three additional peculiarities:

Firstly, the fact that the industrial society achieved predominance as the norm was an evolutionary process, for which there was no 'master plan'. The transformation into a sustainable society, on the other hand, must occur intentionally and under time pressure, to achieve a trend reversal towards a climate-friendly and resource efficient society. There will be no sustainability turnaround without major, strategically targeted efforts by policy-makers, social actors and economy. This is the first great transformation in the history of humankind that has to be consciously effected on the strength of politics and policies.

Secondly, the Great Transformation must take place at a global level, and be embraced by industrialised, newly industrialising and even poor developing countries as otherwise, dangerous climate change cannot be avoided. The Industrial Revolution initially took place in only a few countries, it also took more than a century for it to become an (almost) global phenomenon. Now, the course towards a sustainable global economy must be set within a very short time in order to provide prosperity, stability and security within the planetary boundaries for as many people as possible. This requires an unprecedented level of global cooperation.

Thirdly, the narrative, the guiding principles of social development, must undergo some radical changes. Although the core ideas of the Enlightenment can, on the one hand, serve as inspiration, for example that reason, a sense of responsibility and consideration of other people's interests guide all our actions, it must also be generally accepted that now, the planetary boundaries must serve as the starting point of all social development and prosperity increase (re-embedding). The primary motive of the era of industrialisation, on the other hand, was the overcoming of the boundaries set by nature (dis-embedding). This is not a petition for a romantic return to nature, and not an outright rejection of technological solutions for humankind's future challenges. However, whichever development path is chosen, it must take the boundaries of the global ecosystems into account – as otherwise, the Earth could well become a barren and unsafe place in the course of the 21st century.

Crutzen and Schwägerl (2010) have succinctly made this paradigm change quite clear: 'For millennia, humans have behaved as rebels against a superpower we call 'Nature.' In the 20th century, however, new technologies, fossil fuels, and a fast-growing population resulted in a 'Great Acceleration' of our own powers. Albeit clumsily, we are taking control of Nature's realm, from climate to DNA (...) We now live in 'human systems with natural ecosystems embedded within them.' Long-held barriers between nature and culture are breaking down... (...) It's no longer 'us against Nature'. Instead, it's we who decide what nature is and what it will be. (...) Living in the anthropocene stresses the enormity of humanity's responsibility as stewards of the Earth. (...) Imagine our descendants in the year 2200 or 2500. They might liken us to aliens who have treated the Earth as if it were a mere stopover for refuelling, or even worse, characterize us as barbarians who would ransack their own home. (...) Remember, in this new era, nature is us.'

Following this core thought of the emergence of an entirely new epoch, the anthropocene, not only production and consumption patterns, but also incentive schemes, institutions, normative maxims, and scientific disciplines will have to change (above all the economic sciences).

These three specific characteristics of the Great Transformation indicate that humankind is facing an evolutionary leap for civilisation (as it did during the transition into industrial societies) if the radical change into a low-carbon society is to succeed: it must prove that it is capable of shaping and directing this major upheaval, and this can only be achieved on the basis of thinking and acting with an extremely long-term perspective in mind; it must leave the epoch of nation states behind and foster an unprecedented culture of global cooperation; it must also forge a sustainable and legitimised narrative which will serve prosperity, security, liberty and fairness in a global society of soon-to-be 9 billion people, and which will accept the limitations of the Earth's ecosystems.

3.3 Stages of the Great Transformation – Where are We?

Grin et al. (2010) illustrate the various stages of a transformation by means of a simple S-curve (Figure 3.3-1). Their multi-stage concept helps to describe the basic pattern of transformative change. Transformation progress is determined through the pace of the changes, the scale of transformation, and the stages of the transformation process. Applied to the transition towards a climate-friendly economy (from high-carbon to low-carbon economy), the following picture emerges: the transition from industrial to low-carbon society is, just like the change into an industrial society at the beginning of the 19th century, not a rapid process, as the established economic and social model is initially stable, legitimised through successes in terms of prosperity, and therefore resistant to change. However, since the 1970s critical, at first marginalised, voices have been raised, questioning the sustainability of the established model (Meadows et al., 1972). So, before the accelerated transitional stage commenced (roughly since the beginning of the 21st century), within the scope of the previous model, the dynamics of change already became apparent (preliminaries include the establishment of ministries for the environment in many countries, environmentally-oriented movements emerge, Brundtland Report 1987; Chapter 2). Taking this perspective, the transformation towards sustainability already started around four decades ago, with changes that were initially incremental.

The change from the acceleration of the transitional stage (start phase) to a new social and economic balance and a low-carbon and resource efficient economy will probably take another two decades. This phase is not marked by linear change processes, but by difficult restructuring processes, by the necessity of more rapid and widespread reforms to overcome path dependencies, by chaotic and uncertain changes, and dynamics in different action fields which can trigger positive, as well as negative, feedback loops. The steep progress of the curve (Figure 3.3-1) symbolises that this major break must be achieved in spite of a great number of blockade mechanisms and forces doggedly clinging onto the status quo.

Today, the European economies are in the thrall of this difficult acceleration process. Now, the right course towards sustainability must be set within the next 10 years. This situation can be compared to the 1830s to 1840s of the industrialisation, during which period the new energy system slowly spread, its progress accompanied by innovations, although these dynamics had only spread to some part of economy and society (Box 3.2-1). Box 3.3-1 also shows that the transition to a new balance can also lead to failure. During the acceleration process, the risk of lock-in patterns is high. The energy efficiency of vehicles is improved, however, it is concurrently overcompensated by the even faster growing number of cars (rebound effect, Box 4.3-1); states agree the reduction of greenhouse gases and other 'green reforms', however, far below the level required to avoid dangerous climate change (Section 7.3.9.1); renewable energies become more important, however, they only serve to complement the still dominant fossil energy carriers, not to replace them, This lock-in path leads to a '3–4 °C world' (Figure 7.1-2).

Europe and the global economy are currently at this critical point. Things have already started to move towards low-carbon development; nevertheless, the danger that the current dynamics between the forces of change and the forces of dogged insistence on the status quo will ultimately end in lock-in paths is very high. It is even conceivable that despite the fact that tendencies towards a transformation in favour of sustainability have already progressed for some time, there could

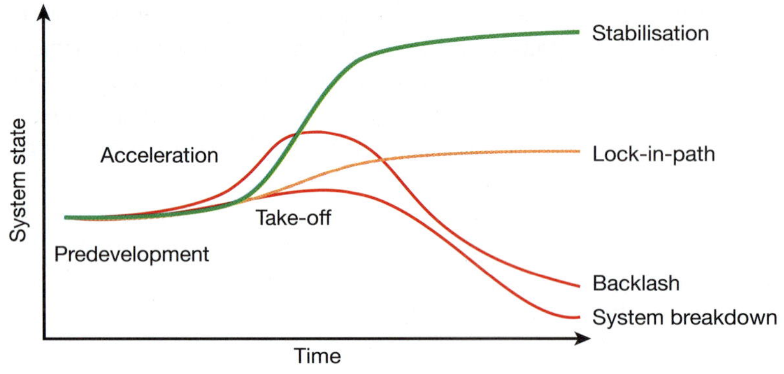

Figure 3.3-1
Illustration of the various stages (preliminary development, start, acceleration) and possible progression (stabilisation, lock-in, backlash) of a transformation. As a transformation process is complex and exposed to various different dynamics, its progress is not really predictable. The multi-stage concept describes the basic pattern of transformative change.
Source: Grin et al., 2010

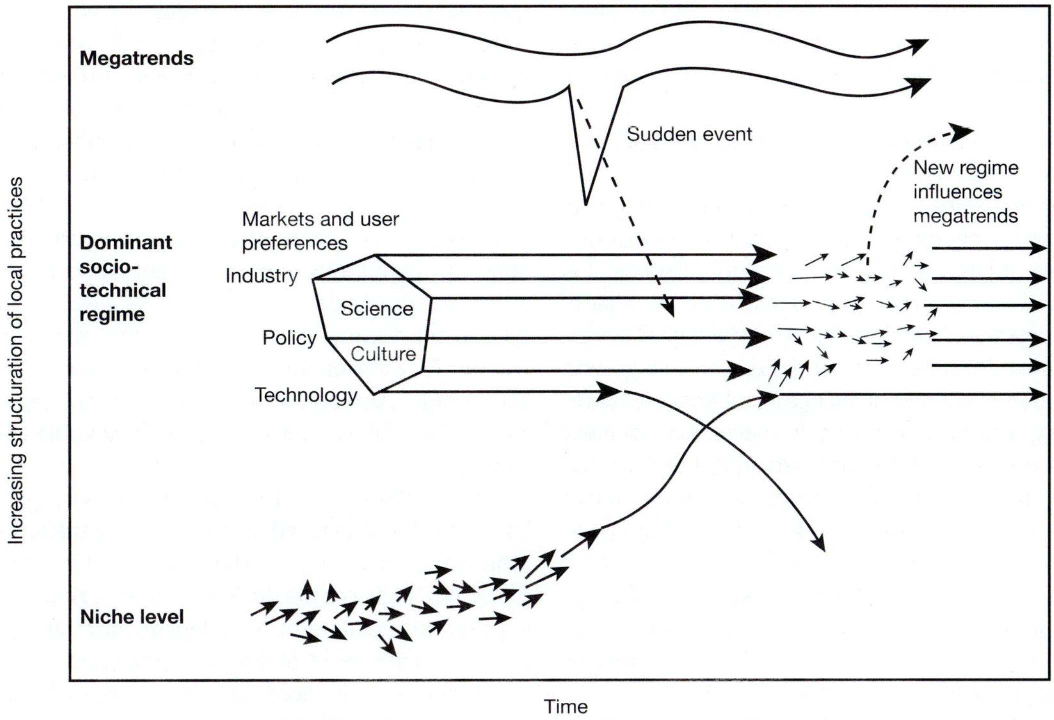

Figure 3.4-1
Multilevel model for analysing transformation processes, example of the substitution of an established technology with a new one. There are three independent but mutually impacting action levels (megatrends, socio-technical regimes, niche level). Changes, the dynamic movement between and within these action levels, and their interaction create the scope the transformation needs.
Source: after Grin et al., 2010

be some serious setbacks. The USA, for example, might reject the low-carbon change on principle, or the majority of the most populous, and currently rapidly growing, newly industrialising countries (China, India, South Africa, Indonesia) that have their own coal reserves might decide to continue to use these, thus seriously impeding the transition towards a low-carbon society. Chapters 4 and 6 empirically examine the elaborated transformation progress in more detail, before the subsequent introduction of recommendations for a successful transformation process in Chapter 7.

3.4 The Great Transformation's Action Levels – Why this Epochal Change can be Shaped

Grin et al. (2010) propose a multi-level analysis approach, as this helps to take the complexities, multi-tiered nature and non-concurrency of the transformation process (co-evolution) into account whilst also making them considerably simpler. The authors differentiate between three initially independent action levels which nevertheless impact each other in turn (megatrends, socio-technical regime, niche level; Figure 3.4-1). Changes and the dynamic movement between and within these action levels create scope for transformation. This can at any given time be extremely minor or major in a country (region, sector).

At the centre is the established socio-technical regime; in our case a global economy based on the use of fossil energy carriers. It creates a system consisting of technologies, policies and institutions, economic sectors, culture and science. As long as this established system is stable, legitimised and economically as well as politically attractive, any change towards low-carbon seems unlikely. At grassroots level, niches and change agents appear: climate-protection oriented entrepreneurs, scientists, architects, NGO members, journalists or change agents in ministries and international organisations (Chapter 6). The more marginal and smaller these pioneering groups, the less likely a low-carbon transformation. Transformative change is not possible without change agents. In Europe, the group of 'climate pioneers' has steadily grown over the past four decades; it has already had an impact outside of its niche, thereby starting to change established regimes. They are no longer merely actors at the margins of the established climate-damaging system, but have also permeated the established economic structures, although the tipping point of system transformation has not been reached as yet: environmentally-oriented industry sectors have already emerged, as have, for example, the European emissions trading scheme, and feed-in tariffs for renewable energies. The discourse on low-carbon development has ceased to be limited to outsiders; it is now almost as accepted as the established growth path, and has possibly already been accorded a higher degree of normative legitimation than the established growth paradigm. The dynamics at change agent level are therefore lively, which also implies that the old development model is no longer stable and hermetic, but that it is gradually being confronted with the pressure to adapt (Chapter 6). This opens a window of opportunity to truly alter the development path, by promoting these 'pioneers of change'. This process is analysed in Chapters 2 (normative reorientation), 4 (core innovations for low-carbon development), 5 (political and institutional change processes), and 6 (change agents).

Besides the two levels for action outlined, megatrends exist, which are difficult to influence but may either impede or promote the transformation process: self-contained technological dynamics and inventions, global power shifts, wars or major disasters (Chernobyl, Fukushima, global financial crisis). The multipolar power blockades could be interpreted as one of these megatrends, considerably hindering international cooperation (for example with regard to the enforcement of an effective international climate regime). The internet and other communication technologies, on the other hand, allow the spreading of knowledge and the organisation of international learning processes at a pace that is unprecedented in the history of humankind. This could make the low-carbon transformation less difficult.

Central global trends impeding a low-carbon ransformation (dynamic urbanisation processes; easy availability of fossil energy carriers in rapidly growing and populous newly industrialising countries; multipolar power blockades hindering international cooperation) were identified in Chapter 1; Chapter 2 elaborates the fundamental normative change processes that tend to favour a transformation; Chapter 4 illustrates that the technological developments make the clean break towards sustainability possible.

In addition, 'shocks' can also be generated at macro-level, significantly influencing the direction and pace of the transformation process. The Fukushima reactor accident in March 2011 and the subsequent, in part radical reassessment of the risks of nuclear energy is a drastic example of such a shock. However, even less dramatic shocks can have a far reaching impact on the transformation. For instance, if any of the rapidly growing newly industrialising countries were to discover further crude oil deposits in the next few years (as has recently happened in Brazil), this kind of 'exogenous shock' could seriously impede the low-carbon transformation. On the other hand, if serious climatic crises (such as increased frequency of weather extremes with unusually high levels of destructiveness) were to occur in the coming years and not at some remote point in time in the future, this could accelerate the transformation. A substantial reduction in the cost of renewable energies through technological innovations would increase the likelihood of climate-compatible investments.

The multilevel model is a helpful analysis grid as a basis for the structured discussion of transformation processes. It combines systemic perspectives (transition from high-carbon to low-carbon regime) allowing the consideration of path dependencies along with processes with more or less self-contained dynamics, which can be influenced, but not 'prevented' (urbanisation, population growth), with an actor's perspective, allowing the exploration of the scope for action (change agents). Political transformation strategies can learn from this: change agents in economy, policy-making and society should receive increased support; the review of economic, innovation and social policies with respect to climate-friendliness is vital, and approaches for redirecting difficult to influence megatrends must be developed (Chapter 7).

By way of a hypothesis, it should be stated here that against the background of the analysis so far, the low-carbon transformation at least appears to be possible. Change agents have already become a relevant group in many societies, and also in the economy (Chapter 6). The established system, largely based on the use of fossil energy carriers, has already been 'unlocked' for sustainability through various reforms. Both positive and negative megatrends do not seem to make a low-carbon transformation impossible, at least in principle. These dynamics will be empirically examined in more detail in the following chapters.

3.5 Lessons from Contemporary History: Medium-Range Transformations

The Neolithic and Industrial Revolutions introduced so far have been the only transformation processes of truly global dimensions. They were also, for the most part, not steered. The following introduces and analyses six historical transformation processes with a medium-range impact, commonly accepted as steered. They are intended to serve the illustration of conditions, steering options, and actor constellations required for the Great Low-Carbon Transformation.

For ease of differentiation, the WBGU divides these historical transformation processes into four types: the abolishment of slavery and the European integration are examples of the type 'vision'. The primary driver was a vision of a better, fairer, and more peaceful future. The 'Green Revolution' and the structural adaptation programmes of the International Monetary Fund and the World Bank have been allocated to the type 'crisis'. In these cases, the transformation processes were motivated by the experiencing of crises (hunger and development crisis). The treaties on ozone layer protection fall into the 'knowledge' category. An unusual aspect here was that irrefutable scientific proof of the fact that fluorochlorinated hydrocarbons are destroying the ozone layer had not yet been offered whilst the Montreal Protocol (1982–1987) was already being negotiated. The international community acted on the basis of theoretical assumptions in the context of correlated impact according to the precautionary principle (Benedick, 1999). Any finally, the IT Revolution exemplifies the type 'technology'. The central aspect here is the vast and rapid proliferation of a technical innovation which, as a key technology, affects far reaching areas of everyday life (multi purpose technology; Grin et al., 2010).

3.5.1
Abolitionism (18th/19th century): Type 'Vision'

The term abolitionism describes the social movement against slavery which spread around the world from the 18th to the early 20th century in several waves. Carried by ethical and religious motives, the incremental change to economic systems and societies resulting from abolitionism was a transformation triggered by a 'vision'. As the abolitionism movement actually achieved the global abolition of systematic slavery, it can also be characterised as a transformation of universal extent.

Abolitionism evolved over more than a century from its initial social organisation at the end of the 18th century into worldwide condemnation and abolition of slavery in the 20th century. Although from a regional perspective, abolitionist transformations certainly also occurred much faster. In England, for instance, the abolition movement achieved an end to the slave trade within twenty years; another two-and-a-half decades finally saw slavery illegalised, and the freeing of all slaves in the royal British dominions. On the American continent, abolitionism spread gradually at first from the north-east to the south, starting in 1776; subsequent to several waves, it was finally successful in 1888 with the abolition of slavery in Brazil.

The exemplary successes and the universal demand of Anglo-Saxon abolitionism led to its transcontinental diffusion from around the middle of the 19th century. By the first third of the 20th century, it finally achieved the global abolition of slavery systems, or at least de jure. Article 4 of the Universal Declaration of Human Rights, dated 10 December 1948, therefore states that: 'No one shall be held in slavery or servitude; slavery and the slave trade shall be prohibited in all their forms.' (UNGA, 1948). By way of example, the following elaboration focuses on the drivers, barriers and impacting factors of Anglo-Saxon abolitionism.

Geographical and Historical Categorisation

Organised abolitionist endeavours were initially made by only a few committed individuals in the United Kingdom, and by those of the United States of America fighting for independence from the British crown. They should be viewed in the historical context of the emancipatory spirit, and the closely related enthusiasm for the ideals of democracy and the rule of law, and against the background of 17th and 18th century colonial expansion policies, and thus the resultant public presence of the slave trade and slavery, almost universally taken for granted.

In England, the Society for Effecting the Abolition of Slave Trade, founded in London in 1787, was one of the organisations that had a major influence on the official abolition of the slave trade in 1807. Subsequent to the Slavery Abolition Act of 1833, all slaves in the British Empire were ultimately set free in 1834. The first abolitionist organisations were also established in the now independent North American colonies, where slavery played a vital economic role particularly on cotton and tobacco plantations; these radicalised especially post-1830, widening their sphere of influence. The North American abolitionists formally achieved their goals in 1865 when the 13th amendment came into force.

Between 1776 and 1804, all of the northern states of the Union had at least taken the first steps towards liberating the slaves. The de jure abolition of slavery followed between 1789 and 1830. As early as 1783, the Supreme Judicial Court of Massachusetts interpreted the Massachusetts Constitution's first Article on equality and freedom as an anti-slavery law, whereas the state of New York did not pass a general anti-slavery law until 1827 (Adams, 2009). The dwindling hope that slavery might equally just gradually 'die out' in the southern states of the USA meanwhile led to the polarisation and radicalisation of both pro- and anti-abolitionists (Raeithel, 1995).

In the 1830s, radical demands for the immediate manumission of all slaves increasingly found social resonance both in Great Britain and the northern states of the American (Finzsch et al., 1999; Drescher, 2009). Some members of the Society for the Mitigation and Gradual Abolition of Slavery Throughout the British Dominions, established in 1823, now lobbied for the universal abolition of slavery, emphasising this goal in 1839 with the establishment of the British and Foreign Anti-Slavery Society. One of the first genuinely transnational movements symbolically and tentatively culminated in the 1840 World Antislavery Convention in London, called by American abolitionists (Drescher, 2009).

Drivers and Innovations

The primary drivers of this public attitude shift towards the rejection of slavery were ethical considerations and their transnational diffusion, especially within the sphere of influence of the British Empire and the Commonwealth. At first, abolitionism purely organised by a civil society organisation operated as the practical realisation of Christian-humanitarian morals which 'very successfully utilised extensive extra-parliamentary campaigns as political means' (Wende, 2001). In contemporary England, the abolition of slavery issue was mainly viewed as a moral imperative, and its successful realisation as an exceptional effort on behalf of society, and was celebrated as such (Drescher, 2009).

The abolitionists' success also represented a partial change in the political structures of England, in which a small, but influential, elite of educated and propertied men repeatedly nudged far reaching reforms by means of targeted information campaigns and skilful organisation (Wende, 2008). During their earliest efforts, the English abolitionists were also given support of the highest judicial kind: in 1772, the Lord Chief Justice ruled that English law did not support the legal status of 'slave'. The thus established precedence case was a benchmark for Anglo-Saxon abolitionism for decades to come (Adams, 2009; Drescher, 2009).

In the USA, the social initiatives for the abolition of slavery progressed more or less synchronously in the northern states. American abolitionism was on par with the British movement not least because the protagonists on both sides of the Atlantic worked closely together. North American abolitionism was also initially advanced by an elite which reasoned on the basis of Christian ethics and emancipatory principles, paving the way for an organised abolitionism movement which gradually became more radical.

However, in what are now the southern states of the USA, which had a strong political-economic interest in upholding slavery, the abolitionists' ethics-based persuasive powers and socio-political methods that had proved so successful in England and the northern states found no resonance. At the close of the 18th century, around 90% of North American slaves lived in the southern states. Combined with new cotton processing methods and the expansion of large plantations, slave labour was the decisive economic factor here, and concern about economic loss overrode any ethical aspects (Raeithel, 1995; Adams, 2009).

Key Actors and Factors

Quakers, Methodists and Baptists played a pioneering role in the large-scale promotion of abolitionism. They opposed slavery on religious and ethical grounds, and had considerable political influence both in England at the close of the 18th century, and in the Puritan colonies of what would later become the USA. Their political aims were also flanked by an open commitment to a capitalist market economy that emphasised the value of paid labour by free men and competitive individuals in the labour market (Adams, 2009).

The Society for Effecting the Abolition of Slave Trade knew how to utilise its members' professional skills for the society's management, the mobilising of financial resources, and in the publishing business, in order to address and inform a wide range of the population's social groups and to successfully mobilise not just the philanthropical elite, but also the English working class (Drescher, 2009). Articles in popular newspapers and pamphlets, social networks, and in particular the presentation of petitions to parliament were the key instruments used to corner supporters of the status quo, forcing them to commit. American abolitionists followed their example closely, and organised specific mutual transatlantic support (Drescher, 2009).

In the course of abolitionist expansion efforts, the American movement grew noticeably more radical during the 1830s and 1840s. On the East Coast, in particular the New England Anti-Slavery Society (renamed the American Anti-Slavery Society in 1833) founded by the newspaper The Liberator's editor William Lloyd Garrison, evolved into an important actor. By 1836, the number of comparable, decidedly abolitionist societies had risen to more than 500 (Raeithel, 1995). Thanks to their passionate propaganda and charismatic public speakers, they managed to effectively advance an ethics-based issue without any form of parliamentary majority within the scope of the overall far more complex constitutional-legal conflict between northern and southern states (Raeithel, 1995; Finzsch et al., 1999).

At the same time, the violent reaction of the slaveholders, the romanticisation of abolitionist 'martyrs', and educational publications such as Garrison's 'The Liberator' and, above all, the 1852 popular novel 'Uncle Tom's Cabin' (Beecher Stowe, 2001) fed the shift in public opinion, which increasingly put pressure on the regime of those in favour of slavery (Raeithel, 1995; Finzsch et al., 1999; Adams, 2009). Finally, by the 1850s, its effect on the shaping of political will and processes, and also on the relatively recently established American party democracy could no longer be ignored: the fact that Abraham Lincoln was elected US president by Republicans was not least a consequence of the polarisation of slavery in the presidential election campaign, leading to a schism within the up to this point dominating Democratic Party (Adams, 2009).

Impact and Barriers

Until well into the 19th century, slavery was deeply rooted in the legal, institutional and economic structures of numerous societies, and in part also sanctioned by religion. In traditional slaveholding societies, social status and the generation of wealth depended almost entirely on the possession of slaves and slave labour. Abolitionist efforts were met with correspondingly fierce opposition.

The censoring of abolitionist publications, draconic law enforcement against abolitionist activities, and the violent repression of individual slave revolts also contributed to delegitimising the slaveholder's regime which ruled in the southern states of the USA. However as such, they initially did not manage to seriously destabilise the hegemony of the southern states' aristocrats. Moreover, the established power structures on the plantations and the resultant living conditions for the slaves also effectively precluded any systematic resistance 'from below' (Raeithel, 1995; Finzsch et al., 1999; Adams, 2009).

The social discourse which sought to opportunistically justify slavery against this political-economic background was fed by an amalgam of cultural-historical, religious, paternalistic and decidedly racist arguments and, particularly in the case of the USA, by the ultimate constitutional-legal issue of whether the federation actually had the judiciary power to prohibit slavery in its individual states (Adams, 2009). The abolition therefore became a decisive factor in the American War of Secession, ultimately violently enforcing the abolition of slavery by linking the issue of the right to possess slaves with the general constitutional conflict raging between 'Unionists' and 'Confederates': the ultimate prohibition of slavery in the territories legally recognising the US constitution was a federal political decision, only enforcable countrywide on the basis of a governmental monopoly on violence.

This example therefore also serves to illustrate the transformative potential of a 'vision' inspired by ethics and morals, and the limits of social change based on normative discourse in the face of material interests and structures. If the abolitionists failed to enforce the abolition of slavery on a federal level by peaceful means, they were nevertheless successful in a transformative sense, as they 'heightened the majority's conscience, thereby also possibly strengthening the readiness to make sacrifices in the war against the Confederate States' (Adams, 2009).

3.5.2
Green Revolution (1960s): Type 'Crisis'

According to the WBGU's transformation concept, the Green Revolution is an example for the transformation type 'crisis'. Subject of the transformation was the 'socio-technical system' of a traditional agriculture with low yields dominant in most of the developing countries in the 1950s, under pressure particularly in southern Asia in the wake of recurring famines. The Green Revolution was a transformation process of agricultural production systems, based on scientific findings and technological advances, actively promoted by western governments and well-funded private foundations since the early 1960s. Substantial research grants allowed the creation of experimental grounds for new agricultural production and productivity increase methods, and the successful breeding of new crop varieties in research institutes. Ultimately, these were able to establish themselves as a 'niche regime' by first practical trials in developing countries taking on a role model character. This transformation was distinguished by scientific actors and a high degree of political steering.

Typical for the new production methods of the Green Revolution were the complementary and precisely timed use of newly developed high yielding cereal grain varieties (HYV), improved irrigation methods, synthetic nitrogen fertilisers, and pesticides and herbicides (complementary input). This was accompanied by agricultural mechanisation (tractors, combine harvesters and threshing machines, irrigation with diesel engine powered pumps). The diffusion of these new production techniques was intensively supported by advisory services (Agricultural Extension Services), production material subsidies and the granting of loans, or the establishment of agricultural banks with numerous branches.

In many countries, the Green Revolution's 'recipe' for increasing agricultural yields became a core element of national rural development programmes (diffusion). Within just a few years, agriculture in these countries was extensively revolutionised (from niche regime to established regime). It must also be taken into account that the Green Revolution took place against the background of the Cold War (megatrends, Figure 3.4-1): from the western industrial states' perspective, it was also about counteracting the political hijacking of developing countries suffering from food shortages and hunger by the competing socialist 'Eastern Bloc'.

Geographical and Historical Categorisation

In Asia (initially in India, the Philippines) and Latin America (initially Mexico), the Green Revolution had resulted in a substantial increase of maize, wheat and rice yields (Cleaver, 1972; Ruttan, 1977; Chapman, 2002). Mexico, for instance, still had to import half of the wheat it needed in 1946. As a result of the Green Revolution, it was completely independent from imports only 13 years later.

As of the 1960s, India became the Green Revolution's prime example. In the past, the country suffered severely from recurring widespread famines, and again faced an imminent food crisis in 1961. The breakthrough started in 1961, when Norman Borlaug, then researching in Mexico, was invited to India in a consulting capacity. Over the next years, the Ford Foundation and the Indian government funded the development of a large-scale programme for increasing area yield for wheat and rice, particularly in the Punjab. In this respect, the programme was very successful: the Green Revolution significantly increased area yield for cereal grain crops. Today, India is one of the major rice exporting countries. However, since the 1980s, India's Green Revolution has increasingly also attracted criticism, because of the subsequent social and ecological consequences, such as salination of incorrectly irrigated soils, contamination due to inadvertent pesticide misuse, and reinforcement of social and geographical disparities (Oasa, 1987; Bohle, 1989; Shiva, 1989, 1991; Conway and Barbier, 1990; Evenson and Gollin, 2003).

Drivers and Innovations

In the 1950s and early 1960s, the governments of many developing countries started to realise that the increasing, population growth driven food demand would forseeably lead to devastating famines, or to extensive and expensive dependency on food imports. Drastic increases in agricultural production therefore appeared to be urgently needed. Chronic food shortages can thus be seen as the Green Revolution's starting point and driving force.

In practical terms, the Green Revolution was ultimately made possible by revolutionary achievements in the cultivation of new varieties of maize, wheat and rice. With the support of the Rockefeller Foundation, Mexico's International Maize and Wheat Improvement Center (CIMMYT), officially founded in 1963, although actually existent since the 1940s, became the world's leading institute for the development of high-yield varieties of maize and wheat (Wright, 1984). At the same time, the development of high-yielding rice varieties was pursued by the International Rice Research Institute (IRRI), founded in 1960 in the Philippines. The institute was established with funds provided by the Ford and Rockefeller foundations (Cleaver, 1972). Norman Borlaug, generally viewed as the father of the Green Revolution, was awarded the Nobel Peace Prize in 1970 in recognition of the groundbreaking importance of his achievements.

Key Actors and Factors

Key actors were the private US American foundations that funded the research efforts. However, in the Cold War context, this research funding was also a geopolitical strategy for the stabilisation of countries which, from a western perspective, could have become particularly 'susceptible' to establishing socialist regimes in the event of disastrous famines, or which might have had to depend on imports from the socialist warehouses (Dowie, 2001). In countries such as India, Mexico and the Philippines, the technological solution was also viewed as a welcome alternative to the agricultural reform debate so often associated with socialist concepts (Ross, 1998). The Green Revolution had therefore clear aspects of political power and vested interests, which certainly helped to significantly advance the transformation process.

The actively steered transformation process of the Green Revolution, primarily controlled by the governments of industrialised and developing countries, was made possible through several converging factors, in particular the involvement of powerful actors with authority to act and a common goal and strategy:

- Large-scale research funding through the establishment of international research centres (Mexico and the Philippines), and the thus accomplished breakthroughs in cultivation research (innovation at 'precisely the right point in time').
- Developing countries under urgent pressure to act due to chronic food shortages and the associated risks of recurring famines and political destabilisation.
- US power political interests in the Cold War context, which helped with research and advice, but also with extensive technology transfer (including expansion of industrial capacities for fertiliser and seed production, pest management, and agricultural machine

engineering), accompanied by substantial financial aid. Major transnational foundations and other governments also helped with additional funding.

- Imposition of large-scale transformation programmes in rural areas, in which complementary measures were implemented at various levels (international, national, regional, local): research, financing, infrastructure, provision of equipment and targeted knowledge diffusion through the setup of advisory networks (so-called Agricultural Extension Services).

Impact and Barriers

The Green Revolution model did not prove to be universally transferable in geographical terms, never gaining a foothold, for example, in Africa. The lack of institutional and infrastructural capacities is cited as reason for this. Moreover, breeding successes were limited to nutritional crops common in Asia and Latin America, and did not include African staples such as cassava or millet.

In addition, the Green Revolution has also tended to heighten already existing socio-economic disparities, rather than lessening them. Large agribusinesses tend to have benefited far more than small-scale producers, leading to intensified land-use competition in some instances, for example because irrigation with the aid of diesel powered pumps had lowered the groundwater level to such an extent that neighbouring farms without access to this technology subsequently suffered from water shortages.

In recent years, new efforts to increase agricultural productivity have been undertaken by the Bill & Melinda Gates Foundation (Gates Foundation, 2010). However, these are surrounded by controversy, particularly because of the heated debate regarding genetically modified plants.

3.5.3
Structural Adjustment Policies (1980s): Type 'Crisis'

In the mid-1980s, the World Bank and the International Monetary Fund (IMF) introduced 'Structural Adjustment Policies' (SAP) in response to the so-called Third World Debt Crisis in developing countries, initially in Latin America. In practical terms, the international financial institutions granted new loans to debt-ridden developing countries within the scope of SAPs, conditionally tied to specific macroeconomic reforms. The reform policies enforced in this manner where strictly guided by the free market principles of liberalisation, deregulation and privatisation, and included concrete economic and financial policy measures such as the privatisation of public companies, the rationalisation of public administration, the restriction of domestic cash flow and the liberalisation of foreign trade. Declared aim of the measures was to restabilise the economy as quickly as possible through a stronger integration of developing countries into the global market. As an attempt of a transformation triggered by a crisis and externally initiated, the SAP can be allocated to the type 'crisis'.

The transformation process is distinguished by the central role played by the two major international financial institutions, the World Bank and the IMF, as agents on behalf of the creditor nations. On the basis of their credit power, they intervened with detailed specifications in national economic and financial policy-making, thereby attempting a fundamental reorientation of the economies of the indebted developing countries. These were to be steered away from the failed model of protectionist domestic market oriented industrialisation policies towards a liberal economic market model of global integration. The impact of SAP, however, was not limited to the economy, the consequence of these enforced cost cutting measures also led to profound changes in social policy. In the short-term, this led to massive increases in unemployment in many developing countries during the 1980s, and social disparities becoming even more pronounced following the decline of the medium-income group (Nolte, 2000; Brock, 2003).

In a global political context, SAPs are an expression of the North-South conflict as well as a result of the conflicting eastern and western systems during the Cold War. On the one hand, they served to reaffirm the western industrialised countries' global economic dominance in North-South relations after the developing countries had been in a position to lend unprecedented emphasis to their demands for a new global economic order through the formation of the G77 and OPEC in the 1970s. On the other hand, SAPs were instrumental in expanding the western industrialised countries' sphere of influence, or rather, in consolidating it: the conditionality of the SAP loans also forced socialist-oriented Third World governments to adjust their economic policies to conform with the preferences of a liberal market economy.

Geographical and Historical Categorisation

At the end of the 1970s, the looming Third World Debt Crisis prompted the leading industrial nations to react with structural adjustment policies in the 1980s. Over the course of this decade alone, Third World foreign debt had sextupled (Brock, 2003). In geographical terms, the SAPs initially targeted the fifteen biggest

Third World debtor nations, primarily in Latin America, the most crisis-stricken region at the time, but also in sub-Saharan Africa (Siebold, 1995; Nolte, 2000). SAPs were also soon expanded to include other debtor nations among the developing countries; at the close of the 1980s, around forty developing countries had taken on IMF or World Bank loans under the Structural Adjustment Policy programme. During the course of this, the SAP regional focus shifted to Africa (Siebold, 1995).

The debt crisis was caused by the fact that many developing countries had pursued economic strategies that were protectionist and domestic market oriented, or import substituting industrialisation mainly financed by foreign loans. These were readily available on the international market at favourable conditions, thanks to the 1973 oil crisis and the oil exporting countries' subsequent liquidity surplus. When, in the early 1980s, international loans suddenly became expensive as a result of US high interest policies, many Third World countries found it increasingly difficult to keep up their repayments to both private and public creditors. The situation was exacerbated by a concurrent decline in raw material prices, which meant a drastic fall in foreign currency income for the raw material exporting developing countries.

Finally, in August 1982, the Mexican government was the first to inform the US Treasury of its inability to pay its debts. Argentina, Brazil, Venezuela and the Philippines soon followed suit (Brock, 2003). World Bank and IMF thus became the central actors in the debt management of the concerned nations. The World Bank had already created the instrument of loans under the Structural Adjustment Policy scheme in 1980, the IMF added a structural adjustment facility in 1986, and an extended one in 1987. Macroeconomic structural adjustment quickly became the development political paradigm of the 1980s: by 1994, a total of 74 developing countries had been granted structural adjustment loans, more than half of these were African countries (52%), and a good quarter went to Latin America and the Caribbean (26%; Siebold, 1995). Regional Development Banks and The European Community followed the Bretton Woods institutions' example with similar loan programmes.

Drivers and Innovations

The radically market-oriented theories by the Chicago School of Economics were the intellectual drivers behind the macroeconomic transformation processes in developing countries that the Structural Adjustment Policies had initiated. During the 1960s and 1970s, these theories became the predominant economics paradigm which later also marked Reaganism and Thatcherism. The incapacity of many developing countries as a result of the debt crisis finally offered the chance to put the theoretical teachings of the Chicago school into international practice.

With increasing saturation of domestic markets, the development model of protectionist industrialisation policies pursued by many African and Latin American countries had unavoidably led to an endogenous structural crisis (Messner, 1993). The external shocks which signified the slump in raw material prices and the sudden rise in interest rates on the international market in the early 1980s finally overtaxed the already debt-stricken developing countries. Their inability to pay meant that no further loans were granted, thus starting the downward spiral of unmanageable debts. Ultimately, the SAP aiming for radical market reforms were forced on the overtaxed governments from the outside as a crisis management panacea. In hindsight, and regardless of the evaluation of the concrete results, this attempt to cure the economic systems of a group of by no means homogenous countries with a generic model prescribed from the outside can certainly be viewed as a rather ambitious political experiment.

Key Actors and Factors

The central actors in the implementation of the structural adjustment policies of the 1980s and 1990s were – apart from the debtor nations themselves – the international financial institutions, the IMF and the World Bank. As agents acting for the international creditor community, they took on the role of 'preceptors for policy-makers' in the developing countries (Wolff, 2005).

As an initial response to the bankruptcy declarations by Mexico and other developing countries, the western creditor nations attempted to hold debt rescheduling negotiations with each individual debtor nation. However, as it became increasingly obvious that this was not just a case of individual developing countries battling temporary liquidity issues, but a (serious) structural crisis of their respective national economies, the World Bank and the IMF basically took over the crisis management. They were mandated by their leading member states to enforce radical reforms in the debt-stricken developing countries, i.e. liberal market-oriented economic policies by means of SAP assistance, de facto fulfilling the role of liquidator in the countries concerned (Herr, 2001).

Due to its hegemonic position in the Bretton Woods institutions, the US Treasury played a key role, supported by its European allies, as also reflected by the retrospective reference to the 'Washington Consensus'.

Impact and Barriers

Because of their one-sided application of macroeconomic criteria and their total disregard of the negative impact on poor and disadvantaged social groups, the Structural Adjustment Policies (SAP) attracted heavy criticism from their inception: whilst the fast successes in terms of economic recovery largely failed to materialise, the extremely serious social consequences were highly visible in many of the countries concerned. The mostly drastic public spending cuts resulted in rising unemployment and the collapse of public health care and education systems. Real wage cuts, implemented to fight inflation, particularly hit employees and workers, widening the income gap between rich and poor and often leading to social unrest.

Growing international criticism of the 'Washington Consensus', its negative social impact, and its failure to achieve the desired economic effects, as admitted by the World Bank, led to a SAP review in the context of the economic crises in Asia and Argentina in the 1990s. Under the motto 'adjustment with a human face', they are now supposed to show increased consideration of the needs of the socially disadvantaged (Siebold, 1995; Tetzlaff, 1996). With the emergence of a transnational anti-globalisation movement in the 1990s, and the Jubilee 2000 'Drop the Debt' campaign, the protest against structural adjustment policies increasingly also found resonance in the industrialised countries (public opinion; Busby, 2010). In 1999, the IMF's structural adjustment facility was finally converted into the Poverty Reduction and Growth Facility (PRGF), which explicitly links economic growth with the fight against poverty and offers the borrowing countries more involvement in developing the loan conditions (Thiele and Wiebelt, 2000; Wolff, 2005).

A sustainable transformation of the global economy in the strictly macroeconomic sense in accordance with the original SAPs obviously failed. However, their failure is not universal. Particularly the example of Latin America makes it clear that the consistent implementation of SAPs certainly helped to create more stable economic framework conditions in the long run, as well as substantially and enduringly lowering the rate of inflation. The positive effects on economic growth and poverty reduction which were hoped for from a development policy point of view, however, did by and large not materialise, despite the powerful economic leverage implemented by the World Bank and the IMF (Tetzlaff, 1996; Thiele and Wiebelt, 2000). This becomes even more apparent when applied to the example of the 'Asian Tigers' which, although generally guided by the benchmark of macroeconomic stability, acted very cautiously when it came to issues of liberalisation and deregulation, and withdrawal of the state from the capital allocation (Wolff, 2005).

The central message to be gleaned from the Structural Adjustment Policies of the 1980s is therefore that political-institutional framework conditions and soft factors such as acceptance, legitimacy and participation are of much more significance than the advocates of radical macroeconomics initially thought. Even the economies of the most dependent developing countries could not be steered mechanically from the outside, as reforms under existential pressure could only be implemented either incompletely or delayed.

3.5.4
Protection of the Ozone Layer (from 1985): Type 'Knowledge'

As a comprehensive reaction to a global environmental problem, the international regime for the protection of the ozone layer is the biggest success story in international environmental policy-making to date. With the effectively regulated production and use of certain ozone-harmful substances, the international ozone policy is therefore an example of a transformation brought about by a science-based suspicion. It concentrates primarily on specific industries and represents the transformation type 'knowledge'.

Geographical and Historical Categorisation

In 1974, the two American natural scientists Sherwood Rowland and Mario Molina warned against the damage chlorofluorocarbons (CFCs) were inflicting on the stratospheric ozone layer. The only one year earlier (1973) established United Nations Environment Programme (UNEP) responded by calling a meeting of scientists and government experts, who drew up a 'World Plan of Action on the Ozone Layer' in March 1977 for further research into the ozone problem.

The 'Coordinating Committee on the Ozone Layer', supported by the UNEP, made up of both governmental and non-governmental actors, continued to intensify the scientific exchange on the impacts of various chemical substances on the stratosphere. However, it was only the discovery of the so-called 'ozone hole' during the course of the British Antarctic Survey in 1985 that led to a widespread public discussion on the risks of increased UV insolation. This increased the pressure to act on the mainly responsible industrialised nations considerably. The speedy establishment of an international legal framework by the Vienna Convention for the Protection of the Ozone Layer in 1985, and the follow-up Montreal Protocol on substances leading to ozone layer depletion (1987), achieved the almost complete discontinuation of production and use of ozone depleting substances at a global level up to the present day (Andersen and Sarma, 2002; Parson, 2003). During the entire negotiation period, there was no sound scientific proof for a causal connection between the use of CFCs and the appearance of the ozone hole. Scientific research merely confirmed the plausibility of this correlation, and produced computer simulations showing the impacts of a damaged ozone layer. The global community acted – for the first time ever both globally and successfully – according to the precautionary principle; the causality was not scientifically proven until later (Benedick, 1999).

The Montreal Protocol, developed under the aegis of UNEP, was signed on 16 September 1987, and has been effective as of 1 January 1989. Initially, it was only ratified by 11 nations, these, however, represented two-thirds of the estimated global consumption of the substances concerned in 1986. Today, the Protocol is legally binding for 196 parties, including the European Union. Due to its extensive range and extreme effectiveness (an almost global ban on all ozone-damaging substances in the meantime), the multilateral regime for the protection of the ozone layer is generally viewed as the biggest success story in multilateral environmental policy-making.

Drivers and Innovations

The initiators and driving force behind the international policy for the protection of the ozone layer were scientists and knowledge communicators like UNEP. The institutional innovations with regard to the formulation of the regime are also remarkable, as they allowed its dynamic further development in response to new scientific findings, and in addition ensured widespread inclusion of the developing countries.

The Vienna Convention for the Protection of the Ozone Layer, in force since 1988, mainly contains institutional and organisational regulations for the negotiation of concrete political measures. In terms of content, the Convention restricts itself in rather general terms to the goal of appropriate protective measures and the overall commitment to global cooperation.

Only the subsequently negotiated Montreal Protocol, in force since 1989, concretised matters further. Besides concrete reduction targets for the production and use of ozone depleting substances, it stipulates trade restrictions in the form of an import ban for the controlled substances from non-party states, and an export ban to such states. Moreover, it was designed as a dynamic instrument from the moment of its inception, and was revised at subsequent meetings of the Parties to the Protocol in London (1990), Copenhagen (1992), Montreal (1997) and Beijing (1999) with amendments.

Through their continued expansion of the list of substances identified as 'ozone damaging', and the one-by-one regulation of their production and use, the Parties to the Protocol acted in a previously unprecedented manner in accordance with the precautionary principle. Not least, this was made possible for the first time in international contracting practice: if a consensus on amendments of this kind cannot be reached, a majority of two-thirds of the present and voting Parties to the Protocol is sufficient under the framework of the Montreal Protocol, provided this majority is equally divided to represent the majority of both developing and industrialised countries. Decisions made in this way are immediately and internationally legally binding for all Parties to the Protocol, regardless of their own vote, without the usually required ratification by individual countries.

In terms of inclusion of the developing countries, who justifiably blamed the industrialised nations for the depletion of the ozone layer in accordance with the 'polluter pays' principle, well-founded exemption regulations regarding the production and use of ozone depleting substances which are difficult to substitute, and the long-term financing of the requisite technology transfers have proved to be effective.

Key Actors and Factors

Three main actor groups were primarily responsible for the successful creation of a global ozone policy, the comparatively speedy establishment of problem solving capable institutions, and the strict implementation of political specifications: scientific experts, committed international bureaucrats, and the powerful industrialised countries which led the international negotiations. Scientific institutions, the World Meteorological Organisation and NASA all played a decisive role, not only because of their research efforts, but also because of their endeavours to raise awareness of the problem in the public sphere and among political decision-makers (Haas, 1992; Parson, 2003).

UNEP's international officials, above all its Executive Director Mostafa Tolba (1973–1992) and the first Montreal Protocol's Secretary General, Madhava Sarma (1987–2000), were also central to the prioritisation of the ozone issue in international environmental policy-making and the dynamic progression of international negotiations (Downie, 1995).

At first reluctant, the governments of the USA and Great Britain subsequently played a decisive role both in international negotiations and in national implementation by demonstrating strong leadership qualities, ultimately leading the other industrialised countries to follow suit and face their responsibilities in terms of ozone politics (Benedick, 1999; Grundmann, 1999). Another factor which not to be underestimated was also the availability of technical substitutes for CFCs and their manufacturers' respective economic interests (Andersen and Sarma, 2002; Parson, 2003).

Impact and Barriers

To what extent the measures for saving the stratospheric ozone layer agreed under the Vienna Convention and the Montreal Protocol are adequate will be revealed only at some point in the future, due to the complexity and inertia of atmospheric physics and chemistry. The level of efficiency in their implementation and the global transformation in handling certain chemicals associated with it, however, is nothing short of radical. But, as this specific transformation only concerns a small and highly specialised industrial branch, i.e. primarily aerosol and refrigeration equipment manufacturers, its significance is limited.

Political barriers preventing unimpeded implementation and further revision of the Montreal Protocol mainly arise from the controversy regarding exemption regulations on production and use of ozone depleting substances which are difficult to substitute, typically following the geographical lines of the established North-South conflicts, as well as new findings and the potentially conflicting goals of ozone layer protection associated with them, and the greenhouse gas balance of various chemical compounds.

3.5.5
IT Revolution and World Wide Web (1990s): Type 'Technology'

The internet is a global network consisting of many smaller, interconnected computer networks. It provides the infrastructure for various communication services such as hypertext, the world wide web, and electronic mail. All of these are capable of providing, managing and transmitting data at a so far unprecedented speed. The development of the internet is a fundamental information and telecommunications technology (IT) transformation, sometimes also referred to as the Digital Revolution. In its wake, the previously dominant communications regime, which was based on analogue technologies, has largely been replaced by digital technologies within just a few decades, and by the communication and action options these allow. The internet is viewed as a key technology, having changed so many different areas of everyday life (a general purpose technology) i.e. a technology that is used across a wide range of economic sectors, in this way contributing to economic growth by productivity increases (Chapter 3). This also helped to rapidly diffuse the basic technology beyond its niche status. The internet-driven IT Revolution therefore represents a transformation of the type 'technology'.

At the same time, the IT Revolution is an example of a transformation where the fundamental technological developments were based on public research. The technology's further diffusion and the associated incremental improvements were driven 'from below' by various different actors, above all from the scientific and private sector, policy-making thereby also made some contributions to this process.

An outstanding characteristic of the IT Revolution is that it spread particularly fast among the younger generation, possibly also the reason why it was able to develop such an extremely high acceleration and penetration potential.

Geographical and Historical Categorisation

Initially developed as a niche communications tool for military and scientific purposes, the internet is now used by almost a third of the global population. Since the mid-1990s, the number of internet users has increased rapidly. In 2009, there were more than 1.7 billion internet users in the world (Internet World Stats, 2010). As its diffusion increased, the internet also became an interesting option for commercial use, and the development of new information and communication technologies has impacted considerably on almost all areas of the global economy in the past years. The generally accepted view is that the global advance of the internet also drove globalisation.

However, as yet, not everyone is in a position to enjoy the benefits of the IT Revolution. Although by now, even poor developing countries are connected to the global network, access is frequently restricted to the urban elites. The majority of people in poor developing countries has not yet joined the world wide web (digital divide; Wittmann, 2006).

As the internet technology was originally developed in a military context, it may well be that the end of the Cold War paved the way for its fast diffusion among civilians. However, what does seem certain is that the accelerated pace of globalisation since the close of the 20th century is directly and closely linked with the availability of new information and communication technologies. On the one hand, economic globalisation processes required and accelerated the diffusion of long-distance communication technologies; on the other hand, globalisation itself gained added momentum through the establishment of these kinds of technologies.

Drivers and Innovations

The requisite key technologies for establishing the internet, in the form of local networks linking university and research institutions, were initially developed in a government niche, i.e. for use in military or scientific research projects. The internet emerged from the so-called ARPANET, a project developed in the 1960s by the US Department of Defense Advanced Research Project Agency (ARPA) (Abbate, 1999). The European Organization for Nuclear Research (CERN) played a major role in the development of a hypertext-based world wide web, making it possible for 'ordinary people' to access the net since the early 1990s.

The invention of the microprocessor and its steadily increasing capacities, the automation of operating processes, the establishment of computers as an everyday household item, and the building of local communication and computer networks all contributed to creating the technological and social preconditions for internet expansion and World Wide Web general use.

However, it gained real momentum and a true global dimension only as a result of the progressive commercial use, particularly among younger people at the start. Both the e-commerce sector and online trade have shown strong growth rates over the past few years, and internet service providers such as the online search engine market leader Google Inc. are now some of the most valuable global brands (Milward Brown Optimor, 2009). The numerous public and private investments in the requisite infrastructure, like glass fibre cables and servers, were not least necessitated by increased demand. Both private and commercial users saw added value in the new internet technology compared to established technologies.

The development and diffusion of broadband internet, allowing the transmission of huge volumes of data, has led to the increased provision of services other than the established digital communication technologies like e-mails, online discussion forums or chats, such as telephone services, online radio and video via the internet. In conjunction with various software innovations, this has facilitated the increasing use of interactive applications, which spread rapidly in the past decade; giving rise to the catchphrase 'Web 2.0'. The traditional media (TV, radio and printed media) are now facing considerable challenges, made even more pressing by the trend towards mobile devices.

Impact and Barriers

In all modern societies, technical information and communication technology innovations have radically changed many aspects of working and living environments over the past few decades. They prove indisputably that a profound, global socio-economic transformation is indeed possible in a relatively short time span. Although the so-called digital divide between the early industrialised OECD nations and numerous developing and newly industrialising countries still exists at a global level, the various information technologies (in particular mobile phone use) are still impressive examples for the leap-frogging of technological development stages (Mehra et al., 2004; Wittmann, 2006).

Apart from the economic importance of information technologies, particularly where the commercial diffusion of mobile devices is concerned, their potential significance as participation and mobilisation tools in political processes must not be underestimated (Perlmutter, 2008). Examples for this are the elections and subsequent protests in Iran in 2009, or the current democracy movements in the Arabic countries. The systematic use of 'Twitter' by Barack Obama during the 2008 US presidential election campaign was viewed as an important factor in terms of mobilising young voters; authoritarian regimes are having considerable difficulties in controlling the diffusion and use of new media. They are also alternative information, participation, organisation and lobbying tools for citizens (Yang, 2009).

Barriers impeding the diffusion of the internet are, on the one hand, development-related. Particularly in Africa, it is still not very widespread, although it must be said that there are still huge disparities in terms of access between rural regions and urban areas. A further barrier, on the other hand, is also the prevention of free communication for political reasons, as practised in China, for example.

3.5.6 European Integration (since the 1950s): Type 'Vision'

The European Union is the concrete manifestation of the success of European integration. The driving force behind it was and is mainly the vision of a more peaceful, economically and politically stable Europe. It represents a comprehensive transformation of the type 'vision'.

Political endeavours for a united Europe were the consequence of experiencing two catastrophic World Wars, the rise and fall of fascist regimes in several European states, the integration and 'taming' of Germany, and the emerging bipolar world order embodied by the rise of the two superpowers USA and Soviet Union. European integration, and particularly the gradual establishment and expansion of genuinely European institutions, has always been a process very much steered 'from the top', as established national state governments pursued a common cause and decided upon the foundation of the European Communities.

During its course, the vision of a peacefully united and prospering Europe led the transformation, even though, in the beginning, the concrete formation of supranational European institutions was by no means a given fact (Haas, 1958; Pollack, 2003). In the not even fifty years that have passed since then, a political, economic and legal project has gained ground on the European continent. It now extends to 27 nation states.

Geographical and Historical Categorisation

Initially, the governments of a handful of founding states – Belgium, Germany, France, Italy, Luxemburg, and the Netherlands – played the role of integration pioneers. Based on the 'Schuman Plan', they agreed the joint management of their coal and steel industries, and to refrain from using either for non-peaceful purposes against one another. Inspired by the success of the European Coal and Steel Community (ECSC), the six member states extended their collaboration to other sectors of the economy. With the 1957 Treaty of Rome, they founded the European Economic Community (EEC); its objective being the free movement of people, goods and services. In 1973, Denmark, Ireland and Great Britain were the first to join the Community, other nations gradually followed: Greece (1981), Portugal and Spain (1986), Finland, Austria, Sweden (1995), Estonia, Latvia, Lithuania, Malta, Poland, Slovakia, Slovenia, the Czech Republic, Hungary and Cyprus (2004), and Bulgaria and Rumania (2007).

The fact that the transformation process of European integration is by no means concluded shows in the EU's need to adapt, and also its ability to adapt in the face of new economic, political and social challenges, with regard to the gradual authority extension of its institutions, and its expansion to encompass new member states (Weiler, 1991; Beach, 2005; Chalmers et al., 2006).

Drivers and Innovations

The determined and purposeful actions of the political elite were considerably influenced by the lasting shock of two World Wars. Against the background of the East-West system conflict, the will to achieve European unity was also driven by the desire to politically and economically counterbalance the Soviet-dominated Eastern Bloc. Post-1990, Europe soon gained major importance in a globalised world, as exemplified by the formulation of a Common Foreign and Security Policy, the introduction of the euro as a common European currency, and not least by the geographical expansion of the community of states.

It had been the integration pioneers' intention to gradually advance the integration process agreed in the ECSC contract economically. The development of today's European Union was therefore based on an evolutionary model of an incremental integration without a comprehensive overall concept. The creation of a common market, the introduction of a common currency and, above all, the conferring of certain rights of sovereignty on the part of the member states onto supranational European institutions has led to the birth of globally unique organisation, unprecedented in international law. With the Treaty of Lisbon, the integration project also formally became the European Union on 1 December 2009.

Key Actors and Factors

Governments of member states have always been the major actors in the European integration process. The former French Foreign Minister Robert Schuman, and the Schuman Plan that bears his name, are exemplary. It provided the basis for the ECSC.

However, with increasing political integration, the European institutions themselves also evolved into integration-advancing factors (Beach, 2005). The European Court of Justice, for instance, on the grounds of its integration-friendly interpretation of Community Law, which enjoys application precedence above national laws as an independent legal system as well as containing contractually intended provisions for extended legal protection, has evolved into a groundbreaking actor in the course of ensuring the enforcement of Community Law in the member states (Alter, 2001). The European Commission has also turned into a 'pro-integration engine', as it frequently makes use of its right to initiate legislation in European legislative procedures.

Impact and Barriers

The growing significance of the European institutions proves that the delegation of national sovereignty is an effective major factor in the transformation. The European Union's member states have gradually ceded their traditional sovereign rights with regard to various areas to a superior, supranational institution, whose authority they submit to voluntarily (Pollack, 2006). In this context, it is also a distinguishing characteristic of this specific transformation that the contractual basis regulates not only the relationship between the EU and its member states, but also that of the EU and its individual citizens.

The failure of a number of projects to communitise certain areas of policy, the laboriousness of the European institutional architecture and its complex internal decision-making and voting procedures, and the continuously growing number of member states can be identified as barriers impeding European integration.

Some of these impediments managed to considerably slow down the transformation pace; however, they could not stop the transformation as such. The member states' growing economic interweaving and the (joint) interests linked to a functioning common market promote European integration. Initially, this became particularly apparent where social policies are concerned, as the domestic market also demanded equal social standards. Gradually, European integration also extended to policy areas which, both from a constitutional and international legal perspective, have always been the preserve of national governments and their actions. This applies especially to the inclusion of foreign and security policies in Community Law, and police and judicial cooperation in criminal cases.

3.6 Conclusions from the Analysis of Historical Transformations

Analysis of these historical medium-range transformations led to the identification of four different types of drivers, developed as types. Transformations of the type 'vision' focused primarily on a better, fairer, or more peaceful, future (value changes). Transformation processes of the type 'crisis' were by and large motivated by the experiencing of crises (hunger and development crises). In the case of the type 'knowledge', the transformation process was advanced above all by knowledge-based considerations (precautionary principle) and research findings. Central element in transformation processes of the 'technology' type is the mass diffusion of a structure-changing technical innovation. With respect to the approaching Great Low-Carbon Transformation towards a low-carbon society, the following six conclusions may be drawn from this historical analysis:

1. The historical transformation processes examined here can be described as collective acts of anticipatory change agents. They were transformations whose outcome could not actually be determined by the actions of individuals or small groups, although these frequently 'get the ball rolling'. The change agents' capabilities in terms of successfully communicating with politicians or the broad public play a decisive role here. The activities of these pioneering change agents are at different times superseded by, or accompanied by, the intensification of economic, cultural, social, and also ecological processes, thereby gaining transformative momentum. An example for this is the creation of the European Union, initially founded in the 1950s by six countries as European Communities to secure peace by promoting intentional economic interdependencies (coal and steel), and to accelerate economic growth by extending the domestic market. With the Maastricht Treaty, the European Community member states founded the European Union in 1992. The EU was given responsibilities that went beyond economic issues. Gradually, the number of member states grew to the current 27 (2011). Most recently, the EU's supranational authority has been extended with the Treaty of Lisbon. Within the EU, the European Economic and Monetary Union currently consists of 17 states. They have introduced a common currency, the euro, thereby transferring their authority with regard to monetary policy to the European Central Bank.
2. It can be said for most of the transformations analysed here that they would not have been possible without the acceptance and support of social actors. That is one of the major reasons, for example, why the Structural Adjustment Programmes were not particularly successful in Latin America, where they were perceived as having been 'imposed' by external forces. With regard to the low-carbon transformation, this means that it is vital that all states and all its citizens join in the cause.
3. The state plays a decisive role in shaping the process. In the case of ozone layer protection, which was organised in a top-down process scientific warnings provided the decisive impulse. It was a knowledge-based transformation, guided by the precautionary principle. The low-carbon transformation belongs to the same category: it is also about 'learning from the future', and acting in accordance with the precautionary principle. After all, based on scientific knowledge and models of future climate change impact, a 'future laboratory' is available to facilitate informed social decisions. Above all, though, the low-carbon transformation – and that is the crucial difference – requires measures of unprecedented dimensions and profundity. Their implementation requires a pro-active state, as the regulatory policies shaping an entire economic system and incentive schemes for investments and innovations must be completely remodelled to change focus from a fossil-fuel based to a climate-friendly economy. Past crises are also a motivator for government actions (EU integration, structural adjustment and Green Revolution). The structural adjustment example shows how difficult it is to nudge a transformation process 'from the outside', despite a crisis and massive financial support, and the Bretton Woods organisations' threat-potential. In relation to

the low-carbon transformation, this background of past experiences is important, as many developing and newly industrialising countries view the international climate protection negotiations and the discourse on low-carbon modernisation primarily as an 'imposed' mechanism which undermines their 'right to development'. The global low-carbon transformation will therefore not be achievable without confidence-building international cooperation. Transformations are usually open-ended processes, the results of a collective steering are never certain, and not clearly foreseeable, despite a defined goal. Transformations are not directly manageable; rather it is a case of allowing the transformation process to develop into a certain direction by creating the respective framework conditions. Exactly how a transformative world will look like at the end of this 'possibility path of many possibilities' cannot be predetermined. Today, the focus must above all be on providing the impetus for a change of course towards the right direction.

4. The speed of transformation processes can vary greatly. Whilst the EU integration process, for instance, by now spans over sixty years, over the course of which it has gradually been institutionally anchored, the world wide web established itself at an almost frenzied speed, by comparison. Independent of this it usually takes a decade for the requisite basic structures of a transformation to become strong enough to create long-term dynamics. However, the establishment of the requisite basic structures relies on strategic political action. It can also be manifestly assumed that the level of intervention with existing established structures is a decisive factor in terms of pace. Whilst in the case of the EU, existing structures tend to be developed further gradually; the IT Revolution evolved independent of existing institutional structures without much resistance. With regard to the low-carbon transformation, it can be concluded that the change of firmly established energy generation and usage structures require a level of interference that will take a very long time.
5. The historical medium-range transformation processes introduced here can only be understood fully if their respective contemporary historical embedment (megatrends, Figure 3.4-1) and the corresponding dynamics are also taken into account (for example Cold War, globalisation, post-war period). The historian Osterhammel describes transformative processes as 'a concurrence of multiple changes', which can progress either ongoing or intermittently; they can occur either additively or cumulatively, either reversibly or irreversibly, either at a steady, or at an unsteady pace (Osterhammel, 2009). These kinds of dynamics are manifestly apparent in the six cases analysed here. For example, the IT Revolution, the abolition of slavery and European integration were continuous, cumulative processes which, from today's point of view, can be considered as irreversible. Typical for most of the processes analysed here is also that they were influenced by a number of actor groups (with by all means different intentions), and occurred simultaneously at several action levels (local, regional, global). One example for this is the Green Revolution, which has been actively promoted by western governments and well-funded private foundations since the early 1960s. Individual countries implemented nationwide programmes to propagate the Green Revolution, supported by international aid donors. The diffusion of these new production techniques was intensively and strategically supported at all levels by advisory services, production material subsidies and the granting of loans, or the establishment of agricultural banks with numerous branches. Change agents took on a key function at all levels.
6. The dynamics required for the low-carbon transformation can only be generated by a combination of measures at various different levels, as the analysis of these historical examples shows. This transformation process
   - must be a process based on knowledge and a common vision, guided by the precautionary principle (Chapters 1, 2, 8);
   - must rely heavily on change agents who help to inspire the requisite social acceptance, and whose concentrated joint activities generate transformative dynamics (Chapter 2, 6);
   - must be accelerated by a pro-active state which creates and actively promotes the appropriate room to manoeuvre, and overcomes the high-carbon economy's framework conditions to develop a climate-friendly system (Chapter. 5),
   - also relies on the cooperation of the international community, and the establishment of supporting global governance structures as an indispensable driving force for gaining the envisaged transformation momentum (Chapter 5, 7).

Technical and Economic Feasibility 4

Only around half of humankind has benefited from the industrialisation that has allowed for great scientific, technical and economic advances during the past 200 years. A precondition for these advances was the unlocking of new energy sources and their diverging use, and substituting animal and human muscle power with mechanical energy (Landes, 1969). Over the past two centuries, fossil fuels have mainly been used for this, as well as for heating and lighting. This has led to more than 1,300 Gt CO_2 being released into the atmosphere, and ecosystem boundaries being reached (Rockström et al., 2009a).

Apart from the energy sector, which is responsible for around two-thirds of current long-lived greenhouse gas emissions, land use is responsible for around a quarter of global greenhouse gas emissions through CO_2 emissions from the ongoing deforestation as well as emissions of methane (CH_4) and the far more persistent nitrous oxide (N_2O) contributed by agriculture. The land-use related emissions are widespread in terms of space, are subject to enormous fluctuations, and are closely linked to natural material cycles (for example soil biology). Improved land-use practices, for instance stopping deforestation, reducing the over-fertilisation of cropland, or better irrigation management would make it possible to significantly reduce these emissions. The respective sectors' institutional complexity, the large number of actors and a still rising global demand for agricultural products, however, add to the difficulties (Section 4.3.4.1).

Fundamental changes in the technological development paths of all countries are necessary in order to provide the chance of achieving elemental development goals like access to food, clean water, basic health care, or poverty reduction, to the 50% of the population so far denied this chance, whilst remaining within the planetary boundaries. The WBGU is convinced that with sufficient political willingness and determination, these objectives are compatible. Central elements of the transformation into a sustainable and climate-friendly society are the comprehensive decarbonisation of the energy system, as well as significant energy efficiency improvements, particularly in end-use efficiency.

The fundamental transformation of contemporary energy and land-use systems will by no means occur unaided. In the WBGU's opinion, however, the determined realisation of a climate compatible development path is possible. This is accompanied by considerable co-benefits which, even taken on their own, justify the efforts required for the outlined transformation. These include, amongst others, facilitating economic development through universal access to safe and modern energy, improving long-term supply security, and a de-escalation of international conflicts with regard to energy resources, positive effects on employment in structurally weak regions, and the reduction of many of the current systems' negative effects on the environment (Section 4.1). Building the transformation-relevant technology and infrastructure requires substantial investments, and the development of new financing concepts and business models for energy services. In the long run, however, these initial investments will be more than compensated by, amongst other things, reduced fuel and security costs, less damage to the environment, and avoidance of costs associated with adapting to climate change, and with the consequences of climate change (Section 4.5).

4.1 Resources, Energy Potentials and Emissions

The WBGU shall commence its analysis of the feasibility of the transformation with an overview of the elements that are of key importance for a transformed, climate-compatible energy, economic and land-use system. Apart from potentials and resources of different energy sources, technological and other options for emissions reductions are analysed, as well as possibilities for creating carbon sinks.

Box 4.1-1

Reserves, Resources, Potentials

Examinations of fossil fuels usually differentiate between reserves and resources. *Reserves* are known deposits that have been determined exactly and, from a technical and economic perspective, can be extracted at any given time. *Resources* also include, in addition to reserves, known deposits or deposits that are believed to exist but which are not yet extractable with current technologies and in current economic conditions. However, they are considered as extractable at some point in the future. Above and beyond this, a distinction is often made between conventional and unconventional reserves: the latter refers to known deposits whose extraction is extremely elaborate, in terms of technology, so that extraction could only become economically viable at some point in the future. Reserves, resources, and other estimated or assumed deposits respectively describe a total volume of stored energy, i.e. they are only sensibly definable for non-renewable energy carriers.

In the case of renewable energies, it is not their overall volume but the potential availability over a certain period of time, their *potential,* that is limited. The *theoretical potential* refers to the physical maximum of energy available from a particular source – i.e. in the case of solar energy, the total solar irradiation on a particular area. Only some of this energy flow can be utilised, from a technical point of view. This is taken into account when considering the *technical potential,* which also includes any boundaries regarding the realistically available areas for energy recovery. The criteria applying to area selection have not been uniformly defined in the respective literature; sometimes further technical, structural and ecological restrictions, as well as legal requirements, are included. The level of the technical potential of the various energy sources is therefore not a clearly defined value, but depends on a number of boundary conditions and assumptions.

The *economic potential* refers to the economically utilisable proportion of the technical potential under the economic framework conditions (at a certain point in time).

Particularly relevant for the WBGU is the *sustainability potential*. This covers all aspects of sustainability. To determine this, various ecological and socio-economic factors must be balanced off against each other, and evaluated. It is difficult to pinpoint the sustainability potential exactly, as individual aspects are evaluated differently, depending on the author.

4.1.1 Energy Carriers

The transformation into a sustainable and climate-friendly society requires a far reaching restructuring of the global energy system. The following summary of the available energy sources and carriers shows that a complete decarbonisation of the energy system is certainly possible. It cannot be expected, however, that such a transformation could be purely driven by resource scarcity. On the contrary, the as yet still available generous volumes of fossil fuels could prove to be an obstacle for the transformation, as, in the absence of a globally applicable price for carbon, they frequently appear nominally cheaper, and deposits are geographically widespread. The long useful lives of existing infrastructures (for example coal-fired power plants, transport infrastructures, buildings), behavioural norms, and established socio-economic interest groups lead to inertia towards rapid changes. Apart from resources and technical and sustainable potentials (Box 4.1-1), the following sections also discuss other transformation-relevant properties of the various energy carriers. The method used to determine primary energy demand is elaborated in Box 4.1-2.

4.1.2 Fossil Energy Carriers

4.1.2.1 Emissions and Properties

Coal is the most greenhouse gas emission intensive of all fossil energy carriers. A hard coal power plant emits around 750–1,100 g CO_2eq per kWh_e (kWh_e = kWh of generated electricity), 850–1,200 g CO_2 per kWh_e is cited for brown coal (Wagner et al., 2007). In relation to energy content (lower heating value), the CO_2 emissions are 94.6 g CO_2 per MJ for hard coal and 101 g CO_2 per MJ for brown coal (IPCC, 2006).

Coal deposits are geographically widespread and, in the absence of a carbon price, frequently the cheapest energy carrier. Potential rises in oil and gas prices increase coal's relative price advantage. Coal is therefore preferred by many national states for reasons of strategic supply security, and frequently enjoys subsidies. Germany and, also, the USA currently generate approx. 48 % of their electric power from coal. In India, the share is 68%, and in China even 81%. The potential greenhouse gas emissions alone from all coal resources and reserves are approx. 58 times the 750 Gt maximum amount of CO_2 emissions from fossil sources that should not be exceeded to protect the climate (Box 1.1-1).

Mineral oil has, with regard to the stored energy, a lower carbon content than coal, its use therefore also causes lower specific CO_2 emissions (around 657–866 g CO_2 per kWh_e for a heavy oil based electricity supply;

Box 4.1-2

Definitions: Primary Energy Equivalents in Energy Statistics

Primary energy refers to the naturally occurring energy form, before the loss-incurring conversion into usable energy such as electricity. In the case of fossil fuels and biomass (together currently more than 90% of the global energy supply), the primary energy content can be directly measured calorimetrically through their combustion. The technical literature usually uses calorific value (lower heating value). For many renewable energy carriers (such as wind and photovoltaic energy, where electricity is generated directly), and for nuclear energy or geothermal power, there is no clear definition as to which stage of the conversion, and which energy form, should be regarded as primary energy. Different institutions use different calculation methods, limiting the direct comparability of statistics (Macknick, 2009). Three alternative methods of calculation are usually applied: the *physical energy content method*, the *substitution method*, and the *direct energy equivalency method*.

1. The *physical energy content method* is used by the OECD, the International Energy Agency (IEA), and Eurostat, for example. It is based on the argument that primary energy should refer to the first energy form for which there are different possibilities of technical application. For one kilowatt hour of electricity generated by a coal-powered power plant, for instance, more than double the amount of primary energy in the form of coal is counted, as the heat released through combustion might also be used differently (for example in heating systems). In the case of electricity generation through hydropower, wind, oceanic or tidal energy, and photovoltaic energy, on the other hand, the energy content of the electricity generated is counted as primary energy equivalent. In the case of nuclear energy, and geothermal or solar thermal electricity generation, the heat is counted as the primary energy form.
2. The *substitution method* is used in various different forms by the US Energy Information Administration (EIA), and BP. It is based on the convention of showing for all forms of secondary energy (for example electricity, or heat) the volume of fossil fuels that would be required alternatively to generate the same amount of secondary energy in conventional power plants. The hypothetical efficiency factors applied can either be fixed (i.e. a uniform 38%, for example), or they can reflect national variations of technologies (and the differences in the installed fossil power plant equipment), or also, in the case of projections, they can vary with time (for example, assume convergence in technical standards, or learning progress).
3. The *direct energy equivalency method* is used by the UN Statistical Commission (UN, 2008a), in numerous IPCC reports, the Global Energy Assessment (GEA, 2011), and also frequently in research literature for long-term energy scenarios. It relies on the convention that all electricity which has not been generated through combustion processes is represented directly as primary energy. It is therefore a standardised variant of the *physical energy content* method. This choice of representation is particularly useful in scenarios which describe a fundamental conversion of the energy system, where non-fossil energy sources gain great significance (Nakicenovic et al., 2000). One of the main advantages is that all energy sources which do not rely on combustion processes are represented in a comparable way. In the *physical energy content* method, for example, one unit of electricity generated by geothermal energy or concentrated solar heat is shown up to five times higher than photovoltaic energy (depending on thermal efficiency); in the direct energy equivalency method, in contrast, it is shown with the same value: in these cases, primary and secondary energy have the same value.

Table 4.1-1 illustrates an example of the differences that result for various energy carriers through the application of the three different methods described above. In scenarios which accord particular significance to renewable energies, the volume of primary energy shown increases most over time when the substitution method is used, and least when the direct energy equivalent method is applied.

Unless marked otherwise, this report used the *direct energy equivalency method,* and figures showing primary energy were adjusted accordingly.

Table 4.1-1

Global primary energy consumption 2008 according to three different calculation methods. For each method, the absolute primary energy contributions of the individual energy carriers are shown, plus their share of the global primary energy supply in percent.
Source: WBGU, based on the data contained in IEA, 2010a

	Physical Energy Content Method		**Substitution Method**		**Direct Energy Equivalency Method**	
	Primary energy demand absolute value [EJ]	Proportion of global demand [%]	Primary energy demand absolute value [EJ]	Proportion of global demand [%]	Primary energy demand absolute value [EJ]	Proportion of global demand [%]
Fossil Energy	418	81	418	79	418	85
Nuclear Power	30	6	26	5	10	2
Renewables	66	13	84	16	64	13
Total	514	100	528	100	492	100

WEC, 2004). In relation to energy content (lower heating value), the CO_2 emissions are 73.3 g CO_2 per MJ for crude oil (IPCC, 2006). Oil is the most important energy carrier for the transport sector. Its substitution through emissions-free alternatives is one of the most difficult elements of a comprehensive transformation.

Methane (natural gas) causes, in relation to energy content, the least CO_2 emissions of the fossil energy carriers. A gas powered combined cycle power plant emits approx. 425 g CO_2eq per kWh of generated electricity (WBGU, 2010a), the bandwidth is around 400-550 g CO_2 per kWh_e (Wagner et al., 2007). In relation to energy content (lower heating value), CO_2 emissions are running at 56.1 g CO_2 per MJ for natural gas (IPCC, 2006). Gas power plants are more energy-efficient than coal power plants, and require lower investments. They can also be controlled quickly, and are therefore compatible with high shares of fluctuating renewable energy sources like wind and solar power. They cause relatively little air pollution, and can therefore also be used in densely populated areas, making a combined heat and power (CHP) use possible. Methane is also eminently suitable for powering small decentralised CHP plants in the form of communal combined heat and power plants.

In the long-term evolution of the global energy system, methane must be seen as a step towards energy system decarbonisation (Nakicenovic, 1996; Grübler and Nakicenovic, 1996; Jepma and Nakicenovic, 2006). Methane storage and distribution systems can potentially be adjusted to include mixed gases with higher shares of hydrogen (a greenhouse gas emission free energy carrier). There is also the option of powering conventional combustion engines with methane, for example, thereby facilitating the technological conversion to low-carbon transport systems that are mineral oil independent.

4.1.2.2 Potentials

Table 4.1-2 shows estimated deposits and current use of fossil energy carriers. Reducing global fossil fuel consumption for reasons of resource scarcity alone is not mandatory, even though there may be substantial price fluctuations and regional or structural shortages as we have seen in the past.

The presently known coal resources and reserves alone probably amount to around 3,000 times the amount currently mined in a year. In terms of resource potential, a current-level demand could therefore be met for many hundreds of years to come. Coal is also relatively evenly spread across the globe; each continent holds considerable deposits. The supply horizon (reserve to production ratio), at 40–50 years, is clearly much lower for conventional mineral oil and gas reserves; the resource potentials, however, when including some resources or deposits which are currently still classified as 'unconventional', again exceed the current consumption rate by far more than one hundred years. However, serious ecological damage is frequently associated with fossil energy mining, particularly of unconventional deposits in oil sands and oil shale.

Over the past few years, new processes have been commercially developed in the natural gas extraction sector, facilitating the affordable unlocking of gas deposits previously considered 'unconventional'. These processes allow the extraction of gas from smaller and more compact deposits with a low pore volume, and from flat coal seams; both are far more frequently found and evenly distributed on a global level than traditional gas fields. Tight gas and shale gas extraction, however, can potentially be accompanied by seismic activities and the pollution of groundwater basins and inshore waters, for example through drilling muds, rinsing agents or the application of hydraulic methods to increase the permeability of the reservoir rocks (hydraulic fracturing). Just like boring into as yet hardly explored depths, it therefore needs special regulations. As a global distribution network for liquid gas already exists, in the form of tankers and loading terminals, it is to be expected that an effective gas market will develop, marked by competitiveness with regard to price fixing, and that oil and gas prices will cease to be linked. The rising share of liquid gas (currently around 10% of overall gas consumption) significantly increases supply security, reducing the danger of supply interruptions that international pipeline networks are subject to, for example.

Gas hydrates, dense, snowy methane aggregates that are solid under high pressure and low temperatures, are another form of gas deposits, found both in the deep sea and subterraneously in permafrost. The possibility of continued greenhouse gas emissions from methane hydrates as a consequence of arctic permafrost soil thaw, or a thawing of the relatively flat Siberian continental shelf, is being discussed as a possible nonlinear disruptive earth system process. The potential extraction of this energy carrier is also being examined. Many states, including the USA, Japan, India, China and South Korea, have launched relevant research programmes. Estimates regarding global deposits vary greatly; however, all are in the zettajoule range, for example 70,000–700,000 EJ (Krey et al., 2009). The Global Energy Assessment report estimates the theoretical potential to be 2,650–2,450,000 EJ (GEA, 2011), i.e. possibly more than a thousand times the current annual total energy consumption.

Table 4.1-2
Global occurrences of fossil and nuclear sources. There are high uncertainties associated with the assessment of reserves and resources.
Source: the representative figures shown here are WBGU estimates on the basis of the GEA, 2011

	Historical production up to 2008	Production in 2008	Reserves	Resources	Further deposits
	[EJ]	[EJ]	[EJ]	[EJ]	[EJ]
Conventional oil	6,500	170	6,350	5,000	
Unconventional oil	500	23	3,800	34,000	47,000
Conventional gas	3,400	118	6,000	8,014	490,000
Unconventional gas	160	12	42,500	56,500	
Coal	7,100	150	21,000	440,000	
Total fossil sources	17,660	473	79,650	503,507	537,000
Conventional uranium	1,300	26	2,400	7,400	
Unconventional uranium				4,100	2,600,000

Approximately a tenth (1,200–245,600 EJ) is rated as potentially extractable, from a technological point of view. In its special report 'The Future Oceans', the WBGU advised against applied research for methane hydrate extraction, as mining bears considerable risks and methane hydrates do not represent a sustainable energy source (WBGU, 2006).

4.1.2.3
Risks and Framework Conditions for Use

Fossil energy carriers cause a wide range of different ecological damages over their entire lifecycle, from resource extraction to disposal. They frequently represent a health hazard to the population, damage natural ecosystems, land used for agriculture and forestry, impact negatively on yields, and are also harmful to buildings, cultural goods and technical infrastructures. The volume of material transported as a consequence of the fossil energy system is gigantic: annual recovery of fossil energy carriers already amounted to 970 million t at the beginning of the 20th century. By 2005, this volume increased to around 11.8 billion t annually (Krausmann et al., 2009); it should be considered that these figures only relate to the direct extraction of resources, and exclude mining dumps, mobilised cap rock or lixiviated oil sands.

Between them, supertankers and coal freighters make up more than half of the total sea freight volume (UNCTAD, 2009). Related accidents leading to oil spillage cause considerable ecological damage, as can chronic leakages during oil extraction, transport in pipelines and processing.

As extraction initially focused on the largest and most accessible fossil resource depots, it has become increasingly necessary to explore energy resources in ever greater depths, offshore, or in remote, partially ice-covered regions. Increasingly, smaller deposits are also being mined. Both the initial resources required, and the energetic return on investment, have significantly decreased over the course of the 20th century (Cleveland et al., 1984).

However, without a doubt, the biggest risk associated with the use of fuels is their climate impacting emissions. Table 4.1-3 shows the CO_2 emissions which would be generated by an exhaustive use of the fossil energy resources, reserves and further occurences illustrated in Table 4.1-2. This is compared with the budget of CO_2 emissions which should not be exceeded in order to avoid a rise in mean temperature of more than 2 °C compared to pre-industrial levels (Box 1.1-1).

Carbon dioxide capture and storage creates possibilities for the use of fossil energy carriers with significantly lower emissions (Section 4.1.3).

4.1.3
Carbon Dioxide Capture and Storage

As a technical option, to gain time for the conversion to emissions-free energy sources whilst utilising at least some of the large fossil energy carrier reserves, technical solutions for separating CO_2 from the emissions of stationary plants are under discussion, as well as options for the subsequent storage of compressed CO_2 in geological formations (Carbon Dioxide Capture and Storage, CCS). CCS is a necessary mitigation measure for countries that continue to use fossil energies, if anthropogenic global warming of more than 2 °C is to be avoided. Beyond this, a combination of bioenergy with CCS is also under discussion as an option for

Table 4.1-3
Potential emissions as a consequence of the use of fossil reserves and resources. Also illustrated is their potential for endangering the 2 °C guard rail. This risk is expressed as the factor by which, assuming complete exhaustion of the respective reserves and resources, the resultant CO_2 emissions would exceed the 750 Gt CO_2 budget permissible from fossil sources until 2050 (Box 1.1-1). The figures refer to CO_2 alone, other greenhouse gases have not been taken into account. They are based on the values in Table 4.1-2.
Source: based on Table 4.1-1 and GEA, 2011

	Historical production up to 2008	Production in 2008	Reserves	Resources	Further occurences	Total: reserves, resources and further occurences	Factor by which these emissions alone exceed the 2 °C emissions budget
	[Gt CO_2]	[Gt CO_2]	[Gt CO_2]	[Gt CO_2]	[Gt CO_2]	[Gt CO_2]	
Conventional oil	505	13	494	386	–	880	1
Unconventional oil	39	2	295	2,637	3,646	6,577	9
Conventional gas	194	7	343	459	27,977	28,778	38
Unconventional gas	15	1	3,987	5,300	–	9,287	12
Coal	666	14	1,970	41,277	–	43,247	58
Total fossil fuels	1,419	37	7,088	50,060	31,622	88,770	118

withdrawing CO_2 from the atmosphere in the long run (Box 4.1-3).

Technologies available today are capable of capturing around 85–95% of the CO_2 generated by a power plant. Taking into account that the energy required to generate a certain amount of electric power increases by around 10–40% through the use of CCS technology, CCS can achieve a net reduction of CO_2 emissions from power plants of approx. 80–90% (IPCC, 2005).

There are already various ongoing projects for compressed CO_2 storage in geological reservoirs such as partially exhausted oil or gas fields, saline aquifers or unused coal seams. In 2007, four such enterprises were active; the longest-running project, Sleipner (carried out by the Norwegian oil company Statoil), has stored approx. 1 million t of CO_2 per year in geological formations below the seabed since 1997. Other projects are Snøhvit (Norway), Weyburn (Canada) and Sala (Algeria). The amounts of CO_2 stored each year by these projects, however, are far lower than the amounts that would be generated by a coal power plant with CCS every year. Even though all of the components have been tried and tested, CCS technology as an overall system is far from fully developed, and carries many risks. The IEA recommended the initiation of at least 20 large-scale CCS demonstration projects in 2010 to facilitate the use of CCS technology by 2020 (IEA, 2008c).

CCS technology increases the investments and operating expenditure required by fossil powered plants, and decreases their efficiency (Herzog, 2010). Capture costs are currently estimated to run at US$ 40–45 per t CO_2 in coal powered, and US$ 50–90 per t CO_2 in gas powered plants (IEA, 2008c). This excludes transport and storage costs, which vary depending on locality, estimated to be in the range of US$ 5–15 per t CO_2 by Herzog et al. (2010). Further excluded are the potential costs for liability. As a consequence, in a modern coal powered plant, the cost of electricity would increase by US$ ct 4 per kWh (Herzog, 2010). The IPCC special report on CCS states increased electricity costs of US$ ct 1–5 per kWh, based on the technology available in 2002 (IPCC, 2005). CCS is also under discussion as an option for process-related CO_2 emissions from the industrial sector. There is a range of technologies available for direct CO_2 capture from production processes. A common factor is that all of these technologies cause additional energetic and economic costs and are only viable if greenhouse gas emissions carry a price tag, or are taxed, as is the case already in Norway, for example. Apart from the four projects named above, plants like these have so far been installed only as pilot projects, with the corresponding scale, including in Germany.

Plants which produce different products simultaneously by means of process integration, for example liq-

Box 4.1-3

Sequestration of Biologically Fixed Carbon: 'Negative Emissions'

Through photosynthesis, plants absorb CO_2 from the air, and store the contained carbon in form of biomass. Long-term storage of this carbon can therefore create a CO_2 sink. A technical option for this would be the use of bioenergy together with capture and storage of the CO_2 produced (CCS). In its 'Future Bioenergy and Sustainable Land Use' report (2009a), the WBGU estimates that the sustainable bioenergy potential would allow the capture and sequestration of 1.8–3.5 Gt CO_2 per year from biomass. In 2009, the use of fossil fuels and the cement industry alone led to emissions totalling 31 Gt CO_2, with deforestation in the tropics causing a further 4 Gt CO_2 emissions (GCP, 2011). If this were used as the benchmark, then it would take 10–20 years to compensate the emissions of a single year with the sequestration of CO_2 from biomass. The WBGU believes that it is extremely difficult to achieve substantial negative emissions.

Another option could be the sequestration of biogenic coal. If this charcoal (biochar) were to be introduced into the soil, *firstly,* the carbon contained would be stored, and *secondly,* a further climate change mitigation effect could be achieved through enhanced plant growth due to improved soil properties. The carbon retention period in the soil, however, is not clear, and it therefore may not be justified to speak of negative emissions here. Research on this subject is still in its infancy, meaning that there are no potential estimates available either. Fundamentally, however, this option, too, is restricted by the sustainably available volume of usable biomass, thus competing with bioenergy use. Both options are therefore neither immediately available, nor can they compensate current anthropogenic emissions. They are therefore long-term and slowly effective possibilities for climate change mitigation, which will gain importance only once anthropogenic CO_2 emissions have decreased to a fraction of current levels.

uid fuels, electricity, heat and CO_2 for storage, do have economic benefits (GEA, 2011). Hybridisation of the raw material basis, for example the mixing of biofuels with fossil energy carriers, can also lead to a cost-effective improvement of process chains in terms of their greenhouse gas balance.

4.1.3.1
Geological Storage Capacity

The IPCC estimates the geological storage capacity of oil and gas fields (including storage options that are not economical) to be 675–900 Gt CO_2, of unminable coal seams 3–200 Gt CO_2, and of deep saline formations 1,000 to possibly 10,000 Gt CO_2 (IPCC, 2005). It should be taken into account that the storage potential of the oil and gas fields only becomes available once the fossil energy carriers have been exhausted. Moreover, the application of extraction technologies which increase the permeability of the reservoir rock formations (fracturing) can impact the tightness of the storage sites. The IPCC estimates this century's total economic potential for CCS to be 200–2,000 Gt CO_2.

4.1.3.2
Risks and Framework Conditions

Particularly important in terms of long-term climate change mitigation is the risk of gradual leakage of the stored CO_2. If we really did store 2,000 Gt of CO_2 this century, then a leakage rate of as little as 0.1 % annually (equal to a retention time of 1,000 years) would lead to 2 Gt of uncontrolled annual CO_2 emissions, which would endanger any stabilisation of the atmospheric CO_2 concentration. The WBGU therefore recommends that only storage facilities with a guaranteed retention time of at least 10,000 years are used (WBGU, 2006). Whilst the WBGU objects to a feed-in of CO_2 into seawater, it estimates that the storage of CO_2 in stores below the seabed is still less risky than the storage in land-based stores.

Since the 1970s, CO_2 has also been injected into oil fields, together with other chemicals, to counteract sinking pressure and increase the yield (enhanced oil recovery, EOR). The Canadian Weyburn project, started in 2000, is the first EOR project with planned subsequent long-term CO_2 storage (IPCC, 2005). Early in 2011, allegations were made that the injected CO_2 had leaked from the store, and already caused damages such as the death of animals (see, for example, the Frankfurter Rundschau, 24 January 2011); other reports, however, doubt this (PTRC, 2011). Undoubtedly, though, there is the risk of leakages, particularly in connection with boreholes, which, among other things, could lead to groundwater degradation. The sealing of boreholes and their long-term monitoring are therefore particularly important (IPCC, 2005).

In 2008, according to the IEA, not a single comprehensive, detailed regulation framework for CCS application had been set up in any country (IEA, 2008c). With its Directive on the Geological Storage of Carbon Dioxide (EU, 2009), the EU has since presented a comprehensive regulation framework for CCS application. Some member states (Belgium, Denmark, Finland, France, Latvia, Lithuania, Luxembourg, Austria, Romania, Spain) have already adopted the requirements of this directive as national law (as at March 2011). The implementation deadline was June 2011.

Apart from the scientific, technical and regulatory questions still open, it is also unclear as yet whether people would accept CO_2 storage in their immediate vicinity (IPCC, 2005).

4.1.4
Nuclear Energy

4.1.4.1
Emissions and Properties

Compared with coal powered plants, nuclear energy causes very low levels of greenhouse gas emissions. Process chain analyses point to lifecycle emissions of around 16–66 g CO_2eq per kWh_e, other references cite a range of 2–126 g CO_2eq per kWh_e. Variations result from, amongst other factors, the quality and concentration of the uranium ore used, and whether it is being assumed that the reactor fuel is reprocessed (WEC, 2004; Lübbert, 2007; Lenzen, 2008; Sovacool, 2008; Kleiner, 2008; GEA, 2011).

As with most renewable energies, most of the costs for nuclear energy are incurred in advance. The operating costs of existing plants are relatively low; the planning and construction costs, on the other hand, are often substantial in comparison with these, not least because cost escalation and delays are common on these projects (Grübler, 2010). The achieved overall running time of the plants therefore impacts their viability, although this not only depends on technical factors, but also on political decisions.

Stringent safety requirements for control systems, cooling, reactor pressure vessels and containment, as well as for the overall quality control, incur average installation costs of between 2,500 and 3,800 US$ per kW_e, depending on reactor type and location (GEA, 2011). These prices are overnight costs, i.e. they do not include financing costs, which, due to the long planning and construction times, are substantial (Schneider et al., 2009).

Globally, 442 reactors with a capacity of around 375 GW_e were in operation in 2011 (IAEA, 2011). 46% of these are located in Europe (including Eastern Europe and Russia), 30% in North America, and 21% in the Far East (Japan and China). Only around 3% of global reactor output is generated in Africa, Latin America, the Middle East and southern Asia. Together, the USA, France and Japan produced around 57% of electricity generated by nuclear power in 2010.

Globally, nuclear reactors provide 8% of installed power generating capacity, and contribute around 13% to power generation, as the output capacity can be utilised approx. 80% of the time. Nuclear energy is therefore often used for base load supply in power grids.

4.1.4.2
Potentials

The raw material supply for nuclear fuels is guaranteed for decades from known geological deposits (Table 4.1-2). Explorative activities have significantly increased recently, and the discovery of further deposits is to be expected. Apart from uranium extraction through mining, there are several methods for using secondary sources, such as existing stores, fissile material from nuclear weapons, or reprocessed waste. Currently, particularly the use of depleted uranium from nuclear weapons has led to power plants using considerably more uranium than is being extracted. The IEA believes that it is certainly possible to triple global nuclear capacity by 2050. India is working on a uranium-independent thorium based reactor type as it has considerably larger deposits of this.

Also decisive in terms of assessing resource supply security is whether spent fuel elements are being reprocessed, the plutonium contained in these is separated, or even whether highly enriched nuclear fuel is propagated in breeder reactors. From an economic point of view, however, there are currently no incentives to do so. Most plants are therefore being run with fuel which is used just once. Some countries are nevertheless pursuing the development of technology for the production of mixed oxide fuel elements (plutonium or uranium, MOX), which have the potential to considerably extend the resource basis. Their use, however, is associated with significant additional risks and far more elaborate disassembly. MOX fuel elements are mainly produced in England and France, and, to a lesser extent, in Japan, Russia and India; China is also pursuing such a programme. 30 of the reactors in Europe use MOX fuel elements, including reactors in Germany, Belgium and Switzerland. Breeder reactor technology for plutonium production is limited to only a few countries, including the USA, Russia, France and Japan, all of which, apart from Japan, are de facto nuclear weapons states. India is pursuing this path, hoping to be able to operate on a closed fuel cycle; China is also pursuing the use of breeder technology.

4.1.4.3
Risks and Framework Conditions for Use

Central events affecting nuclear energy development, significantly slowing down further expansion of the technology since the early 1990s in most countries, have been the disastrous accidents in Chernobyl in the Soviet Union (1986), and Three Mile Island in the USA (1979). The Fukushima nuclear disaster in Japan (March 2011) has rekindled the global debate on the controllability of this technology, and safety standards. At the centre of the discussion are the risk of serious damages, the still unresolved issues concerning final storage, the danger of uncontrolled proliferation, and also, not least, the high costs resulting from these.

Germany – like a range of other countries – has already followed a strategy of phasing out nuclear power for several years, due to a decline in public acceptance, accelerated in the aftermath of the disaster in Japan. As a consequence of the Fukushima nuclear disaster, the German federal government decreed a three-month moratorium for the operation of seven of its older nuclear power stations. Austria outlawed the use of nuclear energy as early as 1978. Other countries view nuclear energy as an essential element of their strategic energy supply, and also of their climate change mitigation plans. Moreover, nuclear programmes are seen as a national status symbol by many developing and newly industrialising countries. Whether this will still apply in future, considering the events in Fukushima, remains to be seen. In China, where 27 new reactors are currently under construction, a moratorium for the building of new nuclear power stations, or those under construction, has been decided on, although a specific timeframe has not yet been given. By now, reactor technology is dominated by light water reactors, which account for around 89% of installed capacity. As these can be operated with low enriched uranium, this technology bears comparatively low proliferation risks.

Globally, there is no long-term repository for highly radioactive waste so far; numerous facilities and different technological approaches are currently under development. Most of the spent fuel material is accumulated in interim storage facilities.

Cost escalation, delays on projects, lack of acceptance by the population and the existence of alternatives make a 'nuclear renaissance' an unlikely prospect in many industrialised states. Due to the unsolved risks (reaching over the entire lifecycle, from mining to the unsolved problem of final storage, in particular also the risk of serious damages) and costs accompanying nuclear technologies, as well as the associated proliferation and security risks and the above described path dependencies, the WBGU rejects a nuclear-based climate change mitigation strategy (WBGU, 2004).

4.1.5 Renewable Energies

4.1.5.1 Emissions and Properties

The use of renewable energies for power generation is usually associated with considerably lower greenhouse gas emissions than the use of fossil fuels. Extremely low specific lifecycle emissions of around 25 g CO_2eq per kWh_e electricity (WBGU, 2010a; 6.8–68 g CO_2 per kWh_e) are generated by wind power, followed by solar power with around 75 g CO_2eq per kWh_e (12.5–360 g CO_2 per kWh_e). Hydropower can also be associated with extremely low emissions of around 25 g CO_2eq per kWh_e (WBGU, 2010a; 3.5–120 g CO_2 per kWh_e), although this depends on location. In some cases of shallow reservoirs in productive tropical regions, methane emissions can lead to higher emissions from hydropower. However, reservoirs acting as a carbon sink were also examined. Particular attention should be called to hydropower's extensive co-benefits: 75% of all dams are primarily built for agricultural irrigation, flood prevention, or to secure the municipal water supply (IPCC, 2007c). Hydropower can also frequently supply flexible balancing power.

Analysis of bioenergy's greenhouse gas emissions balance shows a mixed picture. It can vary greatly according to raw material basis, geographical location, process and final product. Some bioenergy pathways can certainly produce higher greenhouse gas emissions than the use of fossil fuels (WBGU, 2010a). Greenhouse gas emissions from geothermal energy are location-dependent; scientific studies state values of 20–120 g CO_2 per kWh_e (Sullivan et al., 2010). Some very deep water-bearing strata can contain considerable amounts of dissolved carbon dioxide and toxic elements, although this problem can be solved by recirculation of the liquid or the transfer of heat into secondary cycles.

With the exception of geothermal energy, renewable energy sources are characterised by relatively low spatial energy density. Therefore, large areas of land are needed to cover the major share of the energy supply with renewable energy sources. This can be partially solved through the multifunctional use of land, for example by establishing wind farms on agricultural land.

Usually, capital-intensive conversion technologies are necessary to make renewable energy sources usable. The project risk can also be considerable, for example in the case of major hydropower plants. Renewable energies therefore hold little economic appeal in contemporary market models, for example, when comparisons with other energy carriers are made whilst applying substantial discount rates, thereby marginalising the future cost of fossil options. Currently, the prime costs for renewable energies are frequently still above those calculated for fossil energy carriers. As many of the technologies are relatively new, it is to be expected that costs can be significantly reduced through technological learning progress. Well-located hydropower, wind and biomass plants have already achieved cost parity to fossil sources.

Renewable energies can make access to clean, safe and easy to use energy possible particularly in low income countries, thereby contributing considerably to the achievement of the Millennium Development Goals. If the energy carriers were to be integrated into international markets (electricity from hydropower, liquid fuels), they could considerably improve the trade balance of the exporting countries. Renewable energies also contribute to economic development and value creation in rural or structurally weak regions of industrialised countries. They extend the value chain into rural regions (by generating business tax income and jobs), thus reducing regional income inequalities (DENA, 2010).

The various renewable sources have different characteristics with regard to their integration into the energy system. Some of the economically attractive and technically relatively advanced renewable sources such as wind and solar power are also subject to considerable fluctuations in terms of energy availability. Integration of a larger share of fluctuating energy sources into the system requires a conversion of energy infrastructure (Section 4.4.2). As yet, there have been few analyses of the cost implications of such a conversion. In this context, regional studies such as the one carried out by the SRU (2010) indicate substantial potential savings, provided that the international trade with on-grid energy carriers is stepped up. Bioenergy and hydropower are renewable energies that are particularly relevant in terms of system integration, as they can also be used to balance fluctuating feed-in. Pump storage currently represents the cheapest form of electricity storage, although its potential depends on location.

4.1.5.2
Potentials

Not only the theoretical potentials, but also the technical and sustainable potentials of renewable energies far exceed current global energy demand – 492 EJ primary and 345 EJ final energy in 2008. A summary showing the estimated technical potential of the different renewable energies from various literature sources can be found in Table 4.1-4. The technical potential of solar power alone exceeds the current overall consumption by more than one order of magnitude; in some sources, this also applies to geothermal energy. This means that in theory, it is possible to meet the overall global energy demand fully with renewable energies.

From the WBGU's point of view, the decisive factor for assessing the role of renewable energies in a future, sustainable transformed energy system is not their technical potential, but their sustainable potential (Box 4.1-1). The WBGU presented an extensive analysis of this aspect in 2003. Since then, technological and other parameters have developed further, so the figures given in 2003 must be partially updated and reviewed. Table 4.1-4 shows the WBGU's current assessment of the sustainable potential of various renewable energies.

The assessment of the technical potential in some cases varies greatly depending on the author. The range is particularly broad where geothermal energy is concerned. Assessments of wind and solar power potentials also show considerable differences; however, some of these are due to technological advances. In the case of wind power, for example, progress has been made with regard to turbine mast height and rotor area, i.e. individual turbine output capacity. Apart from this, offshore farms, for instance in the form of floating structures, can now be built in much deeper water than the 40 metres frequently used in the past, meaning that the technical potential was adjusted upwards in comparison with earlier studies (IAEA, 2000; WBGU, 2004). Solar power has also seen considerable progress, for example in the conversion efficiency of amorphous silicon and thin film technologies. New experiences have been gathered with plants which generate electricity through concentrating solar thermal processes.

To evaluate the sustainable potential, individual restrictions were taken into account for the various sources.

The main consideration with regard to biomass use is that it must not compete with food production, and that biodiversity must be preserved (WBGU, 2010a). Applications with little impact on climate protection, evident in certain biofuel pathways, have also been excluded. Where geothermal energy is concerned, a distinction must be made between thermal and electrical use. Only locations with a very high supply temperature can be considered for generating electric power, whereas the use of low temperature heat recovery shows by far the greatest potential. Although hydropower is an established technology, its further extension is restricted through, amongst other aspects, the environmental impact on biodiversity, the siltation of large reservoirs, the sediment dynamics, the methane emissions from flooded areas and the effect on the groundwater table.

Solar and wind power also exhibit restrictions in terms of their sustainable potential. Examples are the competition, in terms of land usage, with food production in the case of solar plants, or the noise emissions associated with wind farms.

In comparison to earlier studies, the technical potentials of biomass are now viewed far more critically, owing to land-use competition (Box 4.1-4), and are rated as lower by newer studies than, for instance, in the World Energy Assessment (IAEA, 2000). The

Table 4.1-4
Renewable energies: theoretical, technical and economic potentials. The sustainable potentials are estimates by the WBGU. For comparison: global primary energy consumption in 2008 amounted to 492 EJ.
Sources: WBGU, 2004, 2010a; IEA, 2010a; GEA, 2011

	Theoretical Potential	Technical Potential	Sustainable Potential	Production 2008
	[EJ/year]	[EJ/year]	[EJ/year]	[EJ]
Biomass	2,400	800	100	50,3
Geothermal Energy	41,700,000	720	22	0,4
Hydropower	504,000	160	12	11,6
Solar Energy	3,900,000	280,000	10,000	0,5
Wind Energy	110,000	1,700	>1,000	0,8
Total: Renewable Energies	46,000,000	283,500	>11,000	64

WBGU (2003) specified the annual sustainable potential of biomass at 100 EJ for modern sources and 5 EJ for traditional use. More recently, the WBGU (2009a) estimated the annual sustainable bioenergy potential from energy crops to be 30–120 EJ, plus an additional 50 EJ from waste and residues.

4.1.5.3 Risks and Framework Conditions for Use

The use of renewable energies can impact adversely on environment and society. Major hydropower projects, for example, can require the resettlement of the local population, and destroy valuable habitats. Major biomass projects can also contribute directly to habitat damage, and to soil overuse and water shortages, or impact negatively through indirect effects such as induced land-use changes in other regions of the world, or increased food prices (Box 4.1-4). In the case of wind energy, landscape conservation, bird protection and noise pollution are frequently cited as arguments against expansion. Accordingly, offshore plants in Germany, for instance, are expanded at great water depths and out of sight of the coast, also taking into account bird protection areas, leading to additional costs.

Renewable sources can also be overused: biomass potentials can be reduced through erosion and humus loss, soil salinisation or nutrient depletion. The hydropower potential of reservoirs can sink drastically if these are filled with sediment. Geothermal sources can also lose their potential in the long run as a result of cooling down. These risks are far slighter with wind and solar power; however, their resource potentials could potentially be affected by climate change. Changes in precipitation patterns and meltwater flows from glaciers, for example, can significantly impede the potential of hydropower and biomass.

The temporary support of renewable energy expansion, firmly recommended by the WBGU, must therefore be accompanied by a legal framework which guarantees the sustainability of the use of renewable energies. This applies particularly to the use of bioenergy (WBGU, 2010a).

4.1.6 A Vision as a Thought Experiment: Meeting Global Energy Demand Fully with Renewable Energies

The sustainable potential of renewable energies is fundamentally sufficient to provide the world with energy (Section 4.1.5). The following thought experiment shows that if the expansion of renewable energies were vigorously pursued, from a technological point of view, sufficient renewable energies could be unlocked to meet the global energy demand by the middle of the century. Barriers such as the economic lifetime of existing infrastructures or upfront costs have been consciously excluded from this calculation. This vision relies on a rapid phasing out of fossil-based electric power generation, the replacing of mineral oil in transport systems through electromobility and regenerative fuels, and the replacing of fossil fuels used for heating and cooling through electric heat pumps, solar thermal energy and CHP technology.

If sufficient renewable energies are to be available as early as the middle of the century to fully cover global demand, the economy's final energy intensity must substantially decrease. The vision assumes that, through efficiency measures, the global demand for heating and cooling can be lowered by 1% each year, and that the growth in energy demand for transport systems, as well as the global growth of the demand for electric power, can be restricted to 1% per year. This can be achieved with a range of measures. These include the introduction of electromobility (the conventional combustion

Box 4.1-4

Risks of Uncontrolled Bioenergy Expansion

Bioenergy can be gained either from waste and residues, or from dedicated energy crops. It is the latter variant that bears particular risks, as it is associated with additional and intensified land use. Bioenergy use therefore competes directly with food security, nature conservation, and climate protection. To meet the food demand of a growing global population, global food production must be increased significantly, thereby competing with the cultivation of energy crops (Section 1.2.5). This land-use competition could, for example, result in higher food prices. The cultivation of energy crops can lead directly to a further conversion of semi-natural areas into cropland, or displace the already existing cultivation of foodstuffs, which then has to move to new areas. The conversion of semi-natural areas increases, for instance, the loss of biodiversity, and usually releases greenhouse gases. Whether energy crop cultivation has a beneficial or a damaging effect on the climate therefore depends to a large extent on the type of land that is used. The conversion of forests and wetlands for bioenergy cultivation often releases more greenhouse gases than could be saved over several years through the subsequent use of bioenergy. Nitrogen fertiliser production, production mechanisation, pest control and transporting harvests for further processing often require substantial amounts of fuel and other energy inputs. Therefore, the fact that the quantity of CO_2 released during the combustion is equivalent to the amount previously absorbed by the plants does not imply that bioenergy causes no net CO_2 emissions, in the overall equation. A sustainable bioenergy use is therefore only possible if, at national and international level, policymakers establish framework conditions which ensure the climate mitigation effect and sustainability of bioenergy use. In 2009, the WBGU made detailed recommendations on this topic (WBGU, 2010a).

engine has an efficiency factor of merely 20–25%, the electric motor, on the other hand, 70–80%), the increased thermal insulation of buildings, the use of heat pumps, and the implementation of industrial efficiency measures. Overall, the final energy demand is contained through these measures, to the extent that the fictitious yearly primary energy demand, according to the substitution method (Box 4.1-2), rises up to a maximum of 700 EJ by 2050. The primary energy demand, determined according to the method of direct energy equivalency, even falls, due to the use of renewable energies, which do not cause any waste heat losses (Figure 4.1-1). For the expansion paths outlined in Figure 4.1-1, historical annual growth rates for wind power and photovoltaic energy were initially carried forward, then reduced once larger shares of overall generation were achieved. For the other technologies, for some of which no historical growth rates were known, or which are technologies not as yet established on the market (renewable gas such as, for example, hydrogen or methane, and electromobility), future growth rates were defined according to own assumptions. Biomass is restricted to a sustainable potential of 150 EJ per year (WBGU, 2010a), and is used exclusively in combination with CHP technology in 2050. Traditional biomass use in developing countries should have been fully replaced by modern technologies at this point in time. Hydropower undergoes only minor expansion as its sustainable potential is limited.

The most difficult sector in the transition to renewable energies is the transport sector. This scenario excludes liquid biofuels, as bioenergy can make a more significant contribution to climate change mitigation in the electricity sector (WBGU, 2010a); instead, the introduction of electromobility, gas-powered mobility (hydrogen, methane in natural gas powered vehicles with combustion engine), complemented by fuel cell vehicles, is rapidly accelerated. For specific transport segments (long distance, flight, ship, etc.), the exclusive use of wind and solar fuels is assumed. In this way, by 2050, 70% of the energy demand in the transport sector is met by electricity, and 30% by renewable wind and solar fuels (hydrogen, methane or other fuels from regenerative H_2 and CO_2).

4.1.7
Emissions from Land Use

Only two land-use sectors are the focus here: forests and agriculture. The issue of bioenergy, an important one in this context, was dealt with extensively in the WBGU's 'Future Bioenergy and Sustainable Land Use' report (WBGU, 2010a), and also in Section 4.1.5 and Box 4.1-4.

Around two-thirds of global long-lived greenhouse gas emissions, or 78% of CO_2 emissions, are created through energy generation, i.e. the use of fossil fuels. The majority of the remaining greenhouse gas emissions can be attributed directly to agriculture and land-use change.

When allocating emissions from the terrestrial biosphere to sectors or areas of need, it is important to avoid double counting. CO_2 emissions from deforestation, for example, are particularly significant as they account for just under one-eighth of total global emissions, and are attributed to the sector 'land-use change and forestry', whereas greenhouse gas emissions from the production of agricultural goods, like the outgas-

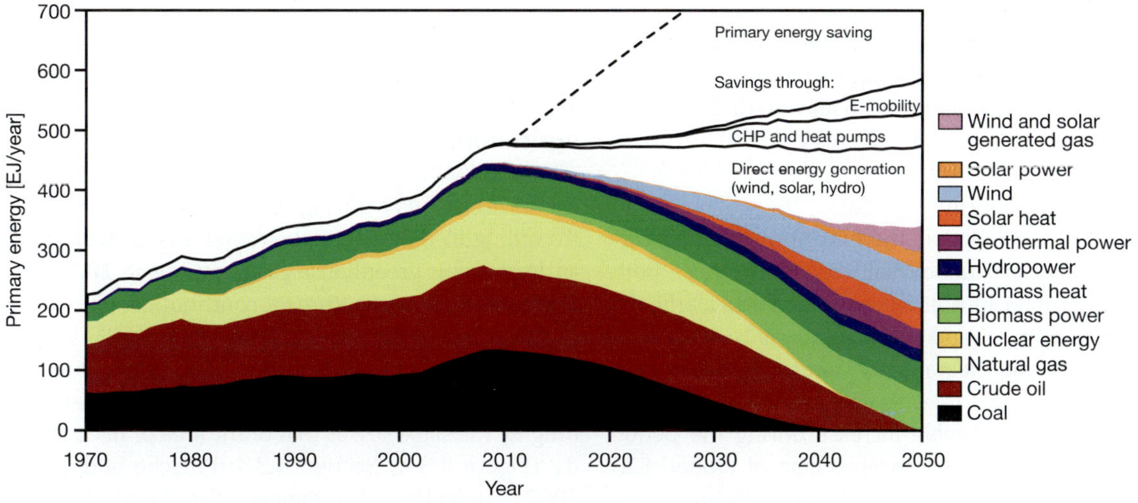

Figure 4.1-1
Vision for a global renewable energy supply by 2050: the figure shows the distribution of global primary energy demand by 2050, using the direct energy equivalency method. The scenario is based on an extrapolation of current expansion rates for renewable energies. Renewables are accorded priority in the energy system, leading to the substitution of existing conventional energy carriers. The economy of existing infrastructures and the availability of key materials have not been taken into account. The dotted line shows the development of global primary energy demand without transformation, based on the GEA baseline scenario (Figure 1.2-4). CHP = combined heat and power.
Source: WBGU

sing of nitrous oxide from the soil, are allocated to the agriculture sector (IPCC, 1996).

An analysis of emissions according to areas of need must include emissions over the entire lifecycle. In the case of food (Section 4.3.4), these are the direct agricultural emissions, but also emissions attributable to the further lifecycle of the products (transport, processing, storage, etc.). In addition to this, there are the associated indirect emissions, for example from forest clearance for the subsequent production of food or biomass for energetic or material use on these areas.

These indirect land-use change emissions play a particularly important role in the production of agricultural goods (WBGU, 2010a). The conversion of forests and wetlands into cropland and pasture releases substantial amounts of greenhouse gases, both immediately and in subsequent years, previously stored in the biomass and the soils (including through soil erosion; Section 1.1.3). From 2000 to 2009, greenhouse gas emissions from land-use changes are estimated to have averaged 4.0 Gt CO_2 per year. A downward trend has led to their respective share of global CO_2 emissions falling from approx. 20% in the 1990s to approx. 11.5% in 2009, primarily due to a decrease in deforestation in the tropics (Friedlingstein et al., 2010; GCP, 2011). In 2005, just under two-thirds of global CO_2 emissions from land-use changes were generated in Brazil and Indonesia (WRI-CAIT, 2011). Furthermore, clearance or draining of natural or semi-natural ecosystems usually turns greenhouse gas sinks into greenhouse gas sources, leading to additional emissions in subsequent years. Altogether, the quantification of emissions from land-use changes is more difficult than quantifying energy sector emissions (Herzog, 2009).

4.1.7.1
Forests and Climate Change Mitigation

Over 4 billion hectares of forests cover around 31% of the global land surface (FAO, 2010a). The FAO's current State of the World's Forests report clearly shows that forest areas continue to be lost. The global deforestation rate of 13 million hectares per year, driven mainly by conversion of tropical forests into agricultural land and forest degradation, has remained at a very high level over the past decade. Large-scale tree-planting in China, India and Vietnam has led to a temporary reduction of global net forest loss over the past decade, down to a total of 5.2 million hectares per year.

Forests are amongst the Earth's largest carbon stores, storing up to 650 Gt C (2,380 Gt CO_2). Approx. 44% of this is bound in biomass, 11% in dead wood and litter, and approx. 45% in the soil (FAO, 2010a). Deforestation and forest degradation are therefore one of the world's major sources of CO_2. Currently, the carbon stocks in forests are estimated to have been depleted by 0.5 Gt C (1.8 Gt CO_2) per year between 2000 and 2010, totalling 5 Gt C (18 Gt CO_2) for the decade (FAO, 2010a). However, emissions due to deforestation could be considerably higher, as the available sets of data on emissions differ in their description of both regional distribution and total quantity, and are not consistent. The Global Carbon Project estimates the emissions caused by the ongoing deforestation and anthropogenic forest degradation alone at between 2.6 and 4.0 Gt CO_2 for the decade between 2000 and 2009 (GCP, 2010).

Trends and Mitigation Potential

It is to be expected that the expansion of foodstuff and bioenergy production will continue to raise both the deforestation rate and emissions. Particularly the number of palm oil and soy plantations is rising fast. The draining and clearance of forested peatlands in Southeast Asia alone releases an estimated 632 Mt CO_2 per year, with a possible increase during the period 2015–2035 to an emissions maximum of around 823 Mt per year (Hooijer et al., 2006). Globally, emissions of over 2 Gt CO_2 per year are estimated to be caused by draining of peatlands and peat fires (Joosten, 2010). As yet, the increasingly negative impacts of climate change, such as droughts, forest and peat fires, intense rain and floods, which all add to peatland deforestation and damage, remain to be seen. The incentives for forest and peatland protection, and sustainable and multifunctional forest management, should therefore become more important on a global level in order to bind and store CO_2. Afforestation programmes must be adapted to the respective location, and must be analysed beforehand with regard to their greenhouse gas balance, as they do not necessarily lead to significant sink formation. Large-scale afforestation can have negative ecological and socio-economic impacts.

Another way of mitigating climate change through forestry-related measures is by increasing the carbon stocks in existing forests through improved management techniques, such as the lengthening of harvest cycles or the reduction of disturbance, e.g. through better protection against forest fires (particularly in sub-tropical latitudes), or by reducing soil compaction caused by heavy machinery (particularly in temperate and boreal latitudes). Also crucial is the development of an effective regime for the reduction of emissions caused by deforestation and forest degradation in tropical forest countries in connection with forest protection, sustainable forest management and responsible afforestation (REDD-plus) within the UN Framework Convention on Climate Change (UNFCCC; Section 7.3.7.2). The various sustainability and development dimensions must be taken into account during this process, such as, for example, the conservation of natural forests and biodiversity, and the participation and rights of local communities and indigenous peoples. The expansion and implementation of policies to support agro-forestry holds further potentials for carbon sequestration and the indirect mitigation of emissions (ICRAF, 2010).

4.1.7.2
Agriculture and Climate Change Mitigation

Direct Emissions from Agricultural Production

According to IPCC (2007c), around 10–12% of global anthropogenic greenhouse gas emissions in 2005 were attributable to agriculture, a contribution of 5.1–6.1 Gt CO_2eq per year, or even as much as 16%, according to WRI-CAIT (2011). The overall greenhouse gas footprint of the area of needs category food alone is roughly the same size as that of the area of need mobility (Figure 4.3-1; Section 4.3.4; Fritsche and Eberle, 2007). Agricultural CO_2 emissions are hardly to blame here; it is nitrous oxide (N_2O) and methane (CH_4) that are responsible for this, in roughly equal measure. Nitrous oxide is a greenhouse gas with an atmospheric lifetime of 114 years. It is formed as a decomposition product after nitrogen fertilisation, and contributes around 2.8 Gt CO_2eq per year to anthropogenic emissions. 84% of global N_2O emissions are caused by agriculture (Smith et al., 2008). With only 12 years, methane has a considerably lower atmospheric lifetime; it is created mainly in the digestive system of ruminating cattle and through the cultivation of wet rice. In total, around 3.3 Gt CO_2 per year, or 52% of global CH_4 emissions, are caused by agriculture (Smith et al., 2008).

Almost three-quarters of direct agricultural CH_4 and N_2O emissions can be attributed to developing countries (Smith et al., 2007; Thorpe, 2009). An increase is apparent, the consequence of agricultural expansion and intensification and increased livestock farming, whilst the agricultural greenhouse gas emissions in industrial countries are stagnating (Smith et al., 2007).

Trends and Mitigation Potential

Agricultural greenhouse gas emissions are expected to rise further, primarily due to population development and changed dietary habits (Section 1.2.5; IPCC, 2007c; Popp et al., 2010). However, the future development of emissions is highly uncertain; estimates range from 6.7 to 10.2 Gt CO_2eq per year in 2020 (Strengers et al., 2004; US-EPA, 2006). The technical greenhouse gas mitigation potential in agriculture by 2030 is estimated at between 5.0 and 6.0 Gt CO_2 per year (Caldeira et al., 2004; Smith et al., 2008). Depending on the CO_2 price, the annual economic potential is between 1.5–1.6 Gt CO_2eq (<20 US$ per t CO_2eq) and 4.0–4.3 Gt CO_2eq (<100 US$ per t CO_2eq; Smith et al., 2008). Roughly estimated, around half of all direct agricultural emissions are therefore avoidable. 89% of this mitigation potential is based on increased carbon uptake of soils through improved cropland and pasture land management (Section 4.3.4.1). Around 70% of the potential is in developing countries, approx. 20% in OECD countries, and 10% in transition countries (IPCC, 2007c). These technical potentials are however not as substantial as the emissions reductions that could be achieved through changed dietary habits (Section 4.3.4.2).

4.2 Insights from Energy Models and Climate Change Mitigation Scenarios

The respective literature encompasses several hundred complex global scenarios by now, elaborating long-term future energy system trends and their corresponding greenhouse gas emissions. So far, however, these include only a few transformative scenarios that have been developed with the ambitious objective of avoiding a global rise in mean temperature of more than 2°C (IPCC, 2007c; Meinshausen et al., 2009). Many models assume strong inertia of the energy system, therefore allowing for only relatively slow, incremental deviations from a projected business-as-usual path. They usually assume, for example, that a conversion can only happen following the investment cycles, i.e. an infrastructure is kept for as long as the economic lifespan allows, or the conventional planning logistics require, say 40 years for a coal-fired power plant. Others are written based on a back-casting strategy, i.e. they assume a future target configuration and elaborate, from this perspective, the changing steps necessary to reach this point. The necessary rates of change, for instance in terms of carbon intensity of the economy or energy efficiency improvements, may under certain circumstances be far higher than the rates known from historical technical learning processes. Paths such as these are therefore also more speculative, and in part linked with optimistic assumptions with regard to technical learning progress or currently not yet developed technologies.

In the present chapter, the WBGU analyses a number of transformative scenarios from the respective literature. The objective of the analysis is not to filter out the 'best', from the WBGU's point of view, of those scenarios, and to suggest that the global community follow it. The initial idea is rather to sketch an overall picture. The scenarios show a range of transformative elements which, depending on their combination, certainly provide the basis for a great number of different possibilities as to how the energy system may be changed towards a sustainable and climate-friendly way of doing business. The answer to the question of whether a transformation is possible that allows compliance with the 2°C guard rail is therefore, at least in the world of models, a resounding yes. And not only that: the analyses suggest that even a transformation such as this, subject to considerable time pressure, still leaves considerable room for political manoeuvring. The exact significance of individual technologies does not ensue inevitably, but allows different options.

4.2.1 Dynamics of the Primary Driving Forces

Demographic trends and economic growth are the primary driving forces behind resource demand and, in the era of fossil energy use, therefore also behind greenhouse gas emissions (Figures 4.2-1, 4.2-2, 4.2-3). Since the beginning of the 19th century, the global population has risen roughly sevenfold to currently just under 7 billion. The average rate of annual growth was 0.9%, peaking at more than 2% between 1965 and 1970. Since 2000, annual population growth has decreased to around 1.2%, and the UN Population Division's prognosis expects a fall down to 0.34% by 2050, meaning that the global population will then number around 9.2 billion people (UN DESA, 2009b; Box 1.2-2).

In the long term, the global GDP between 1800 and 2008 has on average risen by 2.2% per year, i.e. multiplied by a factor of 95 overall, to approx. 51,000 billion US$ (international purchasing power parity; Maddisson, 2010). In contrast to the population growth rate, this growth rate has recently accelerated. Between 1990 and 2008, global GDP has roughly doubled, and the average growth rate between 2000 and 2008 was 4.2 % per year (Maddisson, 2010). In 2000, an IPCC special report extrapolated these dynamics, elaborating the sensitivity of emissions trajectories to variations in primary driving forces (Nakicenovic et al., 2000). The relationship between primary driving forces and environmental consumption has been under systematic discussion since the 1970s (Box 4.2-1).

Global primary energy consumption has risen by a factor of 24 since 1800 (on average 1.5% per year), and final energy consumption by a factor of 17 (1.4% per year). Both parameters have therefore grown at a faster rate than the population, but significantly slower than the rate of economic output. Between 2000 and 2008, years of rapid growth, particularly in Asia, primary energy demand rose by 2.6% per year, final energy demand by around 2.2% per year. The reason for the discrepancy between these core values is the rapidly progressing demand for superior energy carriers such as electricity and mineral oil products, whose production is accompanied by conversion losses.

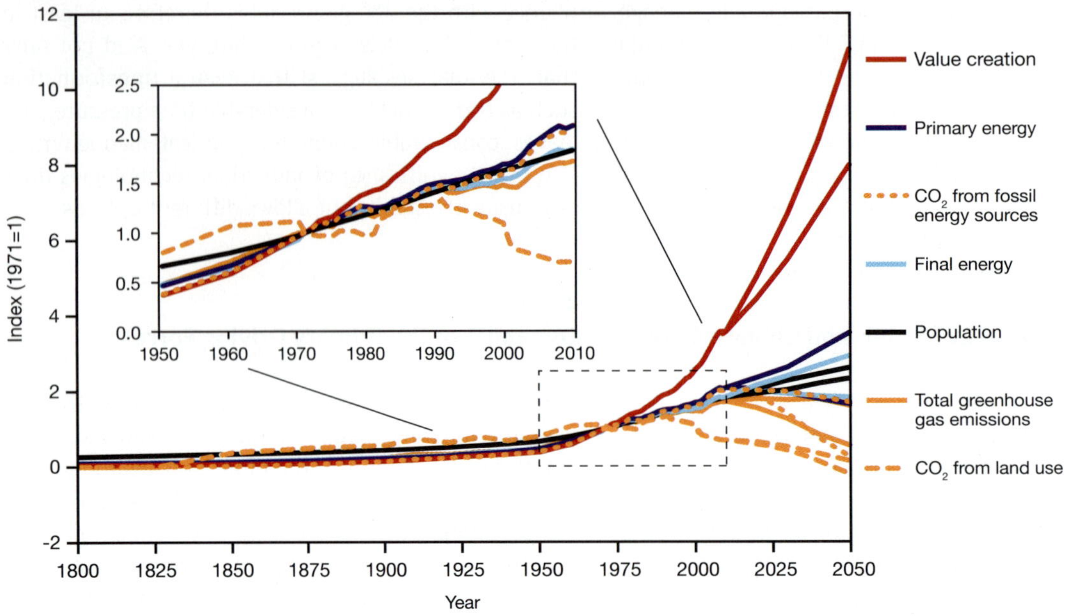

Figure 4.2-1
Global primary driving forces and emissions trends 1800–2008. The insertion shows the period 1950–2010 in larger scale. To afford trend comparison, data are shown as indices that are scaled to have a value of 1 in 1971. Data sources used in the comparison of historical long-term trends up to 2008 are Grübler, 2008b; Houghton, 2008; Schneider et al., 2009; IEA, 2009a; Boden et al., 2010, updated with data from Friedlingstein et al., 2010. Future trends 2008–2050 are shown as a range (maximum and minimum values) of values based on the scenarios described in Section 4.2.3.
Source: WBGU, based on the cited data sources

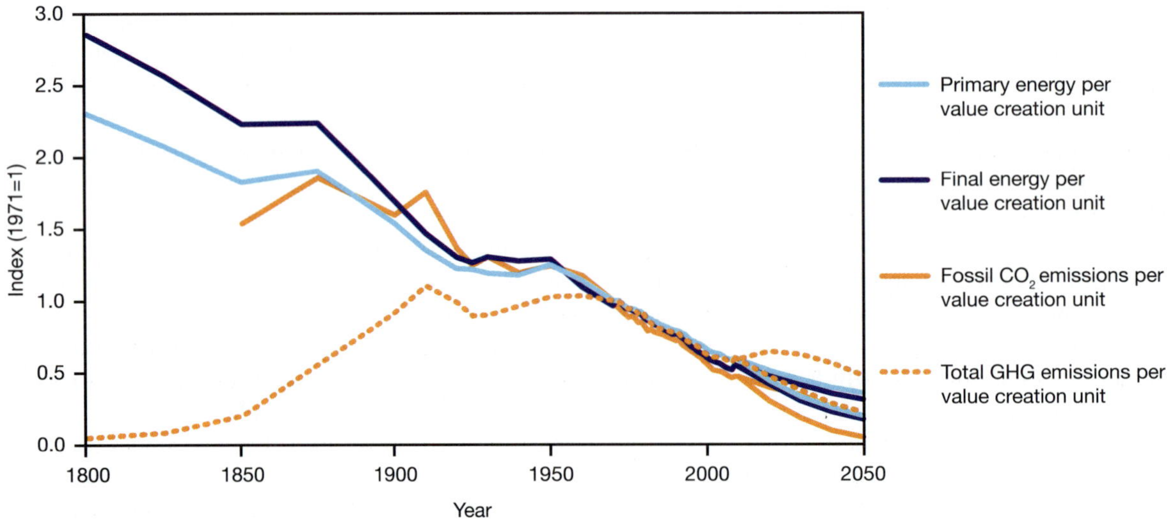

Figure 4.2-2
Global energy consumption and CO_2 emissions per unit of value creation. For trends to be comparable, data are shown as indices that are scaled to have a value of 1 in 1971. Future trends 2008–2050 are shown as a range (maximum and minimum values) of values based on the scenarios described in Section 4.2.3.
Source: WBGU, based on the data sources cited in Figure 4.2-1

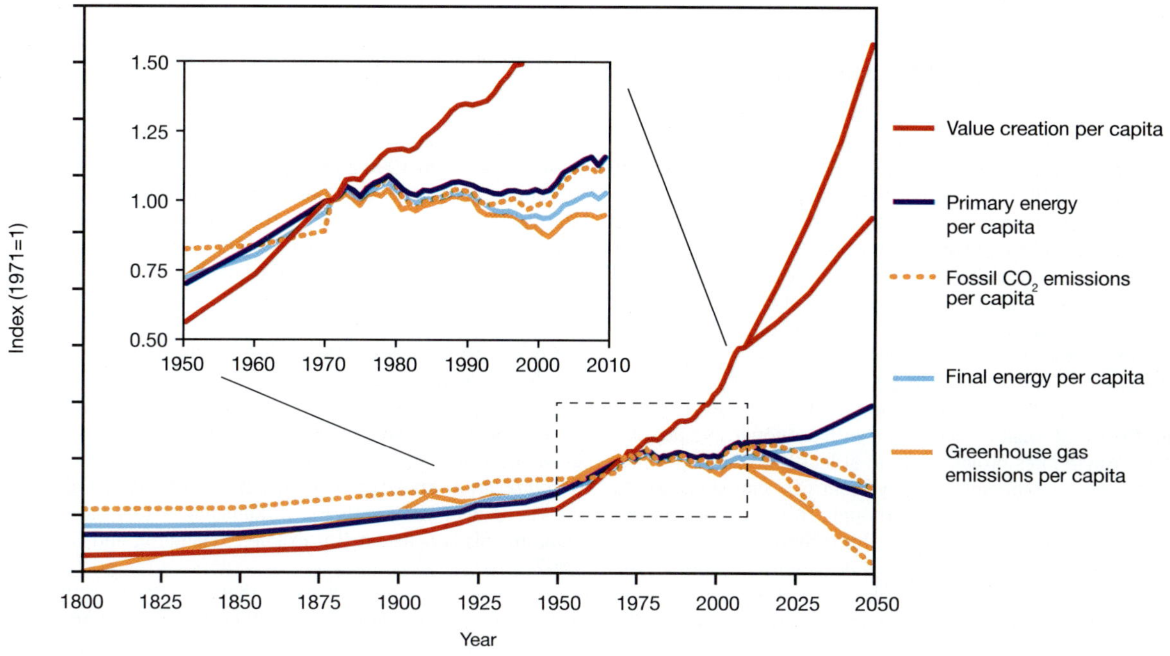

Figure 4.2-3
Global energy consumption and CO_2 emissions per year per capita. The insertion shows the period 1950–2010 in larger scale. For trends to be comparable, data are shown as indices that are scaled to have a value of 1 in 1971. Future trends 2008–2050 are shown as a range (maximum and minimum values) of values based on the scenarios described in Section 4.2.3.
Source: WBGU, based on the data sources cited in Figure 4.2-1

In 1850, CO_2 emissions were still around approx. 2 Gt per year, of which emissions from land-use changes were responsible for around ten times the amount of emissions from the use of fossil fuels (Houghton, 2008). By 1910, both activities were roughly equally responsible, and annual emissions amounted to 6.5 Gt CO_2. Around 1970, total annual CO_2 emissions amounted to 20 Gt, around three-quarters of which were attributable to fossil sources. CO_2 emissions from land-use changes have decreased since 1990. Total CO_2 emissions for the year 2008 were approx. 35 Gt, around a tenth of which is still attributable to land-use changes (Friedlingstein et al., 2010).

Some of the more complex integrated assessment models such as IMAGE or MESSAGE explicitly consider other greenhouse gases apart from CO_2, for example agriculture-generated CH_4 and N_2O, and greenhouse gases from industrial processes; many other models do not feature these.

The energy intensity of global value creation has decreased during the course of the past 208 years roughly by a factor of 4 for primary energy, and a factor of 5 for final energy. The fossil CO_2 intensity of value creation increased until the first decade of the 20th century on a global level, then fell significantly from around 1970 onwards. The overall CO_2 intensity (including land-use changes) has gone down roughly by a factor of 3 since 1850. Since 2000, primary and final energy intensity have been decreasing by an average of 1.5% and 1.9% per year, respectively; CO_2 intensity from fossil sources, or overall CO_2 intensity (including land-use changes), is decreasing annually by 1.2%, or 2.3%, respectively (own calculations based on the sources cited in Figure 4.2-1).

Per capita value creation has roughly risen by a factor of 14 since 1800, an average of 1.3% per year. In the period since 1990, this value has on average been 2.9%.

Final energy consumption per capita in 2008 was roughly 2.5 times the value of 1800, and primary energy demand rose by a factor of 3.5. Primary energy consumption per capita remained more or less constant between 1970 and 2000; since 2000, however, it has again continued to grow at a rate of 1.4% per year.

Overall CO_2 emissions per capita peaked in the early 1970s at around 5.5 t. Since then, emissions initially increased in line with the population, resulting in more or less constant global per capita emissions. However, since 1990, CO_2 emissions attributable to land-use changes showed a considerable downward trend, which initially overcompensated for continually rising CO_2 emissions from fossil energy sources. Between 2000 and 2008, however, per capita emissions from fossil sources have risen by about 1.7% per year, and

Box 4.2-1

Economic Growth and Transformation

On the one hand, economic growth can support the transformation towards a low-carbon society; on the other hand, it can impede it (Box 5.2-1). In the past, at least, there has been a strong correlation between global wealth and CO_2 emissions (Raupach et al., 2007; Edenhofer et al., 2009a). In the context of environmental protection, there has been a long-running debate on the possibility or impossibility of unlimited growth, and on the compatibility of climate protection, or sustainable resource consumption, with economic growth (Georgescu-Roegen, 1971; Box 5.2-1). So far, it remains completely open as to whether the global reduction of CO_2 emissions required for the transformation is possible with economic and population growth rates projected up to at least 2050. An absolute de-linking of economic activity from CO_2 emissions would have to be achieved for this, although, from today's perspective, it remains unclear whether this is feasible.

According to the so-called 'Kaya identity' (Ehrlich and Holdren, 1971; Nakicenovic et al., 2000), there are four main input factors impacting an economy's CO_2 emissions: the population figure, the level of wealth (GDP per capita), the energy intensity of the GDP (energy consumption per unit of GDP), and the CO_2-intensity of the energy generation (CO_2 emissions per unit of generated energy). There is a multiplicatory interrelation between these factors:

CO_2 emissions = population x (GDP/population figure) x (energy consumption/GDP) x (CO_2 emissions/generated energy)

Subsequent to peaking in the 1970s, global population growth has slowed down to a rate of currently 1% per year (Maddison, 2010). In its medium-term prognosis, the UN Population Division assumes that the annual population growth rate will decline to around 0.34% by 2045–2050 (UN DESA, 2009b). Between 1800 and 2008, the long-term average of the global economic growth rate (measured in purchasing power parities) was around 2.2%, between 2000 and 2008, the average was around 4.2% (Maddisson, 2010).

Absolute de-linkage could be considered to have been achieved if CO_2 emissions remained constant, or even if they were to fall, despite an increasing population and continued economic growth. This needs either a reduction in GDP energy intensity (energy consumption/GDP), or a reduction of the CO_2 intensity of energy generation (CO_2 emissions/energy consumption, preferably both. Between 1980 and 2008, the energy intensity of the global production has decreased by around 32%, the equivalent of an average annual reduction of around 1.1% over the past 30 years (van Vuuren et al., 2010; IEA, 2010c). Global CO_2 intensity of energy generation fell by around 0.1% between 1971 and 2005 (US-EIA, 2010; van Vuuren et al., 2010).

The reductions in energy intensity of GDP and the CO_2 intensity of energy generation achieved so far have therefore not been sufficient to achieve an absolute de-linking. Accordingly, global CO_2 emissions continued to rise over the past years. Overall, global emissions increased by around 1% annually between 1990 and 1999, and by slightly more than 3% annually between 2000 and 2005 (Raupach et al., 2007). This emissions trend is expected to continue over the coming years, as soon as the global economy has resumed its growth path, following the financial and economic crisis (Friedlingstein et al., 2010).

Is Complete De-linking Possible? Decomposition Analysis Results

In the past, economic growth has overcompensated the efficiency gains achieved by technological innovations in energy generation as well as production. Various studies that use decomposition analyses to match the development of CO_2 emissions over time with the influencing factors have also come to this conclusion (for example, Hamilton and Turton, 2002).

However, this does not mean that this has to continue in the future. Edenhofer et al. (2009a) have compared various integrated assessment models (REMIND-R, IMACLIM-R, WITCH) in order to examine whether a decarbonisation of the global economy is compatible with an atmospheric CO_2 concentration stabilisation at 450 ppm. In their decomposition analysis, they have reached the result that in the case of an energy systems transformation with the aim of stabilising CO_2 concentration at 450 ppm, technological innovations (i.e. improved energy efficiency accompanied by a decarbonisation of energy production) can overcompensate the global economic growth-related emissions increase. Assuming a long-term average annual global GDP growth rate of around 2.1–2.4% up to 2100, this could lead to a decline in CO_2 emissions as of 2020 or 2025, at least in their models (Edenhofer et al., 2009a; Jakob et al., 2009).

Edenhofer et al. (2010) carried out similar calculations with the models MERGE, POLES, TIMER and E3MG. This model comparison also assumes annual GDP growth rates of around 3% until the middle of the century (Edenhofer et al., 2010; van Vuuren et al., 2010). Overall, the model calculations by Edenhofer et al. (2009a, 2010) show that, assuming average annual growth rates of around 3% up until the middle of the century, or 2% up until 2100, a decarbonisation on the basis of technical innovations is possible, in theory, even if it is a huge challenge. It would require the multiplication of decarbonisation and energy efficiency increase measures at a global level. According to IEA estimates, to achieve a stabilisation at 450 ppm CO_2eq, in the period the decrease rate of 2008 – 2020 the CO_2 intensity of the global economy (t CO_2 per GDP) would have to be twice that of the period 1990–2008, and in the period 2020–2035 it has to be four times of it (IEA, 2010c).

total emissions (including CO_2 from land-use changes) have increased by 0.6% per year (Friedlingstein et al., 2010).

4.2.2
Climate Change Mitigation in Models

Climate change mitigation can be represented differently in models and scenarios. Initially, three roughly complementary strategies for the avoidance of CO_2 emissions can be categorised.

1. Increased efficiency in terms of how energy is provided and consumed is the first, largest and usually most cost-effective greenhouse gas mitigation potential, not least because this saves future energy costs. In the past 200 years, the economy has continuously grown faster than the energy demand (Figure 4.2-2), the energy intensity of the global economic output has therefore continuously decreased. Apart from changes to the economic structure, and the increasing significance of the tertiary sector, technical improvements in energy efficiency are particularly effective. Improvements regarding end-use efficiency are especially relevant, as these have a multiplication effect on the primary energy demand. Every unit of power that is saved replaces three units of primary energy and their emissions, as long as the energy is generated on a fossil basis. However, improvements with regard to end-use efficiency are impeded by the fact that they frequently have to occur close to the consumer. They involve many actors, institutions and technologies, possibly also norms and behaviour patterns. The supply side of the energy system, on the other hand (for example electric power generation), is characterised by a high degree of centralisation, making technical changes easier to implement.
2. Energy supply decarbonisation is a general trend in the technical evolution of energy systems, advancing at a rate of around 0.3% over the past 150 years (Nakicenovic, 1996). In the long term average, energy-related greenhouse gas emissions have risen at a slower rate than energy consumption (Figure 4.2-1). This process is caused by the substitution of high-carbon energy carriers with a relatively low energy density, such as biomass and coal, with energy carriers which contain less carbon and have a higher energy density (such as oil, gas), and forms of energy almost entirely free of greenhouse gases (nuclear energy, renewable sources). The general trend on the demand side towards on-grid energy carriers (electricity, gas), which are safer and easier to use for consumers, supports this movement. A number of technical options are available to accelerate this process, including expansion of the energies low in greenhouse gas emissions (renewable sources, nuclear energy), as well as the technical capture and storage of carbon dioxide (CCS). However, in the years since 2000, a 'recarbonisation' of the global energy system could be observed, diverging from the long-term trend. This was caused primarily by the rapid expansion of coal-powered power plants for electricity generation in China.
3. A number of measures can increase carbon uptake and storage in soils during agricultural and forestry use, and revert soil erosion and humus loss trends (Section 7.3.7). This includes initiatives to stop deforestation, and to protect forest areas from fires. Beyond climate change mitigation, measures such as these offer a great number of social and ecosystem-relevant co-benefits; however, apart from investments in infrastructure, for example in irrigation systems or nutrient supply, they frequently require manifold changes to institutional structures, for instance land reforms. Friedlingstein et al. (2010) report recent progress with regard to the containment of land-use related CO_2 emissions: according to their analyses, these have gone down from 5 Gt per year in 2000 to currently around 3.2 Gt.

The scenarios introduced in the following section can be compared on the basis of the core parameters elaborated above (for example, rates of change in the greenhouse gas emission intensity of the energy, the energy intensity of GDP, GDP and final consumption per capita, etc.), and also on the basis of differences in combining the measures introduced here. Ultimately, it is not only CO_2 emissions that impact climate change mitigation – other greenhouse gas emissions are also relevant. However, these are not explicitly included in the calculation in all of the scenarios featured here.

4.2.3 Scenarios

The following section outlines 14 scenarios and model results that show possible alternative paths for a transformation into a low-carbon energy system. Each of the scenarios consists of a combination of plausible measures, which determine future emissions trends. The models used differ considerably in their complexity, reaching from simple table calculations to fully integrated assessment models that depict the links between the economy, the energy system and environmental processes with a high spatial and temporal resolution. The following introduces the models and scenarios taken into consideration.

Based on the MESSAGE model, scenarios have been calculated for the *Global Energy Assessment* (GEA, 2011) which, apart from the target of climate stabilisation, also examine numerous co-benefits of a transformative change of the energy systems. Apart from the challenge of providing universal access to energy services, implications for supply security and air pollution, for example, are also analysed. To meet all of these requirements concurrently is the normative aim of the scenarios. Three scenarios were developed for the Global Energy Assessment; these are complemented by sub-scenarios featuring technology variants (the numbering of the models in the following sections equals the order of the scenarios shown in Figure 4.2-2, from left to right): GEA-Efficiency (1) is a scenario group that pays special attention to the maximum use of energy efficiency, particularly on the demand side. The scenario group entitled GEA-Mix (2) describes a middle path with a balanced combination of technology elements. It is therefore situated between the two extreme positions of scenario group GEA-Efficiency (1) and GEA-Supply (3). GEA-Supply emphasises the possibilities offered by technology development on the supply side of the energy system, and advances in transport technologies and other growth sectors (Riahi et al., 2010).

In preparation for the IPCC's Fifth Assessment Report scheduled for 2014, Representative Concentration Pathways (RCP) for alternative development trends are currently being developed (IIASA, 2009). The most complex scenario used there was developed with the aid of the IMAGE model, and aims at stabilising the climate at less than 3 W per m² (van Vuuren et al., 2007). It is entitled IMAGE 3PD (4) (peak and decline), and describes a path where the concentration of greenhouse gases peaks in 2040, declining subsequently – reaching a maximum anthropogenic radiative forcing of 3 W per m² during this process, declining to 2.6–2.8 W per m² over the remainder of the 21st century.

The REMIND model (5) was used for the RECIPE (Report on Energy and Climate Policy in Europe) project, sponsored by the WWF and the Allianz Versicherung insurance company (Edenhofer et al., 2009a).

The EU project ADAM (Adaptation and Mitigation Strategies) included, amongst others, a comparison between model results obtained by various European research groups with the models REMIND (6), MERGE ETL (7) and POLES (9) (Edenhofer et al., 2010).

The scenario ETP blue (8) was created for the IEA report 'Energy Technology Perspectives 2008' with the aid of the Markal model.

At IIASA, scenarios entitled 'Global Energy Perspectives' were calculated in cooperation with the World Energy Council, using the MESSAGE model (Nakicenovic et al., 1998). One scenario, named C1 (10), is introduced here.

The energy system model MESAP was used by the German Aerospace Centre (DLR) to develop scenarios on behalf of Greenpeace and the European Renewable Energy Council under the title 'Energy [R]evolution'. The first of these studies was published in 2007, updated in 2008 (EREC and Greenpeace, 2008) (11), and reviewed in 2010 (12). This year, another, more ambitious scenario variant entitled 'Advanced Energy [R]evolution' (13) was added (EREC and Greenpeace, 2010).

The scenario entitled 'WBGU' (14) discusses the vision of meeting the energy demand in full with renewable energy carriers by 2050. It is based on extrapolation of the current expansion rates of these energy sources. The respective assumptions were already described in detail in Section 4.1.5.

Further details on the scenarios are shown in Table 4.2-1. The contrasting respective primary and final energy demands in the various scenarios, analysed according to energy carrier or energy form, respectively, are shown in Figure 4.2-4 and Figure 4.2-5. To allow comparison, the historical development of energy consumption between 1800 and 2008 is also illustrated, and the development path 'GEA Efficiency' from 2010 to 2050. Figure 4.2-6 shows the respective relative contributions of the individual energy sources and types of final use. All representations use direct equivalents to describe primary energy (Section 4.1).

4.2.4 Scenario Comparison

The GEA scenarios (2011), developed using the models MESSAGE and IMAGE, have an aggressive restriction of demand increase to 375–481 EJ final energy in 2050 in common. In the case of GEA-Efficiency, final energy demand in 2050 is hardly more than the current demand level of 352 EJ in 2008. The energy carrier mix, however, shows significant differences: 33–41% of final energy demand is in the form of electricity, more than double the 2008 amount (17%). The relative share of solid energy carriers reduces by around half (from currently 23% to 12–14%). The importance of liquid fuels, which currently dominate final energy with 42%, also falls to 23–37%, most significantly in the scenario GEA-Supply. The category 'other energy forms' includes direct heat use such as solar heating systems, as well as zone and district heating (for instance with CHP technology). These technologies multiply their contribution to final energy in all GEA scenarios from currently 11 EJ (3%) to 17–65 EJ (4–13%) by 2050. The supply side also shows significant shifts: the contribution coal and oil render to primary energy is reduced by around half, the contributions made by biomass and hydropower roughly double, and the category 'other renewable energies' (mainly wind and solar power) shows a growth factor of around 100 over the next 40 years in these scenarios. In the scenario GEA-Efficiency, climate change mitigation can be achieved whilst concurrently phasing out the use of nuclear energy. Current contri-

Table 4.2-1

Comparison of transformative energy scenarios in terms of cumulative CO_2 emissions up to 2050, and the probability of exceeding 2 °C. The scenarios marked with an * do not include all anthropogenic CO_2 emissions. Non-CO_2 greenhouse gases and land-use related emissions were not taken into account in these scenarios. Emissions from international air and maritime traffic, fugitive emissions, and process-related emissions from the industrial sector are also not included in some of the marked scenarios. To include the shares that were not taken into account (which is necessary in order to determine the probability of exceeding 2 °C), corrective factors were used, based on the relative contributions of these activities in 2005. The probabilities of exceeding 2 °C were calculated with the aid of the '2 °C-Check' tool from the supplementary material accompanying the publication of Meinshausen et al. (2009).

§ Carbon Prices in US$ per t CO_2eq.

Source: WBGU, based on the data sources cited in Figure 4.2-4

No.	Model, scenario name	Cumulative CO_2 emissions from fossil sources 2000–2049 [Gt CO_2]	Probability of exceeding 2 °C without CCS [%]	CCS by 2050 [Gt CO_2]	of which bio-CCS [Gt CO_2]	Probability of exceeding 2 °C with CCS [%]	Average growth rate of renewable energies 2010–2050 [%/year]	CO_2 prices [US$/t CO_2] 2030	2050
(1)	MESSAGE, GEA Efficiency	1,496	56	192	4,6	40	3	23	60§
(2)	MESSAGE, GEA Mix	1,391	47	92	4,6	40	3.5	67	177§
(3)	MESSAGE, GEA Supply	1,444	52	259	4,6	34	3.5	53	140§
(4)	IMAGE, RCP 3 PD	1,434	51	164	102	33	3	86	165
(5)	REMIND, RECIPE	1,455	51	77	35	43	4.4	22	92
(6)	REMIND, Adam	1,229	36	172	92	24	4.5	49	75
(7)	MERGE, ETL Adam	1,345	43	83	33	36	2,1	14	45
(8)	MARKAL, ETP Blue	?	?	59			3.6		
(9)	POLES, Adam	1,144	42	310	32	16	3.2	35	135
(10)	MESSAGE, WEC C1	1,138*	53				2		
(11)	MESAP, Energy [R]evolution 2008	?	?				3.7	30	50
(12)	MESAP, Energy [R]evolution 2010	1,107*	50				3.5	30	50
(13)	MESAP, Advanced Energy [R]evolution 2010	970*	38				4.1	30	50
(14)	WBGU	1,017*	41				4.8		

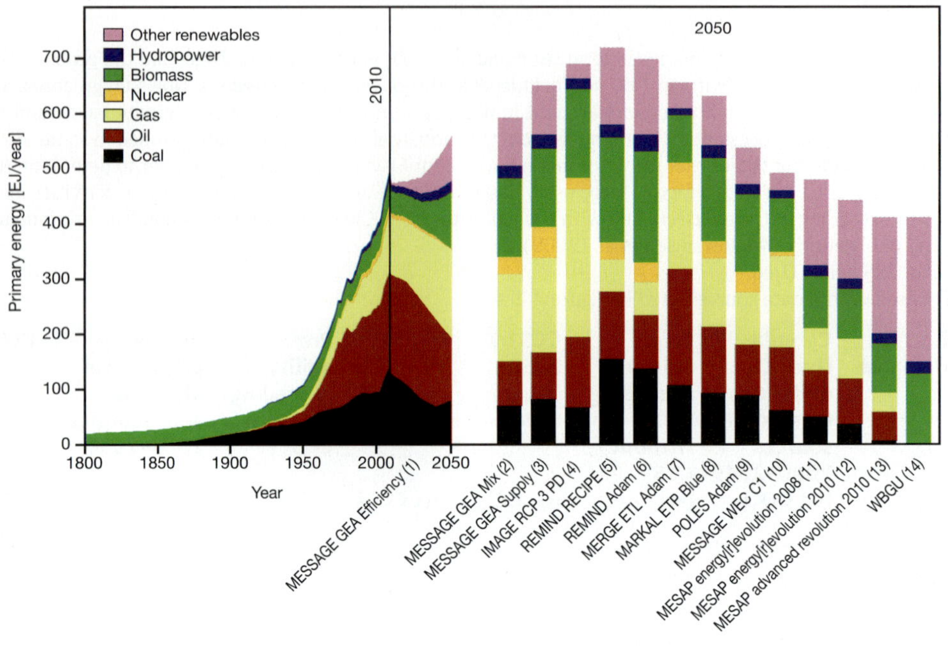

Figure 4.2-4
Global primary energy demand in transformative scenarios, broken down according to energy carriers. For the period 1800 to 2008, actual primary energy demand is shown; for the period between 2010 and 2050, the results from the MESSAGE GEA Efficiency scenario are shown. On the right-hand side, there is an overview of the other scenarios analysed: the figure shows the energy mix in 2050 for each respective scenario. Important characteristics of these scenarios are summarised in Table 4.2-1. Source: WBGU, based on data by Nakicenovic, 1998; EREC and Greenpeace, 2008, 2010; IEA, 2008b; Edenhofer et al., 2009a, 2010; IIASA, 2009; GEA, 2011

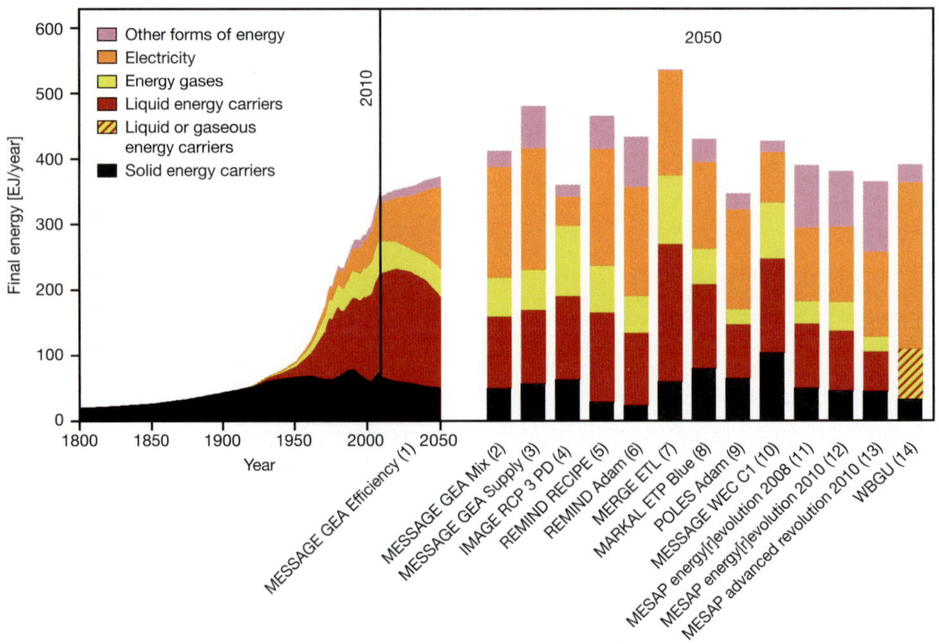

Figure 4.2-5
Global primary energy demand in transformative scenarios, broken down according to energy forms. For the period 1800 to 2008, actual final energy demand is shown, the figures for the period between 2010 and 2050 are taken from the MESSAGE GEA Efficiency scenario; on the right-hand side there is an overview of the other scenarios analysed: the figure shows the final energy demand and its mix in 2050 for each respective scenario.
Source: WBGU, based on the data shown in Figure 4.2-4

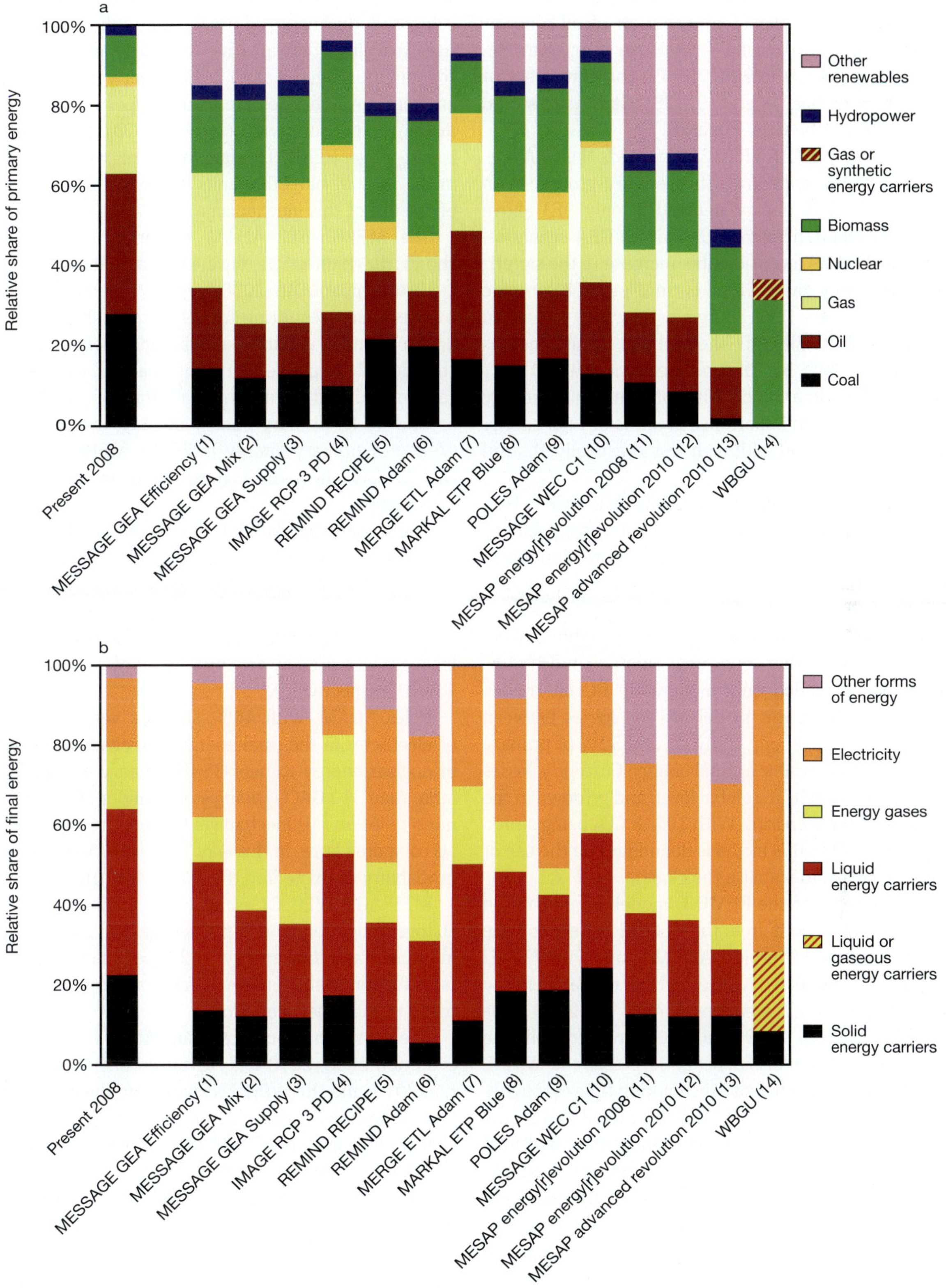

Figure 4.2-6
Current (2008) relative mix of primary (top) and final (bottom) energy, and mix in 2050, on the basis of various transformative scenarios (Table 4.2-1; Figures 4.2-4, 4.2-5).
Source: WBGU, based on the data shown in Figure 4.2-4

butions by fossil energy carriers of 85% are reduced to 63–52%, and the overall contribution of all renewable energies rises at around 3–3.5% per year, from currently 13% (64 EJ) to 205–257 EJ, the equivalent of 37–43% of primary energy. 92–259 Gt CO_2 are stored through CCS in the GEA scenarios.

The scenario IMAGE RCP 3PD exceeds the GEA scenarios in the restriction of final energy growth: with 361 EJ, the final energy demand is only 9EJ above 2008 consumption figures. Unlike the GEA scenarios, this model shows a considerable increase in the significance of energy gases. These currently (2008) provide roughly as much final energy as electricity (around 16%). IMAGE PCP 3PD shows their significance as increasing to 30% by 2050, whereas the share of electricity declines to around 12%. Solid and liquid energy carriers decrease in importance in terms of final energy in this scenario, too, although less drastically than in the GEA scenarios.

With regard to primary energy, IMAGE RCP 3 PD's significant shifts concern the rapid increase of bioenergy: by 2050, their contribution rises more than threefold to around 160 EJ, the contribution made by coal sinks from 28% to 10% of primary energy, and the contribution made by oil products is also roughly halved. By comparison, other renewable energies and hydropower are expanded only moderately in this model. Strikingly high in this model are the losses between primary and final energy: only around 52% of primary energy becomes usable as final energy. Currently, losses are running at 29% at a global level, and go down in the majority of the scenarios. With 102 Gt CO_2 being stored through bio-CCS, this model is dominated by the use of this mechanism to stabilise the climate.

Two versions of the REMIND model were analysed here. Both the results from the RECIPE project and the results from the EU project ADAM show, with 717 EJ and 696 EJ, respectively, the highest primary energy consumption of all scenarios (145% of 2008 consumption figures). At 190 and 200 EJ respectively, the assumed expansion of bioenergy surpasses the IMAGE model's values and current consumption figures roughly by a factor of four. Like IMAGE, this model also shows extensive conversion losses between primary and final energy: only 62–65% of primary energy is turned into final energy. This is due in particular to the relatively high losses in the processing of biomass into superior energy carriers, and the losses through coal-powered electricity generation (including CCS). On the side of final energy use, the REMIND results have many characteristics in common with the GEA scenarios: at 38%, electricity again becomes the dominant energy carrier, whereas solid energy carriers are reduced by a factor of 4 to merely 6% of final energy consumption. In these scenarios, too, the 51–77 EJ contribution made by the category 'other energy forms' (mainly direct heat use) rises to values that are five to seven times the 2008 consumption figures. At 4.5-4.8% per year, renewable energies' growth rates are in the upper region of this model comparison; with 77–172 Gt CO_2, the CCS total is mid-range. REMIND Adam, however, with 92 Gt CO_2 in the form of bio-CCS, ranks in second place in terms of the use of this mechanism.

The MERGE-ETL ADAM scenario, with 535 EJ, shows the highest increase in final energy demand (+52% compared to 2008 level). With liquid energy carriers then accounting for 39%, their share reduces only marginally. Again, electricity and energy gases are considerably expanded, and the share of solid energy carriers reduced to around half that of 2008. With around 50 EJ primary energy of nuclear energy each (7–8% of primary energy in 2050), MERGE ETL and GEA-Supply, show the highest values in this scenario comparison.

The scenario Markal ETP Blue, published by the IEA during the course of Energy Technology Perspectives 2008, is characterised on the demand side by increases in electricity demand to 30% of final energy. On the side of primary energy, both nuclear energy and biomass are increased by around a factor of 3 (to 30 EJ and 150 EJ, respectively).

Poles ADAM, with 44%, shows a very high share of electricity in the final energy, and again an increase in nuclear energy to over 35 EJ primary energy. With more than 310 Gt CO_2 being stored under CCS, this scenario relies on this mechanism the most of all the models compared here. In this way, it manages to reduce the probability of exceeding the 2 °C to only 16%.

MESSAGE WEC C1 is an early, ambitious climate change mitigation model, marked by high shares of gas in primary and final energy. At 2% per year, the growth rates for renewable energy carriers are low here, compared to the other scenarios.

The remaining four scenarios, MESAP Energy [R] evolution 2008, 2010 and Advanced Energy [R]evolution 2010, and the WBGU scenario, are the most ambitious in this comparison. All of them feature a primary energy consumption in 2050 that is lower than the current level, even allowing for a slight increase in final energy demand. This is possible because all four scenarios rely on a massive expansion of renewable electricity generation through wind and photovoltaic energy that surpasses even the REMIND scenarios (annual renewable energy increase rates of between 3.7 and 4.8%). Particularly the scenario Advanced Energy [R]evolution 2010 also features an increase in the use of geothermal energy. In the MESAP scenarios, the increase factors for primary energy production from these sources for the period 2008 to 2050 are somewhere between factors 165 and 228; the WBGU scenario assumes a factor of 284. In all of the four scenarios, the final energy demand is dominated by electricity, with 29–65%. In the WBGU scenario, overall electricity production by 2050 is increased by a factor of 4.2. All four scenarios assume a global phasing out of nuclear technologies, and abstention from CCS.

4.2.5 Discussion

All of the scenarios selected here feature a significant restriction of final energy demand, with only one expecting more than 500 EJ final energy consumption in 2050, whilst some remain below 350 EJ, which corresponds to the current consumption level. There is also a concurrence regarding a considerable transformation of the final energy form, with a massive increase in on-grid energies, i.e. the considerable growth of electricity and gas as final energy. The requisite carbon prices are in the region of 14 and US$ 86 per t CO_2 in 2030, and US$ 45–165 per t CO_2 in 2050.

Without exception, all scenarios feature ambitious expansion rates for renewable energies, most with average growth rates of more than 3%, or even 4% per year over the 40-year period from 2010 to 2050. In four of the 14 scenarios compared, over 300 EJ primary energy per year can be provided by renewable energy sources by 2050. However, this is only sufficient in scenarios with a significantly reduced final energy demand to reach a high percentage of renewable energies in primary energy. The scenarios that feature ambitiously controlled growth of final energy demand thereby create action paths on the supply side that allow the relinquishment of nuclear energy, whilst keeping fossil energy consumption in combination with CCS at a low level.

Technology variants within individual scenarios (knock-out or second-best-world variants), as carried out in integrated assessment models, for example with MESSAGE in the GEA scenarios or in the REMIND model (Edenhofer et al., 2009a; Leimbach et al., 2010), indicate that restricting the technology portfolio would substantially increase climate stabilisation costs, for example if at the same time the biomass potential is limited, CCS is only available to a limited extent, nuclear energy is phased out, and no technical learning progress is made with regard to wind and solar technologies. The consumption losses through climate stabilisation calculated in the models then rise from 1% to up to 4.2% of GDP, and it is doubtful whether the substitution of energy through capital assumed in the models can be solved in reality. Only few of the analysed scenarios stay considerably below the 2°C emissions budget of less than 750 Gt CO_2 from fossil sources between 2010 and 2050 (Box 1.1-1), and achieve a probability of more than 66% with regard to limiting global warming to 2°C. The WBGU estimates that 314 Gt CO_2 have already been emitted in the period from 2000 to 2010. The cumulated CO_2 emissions shown in the first column of Table 4.2-1, less those 314 Gt CO_2, therefore provide a benchmark for the scenarios' cumulated emissions for the period 2010 to 2050. Applying this rough calculation reveals that only MESAP Advanced Revolution and WBGU would comply with the 750 Gt CO_2 budget.

In general, the 2°C target is defined across the whole of the 21st century, and some of the integrated assessment models, for instance (4), pursue so-called overshoot trajectories to allow for an initial overshooting of the safe emissions budget, which is then compensated for later through substantial negative emissions during the second half of the 21st century. Assuming this precondition again allows higher probabilities than those discernible by 2050 to make it highly likely that global warming can be kept below 2°C.

Not all of the models listed in Table 4.2-1 were able to include emissions from land use, and the emission of greenhouse gases other than CO_2. In those cases (marked with an * in column 2 of Table 4.2.-1), the evaluation of climate compatibility featured in scenarios (10), (11), (12), (13) and (14) is based mainly on the analysis of CO_2 emissions from fossil energy carriers - other emissions were estimated based on their relative contributions in 2005 (Table 4.2-1). This meta-analysis of climate change mitigation and energy scenarios allows the conclusion, from the WBGU's point of view, that a complete decarbonisation of the energy systems is possible, and achievable, to allow a roughly 50% probability of compliance with the 2°C guard rail. However, in order to achieve this, the conversion of the energy systems must be considerably accelerated. A conversion that merely allows incremental deviations from a seemingly fixed BAU path will not lead to a transformation.

Whether and how the transformation can succeed, however, is certainly not going to be decided within the energy systems alone. Numerous factors which cannot be illustrated in the current models influence feasibility. The growth of global energy demand, for example, will have a major impact on the room for manoeuvre during the conversion of the energy systems: the more successful we are in limiting the global rise in energy demand over the next few decades, the sooner we can abstain from using risky technologies such as nuclear energy and CCS. In many areas of life, changes which are worth pursuing anyway, or necessary in any case, can be utilised to unlock efficiency and savings potentials. One example of this is the advancing urbanisation: its form will be one of the deciding factors for the demands that a future energy system must meet.

4.3 Implications for Areas of Need

The following intends to take a look at the implications a transformation towards sustainability and climate change mitigation has for the various demand sectors, or consumption fields. It is outlined how current consumption practices and behaviours have to change in order to comply with the guard rail (Section 1.1) whilst ensuring that the whole of the global population has access to the energy-based services associated with prosperity (Section 1.2.4). The focus is, firstly, on the direct and indirect energy demand created by the sectors. The restriction of the global final energy demand, concurrent with the increased provision of energy services (particularly in developing countries) is an important precondition for making the conversion of energy systems, and compliance with the 2 °C guard rail, possible (Section 4.2). In addition, there is also a focus on limiting those greenhouse gas emissions which are not energy-related, but caused directly or indirectly by various consumption fields.

A large part of the global population still has no access to modern forms of energy, i.e. to services in the areas of need defined here. 1.5–2.5 billion people have inadequate or no access to electricity, and around 3 billion people still use traditional biomass for cooking, and sometimes also for heating. This has serious economic and social consequences, as well as having an adverse effect on their health (IEA et al., 2010b). Frequently, there is also a lack of access to sufficient mechanical energy for transport and agriculture. Whilst these figures, without targeted measures, could even increase slightly, the provision of universal access to a minimum level of modern energy is still achievable by 2030, despite the expected population growth in the regions concerned (IEA et al., 2010b; AGECC, 2010; GEA, 2011). The transformation of the energy systems in developed countries and the provision of access to modern energy services in countries where this is not yet universally given can trigger synergies, which should be utilised to achieve these two transformations at the same time (AGECC, 2010). The development and commercialisation of more efficient technologies, for example LED lighting, to lower electricity consumption in countries with universal access to electricity also improves the opportunities for accessing electric lighting in rural areas, as it is easier to cover the lesser need for electricity despite higher capital investment costs. This applies in particular to decentralised stand-alone systems. Although not all technologies are directly transferable, the majority of new technologies, such as smart grids, for example, are also well-suited for establishing decentralised networks for rural electrification. Furthermore, the provision of a sustainable energy supply prevents the acquisition of CO_2-intensive technologies like diesel generators, thereby avoiding path dependencies in terms of increasing costs and greenhouse gas emissions (Casillas and Kammen, 2010).

The following initially elaborates briefly the methods which can be used to allocate the overall direct and indirect environmental impact, such as emissions, to the various consumption activities. Subsequently, the scientific findings with regard to current emissions and short- to medium-term reduction potentials are illustrated for four central needs categories, complemented by an elaboration of some exemplary transformative changes in these areas. These are intended to demonstrate potential and conceivable changes that make the future extension of this particular consumption category possible without impacting on the natural life-support systems.

Lifecycle Analyses to Allocate Emissions

The data on direct emissions of the various sectors is relatively well-known, not least because they are reported by national governments to the UNFCCC on a regular basis. Far more difficult, and also more challenging in methodological terms, is the causal attribution of environmental impact, such as, for example, emissions or water consumption, to consumption fields on the basis of process chains and lifecycle analyses. Hertwich and Peters (2009) analysed the greenhouse gas footprint, i.e. direct and indirect emissions, for eight consumption categories and 87 countries or regions for the year 2001 (Figure 4.3-1). Greenhouse gas emissions from the use of fossil fuels, process emissions, and agricultural methane and nitrous oxide emissions were all taken into account. This analysis does not include CO_2 emissions relating to Land Use, Land-Use Change and Forestry (LULUCF). Production-related emissions have been allocated on a pro-rata basis to the components of macroeconomic demand (household consumption, government consumption, investments, net trade) in order to include spacial shifts of environmental pressure caused by trade. If, for example, a country imports raw materials and industrial goods, the emissions caused by the production are allocated to the end-user in the recipient country. The authors conclude that 72% of overall emissions were related to household consumption, 10% could be allocated to government consumption, and 18% were connected to investments.

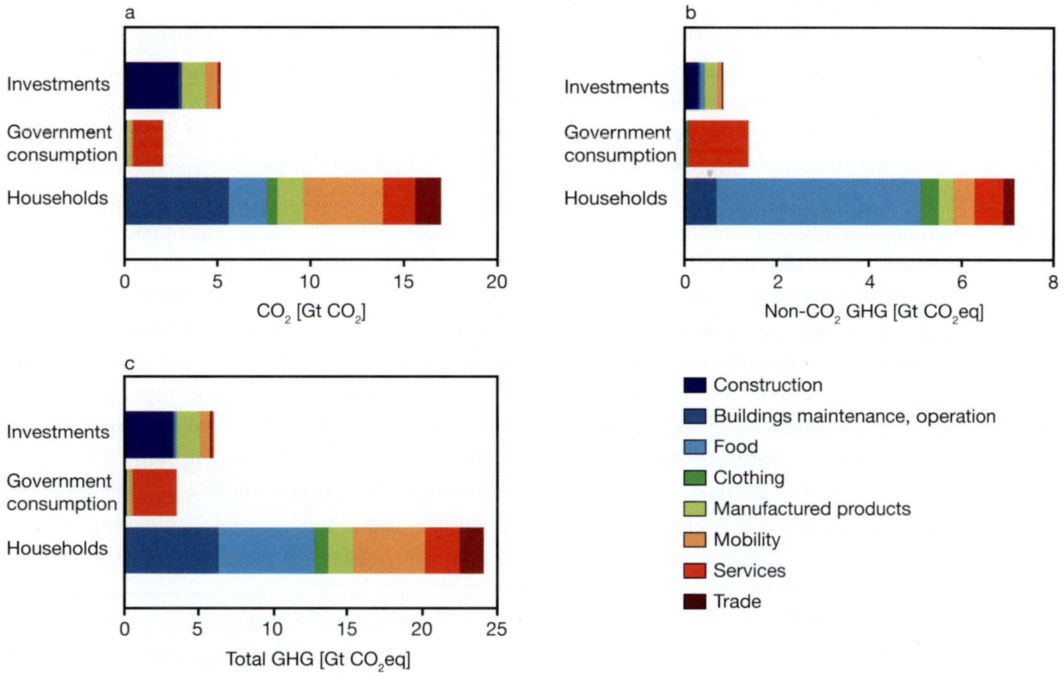

Figure 4.3-1
Greenhouse-gas footprint of various consumption categories in 2001.
Source: Hertwich and Peters, 2009

This analysis shows food to be the consumption field which has the most impact on overall emissions, followed by operation and maintenance of shelter and mobility. If only CO_2 emissions are considered, on the other hand, food has much less influence, with shelter and mobility dominating here. However, it should be kept in mind that this analysis does not include CO_2 emissions from land use and land-use changes (i.e. also those caused by deforestation). But, as particularly for the food category, agriculture is one of the driving forces of land-use changes (Section 4.3.4), the factual relevance of the consumption field food for climate change is higher than represented here.

A consumption-based analysis of the emissions also shows clearly that the influence which consumers, through their consumption decisions, have on climate change mitigation is not limited to their own country. Davis and Caldeira (2010) show that in 2004, 23% of global CO_2 emissions from fossil energy carriers (6.2 Gt CO_2) were related to internationally traded goods. The majority were exports to industrialised nations from China and other newly industrialising countries. The net emissions 'imported' by Germany in this way amounted to 2.8 t CO_2 per capita. Taking this perspective, Germany's emissions responsibility per capita increases from 10.7 t CO_2 to 13.5 t CO_2 for 2004.

4.3.1 Sustainable Production and Sustainable Consumption: Emissions Reduction and Circular Economy

4.3.1.1 Reducing Direct and Indirect Emissions

In 2004, the production of industrial goods generated emissions amounting to 12 Gt CO_2eq, the largest part of which (9.9 Gt CO_2eq) was caused directly and indirectly by energy use. The energy-intensive industries alone (iron and steel industry, metals, chemicals industry, cement, glass) were responsible for around 85% of this (IPCC, 2007c). As the demand for products from the energy-intensive industries will continue to increase over the coming decades due to the high consumption levels in the developed countries, the global population growth and the rapid economic development in the newly industrialising nations, it is vital that production process specific emissions are substantially reduced. In the medium and long term, the transition into a circular economy is inevitable. Apart from reducing the raw materials needed and the raw material intensity, this also allows, in principle, a reduction of energy demand and greenhouse gas emissions. The gradual increase of recycled proportions, particularly of metals, is already contributing to a reduced energy demand (IPCC,

2007c). In the short to medium term, absolute material flows will however continue to increase, such that additional raw materials must be extracted, and significant emissions reductions must also be achieved for the traditional use of raw materials. There are also significant further potentials for efficiency improvement: the universal conversion of production techniques to the best available efficiency technologies alone could lead to an emissions reduction of 12–26% (IEA, 2010a). The use of renewable energies can also contribute considerably. In the light of limited sustainable potentials (WBGU, 2010a), and the other options for biomass use, it must be carefully deliberated to what extent biomass should be used for the generation of industrial process heat. It would therefore be preferable to increase the use of electricity from renewable sources, and energy efficiency, for example through the utilisation of waste heat. In particular with regard to direct, non-energy-related process emissions, which amounted to a total of 1.4 Gt CO_2 for the year 2007 (WRI-CAIT, 2011), CCS should be developed ready for use as an additional mitigation strategy. The availability of this technology could reduce direct industrial emissions (including energy-related emissions) by a total of 1.7–2.5 Gt CO_2 in 2050 (IEA, 2010a).

Consideration of Lifecycle Impact

Even though a substantial reduction of the specific emissions in the industrial production should be achieved as soon as possible, various factors must be carefully considered with regard to the conversion of current production forms. The optimisation of one environmental impact, for example of energy consumption or greenhouse gas emissions, must not lead to the neglecting of other aspects, such as water consumption, toxicity, resource consumption or social impact. The entire product lifecycle should be considered here, i.e. all the impacts of manufacture, transport, use and disposal of the products. Only a comprehensive analysis of lifecycle impact can serve as the basis for informed technology decisions. To furnish such a comprehensive analysis, the data basis for goods production and usage processes should be improved. The collection of all relevant information regarding resource outlay (extraction and use) and environmental impact of production processes should be standardised to achieve a more detailed regional and sectoral breakdown of the data. If uniform databases were to be established, it would allow the comparative evaluation of different products and methods of production.

4.3.1.2
Transition into a Circular Economy

Natural ecosystems are characterised by the functional full circularity and integration of material cycles: the waste products of one group of organisms are usually used by other life-forms as a resource and raw material basis. A forward-looking design makes it possible to organise industrial production processes in the same way, such that secondary products and waste heat from one process, along with used products, can form the basis for further production processes (Braungart and McDonough, 2002). This creates a material flow cycle, so that both the introduction of new raw materials and the disposal of non-usable residue can be reduced to a minimum. The process of applying the energy still required by the various processes should be as efficient as possible and reliant on renewable energies; however, the amount required is generally less than when using raw materials. Manufacturing aluminium from recycled material, for example, requires only 5% of the energy needed for producing the same amount of raw aluminium from bauxite. Recycling also considerably reduces the amount of energy needed for processing a number of other metals, and paper (IPCC, 2007c).

The speedy adoption of this design principle for all production and consumption processes is a prerequisite for expanding industrial production further whilst still complying with the guard rails (Section 1.1). Pioneers in this respect include, for example, 'eco-industrial clusters' such as the city of Kalundborg in Denmark, demonstrating how the proper integration of different branches of industry, communal infrastructure and agricultural user groups can function under the dictum of waste avoidance and improved resource efficiency (Jacobsen, 2006).

Resource efficiency must not be limited to the production phase, even if this part of the lifecycle is frequently accompanied by significant emissions. The actual use is also often, for instance in the case of long-life consumer products like household appliances, electronics or vehicles, associated with considerable operating costs in the form of energy and other resources. The end of the lifecycle – for the consumer frequently the only point in time at which they are confronted with the resource dimension of their consumption – raises the question of how to dispose of a product that cannot be used any longer. Good design makes the extension of product lifecycles through repairs possible, ensures that at least parts of it are directly reusable, and, if that is not possible, enables the materials to be safely recycled. Electronic products in particular often contain heavy metals and other toxins that pose a hazard for both humans and nature, or larger amounts of rare earths and precious metals which, for reasons of resource preservation, should not be wasted.

In most OECD countries, the expansion of recycling systems as part of extended manufacturer and consumer responsibility is a key focus of environmental policy, and an element of 'green growth' and 'green jobs' strategies (OECD, 2009b). Also, numerous newly industrialising countries, such as China and Korea, have presented ambitious plans and legislation with the aim of creating a circular economy (the 'Circular Economy Law of the People's Republic of China', for instance). However, converting to new business models that provide manufacturers with incentives for recycling-friendly product design could make an even more effective contribution to raising the recycling quota than policy-based obligations. One such business model would, for example, be specialising in the recycling of production waste and product components. Toyota, for instance, has initiated a new business model for recycling used nickel-metal hybrid batteries from hybrid cars with the companies Toyota Chemical Engineering, Sumitomo Metal Mining and Primearth EV Energy (PEVE). The nickel part is extracted, so it can be reused for the manufacture of new hybrid batteries (Toyota Motor Corporation, 2010). Similar business models would be conceivable across the whole recycling sector, and, in view of rising energy and resource prices, in the long run, they would be competitive.

However, recycling systems are generally costly in terms of transport and energy consumption, which limits the dimensions at which it still makes sense to recycle. Urban areas, as production site centres and consumer bases, are particularly suitable locations for the functional integration of material flows. The principles of a circular economy can be demonstrated and optimised here with relatively little effort.

Efficiency Gains through New Consumption Models and Technological Trends

There are several comprehensive technological trends and new consumption models that can contribute considerably to resource efficiency improvement in the medium term. Through targeted reinforcement of these trends, making transformative breakthroughs more likely (Chapter 3), they can also contribute to resource conservation.

- *Right to use instead of ownership:* In many fields, object ownership appears to be becoming less important (a car, for example, as a status symbol), whilst at the same time, the focus is shifting from selling towards offering rights of use and provision of services as a business model. Through car sharing, but also through the leasing of car components (for example the rechargeable batteries of electric cars), the overall material need is reduced, whilst the establishment of circular economic structures is made easier.
- *Dematerialisation:* This describes, on an abstract level, the trend towards a lower resource throughput per value creation unit. This is achieved by economic structural change, and through the conversion from industrial into service-based societies (tertiarisation), but also through the long-term substitution of materials, for example replacing the steel used in vehicle manufacturing with carbon fibre, or using aerated concrete instead of bricks in residential construction. Another example is precision farming, which uses geo-information systems and GPS to calculate fertiliser dosage, thus saving fertiliser and reducing water pollution.
- *Industrial use of renewable raw materials:* The replacement of mineral oil products with biogenic materials as industrial base materials, as envisaged in the BioEconomy Research Strategy (BMBF, 2010b; Section 8.1.4.2), reduces resource pressure and import dependency for countries which do not have own oil deposits. Provided that the sustainability criteria for agriculture are adhered to, biogenic materials form part of a closed material cycle, which at the same time contributes to the structural change towards a circular economy. However, in all probability, this will also lead to increased land-use competition (Section 1.2.5). According to WBGU estimates (2009a), if the per capita consumption were half as much as Germany's current consumption, then the area required for bio-based products (textiles, chemical products, plastics, bitumen and lubricants) for a global population of around 9 billion people would equal a total of around 10% of the world's agricultural land.
- *Green chemistry:* This describes a trend in which biological processes are increasingly simulated in applications in technical chemistry. Detergents and cleaning agents, for example, contain synthetically created enzymes (biocatalysts) that clean much more effectively at much lower temperatures than traditional washing powders. These days, the manufacturing processes can also often be carried out under atmospheric pressure, and resulting waste waters are much more biodegradable. This significantly reduces the energy expenditure over the whole lifecycle, as well as water pollution.
- *Nanotechnology:* The drastic reduction of particle and object sizes frequently leads to the creation of completely new properties: surface area is drastically increased in relation to volume, and a fraction of the matter needed for conventional processes can achieve similar catalytic effects. This technology also

Box 4.3-1

Building Services Engineering for Climate Change Mitigation

The energy consumption of existing buildings for heating and air conditioning can be drastically reduced through better insulation (around 80–90%). New buildings can be designed in such a way that they need almost no heating or cooling, generate the energy needed for heating and cooling on site, or can even become net energy producers through the integration of photovoltaic technology. Here, a few of these modern technologies are introduced. Some of these are still in the development stage, but they are promising candidates for the achieving of substantial energy savings.

Vacuum Thermal Insulation, Vacuum Glazing

Vacuum offers extremely good heat insulation whilst needing very little space. To vacuum insulate the facades of buildings, panels made from a microporous silicic acid core material are wrapped in foil impermeable to gas and steam. Vacuum insulation panels have an extremely low thermal conductivity, even with a rough vacuum of 1–10 mbar. Their insulating effect is five to ten times higher than that of conventional insulation systems; therefore, they are far more space-saving than other insulating materials whilst providing the same insulating effect. Vacuum glazing can be an affordable alternative to conventional thermal glazing, which is filled with expensive inert gases. The German Federal Ministry of Economics and Technology supports the further development and testing of vacuum insulation as part of its 'Energy Optimised Buildings – Innovative Building Materials' research programme. Vacuum insulation is not only suitable for facades and windows, but also for roofs and floors.

Transparent Thermal Insulation

Conventional insulation usually reduces the thermal flow from the inside to the outside, transparent thermal insulation additionally imports solar thermal gains into the house. Ordinary insulating materials reflect the sunlight before it hits the masonry. Transparent thermal insulation materials let the sunlight penetrate as far as the masonry, where large parts are collected by an absorption layer to allow solar heat to reach the inside of the house.

Transparent thermal insulation can be particularly useful in the renovation of period buildings. However, without adequate shading, the house can overheat in the summer. In future, this problem will be solved through electrically switchable layers (for example micro reflectors), which will safely avoid overheating by letting only so much solar radiation past as is needed for heating, and reflecting the remainder.

Lighting

LEDs should be used for the needs-based lighting of large areas in buildings. Replacing the sodium vapour lamps currently generally used to provide street lighting with LEDs can save a considerable amount of energy, not least because these are able to light up only targeted areas, and do not waste energy through all-round lighting of spaces where no light is required. Even today, the efficiency factors of some LEDs already exceed those of so-called energy-saving light bulbs (CFLs). LED efficiency factors can certainly be expected to increase even further.

Organic light-emitting diodes can be used for displays and the large-scale lighting of rooms.

harbours major advances for surface coatings, corrosion protection, or semiconductor electronics and photovoltaics, as the materials are often characterised by extremely high specific electrical or thermal conductivity, or stability, which can reduce the resources needed considerably.

4.3.2 Buildings, Living and Land-Use Planning

Energy-Efficient Buildings

In 2004, construction sector emissions amounted to 8.6 Gt CO_2, plus 2 Gt CO_2eq of other greenhouse gas emissions, three-quarters of which were CFC and HFCs (IPCC, 2007c). Around two-thirds of CO_2 emissions were not created in the buildings as such, but in the power plants which generated the electricity and heat used in the buildings. The construction sector transformation must therefore minimise the emissions caused by the complex overall system that is a building. This can be achieved through a combination of energy demand reduction, the use of low-carbon or renewable energy carriers, and the reduction of non-CO_2 emissions. As a consequence of the decarbonisation of the energy supply, measures to reduce energy demand will have less impact than they would have if conventional energy carriers were used. A combination of both strategies is nevertheless necessary in order to minimise emissions. This also has the advantage that delays with regard to technical innovation in the one strategy can be balanced by accelerated progress in the other, which contributes to the solidity of the transformation path.

As room climate control and warm water generation account for two-thirds of global buildings-related energy demand (IEA, 2008c), improved insulation of new buildings and the energy-efficient review and refurbishment of existing buildings (Box 4.3-1), particularly in the higher latitudes and along the equator, must enjoy absolute priority, as this promises substantial potential savings, often at negative costs (IEA, 2010a). Especially in the case of a decarbonised electricity sector, the use of heat pumps and combined heat and power technology can supply the remaining heat needed efficiently and with low emissions. Furthermore, the use of heat storage vessels and smart grids,

Box 4.3-2

Rebound Effect

In the context of energy consumption, the term rebound effect is used to describe increases in energy consumption that are the consequence of a technical innovation which has increased efficiency. A rebound effect can result from the fact that the consumption of an energy service (for example driving a vehicle, or using a household appliance) costs less to use than it did before a technical innovation, due to its subsequent lower energy consumption. This cost saving acts as an incentive for the consumer to increase their consumption of the service in future, or to intensify it (for example, driving longer distances with a more energy-efficient car, more frequent and longer use of an energy-efficient household appliance). This also applies at corporate level, as the improved energy-efficiency of a production process is an incentive to step up production due to costs saved. These direct effects are referred to as 'direct rebound'.

However, another possibility is that consumption of the respective energy service is kept constant despite the cost saving; instead, the demand for another energy service increases as a consequence of the costs saved (for example when the money saved through a more efficient car is invested in flying more frequently). Alternatively, the initial decrease in energy demand caused by the energy saving can lead to falling energy prices, which in turn motivates other consumers to consume more energy. These cases are referred to as 'indirect rebound'. Direct and indirect rebound together make up the total macroeconomic rebound (Sorrell, 2007).

The extent of rebound effects are difficult to estimate, and depend on the measured price flexibility of the energy used by various consumer goods. Direct rebound from residential heating and the use of privately owned cars in industrialised countries is estimated at between 10% and 30%, and varies in proportion with the share of energy costs as part of the operating costs of an appliance (currently still relatively high for running a car or a heating system, rather low for household appliances). Due to indirect rebound effects, overall macroeconomic rebound is probably slightly higher than 10–30% in the industrialised countries, however, certainly below 100%. In developing countries, however, the rebound effect, due to the unmet energy demand, probably even reaches values above 100%; this is called 'backfiring' (Sorrell, 2007; Herring, 2008).

In addition to the cost argument, the rebound effect can also be explained by socio-psychological research findings. According to Thaler's 'Mental Accounting' theory (Thaler, 1985, 1999), consumers usually keep mental accounts to which their consumption in various categories is allocated (for example, money spent on food, clothes, travel, etc.). In the perception of the consumer, the improved energy efficiency of a product can lead to 'credits' being booked to the 'mental account for environmental damage caused', which are now available to be 'spent' for additional environmentally damaging consumption.

The overall macroeconomic rebound effect mitigates the positive impact energy efficiency has on environment and climate, or even, in the worst case, annihilates it. One possibility for reducing the rebound effect is to gradually increase energy prices or carbon prices.

electricity can be consumed primarily in times with peak supply, so that both heat generation technologies contribute to power grid management. In addition, renewable sources such as solar thermal and geothermal energy and biomass can be used for supplying heat to buildings and local heat networks. In the IEA's BLUE Map scenario, the combination of all of these measures allows the reduction of fossil fuels directly used in buildings from 44 EJ in 2007 to only 25 EJ in 2050 (IEA, 2010a).

Even if energy consumption by lighting and other electrical appliances in households and in the service sector represents the lesser part of the energy demand of buildings, the efficiency increase potential of these appliances should be tapped, in addition to the decarbonisation of the electricity supply. As their use continues to increase through new kinds of appliances, and the trend towards more and larger appliances, this is the only way to achieve absolute greenhouse gas emissions reductions in this usage area. Efficiency increases through the use of LED-based lighting (Box 4.3-1), through new, energy-saving refrigeration appliances, improved computers and home media appliances, and the elimination of the stand-by losses of all appliances can lead to considerably less electricity being used in households. However, it must be considered that the effective electricity savings generated through these efficiency improvements may well turn out lower than the expected computed values due to changes in the consumers' behaviour. Usually, in the case of energy supply services, energy cost savings from improved efficiency tend to tempt consumers into increasing their demand for these energy services (for example operation of electrical appliances). In this way, a proportion of the savings is compensated through increased consumption (rebound effect; Box 4.3-2).

Overall, global buildings-related electricity consumption will increase even with these measures applied, due to the increased use of heat pumps and air conditioning; the IEA's BLUE Map scenario, for example, assumes an increase from 8,800 TWh in 2007 to just under 15,000 TWh in 2050. In total, through the decarbonisation of the electricity supply and the simultaneous introduction of cooling and heating measures, this scenario achieves a reduction of CO_2 emissions from buildings down to 2.6 Gt CO_2 by 2050, therefore a reduction of just under 70% compared with 2007.

The Buildings Sector in Germany

In Germany, the electricity needed by private households and the 'commerce, trade & services' sector will decrease by 2050, as calculated by the reference scenario in the energy study compiled for the federal government(EWI et al., 2010). Contrary to the global average, the equipment of households with a great number of electrical appliances is already so advanced that the efficiency increases overcompensate increases in use. Nevertheless, all energy savings efforts should continue, *firstly* to free electricity loads for other uses whilst also covering preferably the entire electricity supply with renewable potentials, which are only limited in Germany, and *secondly* because the development of efficient appliance technologies promotes their global use.

In industrialised countries like Germany, the long usage period of existing buildings is a major barrier when it comes to implementing the outlined conversion in heating. As three-quarters of the buildings currently in use in the industrialised countries will still be in use in 40 years' time (IEA, 2010a), the bigger part of the potential savings can only be realised through active promotion of energy-efficient refurbishment. Particularly the investment barriers in the case of residential and commercial lets (frequently referred to as the 'principal-agent barrier') must be removed, which can be achieved through a combination of tenancy law regulations, financial incentives, information campaigns and standard setting (IEA, 2007).

Transformation of the Buildings Sector and Spatial Planning

Overall, the buildings sector shows pronounced path dependencies, due to the existing building infrastructure. It is therefore particularly difficult to achieve a transformative change of consumption patterns here. The ownership structure of existing buildings is also strongly fragmented: a great number of actors must act to accomplish significant changes. To implement the optimal decarbonisation strategies, the respective actors must also reach a consensus in certain cases (for example local heat network, pedestrian-friendly spatial planning). Economically, the fragmentation of responsibilities has the effect that many of the initially cost-efficient refurbishment measures become uneconomical during the refurbishment planning stage, due to the high transaction costs.

Changes to business models can therefore make an important contribution to realising the transformation in the buildings sector as well. The Energy Service Companies (ESCO) model, or that of energy contracting, are examples of this. ESCOs take over the planning, carrying out, and upfront financing of energy efficiency measures for their clients as contracted partners, with any income generated by capital investment in the form of energy cost savings being passed onto the ESCOs. Accordingly, ESCOs are often trusts. This helps to overcome two further barriers preventing efficiency investments, apart from ownership fragmentation and the corresponding transaction costs: a lack of knowledge about efficiency technologies, and the resultant savings, and a lack of initial, upfront financing options. In Germany, the regional energy agencies and DENA's Centre of Expertise for Contracting provide information and advice regarding energy savings contracting.

Energy contracting, however, plays a role not only in terms of one-off efficiency investments, but also in the efficient continuous provision of energy services. In Germany, the electricity provider Lichtblick, for example, offers customers the installation of small-scale CHP units in their basements in cooperation with Volkswagen. These units are then operated and maintained by Lichtblick. Apart from a one-off payment for the installation, and a monthly service charge, the customer only has the running costs to pay for heating, simultaneously receiving a monthly rental income for the space the unit occupies, plus an annual rebate on their heating bills for the power fed into the grid (Lichtblick, 2010).

Spatial planning path dependencies are even more pronounced, as the usage timeframe for the respective infrastructures is considerably longer even than the timeframe for the capital goods related to buildings and their energy use (Figure 4.3-2). However, as spatial planning and infrastructure have a major influence on transport systems (Section 4.3.3), rapidly growing cities must plan land use in a way that is compatible with sustainable mobility systems. For existing urban structures, on the other hand, framework conditions must be created which allow the transformation of land use whilst largely preserving the major existing structures. Examples of this could be the redevelopment of inner-city areas to feature both residential spaces and workplaces, or the creation of cycle path systems, exclusive bus lanes, and car-free residential and inner-city areas.

4.3.3 Mobility and Communication

In 2007, 20% of global energy-related CO_2 emissions were caused directly by the transport sector, mainly through road transport (WRI-CAIT, 2011). The demand for transport services will grow further in line with the continuing intense economic growth in newly industrialising and developing countries. A sustainable scenario should therefore also include an at least partially decarbonised transport sector, as well as the substitution of

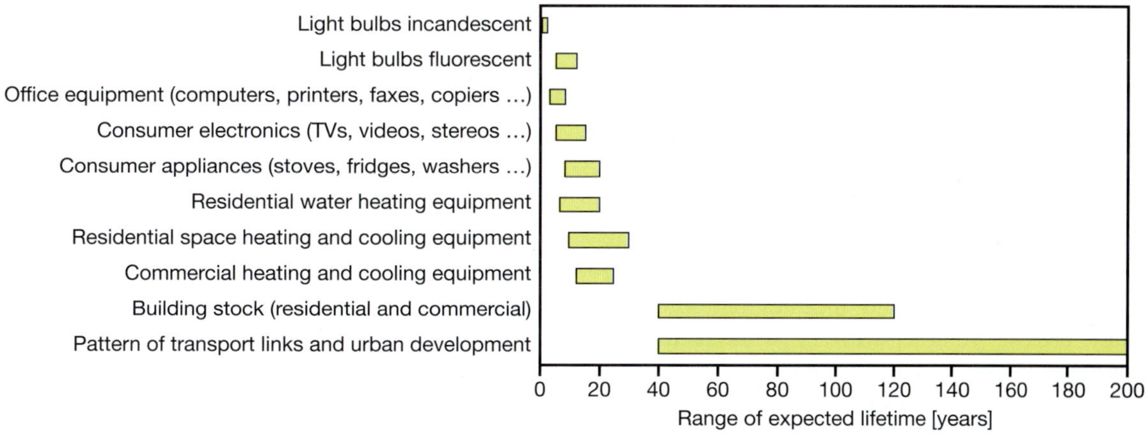

Figure 4.3-2
The economic life-span of various energy-relevant investments.
Source: IEA, 2002

mobility through communication. Core elements of a future sustainable transport system should therefore be developed today, and investments should be steered towards sustainable transport systems. In particular, the goal of emissions reduction calls for substantially reducing the use of fossil fuels, which provided around 94% of the 96 EJ primary energy used for transport in 2008 (IEA, 2008c).

In scenarios like those featured in Section 4.2, where a certain CO_2 reduction target has been set for the entire economy, the reduction of transport sector emissions is disproportionately small, as emissions reductions are cheaper to achieve in other sectors. Fossil fuels therefore still provide more than half of the final energy for the transport sector in 2050, even in ambitious studies. In the Advanced Energy [R]evolution scenario (EREC and Greenpeace, 2010), for example, the proportion of fossil fuels is reduced down to 91% in 2020, and to 57% in 2050; the IEA's ETP 2010 Blue-Map/Shifts scenario (IEA, 2010a) shows 55% in 2050. Important elements of this kind of gradual energy system conversion towards sustainability that are taken into account in these scenarios are:

› *Avoidance of unnecessary and unwanted traffic:* Reducing the volume of traffic is the most effective, as well as the most affordable, measure for reducing negative environmental influences such as energy and land consumption, and noise and greenhouse gas emissions. There is scope for traffic avoidance, both in freight and passenger traffic, especially where traffic is perceived as a burden, or makes economic sense only through distorted incentive structures. Integrated urban and regional planning which prioritises mixed usage (Section 4.3.2), and extending the options for teleconferencing, home working, and other long distance services can contribute to this. In addition, communication technologies are also tasked with reducing journey distances, and avoiding traffic jams, through traffic management. As, over the next few decades, the decarbonisation of current traffic volumes is to be achieved whilst also providing improved access to mobility services for many people, it is vital that resource usage is carefully deliberated. The substitution of individual with public transport is an important element of this strategy.
› *Switching to more efficient means of transport:* As far as short journeys are concerned, particularly non-motorised forms of mobility, i.e. walking or cycling, are encouraged as alternatives, not least because this also impacts positively on health (Woodcock et al., 2009). Local public transport usage can be increased by making it more attractive through the use of modern communication technologies to complement walking or cycling. For long distance passenger and freight traffic, making part of the traffic rail-bound harbours considerable potential for increasing efficiency. To ensure that this potential is fully tapped, the range of available rail-bound services and high speed train routes must be expanded, particularly freight transport routes. Shifting passenger and freight transport away from the road (and away from air traffic) onto rails is a particularly effective measure for reducing CO_2 emissions, as rail traffic is more efficient than road or air traffic. Furthermore, with the decarbonisation of the electricity sector, the CO_2 emissions resulting from rail traffic are reduced even further.

- *Increasing the efficiency of all means of transport:* Increasing engine conversion efficiency, either by improving the current technology, or by changing to more efficient locomotion technologies such as the electric engine, reducing energy demand and changing in part to low-carbon fuels reduces the specific emissions of all means of transport. Mobility must therefore be increasingly based on electricity, making it two to three times more efficient than our current motor vehicles. This includes battery-based, fully electric vehicles with or without a range extender, which can consist either of small-scale combustion engines or of fuel cells in combination with methane or hydrogen. Urban freight transport also relies on hybrid technologies. Cars, railway trains and buses obtain their energy from overhead lines, batteries or fuel cells. Batteries are charged by means of bidirectional charging devices at charging stations. In addition, the storage batteries can be recharged through contactless charging when driving (inductive transmission). For freight and long-distance traffic, and for aeroplanes and ships, renewable fuels (methane or hydrogen) are produced from surplus energy from wind, solar and hydroelectric power. Also conceivable are biomass fuels, which meet stringent sustainability requirements.
- *Promotion of new business models and infrastructures in the area of mobility:* Sustainable mobility should be integrated into the everyday lives of users, with the aid of new business models (for example, car sharing, multimodal transport) and the corresponding infrastructures. It is necessary to optimise the framework conditions for this (for instance, the infrastructure for car sharing), so that the new offers are sufficiently attractive for all users with regard to flexibility, cost, and ease of access to information, and can be easily integrated into habitual daily routines. In this context, information and communication technology solutions are particularly important, as they can considerably increase the flexibility and user friendliness of public and shared means of transport. IT solutions, for example, could provide integrated route planning which includes different modes of transport (electromobility, public transport). In a pilot project in Singapore, for instance, the Bosch group is currently testing a software-based services platform (eMobility Solution) that helps drivers of electric cars to optimise their route by taking charging station locations into account, as well as integrating public transport options (Bosch, 2010).

  In this way, car sharing models could become very important in future. In Switzerland, a country-wide car sharing system for private and commercial customers that can be directly combined with local public transport and railway services has already become established (Mobility, 2010). The Deutsche Bahn's car sharing service can also be booked directly in conjunction with railway tickets, allowing flexibility at the destination (DB, 2010). Systems such as these could be particularly important in urban areas in connection with the introduction of electromobility. On the one hand, they serve to increasingly reduce the dependency on own cars; on the other hand, they can facilitate the introduction of a fleet of energy-efficient cars and electromobility.

Unlike in other sectors, currently available or already advanced technologies are insufficient to fully decarbonise the transport sector in the above described scenarios, which represent comparatively ambitious developments. Whilst rail traffic and motorised individual transport can, for the most part, be decarbonised in the medium term through electrification, there are as yet no sustainable solutions for road freight traffic, or for air and shipping traffic, that are at the stage of being launched commercially. It is certainly possible to run ships and aeroplanes on methane or hydrogen. The annual sustainable biomass potential of 80–170 EJ primary energy (WBGU, 2010a) will probably not be sufficient to completely cover the future energy demand expected in these transport sectors, which will be just under 100 EJ in 2050 (IEA, 2010a; WBCSD, 2004). Furthermore, the WBGU considers the use of biomass for electricity generation and heating as the more efficient climate policy path, as long as these, too, still depend on fossil energy carriers, especially coal (WBGU, 2010a). It therefore seems doubtful whether biomass can offer a sustainable energy supply for these transport sectors.

However, these scenarios merely show possible developments that are plausible from today's point of view, which ultimately means that they generally extrapolate from current consumer behaviour and technical change. Significantly more profound transformations, however, are certainly conceivable. Passenger transport is determined by direct customer decisions, which are not arrived at on a purely economic basis, and could therefore change even without changes in technology. As the speed of technical development also depends on the degree to which a technology is in demand, mutually reinforcing dynamics can develop, which can create completely new mobility systems. The decisive aspect here will be the development of suitable business models which utilise the advantages of technical innovations for innovative mobility products, offering an added value to customers in comparison with the current systems (Box 4.3-3). Which innovations will ultimately become accepted is hardly predictable; a number of options are technically conceivable.

Box 4.3-3

New Business Models for a Low-Carbon Society

According to the transition management approach devised by Grin et al. (2010), the interaction of all actors at all levels of society, including niche actors, experimental spaces and pioneering change agents, is required in order to trigger a system transformation (Chapter 3). Particularly important are change agents, who develop and try out alternative business models in market niches and experimental spaces. As important actors within a social system, companies, supported by the transition management approach, can on the one hand review their own existing business models, whilst, on the other hand, thus triggering important changes to the existing social system (Loorbach et al., 2010). Innovative products and services offer alternatives to current consumption patterns and practices, and can overcome usual action and thought patterns in the entire social system. They therefore have an important part to play in the low-carbon transformation.

Corporate transformations such as these will especially take place once transformative changes are also occurring at meso- and meta-level, for example due to changes in regulations. However, governments can also promote corporate transformations through new criteria in national procurement policies (Section 5.2), and offering financial support for the establishment of new business models (Section 4.5). A public dialogue on paths towards a low-carbon society can increase environmental awareness in companies, and trigger business strategy review processes. According to Loorbach et al. (2010), new business models develop particularly well if they are initially tested parallel to the company's core business, until they are stable as independent business models.

Magnetic levitation trains, or hydrogen-powered aeroplanes, could take over long-distance passenger transport, for example. The major extension of metropolitan public transport networks, along with multimodal systems that allow easy, needs-driven changes between few but fast public railway systems and buses, bicycles or electric bicycles, and electric cars, offers a vision of cities worth living in.

In light of the many local problems, too, it is highly likely that urban mobility systems will change dramatically over the next 40 years. In the WBGU's view, compliance with the guard rails (Section 1.1) also makes a profound change inevitable. However, the long lifecycle of traffic infrastructures and the profound social integration of the prevalent car-ownership based system create strong path dependencies, so that changes require considerable effort.

A stabilisation of the greenhouse gas concentration at a very low level (400 ppm CO_2eq) will probably require a complete decarbonisation of the transport sector by the end of the century (van Vuuren et al., 2010). It is therefore very important to rapidly develop and use those technologies and business models which allow sustainable and zero-carbon mobility. Demonstrating these concepts, particularly in the technologically highly developed and fast growing regions of the world, can begin immediately, and serve as a model and inspiration for leapfrogging technological development phases in rapidly developing regions. Even if the ultimately successful model is as yet not predictable, it is vital to shape the framework conditions now in such a way that innovations can penetrate the market.

4.3.4 Food

In 2005, direct emissions from agriculture amounted to around 14% of global anthropogenic greenhouse gas emissions (WRI-CAIT, 2011; Section 4.1.7). Agricultural emissions are expected to continue to increase in future (IPCC, 2007c). However, to obtain an overall picture of the needs category food, all greenhouse gas emissions 'from field to plate' would have to be taken into account (production, processing, preparation, storage, transport, spoilage and waste of foodstuffs in households, etc.). Indirect emissions, for example CO_2 emissions from the conversion of forests and wetlands into farmland and pasture (land-use changes), must also be included alongside those emissions directly related to the agricultural sector.

Food production (including distribution and trade) accounts for almost half of the lifecycle emissions of food (Fritsche and Eberle, 2007). In contrast to the direct emissions, the indirect emissions consist primarily of CO_2. Around half of the emissions are generated subsequent to agricultural production, for example through storage and preparation. Freight transport accounts for only around 3%, although here, transporting foodstuffs by air is of particular consequence (Wiegmann et al., 2005). Waste-related emissions, through post-harvest losses, through spoilage caused by incorrect storage, or through being wasted in households, should not be neglected. Of the 4,600 kcal per capita per day (including livestock feed) average global harvest achieved in 1990, only 2,000 kcal were ultimately consumed (Smil, 2000; Nellemann et al., 2009). Overall, the greenhouse gas footprint of the needs category food slightly exceeds that of the needs category mobility (Figure 4.3-1).

4.3.4.1
Climate-Compatible Agricultural Management

Roughly estimated, around half of the direct emissions from agricultural production would be avoidable by 2030 (Caldeira et al., 2004; Smith et al., 2008), with around 70% of the potential in developing countries, around 20% in OECD nations, and 10% in transition countries (IPCC, 2007c). The most important measures to achieve this are improvements in farmland, pasture and organic soil management (Section 4.1.7.2).

Since the beginning of agriculture, soils have lost roughly 40–90 billion t of carbon (the equivalent of 150–330 Gt CO_2) (Caldeira et al., 2004). At 89% of the overall technical mitigation potential, the reversal of this process, in other words using soils for carbon sequestration by changing agricultural practices, is the most promising option for climate change mitigation in the agricultural sector (Lal, 2004; IPCC, 2007c). In view of the soil carbon already lost though degradation (erosion, for instance), this will be of particular importance in future (WBGU, 1995a). It includes, for example, refraining from ploughing (Lal et al., 2004), conserving or restoring hedgerows to avoid wind erosion, avoiding the draining of organic soils (peatlands, etc.), restoring degraded land, for instance by adapting soil tillage and crop rotation, improving nutrient and water management, and energy-extensive irrigation (Smith et al., 2008). The remaining technical mitigation potential refers to CH_4 (9%) and N_2O (2%; IPCC, 2007c). A number of these already available management improvement methods have additional benefits, as they increase production, and make adaptation to climate change easier (Smith et al., 2008; FAO, 2009c). However, as these options usually carry no short-term cost benefits for agricultural businesses, additional incentives in the form of pricing or policies are necessary (Schneider and Smith, 2009). The costs for the introduction of these measures differ widely, according to region and option; at project level, they often range between US$ 200–300 per hectare (FAO, 2009c).

This substantial potential must be considered in light of the fact that there has been very little progress made with regard to the reduction of agricultural emissions since 1990. The enforcement of regulations is generally fraught with difficulties in many regions, and many areas of agriculture and forestry, so that the effectiveness of regulatory approaches is limited. A sensible starting point would therefore be additional incentives in the form of pricing or policies (for example, the phasing out of environmentally damaging subsidies, incentives and payments for ecosystem services; Section 7.3.7) for climate protection (Schneider and Smith, 2009; Eger et al., 1996; Section 5.2).

4.3.4.2
Dietary Habits and Greenhouse Gas Emissions

Agriculture's technical emissions reduction potential through climate-friendly management is, however, not as substantial as the reductions which could be achieved through changed eating habits (Popp et al., 2010). The reason for this is that the lifecycle emissions of animal-derived foodstuffs (such as meat, dairy products, eggs) are up to ten times higher than those of the equal weight of plant-derived foodstuffs. However, these values differ greatly according to product and country. Cattle production in the Sahel, for example, causes only around half as many GHG emissions as cattle production in the USA (Subak, 1999).

Livestock farming is the most influential factor of global anthropogenic land use. Overall, around 70% of the world's cultivated land is used for livestock farming (as pasture, or for feed production), which provides only 15% of global calorie supply (Steinfeld et al., 2006; PBL, 2009b). Correspondingly sized, at 18%, is the total, i.e. both direct and indirect, contribution of livestock farming to anthropogenic greenhouse gas emissions (Steinfeld et al., 2006). In addition to the climate impact, livestock farming also accelerates biodiversity loss, causes the overuse and pollution of water resources and environmental nutrient loading, and, not least, promotes the spreading of infectious diseases (for example avian flu, BSE). Due to the significantly lower land intensity, the change towards a healthier diet with less animal products would therefore have a considerable leverage effect not only for emissions, but also for the preservation of biodiversity (PBL, 2010). In terms of the environmental compatibility of eating habits, the consumption of beef makes an outstanding difference (Marlow et al., 2009). On the other hand, this sector provides around 1.3 billion people with employment and an income, and it is often the only practicable option for producing income from marginal land, by pasturing particularly in developing countries.

In accordance with the important part which animal products play in diets, the current ecological footprint of North American and European eating habits is around twice as large as Africa's or Asia's (White, 2000). This ratio is currently changing fast; the per capita consumption of meat in the developing countries has more than tripled over the past 50 years, for example (FAO, 2010b). This trend is expected to continue, so that meat production could double by 2050 (Steinfeld et al., 2006). This is not only the result of population growth, but also primarily of the changed eating habits noted all over the world, in line with increasing prosperity. The diet in developing and newly industrialising countries is becoming richer in fats and proteins, and features more animal-derived foodstuffs, particularly in Latin

America and East Asia (von Koerber et al., 2008). In China, for instance, meat consumption has quintupled over the past three decades (FAO, 2006). The dairy sector contributes around 4% to anthropogenic GHG emissions, with around half of this being accounted for by CH_4 (FAO, 2010c).

Development dependent, these trends can lead to substantial additional GHG emissions (Keyzer et al., 2005; Popp et al., 2010). Conversely, in 2055, global agricultural GHG emissions might even be below 1995 figures, if eating habits were to change towards a diet with a lower proportion of animal products. In combination with the technical mitigation potentials, this could even lead to a reduction of agricultural emissions down to around 2.5 Gt CO_2eq per year by 2055, which would be the rough equivalent of half of today's agricultural GHG emissions (Popp et al., 2010). Reducing meat consumption therefore harbours a considerable potential for mitigating climate change.

From a health point of view, the industrialised countries' prevalent diet contains too many animal products. Stehfest et al. (2009) conclude that a reduction of meat consumption down to a healthy level would also reduce the mitigation costs for achieving stabilisation at 450 ppm by half. Considerable land areas would be released to be used for other purposes. An appropriate change in eating habits would therefore have a twin benefit: it would be beneficial for people's health, and for the environment (McMichael et al., 2007; Tukker et al., 2009).

Another important factor is the losses in households through spoilage and waste of foodstuffs, almost two-thirds of which would be avoidable. This would not only reduce emissions, but also save on costs (WRAP, 2009).

Therefore, the message is: a healthy diet is also climate-friendly. Today's average proportion of animal products in the diet of industrialised countries, and the growing high-income groups in developing and newly industrialising countries, is higher than is healthy. This certainly does not mean that eating habits must become fully vegetarian or even vegan. Even the suggested diet change towards eating less meat in general, and particularly less beef, would have a considerable impact on climate change mitigation (PBL, 2009a). Possible approaches include improved communication, and national framework setting (Brand et al., 2007; Section 7.3.7.4).

4.4 WBGU Exemplary Transformative Path for the EU-27

In the following, the WBGU discusses transformation scenarios for Germany and the European Union that lead to an energy supply which is widely, or even fully, reliant on renewable energies by 2050. For this purpose, existing studies were analysed (EREC and Greenpeace, 2009, 2010; Sterner, 2009; SRU, 2010; Klaus et al., 2010; BMU, 2010c; Roadmap 2050, 2011). As shown in Section 4.1, renewable energies have sufficient technical potentials to achieve this. The following intends to underline the technical feasibility of an energy system that is based on energy efficiency and renewable energies. The realisation of these scenarios depends on political and economic course setting. The objective of this chapter is to illustrate core elements of a decarbonisation of the energy system, and to identify ways of combining conventional and renewable energy management.

Whilst so far, there are few detailed research activities for the technical realisation of a global energy supply that relies fully on renewable energies (for example, Teske et al., 2008), high temporal resolution studies on 100% renewable electricity have already been carried out for Europe, a combined European/North African electricity system, or a combined German/Norwegian system (Roadmap 2050, 2011; Czisch, 2005). Czisch (2005) illustrated that, if the best possible sites for wind farms and solar power plants, bioenergy, and run-of-river hydropower schemes were chosen within the area covered by the scenario, the average costs for electricity generation and transport via a transnational grid would amount to between €ct 5–6 per kWh, even at the price renewable energy carriers were in 2005. They would therefore more or less equal the costs for conventionally generated electricity.

The German Advisory Council on the Environment (SRU, 2010) has shown in a detailed analysis that the potential of renewable energies for power generation in Germany and Europe is sufficient to allow a fully renewable electricity supply in Germany at all hours, and at an affordable cost, whilst meeting stringent nature conservation demands, and avoiding other usage conflicts. Pan-European grid extension and the link-up with neighbouring countries play a decisive role in this. Common to all scenarios is the fact that they are driven by both resources and policies.

4.4.1
A Renewable Energy Supply in Europe

The scenario Energy [R]evolution 2010 (EREC and Greenpeace, 2010) features two exemplary paths that would allow Europe to meet its climate protection targets by 2050. The basic scenario meets the current minimum target concerning an 80% reduction in greenhouse gas emissions by 2050 compared to 1990, or the reduction of CO_2 emissions by around 85%. The ambitious Advanced Scenario even achieves a reduction by 95%, through an energy supply that is almost 100% renewable, and through substantial increases in energy savings. Because of this, both paths lead to considerably more security in terms of Europe's supply than is given today, and focus the energy value creation chain on Europe.

This study's key demographic, structural and economic data, which characterise the economy and therefore also energy demand, largely agree with those on which the IEA World Energy Outlook scenarios are also based.

Significant structural changes appear by 2050. The currently still high conversion losses are considerably reduced through the expansion of renewable electricity generation, and the corresponding sharp decline in condensation power stations. Their contribution goes down from currently 76% (fossil and nuclear) to 57% by 2020, and 32% by 2030. In 2050, only flexible gas power stations (including gas-powered CHP) supplying performance security play a role. The remaining fossil-fuelled power plants (coal and gas) rely on CHP technology. The main contribution is made by renewable energies. Furthermore, transport is mostly electric, and major energy savings measures have been implemented where heating is concerned.

These developments result in a significantly reduced primary energy input, which, in the reference scenario, rises by 3% compared to today, to 76 EJ in 2050, whilst in the Energy-[R]evolution scenarios, it is covered through the widespread use of renewable energies, and therefore considerably lower: according to the physical energy content method, it goes down to 87% of 2007 levels by 2020 in the Advanced Scenario, and down to 62% of the initial value by 2050.

The same level of supply despite a lower primary energy demand stems from the fact that wind and solar energy, as well as hydropower, avoid waste heat, and that a significant intensification of energy savings in all sectors is assumed (Figure 4.4-1).

Energy-related greenhouse gas emissions are reduced by 95% compared to 1990 levels by 2050 in this scenario. In terms of electricity and steam generation alone, emissions of 1.4 Gt CO_2 per year can be avoided through energy savings and the continued expansion of renewable energies. In the medium term, CO_2 reduction is particularly important in the heating sector, as is renewable electricity generation in the long term.

The transformation of the European energy supply is not possible without high initial investments; however, in the long term, these will prove to be cost savings. The additional costs in the Advanced Scenario amount to € 82 billion for 2020, and € 73 billion for 2030; however, it should be considered that these costs, compared to current energy imports of around € 350 billion, remain within reasonable bounds. In the long term, these investments will lead to an energy turnaround through discontinued energy imports and a higher degree of independence from raw materials, savings which will amount to € 85 billion in 2050 for Europe.

Cities are the transformation nuclei: a number of European cities have set themselves the target of a 100% renewable supply. This leads to the creation of beacon projects, which serve as an inspiration in these times of increasing urbanisation in order to make this process sustainable.

Europe's Electricity Supply According to the Energy [R]evolution 2010 Scenario

The transformation of the energy systems rests on the electricity sector. In this sector, decarbonisation is easier to achieve than in the heating or transport sector. However, heating and mobility can also be made more efficient, climate-friendly, and in part also cheaper through the use of renewable electricity. For these reasons, renewable electricity will become primary energy in the long run, with the consequence that, despite energy savings, there is no reduction of the overall electricity demand by 2050.

In the Advanced Scenario, the regenerative share rises from 16% (2007) to 43% (2020), 68% (2030), and 97% (2050), with a capacity of around 1,500 GW by then. Most of this increase can be attributed to wind and solar power. The sustainable biomass potential is used to its maximum extent by around 2030. In this scenario, importing electricity from renewable energy sources (wind, solar thermal power plants) gradually becomes more important from 2030 (Figure 4.4-2).

This scenario, featuring a particularly extensive expansion of renewable energies, would not be obsolete even if some countries choose to continue to employ nuclear energy as part of their electricity mix. Concurrently with the widening expansion of renewable energies, conventional power plants will increasingly have to go into part load operation. This inefficient and uneconomical plant operation, which, in the

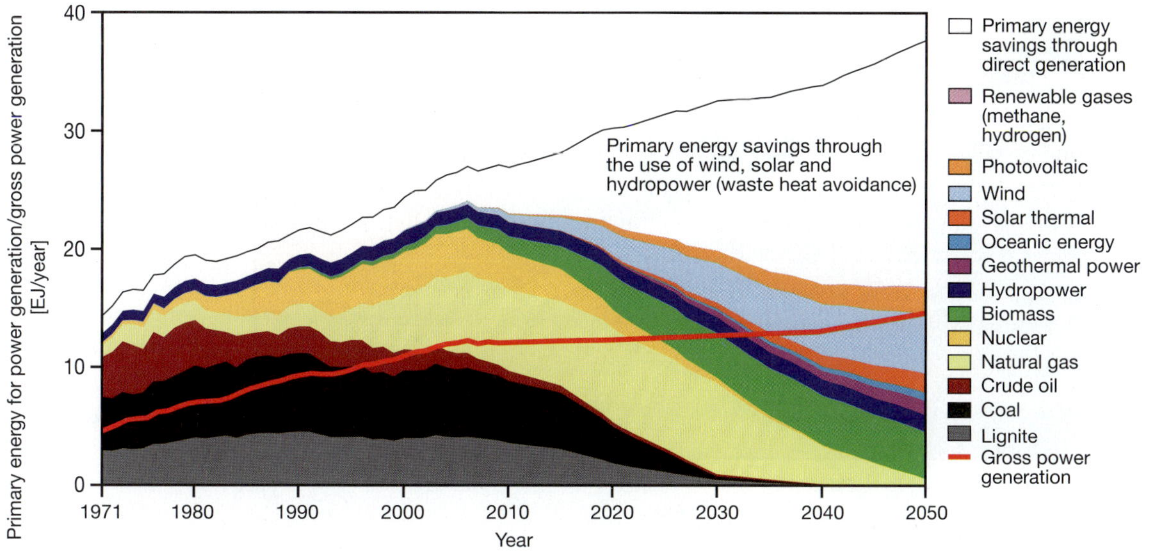

Figure 4.4-1
Primary energy consumption in the EU-27 for electricity according to the Energy [R]evolution Advanced Scenario 2010 compiled by EREC and Greenpeace (2010) for the period 1970–2050. The main contributors are wind energy, solar power, and biomass. Substantial primary energy savings result from the avoidance of waste heat through direct electricity generation by means of wind, solar and hydropower. Gross electric power generation continues to rise moderately until 2050 (red line; Figure 4.4-2). The historical data up to and including 2008 is based on the International Energy Agency's energy balance tables (IEA, 2010d).
Source: WBGU, based on the cited data sources

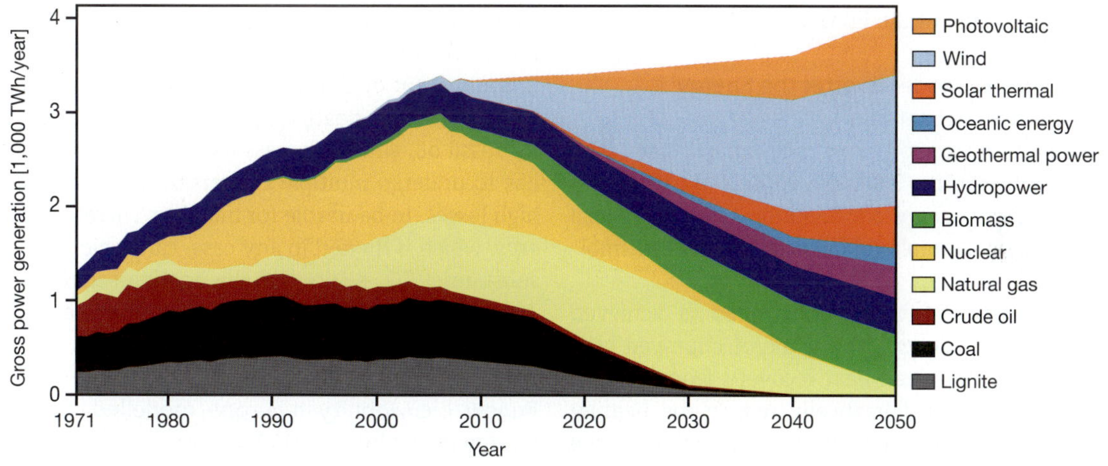

Figure 4.4-2
Gross power generation in the EU-27 according to the Energy [R]evolution Advanced Scenario (EREC and Greenpeace, 2010) for the period 1970–2050. The proportion of renewable energies is gradually increased up to a share of 86% in 2050. Wind, solar and hydropower have the largest share. Electricity transport, energy storage facilities and energy management offset fluctuations in generation and consumption. The increasing electricity demand between 2030 and 2050 is the result of increased demand for electricity for heating (heat pumps) and transport (electromobility) purposes. The historical data up to and including 2008 are based on the International Energy Agency's energy balance tables (IEA, 2010d).
Source: WBGU, based on the cited data sources

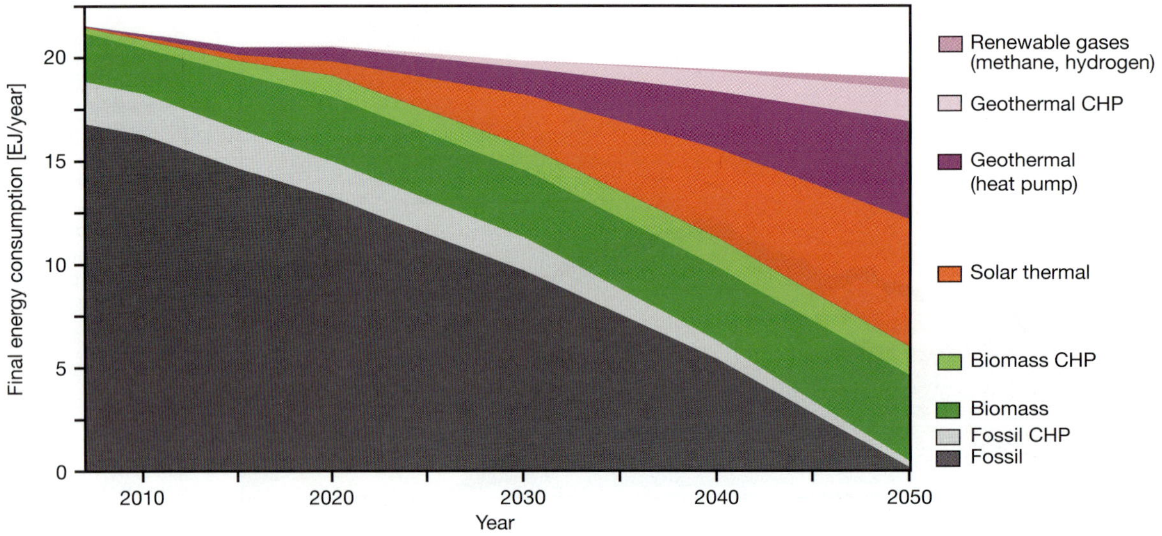

Figure 4.4-3
Final energy consumption in the EU-27 heating sector, with reference to the Energy [R]evolution Advanced Scenario 2010, for the period 2007–2050, showing increased biomass and decreased crude oil reliance up until 2050. Energy saving measures and the introduction of heat pumps, solar thermal energy, CHP technology, biomass and renewable gases (hydrogen, methane) allow 100% renewable heating by 2050.
Source: WBGU, with reference to EREC and Greenpeace

case of fossil-powered plants, leads to added emissions, and may potentially cause technical complications, can be avoided through the construction of storage facilities, and expansion of the European grid.

Heating Europe, modelled after the Energy [R]evolution 2010 Scenario

Europe-wide, the proportion of renewable sources used for heating rises from 13% today to 27% by 2020, and to 95% of final energy consumption by 2050. Fossil energy is gradually replaced by more efficient technologies.

The reduction of the heating need is achieved through energy savings with the aid of improved heat insulation, and improved heat recovery from ventilation. Both measures dramatically reduce the heating requirements of new builds. In existing buildings, the implementation of these measures is tied in with the refurbishment rate, which is accelerated, compared to historical levels.

The remaining heating need and process heat is met through a combination of electrical heat pumps, CHP technology, solar thermal energy, and renewable gases such as hydrogen or methane (Figure 4.4-3). Heat pumps and CHP technology are particularly suitable for balancing power grid fluctuations: whilst the heat pump can be activated when there is surplus electricity, CHP helps to counteract power generation deficits. In both cases, the thermal mass of the buildings, or the suitable dimensioning of heat storage vessels, allows the delinking of the electricity and heat flow.

Deviating from the Advanced Scenario, the variant shown here uses more biomass in the heating sector, as the degree of usage and usage efficiency in this sector is double that of the transport sector. Biomass such as wood is used in heating systems as a 1:1 replacement for fossil oil, whilst biomass for fuel production in part has to undergo multiple conversions, accompanied by high losses, to be usable for mobility. Therefore, bioenergy, which is limited in any case, can achieve far more substantial CO_2 savings in the heating sector (WBGU, 2010a). The mineral oil thus released from heating systems is used as a fuel for mobility.

Renewable Mobility in Europe, modelled after the Energy [R]evolution 2010 Scenario

In the transport sector, the dependence on fossil resources is still most pronounced; accordingly, the transformation poses a challenge (Figure 4.4-4). Due to the considerable freight transport growth rates, combustion engine efficiency increases only slow down consumption growth.

The main efficiency gains are achieved by renewable electromobility, which has an efficiency factor that is three or four times higher than that of fossil combustion engines. The challenge with regard to the widespread introduction of electric vehicles lies in technology development, cost reduction, sustainable raw material cycles, and technical maturity.

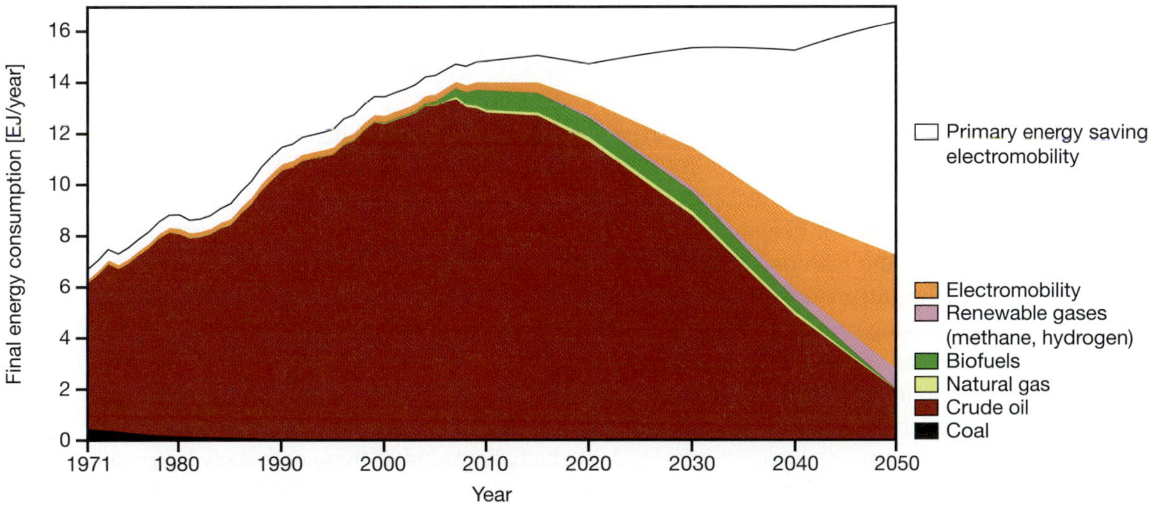

Figure 4.4-4
Final energy consumption in the transport sector across the EU-27, with reference to the Energy [R]evolution Advanced Scenario 2010, for the period 1970–2050, with biomass as interim technology, and including the crude oil that will be released in the heating sector by 2050 (EREC and Greenpeace, 2010). The introduction of efficient electromobility can significantly reduce final energy consumption in the transport sector. Renewable gases (methane, hydrogen) complement biofuels in the long distance segment. The historical data up to and including 2008 are based on the International Energy Agency's energy balance tables (IEA, 2010d).
Source: WBGU, based on the cited data sources

The sustainable potential of biofuels is fully tapped for certain transport systems (long distance, flight, ship, freight transport) that rely on chemical energy carriers with a high energy density. Renewable gases (hydrogen, methane) play an important role in complementing the limited potential of biofuels. On the one hand, the introduction of wind and solar fuels prevents competition over use, which can occur with biofuels; on the other hand, it overcomes the limitations in terms of their availability.

With the speedy introduction of electromobility, the limited use of sustainable biofuels, and the launch of wind and solar fuels, approx. 90% of mobility can be based on renewable energy by 2050. The remaining 10% will continue to be powered by the mineral oil that is released thanks to its replacement in heating systems with biomass.

Transferability of European Conclusions to other World Regions

Europe enjoys the advantage of a well-developed grid infrastructure, and high technology diffusion. These conclusions could equally apply to North America, and some of Asia's densely populated areas. DLR studies (for example EREC and Greenpeace, 2010), which are also used for the IPCC's special report on renewable energies, are suitable for globally differentiated analyses.

4.4.2 The Linking of Energy Systems as the Transformation's Core Element

Integration of renewable energies into the existing energy supply structures requires cross-sector linking. The expansion of electricity and gas grids, their interlinkage, and their smart connection with the IT network are indispensable.

Dynamic Simulations for Integrating Renewable Energies into the Electricity Supply

To analyse a renewable supply with high proportions of wind and photovoltaic energy, the temporal feed-in fluctuations caused by meteorological conditions must be adequately mapped, as these demand the use of compensating measures such as storage or generation and load management, which must be co-analysed in technical and economic terms.

This problematic issue shall be illustrated for Germany on the basis of the study carried out by Klaus et al. (2010), which examines the realisation of a 100% renewable energy supply for Germany in 2050. The study shows that through the ambitious expansion of national renewable energies, the introduction of electromobility for transport, improved building insulation to low-energy standard, the substitution of conventional heating systems with electric heat pumps, and the use of large-scale storage facilities (pump stores and gas network) to compensate for imbalances between generation and consumption, the complete decarbonisation of the energy sector by 2050 is, in principle, technically and sustainably possible. To improve the balance between generation and consumption, load management with the aid of electrical heat pumps, room climate control, and electromobility can make an important contribution: at times when generation exceeds the current consumption, the batteries of the electric vehicles connected to the grid are charged, the thermal storage vessels of the heating systems, which are based on heat pumps, are heated up, or the air conditioning units are switched on to increase current consumption in order to avoid the interim storage of electric energy in electricity storage facilities.

Figure 4.4-5 illustrates the feed-in simulated in Klaus et al. (2010) for the months December and August. Whilst during the summer months, through the combination of wind and solar energy, there are only short periods of differing consumption and generation, confined to a few hours, the simulation shows a fortnight in December with considerable energy supply deficits, which would have to be compensated for in a reliable energy system.

Expansion of Energy Grids

The expansion and linking of the grids allows the Europe-wide transport of energy. Electricity grids must be extensively expanded, both nationally and internationally (DENA, 2010). Today's gas networks could already be described as supergrids, as they feature high transmission levels, and well-developed storage capacities of around 220 TWh_{th} in Germany alone. A strong trans-European high-performance transport grid for electricity and gas is a prerequisite for, on the one hand, facilitating the transport of energy from wind and solar power plants from sites with high yields to consumption centres, and, on the other hand, ensuring wide-ranging compensation of local generation fluctuations. In this way, the power produced by large-scale offshore wind farms and solar power generated in the Mediterranean could be integrated into the European energy supply, and existing possible storage facilities in gas networks or pumped-storage hydroelectric power in Scandinavia, the Pyrenees and the Alps could be unlocked.

Integration of Storage Facilities and Linking of Electricity, Gas and Heat Grids

The need for storage increases in line with the share of wind and solar energy. A distinction must be made between short-term and long-term storage facilities. To compensate output fluctuations lasting only a few hours, pump storage power stations with high efficiency factors can be used. A further expansion of this proven technology is at least in Germany currently limited, mainly due to acceptance issues. An appealing option, however, would be to use the immense capacities of storage power stations, particularly those in Norway. However, high-capacity transmission lines between the European heartland and Norway would have to be built. The currently planned link between Germany and Norway, with a transmissions capacity of 1.4 GW, at a cost of around € 1.5 billion, can only be the first step (NorGer, 2011). The storage capacity can be improved further through the conversion of Norway's already existing pumped-storage hydroelectric power plants, taking into consideration ecological aspects such as the mixing of saltwater and freshwater. Against the background of these extremely large-capacity storage potentials (approx. 80 TWh_{el}), the building of compressed air energy storage plants with considerably lower efficiency factors and higher costs appears secondary (SRU, 2010).

In principle, electrical batteries are also suitable for the stabilisation of power grids. The expected costs of battery storage, however, both today and in the foreseeable future, do not allow competitive use. An exception is the storing of power for electric vehicles, particularly in the case of optimised charging management. Feeding energy from the batteries of electric cars back into the power grid on a regular basis, however, is also not economically viable, although this could become an attractive option during critical times, when a lucrative income could be achieved for grid support.

With the exception of the Norwegian pump stores, however, long-term stop-gap storage, for example if there is a wind lull lasting 1–2 weeks, is not possible with any of the above described types of storage facility (Figure 4.4-5). These gaps could initially be closed with the aid of dedicated back-up power plants, for instance fast-response gas turbines, but also with virtual power stations, consisting of a number of local CHP plants that are synchronised and controlled through smart grids.

Along with the decreasing proportions of fossil energy carriers, natural gas can initially be supplemented by biogas. However, a full substitution requires the generation of renewable methane from wind and solar power. Gas-powered back-up power plants and local CHP units, which are required in any case, are suitable for the reconversion. Overall, this combination results in a long-term store that initially converts renewable electricity into methane, which is the same as natural gas, stores this energy carrier with the aid of the existing natural gas infrastructure, and supplies electricity with the aid of the back-up power plants when it is needed. Gas store storage capacities can close electricity supply gaps of up to two months.

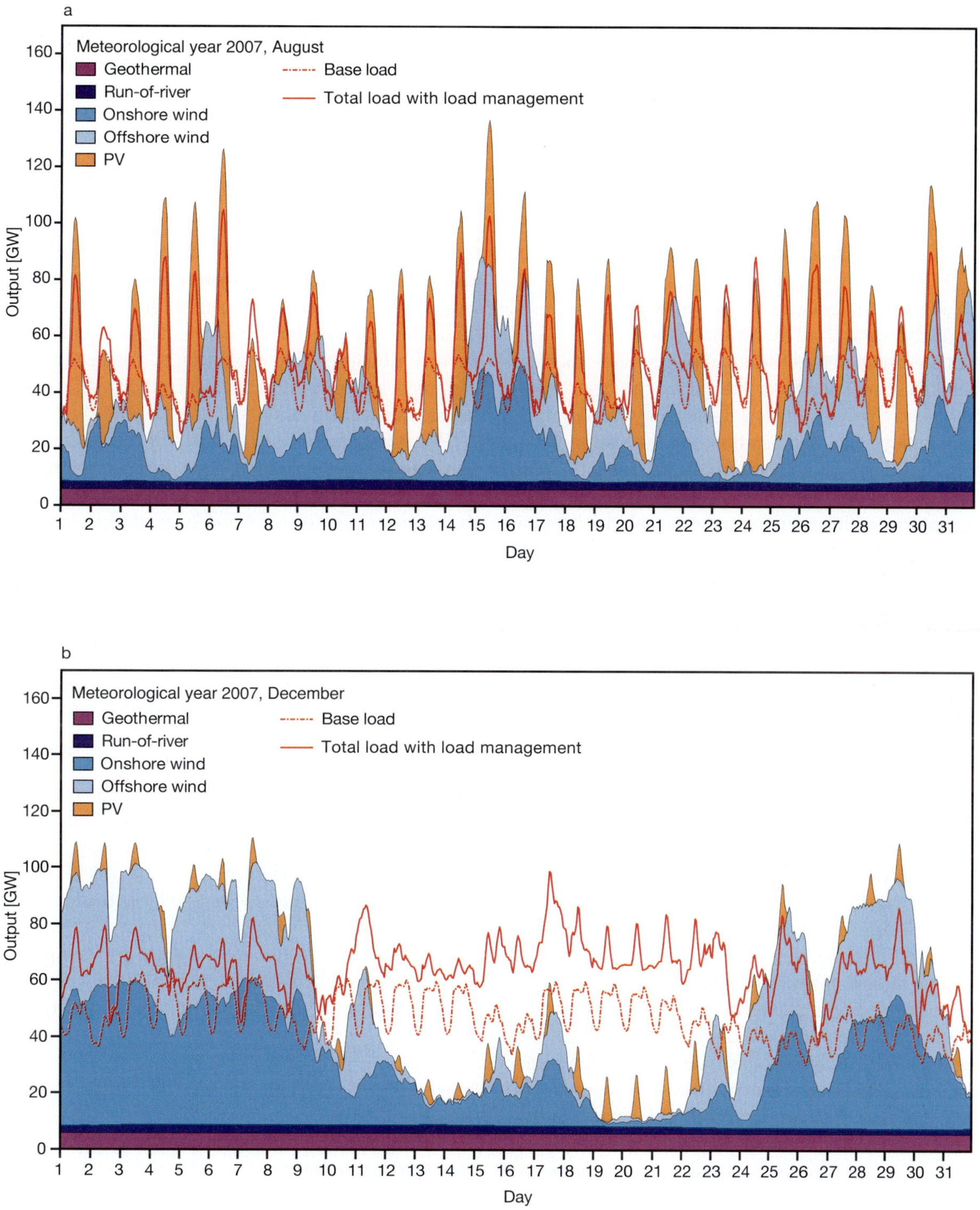

Figure 4.4-5
Simulated renewable energy feed-in (coloured areas) according to the UBA scenario projected to 2050 across one month in relation to basic load (dotted red line), and the resulting overall load with a managed use of electromobility, heating and air conditioning, and heat pumps (continuous red line). Exemplary illustration of one month in summer, and one in winter (a: August, b: December), using the meteorological data for 2007. Extreme electricity supply fluctuations are caused by both wind and solar energy; these can be compensated with the three measures of grid expansion, generation and load management, and storage facilities. Despite ideal grid expansion and ideal load management, gaps in the supply for intervals of one to two weeks occur regularly; these can only be closed through integration of the large Scandinavian storage capacities, or the linking of gas and energy grids.
Source: Klaus et al., 2010

In this way, the electricity grid can be sensibly connected to the gas network. This linking allows the stabilisation of power grids by utilising the storage capacity of gas networks, which is several times higher (Sterner, 2009). The expansion of local heat networks, and their connection to the power grids or gas networks, leads to a further synergy: the electricity generation from stored methane can be carried out in CHP units with high overall efficiency factors, thereby also covering part of the heat supply (Nast, 2007).

Linking Electricity Grids and IT Networks: Production and Load Management

As a precondition for efficient energy services management, all energy networks (electricity, gas, heat) should be linked by information technology (smartgrids). The employment of generation and load management helps to even out electricity supply fluctuations, *firstly* through a needs-based use of electric vehicles, cooling appliances, heat pumps and other electricity-powered devices in households, commerce and industry, and *secondly* through the needs-controlled use of CHP technology. Industrial production, trade and private households offer sizeable potentials for load management (Stadler, 2006).

The Natural Gas Network as a Multifunctional Grid for Energy Transport and Storage

CHP technology in the form of small, local CHP units, or larger gas-steam power plants, is already predominantly gas-powered, which also provides an excellent basis for the linking of the various different energy carriers in future. Today's natural gas network can take over several functions in a networked energy system (Figure 4.4-6). Through CO_2 separation, biogas can be converted into methane, which can then be fed into existing natural gas networks to supply all of the typical natural gas consumers, such as CHP units, gas power plants, gas-powered cars, or conventional heating appliances. Synthesis gas from biomass conversion units can also be synthesised, with the separation of CO_2, into pure methane, and fed in. Similar processes can also be used for the conversion of coal into methane via coal gasification, again with the separation of CO_2 (US-DoE, 2006).

A new alternative is the production of methane from electricity production surpluses. Firstly, hydrogen is produced through electrolysis. This hydrogen is then converted into pure methane in a subsequent conversion process by reacting with CO_2, and can then also be fed into existing natural gas networks (Specht et al., 2010). This path can provide the long-term storage that is needed to shift the various seasonal surpluses from wind-powered and solar-powered electricity production to cover troughs lasting one to two weeks. Another important characteristic of the existing natural gas network can be used during this process: the possibility of storage in existing natural gas storage facilities with a capacity of 220 TWh_{th}, which exceeds the required capacities for power generation compensation several times over (Sterner et al., 2010; Klaus et al., 2010).

A further attractive option provided by methane synthesis from hydrogen and carbon dioxide results from the fact that it enables the initial collection of locally accumulated CO_2 streams, for example from biogas plants, but also from cement and chalk production, which can be converted into methane and subsequently added to large central units, for instance gas and steam power plants, for sequestration via the existing natural gas network.

This strategy also allows the use of coal in combination with CO_2 sequestration, thus generally representing a collection system for locally accumulated CO_2. For the compensation of wind and solar power plant output fluctuations, this allows the delinking of biomass availability, which will dramatically reduce the land-use competition with food production. Using the natural gas infrastructure also allows the long-distance transporting of this energy carrier from biomass, coal and electricity via existing natural gas / liquid gas terminals, and the inclusion of unconventional natural gas deposits (shale gas).

Finally, the Fischer-Tropsch synthesis allows the production of liquid energy carriers for transport use, or raw materials for the plastics industry. The natural gas network is also an ideal basis for the transition stage towards a sustainable energy system: natural gas-based power stations can already be rapidly extended today to compensate for power grid output fluctuations, whilst on the production side, natural gas can gradually be supplemented, and subsequently fully replaced, by biogenic methane or methane from electricity surpluses.

4.5 Financing the Transformation towards a Low-Carbon Society

4.5.1 Investment Requirement for the Transformation of Global Energy Systems

The global rebuilding of energy systems, necessary for the transformation into a sustainable and low-carbon society, including the adaptations required for the different areas of need (Section 4.3), requires substan-

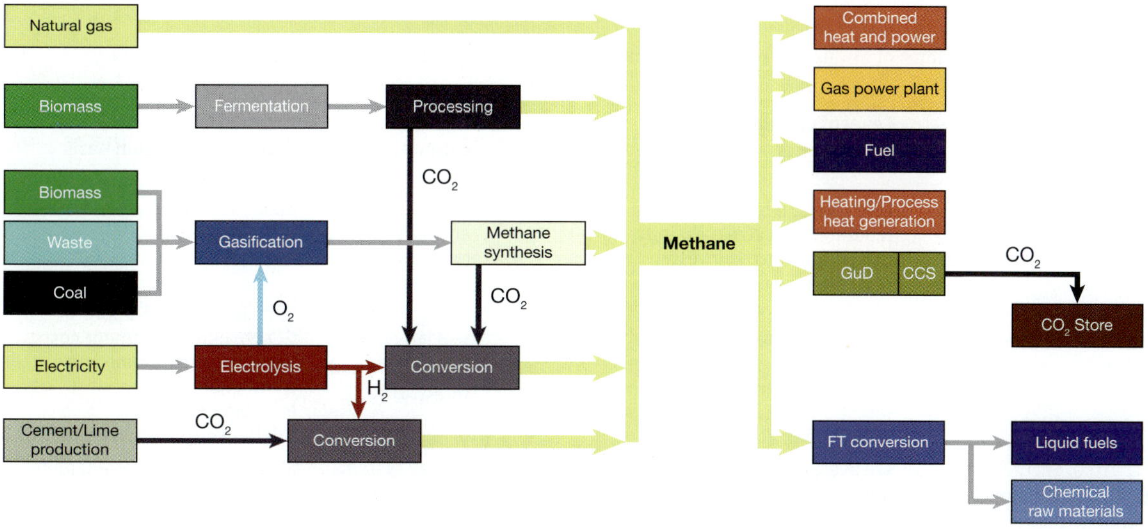

Figure 4.4-6
Possible linking of energy grids, example methane. The existing natural gas grid is used as a central element for the transportation and storage of conventional and renewable energies. This architecture allows CO_2 recycling, or the collection of decentrally captured CO_2 via the natural gas grid, including CO_2 storage after use in power plants. In combination with biomass, this allows the creation of 'negative emissions' in the form of a carbon sink. Renewable energies from wind, solar and hydropower can be stored temporarily in the form of methane in gas storage facilities, and, together with biomass and (in the transition period) coal, fed into all energy sectors – including the transport sector, optionally in liquid form through Fischer-Tropsch conversion (FT conversion).
Source: WBGU

tial additional investments, compared to the continuation of 'business as usual' (BAU). These investments must be made above all in the area of research and development of new technologies (particularly energy-related technologies), as well as technology diffusion, but also into the expansion of renewable energies, into more energy-efficient production technologies, into the rebuilding of communication and transport systems, and into improvements regarding end-use efficiency (including the areas of mobility, housing, communication).

A further important precondition for the transformation is the increase of investments into infrastructures: apart from new transportation infrastructures, additional transmission networks and energy storage facilities are particularly important to allow the integration of large proportions of renewable energies into the energy mix.

The global energy sector is already one of the largest and most important economic sectors, attracting annual investments of at least 1–2% of global GDP. These currently amount to around US$ 740 billion. Annually, US$ 210 billion are invested into electricity generation, US$ 170 billion into transmission and distribution, US$ 130 billion into industry, and a further US$ 3,800 billion in the transport sector alone (IEA, 2010a). This does not include all of the investments in the area of buildings and numerous smaller industries, as these are difficult to distinguish (IEA, 2010a).

4.5.1.1
Comparison of Investment Requirement Estimates

Various studies have reached the conclusion that the average additional global investment requirement for a transformation into a low-carbon society (compared with BAU) per year ranges from at least US$ 200 billion to around US$ 1,000 billion for the period up to 2030, and substantially more than US$ 1,000 billion per year for the period between 2030 and 2050 (UNFCCC, 2008; McKinsey, 2009; IEA, 2010a; Edenhofer et al., 2009a; Project Catalyst, 2010; AGECC, 2010; World Bank, 2010b; GEA, 2011). The various estimates have been summarised in Table 4.5-1.

At the lower end of the global investment requirement range are the UNFCCC Secretariat's estimates (2008), which assume the additional annual investment required in 2030 to reduce global greenhouse gas emissions by 25% compared to 2000 levels to be just over US$ 200 billion, half of which would have to be invested in developing countries. This figure already takes a reduction of investments in fossil-based energy generation into account. Unlike subsequent studies, the UNFCCC Secretariat's estimates only cover the investment costs for the realisation of a technology mix consisting of already existing technologies, whilst all other

Table 4.5-1
Overview of various estimates of annual upfront investment costs for the global decarbonisation of energy systems.
Source: WBGU

Study	Level of estimated investments	Region this estimate refers to	Sectors this estimate refers to	Assumptions for emissions paths or calculation basis
UNFCCC (2008): Investment and Financial Flows to Address Climate Change – An Update	US$ 200–210 billion annually (additional) in 2030, around half of which to be invested in developing countries	Global	Energy systems and land use (agriculture and forestry)	Reduction by 25% below 2000 emissions levels
McKinsey (2009): Pathways to a Low-Carbon Economy	€ 530 billion annually (additional) in 2020 ~US$ 660 billion; € 810 billion annually (additional) in 2030 ~US$ 1,000 billion	Global	Energy systems and land use (agriculture and forestry)	Stabilisation at 450 ppm CO_2eq; pure investment costs, excluding programme and transaction costs; excluding rebound Additionality: compared to BAU
IEA (2010a): Energy Technology Perspectives 2010	On average US$ 1,150 billion annually (additional) until 2050 (overall US$ 46,000 billion up to 2050)	Global	Energy systems in general (including final use in the industry, buildings, transport sector)	Stabilisation at 450–490 ppm CO_2eq; also includes learning and development costs for new technologies; Additionality: compared to basis scenario
Edenhofer et al. (2009a): RECIPE	US$ 480–600 billion annually until 2030; US$ 1,200 billion in 2050 in addition to baseline (assuming decline of investments in fossil energy generation of US$ 300–500 billion)	Global	Energy systems (excluding demand-side investments)	Stabilisation at 410–450 ppm CO_2eq
GEA (2011): Global Energy Assessment	Overall investments: US$ 1,700–2,100 billion annually (in total), equivalent to US$ 65,000–85,000 billion cumulatively between 2010 and 2050 (in total); overall investments for renewable energies: US$ 150–590 billion (in total); Investments in transmissions and storage technology: up to US$ 300–520 billion up to 2050 (in total)	Global	Energy system in general including final use	Climate stabilisation below 2 °C; Universal access and end of energy poverty by 2030; improvement of energy security; significant reduction of air pollution and other emissions
Project Catalyst (2010): From Climate Finance to Financing Green Growth	US$ 290 billion annually (in total) from 2020	Developing countries	Energy system in general	Compliance with the 2 °C guard rail (stabilisation at 450 ppm CO_2eq)
World Bank (2010b): World Development Report 2010	US$ 264–563 billion annually (in total) until 2030	Developing countries	Mitigation measures in general	Stabilisation at 450 ppm CO_2eq (values based on works by McKinsey, 2009; IIASA, 2009; IEA, 2008c, and Knopf et al., 2010)
AGECCC (2010): Energy for a Sustainable Future	On average US$ 35–40 billion annually until 2030 (in total)	Developing countries	Overcoming energy poverty	Goal: addressing energy poverty
GEA (2011): Global Energy Assessment	Around US$ 7–38 billion annually until 2030 (in total)	Developing countries	Overcoming energy poverty	Goal: access to electricity and clean energy carriers for cooking

studies also take the development costs of various (currently not yet developed) technologies into account (UNFCCC, 2008).

McKinsey (2009) assumes upfront investments for the rebuilding of global energy and land-use systems of around US$ 660–720 billion (€ 530 billion) in 2020, or respectively up to around US$ 1,100 billion (€ 810 billion) in 2030; these extrapolations also include the area of land use, unlike other studies. McKinsey's estimates should also be seen as additional investments, compared to the BAU scenario. The additional investments amount to 5–6% of the investments in the BAU scenario (McKinsey, 2009).

The International Energy Agency (IEA) assumes that average annual additional investments for an emissions reduction of 50% compared to 2005 figures (Blue Map scenario) will amount to around US$ 1,150 billion by 2050; the largest part of this (more than 50%) would have to be invested in the rebuilding of the transportation systems (particularly new vehicle technologies). These estimates also include private (demand-side) investments in new low-carbon vehicles and durable products, buildings efficiency, and energy-efficient industrial plants (IEA, 2010a). The IEA reaches the conclusion that the majority of the investments will have to be made after 2030. In 2030, investments totalling around US$ 750 billion will probably be required, rising to US$ 1,600 billion per year between 2030 and 2050. This means that the investments required between 2015 and 2030 in the Blue Map scenario exceed the basis scenario's investments by around 8.6%, and by 16% between 2030 and 2050. However, according to the IEA, these additional investments will be fully offset by savings on fossil fuels. The current value of net savings, i.e. the savings on fossil fuels over the period 2010–2050, less the additional investments over the same period, should therefore still amount to around US$ 8,000 billion, even at a (comparatively high) discount rate of 10% (IEA, 2010a).

The RECIPE study assumes that the energy transformation will require slightly lower investments (Edenhofer et al., 2009a). They are estimated at around US$ 480–600 billion per year until 2030. However, contrary to the estimates provided by McKinsey and the IEA, this does not include demand-side investments (such as new vehicles or buildings insulation). RECIPE's results also lead to the conclusion that the major part of the investments must be carried out before the middle of the century. By the middle of the century, additional investments would have to rise to up to US$ 1,200 billion.

The Global Energy Assessment (GEA) assumes annual supply-side investments totalling US$ 1,700–2,100 billion, thereby presenting the highest figures. However, unlike the figures arrived at in the other studies, these are not just additional investments, but the required overall total. Moreover, the scenarios developed for the GEA are not limited to the objective of stabilising the climate. They also cover the achieving of the Millennium Development Goals, and the overcoming of other negative environmental impacts of the current energy system. According to this, current supply-side investments of US$ 740 billion per year would have to increase to US$ 1,600–2,100 billion per year (the equivalent of US$ 65,000–85,000 billion cumulatively between 2010 and 2050). Investments in renewable energies are responsible for a substantial share of this, as they would have to rise from currently US$ 162 billion (UNEP-SEFI and BNEF, 2010) per year to up to US$ 590 billion per year, and investments in high-voltage grids and storage technology, which would have to rise from currently US$ 190 billion per year to up to US$ 300–520 billion per year in 2050 (GEA, 2011).

Allocating the Global Investment Requirement to Sectors and Regions

The allocation of investments to the various sectors is similar in all of the estimates. The transport sector accounts for around half of the total investments. The buildings sector is in second place. According to UNFCCC estimates, around 44% of global investments would have to be made into the transport sector, a further 25% into the buildings sector, roughly 20% into research and development, around 18% each into industry and agriculture, respectively, and 11% into forestry (UNFCCC, 2008). According to McKinsey's estimate, again more than half of the investments are necessary in the transport and building sectors for energy-efficient buildings and vehicles (McKinsey, 2009; Figure 4.5-1). Around 16%, or 18%, respectively, of the additional total investments would have to be spent on electricity generation from renewable energy sources and nuclear power, and CCS. Regionally, the most sizeable investments are needed in North America, Western Europe, and China (Figure 4.5-1; McKinsey, 2009). According to IEA estimates, as much as 50% of the overall investments required must be made in China, the USA, and the EU (IEA, 2010c).

Investments in transport also dominate in the IEA analysis, with investments into the buildings sector in second place, followed by energy sector investments (IEA, 2010a; Figure 4.5-2).

With regard to the investment cost estimates shown in Table 4.5-1, it must be taken into account that these cannot be compared directly, due to the differing methods used, and different assumptions (for instance in relation to energy mix and stabilisation path). The stated values should therefore be understood as rough indications. More precise and reliable estimates for the requisite additional initial investment costs in the various sectors and areas of need in different countries and regions, and for different decarbonisation paths, should be calculated during the course of research activities for the energy system decarbonisation to provide a solid basis for political decisions (Chapter 8).

However, even if the values shown in Table 4.5-1 are only estimates, they still allow the conclusion that the globally required additional investments over the next two decades will lie in the region of US$ several hundred billion, and can reach values of up to more than US$ 1,000 billion annually by the middle of the

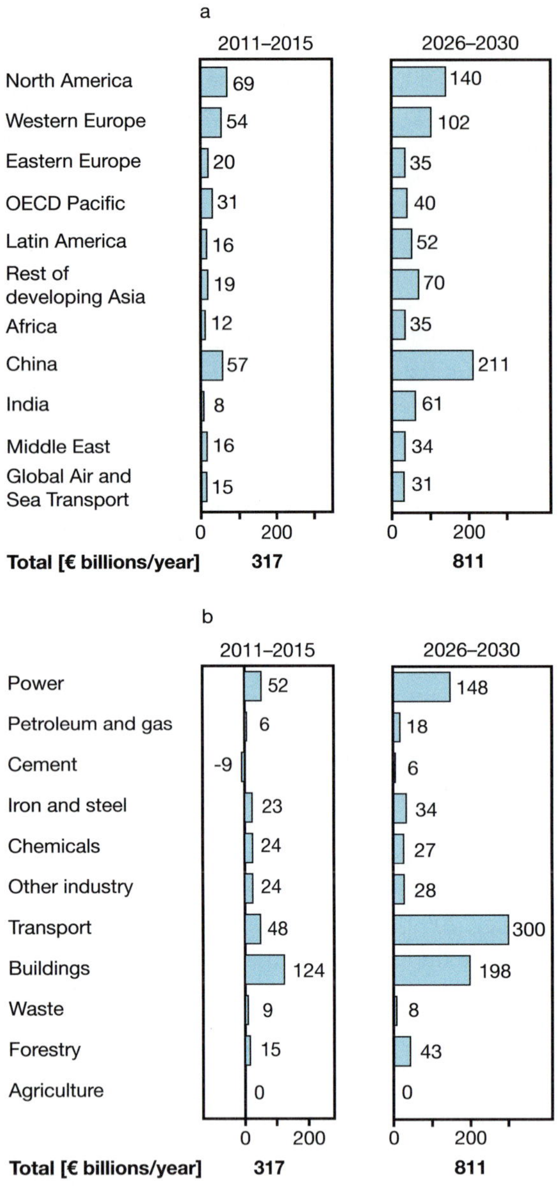

Figure 4.5-1
Additional annual global investments by sector (a), and countries or regions (b) during the stated periods of time (left: 2011–2015; right: 2026–2030) in € billions. The analysis refers to an emission path which allows the stabilisation of atmospheric greenhouse gas concentrations at 450 ppm CO_2eq.
Source: McKinsey, 2009

century. Evidently, two sectors that need particularly substantial investments are transport and buildings. Whilst up until 2015, buildings attract a major part of the investment requirement, this subsequently shifts to the transport sector (McKinsey, 2009; IEA, 2010a; Mehling et al., 2010; Figure 4.5-1).

The increase in investment requirement over time reflects the fact that globally, ever higher emissions reductions must continue to be achieved. Particularly high annual investment flows can be expected from 2030, when many of the low-carbon technologies will be marketable, whilst the demand for consumer goods and energy in the developing and newly industrialising countries will have risen considerably in the meantime (IEA, 2010a; McKinsey, 2009; Mehling et al., 2010). The International Energy Agency estimates that between 2010 and 2035, around US$ 316 billion per year would be needed for the expansion of renewable energies alone, in order to reach the target of stabilisation at 450 ppm CO_2eq. Most of this would have to be invested in wind power and hydropower (IEA, 2010c). According to IEA estimates, total investments into climate-friendly technologies would have to increase around fivefold by 2030, and tenfold by 2050 (IEA, 2010a), which serves to illustrate the dimension of the imminent challenge.

Investment Requirement Estimates for the WBGU's Exemplary Transformation Path

The WBGU's exemplary transformation path, leading to almost 100% renewable electricity in Europe, is part of the global energy transformation (Section 4.4). The expansion of the grid to link European and North African power grids for the large-scale use of solar energy alone would lead to annual investment costs of around € 47 billion in 2020, and these could rise to € 395 billion per year by 2050 (DLR, 2006). Moreover, additional capacities for the generation of renewable energies would have to be installed in Europe.

The authors of the scenario 'Energy [R]evolution – Towards a Fully Renewable Energy Supply in the EU 27', which is more or less comparable to the WBGU scenario, reach the conclusion that in order to achieve an almost 100% renewable energy supply for Europe by 2050, Europe-wide average annual investments into the energy sector would have to amount to € 87 billion (EREC and Greenpeace, 2010). These figures must be considered as overall totals, and not additional to the reference scenario. The investment requirement therefore exceeds the reference scenario's, which estimates annual energy sector investments of around € 45 billion, by around 90%. This must be compared to average annual fossil fuel savings of € 62 billion by 2050. The realisation of the Advanced Energy [R]evolution scenario required cumulative investments amounting to € 3,800 billion by 2050, accompanied by cumulative expected savings on fossil fuels of € 2,600 billion (EREC and Greenpeace, 2010).

Falling Investment Costs for Renewable Energies due to Learning Curve Effects

Due to the learning curve effect, investment costs per kWh generated for renewable energies will go down in

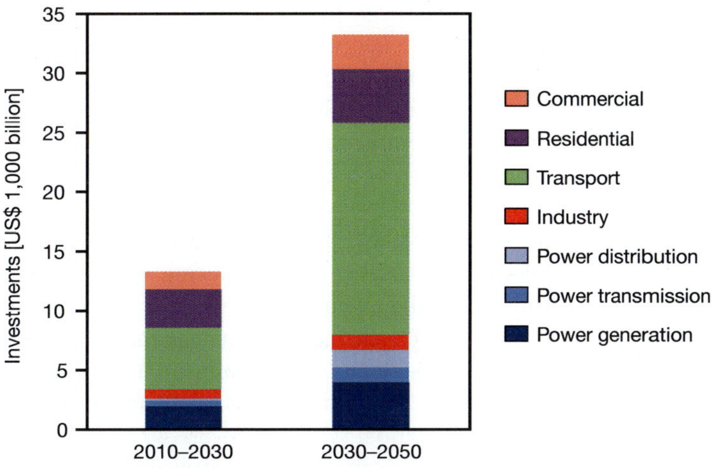

Figure 4.5-2
Breakdown of the additional global investment costs for the various sectors, cumulative over the respective period, in US$. The analysis refers to an emission path which allows the stabilisation of atmospheric greenhouse gas concentrations at 450–490 ppm CO_2eq.
Source: IEA, 2010a

line with an increasing number of new plant installations (Neij et al., 2003). Even when meeting a share of as little as 10–30% of global energy demand, the production costs of renewable energies are generally comparable to those of conventional electricity generation, thus enabling them to compete (Figure 4.5-3).

Figure 4.5-3 shows the cost reduction potentials of four renewable electricity generation technologies in comparison with the cost ranges of conventional coal- and gas-powered electricity generation (€ct 3–5 per kWh). It is estimated that fossil-powered plants with CCS will cost an additional €ct 3 per kWh (IPCC, 2005). The bandwidths of the cost of electricity generation with photovoltaic and wind energy are the result of location-dependence, i.e. degree of solar irradiation, or wind speed. In the case of solar thermal power plants, the bandwidth is not as wide, as it only makes sense to use these in latitudes with a high share of direct radiation, due to the employment of concentrators. The wide bandwidth of biomass electricity generation costs is due to the various different bioenergy technologies.

Learning curves were used for the calculation of expected power generation costs. For photovoltaic and wind energy, these have been recorded for over 20 years, and so far, they are following an extremely stable trend: a doubling of the cumulative globally installed

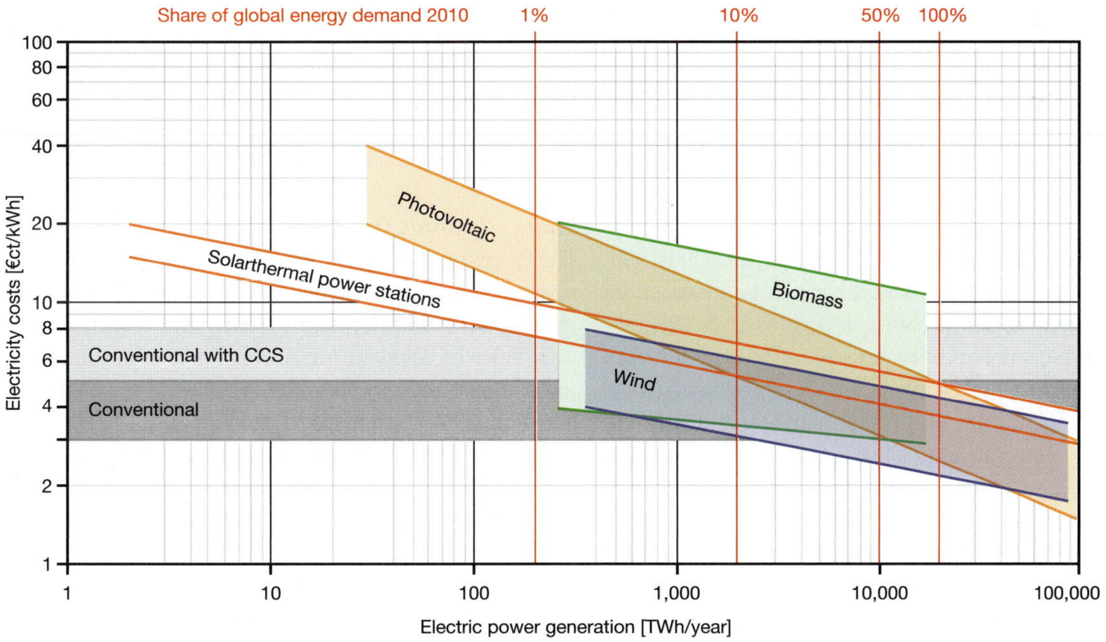

Figure 4.5-3
Global development potential of costs for electricity from renewable energies.
Source: WBGU, own illustration

generation capacity reduces the cost of electricity from photovoltaic energy by 20%, and of wind energy by 10% (Staffhorst, 2006). Up to now, there are too few experiences with solar thermal power plants to allow the determination of a stable trend. Therefore, a learning rate of only 10%, equalling the wind energy rate, has been assumed. In the case of biomass electricity generation, there is a broad mix of fermentation, gasification and combustion technologies. Because of the comparatively conventional technologies, the assumed learning rate is only 5%. The band showing biomass electricity generation is limited to a maximum of 15,000 TWh, or 54 EJ, per year (Figure 4.5-3), which represents the limit of the sustainable potential (with an electricity conversion efficiency factor of approx. 50%). It must be considered here that the electricity generation costs for conventional fossil-powered plants are assumed to remain constant for the purpose of this illustration. On the one hand, learning curve progress is made there, too; on the other hand, it can be expected that fuel costs as well as costs for emissions allowances will rise, which will probably more than compensate any learning progress.

Estimates of Investment Requirement in Developing Countries

The investment requirement for the energy transformation in developing countries is proportional to the global investment requirement, and different studies estimate the amount to range between around US$ 100 and 563 billion per year (Table 4.5-1) by 2030. According to UNFCCC (2008), around half of the estimated global additional US$ 200 billion of investments required must be made in developing countries; the decrease of investments into fossil-fuelled energy generation is already included here. According to the Project Catalyst analysis, around US$ 290 billion will be required annually in the developing countries as of 2020 to finance the investments necessary for a low-carbon economy that is compatible with the 2 °C guard rail. Over half of this (US$ 155 billion) would have to be invested in new energy generation plants, a further US$ 123 billion would be needed for energy efficiency investments, whilst the investments which would have to be made into agriculture and forest management are not particularly substantial (Project Catalyst, 2010). However, the World Bank assumes that in order to achieve stabilisation at 450 ppm CO_2eq, total investments of up to US$ 264–563 billion annually would have to be made between 2010 and 2030 in developing countries (World Bank, 2010b). This estimate includes mitigation measures in all sectors, though, not only those pertaining to energy generation and use, therefore exceeding the Project Catalyst estimates.

In addition, financial transfers for the REDD-plus mechanism for the reduction of deforestation in developing countries are also needed (Section 7.3.7.2). To halve global deforestation, these amount to approx. US$ 20–33 billion per year (Stern, 2008; Strassburg et al., 2008; Project Catalyst, 2010).

Investment Requirement to Reduce Energy Poverty

Reducing the energy poverty in developing countries, on the other hand, requires 'only' two-digit billion amounts. The UN Secretary General's Advisory Group on Energy and Climate Change, for instance, has calculated that up to 2030, investments averaging US$ 35–40 billion per year are necessary in developing countries in order to provide a climate-friendly foundation for local energy systems, whilst also achieving the aim of global universal access to energy services by 2030 (AGECC, 2010). This would allow all households access to basic energy services (AGECC, 2010; IEA, 2010c). These estimates are based on IEA (US$ 35 billion annually for access to electricity; IEA, 2009b) and UNDP (US$ 2–3 billion annually for access to modern fuels; UNDP and ESMAP, 2005) figures. The Global Energy Assessment (2011) arrives at similar amounts, quantifying the required investments for the creation of universal access to energy as US$ 7–38 billion by 2030. Around 50% of this is needed for grid expansion, the remainder for clean cooking facilities, and energy carriers for cooking (GEA, 2011). Each of these investment estimates refers to absolute values – not to additions to business as usual. It must also be taken into account that the reduction of energy poverty cannot be viewed independently of the transformation towards a low-carbon society. Accordingly, the investment requirements overlap, and must not be viewed as an addition.

4.5.1.2 Energy Systems Transformation Cost

The investment requirement for the transformation towards a low-carbon society cannot be equated with its costs. To determine the costs, the resultant savings must be allowed for (lower energy consumption, lower expenditure on fossil energy carriers). As already mentioned, according to IEA estimates (2010a) and McKinsey (2009), the additional investments will be either fully, or almost fully, compensated by savings on fossil fuels. Furthermore, any macroeconomic cost assessment would also have to take the effects on global GDP, caused by the structural changes in the energy and production sectors, into account. This macroeconomic assessment can be carried out with the aid of integrated assessment models that link climate with economic models (Section 4.2). These calculate the development of global GDP with and without climate policies. The difference between both developments at any point in time, discounted to a basis year, reflects the costs of mitigation policies.

Comparing Different Cost Estimates

A comparison of different integrated assessment models yields the result that the aggregated macroeconomic costs of an ambitious decarbonisation strategy (stabilisation of CO_2 concentration at 410 ppm CO_2eq) by 2100 in current values (i.e. discounted on the basis year 2005, assuming a discount rate of 3%) will probably be in the region of 0.7–4% of global GDP (Edenhofer et al., 2009a). A slightly less ambitious stabilisation at 450 ppm CO_2eq would, in current values, result in costs that could even be as low as only 0.1%, up to a maximum 1.4% of global GDP, again calculated over the period up to 2100 (Edenhofer et al., 2009a). The level of costs depends strongly on the model assumptions with regard to technology development. Under the assumption of an endogenous technological change, the models calculate lower costs (Edenhofer et al., 2009a; Fisher et al., 2007). In the ADAM model comparison, the maximum of wealth loss calculated amounted to 0.8% of global GDP by 2100, at a stabilisation of 550 ppm CO_2eq, or, respectively, 2.5% of global GDP by 2100, at a stabilisation of 400 ppm CO_2eq. Again, a discount rate of 3% was assumed (Edenhofer et al., 2010).

A model comparison for the IPCC's 4th assessment report leads to the conclusion that a stabilisation at 445–535ppm CO_2eq would lead to wealth losses amounting to 3% of global GDP by 2030, and 5.5% of global GDP by 2050 (Fisher et al., 2007). This equates to a reduction of annual global GDP growth of 0.12% maximum.

The range of cost estimates for the decarbonisation, depending on model assumptions, timeframe and stabilisation scenario, therefore lies between 0.7 and a maximum 5.5% of global GDP in current values, spread across a period of several years. This must be compared to the high costs of unabated climate change, which, according to Stern (2006) could amount to as much as up to 20% of global GDP.

Cost of a Delayed Transformation

Delaying the transformation will increase the costs further, as this would lead to even more drastic reduction measures having to be implemented over a shorter period of time in order to comply with the 2°C guard rail. Edenhofer et al., (2009a) expect that delaying an ambitious global climate policy (stabilisation at 450ppm CO_2) for another decade alone would cause the cost of emissions reduction to rise by more than 46%. The current IEA scenarios even suggest a doubling of the cost of the transformation in 2035, in the event that only the reduction pledges offered at the UN climate change conference in Copenhagen were to be implemented by the pledging countries in the coming decade. This would demand a drastically accelerated transformation speed after 2020 in order to keep within a CO_2 emissions budget that is compatible with the 2°C guard rail (Box 1.1-1). This target could only be reached through accelerated innovation activities in all transformation areas. A delayed change of course would also lead to economically not justifiable decisions such as the switching off of fossil power plants before the end of their amortisation period. Considering these facts, and on the basis of higher projections for economic growth by 2035, the IEA's cost estimates for the transformation of the energy systems have been revised, and now exceed the 2009 (pre-Copenhagen) estimates by US$ 1,000 billion (IEA, 2010c).

Co-Benefits of the Transformation

However, it is not only costs that go hand in hand with the energy systems transformation; it also offers co-benefits above and beyond the avoidance of dangerous climate change. The integrated assessment models do not take these co-benefits into account. Compliance with the 2°C guard rail also leads to improved air quality, reduces health care costs, and generally reduces the environmental damages caused by pollutant emissions. These advantages would become particularly visible in developing and newly industrialising countries. In a 450 ppm scenario, the global air pollution control costs could be roughly reduced by 23%. Far more than 750 million life-years could be saved through this, especially in China and India. An early transformation would also considerably reduce climate change adaptation costs (IEA, 2010c). Also to be considered are co-benefits resulting from increased energy security and a lesser dependency on fuel imports (GEA, 2011).

Ultimately, it can also be expected that the expansion of investments in sustainable and low-carbon technologies and infrastructure will create new industries, and, correspondingly, employment opportunities. In a global perspective, this could contribute to continued economic growth, and to poverty reduction (UNEP, 2011; Jaeger et al., 2011).

4.5.1.3
Investments so far, Investment Gaps, and Investment Barriers

Current Investments in Low-Carbon Energy Technologies

Compared to the estimated annual investment requirement for renewable energies of at least US$ 150–300

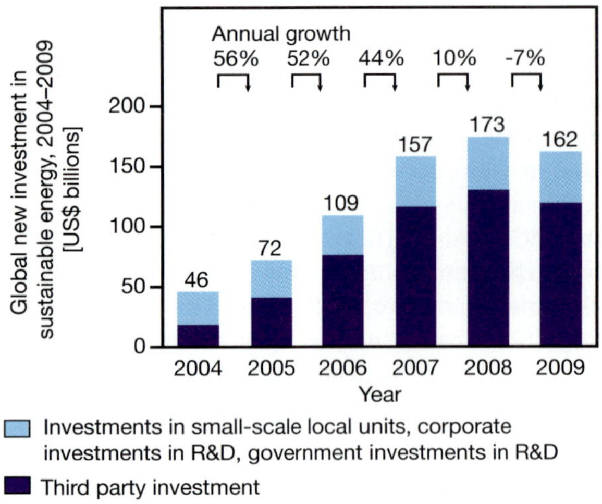

Figure 4.5-4
Global investments into low-carbon energies between 2004–2009 in US$ billions.
Source: UNEP-SEFI and BNEF, 2010

billion per year, new investments into low-carbon energies amounted to around US$ 173 billion in 2008, and around US$ 162 billion in 2009 (UNEP-SEFI and BNEF, 2010; Figure 4.5-4).

The figures shown in Figure 4.5-4 include research and development expenses (R&D), and costs for installation of low-carbon energy generation plants; savings have not been taken into account. A considerable proportion of these investments made in 2009 went into wind energy (56%), followed by solar energy (20%) and bioenergy (15%). Some investments were also made in geothermal energy, small-scale hydropower plants, and other climate-friendly technologies. Most of these were made in Europe, Asia and Oceania, particularly in China (UNEP-SEFI and BNEF, 2010). It is indeterminable whether these were made on top of business-as-usual investments. The positive development of investments into renewable energies in Europe can largely be ascribed to promotion through feed-in tariffs (UNECE, 2010). Globally, feed-in tariffs are currently used in more than 50 countries, and at least 25 regional states or provinces (BNEF, 2010; REN21, 2010).

Investment Gaps

Nevertheless, the global additional investments needed to convert the energy systems (at least US$ 200 billion per year) have overall not reached the required dimensions. An IEA report concludes that there are substantial investment gaps in the area of research and development alone. Annually, another US$ 40–90 billion would have to be invested in R&D of new vehicle technologies, bioenergy, CCS, energy efficiency, efficient coal use, smartgrids, and wind and solar power (IEA, 2010a). And yet, in the IEA member states, government support for R&D in the energy sector has continually decreased since 1979, and this despite the fact that national spending on R&D in general has risen in the last decade (IEA, 2010a). Current R&D expenditure priorities do not seem to focus on the challenge of climate stabilisation at all (Grübler and Riahi, 2010).

During the economic and financial crisis, investments in renewable energies and energy efficiency went down drastically (UNEP-SEFI, 2009b; IEA, 2010b). In future, to comply with the ambitious stabilisation targets, the level of pre-economic and financial crisis investments into energy systems conversion will therefore have to be exceeded many times over. One particular challenge is the rapid generation of the necessary funds for investments in end-use efficiency (IEA, 2008b). The area of energy efficiency in particular is currently extremely underfinanced (IEA, 2010b). New financing and business models can turn this around (Sections 4.3, 4.5.2.2; Box 4.3-3).

Investment Barriers

An important reason for the underfinancing of renewable energies and energy efficiency projects is presented by certain specific investment barriers. For instance, no long-term and binding policy targets for the decarbonisation of the energy systems have so far been set, and investors therefore have to bear high uncertainty regarding future climate and energy policy developments and the resultant market potentials (Holmes and Mabey, 2010; Mehling et al., 2010). Granted, individual countries have set policy targets; however, for the most part only up until 2020, whilst investment horizons for major projects like power plants tend to be much longer (sometimes up to 40 years). As currently a new investment cycle in the field of electricity generation is commencing in most of the OECD countries, the next few years will define the technological course for the coming 40–50 years. The risk of lock-in effects is therefore high (IEA, 2010a).

Moreover, in many cases, the technology development in the area of renewable energies and efficiency technologies is still in its initial stages, so there are risks with regard to the future return on investment (Holmes and Mabey, 2010). There are also often information gaps with regard to efficiency technologies on the part of users and consumers, which leads to profitable investments not being carried out. One of the consequences of this is that many small-scale efficiency potentials, which would nevertheless be significant if taken together (for example in households), are not tapped (Ohndorf et al., 2010). In the area of buildings efficiency, the unfavourable incentive structures for property owners and tenants in the case of rented property, also pose a significant investment barrier (IEA, 2008b; Sections 4.3.2, 5.2).

Moreover, in developing countries, the basic conditions for larger investments in low-carbon technologies and renewable energies are often lacking. In these countries, a regulatory environment must initially be created, which stimulates investments, for example with the aid of market incentive programmes. The promotion of renewable energies with feed-in tariffs, efficiency standards for vehicles, or a fuel tax could be important incentives for low-carbon technology investments. In addition, initial points of contact could be established for companies willing to invest, for example in the form of investment support agencies, and information centres for CO_2 mitigation projects (UNCTAD, 2010b). Many countries will need the financial and technical support of the international community for this. Resources from the bi- and multilateral mitigation funds should be reserved for these purposes.

4.5.2 Financing the Transformation

Due to the necessary extent of the transformation, it can only be jointly financed by states, private companies and investors, international financing organisations (including the World Bank, IMF), and development banks. A major part of the financing must be provided by private companies or institutional investors (including investment funds, pension funds, insurances), as the scale of the investments exceeds government budgets. Many low-carbon investments are hampered by the fact that they require relatively high upfront investments, whilst rather low annual returns on investment are spread across a comparatively long period of time. The amortisation period of such investments is therefore usually longer, and they have a lower rate of return compared to alternative investments. In addition, the expected rates of return have been unrealistically high over the past few years, particularly on the capital markets, which disadvantaged sustainable capital investments even further.

The state, the international financing organisations, and the development banks could provide incentives for private investments (Section 5.2) through long-term and binding policy targets and economic and regulatory measures (including carbon pricing, efficiency standards, technology-specific support), and support these through the provision of loans with favourable conditions or credit guarantees, which would also serve to make investments more profitable (leverage effect). However, the financing of infrastructure investments and large-scale projects, such as the extension of energy transmission grids, above all requires funding by states, national and regional investment banks, and development banks, as such projects frequently have the character of public goods, are accompanied by high risks, and require large sums of capital (Helm, 2010). In order to make sufficient funds available, new financing sources must be unlocked at state level. Developing and newly industrialising countries should be supported by financial transfers in the transformation of their economies (Section 7.3.9). And, not least, new business models could help to reduce the burden of high upfront costs for households and companies.

4.5.2.1 New Financing Sources at State Level

On the one hand, governments can fall back on tax revenue to finance the transformation. Particularly the revenue from carbon pricing, either in the form of taxation or of emissions trading, can generate additional public revenue. Revenues released through the phasing out of fossil energy and agricultural subsidies, levies on international aviation and shipping, and a tax on international financial transactions are also possible new financing sources. On the other hand, governments have the option of obtaining external financing, for example through loans from national banks or the international financing organisations. However, the majority of international financing offers are focused on the governments and financial institutions of developing countries. For these, the UNFCCC financial transfers are an additional important financing source for the transformation.

Public Revenue from Carbon Pricing

At a national level, carbon pricing, in the form of either a carbon tax, or emissions trading, can generate substantial funds (Section 5.2). The UN Secretary-General's High-Level Advisory Group on Climate Change Financing (AGF) estimates, for example, that the introduction of carbon pricing mechanisms in the industrialised countries by 2020, at a price of US$ 20–25 per t CO_2eq, could generate a total annual revenue of US$ 300 billion (AGF, 2010). This could be partly used to finance the transformation in the industrialised countries and partly for financial transfers to developing countries.

The potential revenue can vary considerably, depending on the carbon tax scale, or the amount of emission allowances in an emissions trading scheme. The WBGU believes that in Europe and the OECD countries, the carbon price would have to be a minimum of US$ 40–50 per t CO_2 in 2020, and in 2050 a minimum of US$ 110–130 per t CO_2 to have a transformative impact in terms of achieving compliance with the 2 °C guard rail. In this case, the annual revenue can be expected to be considerably higher than the US$ 300 billion estimated by the AGF. IEA extrapolations confirm this. The IEA expects that an emissions trading scheme involving all OECD and EU countries, which aims at mere compliance with the hardly ambitious mitigation pledges made in Copenhagen, would already yield a revenue of US$ 250 billion in 2020, assuming full auctioning (IEA, 2010c).

A CO_2 tax would have to increase over time, and the amount of allowances in an emissions trading scheme would have to be reduced in order to develop the desired steering effect for compliance with the 2 °C guard rail. The revenue from carbon pricing can therefore be expected to continue to rise over several decades, roughly until 2030/2040. However, towards the middle of the century, the revenue can be expected to fall, as by then, emissions should have gone down drastically, leading to a much lower taxation basis, or a greatly reduced amount of allowances. In the WBGU's view, revenue generated from CO_2-pricing, either through a tax or the auctioning of emissions allowances, would represent a reliable source of revenues for climate financing over a long period, and at the same time develop the requisite steering effect for future investments, as well as for consumption and production decisions (Section 5.2).

Phasing Out Fossil Energy and Agricultural Subsidies

A further potential financing source is the phasing out of fossil energy subsidies, which are currently still widespread, particularly in non-OECD countries, for example, Russia, Iran, China, Saudi Arabia, India, Indonesia, and the Ukraine (UNEP, 2008). According to IEA estimates, worldwide consumption subsidies for fossil energies amounted to US$ 557 billion in 2008, and US$ 312 billion in 2009. Two-thirds of this was accounted for by subsidies for crude oil and natural gas, whilst coal subsidies amounted to a comparatively small amount of US$ 6 billion. Other estimates take the total energy subsidies, both for the producer and the consumer side, to amount to up to US$ 700 billion annually (GSI, 2009). According to IEA estimates, if the subsidies for fossil energy carriers were to be completely phased out by 2020, global energy demand would decrease by around 5–6%, which would lead to a reduction of CO_2 emissions of around 6–7%, compared to the status quo (IEA et al., 2010a; IEA, 2010c).

In either case, fossil energy carrier subsidies far exceed the financial support currently enjoyed by renewable energies, which amounted to US$ 57 billion in 2009 (IEA, 2010c). The public funds which could be released through the phasing out of fossil energy carrier subsidies in the industrial countries within the G20 alone are estimated to amount to around US$ 8–10 billion per year (AGF, 2010), and could also contribute to the financing of the transfers needed by the developing countries. In the non-OECD countries, the funds thus released could be used for extending the electric power infrastructure, and providing energy access based on renewable energies, particularly in rural areas (IEA et al., 2010a).

Taxation of International Transportation and International Financial Transactions

Levies on international aviation and shipping or, alternatively, the introduction of an international emissions trading scheme for these sectors, can generate additional revenue for investments into the transformation. By putting a price on the emissions of to international aviation and shipping, their negative impact on climate would be acknowledged. According to AGF estimates, if 50% of the revenue generated globally through taxation were to be made available for the transformation, this could lead to an annual financial flow of around US$ 10 billion (AGF, 2010).

The AGF estimates further that an equally substantial amount could be generated if a tax of between 0.001% and 0.01% were introduced on international financial transactions (AGF, 2010). However, it is uncertain what impact a financial transaction tax would have on the international capital markets. It could result in the reallocation of substantial amounts of financial flow, which would considerably reduce the taxation basis (Campbell and Froot, 1993; Honohan and Yoder, 2010). If a financial transaction tax were to be introduced, the rate should therefore be kept extremely low, as exemplified in the AGF's sample calculation.

Fund Generation via UNFCCC and Development Cooperation

Apart from grants and loans from international finance organisations, the financial transfers negotiated under the UNFCCC and international development assistance are also important sources of finance for many developing countries. Added to this, there are further bilateral and multilateral funds, which provide resources for mitigation projects in developing countries.

Under the UNFCCC, there is so far only one financing mechanism to support mitigation projects, the Climate Change Focal Area provided by the Global Environment Facility's (GEF) trust fund. Other funds under the UNFCCC umbrella (Adaptation Fund, Special Climate Change Fund, Least Developed Countries Fund) predominantly focus on adaptation financing. In 2010, at Cancún, the UNFCCC agreed the establishment of a new fund, the so-called Green Climate Fund, poten-

Box 4.5-1

The UNFCCC Green Climate Fund

One result of the 16th United Nations Framework Convention on Climate Change in Cancún has been the establishment of the Green Climate Fund to provide funds for mitigation, adaptation, capacity building and technology transfer in developing countries (§ 102–112 of the Cancún Agreements). The fund's Board is to comprise of 24 members, with an equal number of members from developing and industrialised countries; the fund will initially be administered by the World Bank. However, the extent of the fund has not been determined as yet, and nor have its financing sources. The Annex I Countries have pledged a sum of 30 billion US$ for the period 2010–2012 for fast-start financing, and with a view to long-term financing, committed to a goal of jointly mobilizing US$ 100 billion per year by 2020 to address the needs of developing countries. According to the Cancún Agreements, a significant share of new multilateral funding for adaptation should flow through the Green Climate Fund. The fund's exact structure and method of operation has not been determined yet. A Transitional Committee has been suggested to design the fund; this is to comprise 15 representatives from industrialised, and 25 from developing countries (UNFCCC, 2010; Müller, 2011).

tially the most important future multilateral financing mechanism (Box 4.5-1).

The provision of new and additional funds totalling up to US$ 30 billion between 2010 and 2012 for mitigation and adaptation in developing countries (fast-start finance) had already been announced at the climate negotiations in Copenhagen in 2009. As of 2020, US$ 100 billion annually are envisaged to be provided for mitigation and adaptation measures from a range of sources (public, private, bi- and multilateral, including new financing instruments). A proportion of these resources is to be distributed via the future Green Climate Fund, as yet to be established. Particularly funds for adaptation measures are planned to be managed by the fund.

Considering the amounts required for mitigation and adaptation in the developing countries, which are estimated to lie somewhere in the region of three-digit billions for mitigation (approx. US$ 300 billion from 2020; Project Catalyst, 2010; World Bank, 2010c), and in the region of two-digit billions for adaptation (approx. US$ 10–100 billion; Project Catalyst, 2010; World Bank, 2010c), the funds should be allocated adequately to the different areas that require financing (adaptation, mitigation, technology transfer, capacity building). In the WBGU's view, the proportion of the pledged US$ 100 billion that should be used for mitigation projects or measures should average around 60–70%, independent of whether these funds are made available via the Green Climate Fund, or other channels.

Also to be decided is the question of whether the monies provided by the Green Climate Fund should be granted in the form of non-repayable transfer finance, or as loans and credit guarantees. Although loans and credit guarantees are often sufficient to have a considerable leverage effect (World Bank, 2010c; Neuhoff et al., 2010), equitability considerations indicate that a large part of the pledged resources should be defined as true grants or financial aid. This can not least be justified by the high level of cumulative emissions from industrialised countries in the past (WBGU, 2010a).

However, the US$ 100 billion pledged annually from 2020 will not be enough to cover all of the financing needed for the transformation in the world's developing regions. It can be expected that the investments required for the transformation in developing and newly industrialising countries will increase even further after 2020 (Section 4.5.1). Therefore, in addition to establishing the Green Climate Fund, existing bi- and multilateral funds for mitigation projects in developing countries should also be increased. This applies, for instance, to the World Bank's Carbon Partnership Facility, as well as the two funds under the umbrella of the Climate Investment Fund (Clean Technology Fund, Strategic Climate Fund; World Bank, 2010c).

World Bank funds for mitigation and adaptation currently amount to a total of roughly US$ 9.5 billion for 2008–2012 (IEA, 2010a). Apart from the multilateral funds, there are also some bilateral initiatives, for example the Cool Earth Partnership (Japan), equipped with US$ 10 billion of funding, the International Climate Initiative (Germany), with US$ 564 million, or the European Union's Global Climate Change Alliance (GCCA) (US$ 76 million; World Bank, 2010b). However, the millions available in these individual funds, usually to be distributed over a number of years, are hardly enough to cover the required investment volume, which is in the region of billions; they would therefore have to be increased considerably. According to World Bank estimates, the sum total of climate change related transfers (i.e. taking all financial flows for mitigation and adaptation, as well as technology transfer and capacity building into account) amounts to around US$ 10 billion annually (World Bank, 2010c), i.e. still far under the pledged US$ 100 billion to be made available from 2020.

Under UNFCCC, yet another potential financing mechanism is currently developing, independent of the Kyoto Protocol. The developing countries undertake to

Box 4.5-2

Balancing Act between Climate and Development Financing

Since 1992, in developing countries activities to mitigate climate change as well as activities to adapt to the impacts of climate change have primarily been financed from development funds. Contributions by the UNFCCC funds established under the Global Environmental Facility (GEF) have been considerably lower. The focus has always been on climate change mitigation. On the one hand, the relationship between climate and development financing shows marked overlaps and synergies: investments in development can serve climate change mitigation, and also help in terms of resilience against the impacts of climate change. On the other hand, there is some concern that prioritisation of low-carbon infrastructure construction could be at the expense of poverty reduction.

Increased development budgets would decrease the risk that, under the pressure of the climate negotiations, investments in mitigation and adaptation could be accorded a higher priority than investments into poverty reduction relevant areas (aid diversion). However, as the public budgets of most of the contributing nations are strained due to the financial or the euro crisis, respectively, as well as due to the slowing down of economic growth, it seems unlikely, from a political perspective, that developing budgets which do not include climate financing will grow or even remain stable. In the EU, development cooperation budgets are expected to reduce in the medium term: the German Federal Ministry for Economic Cooperation and Development's budget, which represents around 70% of German public development cooperation funds (ODA), will shrink from € 6 billion in 2010 to € 5.6 billion in 2013 (EU COM, 2010d).

The fact that there is no official definition of 'additionality' increases the risk of aid diversion. The Framework Convention on Climate Change does not discount ODA as a financing source. However, the defined targets of ODA and climate financing are not identical: according to the OECD definition, ODA is primarily intended to promote development and welfare in developing countries, whilst climate financing has both global and local benefits. If developing countries are supported in adaptation to the impacts of climate change, this can also directly impact positively on local welfare, whilst the mitigation of their greenhouse gas emissions primarily serves global welfare, as well as indirectly reducing the local need for adaptation. In the OECD, the contributing countries see fast-start financing as ODA; however, there is no joint definition of 'additionality' (Brown et al., 2010). Germany defines all investments that go beyond the level already reached in 2009 as 'additional'. This means that this level remains stable, and climate financing as a whole will increase, although within a shrinking overall budget.

Not least, the lack of transparent procedures and joint criteria for climate financing reporting on the part of the donor countries adds to the uncertainty with regard to the payments made. OECD Development Assistance Committee (DAC) procedures for measuring bilateral climate financing are not satisfactory. Two independent empirical studies have found that the funding countries have a systematic tendency to provide inexact reports. Only 25% of the measures reported as relevant for climate change mitigation by the funding countries could really be classified as such (Roberts et al., 2008; Michaelowa and Michaelowa, 2010). The DAC procedure (the so-called 'Rio markers') relies on the funding countries themselves determining, according to their own criteria, which measures represent a considerable or significant contribution to climate change mitigation. Comparability is therefore not guaranteed, and there is also no subsequent adjustment of data with regard to changed or discontinued measures. A Rio marker for climate change mitigation measures was agreed in 1998, one for adaptation not until the end of 2009. Agreements on definitions and reporting procedures are therefore vital for further negotiations on public climate financing.

However, in the medium term, these issues will lose their relevance, as the impacts of climate change, and their associated investment risks, will in time become common parameters, and an integral part of project planning. Also, a stronger focus on low-carbon infrastructures will become part of mainstream development policies. However, these strategic issues are important in the transitional period, during which the course for the transformation must be set. Uncertainty with regard to aims, instruments and financing are hardly helpful for the strategic redefinition of political aims.

implement appropriate mitigation efforts at national level (Nationally Appropriate Mitigation Actions, NAMAs), which enjoy the support of the industrialised countries in the form of financial and technology transfers. It is not yet clear to what extent these will be project-based measures, and whether and to what extent the supporting industrial countries will be able to offset the mitigations thus reached against their own. One option would be to make payments from the Green Climate Fund dependent on the implementation of planed mitigation measures (NAMAs) (Section 7.3.9). This could then also serve to finance sectoral and mitigation measures of a more strategic nature, such as grid infrastructure expansion or feed-in tariffs, embedded in an overall concept for emissions reduction. The additionality of the resources, and their differentiation to official development assistance, would also have to be verified (Box 4.5-2).

Financing via the Carbon Market

So far, the Clean Development Mechanism (CDM) has been an important financing source for CO_2 mitigation projects in developing countries (World Bank, 2010b). In 2008 alone, it had a transaction volume (primary transactions) of US$ 6.5 billion (IEA, 2010a).

The continuation of the CDM in the framework of the Kyoto Protocol was decided in Cancún– the future of the latter, however, is currently uncertain. The role the international carbon market in its current form will play for developing countries is therefore also unclear.

If, under the Kyoto Protocol, a second commitment period to follow on directly from the first is not successfully agreed, the demand for CDM emission reduction credits can be expected to fall. At best, the demand would be maintained through other emissions trading schemes, such as the EU ETS, or the voluntary market.

The past has also shown the CDM in its current form could not meet a number of the expectations originally riding on it. Various studies have, for instance, reached the conclusion that the additionality of the emissions reductions is, in many cases, not given. According to estimates by Michaelowa and Purohit (2007), and Wara and Victor (2008), the proportion of registered CDM projects that does not fulfil the additionality criterion could be a fifth, or even two-thirds. This would effectively represent an extension of the EU ETS member countries' emissions caps. Vasa and Neuhoff (2011) have calculated that an infringement of the additionality criterion in a fifth to two-thirds of the registered projects in the trading period 2008 to 2009 would have been the equivalent of extending the EU ETS emissions by 30–106 million t CO_2eq.

In addition, the expectations that the CDM would make a guaranteed contribution to sustainable development and would trigger significant technology transfers have not been met. Moreover, it has led to undesirable incentives for the expansion of climate-damaging activities, particularly in the case of CDM projects for the reduction of industrial gases (for example, HFC-23 projects; Vasa and Neuhoff, 2011). There is furthermore the risk that the CDM offers particularly the large newly developing countries incentives to abandon their own climate mitigation policies in favour of the required additionality of projects. For this reason, there are deliberations to limit the CDM to the least developed countries (LDC), which currently profit only marginally from the CDM due to their very low number of CDM projects (UNEP-Risoe, 2011).

From the WBGU's perspective, it would make sense to limit the CDM to the LDC in future, thereby emphasising the CDM's development aspect. In addition, if the mechanism were extended to include sectoral measures – not unlike the programme-based CDM – it would allow, for example, the bundled financing of many small-scale and scattered energy efficiency potentials in microbusinesses and households (Figueres, 2008; Ohndorf et al., 2010). A programme-based or sectoral CDM could also contribute considerably to energy poverty reduction by financing biomass-fuelled cookers, for example, or small-scale solar-powered units for water heating in private households. By adjusting some of the regulations of the programme-based CDM, this potential could be maximised even further in future (Figueres, 2008). The continuance of the CDM restricted to LDC, however, would have to be accompanied by clearly more ambitious reduction targets in the Annex I Countries, and reforms with regards to the accounting of international emissions credits (CER; for instance from HFC-23 projects), as already intended by the EU.

4.5.2.2
Supporting and Mobilising Private Investments

Apart from the government, private companies and investors will also have to take over a major share of the transformation-related investments. On the one hand, this can take the form of own capital due to profits from commercial activities or capital investments. On the other hand, there are various options for external financing available to private investors, for example in the form of venture capital, private equity, or capital provided by institutional investors (such as infrastructure or pension funds), plus debt financing through privately owned financial institutions (mezzanine/senior debt: Figure 4.5-5). Whilst debt financing through privately owned financial institutions is more easily available if an innovative technology has already proven its worth in the field, private equity and venture capital financing tend to be particularly relied on in the initial stages (especially at the second stage; demonstration), due to the high level of uncertainty with regard to the future revenue yielded by the investment (UNEP-SEFI, 2009a).

Private investors frequently have to rely on government support for their investment activities, as there are often investment barriers presented by the size of the project, or the market risks which accompany the launch of any new technology. These barriers can be overcome through public financing mechanisms (including low interest rate loans, credit guarantees or technology-specific subsidies).

Depending on the stage of technology development (R&D, demonstration, deployment, diffusion, commercial maturity), different forms of government support for private investors make sense (UNEP-SEFI, 2008). Figure 4.5-5 shows the financing offers of private financial institutions and capital providers (commercial financing mechanisms), along with the financing offers of government institutions (public finance mechanisms). This also graphically illustrates the fact that government financing is particularly called for from the initial research stage to the diffusion stage.

Government Support of Investments and Strengthening of the Venture Capital Market

Whilst direct governmental support appears to be a sensible option for the research & development stage, loans and credit guarantees can have a considerable

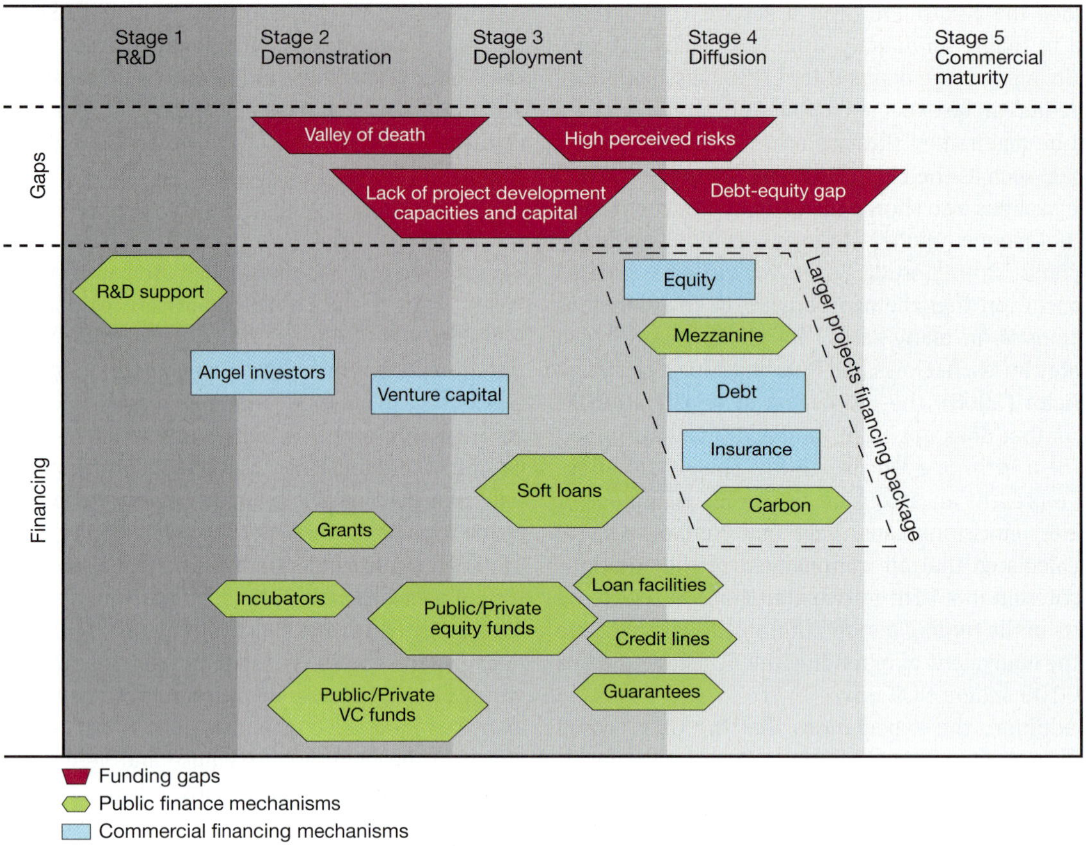

Figure 4.5-5
Public and private financing mechanisms according to technology development phase.
Source: UNEP-SEFI, 2008

impact at other financing stages. One particularly wide financing gap ('valley of death') in any project cycle is usually experienced during the demonstration and deployment stage. During these phases, the technology innovation is already on the way to commercialisation. However, further development often means high costs, and technological risks also remain an issue due to the lack of practical experience (UNEP-SEFI, 2008; IEA, 2010a). This is where government grants, low-interest loans and credit guarantees allow the acquisition of funding from private venture capital providers, who would otherwise not invest without government aid. Additional funds can also be unlocked by the combination of government and private venture capital in one fund, such as the UK Carbon Trust Venture Capital Fund, or the California Clean Energy Fund (BASE and SEFI, 2006). In this case, government funds enhance the attractiveness for private venture capital providers.

In the diffusion stage, access to private financial capital can also be improved through the provision of soft loans and credit guarantees, helping to make extended commercialisation easier (UNEP-SEFI, 2008; Figure 4.5-5). However, access to financing for commercialisations is only a necessary condition, and not a sufficient one. Also decisive is the demand side. In order to generate the appropriate market demand, the government can ultimately also support the market entry of a technical innovation through information policies, a policy framework, and incentive schemes (Section 5.2).

Improving the General Investment Climate

In many OECD countries, particularly in Germany, there are considerable deficits in terms of investment dynamics. The net investment ratio (i.e. the ratio of gross domestic investments minus depreciation to the NNP) in Germany, for example, between 1995 and 2008 amounted to only 5.3%, significantly below the European and OECD average (Figure 4.5-6; Sinn, 2010; SVR, 2008, 2010).

The investment climate has not been particularly dynamic between 1995 and 2008, both in terms of public and private sector investments. Particularly public net investments have been at an extremely low level, even running at negative values since 2003 (SVR, 2010; Priewe and Rietzler, 2010). The share of

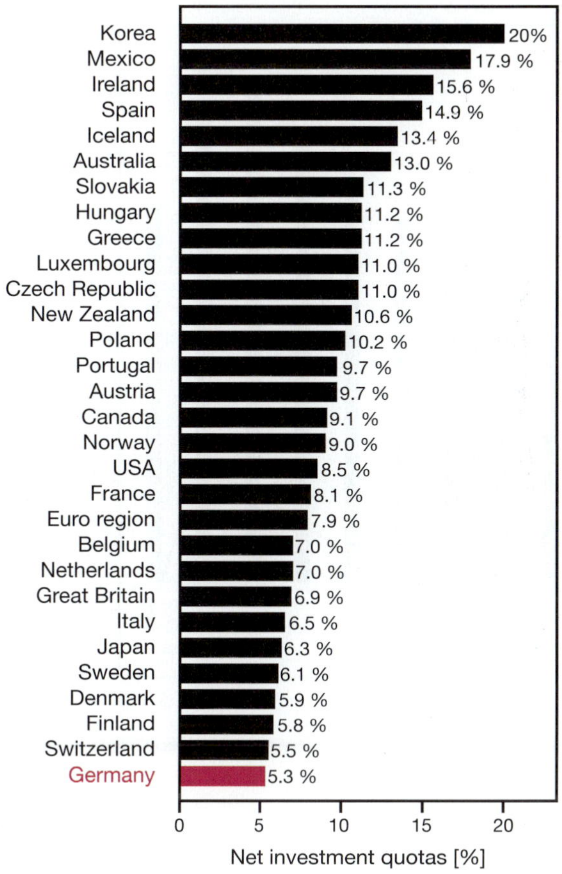

Figure 4.5-6
Comparison of international net investment ratios 1995–2008 (in % of NDP).
Source: Sinn, 2010

net investments in business profits has fallen dramatically since 2001, remaining at this low level ever since (Priewe and Rietzler, 2010). The low net investment ratios have been accompanied by rising business profits across the same period (Figure. 4.5-7; Priewe and Rietzler, 2010).

The business cycle is one explanation for the low net investment: the private sector investment ratio had gone up significantly between 2005 and 2008 as a consequence of economic recovery (Figure 4.5-7; SVR, 2010); however, due to the poor global economic development in 2009, it broke down again. Independent of the business cycle, the long-running low level of investment activities can also be explained by the fact that Germany, like many other industrialised countries over the past few decades, has undergone a structural change away from investment intensive industries towards service industries. One of the further causes for Germany's sluggish investment dynamics can also be seen in the introduction of the euro, the announcement of which already led to the harmonisation of interest rates at the end of the 1990s in the euro-countries, thereby triggering an investment boom in former high-interest countries, whilst capital from the former low-interest country Germany tended to go abroad (Sinn, 2010; Priewe and Rietzler, 2010). The increasing opening up of factor and goods markets in the course of globalisation and the European integration have led to private sector investment decisions being generally more likely to be influenced by more profitable opportunities abroad, where investments frequently yield higher profits, which in turn impacts the return on domestic investments (Hinze and Kirchesch, 1999). This trend has probably grown stronger due to the deregulation of the capital markets.

Above all, Germany's structural weakness in terms of investments should be addressed with changes to monetary and fiscal policies (SVR, 2009, 2010; Priewe and Rietzler, 2010). With regard to the transformation, extraordinary depreciation, for example, or the introduction of investment-related business, trade and income tax allowances, investment subsidies, or government soft financing offers could all help to create a specific incentive for transformative investments. At the same time, non-transformative capital investments would be made less attractive (Jaeger et al., 2009). Favourable taxation of 'green' investments could be a further element of a transformation-promoting fiscal concept. However, above all, to steer the fundamentally available capital towards transformative investment projects in particular, long-term and stable policy framework conditions are crucial for increasing the return of transformative projects, and expectation security for companies. The uncertainty regarding the government's future energy and climate policy continues to be a considerable barrier against investments. Long-term and stable policy framework conditions should, most importantly, include a carbon price, the phasing out of fossil energy carrier subsidies, technology-specific support, and energy efficiency standards (Section 7.3).

Establishment of National Green Investment Banks

A further option for governmental support for private investments is the provision of public funds through national Green Investment Banks. Public and private sector deposits could be combined here to support private investments in transformative fields with low-interest loans and credit guarantees. A good example of this is the UK's Green Investment Bank, with a planned £ 2 billion (approx. € 2.3 billion) of funding to finance renewable energy projects in the UK (Green Investment Bank Commission, 2010). Together with the KfW Development Bank, the German federal government has also established a revolving global climate protection fund for developing countries (KfW, 2010). The

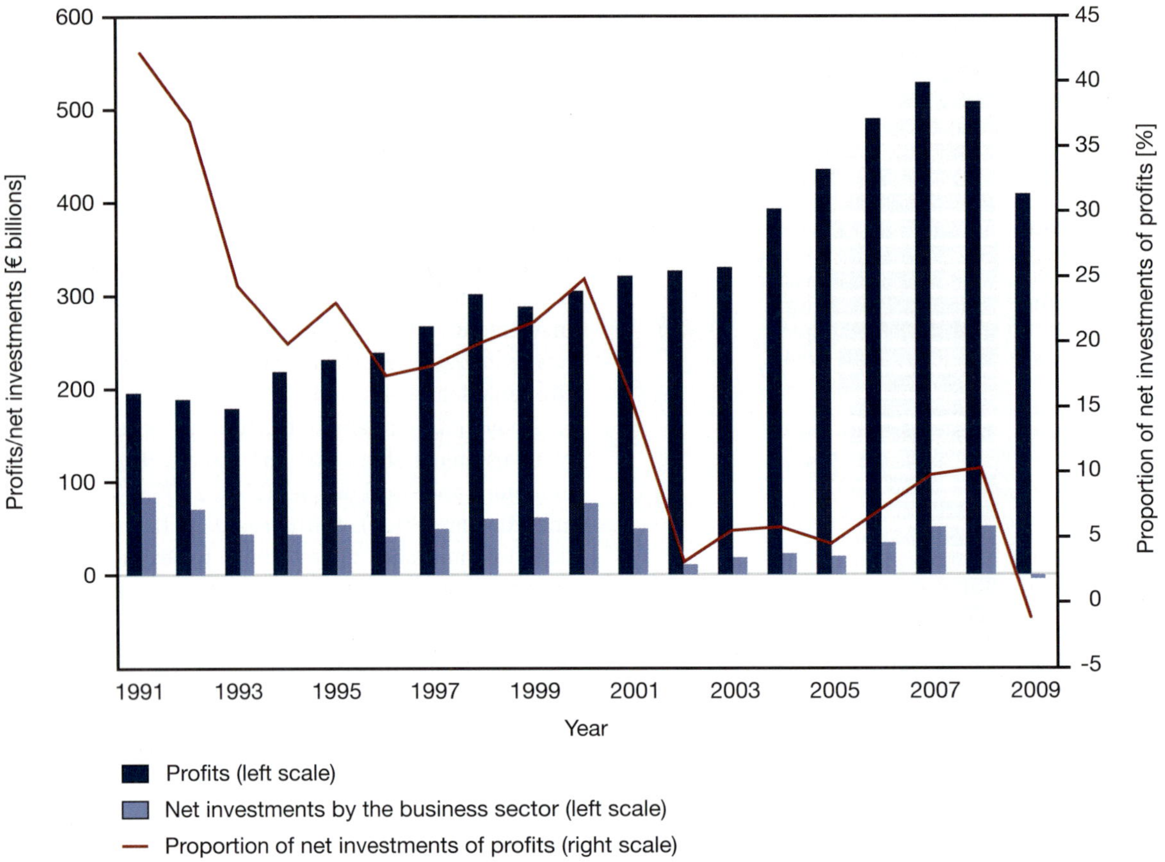

Figure 4.5-7
Profits and net investments of German companies between 1991 and 2009.
Source: Priewe and Rietzler, 2010

fund provides financial support to small and medium-sized enterprises and private households in developing countries for renewable energy and energy-efficiency projects. The fund also pays for corresponding consultancy services (KfW, 2010).

The combination of existing funds, and various funding sources – to finance both national and international transformation-related projects – in a Green Investment Bank such as this could generate the requisite order of magnitude of resources needed for the transformation. National and supra-regional investment banks (such as the European Investment Bank or the regional development banks) would have a particularly major role to play in financing infrastructure investments. It is also important in this respect that the financing criteria are sustainability-oriented, and that they are transparent.

Integration of Institutional Investors and Issuing of Climate Bonds

In particular institutional investors, such as pension schemes and insurance companies, could be approached to generate deposits into Green Investment Bank funds. They could make a considerable contribution to financing the transformation towards a low-carbon society, as they command the necessary capital, and tend to work with long-term investment horizons. Their deposits into the fund could yield revenue in the form of a fixed rate of interest. Funds such as these would provide institutional investors an opportunity to make low-risk capital investments with a steady interest rate whilst also providing a way of investing into a low-carbon future (Caldecott, 2010).

One option for additional fund generation for the Green Investment Banks would be the issuing of climate and energy project specific bonds (for example, in the form of climate bonds issued by the EU, the World Bank and the USA). There are already some successful models for this. The European Investment Bank (EIB), for instance, issued its first climate bonds onto the capital market in 2007 (EIB, 2007). The bonds, with a maturity period of five years, serve climate protection twofold: in terms of allocation of the deposits and also in terms of the rate of return. The € 600 million bond issuance proceeds were used exclusively to finance projects in the area of renewable energies and energy efficiency. The rate of return relies on the 'FTSE 4 Good Environmental Leaders Europe 40' index, which is made up of 40 major European corporations chosen for their sustainability criteria.

In 2009, the EIB launched further Climate Awareness Bonds, together with the Swedish bank Swedbank, i.e. capital market securities in Swedish Krona, whose proceeds also go towards EIB projects in the area of renewable energies and energy efficiency (EIB, 2009). Other climate bonds are currently issued by the World Bank, and the US government (Clean Renewable Energy Bonds), for example (World Bank, 2011a; US-DoE, 2011).

Support through Development Banks and International Financing Organisations

In developing countries, and particularly in the least developed countries, the financial markets are not appropriately developed, so that frequently, there is insufficient liquidity to finance large-scale projects; moreover, due to the LDCs' low credit rating, markets are also reluctant to supply capital. For this reason, the international financing organisations (IMF, World Bank) are particularly important for these countries. The institutions' various financing mechanisms (including loan programmes, credit guarantees) could enable local private financing intermediaries to grant loans for projects, even though they would not usually have granted these due to particular high risks (for instance political risks, currency risks, technological risks). Public monies (grants, soft loans, credit guarantees) are usually transferred via development banks to private financial institutions, which then use them to finance projects, frequently also attracting additional funds from institutional investors. Public resources therefore act as a catalyst (UNEP-SEFI, 2008).

In developing countries, financing must also be complemented by technical cooperation and human resources, as often, there is limited local experience available in project development and realisation. Financing commitments should therefore be combined with consultancy services. Especially where energy efficiency investments are concerned, private financing intermediaries often overestimate the risk represented by the lack of relevant expertise. Financing via Development Finance Institutions (DFI) and intermediaries such as Energy Service Companies (ESCO), who have the relevant technical expertise, are therefore most effective (Taylor et al., 2008; Ohndorf et al., 2010).

A probable leverage effect of between 3:1 and 15:1 is attributed to government resources, depending on the financing mechanism. Accordingly, making US$ 10 billion of public monies available could attract private investments of between US$ 50 and 150 billion (UNEP-SEFI, 2008). The empirically determined leverage rates vary, from 1:1 for the GEF Small Grants programme, to 3.6:1 for the Forest Partnership Facility and the World Bank's Carbon Partnership Facility, 6.3:1 for the GEF Trust Fund (climate focal area), and 8.3:1 for the Clean Technology Fund to 15:1 for the IFC Partial Credit Guarantee for Energy Efficiency (Norad, 2010; World Bank, 2010c). The leverage effect of government funds generally increases in line with the risk, and therefore at the rate at which government funding reduces the risk for private investors (Neuhoff et al., 2010).

Microfinancing to Overcome Energy Poverty

Microfinancing also plays a major role in transforming the energy systems in developing countries, particularly in the rural regions. Through microfinancing offers, energy poverty can be overcome with the help of renewable energies. Microfinancing has been used in developing countries for the past 25 years. The basic concept of this instrument is providing access to capital to poor and people on low-incomes who, due to a lack of securities, have no access to formal financial markets and banks (Terberger, 2002; Rosenberg, 2010). Microloans granted are usually used for enterprise-related investments, and paid back from the resultant profits generated, monitored by the community. Over time, this financing model has been extended to include personal loans, savings and insurances (Bunse et al., 2007).

At the same time, a grid-independent micro-energy-system has evolved in developing countries, particularly in rural regions (MicroEnergy International, 2008). Apart from the traditional biomass use, this includes rechargeable car batteries, kerosene and diesel generators. The Grameen Shakti company, a subsidiary of the Grameen Bank in Bangladesh, has managed to substitute fossil energy usage by combining microfinancing with renewable energies for micro-energy-systems. The company offers small-scale solar power units for homes, with the purchase being financed through loan repayment in instalments over two to three years. The company also specialises in technical advice and the maintenance of these solar power units, and so the purchase also includes a service package (advice, installation, maintenance). The instalments are equivalent to the monthly costs of alternative energy sources such as diesel or kerosene. Once the consumer credit is repaid, the household can generate a profit, and use the money that would have been spent on energy for other purposes (MicroEnergy International, 2008; Kamal, 2010; UNEP, 2011).

The microfinancing model is also used in a business environment, for example by using solar energy to light business premises, or in order to provide new kinds of energy services such as telephone, internet, or the recharging of batteries (Mohiuddin, 2006; USAID, 2009). Larger rural electrification projects would be small-scale hydropower or biogas plants, requiring both larger sums of capital and community cooperation (WI, 2006; Bunse et al., 2007). Projects such as these can also be financed through microfinancing institutions (Mohiuddin, 2006).

An important precondition for the transformation in developing regions is that the microfinancing institutions take rural electrification into account as an objective, and build up a pool of expert consultants (Mohiuddin, 2006; Bunse et al., 2007). It is also helpful when national governments initiate programmes for the diffusion of renewable energies, and information campaigns. Microfinancing makes it possible to supply wealthier villages and villagers, who are already using energy services, with renewable energies that do not necessarily have to be on-grid.

4.5.2.3 New Business Models to Reduce Investment Barriers

The burden of high upfront costs can be reduced for individual investors – whether in developing or industrialised countries – by spreading the capital invested 'across several shoulders'. This can for example be achieved by turning traditional buyer-seller models into new business models, with new ownership and financing structures, which reduce investment barriers and change incentive structures.

Rental, Leasing and Shared Use

These kinds of models are characterised, for instance, by the fact that they offer their customers combined packages in certain areas (for example mobility, housing, production and consumption) which include services as well as real assets, instead of just tangible goods. The property rights to the goods remain with the provider, who is committed to efficient resource utilisation and reintroduction of the goods into the recycling cycle. Concepts such as car sharing, in the mobility sector, and energy contracting, through so-called Energy Service Companies (ESCO), in the energy supply and energy efficiency sector, are already established (Section 4.3.2). The tangible goods (i.e. car, heating system, energy raw material) again remain the property of the provider, whilst the goods required to meet user needs are only rented, or leased, or used communally together with other customers. Customers thus pay primarily for the actual mobility or energy services they have used, rather than for a larger package' of potential future uses.

This reduces several investment barriers at the same time. Users of mobility or energy services are not faced with upfront investment costs, and the investment risk is carried fully by the provider, who is usually better placed to carry such risks than individual households or individual people. The users' information and transaction costs are minimised, as the provider has the relevant knowledge, and is usually also responsible for product maintenance and repair, as well as for reintroducing any tangible goods into the recycling cycle. This also has the effect that, as the subject of the contract is not the sale of tangible goods, but the fulfilment of mobility, energy or similar needs, raw material and energy efficiency directly benefit the provider.

These kinds of services, or integrated product-service systems, should be increasingly advertised and promoted during the course of the transformation, for example also tax incentives. In order for the use of such business models, oriented to results rather than consumer goods, to become widespread among potential users, a fundamental value change is required, both on the part of private customers (for example with regard to the status value attached to consumer goods), and in the business world.

Cooperative Financing Models

A further important business and financing model for the transformation is cooperative society financing. As early as the beginning of the 20th century, cooperative societies were founded for the electrification of rural areas (Holstenkamp and Ulbrich, 2010). The cooperative society is a society which serves the purchase or management of a business by its members through collective operation. Cooperative society members all have equal rights, and the self-administration is independent of the contribution of capital, i. e. each member has one vote. Cooperative societies are usually communities of value, i. e. they do not operate for profit, but understand themselves as self-help organisations for their members. As solidary enterprises, cooperative societies operate all over the world, and are represented by the International Co-operative Alliance (ICA) (UN, 2009b).

In Germany, an increasing number of renewable energy cooperative societies have been established over the past few years. They usually concern photovoltaic energy units (Holstenkamp and Ulbrich, 2010), for example installed on public buildings, such as schools. They are financed by both own and debt financing, to which a cooperative society is more likely to be given access than individuals. In many cases, cooperative banks also participate in energy cooperatives. Through the feed-in tariffs under the law on renewable energies (EEG), such joint investments in renewable energies can refinance themselves (Holstenkamp and Ulbrich, 2010).

Because of this, energy cooperatives are also a possible model for developing countries for the electrification of rural areas with the aid of renewable energies.

4.5.3 Interim Conclusion

The level of the investments required is at least known, and a substantial investment level has already been reached in the area of renewable energies and energy efficiency. However, the further mobilisation of financial means for the transformation of the energy systems requires considerably improved policy framework conditions for private investors for investments into low-carbon technologies. In particular, this requires a clear commitment on the part of governments to the rebuilding of energy systems, and the acknowledgement of this commitment through concrete policy framework conditions, which create investment security for private capital investors (Chapter 5).

4.6 Conclusions: Central Elements and Framework Conditions for the Transformation

The preceding analysis shows that a transformation towards a global low-carbon economy is technically feasible, and economically achievable. The transformation's central element is a global energy turnaround; however, this must also take current global dynamics of development into account. Almost 3 billion people still have no access to essential modern energy services, particularly for cooking, heating and lighting. At the same time, more than 80% of the global energy supply still relies on environment and climate damaging fossil fuels. The challenge lies in giving these people, so far excluded, access to clean and safe energy services as soon as possible, whilst at the same time rapidly and drastically reducing CO_2 emissions from the use of fossil fuels.

The long-term economic costs of a global decarbonisation of the energy systems amount to just a few percent of global GDP. If the transformation is to succeed, a vastly accelerated reduction of the global economy's CO_2 intensity is indispensable. Assuming an economic growth rate of 2-3% and an emissions path leading to emissions of no more than 750 billion t CO_2 from fossil sources by 2050, the CO_2 intensity of the global economic output would have to decrease at least twice as fast as it has done in the past over the next few years.

The technology portfolio for such an ambitious decarbonisation of the energy system differs greatly in various analyses; there is more than one way of transforming the energy systems to become low-carbon. The actual energy path followed will differ between states and regions, depending on political, technological and cultural circumstances and preferences, and individual geographical features. Particularly the use of nuclear energy and the significance of CCS (Carbon Dioxide Capture and Storage) have attracted much controversy and heated debate, both globally and within the EU. The extent to which these technologies are used could develop in very different directions, regionally and nationally, primarily on the basis of policy decisions.

The WBGU generally advises against the expansion of nuclear energy use, above all because of the risk of serious damages, the still unresolved issues concerning final storage, and the danger of uncontrolled proliferation, and not least also because of the resultant high costs. CCS is a necessary mitigation option for countries which continue to use fossil energies if the 2 °C climate protection guard rail is to be complied with. CCS could also play an important role in the active withdrawal of CO_2 from the atmosphere at a later point in time. Even though the WBGU rejects a path that relies primarily on the expansion of CCS, it nevertheless recommends stepping up research and in-depth examination of the risks. Germany should also participate in the drafting of standards. In its recommendations, however, the WBGU focuses on development paths that accord nuclear energy and CCS only a marginal role. Rather, the WBGU recommends a strategy that relies primarily on an accelerated expansion of renewable energies, with the prospective aim of covering 100 % of demand with renewable energies. An important characteristic of the energy systems transformation, from the WBGU's point of view, is the general switch to on-grid energy carriers as a major share of the energy mix. Electricity and gas should prevail as the dominating energy forms. A precondition for the transformation's success is therefore the expansion of transcontinental energy infrastructures (supergrids, gas pipelines and terminals), and smartgrids.

The rapid expansion of renewable energies unlocks opportunities that allow the achieving of climate mitigation targets, without burdening society with high risks in the form of unresolved final storage issues, or the risk of nuclear material proliferation. However, particularly the expanding use of bioenergy also bears significant risks for various sustainability dimensions (Box 4.1-4). The international trade with agricultural goods leads to the creation of non-obvious effects that, for example, accelerate deforestation and lead to rising food prices. Only the establishment of a global regulation framework can guarantee the sustainability of bioenergy use (WBGU, 2010a). Until this is established, the expansion of bioenergy should therefore be advanced only very carefully.

The analysis further shows that the global final energy demand should not rise to more than 400–500 EJ per year if the transformation is to succeed; current global final energy demand is around 350 EJ per year. Without additional political measures, the final energy demand could more than double. Limiting final energy demand, particularly in the industrialised countries, is therefore a major challenge, and corresponding strategies are extremely important. That is one of the important factors leading to the WBGU's conclusion that the transformation will concern all areas of human need (Section 4.5). As CO_2 emissions accumulate in the atmosphere, a lower energy demand in the current high-carbon energy system will afford more room for manoeuvre with regard to the emission reduction rates that will be required in future. Therefore, a lower energy demand also automatically allows more freedom in relation to the choice of energy generation technologies.

Due to catch-up development, rapidly progressing urbanisation, and population growth, developing and newly industrialising countries are responsible for most of the current rise in energy demand (IEA, 2010a). The transformation is therefore not only about restructuring of existing energy systems, but also about steering investments in energy infrastructure expansion necessary due to rising demand into sustainable infrastructure right from the start.

Many low-carbon technologies still do not fare well in an energy generation cost comparison. One major reason for this is that the negative externalities from fossil and nuclear energy generation do not appear as costs. To promote the transformation, and the switch to low-carbon energy systems, policy-makers are called upon to make the impact that energy generation has on environment and climate visible for the market, for instance through carbon pricing, or a cap on emissions accompanied by the introduction of tradable emissions certificates. The transformation can succeed only if the use of climate-damaging technologies becomes economically unattractive. At the same time, many sustainable technologies are still at a stage where high cost reductions can be expected through learning effects. Moreover, renewable energies (not unlike nuclear energy) are associated with comparatively high upfront investments which amortise only after a longer period. For these reasons, the WBGU believes that the technology-specific promotion of renewable energies for a limited period of time is important in order to make the transformation possible. The instruments mentioned above are also very important for steering the transformation in newly industrialising and developing countries. However, this does not imply that these countries must bear the cost of the transformation on their own; on the contrary, mutual interests are served best by intensifying international cooperation, and increasing the supporting measures offered by the industrialised nations.

Other than decarbonisation, the second objective of a conversion of the energy systems is the overcoming of energy poverty to provide universal access to modern, clean and safe energy in the form of electricity or gaseous energy carriers by 2030 (WBGU, 2004). To meet this target, the developing and newly industrialising countries primarily need support to leapfrog past stages of technological development, both for the overcoming of energy poverty, as well as general support for the establishment of a sustainable energy infrastructure. If this does not succeed, there is a risk of path dependencies on emissions-intensive, fossil-based energy systems that would be very difficult and costly to overcome, and it would take decades to do so. Access to energy services is also a precondition for achieving the majority of the Millennium Development Goals. In the WBGU's view, the limiting the global final energy demand is compatible with the aim of overcoming energy poverty. If efficiency potentials were exploited worldwide, and the current focus on the amount of available energy were replaced by the goal to provide certain energy services, the energy demand in regions with currently high energy use can decline without the loss of comforts, thereby compensating for the rising energy demand in currently energy-poor countries.

A development path as outlined by the WBGU can hardly be reached with the currently predominant energy infrastructure financing patterns. For example, there is no inherent incentive for current energy suppliers to improve energy efficiency. Their turnover grows in line with rising energy consumption. New approaches, such as energy service companies (ESCOs), on the other hand, make the unlocking of energy potentials one of the central elements of their business model. Similar incentives for the exploitation of efficiency potentials are offered by business models such as car sharing, where, instead of a commodity or a consumer good, an energy service is offered for sale.

Further important approaches to promote private investments in renewable energies and energy efficiency are financing mechanisms that reduce investment risks, and increase the yield of transformative investments. These include, for instance, government loan programmes with particularly low-interest, long-term loans, and government credit default guarantees – consolidated in so-called national Green Investment Banks, the establishment of venture and equity capital funds with contributions by the state, and the promotion of cooperative financing models and micro-financing.

Cities, as focal points of energy demand, are areas where partial aspects of the transformation would have to effectively interact. They are places of innovation and investment in new infrastructures and (together with the private sector) are increasingly becoming multilevel governance actors (Corfee-Morlot et al., 2009) who, because of their dimension, can achieve their own scaling and agglomeration effects. Through the spatial integration of urban functions, traffic can be reduced whilst at the same time achieving a high quality of life for inhabitants. Energy infrastructure integration (CHP technology, heating and cooling systems, smartgrids, electromobility, etc.) can benefit considerably from the spatial density.

Around a quarter of worldwide greenhouse gas emissions are direct emissions from agriculture and land-use change. These can be substantially mitigated, but land-use systems cannot become completely emissions-free, or at least, not in this century, alone because of the nitrous oxide resulting from the use of nitrogen fertilisers. However, as climate stabilisation cannot succeed without a significant contribution from land use, all of the available mitigation options should be utilised. Emissions reduction should become another core element of new strategies for global, integrated land-use management. The most important starting points for this are stopping deforestation and switching to sustainable forest management, as well as the promotion of climate-friendly agriculture and dietary habits.

Transformation Governance 5

5.1 Introduction: New Problems, New Statehood!

In contrast to the civilisation leaps described in Chapter 3, the forthcoming transformation is hardly likely to occur gradually and successively. Rather, it must be driven forward actively and simultaneously all over the world within a very short period of time. The transformation towards a low-carbon society must include industrialised and newly industrialising, the poor, and even the poorest, developing countries if dangerous climate change and the loss of natural life-support systems is still to be averted. To achieve this, a new level of statehood, and a level of to date unprecedented international cooperation must be achieved.

In Chapter 4, we showed that the transformation towards a low-carbon society is both technically and economically feasible. In this chapter the WBGU examines the opportunities and limits of governance. Each of the transformation fields analysed – energy, urbanisation and land use – constitutes a different global challenge in terms of governance:

1. The availability of the relatively cheap, but most carbon-intensive fossil energy source coal is a great obstacle to the transformation of the energy system (Section 4.1.2). As coal is found in many countries, it is the number one local energy source. The countries with the largest coal deposits are the USA, Russia, China, Australia, India and Indonesia (IEA, 2010c; Heinberg and Fridley, 2010). The continued intensive use of coal around the globe thwarts any policy-making with regard to the transformation towards a low-carbon energy system.
2. Today, 50% of the world population already lives in cities and a dynamic, uncontrolled urbanisation process is emerging, particularly in the newly industrialising and developing countries. At present, three-quarters of the global final energy demand originates in cities, as does the same proportion of greenhouse gas emissions (Section 1.2.4). Cities therefore play a decisive role in the transformation process (Chapter 4). If this rapid urbanisation does not increasingly take the transformation perspective into account, urban growth processes could become one of the main barriers on the course to a low-carbon society.
3. Demand for forestry and agricultural products and the importance of ecosystem services will rise considerably in future. At the same time, climate change and soil degradation are reducing cultivation areas, and respectively productivity. Land-use competition will therefore increasingly become a global field of conflict (Section 1.2.5; WBGU, 2008, 2009a). There is largely a consensus concerning the scale of the challenges and the need for reform and development. In contrast, there is no broad scientific or political consensus on which strategies are best suited to ensure sustainable global land use.

So what do these three main issues typically lack? The scale and speed of the already initiated transformation processes are a long way from meeting the challenges outlined. 'Slowly drilling of hard boards' (Max Weber) is not a practicable route in climate policy-making if global warming is still to be halted at a maximum of 2°C. Political processes at national, European and global level must therefore be considerably accelerated and actively advanced.

Evidently, any illusion that a regime change on a global scale can be purely technocratically organised and steered top-down must be avoided. Certain individual aspects of transformations of the kind described can be managed, but overall, they are not directly steerable (Chapter 3). Active political steering is also not necessarily a guarantee for a successful transformation. Rather, the progression of the transformation process must be steered in a certain direction by means of appropriate framework setting, and the setting of a decisive course towards structural change (Chapter 3). The transformation towards a low-carbon society is a complex process, as it will continue to be characterised by uncertainty. We are aware of the signs of damage, and the damage to be expected, but nobody can predict what a climate-friendly system will look like exactly, and above all how to proceed politically in a way that will prove to be effective and legitimate on a global scale. Anyone wanting to shape the transformation practices the 'multilevel architecture' politics of global governance, as the forthcoming changes concern all political action levels, from local through national to global level, and involve numerous government, civil society and private sector actors with varying interests, beliefs and resources (Messner, 1998). This is both about the reorganisation of markets and the restructuring of institutional systems and, in equal measure, 'hard' technological innovations and 'soft' socio-cultural mindset changes. Such a transformation process will ultimately have to be pushed through, despite the many blocking mechanisms and forces persisting on the status quo. Policy-making to achieve a climate-friendly society is therefore a highly demanding, long-term and comprehensive goal.

In the following sub-chapters, the WBGU examines the opportunities and limits of governance, identifies barriers impeding the transformation process, and reveals approaches to solve these problems. In this respect, Chapter 5 concentrates on sub-national, national and international government measures and actors, whereas Chapter 6 primarily focuses on actors from civil society, such as companies, consumers and citizens. Chapter 5 initially discusses the structural factors impeding change. It then elaborates how political barriers in democratic systems and at international level can be overcome with improved statehood. Requirements and problems with regard to accelerating political processes in the light of a lack of long-term orientation are elaborated, as are the legitimacy foundations for a global transformation policy. And finally, this Chapter evaluates the current governance structures in the three transformation fields. Here, the WBGU principally looks at the altered role of the state in the transformation process; the Herculean task of a global transformation requires new normative foundations, improved instruments and unusual approaches on all levels of governance.

5.2 Political Instruments for Managing the Transformation

Managing the transformation by means of governance is about correcting various forms of market failure (e.g. positive and negative external effects, public goods, information asymmetries, market entry barriers and natural monopolies). The WBGU assumes that essentially, the political instruments, such as administrative command-and-control, taxation, tradable permits, market regulation, or regional and urban planning, needed to correct the present market failure and to manage the transformation are known and available. All of the political instruments applicable in the transformation fields analysed here, namely energy, urbanisation and land use, have also been recommended in other transformation studies.

For a transformative effect on production and consumption, the simultaneous use of various instruments is required for a policy mix to initiate systemic and fundamental changes in the economy and society. The WBGU recommends designing transformation policy in a way that initiates systemic structural changes, avoids path dependencies, and overcomes existing structural impediments. This calls for taking a long-term course on a global scale today to achieve broad legitimisation (Sections 3.4, 5.4). As there is considerable time pressure to achieve the transformation, the policy mix should include instruments that can be introduced quickly and take effect within a short time. At the same time, political instruments are required which provide incentives for medium to long-term transformative changes, and which promote social and technological innovations.

First of all, this chapter introduces recommendations for action from selected transformation studies, each with a different focus, in order to demonstrate that essentially, the range of political instruments needed to achieve the transformation towards a low-carbon society is known. A policy mix is then derived from this, with elements which the WBGU considers necessary and appropriate for the transformation fields of energy, urbanisation and land use.

5.2.1 Recommendations for Action from Selected Transformation Studies

Various studies on the transformation of economy and society towards a low-carbon economy and lifestyle include recommendations on how the transformation process outlined in Chapters 3 and 4 can be initiated and promoted. The transformation studies considered here can be roughly divided into four groups: there are for instance many studies on the transformation of energy systems with the primary aim of decarbonising the economy, presenting a pragmatic and more functionalistic view of the associated governance processes (Group 1). Other studies emphasise the compatibility of economic growth and decarbonisation (green growth) and underline the potential benefits of a transformation (Group 2; Box 5.2-1). In contrast, other studies yet again assume that a transformation can be achieved only through a new economic and growth paradigm, therefore presenting new approaches to make the predominant economic system a thing of the past (Group 3; Box 5.2-1). The fourth type focuses on governing the transformation politically under inclusion of all social groups (Group 4).

Group 1 studies on the decarbonisation of the economy view the transformation of the energy system as a central lever for achieving significant emissions reductions (WBGU, 2004; Stern, 2008; Jochem et al., 2008; McKinsey, 2009; UKERC, 2009; Ziesing, 2009; Edenhofer et al., 2009a; Knopf et al., 2010; GMF and Ecologic, 2010). They focus on political measures in the areas of climate, energy and innovation policy. Most of these studies recommend market-based instruments such as taxation, subsidies, feed-in tariffs or an emissions trading scheme to accelerate the development and diffusion of low-emission technologies. They also specify efficiency standards in industry, for buildings, and for vehicles. Technology promotion should also include both direct support for research and development (R&D) and targeted support for investments. These studies emphasise the need for intensified technology and financial transfers to developing and newly industrialising countries to extend the transformation of the energy system to an international level.

Group 2 studies on green growth recommend a policy mix that is similar to those in Group 1, with incentive and regulatory instruments (UN DESA, 2009a; PBL, 2009a; UNEP, 2009; UNCTAD, 2010a; OECD, 2010a). However, these studies take additional crises into account, such as the global financial market and economic crisis (2007–2009) and the energy and food crisis in 2008. Accordingly, the recommended measures are selected from a broad spectrum of policy areas. Apart from climate and energy policy, they also include economic, trade, labour market, social and development policies, as well as agricultural policies in developing and newly industrialising countries. Most of these studies describe a structural change that creates new employment opportunities, strengthens new sectors and reduces social inequalities, all in the course of energy systems decarbonisation. Under the premise of further global economic growth, resource consumption and CO_2 emissions should be decoupled from economic growth through efficiency improvements in production and consumption.

Group 3 studies take an entirely different view, as they assume an irresolvable conflict between economic growth and decarbonisation (Adler and Schachtschneider, 2010; Bread for the World et al., 2008; Jackson, 2009; NEF, 2009; Raskin et al., 2002; Rosen et al., 2010; Ulvila and Pasanen, 2009). They advocate a transition to a new economy which operates within clear ecological limits, and focuses on social equity and environmental compatibility. Primarily recommended is a government information and communication policy that triggers a value change towards frugality, towards solidarity, a pronounced environmental consciousness, and greater social participation (Chapters 2, 6). In the opinion of the authors, any steering by means of state policies must be legitimised through participation and social debate. Management by governance should encompass social redistribution, the democratisation of decision-making processes, renunciation of the present consumer behaviour, and the introduction of new welfare indicators and new narratives for a 'good life'. The differing recommendations of Groups 2 and 3 studies with respect to the transformation towards a low-carbon economy and society are rooted in the long-controversial scientific and political debate on whether unlimited economic growth is possible within the guard rails, and whether it is in fact essential for solving social and ecological problems (Box 5.2-1).

Group 4, represented by a joint study of Atomium Culture and Lund University, points out important factors of a political and social governance of the transition towards a low-carbon society. Here, the importance of information and communication between government and citizens, the involvement of all actors in the processes of change (multilevel/multi-actor governance), an interdepartmental system-oriented approach, and innovation and learning processes are highlighted (Atomium Culture and Lund University, 2009).

The recommended action options vary depending on the transformation studies' focus. Group 3 and 4 studies concentrate primarily on the political and social framework conditionsthat are crucial for a transformation towards a low-carbon society. This is elaborated in Section 5.4, also particularly in Chapter 6. By contrast, Group 1 and 2 studies focus on political instruments, such as carbon pricing and other measures for realising and accelerating a transformation. In the WBGU's view, both the use of governance instruments and the creation of new political and social framework conditions are indispensable for the transformation. The following presents the mix of instruments recommended by the WBGU to overcome various forms of market failure and to accelerate the transformation.

5.2.2
Carbon Pricing as a Necessary Political Measure for the Transformation

Groups 1 and 2 studies show that CO_2 pricing is a necessary precondition for a transformation towards a low-carbon, sustainable society (Section 5.2.1). Through

Box 5.2-1

The Debate on Growth

Since the 2007 – 2009 global financial and economic crisis, the growth debate has been rekindled in political and public discussion (Chapter 2; Group 2 and 3 studies). The debate focuses on the economic growth of a national economy measured by gross domestic product (GDP). Since the Second World War, after which the industrialised countries showed high growth rates, their economic policies have focused on the aim of increasing GDP. Apart from rising wealth, economic growth is associated with sufficient employment opportunities, equitable distribution of wealth, stable social security systems, and technical progress (Seidl and Zahrnt, 2010).

The first debate on growth

The first growth debate in 1972 was inspired by Meadows et al. with their study 'The Limits to Growth'. It focused on the limited availability of natural, non-renewable resources. At that time, conventional economic models taking into account only the production factors of capital and labour were criticised from an ecological perspective. The economic macromodels used considered neither natural resources as input into the production process, nor emissions or waste as output (Daly, 1996; Irmen, 2011). As such, the models featured no ecological limits to national economic growth. However, even when conventional macromodels did take natural resources into account as a production factor, growth could be maintained in the models, as the production factors could be substituted for each other, and technical progress took place exogenously (Daly, 1996; Irmen, 2011).

This kind of modelling was criticised time and again by various different ecological economists, and alternative models were developed. Starting with the laws of natural science, particularly thermodynamics, attention was called to the fact that, as a subsystem of the Earth system, the economic system is also subject to its principles and can therefore not grow indefinitely (Georgescu-Roegen, 1971; Box 1-2). Daly's 'steady-state economy' exemplifies this (1974; Czech and Daly, 2009). According to this approach, the material and energy flows, respectively the throughput of an economy, should be in balance with the natural system, i. e. resources should not be overexploited. Assuming a constant population, a constant capital stock, and a constant throughput volume (energy, material), a steady state is theoretically achievable (Daly, 1974; Czech and Daly, 2009). However, in terms of sustainable development, a steady-state economy can grow qualitatively, but not quantitatively (Daly, 1996).

At that time, Hirsch (1977) was the first scientist to note that there were also social limits to economic growth. The new debate on growth revisits his scientific findings.

Binswanger recognised the economy's ecological limits at an early stage, and wondered whether monetary economies imply the 'necessity to grow'. According to Binswanger (2006), the expansion of the money supply through private banks which can borrow from central banks, and the predominant system of joint stock companies leads to 'the necessity to grow'. The joint stock companies have to make profits in order to pay back loans and the interest thereon, and distribute dividends to the investors. In his model, investment, production and sale diverge temporally, up-front financing is therefore required for the investments. A discontinued growth process results in a cumulative shrinkage process. Based on his model, Binswanger calculates that 1.8% is the maximum global growth rate at which a monetary economy does not shrink, but rather continues to grow moderately. Irmen (2011) has criticised the model, reaching the conclusion that the monetary theory perspective affords no compelling argument for the necessity to grow in market economies. A functioning credit system is not a sufficient condition for economic growth. Tichy (2009) also points out that growth is not an imperative for capitalist systems. Victor (2008) has developed a growth simulation model for Canada in which he demonstrated that Canada's wealth could be maintained and increase even if the economy were to grow only moderately, or not at all.

The new debate on growth

Natural scientists, economists and social scientists have introduced critical arguments and alternative ideas to the current growth debate, questioning the concept of 'qualitative' or 'green' growth (Adler and Schachtschneider, 2010; Seidl and Zahrnt, 2010; Martinez-Alier et al., 2010; Group 3 studies). The French 'décroissance' social movement, which now also has followers in other European countries, fundamentally questions economic growth, and particularly the political fixation on it (Latouche, 2010; Martinez-Alier et al., 2010). Those following this movement are of the opinion that the political promises made by economic growth, such as greater wealth and equity, have not been fulfilled in recent years. To date, however, there is no alternative model for the economy. Other growth critics assume that, as long as there is continued economic growth with the associated rising demand for consumer goods and services, the global consumption of energy and resources will also continue to increase, despite improvements in efficiency, and that it cannot be reduced to a sustainable level (Jackson, 2009). This particularly applies if not only CO_2 emissions are taken into account, but also finite natural resources in general. Decoupling economic activities from the consumption of natural resources requires not only technical efficiency, but also improved recycling systems and changes in consumption behaviour. Several studies (Jackson, 2009; Simms et al., 2010; Adler and Schachtschneider, 2010) therefore assume that is not possible to totally decouple economic growth from resource consumption, and that it will not be possible in future, either. This is mainly due to the rebound effect (Box 4.3-1).

The model and scenario analysis in Chapter 4 has shown that decarbonisation can be consistent with positive, although moderate, economic growth (Box 4.2-1). Nevertheless, according to Jackson's calculations, the global economy's carbon intensity would need to fall by an average of 7% per year in order to limit the CO_2 concentration in the atmosphere to 450 ppm. According to his data, global carbon intensity has improved by an average of only approx. 0.7% per year since 1990. This would mean that efficiency increases would need to increase by a tenfold in future to ensure compliance with the 2 °C guard rail (Jackson, 2009). However, other authors specify the average decline in carbon intensity during recent years at 1.2–1.3% (Section 4.2.1; Canadell et al., 2007; IEA, 2010c), which would mean that current reduction rates would need to increase by a fivefold.

These figures must nevertheless be interpreted with caution: in order to comply with the 2 °C guard rail, the economy's carbon intensity does not necessarily have to fall over a long period at a constant rate that is relative to the percentage rate of the previous year, as could be inferred from Jackson

〉

(2009), nor would this be sensible. In fact, this would actually result in extremely unrealistic emission paths with initially very high absolute reduction rates. In order to roughly follow the emission paths illustrated in Box 1.1-1, where emissions will peak in the next few years, and no more than 750 Gt CO_2 are emitted by 2050, a more or less linear decline in carbon intensity would be necessary if the economic growth rate were 2–3 %. Carbon intensity would therefore need to decline around 3–4 % per year, relative to the present. Accordingly, the past 45 years' average abatement rate of approx. 1.2 % (Canadell et al., 2007) would have to be more than doubled in the coming years.

Using a similar approach, the International Energy Agency (IEA) also concludes that doubling the average 1990–2008 abatement rate in the period of 2008 – 2020, or quadrupling this rate in the period 2020 – 2035 would be sufficient to achieve a 450 ppm path.

What are the impacts of an economy without growth?
Essentially, a market economy with little or no growth is conceivable; however, from a social perspective, this would have some problematic impacts, and require respective, supporting policies (Tichy, 2009; Victor, 2008). Many economists point out that even in the case of population growth stagnation without economic growth, redistribution could no longer rely on increment of growth in material wealth, but would have to come out of the existing capital stock. This would be accompanied by distributional conflicts. Either way, there would be losers. A fundamental structural change such as the transformation towards a low-carbon society would also be much more difficult to achieve in an economy without growth, as a nominal wage renunciation would also be accompanied by structural unemployment in the shrinking sectors. Overall, an economy without growth provides fewer incentives, particularly with regard to investment and innovation (Schneider, 1991; Tichy, 2009).

If an economy without growth in GDP were the theoretical goal, investments would have to be reduced to pure replacement investments, and profits would have to be cut back to a minimum, barely enough to cover these replacement investments. Consequently, production capacity would stagnate at a certain level. Consumption would adjust to this stagnant production capacity. Given production capacities and an increasing world population, the global per capita consumption would decrease, and the global GDP would have to be redistributed. This would require a cultural change towards foregoing consumption, a shortening of people's working lives in the industrialised countries accompanied by increases in household production, and acceptance of intensified national and international redistribution (Tichy, 2009).

The above impacts of an economy without growth are not insignificant, and would require the broad acceptance of the population. At present, it is difficult to imagine that an individual country in this globalised world could simply 'decide' on an economy with slow growth, or even no-growth. This would mean that a country would have to largely withdraw from international competition and the international financial and product markets. For ethical reasons, slowing down, or foregoing growth cannot be demanded presently, particularly from the developing and newly industrialising countries. It would run contrary to the development goal of poverty reduction, as established in the Millennium Development Goals, for example (MDG; Section 1.2). Slowing down the growth rate would therefore essentially be conceivable only for industrialised countries. However, in this respect, it has to be considered that slowing down economic growth in the industrialised countries would also impact considerably on the economic activities in developing countries as a result of the interdependency of global trade, as recently seen in the course of the 2008 financial and economic crisis (ODI, 2008).

Economic growth and the transformation towards a low-carbon society
The capital need for the global transformation of the energy system, urbanisation and land-use systems will run into billions (Section 4.5). Economic growth can therefore provide the financial resources and incentives needed to reduce CO_2 emissions and resource consumption by means of technical innovations. Urgently required investments in technical innovations (energy and efficiency technologies, recycling systems, etc.), for example, could thus be financed more easily. Furthermore, workers released as a result of the transformation in certain sectors (e.g. fossil energies) could take advantage more easily of newly created employment opportunities in other sectors. Potential decarbonisation losers could be compensated more easily from additional national revenue (for instance from taxes, emissions trading).

If a national economy can successfully produce goods and services whilst keeping the consumption of energy and natural resources low, economic growth need not necessarily conflict with decarbonisation. A suitable framework can advance the desired decoupling of resource and energy consumption from economic growth. Consumption patterns observed today would need to be redirected to increase the demand for less resource and energy intensive goods. Profit-oriented companies would be forced to adapt their production methods to the new market conditions. Current insights do not allow predictions as to whether decoupling can actually be achieved in this way.

the introduction of a price for negative external effects, such as CO_2 emissions, their social costs are internalised, triggering changes in the behaviour of market players. Carbon pricing can essentially be introduced through a CO_2 tax or the restriction of CO_2 emissions and introduction of an allowance trading scheme (cap and trade) (Box 5.2-2). Both are market-based instruments which, compared to regulatory instruments, can archieve the emission reduction target more cost efficiently.

CO_2 pricing can systematically guide production, consumption and investment decisions towards low-carbon and accelerate the decarbonisation of energy systems, as well as climate-friendly urbanisation and land use. On the one hand, CO_2 pricing increases the incentives on the supplier side to expand renewable energies and increasingly use low-emission production technologies. Moreover, an appropriately high CO_2 price is a prerequisite for the earning power of many

Box 5.2-2

A CO_2 Tax versus CO_2 Emissions Trading

Essentially, external effects resulting in market failure can be internalised with price control (taxes, subsidies) or quantity control (tradeable permits). For a detailed elaboration on the choice between price or quantity control, see Weitzman (1974). With full knowledge of both the damages from emissions on the one hand, and of emissions abatement costs on the other, a CO_2 tax and CO_2 emissions trading are equivalent, in theory. A welfare-maximising emissions volume, or a price leading to this volume, can be identified in a static analysis. However, due to existing uncertainties in the area of climate, an accurate assessment of damage costs and abatement costs is not possible, either statically or dynamically.

Price control – in the form of an emissions or CO_2 tax – gives companies and consumers certainty about the costs incurred, for example the costs of a tonne of CO_2 emissions. Nevertheless, the desired emissions reduction can be achieved only in a trial and error process through carbon tax adjustment. In other words, ecological effectiveness is not necessarily given with this instrument. This applies even in the case of rather high taxation rates (Sinn, 2008; Edenhofer and Kalkuhl, 2009). Greater effectiveness in terms of the goal of emissions reduction is therefore to be expected from quantity control.

Pursuing the guard rail concept outlined in Chapter 1, which defines the still acceptable dimension for anthropogenic intervention in nature, the more sensible strategy seems to be quantity restriction in the sense of a global CO_2 budget (Box 1.1-1; WBGU 2009b). It may prove to be a disadvantage that emission allowance price development is unpredictable, therefore calculating the cost may be difficult for market players.

As a global instrument, CO_2 emissionss trading has advantages over taxation, as 'only' one market place needs to be established for trading, rather than a global fiscal authority to collect and redistribute the tax. A further political advantage of emissions trading is the option of allocating emission rights on the basis of a politically negotiated distribution key (WBGU, 2009). In this way, the principle of 'common but differentiated responsibilities' anchored in the 1992 Framework Convention on Climate Change, for instance, can be put into practice whilst maintaining the advantages of clear emission restrictions and cost-efficiency. The WBGU believes that financial transfers could be generated much more reliably through tradable emissions rights as a fraction of a global emissions budget (WBGU, 2009). They would be an indirect result: whilst maintaining the advantages of a uniform carbon dioxide price in all countries involved, auction revenues could be allocated to countries in proportion to their share in the global emissions budget.

investments in low-emission technologies (Garz et al., 2009; Section 4.5). It accelerates the substitution of fossil with renewable energy sources, for example, which also, in a dynamic perspective in the context of renewable energies expansion, not least in the field of urbanisation, leads to learning effects and cost reductions.

On the other hand, it causes changes on the demand side. A high CO_2 price thus leads to rising energy and product prices, thereby reducing energy consumption, and the consumption of goods which are carbon intensive. This stimulates an increased tapping of (energy) efficiency potentials (Fischer and Newell, 2008). The higher the CO_2 price, the stronger the incentive for investments in energy efficiency and other measures to reduce energy consumption. Moreover, in the long run, a CO_2 price signal provides investors and consumers with planning security and prevents lock-in effects with respect to long-term investment and consumption decisions. The greater the number of countries opting for carbon pricing, the more comprehensively and effectively this measure can impact. For carbon pricing to achieve maximum impact, the subsidies for fossil fuels which still exist in many countries should also be phased out at the earliest opportunity (Section 4.5).

Emissions from land use and land-use change should be dealt with separately from the emissions generated by fossil energy use. The CO_2 dynamics associated with the terrestrial biosphere differ substantially in many fundamental aspects – such as measurability, reversibility, long-term controllability, interannual fluctuations – from the CO_2 flows associated with the industrial use of coal, crude oil or natural gas (WBGU, 2010a). It is therefore appropriate to develop specific instruments and measures for this sector, rather than linking it with solutions for fossil sources.

Subsequent to considering the advantages and disadvantages of price and quantity control, the WBGU argues in favour of quantity control, i.e. restricting the emissions from fossil sources whilst introducing tradable emissions rights. The establishment of a CO_2 emission trading scheme that is as global as possible is recommended at corporate level in order to generate a widely impacting, uniform price signal for the transformation. The WBGU suggests moving towards a global CO_2 certificate trading scheme in three stages: by developing the European emissions trading scheme further, linking existing national emissions trading schemes, and through supranational agreements on emissions restriction in high-emission countries (Section 7.3.2). In those countries where the requisite administrative structures and institutions, such as legal security, are not in place, a national CO_2 tax may prove to be the more appropriate instrument (Goldblatt, 2010; OECD, 2009a).

Ultimately, however, a CO_2 emissions trading scheme can only guarantee an adequately high CO_2 price and secrurity in terms of long-term expectations through very strict restrictions in order to develop transformative impact. Where the requisite institutional opportunities are not given, a CO_2 tax at a corresponding level represents an alternative instrument for effective, transformative management by governance. As a guideline, the WBGU assumes that the carbon price in Europe and the OECD countries will have to be at least US$ 40–50 per t CO_2 in 2020, and at least US$ 110–130 per t CO_2 in 2050 in order to comply with the 2 °C guard rail (Sections 4.2, 7.3.9; IEA, 2010c). According to IEA estimates, the CO_2 price in developing and newly industrialising countries will need to reach approx. US$ 60 per t CO_2 by 2030, and at least US$100 per t CO_2 by the middle of the century to achieve stabilisation at 450 ppm CO_2eq. These conclusions were derived from IEA's model calculations (2010c) and the scenarios in Section 4.2.4; however, they probably at most denote the lower limits for the required overall total.

Globally uncoordinated carbon pricing holds the risk of distoring the competition in international trade, and a risk of carbon leakage as a result of production shift (Box 5.2-3). Both problems have been discussed intensively in the context of the further development of the European emissions trading scheme. One solution to these problems may be border adjustment measures (for example border tax adjustment on imports). Measures such as these are intended to prevent any freeriding by individual countries and distortions of competition as a result of higher costs due to carbon pricing, and to increase the incentives for cooperative behaviour (Edenhofer et al., 2009a, b; Box 5.2-3). However, border adjustment measures only have a limited impact and carry a high potential for causing trade disputes. They can therefore at most be applied as an accompanying measure, rather than as an independent instrument within any policy mix for the transformation. At best, extremely moderate border adjustment measures should be introduced in order to reduce the competitive disadvantages suffered by energy-intensive companies (Section 7.3.2).

Phase Out Fossil Fuel Subsidies

The introduction of carbon pricing should be accompanied by the phasing out of all subsidies for fossil energy carriers as these artificially maintain their competitiveness and weaken the impact of the CO_2 price signal (Section 4.5). This also includes all direct payments, tax concessions, fixed prices, import financing, or public assumption of risks from fossil energy use. The majority of fossil fuel subsidies is currently paid in non-OECD countries, including China, India, Saudi Arabia, Indonesia, Russia, Egypt and Iran. The phasing out or reform of these subsidies was decided at the G20 summit in Pittsburgh in September 2009. It was to be ensured that poor population groups were not disadvantaged (IEA et al., 2010a; Section 4.5).

5.2.3 Policy-mix for the Transformation

Carbon pricing encourages market players to consider the social cost of CO_2 emissions in their decision-making. However, carbon pricing alone is not sufficient to induce changes in market player behaviour in the transformation fields of energy, urbanisation and land use, as the relevant markets show various forms of market failure, such as positive and negative external effects, information asymmetries, market entry barriers, natural monopolies and the supply of public goods. These cases call for state action; including legislation (administrative command-and-control, planning), money (market-based instruments) and 'good words' (information, voluntary agreements with the threat of regulation). These political instruments acts as direct or indirect incentive for market player behaviour and coordinate changes in behaviour (Section 5.4).

For a transformative impact on production and consumption, the simultaneous use of various instruments is required in the context of a policy mix to initiate systemic and fundamental changes in the three transformation fields. The design of a transformation policy should trigger fast and long-term oriented structural changes, avoid path dependencies, and help to overcome present obstructive short-term orientations.

McKinsey (2009), for example, discuss on the basis of its global greenhouse gas abatement cost curve the political instruments which have to be enforced to overcome present market imperfections whilst exploiting existing abatement cost potentials (Figure 5.2-1).

In the first third of the cost curve, which includes abatement measures that could generate profits, if implemented, market development and the demand for known technologies, techniques and land management methods can be promoted through regulatory instruments such as standards or requirements. These are generally efficiency measures, currently not implemented due to lack of information, for reasons of convenience, because of a lack of long-term orientation, or loss aversion on the part of the agents. In terms of investments at the increasing part of the cost curve, various political instruments are required in order to develop a long-term international regulatory framework to facilitate the introduction of emerging technologies, techniques and management methods. This particularly applies to the currently expensive abatement measures. With the aid of market-based instruments and policy-based technology support, the com-

Box 5.2-3

Distortions of Competition, Carbon Leakage and Border Adjustment Measures

Competition and Carbon Leakage

Until a global price for CO_2 exists, and until all countries have introduced climate policy measures, a country's unilateral climate policy may result in competitive disadvantages for companies based in this country but operating internationally. This particularly concerns companies in energy intensive sectors with strong international competition, for example companies in the lime, fertiliser/nitrogen, iron/steel, aluminium, paper and chemical production sectors. This could lead to the problem of carbon leakage, caused by three different aspects: firstly, it can be related to the potential relocation of companies suffering a competitive disadvantage in the form of higher production costs as a result of climate policy. However, their relocation to a country without a climate policy does not impact the high level of global CO_2 emissions. Secondly, products from countries with a climate policy may be substituted by products from countries without a climate policy, produced with less efficient production technologies, therefore leading to a rise in global CO_2 emissions. Thirdly, global CO_2 emissions can rise as a consequence of the declining demand for fossil fuels in industrialised countries in the course of climate policy ; world market prices for fossil fuels would come down, leading to an increased demand for fossil fuels in countries that have not adopted a climate policy. This effect is also known as the 'green paradox' (Sinn, 2008; Edenhofer and Kalkuhl, 2009). The relocation of energy intensive companies abroad to unregulated countries is also associated with job losses and a decline in profits and tax revenues. This represents a not insignificant negative incentive with regard to implementation of national climate protection measures (Babiker and Rutherford, 2005).

Border Adjustment Measures

The introduction of border adjustment measures is one possible option for maintaining the competitiveness of energy intensive production companies and preventing carbon leakage (WTO and UNEP, 2009; Dröge et al., 2009). These were already discussed in the context of the GATT in the 1960s. They can be divided into direct and indirect adjustment measures. In the context of the introduction of an emissions trading scheme, indirect measures include, for example, a free of charge allocation of emission rights to energy intensive companies in international competition. As an additional incentive for investment in more energy efficient technologies, the companies can also be offered subsidies in the form of soft loans (Dröge et al., 2009). Direct measures would for instance be: an import tax on high-carbon goods; the compulsory purchase of CO_2 permits for importing goods in accordance with the CO_2 emissions generated in the course of their production; the corresponding subsidisation of exported products; or the introduction of production technology standards backed up by international treaties (Dröge et al., 2009). In the case of import taxation, the tax rate can be based either on the actual CO_2 emissions attributable to the production of the goods, or based on a fixed value, for example a product's CO_2 emissions assuming the best available technology (BAT), or the CO_2 emissions attributable to the production of a similar domestically produced product (Ismer and Neuhoff, 2007; Fischer and Fox, 2009). This also leads to technical problems, as the production carbon intensity would have to be determined for all products and all countries under consideration of all preliminary products.

Calculations using general equilibrium models show that the problematic issue of carbon leakage can generally be classified as not quite so significant, whilst the competitive disadvantages can turn out to be quite considerable for certain energy intensive industries (Burniaux et al., 2010). Various authors conclude that the introduction of border tax adjustments (BTA) would have little impact on the problem of carbon leakage. On the other hand, the introduction of BTA could substantially improve the reduced competitiveness of energy intensive companies (Babiker and Rutherford, 2005; Ismer and Neuhoff, 2007; Fischer and Fox, 2009; Mattoo et al., 2009; WTO and UNEP, 2009; Böhringer et al., 2010). However, they must also be assessed differently in terms of their compatibility with WTO law (Dröge et al., 2009; WTO and UNEP, 2009). Equally, it is not clear whether they could provide cooperation incentives for countries previously unwilling to cooperate with regard to climate policy.

Border Adjustment Measures and WTO Law

The issue of whether border tax adjustments are combatible with WTO law is highly controversial in academic legal literature (WBGU, 2004) and must not be assumed to be finally resolved until a relevant decision is made by the WTO dispute settlement bodies. There are nevertheless good arguments for their compatibility with WTO law, providing the requirements formulated by the WTO dispute settlement bodies in other cases are observed in the design of border tax adjustments (UBA, 2008): essentially, the purposeful introduction of a fee for the import of goods produced in countries with less stringent environmental standards does not contravene the General Agreement on Tariffs and Trade (GATT) principle of non-discrimination. In particular, it does not contravene the principle of national treatment (Article III: 2 GATT), providing the border tax adjustments for imported products is not greater than the costs created by the higher environmental standards for similar domestic products (Ruddigkeit, 2009). The production costs of domestic products should therefore be assessed such that they cause no discrimination. Appropriate as a basis would be the costs generated by the use of best available technology. Should these fees nevertheless contravene the non-discrimination requirement, the contravention would be justified in accordance with GATT Article XX lit. (b) and (g): pursuant to these, measures can be taken to protect the climate as a global environmental good (Epiney, 2000; Ismer and Neuhoff, 2007) if no less moderate measures are available, and the duty of cooperation as defined in Article XX GATT has been sufficiently exercised to a minimum, i.e. through international climate protection negotiations (UBA, 2008). The reimbursement of additional costs due to climate protection when exporting domestic products (so-called export refund) causes no concerns with regard to WTO law; this merely requires compliance with the duty of notification pursuant to Article XVI: 1 GATT.

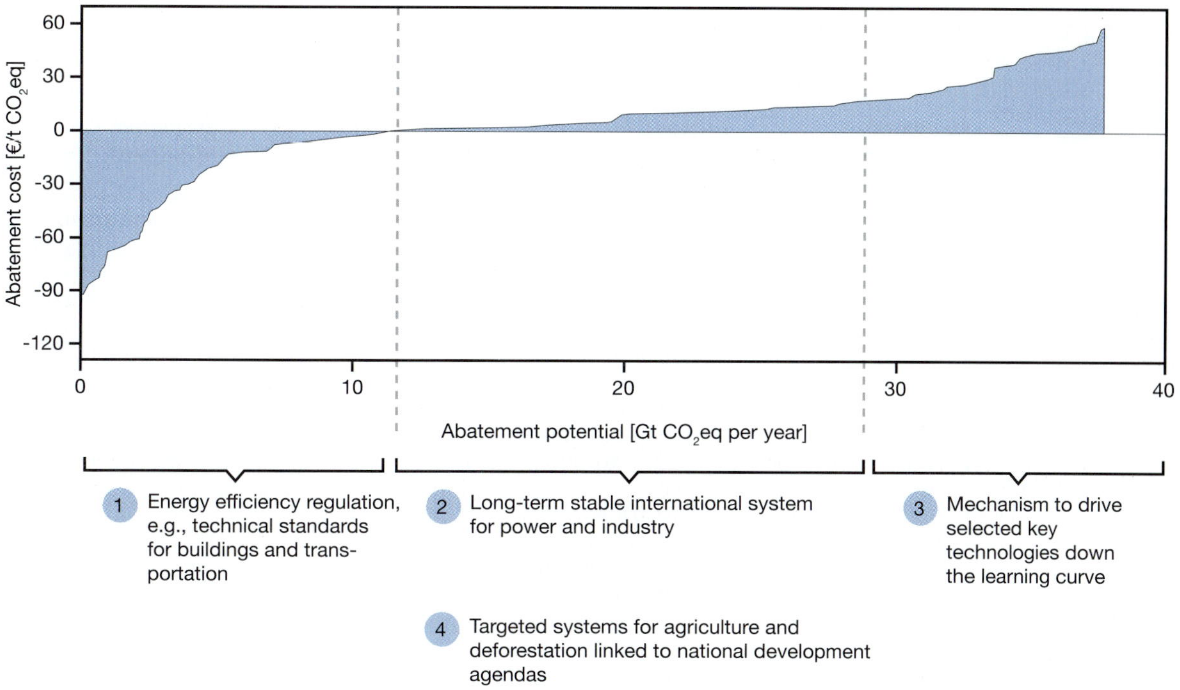

Figure 5.2-1
Proposals for regulations in four areas (energy efficiency, power and industry, agriculture, key technologies) according to the greenhouse gas abatement cost curve for the cost efficient reduction of CO_2 emissions.
Source: McKinsey, 2009

mercial launch of these technologies and the further development of technical solutions should be accelerated through learning curve effects (McKinsey, 2009). In the field of land use, it is important to establish the necessary political and institutional capacities for sustainable land management internationally and to integrate this goal into international cooperation as land-use policy is too fragmented in many countries (Chapter 1, Section, 5.4).

The abatement cost curve in Figure 5.2-1 clearly shows that in the short term, demand for new technologies in the areas of durable consumer goods and the building and transport sectors can be generated through a combination of administrative command-and-control as well as market-based instruments, and information. The transformation towards greater energy efficiency can therefore commence.

For systemic and long-term changes in the transformation fields of energy, urbanisation and land use, a combination of political instruments is required to also contribute to stable framework conditions with a transformative impact at an international level. The WBGU recommends to focus not exclusively on technologies here, but also on encouraging changes in behaviour and social innovations.

Usually, not just one policy instrument but rather a portfolio of measures (policy mix) should be used if the various market imperfections and barriers are to be overcome (Gupta and Tirpak, 2007; Edenhofer et al., 2009a; McKinsey, 2009; Knopf et al., 2010; Matthes, 2010; OECD, 2009a, 2010a). The measures should mutually support one another, rather than impede each other's impact. The policy mix can be used on all political levels, from local authorities through to regional states/provinces, to national and supranational level. National governance measures should be flanked by international agreements for the transformative impact to develop globally. The measures in the policy mix can continue for very different lengths of time, as some instruments, such as technology-specific support, for example, should be used only temporarily. The policy mix for the transformation should concentrate primarily on the following three areas: firstly, it should support the development of new markets for innovations; secondly, it should provide incentives for climate-friendly market behaviour; and thirdly, it should target the supply of public goods such as infrastructures and ecosystem services.

Table 5.2-1 on political instruments in the three areas specified (innovations; investment, production and consumption decisions; supply of public goods) illustrates a suggested policy mix the WBGU considers sensible. This policy mix principally applies to the industrialised countries, as these already have the requisite

Table 5.2-1
Exemplary policy mix for the transformation towards a low-carbon society.
Source: WBGU

	Regulatory instruments	Incentive instruments	Government investment	Informative instruments
Promotion of Innovation	› Technology and Efficiency Standards (for example for vehicles, buildings, durable consumer goods) › Production standards › Sustainability standards in land use › Government procurement policy › Regulation of capital markets › Prohibitions (for instance of certain land uses or products, F-gases) › Regulation (for example bioenergy quotas) › Urban, regional and infrastructure planning › Patent law	› CO_2 tax › CO_2 emissions permits › Public support for research and development › public venture capital › soft loans and credit guarantees by the government › Fiscal innovation incentives › Promotion of new business models as experimental projects (for example Energy Contracting) › Competitive promotion of experiments	› Public infrastructure provision › public demonstration projects	› Staging of competitions and granting of awards (Jugend Forscht, encouraging young people to engage in research, Low-Carbon City, innovation prizes) › Voluntary agreements with a threat of regulation
Investment, production and consumer decisions	› Technology and efficiency standards › Production standards › Sustainability standards (biomass, land and forest management) › Emissions capping › Nudging ('libertarian paternalism') › Government procurement policy › Regulation (bioenergy quotas, organic products) › Market regulation (energy law, Tenancy law) › Urban, regional and infrastructure planning	› CO_2 tax › CO_2 emissions permits › Technology-specific market entry promotion (for example feed-in tariffs) › Promotion of new business models › Fiscal investment incentives › Phasing out of distorting subsidies (fossil fuels, agricultural subsidies) › Payment for ecosystem services › Road use charges › Public transport tariff structure	› Public infrastructure provision › Public-Private Partnership	› Information campaigns (on energy efficiency, dietary habits, new forms of housing and mobility) › Labelling (organic products, carbon footprint, sustainability) › Voluntary agreements with a threat of regulation
Availability of public goods	› Urban, regional and infrastructure planning › Certification › Market regulation › Bans	› Payment for ecosystem services	› Governmental infrastructure provision	› Information campaigns, labelling › Voluntary labelling › Voluntary agreements with a threat of regulation

political and institutional capacities for implementation and enforcement (OECD, 2010a). However, a transformation policy must also be introduced concurrently in developing countries. It has to be supported by capacity building and international cooperation, technology transfer and financing. Compared with the industrialised countries, measures which are particularly promising in the developing countries, other than carbon pricing approaches, are state regulations (for example in the form of efficiency standards for buildings, vehicles and appliances), the subsidising of renewable energies, financing support and information policy (UNCTAD, 2010a; UNEP, 2009).

5.2.3.1
Promotion of Innovation

Developing a national innovation strategy in which all subsystems of the national innovation system focus on solving a particular problem supports innovation. In this case, this includes the transformation of the energy system and steering urbanisation and land-use systems towards climate-friendlyness. The areas of education and research, capital markets, the legal framework, the corporate structure, and the entire economic structure should be integrated into such an innovation system (OECD, 2010b).

Moreover, public support of research and development through the use of subsidies or tax concessions for businesses can provide incentives to develop more innovations. Government-financed cooperation between science and industry and international research and technology cooperation can ensure that new, low-carbon technologies are diffused and deployed all over the world as quickly as possible.

Temporary, direct government support for private sector investments is also necessary in order to accelerate innovation. Depending on the stage of technology development (research, demonstration, deployment, commercial roll out, diffusion), different forms of government support for private investments would be sensible measures (UNEP-SEFI, 2008). In the research phase, direct public support for research projects is important. Likewise, the promotion of public-private partnerships in applied research and development is also of major importance. The greatest funding gap (valley of death) is often at the demonstration and deployment stages, as the invention is already on the way to commercialisation, yet further development is frequently (for example due to limited numbers of unit quantities) associated with high costs, and high technological risks due to little practical experience (UNEP-SEFI, 2008; IEA, 2010a; Figure 4.5-5). This is where government grants and guarantees could further the acquisition of private venture capital providers who would otherwise not invest without public support. Additionally, the state should create an environment that is attractive to venture capitalists. One option would be the combination of public and private risk capital in venture capital funds, examples of these are the UK Carbon Trust Venture Capital Fund or the California Clean Energy Fund (Section 4.5; BASE and SEFI, 2006). Government demonstration projects or the provision of infrastructure by the government could also help to reduce the risks for private investors in the deployment stage. In the diffusion stage, access to private capital for financing can also be improved through the provision of soft loans and credit guarantees, helping to facilitate extended commercialisation (Section 4.5).

Apart from CO_2 emissions pricing, regulatory instruments such as dynamic technical standards in the transport sector, the building sector or for durable consumer goods can provide incentives for investment in research and development. These also include policy-based standards for the transformation of systems, such as the introduction of electromobility, which requires new solutions along the entire private transport value creation chain, thereby offering incentives for private research spending. The introduction of sustainability standards in agriculture will provide incentives for research and development spending in this sector. This applies not only to technological innovations, but also to social innovations such as new business models, for example energy contracting (Sections 4.3, 4.5).

5.2.3.2
Investment, Production and Consumption Decisions

A policy mix is also needed in order to achieve changes in market players' behaviour. Again, various financing choices should be an element. The transformation of energy systems, of urban infrastructures and of land-use systems is usually associated with high up-front investments which generate returns only in the long term. Such investments therefore often require long-term and low-interest financing, which is, however, not always available through commercial financial institutions (Section 4.5). Here, the government can support private investments with soft loans or credit guarantees.

Energy efficiency investments in buildings, heating systems and production technologies, generally also characterised by high up-front investments with continuous long-term returns, can also be accelerated through soft loans and grants by the government. In addition, regulatory instruments such as efficiency standards for consumer goods, buildings, machines, vehicles or entire production processes are also appropriate.

In the area of land use, minimum standards and a certification scheme can ensure that climate-friendly management processes are applied in agriculture and forestry or in the provision of bioenergy. The European Union's minimum bioenergy standards could, for example, be extended to all biomass products (WBGU, 2010a).

And finally, a government procurement policy that focuses on efficiency or low-carbon products, and a targeted information policy (campaigns, road shows) can advance technology development and investments in efficiency quickly and extensively, and promote changes in behaviour on the part of consumers.

The commercial attractiveness of investments in low-carbon technologies should also be ensured with a long-term oriented, stable regulatory environment. Besides the introduction of a CO_2 price signal, technology-specific support increases the return on investments in low-carbon technologies and minimises their risks (Box 5.2-4). To make investments in renewable energies particularly attractive, targeted support for the commercial roll out of renewable energies in the form of a feed-in tariff (FiT) has proved to be very effective in the past (Box 5.2-4).

Regulations on market access, prices, quality, natural monopolies or the obligation to contract into public utilities guide market player decisions. For example, the German Renewable Energy Source Act (EEG) made large-scale market entry possible by obliging grid operators to purchase electricity from renewable energies. The liberalisation of energy markets has led to competitiveness in production, trade and distribution to end customers. However, the grid-bound electricity and gas markets networks are still subject to regulation.

Network operators in Germany, for example, have so far been subject to incentive regulation (revenue-cap regulation) in order to provide incentives for cost-effective production through an upper revenue cap for the duration of a regulation period. Efficient companies thereby receive a higher rate of return on theit investments. This keeps the transmission fees low. However, incentive regulation bears the risk that network operators are not adequately encouraged to expand networks and ensure grid quality. There is therefore also an additional obligation to prepare replacement and expansion investment plans, and to have these investment budgets approved by the regulatory authority (Monopolkommission, 2009).

Because of a lack of investments, a regulation review is under consideration (von Hirschhausen et al., 2010; Helm, 2009). Apart from aspects of operating efficiency, the regulatory design should also include long-term objectives serving the development of a sustainable infrastructure. In addition to the imputed interest rate on own capital as an incentive for investments into the grid, competitive tendering for network development could be considered. The specific design of markets allows the state to provide incentives for a systemic transformation in the three transformation fields.

Changes in consumer behaviour, for example when purchasing food or even timber-derived products such as furniture, can be supported further through information measures such as product labelling, product standards and targeted communication policies (for instance information campaigns). This applies to energy efficient appliances as much as to encouraging low-carbon eating habits. Carbon footprint labels on groceries or campaigns to encourage a low-meat diet, for instance, or the purchase of regional and seasonal products can lead to changes in behaviour. In the area of mobility, campaigns for new services such as car sharing, for example, can encourage climate-friendly behaviour (Section 4.3).

Consumer decisions can also be influenced in the direction of sustainability by the specification of so-called 'default' options. One option for overcoming barriers for behavioural changes not caused by a lack of environmental preferences but by loss aversion, a lack of long-term orientation, or barriers present for reasons of convenience (Section 2.4) could be so-called 'nudges'. This strategy is also known as 'libertarian paternalism' (Thaler and Sunstein, 2008). One prominent example for nudges are default options, i.e. those that would also be preferred by the majority of consumers even after careful consideration of all arguments, yet are still not selected because of the above mentioned barriers and a lack of information. At the same time, the option of selecting another alternative (opt out) is always kept open. When there is a divergence in terms of time between the costs and benefits of an action, nudges can help individuals to make their decisions in such a way that the resultant benefit is optimised in the long run (Box 5.2-5).

5.2.3.3
Supply of Public Goods

There are various political instruments available for public goods such as ecosystem services or technical and social infrastructures, which are important for a low-carbon economy.

All transformation fields (energy, urbanisation, land use) have a common problem: how, in the long-term, can spatial requirements be met at different levels (local, regional, nationwide, cross-nationally). The necessary infrastructure changes and low-carbon land use require the coordination of different interests (mobility, supply, economic development, population development, nature conservation), the settlement of

Box 5.2-4

Feed-In Tariffs for Renewable Energies

Feed-in Tariffs (FiT) provide investors with long-term planning security, thereby overcoming investment barriers. Technology-specific feed-in tariffs also allow the parallel promotion of different forms of renewable energy, thereby unlocking various options for securing the future energy supply. In these respects, feed-in tariffs are preferable to instruments such as quotas and tradable permits for renewable energies (Neuhoff, 2005; Lesser and Su, 2008). In the past, expansion of renewable energy has tended to be faster in countries with feed-in tariffs than in countries with quota-based promotion (IEA, 2008a). Germany is generally regarded as a role model in terms of accelerated expansion of renewable energies because of its early introduction of feed-in tariffs (Sijm, 2002; Ragwitz et al., 2007; Rickerson et al., 2007; IEA, 2008a; Fulton et al., 2009).

Feed-in tariffs are usually paid out differentiated according to the various energy technologies over a set period of approx. 15–25 years, ideally subject to degression over the entire term. They therefore afford investors sufficient planning security and long-term, secure returns on their investments (Fulton et al., 2009). However, the degression also provides an incentive for technological innovations. Learning effects impact favourably on reduction of the prime costs (IEA, 2008a; Klein et al., 2008; Lehmann, 2009; Fulton et al., 2009).

To ensure that feed-in tariffs are cost-effective, yet also effective in terms of their impact, various aspects must be taken into consideration during their design. The rate of tariff, or the premiums paid, for example, and the payment periods should be set technology-specific. As already noted above, the feed-in tariff should be subject to a gradual degression over time which takes into account changing market conditions (including prime costs, CO_2 price) along the lines of the German Renewable Energy Source Act (EEG). However, on the basis of the experiences regarding the various market dynamics gained there, the degression of feed-in tariffs should not be linked to a certain number of years, but rather to the cumulative installed capacity of the respective technology. This would provide additional cost-reduction incentives, making the operating efficiency for renewable energies financially viable sooner. At the same time, in order to provide planning security for investors, the tariffs applicable in the year of investment should be guaranteed over a fixed period of 10–25 years. Tariffs or premiums should be used as supporting instruments for new capacities only until the technologies have become competitive.

At present, feed-in tariffs have been introduced in over 50 countries and 25 regional states or provinces (REN21, 2010). These include many developing and newly industrialising countries, such as China, India, South Africa, Thailand, Indonesia, the Philippines, Uganda, Kenya, Tanzania, Argentina, Ecuador and Nicaragua. Through the use of appropriate technologies, feed-in tariffs can also be introduced in small, local island networks, which is why they are so important, particularly for overcoming energy poverty in developing countries (Moner-Girona, 2008).

The wide-spread use of feed-in tariffs at a global level would significantly accelerate renewable energies expansion. To support the further diffusion of feed-in tariff systems, Germany should start a global political initiative and encourage an ongoing exchange of experiences between countries with feed-in tariff systems to facilitate system effectiveness and efficiency improvement (Section 7.3.4). For the least developed countries, funds would have to be made available for both the feed-in tariff itself, and for renewable energy capacity building. According to estimates, a comprehensive funding of renewable energies in developing countries (including the BASIC states) through feed-in tariffs could require gradually increasing financial transfers of up to US$ 250–270 billion per year between 2025 and 2030 (funding peak). Prior and subsequent requisite transfers would be lower, although still in the region of several billion US$ per year (DeMartino and Le Blanc, 2010). If nothing else, at least the payments during the funding peak far exceed the sums currently flowing into these areas in the form of loans. They are also far in excess of the annual US$ 100 billion financial transfers as of 2020 agreed to by the Annex I countries in the Cancún Agreements. By way of comparison: in 2009, global annual investments in clean energy technologies were somewhere in the range of around US$162 billion, of which around a third was in developing and newly industrialising countries (UNEP-SEFI and BNEF, 2010). What a financing mechanism for the global diffusion of feed-in tariffs could look like has been elaborated in the Deutsche Bank Climate Investment Research's draft concept 'Get FiT', for instance (Fulton et al., 2010). This could form the basis for a political initiative to support feed-in tariffs in developing countries.

conflicts and precautionary provisions for spatial function and spatial use. As a coordination instrument, public planning allows forward-looking, formative management of these areas of government responsibility. It serves the embedding and coordination of individual projects into an overall strategy. In the context of a transformation towards a low-carbon society, planning primarily concerns the areas of environmental, regional and urban planning, as well as infrastructure planning. Regional value creation chains and the integrated management of land, energy and material flows are of great importance, for example, for planning sustainable land use. Another specific challenge is the planning of infrastructures such as new supra-regional power grids (for example the supergrid; Chapter 4). Infrastructure and land-use planning must increasingly be carried out supra-regionally, for example at EU level (Section 5.4.3). Transnational planning processes within the EU must therefore be reinforced (EEAC, 2009). In the case of infrastructure investments, planning law is vital in order to obtain quick approvals for private investments, thereby providing an adequate incentive for these (Matthes, 2010).

Box 5.2-5

'Nudges': Green Electricity as Default Option

One example of how 'nudging' can be useful in the context of the transformation towards a low-carbon society is the offer of eco-electricity as the default option, as introduced, for example, by the Zurich electricity company Elektrizitätswerke der Stadt Zürich (EWZ). In the course of a tariff adjustment in October 2006, the EWZ introduced a combined product, consisting of ecologically certified hydroelectric power and a small proportion of certified eco-electricity from wind or bioenergy as their standard electricity product. This new standard product met sustainability criteria to a far higher degree than the previous, cheaper standard product. Furthermore, various high quality eco-electicity products (water, solar) were offered as well as an ecologically less valuable option with electricity from nuclear power, waste incineration plants and non-certified hydroelectric power plants. The new eco-electricity mix was delivered as a standard. If customers wanted to use one of the other products, they had to give notice of this in writing. In consequence, around three-quarters of private customers opted for the eco-electricity mix, i.e. the standard product following the tariff adjustment, and only around 20% deliberately selected the option with nuclear power. A further 3% of customers deliberately opted for an ecologically higher quality electricity product. Once the increased eco-electricity demand from business customers is added, the total proportion of certified eco-electricity supplied by the EWZ rose from 40 to 60% (EWZ, 2007).

On the one hand, these kind of projects are successful due to the fact that those purchasing electricity tend to be less than willing to change their electricity company or their electricity products on their own accord. Reasons given are time-consuming procedures, products that require explanation, non-transparent tariff systems and long-term contractual relationships (Kosakova, 2005; Burkhalter et al., 2009). On the other hand, there are indications that electricity customers in Switzerland, at least, wanted an ecologically higher quality electricity product even before the tariff adjustment, and that the new standard product responded to their preferences, in contrast to the old electricity product from conventional hydroelectric power plants, nuclear power and electricity from waste incineration plants (Burkhalter et al., 2009). What is certain is that, if default options are offered, the probability that this option will be kept is very high. One reason for this is that it takes less effort to make no decision. Moreover, particularly with regard to complex products that require explanation, decision-makers tend to feel that certain default options already contain elements of a recommendation representing the best choice for them (Thaler and Sunstein, 2008; Dinner et al., 2009).

The provision of environmental goods can also be managed by governance. Sustainable agricultural or forestry production supports the conservation of regional and global public environmental goods (for example air pollution control, climate, water and soil protection). Ecosystems can be economically valued based on their various functions: provisioning (production of food and feed, biomass, drinking water, genetic resources), regulating (air pollution control, climate, water and soil protection) and cultural (aesthetic value, recreation and tourism, social networks) in order to supply a price signal. Reward systems in the form of Payments for Environmental Services (PES) can accelerate the transformation towards low-carbon land use. Farmers and forest managers are rewarded for providing certain ecosystem services, such as carbon sequestration, water cycle regulation, soil formation or primary production, in order to create economic incentives for their long-term provision (Wunder, 2005). The EU agricultural subsidies should therefore be reformed and carried over to a system of payment for ecosystem services (SRU 2008). Initiatives based on this principle, in which even private beneficiaries pay either directly or voluntarily for ecosystem services, are currently evolving all over the world. These include hydroelectric power stations, for example, which are dependent on the regulation of the water cycle in their catchment areas.

5.2.4
Conclusion

The majority of the political instruments required to shape the transformation are already available. The policy mix should comprise carbon pricing in combination with other political measures to overcome market imperfections and transformation barriers in the three transformation fields. The policy mix must promote innovation, guide investment, production and consumption decisions, and ensure the supply of public goods. Due to the tight timeframe for the transformation, the various political instruments must be implemented and enforced quickly for the transformation to commence simultaneously in all markets and transformation fields. Market player planning reliability should be created by taking long-term objectives into account.

5.3
Transformation Impediments and Barriers: It's Politics, Stupid!

Although there has been an awareness of Earth system crisis tendencies and the finiteness of natural resources for over 40 years now, and these problems have been discussed at various international conferences (Meadows et al., 1972; UN Conference on the Human Environment in Stockholm, 1972; UN Conference on Environment and Development, 1992, etc.), and numerous measures have been taken to implement a more sustainable economic order and lifestyles, these efforts have so far yielded only limited success. In the key problem areas (climate change, loss of biodiversity, desertification), the situation has even become exacerbated (Section 1.1). Most recently, the issue of change resistance has become a focus for sustainability and transition research (Harich, 2010; Kastenhofer and Rammel, 2005). The fact that the doubtlessly existing transformation willingness of people in OECD, newly industrialising and developing countries (Chapter 2), which has increased over the decades, has not automatically been translated into sustainability transformation is primarily due to the objection of influential social forces and barriers and institutional impediments deterring, frustrating and ultimately putting off actors who are willing to change. The WBGU has identified these barriers as mainly political, i.e. on the level of political debate, interest intermediation and implementation.

5.3.1
Political Barriers in a Multilevel System

The transformation towards a low-carbon society is a global task in which nation states continue to play a central role. In democratically structured constitutional states, public policies are based on a collective will which essentially depends on national association but also requires a transnational perspective. International law, particularly the Law of Treaties (still) does not have the necessary effective regulation and sanction mechanisms at its disposal. The scope for determining an effective transformation policy must therefore largely be sought and sounded out at a national level (Giddens, 2009; Ostrom, 2009), however, concurrently also at a sub- and supranational level and in non-national and para-state transnational networks (for example major cities and non-governmental organisations; Leibfried et al., 2010).

On this level of politics, the WBGU has primarily identified four factors overshadowing the problem horizon of state actors in multilevel systems which reduce their problem-solving capacity: the huge time pressure that climate change has placed on the tried and tested mode of the incremental and dilatory policy of 'muddling through' and procrastination (Section 5.3.1.1); existing path dependencies and the veto power of high-carbon regime interest cartels (Section 5.3.1.2); the inadequacy of a cooperatively moderating government organisation to deal with new problems (Section 5.3.1.3); and a representation deficit (Section 5.3.1.4). The clear strengths of modern statehood – gaining time through compromise, integration of well-organised interests into the political decision-making process (neo-corporatism) and a well-meaning balancing of these on the part of a moderating state – have become weaknesses endangering the future viability of post-industrial societies.

5.3.1.1
Short-Term Orientation and Politics of Delay

The politics of transformation requires public policies that focus on the long term, and which are valid over a number of years or even decades, thereby traversing cyclical government changes and political opinion swings (Giddens, 2009; Nullmeier and Dietz, 2010). By contrast, politics in democracies naturally focus on short parliamentary terms and the current constraints of staying in power (Weber, 1992; Downs, 1968). More or less the same applies to economic elites, particularly under the conditions of the financial market economy (Windolf, 2005). They also neglect longer-term developments, instead focusing on quarterly balance sheets, annual financial statements or stock-market quotations. This sometimes extremely short-term focus favours concentration on fast impact measures which are easily communicated in the mass media; it has, however, an adverse effect on issues where both short- and long-term effects have to be taken into account (Sprinz, 2009; Hovi et al., 2009). To date, our societies' social, economic and political institutions are not capable of responding to these challenges. Solutions need to be found which enhance the capacity for long term policy-making and establish institutional continuity.

The 'short-termism' (Giddens) of political attention is coupled with dilatory (delaying) methods of handling dissent and finding compromises in political negotiation arenas: difficult to solve problems tend to be shelved. This applies without a doubt to the big reform agendas of western democracies, such as demographic change, exploding healthcare costs, or mass unemployment and national debt. Adressing climate change also falls into this category. Many of the harmful effects of global warming will impact fully only at some point in time in the future; the policy-making system therefore favours delays in tackling dangerous situations such as these.

Contemporary politics like this are not objectionable per se. Gaining time is often necessary in order to maintain stability, and the struggle to do so is an appropriate reaction to the contingencies and risks of modern societies (Günther, 2006). However, the combined ecological and fiscal crisis increasingly calls the positive effects of a policy functioning on the principle of 'muddling through' into question. Responding to uncertainty and mitigating conflicts with procrastination reaches its limits when risks (believed to be far off) revert into (present and close) fundamental dangers. This new situation's difficult consequence is, on the one hand, 'deceleration' whilst the political process shakes off its media-driven shortness of breath, and, on the other hand, 'acceleration', as the clear requirement that certain climate stabilisation or land-use change targets set at intervals of five, ten or twenty years must not be missed results in the need to draw up more realistic schedules for current decision-making. Impediments are the braking influence of veto groups and an ineffective administrative structure.

5.3.1.2
Opposing Forces and Resistance: Lobby and Interest Groups

In addition to the institutional factors determining the chances of political change, interest and ideology-based differences play a central role. The transformation towards a low-carbon society is only achievable if social and political majorities are in favour of it. It is the only way to initiate and develop the changes that are the basis for the transformation on a legislative level and in civil society. It requires an extremely broad cross-party coalition far beyond a simple majority. Not surprisingly, the most obstructive groups impeding the transformation process are those which will experience material or status losses as a result of the intended change (Section 2.4.1). The positive impact of interest group activities in liberal democracies is undisputed; without the contribution of these intermediary agents in negotiations between specific core constituencies and the government, the specialist knowledge required for legislative and administrative actions in complex societies would hardly be available. Furthermore, society tends to respond better to the communication of government measures through interest groups, which not least also relieves governments of yet another task (von Alemann, 1989).

Unfortunately, however, neo-corporatist power constellations dating from the zenith of industrialisation still enjoy a particularly high level of consolidated power and informal political influence. Associations from the economic sector have far greater conflict handling capacities than associations in socio-ecological cross-sectional areas representing general and public interests. There is also a lack of transparency in the interaction of ministerial or local bureaucracy and certain interest groups, some of which seem to have evolved into downright 'private interest governments' (Streeck and Schmitter, 1985), leading to lobbyists excessively influencing legislation (Maras, 2009). At the same time, an increasing reluctance on the part of both employers and employees to join in these capital and employment interest groups can be observed in most OECD countries. In his 'Post-Democracy' analysis, Crouch identified the growing direct political influence of corporations as the 'driving force' of the democracy crises in Europe and the USA (Crouch, 2004). According to Crouch, one characteristic of the state of post-democracy is that politics increasingly function on the liberal model basis of lobby work and interest representation. From a democracy theory perspective, this development is problematic as the resources individuals can draw on to defend their interests differ widely. Firstly, lobby groups can effectively threaten with the fact that one sector currently assigned a high level of 'system relevance' is going to make losses, and will potentially migrate. As long as economic success is one of the most important parameters in the evaluation of a government's political performance, this argument is extremely effective with politicians (Crouch, 2004). Secondly, business representatives can spend huge sums of money on their lobbying work.

In the problem areas of sustainable development analysed by the WBGU, the influence of lobbyists representing oil and coal manufacturers or energy-intensive industries and the automotive industry is currently significantly greater than that of civil society organisations or the 'green industry' (Streeck, 1994; Brunnengräber, 2009). A prime example for this was the 'scrappage premium' introduced in Germany and other countries (2008), where the interests of the automotive industry – usually an alliance of both employer and labour organisations – were easier to express and more forceful than more 'general' environmental interests, which would have favoured linking the premium with environmental requirements.

Transformation objectors and lobbies opposed to decarbonisation strategies on the grounds of short- and medium-term interests can be found in various different industries and other areas of society. An imminent renunciation of fossil energy carriers, for example, means huge reductions in profit for the oil, gas and coal industries, and for energy suppliers with a large portfolio of coal-powered power stations. Accordingly, oil industry lobby groups in the USA and Europe have campaigned particularly intensively and persistently against any political handling of the climate problem in the past – even to the extent of challenging the scientific proofs for anthropogenic global warming with 'counter assessment' campaigns (Brunnengräber, 2009; Levy and Egan, 2003). Without international climate protection regulations, energy-intensive industry and production sectors (for example the cement, steel, glass, and paper industries) fear competitive disadvantages on the world market (Box 5.2-3). Automotive industry representatives, particularly the manufactures of large cars with high fuel consumption, have also repeatedly influenced political decision-makers in the past, for example with respect to changing the CO_2 guide values for car emissions in their favour (Brunnengräber, 2009). Certain political formations (for instance some elements of the Republican Party in the USA) also reject climate protection measures for ideological reasons (as indeed they fundamentally object to any kind of intervention in the economy). Not least, the growing 'global consumer class' (Worldwatch Institute, 2004; Bread for the World et al., 2008) also features groups of people who object to change because a climate-friendly lifestyle means deprivation, or is perceived as such (Urry, 2010; Ulvila and Pasanen, 2009). Socially disadvantaged groups could also become potential opponents of the transformation as a result of price increases.

Functional regulations and institutions are structural preconditions for implementing a transformation policy. In this respect, from a global perspective, corruption – i.e. the abuse of entrusted power for private gain (Transparency International, 2005) – is a serious barrier and represents a further, illegitimate scope of influence for lobby groups or veto players (von Alemann, 2005). Corruption is particularly prevalent in the areas identified as central transformation fields by the WBGU: the construction sector (urban planning), the energy sector, and land use (here particularly in forestry and agriculture; Transparency International, 2005, 2008, 2011; Kenny, 2007). In these sectors, corruption is not merely a temporary phenomenon during a transitional period of modernising societies, and therefore particularly virulent in weak states or developing and newly industrialising countries (Giannakopoulus and Tänzler, 2009). Corruptive interrelations in society, economy and politics are also present in the democratic systems of OECD countries, as 'corruption in affluent countries frequently takes forms that are as equally 'advanced' as the countries themselves' (Piepenbrink, 2009).

Even more important than the subjective attitudes and preferences of the economic elite, which can be, and are currently already being, corrected with a view to the advantages of a 'green development path', are political and economic routines and path dependencies. Past developed and established procedures and problem solving paths are blindly followed, even if they no longer adequately address the problem, and problem case contexts have changed. The reason for this persistence on the part of actors and the institutional conservatism lies in the assumption that a path change is associated with uncertain and potentially expensive risks. It is difficult to estimate the impacts of a path change (Pierson, 2000; Lehmbruch, 2002, 2003). Administrations in political bureaucracies and commercial corporations spontaneously rely on the familiar, and on the benefit expectations of the old path; on the other hand, the disappointment of such expectations, a greater willingness to take risks, and 'creative destruction' (Joseph Schumpeter) are everyday aspects of corporate decisions and generational change. Contrary to the convenient preconception, administrations are institutions continuously undergoing a learning process. Yet the rigidity of administrative routines is fostered through inadequate problem perceptions and departmental architectures.

5.3.1.3
Institutional Fragmentation and Lack of Coherence and Coordination

According to a widely-followed theory by Tsebelis (2002), the feasibility of reshaping a policy area generally depends on policy stability. Political innovations are therefore condemned to failure if objected to by actors whose approval is essential either under the constitution or in real political terms. The more collective or independent veto players emerge, and the more uniformly and competitively they act, the less likely a status quo change. So political systems differ according to how many veto players they feature. Horizontal and vertical policy integration and fragmentation into different levels, such as federal state and individual states (Länder), in the case of Germany, or nation states and the EU therefore also result in self-imposed horizontal and vertical barriers in the state system.

The problem of institutional fragmentation is exacerbated by a lack of coherence and coordination (Scharpf, 1993; Mayntz, 1997; Blanke et al., 2002). An effective transformation strategy needs a new, coherent, integrated policy. Applying an understandable yet factually problematic kind of conflict prevention and resolution strategy, however, modern policy-making tends to adhere to the maxim of 'good for everybody and harming nobody'. As everyone's interests are more or less served, this results in, for example in Germany, the extensive promotion of renewable energy expansion whilst continuing financial support for fossil and conventional energy carriers. This impedes the expansion of renewable energies and dilutes the political goal of a true energy system transformation.

A further barrier arises from the poor coordination of individual departmental policies. Obviously, transformation policy cannot be the remit of a single department, but must be systematically taken into account in all governance branches (Giddens, 2009). Admittedly, there are now a number of government agencies tasked with climate protection and decarbonisation, but there is a lack of effective coordination and no appropriately strong anchoring in the state apparatus.

Nowadays, climate protection, biodiversity conservation and sustainable urban planning are addressed and taken into consideration by government agencies far more than they were in the early stages of environmental policy-making. However, what remains unchanged is the institutional marginal nature of these departments in comparison to policy areas dedicated to the historic core problems of industrial and welfare societies which, accordingly, occupy the key departments, claiming respective reputations and the corresponding budget shares. Central in most OECD states and many newly industrialising countries are the financial, infrastructure and social departments that deal with the development of the industrial infrastructures of 'labour societies' and handle any associated social problems (such as mass unemployment, demographic change, etc.) by means of distribution and compensation measures. In comparison with these, environmental policy is generally positioned to take into account externalised damages in industrial processes and services either subsequently or preventively, and attempts to keep them within limits. In the WBGU's view, the current departmental architecture prevents climate protection, nature conservation and urban planning from reaching the status they should have, not least with respect to shaping a post-fossil future and establishing a sustainable economy.

5.3.1.4
Representation Deficit and Lack of Acceptance

A perceived participation deficit on the part of the citizens – irrespective of whether this is actually the case, in legal terms – can be another significant barrier to transformation implementation and result in a lack of acceptance. A growing representation deficit is becoming apparent in political systems that are incapable of identifying, consolidating and programmatically implementing the environmental and climate policy related demands and expectations of an increasing number of the electorate. At the same time, the population's willingness to take grassroots action, and to become active predominantly outside of the parliamentary system, is increasing. A general mood in favour of sustainable environmental and climate policy – as documented for example by World Values Survey (2010) data (Chapter 2) – therefore often stays locked in the 'pre-political' domain. What is therefore lacking is appropriate consolidation and representation on a parliamentary level, and other options for productively realising citizen commitment (Section 5.4).

Participation (as an 'input legitimisation' tool) is generally viewed as the normative foundation, and a precondition in practical terms, of democratic communities, which in turn are tasked with providing the structural requirements. In this interplay, the quality of democratic politics is highly dependent on whether citizens have the opportunity to make themselves heard, whether they feel taken seriously or patronised, whether they feel mistrust in their activity or can trust their representatives. Social capital and political action in the life-world environment, and legal institutional guarantees of civic autonomy are closely linked. They have to be well-balanced in order to avoid a tight, legalistic interpretation of the status of citizen and its distention into activism (Seubert, 2009).

Overall, in view of the ecological problems, an outdated administrative culture is predominant in most states, which integrates too little, is not sufficiently open and transparent, and is lacking in innovative ability and permanence, instead relying on ad-hoc solutions and isolated or extremely formalised negotiation arrangements (Jann, 1983). In contemporary policy-making, a short-term orientation and playing for time predominate where quick and long-term decisions are needed. The primacy of structurally conservative interests remains in place even though a forward-looking and pro-active policy would be what is needed to secure the life-support systems and living conditions of future generations. A political administrative structure is required which operates in the 'future II' tense – asking today what politics, the economy and civil society should have done in 2011 to achieve goals in 2020 or 2050 that a consensus can fundamentally be reached on. Vested interests systematically dominate the interests of what is understood to be the global common good. This tendency, consistent in the history of modern states despite repeated periodical interruptions, is now growing even stronger in the face of 'natural dangers' such as climate change and biodiversity loss.

5.3.2
Dare more Democracy!

The world's nations are at different development stages, and have different politico-institutional and socio-economic action capabilities for coping with the transformation. In the WBGU's view, the democratic constitutional state forms the reference frame for transformation assessment. The Great Transformation goes far beyond greenhouse gas reduction, it is about establishing legitimate, fair, creative and durable problem solutions. The democratic process provides exactly those institutions that are needed for a sustainable transformation.

As this is frequently disputed in the current debate, and autocratic regimes are sometimes considered more suitable, for example in terms of developing and implementing large-scale energy efficiency and infrastructure programmes, a brief reminder is required of the structural elements and advantages of democratic governance and life-worlds: democracy's core element is the congruence between rulers and ruled – or, as Abraham Lincoln so famously said, democracy is 'government of the people, by the people, for the people'. Its most important achievement is therefore the legitimation requirement for all acts of governance, which in democratic systems is guaranteed by the political equality of all (inclusion). For 2500 years, democracies have put their trust in the (political) 'wisdom of crowds'. That is why they function according to different variants of the majority rule, which must, however, not be construed as a 'tyranny of the majority', but must rather effectively and fairly allow minorities to have a say, to be involved, and to be protected. Moreover, democratic political systems are embedded in legal orders and the rule of law; fundamental constitutional standards are explicitly eliminated from revision by majority decision.

Effective decision-making advantages such as the reversibility of decisions and effective stakeholder participation on the part of the citizens, instigated through direct and indirect involvement in the decision-making process and public multi-level communication, go hand in hand with these principles. Improved consolidation of preferences and interests, best-possible use of widespread knowledge, and the highest level of 'input legitimation' of any political system therefore reflect the rationality and comparative advantage of democracies. What this effectively means is that citizens do not merely receive services from an authoritarian state, but make a sovereign contribution to their composition and direction. In this respect, modern democracies respond to the general decoupling of modern societies from hierarchies and the proven ethical impact of public discussion and deliberation; both ensure that each individual develops a relatively strong awareness for the (notional) common good whilst also enjoying the chance to pursue and assert their own individual interests.

It is obvious that no democratic system has ever achieved this ideal, and the theory of a 'post-democratic' development of liberal systems with a long democratic tradition is widely discussed in socio-scientific literature (Crouch, 2004; Jörke, 2010). Essentially, there are three problematic factors: (1) the growing social inequality in many developed societies, impacting negatively on participation opportunities and willingness; (2) the discouragement of civic activity caused by global economic imperatives undermining the civil culture of cooperation, responsibility and solidarity by providing incentives for individual competition; and (3) the empirical linking of welfare state systems with the paradigm of an economic growth that erodes the natural foundations of democratic societies through disproportionate consumption of resources (Section 2.3; Box 5.2-1). Despite such by all means serious crises tendencies, the general democratisation trend outlined in Section 1.2.2 continues worldwide beyond the western core countries. Democracy could, then, be considered as a system model for political order which has become globally established; it would therefore have to prove its effectiveness with a view to the forthcoming Great Transformation.

Democratic Performance

At present, democracy has certainly not yet proven its future viability (Box 5.3-1). Time pressure and the complexity of the transformation inevitably lead to the question of the performance and suitability of democratic systems. The quality and the performance of democracies are usually measured by their input, i.e. by effective citizen participation and the willingness of policy-makers to respond to citizens' interests and aspirations, and by their output, i.e. their political effectiveness in the form of effective and efficient action by the executive powers (Brusis, 2008). The measures required by a transformative policy place the usual form of democratic governance under pressure, both in terms of time and space. Democratic processes generally need time, as they take many different interests into account. Moreover, they usually focus on the short-term achievement of political objectives, making the handling and resolution of long-term problems difficult (Section 5.3.1.1). Slowness is, however, not an inherent property of democratic systems and institutions. As demonstrated by the handling of the financial and economic crisis in the autumn of 2008, democracies are certainly able to react quickly to financial and economic crisis situations and to make far-reaching reform decisions. Under the pressure of financial and economic crisis, multi-billion bank bailout and economic stimulus packages were adopted within a very short time (Meyer-Ohlendorf et al., 2009). In summary proceedings, the passing of the German financial market stabilisation act (FMStG) and the establishment of a € 480 billion fund were decided by the Bundestag and the Bundesrat, i.e. the German parliament, and signed off by the German Federal President within a week (BMF, 2008). If the requisite legislative coalitions are in place, democratic systems also allow far-reaching reform decisions to be made within a very short period of time.

However, as far as a transformation policy is concerned, there is no sign of any such blanket coalitions and rapid decision-making processes, despite awareness of the grave consequences of global warming. This fuels the democracy scepticism mentioned earlier, and a belief in the allegedly greater efficiency of autocratic

Box 5.3-1

Environmental Performance of Democratic and Autocratic Regimes

In view of the present ecological crises and more far-reaching disaster scenarios, the ecological problem solving capacity of democracies is under review. Autocratic regimes are, sometimes openly, sometimes covertly, credited with a greater capacity for limiting environmental and climate change and overcoming its consequences (Meadows et al., 1972). It was long assumed that the structuring of political institutions and policy processes played a minor role in solving environmental problems – or rather, this aspect was considered less important than economic factors or (im Original falsch) technology, population growth, geographical location, etc. Since 1989/90, researchers have increasingly focused on the environmental performance and ecological problem solving capacity of both democratic and autocratic regimes.

To date, the various studies have yielded no clear result. Payne (1995) states that a democratic regime type has a positive impact on the condition of the environment, as democracies usually showed a higher level of responsiveness to environmental concerns, their citizens had unrestricted access to information about environmental problems, and democratic systems generally demonstrated greater capacities to adapt. Other studies (such as Gleditsch and Sverdrup, 2002; Li and Reuveny, 2006) have also empirically proven a positive relation between democracy and environmental performance, and have shown that – relative to the level of economic development –democracies have a lower CO_2 output than autocratic regimes. Zahran et al. (2007) and Bättig and Bernauer (2009) have furthermore shown that democracies are more willing to embrace international cooperation on matters of environmental and climate protection. In the Climate Change Performance Index (CCPI), which measures the climate protection performance of countries, the ten top positions in 2009 and 2010 were also held exclusively by democracies (Germanwatch and Climate Action Network Europe, 2008, 2009).

Midlarsky (1998), on the other hand, argued that a democratic governmental system has a negative impact on the ecological problem solving capacity of a society, as it is more difficult in democracies – which strive more for consensus and compromise – to overcome self-serving interest groups that block effective environmental protection. Essentially, the proponents of environmental interests have to battle against dominating, purely profit-orientated lobby groups. Based on a random sample of 98 countries in relation to three indicators for measuring environmental performance (including CO_2 output and deforestation), Midlarsky (1998) has empirically proven a significantly negative relationship between democracy and environmental protection.

Although the results of the research with respect to a positive effect of democracy on ecological performance remain ambiguous, it should nevertheless be noted that to date, there is no evidence whatsoever for the assumption that the environmental performance of autocracies is better than that of democracies (Saretzki, 2007). Above all, there are so far no empirically well-founded arguments for seeking political systems outside the realm of democracy promising a better environmental performance.

or expertocratic systems (Shearman and Smith, 2007; Friedman, 2009; Pötter, 2010; Siller, 2010): the non-consideration of lengthy parliamentary procedures and individual rights can considerably accelerate government action, so the critics say. Extraordinary legal authorities, such as emergency laws to overcome existential crises, are therefore common even in democracies (Nullmeier and Dietz, 2010). They represent a regulated and temporary extension of the executive authority. In its initial phase in the 1930s, the 'New Deal' policy under US President Roosevelt also used the unparalleled extension of federal government authority over that of the individual states and in new areas of policies in order to expand the government's capacity for action (Adams, 2008). The use of emergency law or other dirigiste measures for accelerated redirection can, however, hardly claim democratic legitimisation. The acceptance and implementation of the planetary guard rails for maintaining the natural life-support systems in a politico-economic system can therefore not proceed on the strength of authoritarian regulatory policy, but must in the long term be based on broad public approval (Section 5.4.1.2). In the contrary, a policy which does not appear to have been legitimised by the public can seriously damage said transformative policy's prospects of success (Nullmeier and Dietz, 2010; Leggewie, 2010).

In addition, there is no empirical proof for the problem-solving capabilities of authoritarian systems or processes in the context of the necessary transformation (Box 5.3-1). The Great Transformation can succeed only if the systems produce innovative solutions and involve as many actors as possible from all areas of society. It is dependent on active, interested and responsible citizens. Only an open, democratic society is able to develop the kind of creativity and innovation demanded by the transformation. The question is therefore not whether, but rather how the transformation is to be carried out democratically. The main problems are the time pressure, and the Great Transformation's transnational nature. As democratic processes are inevitably time-consuming, the political redirection must commence immediately.

There is no lack of political programmes and policies with regard to the transformation into a sustainable society; the problems lie in the political process with its political competitiveness and power struggles. Transition-impeding barriers such as these must now be overcome in national systems and at a global level; political processes must be accelerated and take a long-term perspective whilst also increasing the legitimisation basis for these decisions (Leggewie, 2010). Not least, the Great Transformation is therefore a test of the future viability of democratic systems (Leggewie and Welzer, 2009).

5.3.3 The Transformation in Newly Industrialising Countries – Affluence and Political Trends in China, Brazil and India

Analysis of the institutional and political requirements for the transformation towards a low-carbon society highlights the high demands this process places on societies. Considerations to date have concentrated primarily on transformation potentials and barriers in western industrialised societies and democracies. For the global transformation to succeed, however, particularly the newly industrialising countries must become actors in the low-carbon transition. A detailed policy analysis of the transformation dynamics in newly industrialising countries cannot be carried out here, but the respective developments in China, Brazil and India are briefly outlined to illustrate the very different basic patterns of socio-economic change in typical newly industrialising countries. If Germany and Europe intend to nudge newly industrialising countries towards the transformation, or hope to build on any already existing reform tendencies, they must take into account these countries' very different starting positions and framework conditions (Section 5.3.3).

5.3.3.1 China

Economic growth and energy demand in China continue to rise strongly despite the worldwide economic crisis of recent years. At present, a good 70% of the energy supply is covered by coal-powered power stations. Due to the rapidly increasing energy demand, the government is also investing heavily in the expansion of nuclear energy and renewable energies. The country's institutional efficiency is high for a country with an authoritarian government, and has constantly improved in the growth regions on the east coast of the country. They are roughly comparable with the governance capacities of South Korea or Taiwan in the 1980s, and therefore in clear contrast to the institutional sclerosis currently apparent in the North African autocracies.

High investment dynamics and the investment structure show that national and international investors are willing to realise long-term projects in China (Winters and Shahid, 2007; Kaplinsky and Messner, 2008). This willingness would probably continue even if the future course were set in the direction of decarbonisation. Initially, the government's own interests and its political will to make 'green reforms' are crucial for the transformation's chances of success. It must be noted here that there are strong interest groups corresponding to the sheer size of the fossil-based energy industry – just like in many OECD countries – lobbying for the continuation of the established development path. There are also many reasons that speak for China becoming a low-carbon development driver: certain elements of the Chinese government and economy, for instance, believe that China has a much better chance of making the technological change towards climate-compatibility and sustainability, and to make it faster, than western industrialised countries. It could therefore unlock associated competitive advantages for itself. The serious consequences China might suffer from climate change are now systematically considered in discussions on the country's future development strategies. Foreign policy thoughtleaders at Chinese universities and in its ministries consider the potential pioneering role of China in the area of 'green development' a central element for enhancing the emerging superpower's reputation abroad, as it currently still enjoys only limited international approval on the grounds of its democracy and human rights deficiencies (Gu et al., 2008; Wang, 2009). The linking of these discourses could lead to the development of a transformation momentum which the Chinese government's 12th Five-Year Plan, published in early 2011, appears to promise (Chinese Government, 2011).

Whether such a transformation could meet with the support of China's civil society, or even be advanced by it, is difficult to assess. Classic environmental issues (for example air and water pollution) and concern regarding food safety (contamination from chemical fertilisers, contaminated drinking water) play an important role in public debate and the media. At the same time, social advancement is at the very top of the personal agenda for many Chinese people, so a 'green transformation' could be perceived as slowing economic progress (Heberer and Senz, 2007). Nevertheless, there is no reliable data that could provide reputable information on the actual views of the Chinese population. Indeed, the fragile acceptance and legitimisation of the Chinese government is the Achilles' heel of Chinese development: the fact that the Chinese government suppressed any news in the media on the democratic movements in North Africa in early 2011 and the seriousness of the nuclear accident in Fukushima proves its incapability of holding public discussions on the future in 'sensitive areas'.

It is difficult to say how long China's dynamic economic development will function without radical political reforms. Since the Industrial Revolution, there have been no relevant historic examples of autocracies that have enjoyed sustained economic success. As of a certain development level, considered by many authors to be reached at an average income of 5,000 US $ per capita, modernising autocracies must either liberalise politically in order to continue to be economically successful (as Taiwan, South Korea, Chile and a few other former socialist countries did in the 1990s), or fall into stagnation traps in the medium term (as is the case in the former Soviet Union, Russia, Egypt, Tunisia; Sen, 1999; Faust, 2006; Reinert, 2007). The Chinese government is presently already experiencing problems with implementing central state decisions in the regions and local communities (Heberer and Senz, 2007).

The Chinese government is therefore facing the challenge of combining the continued fight against poverty and increasing economic welfare with a transformation to sustainability and a gradual political opening. Indicative of progress towards climate-compatibility is the fact that these challenges have been recoded in Chinese discussions in recent years, from an environmental to an economic and innovation issue (CCICED, 2009). Herein lies the relevant starting point for climate partnerships with this huge Asian country.

5.3.3.2
Brazil

In Brazil, the current situation is completely different. Political legitimisation and government acceptance by the population have risen constantly in the last two decades. The comprehensive modernisation of public institutions, advances in democratisation, and socio-economic improvements impacting even the weakest social stratas have all contributed to this (Schirm, 2007). Brazil can also already meet around 40% of its energy needs from renewable sources, primarily hydropower. Moreover, with political support, the Brazilian economy has established a high-performance ethanol economy. The initial situation would therefore be favourable for developing Brazil into a pioneering low-carbon economy. On the one hand, the natural geographical conditions for the use of renewable energies are very good; on the other, the international community shows significant willingness to support Brazil in protecting the Amazon rainforest: 70% of the country's greenhouse gas emissions can be attributed to deforestation.

However, Brazilian policy-makers, its economy, and its society are currently still guided predominantly by the industrial era's established modernisation paradigms. The discourse on climate-compatibility is less pronounced than in China (Stuenkel, 2010). In addition to this, there are large oil deposits off Brazil's coastal areas, triggering economic desires and hopes of increasing Brazil's role in the global economy. Brazil is therefore a 'potential low-carbon economy: on the one hand, it has excellent natural geographical conditions and enjoys favourable political conditions for a post-fossil transition (democracy, institutional capacities, high government legitimisation); on the other hand, its social transition does so far not seem to have promoted such a transformation. The most important driver of a development like this would therefore probably be a change towards sustainability in the important centres of the global economy, for example Europe and China. This would create incentives to see the green transformation as an economic opportunity, thereby generating signals which to date seem to lack majority appeal in Brazilian society.

5.3.3.3
India

Until a few years ago, the Indian government essentially argued that the low-carbon restructuring of the economy was a challenge and an obligation to be met by the OECD countries, rather than by developing countries. This discourse has ultimately changed. Just recently, the government announced energy efficiency programmes and placed the issue of controlling emission increases on the political agenda (ADB, 2009). At 1,180 US $, the average Indian income (net domestic product per capita) in 2009 was significantly lower than the average income in Brazil, at 8,040 US $, and in China, at 3,650 US $; the central issue of political debate in India in the foreseeable future is and remains increasing economic performance and reducing the still high level of poverty (World Bank, 2011a). It is therefore unlikely that India will provide any strong impulses for a low-carbon transformation of the global economy. However, if relevant national economies can demonstrate that low-carbon development pathways, competitiveness and poverty reduction can be combined, the conditions for learning from their experience would be particularly favourable in India. Despite the high economic growth of the past two decades, India's per capita CO_2 emissions from fossil sources were only 1,3 t in 2007 (China 5,1 t; Brazil 2,0 t; WRI-CAIT, 2011). The fossil path dependencies impeding the transformation in the OECD countries and in China are therefore significantly lower. In contrast to China, India still has a chance of steering its modernisation process without taking the 'fossil detour', and to rely on a low-carbon development path early on in the process.

5.3.4
Supranational Expansion and Further Globalisation

In addition to the limited timeframe normally applicable in democratic governance, the problem also lies in the transgression of global boundaries and the democracy deficiencies of supra-, trans- and international regulation. Governments make their decisions with a view to the interests and expectations of their local, national clientele and electorate. And this consideration of their immediate interests again disregards the consequences which decisions made today have for future generations. Democracy again runs into structural deficiencies in this respect. For some time now, these 'limits of majority democracy' (Offe and Guggenberger, 1984) have been subject to discussion, as, in good conscience, majorities must not be allowed to make far-reaching and irreversible decisions which not only potentially deprive future generations of the freedom to act, but also have a huge impact on populations beyond their borders. In terms of both space and time, the gulf between those with decision-making authority and those affected by those decisions (or authors and recipients of legislation and jurisdiction) has grown, which is untenable in democratic politics.

This is particularly true for policy areas concerning climate protection and other Earth system boundaries, as democratic participation also determines the chances for survival (Möllers, 2010). A high-carbon lifestyle in western industrial societies threatens the interests of people whose very existence is threatened by the consequences of climate change. To date, most of these live in developing and newly industrialising countries. The transformation can therefore succeed only if liberal societies impose self-restrictions, as elaborated in Section 2.5, and show a greater awareness of the geographical effects and temporal consequences of their decisions than they have done so far. Any policy that seeks to manage the global agendas merely at nation state level is therefore an anachronism. Because it is not only financial markets and transnational corporations that are globalised; many environmental problems are also of a planetary scale.

As there is no world government (or even a world state), global politics must promote supra- and transnational approaches offering regional formats for risk identification and problem solving below this level. In this respect, the EU is exemplary: as a sui generis polity somewhere between a union of states and a federal state with 27 member states (Landfried, 2002; Jachtenfuchs and Kohler-Koch, 2003; Lepsius, 2000). As described in Section 3.5.6, it is an example for, and the result of, a transformation. As a supranational association of states, it offers its member states – and also effectively included non-member states such as Switzerland, neighbours such as Norway, and candidate countries such as Croatia and Turkey – the chance of transnational problem solving with regard to energy, environmental and climate policy, both through the application of supranational law in 'communitised' policy areas and through intergovernmental cooperation on common issues. Interestingly, the classic policy areas of social security are less 'communitised' than structural policies such as agricultural and environmental policy, they are therefore largely a matter for the member states. Thus, the EU represents a historically unique removal of a national sovereignty which has become anachronistic by means of a supranational horizontal and vertical policy integration, and through its convergence into a transnational European society whilst still preserving each country's local characteristics and traditions. Both tendencies are counteracted by the dysfunctional consequences of horizontal and vertical policy integration (Scharpf, 1985), and tendencies towards (symbolic and actual) renationalisation.

Impediments for a Common European Energy Policy

The EU is potentially going to play an important role in the Great Transformation, as the expansion of the energy infrastructure to link new power sources in northern and southern Europe with energy storage facilities and (primary) consumption centres, for example, requires an EU-wide process for cost-effective and efficient implementation (EU COM, 2010e). Apart from the barriers already described (Section 5.3.1), the institutional framework and the relationship between the EU and its members states represent further impediments preventing the EU from embracing its transformative tasks. Regulations and directives, fundamentally available to the EU, are the appropriate tools for initiating transformative measures in its member states to serve a common, EU-wide goal. From the perspective of the member states, a directive is the more moderate method, as it only specifies a binding goal. The means needed to achieve this goal, including the structuring of the administrative process, are up to the member states themselves. By contrast, a regulation and all of its provisions apply directly in the member states (art. 288 TFEU).

The means for implementing a supranational infrastructure policy are therefore essentially available; however, the fact that the EU, as a supranational institution, can use these means only if it has the power or authority to act in a respective area, as stipulated by the basic principle of limited individual authorisation (art. 7 TFEU), is proving to be a hindrance. In the three transformation fields of energy, urbanisation and land use, it does not have the requisite competencies. With respect to energy systems, the EU lacks the authority for regulating the establishment of a comprehensive transnational energy network, and setting the legal framework for an energy mix leading its members states towards a low-carbon future without nuclear energy (Chapter 4). Since the Treaty of Lisbon came into force, the EU has been given the (explicit) authority for energy policy decisions and, within this context, also the chance to support energy network interconnection (art. 194 par. 1 lit. d TFEU). Under the treaty, however, the EU can only initiate its own projects, although it has been given general competence for tasking its member states with implementation ('whether'). In terms of the mode of implementation ('how'), for example with respect to specific power cable routing, it is unable to act due to its lack of planning authority. This remains with the member states. An EU-wide energy network expansion, however, involves not only the 'whether' but also the 'how' to ensure the effective linking of networks.

Moreover, the energy policy competency recently inserted in art. 194 TFEU also does not include the authority to determine the legal framework for the energy mix in the member states. On the contrary, art. 194 par. 2 sub-par. 2 TFEU explicitly excludes measures from EU competence in areas that touch on a member state's right to define the conditions for the use of its energy resources, to choose between various different energy sources, and to determine the general structure of its energy supply. This clearly limits EU authority (Calliess, 2010); the determination of the energy mix therefore remains solely a sovereign matter for the member states. The EU's lacking energy political authority to determine the energy mix is a consequence of the lack of the member states' political will to hand over this area to the supranational level, and to thereby expose it to the influence of other member states (Fischer, 2009).

Ultimately, the EU also has only a limited influence on national energy mix standards on the grounds of its environmental policy-making authority, as this primarily serves the protection of the environment and human welfare and the careful handling of natural resources (art. 191 par. 1 TFEU). This also includes any ecologically motivated promotion of renewable energy carriers, the reason for passing the Renewable Energy Directive (2009/28/EC) on environmental policy. It determines the proportion of renewable energy carriers to be achieved by the member states in their gross final energy consumption and their transport sector by 2020, thereby at least partially regulating the energy mix with respect to these energy carriers. However, even with such an ecologically-motivated influence over the energy mix, the EU can use its environmental policy authority only under extremely difficult conditions. Measures resulting from this authority which have a considerable impact on the energy sources and general energy supply structure of a member state require a unanimous decision of the member states, and are therefore subject to national veto (art. 192 par. 2 lit. c TFEU). Ergo, the authority does not extend to determining the legal framework for the energy mix. EU competency in terms of environmental policy determination only allows any influencing of the energy mix solely under the aspect of ecological impact as approved by all member states.

The EU cannot obtain the authority to determine the legal framework for the energy mix by means of treaty interpretation, either, as the basic principle of limited individual authorisation still applies to the EU, as a supranational organisation. According to this, the EU only has the authorities it has been specifically assigned by treaty, which it can also not expand autonomously. As it has no treaty competency, it cannot authorise itself to regulate.

5.3.5 Global Governance in a Multipolar World

Just like the physical climate system, the global political constellations are currently also undergoing radical changes. The system is in transition from a US-dominated, unipolar world order to a multipolar global system, conceivably marked particularly by the relative growth in the importance of China and India (Messner, 2006; Zakaria, 2008). It is also to be expected that other emerging regional powers such as Brazil or South Africa will in future equally play a more important role in the world than they have in recent decades, whereas the relative importance of the established 'western powers' will diminish (Khanna, 2008; Flemes, 2010; Kappel, 2011). In view of the rise of large, newly industrialising countries and the growth in importance of new political forums such as the G20, one cannot speak unconditionally of a western-dominated global system even today (Cooper and Antkiewicz, 2008; Nuscheler and Messner, 2009; Kumar and Messner, 2010).

In consequence, serious conflicts of interest can be expected; overcoming these peacefully will be a further Herculean task for global governance in addition to conserving or providing global public goods (Bauer, 2009). National demands and international distribution issues in the context of 'peak oil', 'peak soil', or atmospheric pollution rights are prime examples for this. The multipolar constellation here is far less clearly arranged than the bipolarity of the Cold War. This is also backed up historically by the insight that power shifts in the

Box 5.3-2

Sino-American Relations as the Parameter of Future World Politics

The summit meeting of US president Barack Obama and Chinese president Hu Jintao in January 2011, accompanied as it was by all the insignia of high intergovernmental diplomacy, demonstrated the mutual increased awareness of the fact that the fate of the world cannot be determined without consideration of the respective other nation to the entire global public. The questions of whether this will result more in rivalry, or in partnership-based bilateral relations, and which implications this will have for the rest of the world, remain open. A new 'Cold War', or even a 'Hot Escalation' of conflicting interests between the old superpower and the new one is just as conceivable as a 'Cold Peace', or the continuous expansion of constructive bilateral relations for the good of all (Figure 5.3-1).

On the one hand, the US-American fear of an ever stronger growing China and the loss of sole superpower status, and of a distinctly confident Chinese nationalism is growing stronger and threatening to escalate. This would accentuate the rivalry of the two states, increasing the likelihood of a conflictive 'realpolitik' style of foreign policy that could certainly escalate, for instance when it comes to the Taiwan question, or in the course of the exploitation of scarce raw material deposits. On the other hand, not only the demands of global problem solving, but also the close links in trade, fiscal and economic policy of the two states in the context of a globalised world economy suggest the route of greater communication and cooperation. Stable trade and financial relations, for example, are essential for the development prospects of both national economies. This would favour the incremental institutionalisation of constructive intergovernmental relations.

Ignorance, prejudices and mistrust favour the first route; communication, transparency and confidence-building facilitate the second. If the decision-makers in the USA and China opt for conflictive strategies, the chances for a constructive reform of global multilateralism would accordingly fall. It is therefore in the interest of all other nations to support both superpowers in choosing the route of trusting cooperation. Europe could play the constructive role of mediator here on the global political stage: traditionally, it enjoys close relations with the USA, has comparatively less to lose with regard to China, and as a central global economic market, it is of vital interest to both the American and the Chinese national economies. The overcoming of the Franco-German 'hereditary enmity' after the Second World War, and the defusing of the Cold War through confidence-building measures can provide some important lessons here.

international system are generally turbulent and frequently violent (Kennedy, 1988; Kupchan et al., 2001; Münkler, 2005). As a result, the trend towards multipolarity threatens to become a fundamental barrier to transformation-conducive global politics. In any case, it will significantly co-determine future framework conditions for global governance (WBGU, 2008; Chapter 4). In the light of international relations theories, four alternative global political order models appear to be particularly plausible scenarios:

1. A multipolar structured world order, within the framework of which a geopolitical power struggle moves between the poles of 'cold peace' and 'hot conflict';
2. A strained, possibly violent transition to a new, unipolar, hegemonial order, for instance under the leadership of China;
3. A largely peaceful, cooperative further development of a multilateral order based on international law and the United Nations with the familiar shortcomings and limits in terms of global problem solving capacities and power to act;
4. A progressive erosion of the international political order as a result of cumulative policy disasters and global policy failures.

Accordingly, it remains to be seen how an order model that is normatively desirable and effective in terms of the transformation into a low-carbon global society could manifest itself, facilitating a peaceful, legitimate and, not least, effective global governance.

5.3.5.1 Altered Framework Conditions Through Multipolarity

In the scientific debate on global governance that followed the end of the East-West conflict, the growing importance of China and India was initially not recognised, or largely dismissed (Messner, 2006). If China and India actually do rise to become major global power poles alongside the USA, however, they will decisively determine the system's further institutional architecture and organisation (Box 5.3-2). Particularly from a European perspective, this leads to the question of the extent to which the protagonists of world politics will contribute to a functional multilateralism, or whether they will impede global governance efforts (Bauer, 2009; Nuscheler and Messner, 2009).

If the USA, for example, insist on defending the status quo and, by contrast, China, India or Brazil pursues a decidedly unilateral foreign policy, this would conceivably result in supposedly outdated balance-of-power politics, and tie up considerable capacities and resources, accordingly impeding global governance (Messner, 2006). In this respect, the multipolar constellation emphasises the classic 'security dilemma' of international politics (Herz, 1950): correspondingly, relative shifts in power potentials in an anarchic, international system can trigger self-powering dynamics

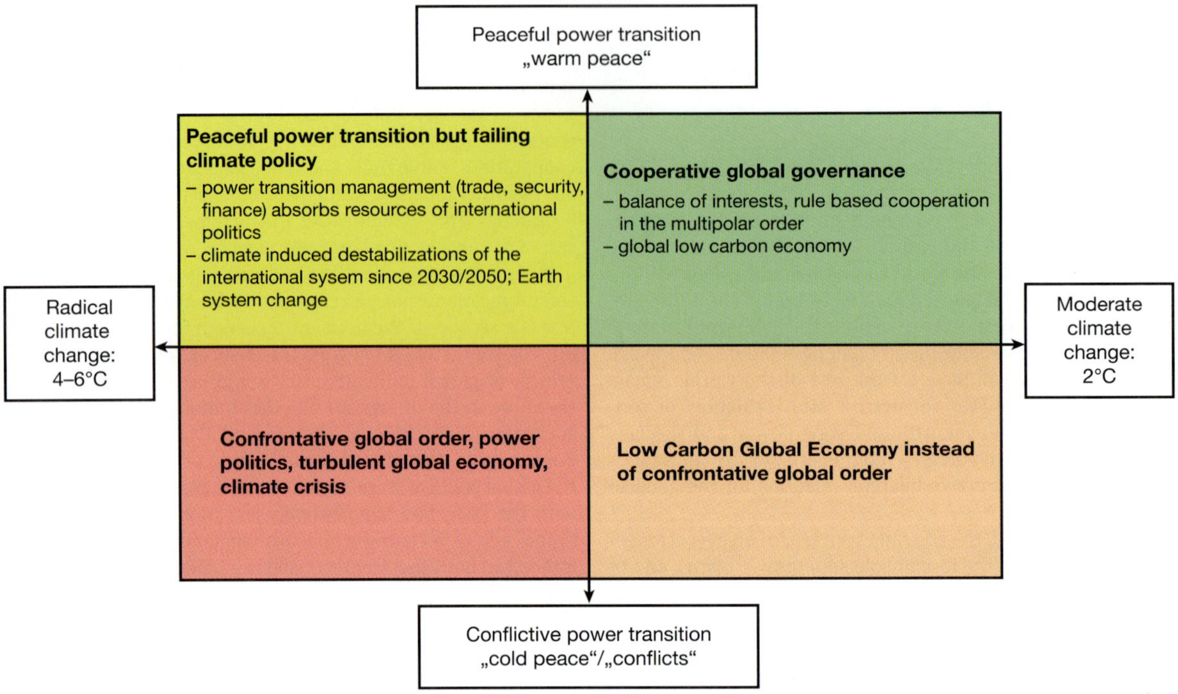

Figure 5.3-1
Scenarios of world political futures in the context of international power shifts and global climate change. The multilateral architecture is under strong pressure to adapt. This can be schematically demonstrated using the axes of the international power shift (cooperative/conflictive) and global climate change (moderate/radical).
Source: Messner, 2009

that undermine cooperative behaviour and make uncooperative or even aggressive behaviour towards less powerful states appear rational.

The demands of an effective, steering global governance would run contrary to such action logics, and subvert the goal of transformation. Against this background, the answers found by the community of states to problematic issues with regard to collective action will therefore show whether the applicable conflicting interests mean a return to a 'world of superpowers', or create a world that is a network of international cooperation, where 'global governance islands' can unite to form a structuring system model for global governance (Kohler-Koch, 1993; Messner et al., 2003).

In any case, the present, multilateral architecture is under strong pressure to adapt. To be able to act for global transformation purposes, it must be guided by the demands of the planetary guard rails (Box 1-1), and take the power shifts in the international system into account. The growing tensions this leads to can be schematically positioned along the axes of the international power shift (cooperative/conflictive) and global climate change (moderate/radical) (Figure 5.3-1).

Irrespective of how new global system models and cooperation patterns balance out within this system of coordinates, they will become an inherent element of a world in transition. The sudden importance of the G20 in the course of the global financial crisis appears to illustrate this, in line with the 'form follows function' principle. At the same time, however, the international summit diplomacy of the G8, G8+5 and G20 shows increasingly clearly that there are not only changes in the traditionally difficult relationships between industrialised and developing countries, and established and emerging powers, but that there are also important changes in South-South relations: together with the industrialised countries, emerging economies such as China, India, Brazil and South Africa are increasingly experiencing an 'explanatory crisis' when facing small and particularly poor developing countries (Bauer, 2009; Conzelmann and Faust, 2009).

However, exactly how a lasting functional adaptation of the international system that meets the challenges of a politically steered global transformation and of a multipolar world order might look like remains to be seen. The fundamental structural problems of global governance will vanish neither through a renunciation of the slow business-as-usual multilateralism of the United Nations, nor through focusing all hope on the G20 as the carthorse of global problem solving authority. Individually, neither the United Nations nor the G20 can guarantee a satisfactory global governance: on one side, the United Nations' inadequate capacity to act, on the other, the limited legitimacy of the G20 summit structure (Bauer et al., 2011). The development of the G20 is a further expression of the former G8's limited powers to act and faded legitimacy. The global community of states and the world society thus see themselves confronted by a cooperation paradox that has led to a huge gap between the increased awareness of global problems and the global ability to act.

5.3.5.2
Structural Problems and Democracy Deficits of Global Governance and International Organisations

Whilst world markets and the world society have changed rapidly in the age of globalisation, particularly since the end of the East-West conflict, standards and regulations for global political steering have kept pace only in some sectors, and to a very limited extent. New actors have also entered the playing field of transnational politics. They have changed the action constellations of global governance (Keohane and Nye, 2000; Pattberg, 2007; Reinalda, 2011). This has, however, not affected the fundamental structural problems of the international system and the multipolar community of states: namely the lack of a global sovereign and a global monopoly on the use of force. For this reason, both political and scientific actors have progressively distanced themselves from the idealistic concepts of a global state or a global government over the decades, gradually replacing these with conceptual and normative discourses on global governance (Rosenau and Czempiel, 1992; Dingwerth and Pattberg, 2006; Weiss, 2009).

Despite the academic paradigm shift, there remains a fundamental deficit of democracy in the many different international organisations embodying the classic locus of intergovernmental cooperation and global governance (Karns and Mingst, 2004; Neyer and Beyer, 2004). The tangible consequence of this deficit, arising from the delegation of nation state sovereignty to international governmental organisations, is the growing decision-making power of international bureaucracies, the relative loss of importance of national parliaments and decision-making bodies, and the intergovernmental nature, i.e. domination by executive actors, of negotiations between states (Neyer and Beyer, 2004; Barnett and Finnemore, 2005; Hawkins et al., 2006). With respect to the advancing juridification of international political processes, international courts are also acquiring a special role, as states seem to delegate sovereignty to supranational actors here, sometimes without any rational need to do so (Alter, 2006; Zangl and Zürn, 2004).

The questions of the legitimacy of global governance and the power of international organisations to act largely revolve around the significance of sovereignty transfer and technocratisation, or the balance between a participative 'input legitimacy' and an 'output legitimacy' that is based on efficiency and effectiveness (Scharpf, 1999). This balance can differ considerably on local, national or intergovernmental level, between private and public areas, and between democratic and authoritarian actors. In the international field, however, legitimisation chains are per se more complex than at local or national level (Nullmeier and Dietz, 2010). Although intergovernmental interactions are formally legitimised by the principle of state sovereignty under international law, there are also, understandably, some doubts with regard to the subtle politicisation and the effectively supranational influence of international organisations (Barnett and Finnemore, 2004; Keohane, 2006; Zürn et al., 2007).

The opening of international organisations to non-governmental actors, and the efforts for greater transparency are only little compensation for the inherent structural deficits of democracy (Dingwerth, 2007; Müller, 2008; Gupta, 2010). Furthermore, precisely these efforts to improve input legitimacy are frequently made at the expense of the efficiency and effectiveness of international processes. The consequence is that output legitimacy is often undermined. In the absence of a democratically legitimised world government or a cosmopolitan world state, this dilemma is impossible to solve. As the subjects of global governance, nation states will remain the central actors for the time being in view of the existing international system and its transnational steering requirements. Consequently, international governmental organisations, particularly within the framework of the United Nations, and despite all inherent autonomy efforts of their sometimes certainly influential bureaucracies remain an expression of collective nation state politics and the basis for future global governance (Messner, 1998; Hawkins et al., 2006; Weiss and Daws, 2007; Biermann and Siebenhüner, 2009).

The multilateral system represented by the UN is therefore the international political action framework within which the requisite course for the transformation to a low-carbon global society must be set, even though it was founded more than seven decades ago, and despite all its institutional failings. International climate policy, international environmental policy and international development cooperation are given important impulses through actors such as the G20 and transnational networks or strategic 'sub-global' alliances of powerful states, whilst their concrete form and implementation remain the subject of the community of states, universally organised only in the form of the United Nations. Apart from urgent institutional reforms and an improved financing base, this world organisation, dominated by the victorious powers of the Second World War (and originally founded by only 51 states) must above all allow the developing and newly industrialising countries a level of participation that is appropriate to the empirical realities of the 21st century in order to increase its effectiveness (Bauer et al., 2011). The great number of more or less detailed UN system reform efforts proves that the international system is apparently almost impossible to reform under the present conditions (Malloch-Brown, 2008).

This inventory of the structural problems of global governance does not look quite as gloomy if viewed in the context of the 'longue durée' of the civilisation process. Compared with the era of the League of Nations or the post-WWII founding era of the United Nations, the institutionalisation of international cooperation and the associated containment of classic power politics has undoubtedly been relatively successful (Kennedy, 2006; Müller, 2008). Irrespective of all their functional deficiencies, the present importance of international organisations is based on a fundamental insight into their value, and the resultant willingness to delegate, if not to transfer national sovereignty in a way that would have been almost unimaginable even as recently as in the first half of the 20th century. The evolution of the European Union, or the virtually supranational role of international courts such as the International Maritime Court or the International Criminal Court, would be virtually inconceivable without the long-term regulation and juridification of a wide range of different policy areas, not to mention the concept of a universal claim for Human Rights.

With their ideas on nation formation, separation of powers, democratic rule and an international law of treaties, the state theoreticians and philosophers of the 17th and 18th centuries were also far ahead of the political realities and conjectural feasibilities of the feudal age (Chapter 3). The historic transition from different kinds of feudal systems to more democratic forms of society, however, needed the Enlightenment's preliminary intellectual groundwork as a foundation (Chapter 3). Immanuel Kant's reflections on 'Perpetual Peace' and a world citizenship, for instance, are now viewed as important basic principles in modern international law and international organisation (Rochester, 1986; Delbrück, 1998). In terms of the demands on international politics to be expected from a global transition, the crux of the matter is therefore not so much its utopian character, but the inertia of civilisation processes and the difficulty of steering and accelerating social change (Sommer, 2011).

5.3.5.3
Interim Conclusion

The central, but by no means new, problematic issue of global governance lies in the fact that although the necessity for global governance to effectively tackle genuinely global problems is widely recognised in international politics, the structural foundations and the resultant action incentives for intergovernmental cooperation continue to impede effective global governance. A great deal therefore speaks for the fact that the established basic pattern of international politics – the interaction between nation states on the basis of sovereign national interests, either whittled down to the lowest common denominator through lengthy negotiations or determined by the most powerful actors according to their preferences – is not suitable for resolving the problems of a global society of soon-to-be almost 9 billion people, characterised by an unprecedented level of global interdependence and a wide range of risks to the global system (including the planetary guard rails outlined here; Section 1.1).

In view of this, there is no alternative but the pursuit of effective and legitimate global governance: the world desperately needs a higher level of international cooperation if climate- and environmentally-friendly global development is to be achieved in the long-term.

Firstly, from a functionalistic perspective, it is not clear how the interdependent problems of humankind in the 21st century, characterised on the one hand by the incongruity between transnational problem constellations, particularly climate change, and on the other by the geographically limited reach of nation states, could be tackled at all without overcoming the traditional concepts of sovereignty in favour of increased international cooperation and global rules.

Secondly, this conversely implies that there is a risk that the lack of international cooperation will advance counterproductive conflict dynamics to the same extent as the unresolved problems will lead to distributional conflicts and recriminations with regard to the causes and impact of environmental damage and climate change.

Thirdly, international cooperation is rational in as far as it reduces the problem solving costs; or rather, non-cooperation increases the costs unnecessarily. This is particularly true of cooperation with respect to the establishment and modification of the transformation fields identified by the WBGU (energy, urbanisation, land use; Section. 5.4.5).

Fourthly, international cooperation is needed in order to nudge political, economic and social learning effects to be able to exploit the resulting economies of scale for the global transformation. National and unilateral action approaches necessarily lag behind the potentials offered by transnational and transregional learning processes.

Fifthly, a cooperative international spirit is one of the most elementary requirements for the development of a global 'we' identity. Without it, a permanent, successful global transformation seems hardly conceivable.

Although awareness of global problems has increased dramatically all over the world, national decision-makers continue to waver between helpless incrementalism (see United Nations Environmental Programme), major symbolic global management events of limited scope and effect (see G20), sheer fatalism (all notions above and beyond the established international system are utopian global governance fantasies), and relapses into classic, nation state power and interest-driven politics. Almost seventy years after the founding of the United Nations, the international community of states is still helpless and at a loss when faced with the cooperation paradox and urgent global challenges. If this cooperation paradox is not overcome, a steered transformation towards a low-carbon global society cannot succeed. It requires a global evolutionary leap towards a greater willingness for global cooperation and the appropriate coordination skills. Its scale would be comparable with the substitution of feudal societies with democratically structured constitutional states during the course of the 18th and 19th centuries (Section 3.2). The community of states in the still very young 21st century will therefore manage this profound historic change cooperatively. Alternatively, the global society will founder on the demands of the transformation.

5.4 A New Statehood within the Multilevel System

In political terms, the major transformation process challenges are the acceleration of politico-administrative procedures and processes, improvements with regard to the implementation of a long-term orientation in policy-making, the resolute overcoming of path dependencies, the empowerment and involvement of the civil society, and a historically unparalleled expansion of international cooperation. The following chapter develops solution approaches to overcome the impediments and barriers highlighted in Section 5.3.

5.4.1 Proactive State with Extended Opportunities for Participation

5.4.1.1 The Vision of a Proactive State with Extended Participation

The state plays an important role in the transformation process. Legislative, executive and judicative must create or extend the regulatory framework required to empower the economy, science and the civil society to use their resources and apply their capabilities to developing, implementing and using measures such as the expansion and reorganisation of the energy supply, the redesigning of urban spaces, and changes in land use (Chapter 4), rather than merely paying a rhetorical, symbolical lip service to putting the spotlight on innovations development. In the opinion of the WBGU, the present situation generally requires states to return to playing a more active role. Particularly since the 1970s, a liberal-libertarian philosophy of extensive denationalisation and deregulation has become prevalent as a reaction to certain bureaucratic excesses and rising public spending. Parallel to this, many OECD states' resources for fiscal intervention have diminished whilst average public spending has not decreased. At the same time, the governmental regulatory and steering capacities in the newly industrialising countries have grown as a result of economic success whilst in many developing countries, statehood as such has largely or entirely failed, even breaking down completely in some places. States have been perceived as both powerless and overpowering in these conflicting developments; as colossi with feet of clay.

The global economic and financial crisis (2007–2009) emphatically demonstrated the failure of deregulated market mechanisms. The disadvantages of deregulated market mechanisms become particularly apparent not least also with respect to environmental quality: the inability of companies in free markets to consider the long-term dimensions of their business models and technology applications makes environmental regulation on the part of the state inevitable (Winter, 2010). However, it should be noted that top-down government planning is an illusion. The state itself does not know the best options, but is tasked with activating both corporate and civil society, and politico-administrative system potentials whilst also refraining from restricting itself to the purely moderating and remedial role that is typical for pluralistic negotiation democracies. The WBGU therefore encourages its further development, without underestimating the risks of interventionist politics or subscribing to yet another illusion with regard to policy-based steering, from a moderating to a 'proactive' state that also pursues a proactive transformation policy itself. This 'more' in state interventionism must be offset by a 'more' in citizen involvement in the form of a new social contract (Section 7.2). The key aspect of this (virtual) contract is that it confers rights and obligations to government and civil society actors by giving them responsibility for the ecological future with a view to common welfare goals and global collective goods.

Historic Role Models for Statehood

The chequered history of modern state intervention illustrates the opportunities and architectures of such a proactive state with extended opportunities for participation. The (European) state is an 'acting subject with a will of its own' (ad-hoc translation by the WBGU, Koselleck, 1990) which takes on the organisation of political authority in modern societies. Within this state, the separate public political institutions of government, legislature, administration and jurisdiction as we know them today have been combined on a basis of division of labour. For this purpose, the state has been awarded a monopoly on the use of force over its citizens, and the authority for making collectively binding political decisions. In order to avoid despotism and the abuse of this power, government actions are subject to laws and the constitution. States interact with third parties and each other by tangible and intangible means, including: law (mandatory regulations and bans), money (positive and negative monetary incentives) and 'good words' (persuasion, and also orders and deterrents). These instruments impact as direct or indirect governance impulses on the environment and the legal relationships in the economy, families, religious communities, etc.

The intervention capacities of the modern state are defined and structured in very different ways, depending on politico-cultural tradition, economic capacity and social level of modernisation. In the liberal model of the minimal state, state duties are intended to be limited to ensuring international and national peace and providing a basic technical-economic infrastructure and elementary education, whereas in socialist systems, the state had a command and control function that affected all areas of life, including those usually private and intimate. Between these two models, there have been countless variants of state intervention primarily of a socio-political nature, called for and also implemented by both social democratic and conservative powers.

In the affluent industrial labour societies, as well as in some newly industrialising countries, the concept of the welfare state is central. Until the 1970s, the consensus was to transfer the responsibility for collective action with regard to common goods not available to individuals at an acceptable level as a matter of course to the welfare state, including access to comprehensive health care, education and culture, public transport, security against unemployment and old-age poverty. Even in countries where a 'neoliberal' countermovement started to question the expansion of state duties and increased state spending during the 1970s, public spending and borrowing have generally remained at a high level, primarily for crisis management reasons. Since the 1970s, state intervention has largely consisted of preventing the consequences of any kind of crisis, rather than consistently and sustainably encouraging social self-organisation. The concept of the 'enabling state', mainly discussed in socio-political debates in the United Kingdom and Germany, can therefore be viewed as something of a departure from the classic interventionist state (Giddens, 2009). The enabling state combines support of disadvantaged social groups with demands for their greater self-reliance and self-help.

Proactive state action features neither in the liberal constitutional state model, which primarily focuses on maintaining public safety and order, nor in that of the welfare-oriented fulfilment state, which first and foremost governs its population's welfare improvement. Likewise, the new role model of the guarantor and regulatory state, which the EU member states, particularly Germany, seem to aspire to at least in part does not do justice to the state's enabling and proactive function. It is rather an expression of retreat on the part of the state to ensuring the functioning of public utility markets (for example the supply of water and energy, the provision of telecommunication networks and public passenger transport). For decades, the provision of public utilities has been one of the classic duties not delegated by the state; as the sole infrastructure and service provider, the state therefore held a monopoly position. The creation of a common EU market and the requisite liberalisation of network management hailed the end of this monopoly position. The public utilities market was opened up to private suppliers (Hoffmann-Riem, 1999b). The guarantor state is now therefore merely obliged to ensure, through the creation of appropriate regulations, that the duty to the public of providing said public utilities is exercised by private sector companies under the aspect of 'common good' (Schoch, 2008). The current role models for statehood therefore do not adequately describe the kind of proactive and enabling state considered necessary for the transformation by the WBGU, and must be redefined.

5.4.1.2
The Responsibilities of a Proactive and Enabling State

The WBGU believes that the state must act proactively yet also enabling, particularly in the areas of climate, environmental and energy policy, and that these policy areas should be key to a new perception of the welfare state. To fulfil their proactive role, the nation states should set clear national and international climate and energy policy goals. They should establish a climate-friendly macro framework and create an effective set of legal instruments supported by an appropriate policy mix involving private sector, public-private and public actors (Section 5.2); ensure transparency and, not least, make suitable spaces at various levels available for experimentation and ensure leeway (Box 5.4-1; Chapters 3, 6) to allow the progressive consideration of scientific insights and technological innovations requisite for the implementation of the transformation, and incorporate these into social life-worlds. Nation states should – within the scope of their competencies – work towards regulating the measures needed for the transformation by international law in a multilevel system. Furthermore, the steps already taken towards the transformation must be continuously evaluated, not least also through participative research (Chapter 8).

In fulfilling its proactive role, the state must promote the innovations necessary for the transformation, mobilise the actors important for this process, and remove barriers (Jänicke and Lindemann, 2009; Section 5.2). One of the central components of such a proactive state open to innovation are regulations that encourage innovation. Of the three organs of state, the legislature is therefore the first one tasked with action (Eifert, 2009). This could take the form of, for example, incorporating climate protection in the German constitutional law as a national objective whilst also stipulating that this goal should be achieved particularly through regulations which encourage innovation, to be supported by the appropriate legal rights to bring action. Moreover, the fulfilment of this duty to establish national objectives also tasks ordinary law-makers with the creation of a legal infrastructure which promotes the development and diffusion of innovations. This includes a mix of instruments covering the entire innovation cycle (Sections 4.5.2, 5.2.3.1). However, the 'more' in state governance resultant from regulations encouraging innovation does not automatically mean less market, or fewer private initiatives. On the contrary: state action should be aimed at using and supporting market forces and civil society commitment for the purpose of the transformation.

Equally, a proactive legislature open to innovations should remove (legal) impediments or barriers preventing the implementation of innovations. This includes, for example, the long time outlay between planning and implementation of innovative projects. However, the necessary acceleration of approval and infrastructure authorisation processes must not result in the sacrificing of public participation (Section 5.4.1.3). Empirical analyses have shown that, contrary to all assumptions, this particular step in the process does not contribute to the considerable delays experienced in approval processes (Zschiesche and Rosenbaum, 2005). In fact, effective public participation at the earliest possible stage, i.e. participation at a point when all options are still open (Article 6 Section 4 Aarhus Convention) can actually improve the decision-making process and its result (von Danwitz, 2004). Public participation is therefore an expression of the communication process in an enabling state in which the citizen is mobilised to enforce the law (Masing, 1997).

However, a proactive state open to innovation must also not push innovations through at any cost. In the promotion of innovation, the constitutional obligations of the state continue to apply – above all the basic rights, constitutional procedural law and the establishment of national objectives to take environmental protection into account. This may be described as the state's responsibility for innovation (Hoffmann-Riem 1999a; Eifert, 2009), which must of course be offset by its 'responsibility for the future'.

5.4.1.3
Legitimisation Through Participation

The WBGU agrees with the demand for 'bringing the state back in' (Skocpol, 1982), under discussion for a number of years now in the expert community. However, a strengthening of the state's enabling function can only claim legitimacy if the citizens participate in the decisions to be made, rather than being merely expected to give their consent or accept them ex-post. Not only must every individual share in the greater ecological responsibility, the transformation towards a low-carbon society also requires a new culture of participation. The democratic legitimisation of state control and planning has been a subject for debate in political science since the end of the 1960s (Offe, 1972). Political decisions in representative democracies can be considered legitimate firstly through the input of citizen participation, which amounts to far more than just elections and votes (or party membership), also including various non-parliamentary formats, from signing petitions to demonstrating (Barnes and Kaase, 1979; Verba et al., 1995), and secondly through the output, i.e. the performance and quality of a decision made on this basis (Scharpf, 1999).

Box 5.4-1

Experiments: Promotion and Acceleration of Transformative Innovations

Social and technological innovations are a prerequisite for the transformation. Innovations are also based on experiments, which can be locally-focused search processes, for example. Innovative, climate-friendly technologies, behaviours, processes and forms of organisation for the various elements of the Great Transformation are developed and tested in experiments. Successful innovations provide climate-friendly alternatives, and can challenge the established high-carbon regime alone on the strength of their existence (Chapter 3). To support innovations, policy-makers should create room for experiments, consolidate promising innovations into niches, and support their rapid diffusion beyond these. Experimental spaces should be given certain time limits in which they are protected from market selection pressure and conventional funding evaluations in order to be able to develop successfully (van den Bosch and Rotmans, 2008).

Political and Legal Steering of Experiments

In order to successfully develop and realise experiments, the first step should be the choosing of certain low-carbon transformation action fields and their associated problems with regard to the tranformation. In order to minimise wrong decisions on the part of the state and secure the support of central actors from the outset, this selection process should take place in cooperation with the relevant stakeholders. In the Netherlands, for example, the government established 'transition platforms' in 2001, providing representatives of companies, the government and NGOs, as well as scientists, with a space to discuss not only policies, the barriers blocking innovations, and demonstration projects, but also to jointly decide on the development of experiments, and the potential options for their diffusion (Rotmans et al., 2001).

The second step should be the development of goals and visions, possible paths to achieve these goals must be highlighted, and specific room for experimentation outlined. Experiments can then be realised. Depending on the action field chosen (energy system, urbanisation, land use), there could be experiments with regard to new technologies, innovative production processes, new types of housing and living, or new business models. Policy-making establishes a framework for this, and the relevant actors develop alternatives (Chapter 8). The British National Endowment for Science, Technology and the Arts, for instance, has suggested experiments in the form of special innovation zones. These are specific geographical units, such as a city district, a community, a power plant network or a business park. By means of the respective policy-making, they are afforded a certain scope by innovative political framework conditions and given generous financial support. In return, they must meet an ambitious greenhouse gas reduction target as a result, or their further funding depends on achieving this goal (Willis et al., 2007).

Once their relevance has been assessed, existing experiments started on the initiative of companies or the civil society should also be given the same level of support as completely new ideas (Chapter 6). The fundamental principle is that policy-makers should establish a framework, provide funding, initiate dialogues, facilitate processes, and document the results. In this way, experiments enjoy political backing, and learning processes are supported. Learning objectives include the extent to which experiments actually contribute to the transformation, and under which conditions the solution assessed during the course of the experiment can be repeated and diffused. Costs, markets, and social, infrastructural, legal and cultural requirements for further diffusion are issues to be addressed with regard to innovations. Learning processes can be supported through dialogue between the parties involved, the establishment of networks, and accompanying research (Chapter 8). If progress becomes apparent with regard to alternatives, learning processes can be intensified through niche creation, which also increases the chances of a further diffusion of the innovation. Niche establishment requires the repetition of experiments in various contexts, linking experiments to various problematic situations (national and international), and the integration and broad communication of the experience made.

Through niche establishment, innovations can also increase their social relevance (Chapters 3, 6), which on the one hand means that the alternatives gain greater political and economic significance through increased publicity, incentives for network and interest-based organisation establishment, and increasing funding. On the other hand, however, it also means that innovations must adapt more to requirements beyond the niche, for example through cost reductions or adaptation to the preferences of a broader demand. The promotion of a range of variants allows selection of the best solution.

In legal terms, incentives for innovations can be created in different ways, some of which can be seen as spaces for experimentation. These include:

- Easing the legal admission requirements for research projects, or dispensing with them altogether. For example, plants serving the development or testing of new products or processes do not require approval under air pollution control law.
- Establishing explicit research laws that apply only for a limited period of time, again also to allow research projects to go ahead under less stringent conditions. A law such as this was endorsed, for example, for CCS technology (Hellriegel, 2008).
- Formulating dynamic technical standards: this is generally achieved through the use of vague legal terms in so-called technical clauses, for instance 'Best Available Technology'. These abstract legal concepts are then usually met with references to statutory instruments and administrative regulations, or complemented by extra-judicial standards which have been developed by private-law organisations. Both methods of reference are accompanied by constitutional concerns: with respect to the standards created by private-law organisations, for example the German Institute for Standardization (DIN), there is the issue of how democratically legitimised the enacted law-making authority is. Referring to regulations established by the government turns out to be problematic in the light of the constitutional principle of legal certainty, if this takes place not in the sense of a static reference to a specific technical standard, but rather to the latest version of the technical standard (so-called dynamic reference) (Erbguth and Schlacke, 2009). However, these constitutional legal deficits can be offset through reinforcement of reporting obligations towards citizens, and the citizens' statutory right to information, as well as public participation and legal protection.

If innovations have essentially proved themselves to be a

potential solution for a particular problem in the experimentation phase, policy-making should also in many cases support their further diffusion (scaling up; Chapter 3). Additional political measures are necessary as niche innovations may still prove to be incompatible with the structures and demands of the established socio-technical regime despite initial development in a niche environment (Chapter 3).

Many innovations cannot establish themselves because they are incompatible with the existing political and economic framework conditions (Chapter 4). They require changes in established perceptions, thought patterns and routines (Chapters 2, 3, 6). This applies, for instance, to alternative means of transport in comparison with fast, big, fossil-fuelled cars and their status symbol function (Chapter 4). In order to also advance changes in these areas, respective policy-making can involve central actors with sufficient authority to act in the discussion on experiment results, and initiate social debates on a broad level. The aim is to change the interpretation frameworks of established actors, gain political and social majorities, and highlight the benefits of the greater diffusion of innovations by discussing 'narratives'.

Further diffusion can be promoted by supporting transformation-friendly actors, and creating framework conditions that are conducive to transformation (Section 5.2, Chapter 6). These include investors willing to take risks, innovative companies, cultural norms and values and a legal framework, as well as scientific and technological capacities (Chapters 2, 8, Sections 4.5, 5.4).

The usual form of democratic participation in elite and negotiation democracies is the subsequent evaluation of government action, reflected in the bestowing (or denial) of political advance credits for the next legislative term. This mechanism of latent direct participation is obviously impaired at present; there is a lack of particular confidence in the effectiveness of government action both with regard to specific legislative matters, and the credibility of the politico-administrative system and its representatives in general. Over the past three decades, the classic instruments of democratic participation and control have been embraced to a significantly lesser degree by the majority of the population in virtually all OECD countries. This reflects an encroachment on one of the central mechanisms of recognition of rule by the ruled. Not only has the respect for (party) political elites diminished in the established democracies of Europe and America, but the general acceptance of the democratic process and system also appears to be gradually waning; in fact, there is a risk of its complete erosion.

In Germany, the most recent lesson on the lack of legitimacy of government decisions (despite the legality of both project and process) is to be learned from the intensive dispute surrounding the reconstruction of the main railway station in Baden-Württemberg's state capital Stuttgart ('Stuttgart 21' project) in 2010 (Box 5.4-2), which had a nationwide impact. It shows that where (major) infrastructure projects are concerned, the parliamentary political process is evidently no longer capable of raising the required level of credibility in order to realise large-scale construction projects, even though they have been decided on entirely above board and with a large parliamentary majority. As soon as the reconstruction commenced, i.e. became visible, the non-parliamentary protest expressed for a number of years escalated. Concurrently, the longstanding resistance to the transport of nuclear waste into temporary storage facilities at Gorleben in Lower Saxony became topical once again. Taken together, these events gave the impression of a growing, widespread legitimisation crisis across the (apostrophised!) 'anti-republic' confirmed by spokespeople for the political decision-making elite (Bartsch et al., 2010).

In conjunction, various opinion polls and studies on 'disaffection from politics' ('Politikverdrossenheit') do not really reflect a general legitimisation crisis, but they do indicate a growing disappointment with the effectiveness and accountability of democratic systems. The misgivings triggered by unresolved issues such as the labour market (structural mass unemployment since the mid 1970s with a growing shortage of skilled workers), demographic change (exploding healthcare costs, uncertainties regarding old-age pension provision) and the consequences of financial market volatility (accompanied by a growing fiscal crisis in the 'taxation nation') are now increasingly joined by concerns regarding the risks arising from anthropogenic climate change and other environmental burdens.

The colossal challenge with regard to the modernisation of representative democracies now lies in institutionalising more formal opportunities for participation in order to gain additional legitimacy whilst also linking these to a value consensus regarding a policy-making that focuses on sustainability to ensure that the 'more' in participation does not result in a 'less' with regards to sustainability issues. Because (both legal, and in principle legitimate) political protest would fall short of the normative foundations of sustainability and the ethics of ecological responsibility if there were only a 'general mood against' any form of large-scale technology, and if the benchmark for infrastructure projects designed to explicitly secure a sustainable future were also solely the level of disruption they cause in local contexts.

Resolving this dilemma is like squaring the circle, yet it must be the central task in any democratic

Box 5.4-2

New Forms of Direct Democracy: Insights from the 'Stuttgart 21' Mediation Process

In 2010, the long-planned conversion of Stuttgart's main railway station from a terminus to an underground through station ('Stuttgart 21') finally got under way. Once construction work started, resistance against this major project developed into a mass protest also joined by the urban middle classes. In order to de-escalate this social conflict, public arbitration talks were held in the autumn of 2010. According to arbitrator and former German federal minister Heiner Geißler, this mediation process was a 'democracy experiment', showing how future forms of direct democracy can be structured in Germany (Geißler, 2010, all comments quoted ad-hoc translations by the WBGU). In his November 2010 arbitral verdict, Geißler outlined essential elements of new forms of direct democracy, elaborated in the following.

Transparency and Involvement from the Outset

Once major projects are being planned, a civil democratic process should commence, including the discussion of alternatives. It is important here that equal consideration is given to the critics and the proponents of a project, for example through the public financing of expert's reports and assessments, also those commissioned by the opponents. It is of fundamental importance that not only some selected aspects are communicated to the public in the context of political opinions, but that the 'provenance of all arguments' and the 'overall technical narrative' are revealed to everyone involved. A comprehensive public presentation on the internal context of major projects – if applicable with media involvement to a public of millions – can furnish transparency and counteract the growing mistrust citizens feel towards policy-makers and the economy ('modern enlightenment'; Geißler, 2010).

In Heiner Geißler's view, planning approval procedures are the 'most bureaucratic form of democracy'; citizens can only object to the plan once it has been submitted. 'They can do that even in a dictatorship,' Geißler continued in the Süddeutsche Zeitung newspaper (SZ, 2010). Although, according to §3 of the German federal construction law code, the public must be informed at an early stage of plans and alternatives,'...this proviso is made only on paper, but not actually observed, or interpreted too narrowly. However, what should be the case is that alternatives are considered and assessed *officially*' (Geißler, 2010). 'The completely outdated building law needs renovation; above all, it must be accelerated' (Die Welt Online, 2010).

Increasing Direct Democracy

Considering the present media democracy, where tens of thousands can be reached and mobilised online at a mouse click, decision processes in representative democracies can no longer work the way they did in the 20th century; 'the age of full-stop politics is over' (Geißler, 2010). Even parliamentary decisions were now questioned, particularly if they took years to implement. In this day and age, such decisions would need to be repeatedly justified and elaborated. The deadlines between planning and realisation were also far too long.

Geißler calls for a 'reinforcement of direct democracy'. Admittedly, the Swiss model could not work in Germany, but 'the Swiss participation procedures should be adopted, at least for major projects.' To achieve this, he proposes dividing the execution of major projects into three participative planning segments. In the first phase, the objective should be formulated (for example construction of a base tunnel through the Gotthard), then the project should be voted on. In the second phase, the plans should then be developed, if applicable also including alternatives. Then there should be another vote. The project is realised in the third phase, with accompanying justification and information.

'For as long as a participation procedure such as this is not possible with regard to decisions made by the German federal government and the regional states, the Stuttgart model should serve as a prototype for institutionalised citizen participation that is on par with planning authority's', Geißler continues. Arbitration should remain the exception once all democratic and legal processes have been completed. In future, new forms of early citizen participation could help to prevent an escalation such as the one seen in Stuttgart.

and civil society actor self-modernisation process. In order to achieve effectiveness, these actors can on no account do without intermediate organisations such as political parties and organised special interest groups, which consolidate political interests in mass democracies (aggregation), escalate them programmatically, and integrate groups that are drifting apart. Because it is in this so-called pre-political sphere that the positions which can result in the formation of a consensus must be established and developed. The waning respect for 'intermediary organisations' such as parties, organised special interest groups and citizens initiatives, and their diminishing importance should be counteracted, as they do indeed have a significant mediating and aggregating function when there are tensions between state institutions and society. Apart from serving the articulation of interests, particularly political parties have so far undertaken the aggregation of political interests and the integration of various social groups (Schultze, 2010). And, not least, it is in the context of party political programmes that more comprehensive, long-term focused visions about the way we live together beyond short-term political events are developed. In the past, they have therefore contributed considerably to the formation of opinions and political will.

As a result of the growing disaffection with the way career and party politics are run, the population has become increasingly willing to take grassroots' action (Chapter 6). What is lacking is a 'citizenation' (Tully, 2009) of this commitment, i.e. its adequate consolidation and representation at a parliamentary level, or in other arenas, to allow the productive input of this action on the part of the citizens. A democracy with future sustainability must therefore not only accelerate its procedures, it must above all expand the basis for its legitimisation. As the appeal of a long-lasting commitment to parties and interest groups and the respect for these have severely declined in the last three decades under pressure of social individualisation and individual benefit calculations, they must be supported by more flexible networks and focused alliances that respect the autonomy demands of individuals, and encourage change agents' own initiatives whilst also providing them with stability and continuity (Box 5.4-1; Chapter 6). Interestingly, the intermediating organisations must also show themselves to be more responsive and yet decisive, not unlike the enabling state. Once parties have largely handed over agenda setting to the (electronic) media (or rather, share it with these), subsequently fulfilling virtually no further programmatic orientation functions, they are able to concentrate on service and coordination functions whilst rebuilding their reputability through programmatic clarity. Parties could therefore become essential actors in the 'triangulation' between active civil society citizens (Chapter 6), the proactive state and actors from the economy. Parties and organised interest groups, which are now perceived much less as actors with a focus on the common good than in the past, must appear modest and avoid the impression of wanting to usurp and channel citizen commitment.

A proactive state with extended participation opportunities in a multilevel system of global cooperation therefore conveys two aspects frequently thought of as separate or contradicting: on the one hand, the empowerment of a state which actively determines priorities and underlines them with clear signals (for example bonus/malus solutions) whilst providing citizens with more extensive opportunities to have a voice, to get more involved in decision-making processes, and to take on a more active role in politics. A powerful (eco-)state is often thought of as restricting the autonomy of 'the man in the street', whilst at the same time, any meddling on the part of precisely these 'ordinary citizens' is viewed with misgivings as a disturbance factor to political-administrative rationality and routines. Precondition for a successful transformation policy, however, is the simultaneous empowerment of state and citizens with regard to the common goal of sustainable policy objectives. The proactive state is therefore firmly anchored in the tradition of a liberal and constitutional democracy, but it develops this democracy further with a view to achieving a sustainable democratic polity and free civil societies. Whereas climate protection measures are often regarded as imposing limitations and requiring unreasonable levels of self-deprivation, the aspects of a proactive and enabling form of government elaborated in the following relate to a governance that is explicitly tasked with preserving and extending available choices and the room to manoeuvre for future generations.

A successful transformation policy should be pursued on four interconnected levels: (1) constitutionally, by setting climate protection as a respective national objective, (2) materially/legally, by embedding climate protection targets in climate protection legislation, (3) procedurally, be extending the opportunities available to citizens and non-governmental organisations for participation and improving access to information and legal recourse, and (4) institutionally through government institution climate policy mainstreaming. All of the measures elaborated in the following express and concretise the national objective of climate protection, forcing legislators, executives and the judiciary to act.

5.4.2 Proactive Options at National Level

5.4.2.1 Constitutional and Legal Climate Policy Self-Commitment on the Part of the State

The general climate political responsibility of the state and its proactive and enabling role in the transformation must be firmly established by law. To emphasise the state's extensive self-imposed commitment, it should be embedded in constitutional and administrative law.

Increased Protection by a New National Objective: Climate Protection

In constitutional law, the state's responsibility for climate policy can be highlighted and thus strengthened by an explicit reference to climate protection in the constitution. A national objective of 'climate protection' could conceivably be included in the German constitution as a supplement to Article 20a. Although the national objective of 'environmental protection' formulated here already defines natural resources as protected, thereby including the climate (Groß, 2009; Maunz and Dürig, 2010), the explicit inclusion of climate protection in Article 20a of the German constitution would nevertheless emphasise its outstanding importance, and the commitment on the part of the state. A national 'climate protection' objective would emphasise the common goods character of climate, i.e. take into account the fact that it is a supra-individual, protected property. By contrast, anchoring climate protection in the constitution as a basic right is not advisable as basic rights are primarily subjective, defensive rights protecting citizens ('negative liberty'). They therefore serve the protection of the individual sphere but cannot afford the supra-individual protection required in the case of climate protection (Maunz and Dürig, 2010).

National objectives provide basic principles and guidelines for state action. They contain a commitment to certain values, decisions made by government bodies must in fact update and concretise these (Maunz and Dürig, 2010). A national 'climate protection' objective would therefore oblige the state and its institutions to pursue an active and appropriate climate protection policy whilst retaining a broad decision-making scope. Concrete action on the part of the state can therefore not be demanded on the basis of a national objective, it is rather a case of the legislature being initially and primarily required to effectively implement the setting of a national objective. The requisite decision-making process must take climate protection into account (so-called mandatory consideration; Groß, 2009). Executive and judiciary fulfil their constitutional responsibility for environmental protection by interpreting the existing regulations created by the legislative as a concretisation of the national objective in a climate-friendly way, thereby particularly using their scope of discretion and scope for judgment evaluation to implement low-carbon solutions (Groß, 2009).

Introduction of Climate Protection Legislation

At the administrative level, the national objective 'climate protection' should be concretised in the form of climate protection legislation. The core element of a climate protection law is the establishment of legally binding mitigation targets. Beyond these, targets should also be set for the share of renewable energies in primary energy consumption, energy consumption reduction, and energy efficiency increase rates (UBA, 2011). Furthermore, the climate protection law should include an obligation to preserve terrestrial carbon stores, and measures for reducing greenhouse gas emissions from agriculture. The reduction of emissions of climate-damaging industrial gases should also be obligatory.

The WBGU's budget approach (WBGU, 2009) could serve as an orientation for the quantitative aspects of the mandatory targets to be set in the climate protection law (Section 7.3.9). It must be differentiated here between Germany's overall responsibilities on the basis of international fairness considerations, and the emission reductions to be achieved nationally. A climate protection law should include Germany's binding commitment to the complete decarbonisation of its energy systems by 2050, equalling a 100% reduction of CO_2 emissions from fossil energy sources. Some flexibility can be afforded by emissions trading schemes, although the WBGU advises against credits from offset-schemes such as the CDM (Sections 4.5, 5.2, 7.3.8, 7.3.9). Even with the stated reduction, Germany would still exceed its CO_2 budget as per the WBGU budget approach. However, as the WBGU believes that the government should focus on general fairness considerations, additional reliable payments would have to be made in the context of international climate financing in order to support the developing countries in their transformation, these would need also to be established by law (Sections 4.5, 7.3.9).

As such a climate protection law only contains the general obligation of all government bodies to implement climate protection measures, further-reaching legal regulations are necessary to specify concrete measures for achieving the respective interim targets. In addition, a regular reporting duty on compliance with the interim targets should be introduced in the climate protection law to transparently and verifiably prove road map compliance. Furthermore, the climate protection law must include (sanction) mechanisms to prevent target shortfall and, if necessary, take corrective action. With regard to the latter aspects, the British Climate Change Act (2008; CCA) could serve as a model for a German climate protection law: above and beyond long and medium-term climate protection targets (the so-called carbon budget) already mentioned, it also stipulates the establishment of an important institution for climate protection in the form of the Committee on Climate Change. This committee plays an important role not only in establishing climate protection targets; it also publishes annual progress reports with an assessment of adherence to climate protection targets to which the government must respond. The British Committee on Climate Change is therefore a neutral regulatory body monitoring the government. The act stipulates that in the event of target shortfall, the responsible minister must inform the British parliament of the reasons for this shortfall, and make proposals for offsetting the excess emissions during the following period.

5.4.2.2
Extend Opportunities for Information, Participation and Legal Protection

A transformation process is condemned to failure if policy-makers make decisions which force citizens to accept the corresponding measures subsequently. Policies that rely on the early and active consultation and participation of those concerned to legitimise political-administrative measures are more successful than any attempts to obtain acceptance after the event.

Extended Participation Opportunities in the Administrative Process

The implementation of large infrastructure projects, for instance the expansion of the high voltage grids, could fail – even though it appears to present no problem in terms of legality – due to a lack of participation and acceptance on the part of the population. As defined in the second pillar of the Aarhus Convention, involvement of the public is the central instrument for promoting participation in official infrastructure planning decisions, and for their acceptance. It makes the administrative and planning process more transparent and contributes to structuring it democratically (Fisahn, 2004; Schlacke et al., 2010). However, this requires the public become involved at an early stage, as citizens only have a realistic chance of influencing administrative decision-making with their arguments when all options are still open (Fisahn, 2004). Involving the public at an early stage can make the decision process more effective, as unwelcome projects are identified as such much sooner, thus avoiding expensive conflicts. Not least, relying on the specific expertise of participating environmental protection associations can improve the overall quality of the decision (von Danwitz, 2004). This kind of 'legal remedy in advance' can prevent infringements on any rights from the outset, therefore also contributing to easing the burden on the courts (von Danwitz, 2004).

In Germany, the present planning and approval procedures, for example, so far hardly meet these requirements (Walk, 2008; SRU, 2010). The public does not become involved, for instance, until after an agreement between the respective authorities and those responsible for financing public projects has already been reached. At that point in time, there is no longer room for alternatives. It is also doubtful whether the legally required public announcement regarding a planned project, and the way in which notice of a planned project is in actual fact given to the public, serve to motivate citizens to participate in the decision-making process. Often, the pros and cons of the planned project are not adequately explained, as prescribed by law – although in part, this may also be due to the accelerated legislation ('Beschleunigungsgesetze') in recent years. The present procedure's deficiencies were described in detail, for example, in CDU politician Heiner Geißler's arbitral verdict on the disputed 'Stuttgart 21' railway station project in November 2010 (Box 5.4-2). Key task for a proactive and enabling state is the establishment of structures that allow effective participation, and to organise a 'constructive communication process' just as required by the Aarhus Convention.

The preconditions for successful citizen and local participation in decision-making processes, particularly where large-scale projects are concerned, are: (1) extensive and continuous public and local involvement from the earliest possible stage, including the unbiased examination of alternative concepts; (2) greatest possible process transparency, for example through increased use of radio and television broadcasting, the new media, or additional information campaigns/platforms; (3) the involvement of independent parties in cases of conflict. Government agencies must be given more scope for mediation efforts.

Financial involvement is also an important driver of participation. Projects such as wind farms, for example, are more likely to win approval if they are jointly organised and run as cooperative societies, i.e. if citizens participate in the planning process and reap some of the profits (Section 4.5). In certain cases, compensation payments can generate acceptance of unavoidable impositions. Financial involvement creates a 'win-win' situation in the form of enjoyment of tangible benefits ('everyone must be a transformation winner'; Section 2.4).

Extending the Scope of Collective European Legal Action

Collective legal action means the right to appeal to the courts as a group, for example in the form of an officially recognised association, i.e. legal remedy can be sought without the infringement of any subjective rights (supra-individual collective legal action; Schlacke, 2008). In Germany, this option is available in only a few areas of public and civil law. However, specifically in the area of environmental law, and there particularly in nature conservation law, lawmakers have empowered collectives, such as interest-based organisations, to exercise and legally assert rights for the protection of the general public or individuals. Essentially, only individual people concerned (such as neighbours) can bring legal action against the approval of environmentally hazardous industrial facilities in Germany. Interest-based organisations that view themselves as advocates for the environment cannot. The right to file collective European legal action – formerly dealt with at German individual state (Länder) level – has been bindingly regulated in the Federal German Nature Conservation Act (BNatSchG) since 2002. Environmental protection associations which have registered with the German Federal Environment Agency (UBA) or the responsible local German state authorities may seek legal remedy, i.e. they are permitted to file an appeal against official decisions by government bodies with the administrative court, for instance. At the end of 2006, the Environmental Appeals Act came into force, providing environmental interest-based organisations with more scope to file collective European legal action (Schlacke, 2007). They now have the option of initiating legal proceedings against certain approval decisions for industrial plants and infrastructure measures under environmental law, for instance if an environmental impact assessment has not been carried out. This is an implementation of EU Directive 2003/35/EC, which in turn served the implementation of the Aarhus Convention (UN/ECE Convention on access to information, public participation in decision-making processes and enforcement of environmental laws). However, any interest-based organisations with the right to lodge an appeal under the Environmental Appeals Act can only include the same content that a subjectively concerned individual could include in their appeal. Climate protection aspects cannot be included, for instance, not even in the case of a project proposal, such as the construction of a new coal-fuelled power station. This circumstance has increasingly attracted criticism (Genth, 2008), as the aim of the Aarhus Convention, and therefore also of the EU directive implementing the same, was the mobilisation of citizens, and of organisations that represent citizen interests, to encourage them to campaign more intensively for environmental protection, thereby countering enforcement deficiencies particularly in this area. Extending the right to file collective action in this direction could encourage the responsible authorities to actually respect climate protection as a national objective.

Using Ombudspersons

The use of expert ombudspersons with monitoring authority and the right to launch legal action with the judiciary complements can improve the existing information, participation and monitoring rights of the public and interest-based associations. In a broader sense, legal protection – apart from the judicial right to bring legal action – also includes extra-judicial, alternative monitoring procedures. These can serve the assertion of supra-individual interests such as climate protection whilst also providing a means of monitoring government agencies. Apart from mediation procedures in areas governed by public law, particularly in environmental matters (Hellriegel, 2002; Sünderhauf, 1997), and the petition procedure, this also includes the institution of an ombudsperson (Schomerus, 1989), a concept originally conceived in Sweden. Ever since the Treaty of Maastricht, the European Union also employs an ombudsperson: the European Ombudsman (Article 24, Subsection 3 in conjunction with Article 228 TFEU; Magliveras, 1995; Cadeddu, 2004). The institution of ombudspersons primarily aims at extra-judicial arbitration under administrative law conditions, thereby complementing the system of administrative courts as it serves the observance of legal order.

A Societal Discourse Initiative for the Great Transformation

The transformation towards a low-carbon society is only achievable if it can gain the support of a wide spectrum of social and political majorities. Only then can the changes that are the basis for the transformation be initiated and developed both at a legislative level and in the civil society. This requires an extremely broad coalition far beyond a simple majority, possibly a new 'social movement' (Nullmeier and Dietz, 2009). According to Giddens (2009), sufficient support from the social stratas considered as central will result in a 'depoliticisation' of climate policy to the extent that it is lifted out of the usual right-left context. On the other hand, developments that are often viewed as merely natural hazards, such as biodiversity loss and climate change, will thereby become the subject of eminent political debate.

An awareness of the necessity of a profound transformation to safeguard future prospects and fair global burden sharing should permeate all areas of society. A fundamental societal mood of taking the issue seriously should be strived for, and inertia or a 'business as usual' attitude must increasingly be viewed as socially not acceptable. The more pronounced the discourse hegemony on the interpretation pattern 'the transformation towards a low-carbon society is necessary and achievable, transformation safeguards our welfare' the more likely it will be that the potential social resistance, and powerful veto players, can be overcome in the political arena, and that political and economic elites can be convinced to act (Nullmeier and Dietz, 2009; Hajer, 1995). The requisite course can be set only on the strength of this deliberative discourse.

Policy-makers should now be tasked with the initiation of such a wide-reaching social dialogue. Article 6 of the Framework Convention on Climate Change also refers to the role of government institutions in raising public awareness with respect to climate change (Walk, 2008). The issues of climate change, lifestyles, decarbonisation and transformation should be presented and discussed in public at the widest possible range of levels (global, national, regional, local) and by a variety of means (conferences, campaigns, education opportunities etc). This process of wide-ranging participation by all influential actors from the areas of policy-making, science, the economy, interest-based organisations and groups, the media, etc. can create the opportunities needed for a scientific and social debate that contains all facets, perspectives and assessments, and leads to the cooperative development of solution options or channels. To avoid addressing sustainability issues merely symbolically, or the danger of missing the point through inter-party squabbling, a carefully moderated debate under the patronage (and with active participation) of the German Federal President and the above mentioned ombudspersons, with involvement of the 'future chambers' elaborated in the following, should be instigated in Germany, using mainly digital information and communication media.

Deliberative Participation Processes

Peter Dienel (1978, 2002), James S. Fishkin (1991, 1995, 2009) and a range of other social scientists have conducted experiments and pilot studies they described as 'planning cells' or 'deliberative opinion polls'. A comprehensive overview is provided by Buchstein (2009, 2010) and Buchstein and Hein (2009). They follow the same basic pattern: first, a representative group of citizens from a region (or country) is invited to meet for several days. They are paid expense allowances in order to consult on a specific current political issue, research the different available options in detail, and develop a decision recommendation on the basis of their discussion and the information they have gathered. To date, pilot studies have been conducted on issues related to family affairs (USA), fiscal policy (England), the introduction of the Euro (Denmark), the abolition of the monarchy (Australia), and the distribution of extra fiscal revenue at local level (China). The term 'deliberative opinion poll' was chosen to distinguish these studies from the classic opinion poll.

In classic opinion polls, for the most part uninformed citizens are interviewed on issues in which they had no prior interest in. They are confronted with a set of predefined response options, and the social scientists conducting the study present the poll result arrived at on the basis of the responses as 'expressing authentic citizen preferences'. Such poll findings are not a genuine expression of political volitions, they merely represent social scientific artefacts. As 'pseudo-opinions in the echo-chamber' they have no true bearing on political decision-making – in contrast to everyday political practice, which relies heavily on polls.

Proposals for greater participation of ordinary citizens are often countered with claims that ordinary citizens are poorly informed and easily manipulated, and that, in crisis situations, the majority would even support serious violations of basic rights. By contrast, the initiators of the deliberative opinion poll want to determine the political volition of citizens once they have had the chance of gathering detailed information on the issue in question, and deliberating on it. In practice, this requires two factors: on the one hand, the representative selection of these citizens under consideration of local social statistics (in this respect, the deliberative opinion poll does not differ from the conventional opinion poll), and, on the other hand, a deliberative process quality that actually leads to gains on the basis of information and reflection.

The requirement of representative selection under consideration of local social statistics is met directly by resorting to random sampling by drawing lots. All of the studies conducted to date selected potential participants with the aid of computerised randomisation. They were then contacted by telephone and invited to take part. The second requirement for providing a deliberation setting that is as constructive as possible is met by intensive content preparation and discursive choreography of the meetings. Random sampling by drawing lots is again employed for this. The national level pilot studies conducted by Fishkin and his team assemble 300 to 500 participants for a long weekend at a specific location. The number of participants should be large enough to obtain a certain statistical representativity but small enough to be able to organise discursive processes in small groups and plenary assemblies with the support of professional facilitators. Experience to date demonstrates that random sampling by drawing lots is a reasonably accurate method for achieving the intended social statistical representativity. Although numbers vary between the various studies, the overall social statistical distribution ratio was still above that of conventional opinion polls before their subsequent 'adjustment'. Even if the assembled groups did not exactly match the social statistical cross-section, they nevertheless did have a significantly higher level of social heterogeneity than all of the institutions of the regular political establishment.

One robust empirical finding in the 'deliberative opinion polls' held to date is that there were significant changes in participants' opinions in consequence of their deliberations at aggregate data level. These individual opinion changes were a 'political learning' process with cognitively matured, new positions. They are based on increased factual knowledge, are more coherent in terms of logic, take the complexity of the problem into account, and are also consistent with respect to the participants' own value basis. This is a finding with positive significance for the suitability of a 'House of Lots' – a kind of deliberative chamber for decisions concerning the future (Section 5.4.2.4) – for recommendation, consultation or even decision-making on climate policy issues.

5.4.2.3
Climate Policy Mainstreaming in Government and Parliament

The low-carbon transformation requires the commitment and participation of many actors (state, civil society, private economic sector, etc.). As a state actor, the German federal government has the opportunity of improving the framework conditions through institutional reforms in such a way that transformation issues are accorded high priority, and are firmly anchored in government and parliament. Decarbonisation would need to be 'mainstreamed' to achieve this. 'Mainstreaming' refers to an organisational principle targeting the consideration of a specific aspect in all decisions – with respect to products, public image, human resources, organisation, etc. A kind of climate policy mainstreaming that is not unlike gender political mainstreaming would be conceivable, i.e. all government departments and all legislative proposals take decarbonisation issues into account.

Obligatory Climate Impact Assessment Scheme

A climate impact assessment scheme can ensure that measures presented for decision-making do not jeopardise the achievability of climate protection targets. Austria already plans to introduce such a climate impact assessment scheme in order to determine whether specific proposed regulations are relevant in terms of climate protection target achievement. In any case, the respectively more climate-friendly alternative must be chosen to meet the regulation objective. Assessing the consequences of laws is generally not a new concept, also in Germany. For the past few years, for example, it has been mandatory to include an ex-ante administrative burden assessment involved in each draft bill prior to its being laid before the Bundestag. In the context of the so-called sustainability assessment, a mandatory requirement since May 2009, all draft bills and regulations presented by the German federal government have first been assessed by independent advisory councils with respect to the costs of the companies' duty to inform, as stipulated by the sustainability assessment (= bureaucracy costs), and with respect to compatibility with the national sustainability strategy. However, this procedure has the disadvantage that subsequent amendments to the draft are not included in the assessment. Moreover, it should also be taken into account that the climate impact assessment must be distinctly separate from the sustainability assessment with regard to its area of application in order to avoid duplication: even though climate protection is an element of sustainable development and a national sustainability strategy goal. However, the sustainability assessment includes numerous other aspects of intergenerational fairness, for example social and demographic changes and the use of resources in general. It is therefore not an instrument that is used solely to determine the climate compatibility of legislative measures in the sense described above.

Other measures are already in place besides the climate impact assessment of proposed legislative measures, such as the environmental impact assessment for specific planned projects and the strategic environmental assessment for proposals and programmes to assess their climate-relevant impact. However, between the climate impact assessment of proposed legislative measures on the one hand and the environmental impact assessment for planned projects and the strategic environmental assessment for proposals and programmes on the other, duplicate assessments must be avoided. This can be achieved by tiering, i.e. aspects which have been adequately analysed during the previous stage of the assessment do not need to be reassessed at the next stage.

Empowering Executive and Legislative for the Transformation

To ensure that all political departments in Germany address the low-carbon transformation, and to improve harmonisation of interdepartmental policies, the issues of energy systems decarbonisation, land-use related greenhouse gas emissions reductions and climate-friendly urbanisation should become a priority focus for the Federal Committee of State Secretaries for Sustainable Development. This committee's role should also be stronger defined as an independent panel. All German federal ministries should develop strategies for the low-carbon transformation. These should systematically establish the state's climate political responsibility in administrative organisation and procedure.

To emphasise the transformation issue in German foreign policy, the creation of the post of foreign office state minister for global sustainability issues, energy systems decarbonisation and raw materials strategy could be an expedient measure.

Climate protection, biodiversity conservation and sustainable urban planning are now addressed and taken into consideration by government agencies to a far greater degree than they were in the early stages of environmental policy-making. In the WBGU's view, however, the current departmental architecture prevents these issues from reaching the status they should have, not least with respect to shaping a post-industrial future and establishing a sustainable economy. Therefore, in the long term, the partial modification of the current departmental architecture should be considered, for example by establishing a ministry for environment, climate and energy.

Increasing awareness of the global contexts of policy-making can represent another form of executive climate policy mainstreaming. Means to the end of 'global education' can be the 'internationalisation' of ministerial departments, for example by staffing them with 10–15 % of staff hailing from other OECD nations, developing, and newly industrialising countries whilst

Box 5.4-3

Parliamentary Support for the Transformation

One of the most important advocacy tasks' of the German Bundestag's Parliamentary Advisory Council on Sustainable Development is the evaluation of the sustainability assessment in parliamentary legislative procedure. The Parliamentary Advisory Council on Sustainable Development was constituted on 21 January 2010, after the Bundestag had decided its establishment on 17 December 2009 (Bundestag printed matter 17/245). The Advisory Council has 22 members: nine from the Christian Democratic Union/ Christian Social Union (CDU/CSU), five from the Social Democratic Party (SPD), three each from the Free Democratic Party (FDP) and The Left (Die Linke), and two from the Alliance 90 / The Greens. It is chaired by Andreas Jung (CDU/CSU), deputy chair is Gabriele Lösekrug-Möller (SPD). The Advisory Council is tasked with accompanying German federal government's national and the European sustainability strategies, and submitting recommendations.

also supporting and intensifying the adequate capacity building in these. In this way, national interests and perspectives could be brought into line with international perspectives and discourses from the outset, accelerating interactive learning processes and generating multilateral trust. A concrete step in this direction would for example be the establishment of exchange programmes for departmental specialists, comparable to the present DAAD German Academic Exchange Service.

In addition to the existing administrative assessment of the impact of legislative measures on sustainability, options for strengthening the role of parliament should be considered. Turning the Parliamentary Advisory Council on Sustainable Development (Box 5.4-3) into a permanent committee within the German parliament (Bundestag) would place the council in a far better position to act and assert its objectives in parliament, thereby strengthening its climate political role. The following elaborates and gives reasons for the institution of 'future quorums', or a 'future chamber' to improve citizen representation.

5.4.2.4
Improve Representation of Future Interests: Electoral Law Reform and House of Lots

One open question that needs to be re-examined from both democracy theory and constitutional policy perspectives is whether, in a proactive state with extended participation, citizen representation should be permitted to change, and indeed should change, by establishing 'future quorums'. This examination involves all instruments that anticipate the assumed interests of future generations (implicit: in greater sustainability of present-day politics) in the current decision-making process in consultative panels or additional chambers to give future generations a (virtual or vicarian) voice.

This touches on the fundamental concept of representativity, a core issue in European political-administrative architectures since the Middle Ages: beyond a polis or urban community that is workable in terms of its number and its susceptibility to problems, how can a collectivity of people (the entire population) be represented fairly and appropriately by an assembly comprising members that are either appointed, drawn by lot, or, preferably, have been elected by means of universal, equal and fair processes?

The present standard type of representative democracy contains a wide range of answer variants to this question that come close to this ideal, yet never quite achieve it – representation is 'not necessarily true' (Sartori, 1992), and 'under any system ... biased' (de Grazia, 1951). Distortions particularly stem from the fact that the political elite does not represent a cross-section of the social architecture. They are also the result of electoral processes, or lie in the lack of balance between the autonomy of the people's representatives – who take the mandate of their voters on trust and may interpret it as they wish – and the delegation of the will of the people by means of election. Furthermore there are aspects such as party political discipline in parliamentary chambers, 'perquisites of power' as a result of frequent re-election, and suchlike.

With respect to the future interests outlined in this report, 'surrogate representation' (Mansbridge, 2003) is a particularly interesting concept. It describes the representation of electorates which reside outside the usual constituencies of the representatives both in terms of time and space. It concerns people who do not belong to the respective nation state but are affected by its actions, and those who are currently not yet eligible to vote or have not even been born yet, but whose living conditions will be influenced by decisions made or refrained from at the present time (Section 5.3).

Particularly two political experiments are designed to get a measure of how the latter assertion of volitions, paraphrased as 'future interests', can be anticipated:

1. The direct or indirect representation of children and adolescents in electoral processes;
2. House of Lots.

Voting Rights for Children, Families, and Demeny Voting

In order to take both the actual and the presumed preferences of children and adolescents into account in the political process, or ensure their parliamentary representation, three reform options are under discussion: (1) the introduction of an original child voting right (i.e. a reduction in the voting age or, in the most radical form, a voting right from birth); (2) the introduction of an original parental voting right (also family voting right) and; (3) the introduction of a Demeny (vicarian) parental voting right, according to which parents exercise the voting rights of their children on trust until these have reached voting age (Grözinger, 1993; Goerres and Tiemann, 2009). The Demeny parental voting right is also under discussion as a form of child voting right, or as a compromise between an original child and a parental voting right, and dominates the current German debate (Goerres and Tiemann, 2009). It presumes that parents will consider their children's interests with regard to sustainability policy-making when placing the votes they hold in trust (Steffani, 1999).

In Germany, the introduction of a Demeny parental voting right is supported by a heterogeneous social and political spectrum, including prominent advocates such as Rainer Eppelmann, Olaf Henkel, Roman Herzog, Paul Kirchhof, Cardinal Karl Lehmann, Werner Schulz, Wolfgang Thierse and Antje Vollmer (Westle, 2006). In recent years, the Bundestag has also repeatedly addressed cross-party motions calling for the introduction of the child voting right (German Parliament, 2003, 2008; printed matter 15/1544 and 16/9868). The 'Foundation for the Rights of Future Generations' (SRzG) calls for a voting right by registration, whereby every national should be entitled to vote, irrespective of age, as soon as he or she communicates a corresponding desire to do so to the government body responsible (SRzG, 2009).

Assessments regarding the level of impact this proposal might have on the constitutional order and the right to vote differ. Both the introduction of a child voting right and the introduction of a Demeny parental voting right would necessitate an amendment to the German federal constitution (Grundgesetz, GG) and various German state constitutions. According to Article 38 Section 2 of the German federal constitution (GG), anyone 'over the age of eighteen' is eligible to vote in Germany. The introduction of a Demeny parental voting right would be contrary to the principles of equality and directness of elections established by Article 38 Section 1 of the federal constitution, and in the German state constitutions. In constitutional appeals with respect to the electoral participation of adolescents, the German Federal Constitutional Court has so far always reached a negative decision, citing the argument that the current voting age were 'historically substantiated' (BVerGE 36, 139, 141), and concluding that the introduction of a minimum age did not infringe on the principles of democracy and the universal right to vote (BVerGE 42, 312, 340). Whilst Schreiber (2006), for example, argues that a constitutional amendment would infringe the principle of democracy and the constitution's 'eternity clause' (Article 79, Section 3 GG), former German Federal Constitutional Court judges such as Roman Herzog and Paul Kirchhof consider the introduction of a family voting right that complies with the respective formal constitutional requirements possible in constitutional legal terms (Deutscher Familienverband, 2003).

In addition to objections citing national and constitutional legalities, there are serious empirical arguments against the possible political-material consequences of introducing a Demeny parental voting right, whether presumed or possibly sought intentionally. So far, it is only a hypothesis that parents' voting decisions would be genuinely motivated by an increased consideration of future interests, which, incidentally, feature a high level of uncertainty and ambivalence when it comes to concrete decision alternatives.

Critics primarily argue that the vicarian parental voting right might not be used to promote long-term sustainability policies but rather to effectively assert the parents' own, short-term interests (example: a significant increase in child benefit and parental allowances financed through additional state borrowing). Likewise, the assumption that non-parents or older voters will focus less on altruistic interests in their voting decisions can also be viewed as extremely questionable, from a sociological perspective (Szydlik, 2000). Furthermore, empirically well-founded simulations show that, despite a number of systematic differences in the voting behaviour of parents and non-parents, the overall results would have differed only slightly if a Demeny parental voting right had been introduced for the Bundestag elections between 1994 and 2005 (Goerres and Tiemann, 2009).

One variant of the vicarian child voting right is a reduction of the age of majority in terms of entitlement to vote, or thematically specific agreements on 'maturity' (analogue to the religious age of majority at 14). From a normative perspective, the current legal provision is problematic for two reasons. For one, it is difficult to cite convincing reasons for a very specific age limit over any other. The differing perspectives with respect to this issue have already been illustrated by the trend of a secular reduction of the voting age since the 19th century. In 1814, the voting age in France was 30. In 19th century Germany, it ranged between 30 and

23. In some German regional states, citizens are today eligible to vote in local elections once they are 16 years old, scientists are calling for a further reduction to 14 in the near future (Hurrelmann, 1997). Ultimately, an age regulation is plausible only if a specific minimum qualification to appreciate civil rights is assumed and this is linked to an age-dependent maturing and education process. And indeed, this is where the question arises of whether reducing the age at which young people are permitted general or partial decision participation rights might not improve the parameters and quality of these decisions, particularly in the area of sustainability policy.

House of Lots

Deliberative policy-making stands for, on the one hand, making knowledge society findings more accessible through consultation mechanisms, and on the other, giving citizens responsibility through participation in future decisions, and by taking them seriously. Deliberative 'future chambers' could be conceived for this purpose. This concept draws on an idea that is not new in the history of democracy, yet it has always tended to be marginal in contemporary representative democracy. This 'future chamber' is an institution whose members have been selected on a random basis. It is given political proposal, consultation or decision-making competencies (Buchstein, 2009, 2010; Hein and Buchstein, 2009). Already practised in antiquity, the approach was revived by US American political scientist and leading democracy theorist Robert A. Dahl. With a view to the positive experiences made with employing a lottery-style system of randomised jury selection for US American jury trials, introduced in the late 1960s, he suggested restoring the 'democratic device of the lot' (Dahl, 1970). 'Advisory councils', randomly chosen by drawing lots and financially reimbursed for their efforts, should be set up to support important political offices in modern democracies, from the mayors' offices of large cities through to the US congress, and even the White House. These councils should meet every few weeks at regular intervals to discuss issues important to them with the respectively responsible politician in office, to confront the politicians with the council's perception of a specific problem, to ask questions, and to give advice. These councils should be of a consultative nature and complement the representative system by 'improving the development conditions of an (everyday) political practice that is essentially deliberative' (Schmalz-Bruns, 1995, own ad-hoc translation by the WBGU).

Dahl developed this idea further into a 'minipopulus' (Dahl, 1987, 1992). A 'minipopulus' would, for example, consist of a thousand citizens of a country, selected by computerised randomisation. They are tasked with in-depth consultation on a specific issue, determined by parliament (or another responsible institution), over a longer period of time to develop various decision options. The members can meet face to face or communicate with each other electronically. Conceivable is a network of several minipopuli debating various topics at the same time and at different government levels. The outcome of the consultation process should be a 'policy recommendation' for the legislative.

The intention behind this is that the political system as a whole gains from the fact that career politicians are confronted with votes by well-informed citizens, accompanied by the hope that the legitimisation chain between citizens and career politicians is strengthened to counter political (politician) disaffection. Although the experiences at individual state level in Germany with regard to participatively- and deliberatively-structured technology assessments in the 1990s did not turn out particularly encouraging, this can primarily be traced back to precisely the fact that they were not decision-making, but exclusively recommendation-based processes, and that the recipients – predominantly official authorities – were very hesitant in taking these recommendations on board. Among the members of deliberative bodies, there is clearly a manifest problem with regard to motivation if the entire event bears little reference to decision-making, or this reference is not easily identifiable for the participants.

In view of this, it would be interesting to know what happens if randomly chosen panels drawn by lot are brought on a par with the other political actors on the power circuit of modern democracies. However, to date, there is an extensive lack of practical experience with regard to panels with binding political weight chosen by the drawing of lots. Because all of these examples in politics differ in one essential point from the judiciary's classic trial by jury method: even if called by parliamentary committees or other government agencies, their conclusions do not lead to a votum that would be equivalent to a decision with binding consequences. They merely give recommendations to elected holders of office and mandated representatives, effectively functioning as a method for political elites to attempt to determine the will of well-informed citizens. At best, all of the projects to date have moved in a kind of grey area between directly impacting political decisions and indirectly providing feedback which is fed into the political process through communication by the public.

Since the 1990s, there have been experiments with new forms of political consultation, such as 'consensus conferences' or 'scenario workshops' comprising representatively compiled groups of citizens, for example, particularly in some European countries. Evaluations have shown that in Denmark, consensus conference recommendations have impacted considerably on policy decisions in that country. In other countries, however, similar models have not shown any real practical impact. On the contrary, political actors emphasised the recommendations when they saw fit to support their own positions or – in the opposite case – ignored them completely. Their more substantial impact in Denmark is explained by the quasi-official status of the consensus conferences under the aegis of the Danish Ministry of Science, Technology and Innovation.

Current plans and projects with randomly generated panels therefore need further revision in order to be able to become a promising reform option. What is needed above all is the clear establishment of binding assignments of competence within the scope of the political system of modern democracies. Otherwise, there would be an almost unavoidable risk of the appointment of randomly generated advisory councils becoming an instrument to be used by a government or the opposition – depending on the general political situation and ad-hoc requirements – to add legitimacy to its parliamentary policies. Also requisite is a clear definition of the constitutive conditions and sectoral competencies of panels randomly chosen by drawing lots, as consultation matters can otherwise be fragmented into so many issue aspects that councils meeting concurrently would impede each other. In the case of regional or thematically focused councils, a further requirement would be the definition of the basic population sample to be entered in the random selection process. There are no general answers to questions such as the latter ones; they can only be answered in the course of concrete reform proposals.

The establishment of a 'House of Lots' as an institutional response to the problems of political programming in the area of climate policy is one element of a proposal for 'democratic innovations' (Smith, 2009). In terms of the particular suitability or otherwise of a 'House of Lots' as an innovative political institution that could have some input in future climate policy decisions, the following theses can be formulated with regard to the current status quo:

- 'House of Lots' consultations are fundamentally appropriate for issues with a high level of intergenerational relevance, as past research attests not only considerable cognitive changes on the part of the participants but also a certain 'force of universalism' with regard to cited arguments, as the actors selected by randomly drawing lots have less strategic incentives for arguing purely on the basis of interests than political actors who are firmly embedded in political networks. Empirical research over the past few years has shown that representatives selected by drawing lots ('LotReps') exhibit a high focus on the common good (although this does not solve all of the problems, it does reduce their number).
- A 'House of Lots' should be strictly separated from elected bodies, as actors from elected institutions (have to) follow a different operational logic than representatives selected by lot. As a minority in an elected chamber, they would also be susceptible to party political classification and constraints.
- Compared with the current model projects, the development potential for randomly generated councils ultimately hinges on deciding between two options: one is to pursue this recently established route by carrying on with the experiments and projects described, and their frequently non-binding status. This would support the commendable intention of teaching more democracy. Such projects would, however, tend to remain a purely ornamental embellishment of the political system's routines in which participants would expect the exertion of a very low degree of real influence evoking the motivational problems described. The alternative route would be a randomly generated, empowered chamber as a new political institution with limited but real opportunities for influencing policy-making. A reform policy in this direction would ultimately lead to the incorporation of a 'House of Lots' into the existing institutional arrangement with a clearly assigned and binding competence profile. This can range from an obligatory requirement to give an advisory opinion through to having the authority to call a moratorium, or having certain veto functions, and would need to be carefully structured according to governance level (local, regional, national, EU, worldwide).

5.4.3 Proactive Options at EU Level

As a supranational institution, the EU has a decisive (pioneering) role to play in the transformation: on the one hand, it can initiate transformation-promoting measures in its member states through ambitious legal and political requirements. And on the other, the EU can aid the diffusion of advanced developments beyond its member state area through cooperation with non-member states.

5.4.3.1
Possible Courses for Action in the Member States

Emphasising Climate Protection in EU Treaties

In order to ensure the comprehensive consideration of climate protection in the establishment and implementation of all Union policies and measures, this objective must first be established in European primary law, i.e. anchored in the Treaty on European Union (TEU) and the Treaty on the Functioning of the European Union (TFEU). Currently, climate protection is listed only as one of several EU environmental policy objectives in Article 191 Section 1 No. 4 TFEU. Although the current horizontal clause in Article 6 TFEU, calling for the general consideration of environmental protection as per Article 191 TFEU in all Union measures, indirectly implies an obligation to protect the climate, it is not explicit (Calliess and Ruffert, 2007; Schwarze, 2009), and should be amended to ensure further protection, as should Article 3 TEU.

EU Climate Policy Mainstreaming: Anchoring the Transformation Institutionally

Inspired by the symbolic, constitutional anchoring of climate protection at Union law level, climate protection matters and the resultant transformation issues must also be taken into account when structuring institutional architectures. Climate policy mainstreaming should therefore also be introduced at Union law level, in line with the options available at national level (Section 5.4.2.3), to ensure highly prioritised anchoring of climate protection and transformation issues in all government departments and planned legislative processes. In the Directorate-General for Energy, this kind of transformation-oriented climate policy mainstreaming can already be observed in the form of a transformative energy policy: based on the 'Europe 2020' strategy (EU COM, 2010f), the Directorate-General is developing a European energy policy with the particular goals of promotion of sustainable energy production, sustainable energy transport and consumption, and innovative energy services (EU COM, 2011e). This facilitates technological innovations in the energy sector and ensures compliance with the energy and climate objectives, particularly in the area of energy efficiency and renewable energies. Successful implementation of the climate protection objective at Union level nevertheless needs a stronger commitment to transformative policies across all organisational units, i.e. a mainstreaming of climate policies.

Common Energy Policy as a Chance for Europe

One core element of the transformation is the decarbonisation of the energy system. Fossil energy carriers and nuclear power currently still dominate the energy mix in the EU member states. The EU contributes almost 15% of worldwide CO_2 emissions (excluding land-use changes). Moreover, there is a high dependency on imported fossil energy carriers, particularly oil and gas. As an important element of the transformation, developing the sustainable potential of renewable energies by the middle of the century can credibly substantiate the EU's self-proclaimed leadership position in terms of energy and climate policy (Chapter 4).

The formation of a future, functioning common internal energy market can have an integrative effect as strong as that of the European Monetary Union, thereby deepening identification with Europe on the part of the citizens. The EU currently needs a new project to convince, motivate and inspire its citizens. The general mood is one of euroscepticism and, in part, euro-apathy. Developing and implementing the vision of a common European energy policy could lead the way into a new era in terms of energy supply, and prove to the world the feasibility of a continent-wide, sustainable energy supply. No other actor could achieve this much.

The WBGU believes that the development of a common internal energy market should include the following elements: the regulation of grid access, targets for the reduction of carbon dioxide emissions, the expansion of grids and storage facilities, and, with regard to this, the appropriate EU foreign policy competence to enter into agreements with non-member countries. Important directional changes are currently taking place with respect to the further development of the European energy market and, in particular, regulation of grid access and expansion of energy infrastructure. The EU Commission has proposed important steps towards decarbonisation of the energy supply by announcing its energy infrastructure priorities (EU COM, 2010e), the 'Energy 2020' strategy for competitive, sustainable and secure energy (EU COM, 2010f), the Roadmap for moving to a competitive low-carbon economy in 2050 (EU COM, 2011a), and the Energy Efficiency Plan 2011 (EU COM, 2011b). However, the Roadmap 2050 assumes goals that are far less ambitious than the actual opportunities for renewable energy expansion, and nuclear energy continues to occupy a dominant position. As shown in Chapter 4, more ambitious objectives for the energy mix can be pursued here without the forced acceptance of the inevitable risks of nuclear power. Based on these political proposals, legally binding measures should then be taken to advance the expansion of renewable energies.

Expansion of EU Competency

Transformative action on the part of the EU in the area of energy policy demands the granting of the respectively necessary competences. In accordance with the principle of conferral of power, Article 7 TFEU, the EU can take action only to the extent to which it has been conferred its member states' sovereignty rights as a supranational institution. As it can take action for environmental protection under Article 191 TFEU, in which it is also tasked with realising climate protection targets, it already has the requisite competency bundle at its disposal. However, the implementation of the Great Transformation requires additional competences not yet conferred on the EU. This also and in particular applies to the area of energy policy, which is now explicitly included in the EU competences (Article 194 TFEU). Nonetheless, its authority does not extend to the right to determine the legal framework for the member states' energy mix, for instance. To a large extent, this legal framework effectively controls the member states' decisions with regard to their choice of energy carriers per se, i.e. not with regard to renewable energy carriers only. Equally, it does not include the authority to oblige member states to establish energy grids, and to enforce grid expansion plans in cooperation with non-member states (Kahl, 2009; Calliess, 2010; Nettesheim, 2010).

If the EU were granted these competences, it would subsequently be in a position to regulate climate protection measures and energy policy in its member states at delegated legislation level. It could issue a climate protection and energy directive to this effect. In terms of procedure, this would have the advantage that the member states would retain their own scope for decision, as directives are binding only with respect to the result to be achieved, leaving to the national authorities the choice of form and method required to achieve the stated objective (Article 288 TFEU). In terms of content, such a directive could include energy strategy requirements and requirements for the expansion of electricity supply and distribution grids.

Despite the present competency situation, the EU Commission has presented various proposals for a competitive, sustainable and secure energy policy. However, these are initially only political proposals which do not yet have a legislative form, they are therefore also not yet mandatory.

EU Promotion of Accelerated Renewable Energies Expansion

At present, there are de facto 27 different energy mixes and 27 different import dependency structures within the EU. In view of the different geographical and economic factors for the production and storage of renewable energies, e.g. suitable locations for wind or solar power generation or cropland for bioenergy production, the EU member states' expansion requirements differ widely.

However, the long-term rebuilding of the European energy supply to renewable energies is hardly achievable within national boundaries. The EU should continue to provide incentives and set targets so that renewable energies are promoted and expanded whilst the use of fossil energy carriers is gradually phased out. In order to be able to do so, the EU needs to be given the option of prescribing the member states' legal framework for their energy mix. Although its present environmental competences allow the EU to govern the promotion of renewable energies, provided it is ecologically motivated, neither this competence, nor the energy competence explicitly applicable since the Treaty of Lisbon came into effect (Article 194 TFEU) give the EU the right to determine the legal framework for the Union-wide energy mix. This area remains solely a matter of member state sovereignty. The EU's competence must therefore be expanded in this respect.

Moreover, the present EU approaches for the promotion of renewable energies (Renewable Energy Directive) are inadequate: instead of a restriction to (overall) targets to be achieved by 2020, ambitious goals up to 2050 are needed. Interim targets subject to reassessment under consideration of new scientific and technological findings should be established.

Non-compliance with these targets should be subject to sanctions. These should not only take the form of treaty infringement proceedings brought by the Commission, but also of collective European legal action – as yet not included in the EU Treaty – before the European Court of Justice. In addition, the incentives should be structured in a way that encourages investments to be made where they are profitable on the basis of local geographical conditions. The WBGU recommends the introduction of a standard EU feed-in tariff (Box 5.4-4). To increase the effectiveness of this financial promotion of renewable energy carriers, the subsidies for fossil and nuclear power fuelled energy generation should be phased out. Moreover, the further development of the European climate protection targets also represents an important frame of reference for the dynamics of renewable energies expansion. Finally, accompanying and binding energy efficiency targets should be established. The EU already has the competence to do so under Article 194 Section 1 TFEU.

Construction of Continent-Wide Energy Grids

The cost-effective expansion of renewable energies demands a continent-wide production, consumption and storage network. This requires the expansion and rebuilding of transnational infrastructures. A trans-

Box 5.4-4

Europe-Wide Harmonisation of Renewable Energies Promotion

In recent years, the proposal of a Europe-wide alignment of renewable energy promotion schemes has been discussed repeatedly, although it has not been introduced as yet (SRU, 2011). This harmonisation could be realised with standard feed-in tariffs, a quota system (renewable portfolio standards) and tradable certificates (renewable/green energy certificates), and with competitive tendering, although it must be considered that the choice of promotion scheme would impact the various renewable energy technologies' expansion rates (Box 5.2-4; IEA, 2008a). A standard EU renewable energy promotion scheme would ensure that renewable energy generation would take place at those locations within the EU that provide the most favourable conditions for the different renewable energy technologies. In theory, harmonised promotion could unlock efficiency potentials within the EU, due to the different conditions of various geographical locations, and the varying potentials for renewable energy generation.

The proposal of harmonising European promotion schemes was most recently addressed in the European Commission's 'Energy 2020' energy strategy in November 2010 (EU COM, 2010f). The German Advisory Council on the Environment (SRU) has also discussed the full harmonisation of promotion schemes across the EU in its latest report (SRU, 2011). In this report, the theoretically existent efficiency benefits of a Europe-wide harmonisation of promotion schemes are contrasted with the practical disadvantages. In the case of a decision in favour of standard feed-in tariffs across Europe, there is a conflict of objectives between exploiting the cost saving potentials, i.e. focusing on optimum locations with correspondingly low subsidy rates, and a promotion policy that also encourages investments in countries where the geographical situation is less favourable. However, the latter would require higher feed-in tariffs, which in turn – assuming standard rates – could result in freerider effects in the more favourably placed regions. Furthermore, during the transition from national systems to a European scheme, a period of investment uncertainty could ensue. The report also highlights possible acceptance issues on the part of politicians and society if the promotion were concentrated on just a few selected locations. The SRU ultimately recommends that the introduction of a pan-European standard range of promotion instruments should not be considered earlier than 2020, due to the still non-existent network and storage facility infrastructure (SRU, 2011).

The WBGU shares these concerns with respect to the present technical, political and social barriers against the harmonisation of the nevertheless appropriate promotion instrument of feed-in tariffs, whilst also suggesting the deliberate pursuit of a pan-European feed-in tariff as of 2020, and to have European energy policy adjusted accordingly by 2020 (Section 7.3.4). Essential precondition for a standard feed-in tariff is a stepped-up grid expansion and increased transmission capacities between the EU member states, as well as the availability of new infrastructures to manage fluctuation (including storage capacities, load management systems). An immediate, pan-European standardised feed-in tariff would conceivably slow down the expansion of renewable energies in some regions, particularly in Germany, without the ability to import sufficient electricity from renewable sources. Without the respective infrastructure, it seems probable that recourse would again be taken to less sustainable forms of energy. A European common electricity market with unhampered grid access is a further precondition which has to be given.

Another consideration once these prerequisites are fulfilled is the inclusion of North Africa in a standard European feed-in tariff system. The requisite (external) competency the EU would need for a binding integration of North Africa into a European feed-in tariff system, from a legal perspective, has already been granted (Section 5.4.3). The (internal) competency for ecologically motivated funding of renewable energies, Article 191 TFEU, also gives rise to the corresponding – although not explicitly stated – authority to bindingly act for the member states in external relations, i.e. towards third countries (so-called AETR ECJ judgement, judgement 22/70, decision dated 31/03/1971, Court of Justice Reports 1971, p. 263). However, this would also require further network expansion in the form of a transcontinental power grid, which is probably not going to be realised before 2030.

continental high performance electricity supergrid should be created in Europe to allow the pan-European exchange of electricity. The grid should also be linked to neighbouring countries that produce power or store it, for example connections to Norway's power plant storage capacities, to offshore wind farms, or to solar thermal plants in Africa. Apart from offsetting regional and temporal energy supply fluctuations, this contributes to the efficiency and improvement of the strategic supply situation, as it allows optimum use of locations particularly well suited to the respective resource, and compensation in the event of import shortfalls. Such division of labour would be more cost-effective than respective individual national decarbonisation strategies with a need for self-supply.

The EU's Third Internal Energy Market Legislative Package creates a new legal framework for the cross-border management of grid operation, unlike previous EU liberalisation steps, and focuses on the problematic issue of grid planning. One aspect is that network operators are obliged to produce regional and EU-wide10-year grid development plans. There is no obligation to expand the supply networks, and there are no substantive criteria or procedural specifications. In order to guarantee the timely construction of new grids and ensure the promotion of electricity feed-in from renewable sources, the EU's legally relevant acts (for instance the Electricity Directive) must be updated as soon as possible to include obligations with regard to not only grid planning, but also grid construction and expansion, accompanied by the substantive objectives of renewable energies promotion. In procedural terms, the Union's citizens must be involved and participate in the EU-wide planning process at the earliest opportunity. A later participation in the planning of individual grid sections only is too late and distorts the overall planning perspective.

However, in terms of competency, the EU is still not authorised to accelerate its grid expansion promotion: since the Treaty of Lisbon came into force, the EU has been given the authority for energy policy decisions and, within this context, it also has the option of promoting the interconnection of energy networks (Article 194 Section 1 (d) TFEU). In the absence of a limitation to this authority, the EU can initiate its own projects based on this, and oblige its member states also with respect to the 'whether' with regard to implementation. Alone in terms of the mode of implementation ('how'), for example with respect to specific power cable routing, it is currently unable to act due to its lack of planning competency. The competency therefore rests with the member states. As the EU-wide expansion of the energy grids requires extensive commitment on the part of the member states, this EU competency should also be extended. As per the European Court ruling on the European Agreement on Road Transport (AETR), this would also simultaneously grant the EU the competency it needs to push ahead with grid expansion beyond EU borders.

Despite the current competency situation, the EU Commission has already presented a concept for an integrated European energy grid. It proposes the identification of energy infrastructure priorities, and measures for their prompt implementation (EU COM, 2010e). This must fundamentally be viewed as positive. However, effective implementation still requires legal obligation.

Grid expansion also requires substantial investments, particularly in regions which are unable to attract private investors. These regions therefore require public aid. The requisite funds should also be made available at European level. In addition, government incentives are called for (for example the offer of low-interest loans) and, possibly, the introduction of a legal obligation to expand the grids, assuming this is economically feasible.

EU-Wide Grid Access

A continent-wide, sustainable energy supply requires the creation of a functioning European internal energy market. The WBGU supports the liberalisation of the member state energy markets under Union law, characterised by a regulated network access model which essentially requires the establishment of an appropriate regulatory authority.

The liberalisation of the Union-wide energy market must be stabilised and advanced further. For the purpose of decarbonisation, the legal framework conditions should be structured in a way that allows the internalisation of externalised costs, for example those caused by greenhouse gas emissions (Section 5.2). Applying the 'polluter pays' principle, these costs must be covered by the energy supply companies to prevent the continued support of existing climate-damaging structures through progressive liberalisation (Section 5.2). The EU should therefore use its existing competences to realise a low-carbon internal energy market, and formulate the appropriate framework regulations.

In the absence of adequate implementation of the measures envisaged in the Third Internal Energy Market Legislative Package, the European internal energy market has as yet not been sufficiently liberalised to allow demerging, unlimited grid access and transnational trade. It continues to be dominated by the established energy supply companies. In order to open up opportunities for new energy market actors and remove the existing legal and actual barriers to European energy network access, member states must ensure implementation of the Third Internal Energy Market Legislative Package's already extensive demerger regulations. Furthermore, the Agency for the Cooperation of Energy Regulators (ACER) established by the Third Internal Energy Market Legislative Package, the European Network of Transmission System Operators for Electricity (ENTSO-E), and the European Network of Transmission System Operators for Gas (ENTSO-G) must be supported, not least to facilitate coordinated EU-wide energy grid expansion.

5.4.3.2
Possible Course of International EU Action

Expansion of External EU Competency

The promotion of renewable energies, construction and expansion of grid infrastructures, and decarbonisation of the EU-wide energy system by 2050 all require the involvement of countries bordering on Europe. In the WBGU's view, the EU should therefore exploit its existing external competences with regard to the agreement of international law treaties fully, and be granted further external competences beyond those it currently has. In addition to its explicit external competences, the EU also has an implicit authority to agree treaties that runs parallel to its internal competencies, according to settled European Court of Justice (ECJ) case law, now established in Article 216 TFEU. As Article 191 et seq., 194 TFEU authorises the EU to promote renewable energies internally, and Article 194 TFEU confers the authority for grid infrastructure construction and expansion, the EU does have the respective external competencies. However, the EU-wide decarbonisation of the energy system requires competency for setting an EU-wide energy strategy (particularly with respect to choice of energy carriers and transnational grid expansion). In this respect, the EU does not have the necessary internal authority. The agreement of respective treaties under international law therefore requires a currently not existing, corresponding internal competency.

Promote Cooperation with Neighbouring Countries

The decarbonisation of the EU-wide energy system by 2050 can be achieved more cost-effectively if Europe cooperates with its neighbouring countries. Core element would be the initiation of broadly impacting energy partnerships between the EU and North Africa (analogue to the EU partnerships with major newly industrialising countries), in order to utilise the favourable local conditions for renewable energies (wind and solar power) (WBGU, 2009, 2010b). European-African energy partnerships should firstly contribute to the European energy supply, and secondly help to establish sustainable energy supply infrastructures in Africa to effectively combat energy poverty (Section 7.3.5). A future project such as this could also put any cooperation between Europe and Africa on a completely new footing on the basis of common interests. Development, energy and stability policies would be bundled. An African-European energy alliance could be a central element in the transformation to a low-carbon global economy. Africa would thus gain entirely new, long-term development opportunities. Overall, EU development policy should consistently combine the poverty reduction target system (Millennium Development Goals) with decarbonisation strategies. European development policy should take on a pioneering role with regard to this kind of strategy change, not least in order to gain credibility on the international stage (Sections 7.3.9, 7.3.10).

5.4.4
Global Governance through International Cooperation

Although many of the elementary action fields for a transformation towards a low-carbon society, such as transformation of the energy systems or urban planning and land-use issues, above all require local and national solutions, a successful transformation is almost inconceivable without genuinely global action. A high level of international cooperation and global governance is therefore an important premise for the success of the transformation advocated by the WBGU. Without close harmonisation and international policy coordination in the policy areas that are essential to the transformation, the requisite trend reversal in global development dynamics will be impossible.

However, the complex challenges of climate change, the now tight planetary guard rails of the fossil age, and the multipolar restructuring of the international community of states appear almost unmanageable with the established means of multilateral politics. In view of the snail's pace of the current negotiation round of the World Trade Organisation, the stagnant state of international climate negotiations, or the G20's new activities, there are numerous claims that multilateralism is in a crisis, including postulations that its end is nigh (Section 5.3.5). At the same time, transnational cooperation remains essential for managing global problems, not least one of the reasons for the WBGU's demand for an 'international cooperation revolution' (WBGU, 2009, 2010b). To name but one concrete example, decision processes based on the majority principle should be allowed in the context of the UN Framework Convention on Climate Change (UNFCCC) in order to overcome the crippling consensus formation at lowest common denominator level (WBGU, 2010b).

A transformative cooperation revolution for the purpose of effective and legitimate global governance must have a broader spectrum, and a more profound effect than merely overcoming the established consensus principle of multilateral negotiation processes. The International Human Dimensions Programme on Global Environmental Change advocates the need for 'Earth System Governance', developing conventional notions of global governance further and transcending them with a dedicated consideration of global environmental change (Biermann, 2007, 2008). Irrespective of this it is still difficult to imagine that the necessary level of universal cooperation can be achieved in the present international system outside of the established institutional structures of international law and the United Nations (Section 5.3.5).

This does not mean that the United Nations should be turned into a global super-government hierarchically superordinate to the sovereign nation state world. However, as a multilateral platform for action which links international organisations and transnational actors from civil society and the private sector and reduces the complexity of international and regional political processes at the global level, thereby improving the framework conditions for intergovernmental cooperation, it remains indispensable. It will not effortlessly evolve into an integrated, multilateral world order, but represents a foundation for the global society to legitimately pursue aspirations of global governance.

In this context, a number of sometimes contradictory myths regarding the nature of multilateralism must be dispelled, as these have to date prevented the 'cooperation revolution'. Multilateralism is, for example, often described as the 'soft' option in comparison to unilateral foreign policy and bilateral cooperation, subscribed to by states only in 'good times', when there are only 'moderate' coordination and cooperation problems. However, it did not just take climate change to show that the global interdependencies already observed in the 1970s, making the distinction between 'high politics' and 'low politics' seem increasingly artificial, are real (Held et al., 1999; Keohane and Nye, 2001; WBGU, 2008).

Another myth is the assumption that multilateralism could virtually replace 'leadership' in global problem management as the pressure is shared by so many. This curtate perception of international cooperation fails to recognise that multilateral politics become effective above all when one or several of the cooperating partners have the power to act, taking over the leadership and showing a serious commitment to resolving the problem concerned (Lake, 1993; Underdal, 1998; Brzezinski, 2004; Lindenthal, 2009). A third myth, frequently cited as an argument against entering into multilateral obligations, is the fear of giving up too much sovereignty, thereby encouraging the formation of supranational bureaucracies with decision-making power but without democratic legitimacy – 'institutional Frankensteins terrorising the global countryside' (Hawkins et al., 2006). Despite international organisations' pursuit of autonomy and rational-legal authority, this is ultimately prevented by the national sovereignty of their member states, as in practice, their conflicts of interest tend to be moderated, rather than overlooked (Barnett and Finnemore, 2004; Vaubel, 2006; Biermann and Siebenhüner, 2009).

Not only do myths such as these, inhibiting cooperation, need to be dispelled, but further and ongoing clarification is needed concerning the global system risks resulting from ecological, technological and socio-economic megatrends now faced by the global community (Chapter 1; Beck, 2007; Messner et al., 2009). Granted, the fundamental problem awareness, particularly with regard to the ecological risks, has risen worldwide continuously since the beginnings of the 'green movement' in the 1970s, augmented by the climate policy debate in recent years (Chapter 2; Sommer, 2011). Nevertheless, there is still little awareness of the fact that today's evident juncture between technological and economic change represents a civilisation threshold rivalling the Industrial Revolution, and of the resultant needs for political transformation (Chapter 3). This is proved by the parallelism between rapid technological and social innovations in transformation-friendly niches and a conventional society dedicated to the fossil age and a logic of constant growth (Chapter 3). It can safely be assumed that this is also the catch when it comes to the transition from a 'world of possibilities' to a 'world of necessity' (Ostrom, 2003).

This does by no means suggest that the global transformation represents a primarily technocratic challenge which could easily be implemented solely with power politics and financial efforts (Messner, 2011). On the contrary, it is a profoundly social challenge. It demands long-term focused action from political and economic decision-makers, based on sound scientific insights, i.e. not merely action in response to events that have already occurred, such as the 2007 to 2009 global financial market crisis or the serious nuclear disaster in Fukushima, Japan, in 2011. It implies profound social innovations, starting with the prevalent 'mental maps' in politics, economy, and society (Leggewie and Welzer, 2009; Messner, 2011). An international policy failure with regard to the transformation, and particularly with regard to the prevention of unabated climate change, would inevitably result in a radical change of the global economy, and consequently a change of global politics – so the global community is facing some form of global upheaval in any case (WBGU, 2008; Leggewie and Welzer, 2009; Messner and Rahmstorf, 2009).

If the international political protagonists continue to cling to primarily asserting their unilateral interests, the global transformation will fail altogether, and there will be other impediments besides unabated progressive climate change preventing an international cooperation that is based on trust (Figure 5.3-1). In all probability, global environmental changes could then increasingly become a security-relevant matter, completely bypassing the underlying problems. Conversely, a comprehensive and credible international decarbonisation policy could not least serve as a confidence-building measure between the superpowers, and become one of the important pillars of a completely remodelled multilateralism in the coming years and decades (Bauer, 2009). Essentially, the global decarbonisation would become the disarmament diplomacy of the future (Figure 5.3-1).

The WBGU believes that there are four key starting points for progressing towards a global cooperation revolution despite the adverse global political conditions: overcoming the emerging power vacuum in international relations (Section 5.4.4.1); setting transformation-friendly priorities at the highest political level (Section 5.4.4.2); approaching the overriding objective of global fairness by establishing credibility, particularly on the part of the affluent industrialised countries (Section 5.4.4.3); and redesigning the institutional framework for multilateral political processes (Section 5.4.4.4).

5.4.4.1
Managing the International Power Vacuum

The international power vacuum associated with the trend towards the multipolar restructuring of global politics and the resultant barriers preventing intergovernmental cooperation must be overcome (Section 5.3.5). Geopolitical alliances, coupled with strong political leadership, can take on a defining role in this respect to progress towards the international policy quadrant of cooperative global governance in a decarbonised global economy (Figure 5.3-1).

The WBGU believes that a geopolitical strategy, using climate policy decidedly as the groundbreaking vehicle for establishing mutual trust between the global superpowers, and for the constructive development of global interdependence, serves best here (WBGU 2009b, 2010; Bauer, 2009; Messner, 2010). Subglobal alliances that display influential pioneering spirit in the relevant policy areas – such as forest policy or emissions trading – in the context of privileged geopolitical partnerships could become confident drivers of a sophisticated, cooperative multilateralism. In line with the model of the six core countries of the European Community, such alliances could gradually expand (Messner, 2010; WBGU, 2010b).

An approach such as this would particularly provide ambitious states willing to cooperate with the opportunity of reaching a pole position in the transformative innovation race beyond the G2 (China, USA), which take turns in blocking each other. Current research on common pool resources as the subject of international regimes and based on the example of climate policy reveals that at least four potentially advantageous situations can be construed from this at international level for the cooperating states (Keohane and Victor, 2010): (1) 'first-mover advantage' situation; (2) common pool resources co-benefits situation; (3) common pool resources benefits exclusion situation; and (4) small group reciprocity situation. Various different strategies are appropriate here, depending on incentive structure, to establish certain cooperation situations and action alliances (Bauer and Sommer, 2011).

The need for rapid global transformation means that the global community cannot sit back idly and wait until the USA and China have 'got it together' in a multipolar world order, so the European Union should seize the chance to form ambitious transformation alliances with key countries such as Brazil, India, Indonesia, Malaysia, Egypt or South Korea. As the WBGU has already demonstrated in the context of international climate policy, deforestation and its prevention, the modernisation of transformation-relevant systemic infrastructures in the energy and mobility sectors, and the expansion of the European Emissions Trading Scheme are all suitable issues to serve as a basis (WBGU, 2010b).

5.4.4.2
Transformative Prioritisation

The inertia of multilateral negotiation processes associated with the blockades described above must be overcome by accelerating global decision-making processes. The international community's reaction capability in response to the global financial crisis of 2008, and the impulses given by the G20 in this context are signals allowing a cautiously optimistic view where this is concerned (Berensmann et al., 2011). In the short term, the pressure to act in response to ecological and socioeconomic megatrends (Chapter 1) must be translated into political decisions with specific strategies for their implementation in the long-term. This needs clearly defined policy-based targets, an explicit timeframe, corresponding innovation efforts and prioritisation (Messner, 2010). However, this nevertheless assumes that these priorities are taken seriously, and not counteracted by diffidence in the light of supposed competitive disadvantages or other considerations with a short-term orientation.

In the 'Palais-Royal Initiative', eminent figures active in international finance and economic policy recently spoke out clearly in favour of such prioritisation on the part of heads of state and government, issuing a forceful reminder of the need to give the 'global interest' its own authoritative voice beyond parochial national interests (Camdessus et al., 2011; Köhler, 2011). Although this specific initiative may be limited to issues of international financial and monetary policy, the underlying logic of putting global system risks forward as an argument can still be generalised for global public goods: these urgently need legitimate and effective decision-making structures to provide a framework for 'global interest' advocates to be able to identify priorities for international action (Messner, et al., 2009; Camdessus, et al., 2011).

5.4.4.3
Credible Pursuit of Fairness

Overcoming the international power vacuum cooperatively and setting transformative priorities will be considerably easier to achieve if particularly the industrialised countries, as the main consumers of planetary resources to date, credibly fulfil their obligation towards the developing countries in this respect to allow fair burden sharing for the purpose of sustainable development (Section 7.3.9). In a world of extreme inequality, goods distribution is a central aspect of fairness; accordingly, the distribution of global goods is an integral element of the international discourse on the establishment of global fairness (Parks and Roberts, 2006; Roberts and Parks, 2007; Müller, 2008).

In the context of international climate policy, the WBGU developed its own proposal to combine political pragmatism with global fairness by means of emission rights trading (2009b). Assuming a global emissions budget, national emissions budgets can be allocated on a per capita basis (Box 1.1-1). Countries with high greenhouse gas emissions could therefore extend their remaining national emissions budgets by buying emission rights, whilst countries with low emissions would obtain financial resources and technologies for low-carbon development by selling some of their rights. This proposal rewards greenhouse gas efficiency and the establishment of low-carbon energy structures and infrastructures in developing countries (WBGU, 2009). The WBGU views this as an excellent opportunity for a fundamental restructuring of the cooperation relationships between industrialised and developing countries, particularly as the newly industrialising and developing countries also need to decarbonise their economic systems in the long term with respect to the global transformation towards sustainability (WBGU, 2009). The common vision agreed by the community of states in Cancún focuses on the principle of equitable access to sustainable development instead (UNFCCC, 2010).

Apart from the urgent demand to promptly translate such a vision into concrete action, the fulfilment of commitments already voiced – particularly on the part of the industrialised countries, for instance in the context of the Kyoto Protocol or the CBD – is an absolute imperative for the preservation, or restoration, of credibility. The rise of large newly industrialising countries such as China, India or Brazil is associated with substantial resource consumption. On the one hand, this demands continued differentiation in the discussion on distribution in the sense of 'common but differentiated responsibilities', which must extend beyond a subcomplex North-South dichotomy (Bauer and Richerzhagen, 2007). On the other hand, the fundamental obligation the industrialised countries hold towards the developing countries cannot legitimately be questioned in the context of global environmental change and global fairness.

The principle of credible burden sharing should accordingly also be applied to other policy areas, and should be accompanied by an appropriately generous transfer of financial resources or technologies to prove its credibility (Section 7.3). The breakthroughs in the long deadlocked multilateral negotiations on climate and biodiversity in 2010 show that this could well be one of the keys to success.

5.4.4.4
Improving International Cooperation Institutional Framework Conditions

In order to sustainably improve the preconditions for international cooperation for the purpose of global governance, it appears inevitable that substantial institutional changes must be made. For future global governance to be effective in terms of the transformation into a sustainable world society, the international community of states will need to take the planetary guard rails seriously, as they are the long-term parameters for multilateral cooperation across all sectors.

In spite of all its institutional deficiencies, the United Nations continue to provide an action framework that is fundamentally suitable for this, as the striving for a global transformation must include all countries, at least in the medium term. Exclusive alternative models such as the G20, for example, inevitably face restrictions in terms of achievability. Any country can potentially shift the significant parameters for global environmental change towards the planetary guard rails, and no superpower has the authority to prevent this (Bauer, 2009). The unlimited exploitation of atmospheric space through the emission of greenhouse gases is only the most prominent, but certainly not the only example of this (Chapter 1). In the long term, exclusivity would be as self-damaging as deliberate non-compliance – for example with regard to deforestation issues.

The extent to which the present hodgepodge of established and new multilateral processes and structures can have a catalytic effect on global consensus formation remains to be seen – it could transpire that G20 or transnational actor network models serve to accelerate decision-making processes within the UN, and inspire it with more unconventional ideas. Conversely, however, the formation of parallel structures could increase transaction costs, promote competitiveness and encourage institutional fragmentation, counteracting global political objectives. Evidently, it must be understood that in view of the realities of fragmented regime complexes, coordination must not be an end to its own means, to be used to enforce multiply attested 'synergies' or greater effectiveness by use of an organigram (Oberthür and Gehring, 2005; Biermann et al., 2009; Keohane and Victor, 2010; Zelli et al., 2010). Viewed from the perspective of a transformation logic, it is far more essential that the individual elements of complex governance regimes do not have an impeding effect on cooperation; ideally, they can reinforce each other for the purpose of 'polycentric' governance (Ostrom, 2010).

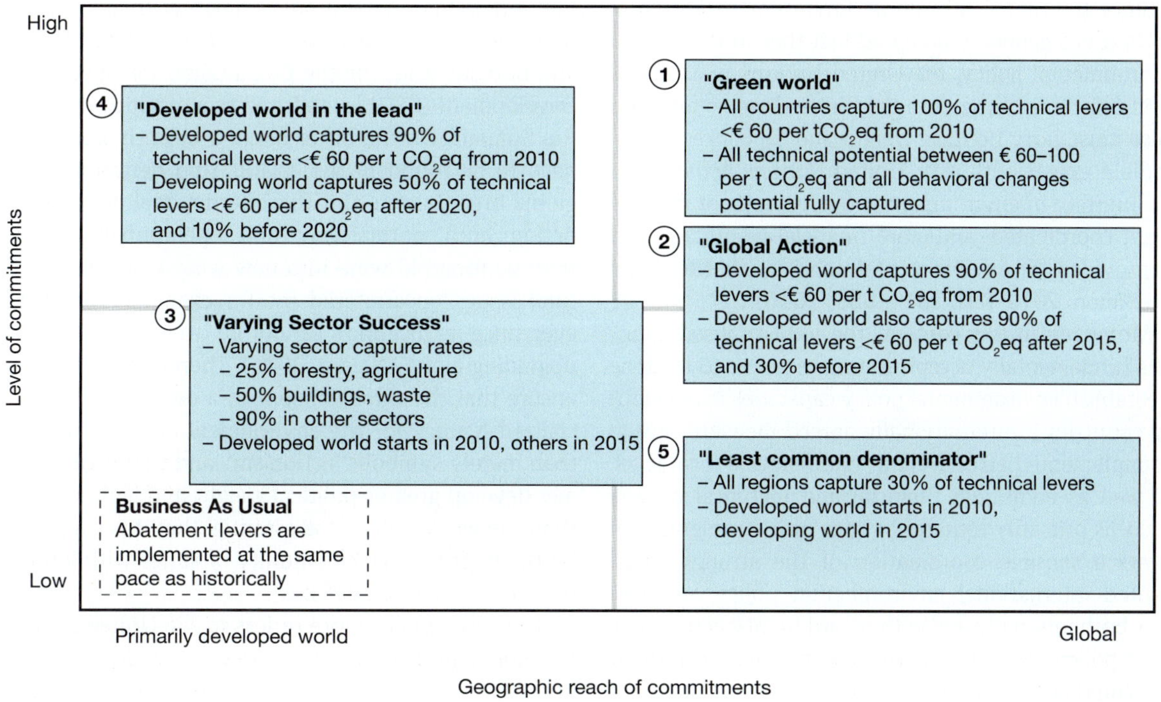

Figure 5.4-1
Integrated realisation scenarios 2010-2030. Only the scenarios 'Green World' and 'Global Action' would achieve emission paths with a high probability of compliance with the 2 °C guard rail as a consequence of drastic measures by industrialised and developing countries.
Source: McKinsey, 2009

Particularly the further developments in international climate policy have the potential to become both a testing ground and a gauge for global politics in coming years and decades. Initially only a hypothesis, global multipolarity has long become a reality in this context: without the cooperation of the USA, the EU, China and India, it will not be possible to restrict global warming to a level that is – just about – manageable. Numerous other countries – particularly the forest-rich developing countries in Latin America, Central Africa and Southern Asia – could also endanger the 2 °C guard rail by refusing to cooperate. Sooner rather than later, even poor developing countries must choose a low-carbon development path (Bauer, 2009; WBGU, 2009).

Analyses by the consultancy firm McKinsey (2009) also show that a 2 °C scenario can realistically be achieved only by means of global cooperation: of the climate policy scenarios summarised in Figure 5.4-1, only 'Green World' (1) and 'Global Action' (2) can still stop dangerous climate change – although they differentiate between industrialised and developing countries with regard to the relative importance of measures, they both require universal participation.

In international environmental policy, an elaborate, multilateral consultation process with the aim of institutional reforms is already in full swing. This momentum was triggered by the realisation, proven by the recurrent respective declarations of intent on the part of the member states, that the United Nations' capabilities for action are evidently not commensurate with those needed to solve obvious regional and global environmental problems, although the current process is closely linked to previous discussions on the ifs and buts of a more forceful international environmental governance (WBGU, 2001b; Bauer and Biermann, 2005).

Although the Cartagena Package agreed by the UNEP Governing Council in 2002 and the Bali Strategic Plan passed in 2005 represent considerable progress, also functioning as a benchmark to prove the seriousness of current reform efforts (Bauer, 2008; Simon, 2010), they still represent the incrementalism that characterises the United Nations. This incrementalism does not seem to be suitable for bringing about the profound institutional and procedural adjustments in the international environmental architecture needed to actually lend greater weight to international environmental policy actors in the complex web of interests that is global politics.

Since the Global Ministerial Environment Forum in 2010, it is a generally accepted fact that in the area of environmental policy, the United Nations must speak up in unison far more than they have done so far, their voice must carry political weight and be backed up by credible expert authority. United Nations activities at the interface of environment and development must be better coordinated, and more financial resources must be provided for environmental policy goals (Beisheim and Simon, 2010; IEG, 2010; IISD, 2010).

Moreover, in this context, the industrialised countries fundamentally accept that more needs to be done to establish environmental policy capacities in developing countries if internationally agreed measures are to be implemented effectively at national and local level. As well as additional financial and technical capacities, this primarily requires a range of instruments that allows a sensible coordination of the strongly fragmented international environmental policy architecture, both internally and with regard to interaction with other policy areas. One form this improved coordination could and should take is the targeted reduction of the 'multilateral travelling circus' (Munoz et al., 2009). The countless Conferences of the Parties, and the associated preparatory and working group meetings, not only overtax many developing countries in terms of human resources, they are consequently also de facto disadvantaged in concrete negotiation situations.

A corresponding reform of international environmental policy should pursue the replacement of the UN Environment Programme (UNEP) with a dedicated, newly to be established UN Specialised Agency for the environment with far-reaching competencies, or the transformation of the UNEP itself, for instance its expansion and upgrading to a key global organisation along the lines of the World Health Organisation (Section 7.3.10; Biermann, 2005). In the past, corresponding initiatives have regularly fizzled out, although they did ultimately not only succeed in gaining increased political attention, the debate also became more focused on the seriousness of the situation, and won the support of central actors such as the EU and Brazil (Simon, 2010). This becomes apparent not least through the particular emphasis on the development policy dimension of any potential environmental policy institutional reform.

As it is particularly the point where international environmental and development policy meet that highlight the difficulties of potential organisational reforms. On the one hand, these lie in the restructuring of the relationships between the proposed dedicated UN Specialized Agency for the environment and existing environmental policy institutions. They each have their own particular foundations under international law, particularly the Global Environment Facility (GEF), the various multilateral environmental treaty regimes with their own respective Conferences of the Parties and bureaucracies, or the Commission for Sustainable Development (CSD) established as a result of the 1992 Rio Summit. On the other hand, a balance would also have to be found in the relationship between a new global organisation and the international actors competing both normatively and operationally, rather than pouring old wine into new wineskins. The structural issues encountered by, for example, the UNEP ever since its inception cannot be overcome by formal upgrading alone (Najam, 2005). Therefore, in order to ensure that the establishment of a dedicated UN Specialized Agency for the environment amounts to more than merely symbolic 'actionism', and that it can actually develop greater political weight and legitimisation than the weak UNEP, it is essential that it is supported by the international community of states with a broad consensus (Simon, 2010).

This also applies more or less to the United Nations Development Group reform debate, which has also become bogged down by detailed incrementalism (Weinlich, 2011). Although the expansion of efficient and result-driven management approaches combined with UN-wide harmonised procedures along the lines of the 'Delivering As One' initiative do offer some interesting starting points, they cannot meet global governance requirements. Indeed, many donor countries seem to regard the United Nations as nothing more than a service provider for multilateral development cooperation (Weinlich, 2011).

The UN Conference on Sustainable Development (UNCSD, Rio+20 Conference) called for 2012 provides the United Nations with an excellent and timely opportunity to overcome the typical reform incrementalism in favour of radical institutional reforms. The thematic focus on the two key aspects of 'Green Economy in the Context of Sustainable Development and Poverty Eradication' and 'Institutional Framework for Sustainable Development' unanimously agreed by the international community suggests not least a desire for better programmatic and operational dovetailing of the United Nations' environmental and development policy activities (Section 7.3.10). If this were to succeed, the Conference could become an important milestone on the road to a comprehensive cooperative global governance architecture, without which the global transformation to sustainability cannot succeed.

5.4.5
Transformative Governance in the Three Transformation Fields

The transformation process in the transformation fields analysed, namely energy, urbanisation and land use, must be designed within the multilevel system. To date, any political decision-making has at best taken place at national and local level. It lacks the necessary political attention at international level, although a distinction must be drawn here between OECD and non-OECD countries. It appears to be the case in all three transformation fields that the necessary technologies, techniques and political instruments are already known; however, an international coordination process is required for the three fundamental infrastructures identified for a low-carbon world economy. To date, no global governance mechanisms exist for the establishment and rebuilding of these fundamental infrastructures to allow a course change towards a low-carbon economy and society by 2020. In all three transformation fields, international cooperation and coordination is called for in order to agree goals/targets, generate an enforcement of rules, and prevent freeriding. Through international cooperation, positive incentives could be provided in developing and newly industrialising countries to ensure that these are also in a position to implement a transformation policy.

5.4.5.1
Transformative Governance of the Energy System

Access to safe, clean and affordable energy for all people worldwide whilst also achieving decarbonisation are the global energy system of the 21st century's key challenges. Currently, more than 80% of global energy use continues to rely on environment and climate damaging fossil energy carriers. Almost 3 billion people still have no access to the basic necessities afforded by essential modern energy services. In order to transfer existing energy systems and meet the increasing energy demand in developing and newly industrialising countries, technological development paths must be fundamentally changed. Increasing energy efficiency substantially is vital, as is a massive expansion of renewable energies (Chapter 4).

Energy system tranformation towards low-carbon has gained in importance all over the world. For a long time, supply security and low prices (operative efficiency) were the foremost objectives of energy policy. This has changed in the light of dwindling oil resources (peak oil) and in the context of the global climate discourse (Prugh et al., 2005; Homer-Dixon, 2009; Sterner, 2010). There is now a global awareness that climate protection is one of the greatest challenges of energy policy (Scrace and MacKerron, 2009).

Nevertheless, there are still great barriers on the road to the transformation. The fossil energy carriers still available in large quantities, for example coal, which is also relatively cheap, make alternative energy paths seem expensive in comparison. High investment requirements impede the establishment of a sustainable energy infrastructure, particularly in newly industrialising and developing countries. As long as carbon dioxide does not have a sufficiently high price, there are few incentives to invest in relatively expensive zero-carbon technologies (Section 5.2). Multi-billion subsidies and interests established over decades also support the fossil-fuelled system (Sections 4.5, 5.3.1.2). Altering incentive systems to permit the establishment of a low-carbon, sustainable energy system therefore becomes one of the most important governance tasks for the transformation.

As elaborated in Chapter 4, there are basically sufficient sustainable renewable energy potentials to provide the whole world with energy (Section 4.1.5). From a technological point of view, a radical expansion of renewable energies could unlock sufficient renewable energy sources to cover the entire global energy demand by the middle of the century. Extensive decarbonisation of the energy systems is possible with various technology mixes, and it is achievable in a period that allows compliance with the 2 °C guard rail with a probability of around 50%. So there is nothing much to prevent a radical energy turnaround, from a technical perspective.

As illustrated in Section 5.2, the political instruments for implementation and acceleration are also already known. A CO_2 emissions trading scheme is already established in the EU, it could easily be expanded. Around the world, more than 50 countries, including numerous developing and newly industrialising countries, have already introduced feed-in tariffs for renewable energies (Box 5.2-4). There are also other established, proven instruments available, such as administrative command-and-control, taxation, tradable permits, and planning and market regulations to facilitate the introduction of a transformation process and its acceleration. The rapid and concurrent use of various different instruments can initiate the systemic and fundamental changes in the economy, and in society, towards transformation.

Energy Governance in a Globalised Multilevel System

In a globalised multilevel system, energy system governance involves many private sector actors, from individual energy consumers to powerful energy companies, and it is impacted in turn by complex market dynamics and geopolitical interests (Scrace and MacKerron, 2009). Whether and how the transformation can succeed does therefore not depend solely on energy policy. In the past, energy policy was perceived primarily as a task for nation states, not least because of the energy sector's strategic significance. The liberalisation of the energy sector, economic and technical interrelations between the states, the transnational consequences of energy use and, not least, the climate and development issue have led to a pronounced internationalisation of energy policy (WBGU, 2004).

However, the nation state remains a central political action level (Reiche, 2005; Giddens, 2009). National policies for the expansion of renewable energies and decarbonisation have been implemented in various countries, although they differ in weight. Certain newly industrialising countries, for example China and South Africa, are pursuing the expansion of renewable energies with great ambition (REN21, 2010; IEA, 2010c). However, with the exception of a few countries, for instance states with a high level of hydropower potential, the proportion of sustainable energy forms in the energy mix remains very low overall. Fossil portfolios continue to dominate. Whereas in essence, the financial and technical means for the transformation would actually be available to the industrialised countries, most developing and newly industrialising countries require financial and technical support in order to be able to sustainably establish or modernise their energy systems (Section 4.5). Such global cooperation is also needed to achieve international climate protection as cost-efficiently as possible (IEA, 2010c; World Bank, 2010b).

Regional approaches may act as a bridge between national and global solutions, and can facilitate the implementation of the global transformation and offer successful solutions for other (groups of) states. The EU could be a model for such regional cooperation to create a sustainable European energy market if it succeeds in deferring national interests for the benefit of an ambitious, common climate and energy strategy (Section 5.4.3).

Governance Deficit at Global Level

Climate protection and the establishment and transformation of energy systems can be successfully advanced only on the basis of effective cooperation (Section 7.3.9). Particularly in the energy sector, however, there are evidently blatant deficits with regard to governance at global level. There is a lack of the legal and institutional foundations required for an effective international energy policy for the transformation (WBGU, 2004; Steiner et al., 2006; Scrace and MacKerron, 2009). In contrast to international climate policy, where a central regime with rules and instruments (for instance the CDM) has slowly evolved and is now in place, global energy policy institutions are severely fragmented. Numerous UN organisations, multilateral financing institutions and other processes, mechanisms and treaties deal either directly or indirectly with the issue of energy, even though energy policy is not an actual key issue addressed by either the UN or a similarly comprehensive international organisation. The Commission for Sustainable Development's (CSD) Energy cycle (2006/2007) or UN-Energy, as the UN system's coordinating mechanism for energy, have so far succeeded only moderately in increasing the energy policy focus. It remains far removed from systematic institutionalisation (UN-Energy, 2010). An exception here is the International Atomic Energy Agency (IAEA), as an energy-related institution within the United Nations system with the mandate to promote the peaceful use of atomic energy.

At a global level, the link between energy and development policies has also long been neglected. With the establishment of the Advisory Group on Energy and Climate Change (AGECC) in 2009, a high level UN expert commission is finally focusing on the link between decarbonisation and the future provision of access to energy services in developing countries (AGECC, 2010). The Commission's recommendations, and an institutional upgrading of UN-Energy can contribute to strengthening the UN system's sustainable energy policy, and ranking the issue higher on the global agenda. Overall, a systematic linking of climate, energy and development agendas is urgently required (UNDP, 2007; Bauer, 2008; WBGU, 2010a).

An influential international energy institution does exist in the form of the International Energy Agency (IEA). However, membership, role and energy policy objectives leading towards sustainable energy have so far been restricted. As an OECD institution, it is perceived as an organisation that focuses on the interests of the industrialised countries – along the lines of OPEC, a group representing the interests of crude oil exporting countries. For many developing and newly industrialising countries, it is therefore a rather difficult partner to consider. Over the years, however, the organisation has built up relevance and credibility in global energy policy and with regard to the issue of decarbonisation, and has slowly become more open towards non-OECD countries (Lesage et al., 2010). This has led to the establishment of the 'Low Carbon Energy Technology Global Platform' in 2009, with the intention of strengthening global cooperation for the development of low-carbon technologies. The WBGU believes that this process of change and increased accessibility should be pursued further, and intensified.

The growing significance of renewable energies worldwide is reflected in the expansion of international initiatives in the UN context, within the framework of conferences (e.g. the Renewables series), network building (e.g. REN 21) and so on (Oberthür and Gehring, 2005; Sterner, 2010). With the founding of the International Renewable Energy Agency (IRENA) in 2009, a new international organisation was established, tasked with advising and supporting both industrialised and developing countries with regard to renewable energies introduction. Of the 149 signature states to date (including the EU), 65 have now ratified the founding treaty (as at March 2011). However, countries which are as central to global energy demand as China and Brazil are not among these. In future, once the initial problems have been overcome, IRENA can play an important role in the promotion and diffusion of renewable energies and the respective industries (Section 7.3.9). IRENA could then take on the important role of 'transition coach', particularly for the developing countries (Najam, 2010). Still, due to the current restrictions in terms of its mandate, the organisation is hardly in a position to advance a global transformation of energy systems. This would require an organisation which includes all energy systems and low-carbon energy options, as well as issues of energy efficiency on the demand side and systemic solutions, in the reform process. In the long term IRENA could nevertheless gradually develop into an international sustainable energy agency, as previously suggested by the WBGU (2003).

Important Role of Subglobal Alliances

Subglobal alliances increasingly play a leading role in the present multipolar system of global energy and climate governance (Lesage et al., 2009, 2010; Section 5.4.4). In terms of content, particularly the (extended) G8 have recently begun to intensively address the issue of energy and climate. In Gleneagles, under British presidency in 2005, and in 2006 under Russian presidency, a global debate on energy started that has since continued, also in the context of the G8 and the G5 dialogue process (Heiligendamm process; Lesage et al., 2009, 2010). Consequently, the Heiligendamm summit in 2007 became an important step on the way to international recognition of the 2 °C target (WBGU, 2007b), ultimately confirmed by the leading economic powers in 2009 in L'Aquila (Major Economies Forum on Energy and Climate, of which the G8 are also members; WBGU, 2009). The founding of the Global Bioenergy Partnership (GBEP) in 2005 to promote the use of bioenergy was also initiated by the G8. This was followed in 2008 by the International Partnership for Energy Efficiency Cooperation (IPEEC), which is open to non-OECD countries, despite its institutional affiliation with the IEA. The G20 states also decided the reform of fossil subsidies in 2009 in Pittsburgh (IEA et al., 2010a; Section 4.5).

The IEA, as the G8's preferred partner on energy issues besides the World Bank, has undergone a political upgrading. The G8 have so far not campaigned for a strengthening of the United Nations when it comes to energy issues, the promotion of renewable energies, or the expansion of the energy debate to include issues of sufficiency and lifestyles (Lesage et al., 2010). In the context of the G8, G8+5 and G20, progress has nevertheless certainly been made with regard to global energy governance. Because of its economic and international political weight as well as its relevance for global climate protection (the G20 are responsible for approx. 80 % of global greenhouse gas emissions), this alliance continues to play a major role as a driver for sustainable climate and energy policy (Lesage et al., 2010; Lindenthal, 2010).

5.4.5.2
Transformative Urbanisation Governance

In countries with rapid economic growth, particularly in Asia, a dynamic urbanisation trend can currently be observed (Chapter 1), with investments in non-sustainable infrastructures leading to lock-in effects. This can undermine the transformation towards a low-carbon society. This urbanisation trend is frequently market-driven through land and real estate speculation, it is very rarely governed (UNEP, 2011). In many cases, the energy supply is based on fossil fuels and priority is given to private transport, even though alternative technologies and, for example, low-carbon options for mobility would be available. This undesirable development can be counteracted only with various, already well-known political measures, particularly at local government level (Section 5.2). In many OECD countries, but also in Latin America, the low-carbon rebuilding of cities is required, calling for integrated and controlled urban development.

The UN defines urban governance as the sum of all possible measures by governmental and non-governmental actors to plan and manage the public affairs of a city (UN Habitat, 2002). Urban planning is the main instrument. It is at various development stages in industrialised, newly industrialising, and developing countries. Formal urban planning, which has traditionally pursued a top down approach, increasingly adopts more participative approaches (UN Habitat, 2009). Many cities, especially in the industrialised world, use management and formal planning systems to shape urbanisation. These need to be reorganised in order to reduce urban energy and material flows, and to ensure that further urbanisation takes the required transformation into account. Urban planning systems have also been developed in numerous transition and newly industrialising countries. The most obvious example is China, where the state is currently planning a number of new cities and districts. Low-carbon aspects, however, continue to play a minor role. Nevertheless, the Chinese government has started to recognise the importance of the issue, initiating a range of climate-friendly urbanisation programmes and projects (UN Habitat, 2010b).

In many developing countries, formal planning hardly exists. In such countries, planning capacities must first be built; and transformation aspects must be considered right from the outset. The planning processes must avoid path dependencies and lock-in effects, as these would block the low-carbon development of cities for decades. This applies particularly to infrastructure investments in the areas of energy generation and distribution, waste disposal, and mobility. In a range of cities in developing countries, climate protection measures – often embedded in the context of sustainable development – are already an issue in urban planning (UN Habitat, 2009). However, the vast majority of cities are still much further away from climate policy mainstreaming than cities in industrialised countries are.

The challenges in developing countries are a different set of problems; for a start, many urban administrations lack the finances, human resources and institutions required on all levels of government to successfully shaping urbanisation. The stronger integration of climate protection would therefore need to run parallel to the building of institutional capacities. Urbanisation in developing countries is characterised by the increasing migration from rural areas into cities (Africa has the world's highest rate of urbanisation), by a high population growth with a high proportion of adolescents and young adults, by a concentration of urban growth in peri-urban areas (just beyond the limits of local government planning competence), the extreme importance of informal urban economic sectors, and exploding land prices, as well as extensive social inequality, marginalisation, and the rapid growth of shanty towns (slums, favelas, bidonvilles). This is exacerbated by a lack of qualified urban planners and a civil society that has few options for action, and lacks the organisation often so important in planning issues. With respect to climate protection, there are frequently no local educational and administrative capacities with experience in these issues, or there are no climate protection strategies in place, or they are not being implemented (UN Habitat, 2009).

Planning as a Key Instrument

Two types of municipal level planning are relevant for climate protection: firstly, the development of climate protection concepts and strategies, and the use of urban planning as a superordinate management instrument (Masterplan; UN Habitat, 2009). Urban planning provides opportunities for climate protection by means of compact settlement structures, the careful selection of settlement locations, requirements for buildings and structures and the use of energy-saving construction methods, and traffic avoidance (EU COM, 2010a). Overall concepts of urban planning for low-carbon urban living can be developed, for example cities that are particularly compact, with short distances between home, work and leisure venues, to allow inner-city mobility largely by public transport (BMVBS, 2010a). The development of overall concepts must take participation and communication into account (Sections 5.4.1, 5.4.2, Chapter 6) to find acceptance, and convince particularly private actors and city dwellers (UN Habitat, 2009). Urban planning which integrates climate protection measures also requires cities to cooperate with their surrounding communities at a regional level. In many countries, however, there is still little evidence of cooperation between different municipalities. There is often no procedural framework for cooperation, and the interests of the individual communities or municipalities oppose each other. In Germany, the regions, or the administrative districts, are not in a particularly strong position, compared to the local authorities. In countries with the relevant legislation, however, intermunicipal planning takes place (for example Denmark; BMVBS, 2009a, b; EU COM, 2010a).

In Germany, the climate, as a protected public good, is already taken into account in the context of urban land-use planning in form of the environmental impact assessment. Climate protection has also been assigned increased importance in urban planning legislation (BMVBS, 2010a; BMVBS and Difu, 2010). The introduction of low-carbon urban development, the climate-friendly improvement of existing buildings, or low-carbon urban land use could be regulated here in future. Moreover, particularly in Germany, building regulations or the building law (Bauordnungsrecht) are an important instrument in urban planning legislation, as they contain concrete requirements for individual construction projects.

Embedding of Low-Carbon Urban Development in National and European Climate Protection Policy

In Europe, the implementation of local climate protection measures is generally legally embedded in national or, within the EU, in supranational law. One the one hand, this limits such measures, on the other, however, this circumstance supports them (Corfee-Morlot et al., 2009). In many cases, significant emission reductions decided at nation state or EU level can be achieved only through their implementation in cities, and local administration. It is also helpful for local authorities if there is a national climate policy in place, with set emission reduction targets for guidance. A national climate policy frequently also includes financial support for municipal low-carbon development objectives, or provides the space needed for experimenting with different strategies for a low-carbon city from which other cities can learn (Chapters 3, 6, Box 5.4-1).

However, it appears that to date, neither climate protection nor the integrated planning processes required for it are considered in urban planning processes to the extent they should be (Alber and Kern, 2008). Climate protection activities are primarily limited to membership of city networks, the adoption of objectives and the initiation of demonstration projects and information campaigns.

If integrated planning processes are implemented in Germany, they rarely relate to climate protection, and are usually linked to nationwide support measures. Similar conditions are indicated for other European cities, despite different legal premises (BMVBS, 2009a, b). National and international actors should fundamentally take into account that climate protection measures must largely be realised at the local level, but cannot be achieved with local capacities alone.

Urban Climate Protection in Practice

The issue of climate protection in cities is gaining in importance at a global level, as not least expressed by numerous city partnerships, local government projects, the formulation of city-specific climate protection targets, and city networks. Around the world, there are many cities with a commitment to specific climate protection targets, such as the goal of general reduction of greenhouse gas emissions (Hamburg, Kitakyushu), the reduction of greenhouse gas emissions per capita, the aim of carbon neutrality (Austin, Vancouver), the target of using exclusively non-fossil fuels (Växjö, Stockholm), or the general goal of sustainable development (Freiburg im Breisgau, Dubai; IEA and OECD, 2009).

In addition to general climate targets, many cities have also set themselves sectoral targets for the promotion of renewable energies, for example the goal of achieving a certain proportion of renewable electricity (Adelaide, Taipei) or the target of generating a certain proportion of thermal heat or cooling on a renewable basis (Beijing, Tokyo). Other sectoral targets include, for instance, increasing the proportion of biofuels in the transport sector (Betim, Stockholm) or the proportion of electric vehicles (Oslo). Such energy targets are also set for public buildings (such as government buildings: Leicester, Toronto; IEA and OECD, 2009).

Further Governance Mechanisms

The remit of cities and communities (local authorities) generally includes self-government and the carrying out of delegated state functions. Self-government can generally be divided into compulsory and voluntary matters, although local authorities are in principle subject to the general laws.

With respect to the transformation process towards a low-carbon society, there are also other concrete action fields at city-level besides low-carbon urban planning: (1) energy management and investments in energy efficiency; (2) investments in renewable energy sources and in combined heat and power; (3) environmentally friendly transport development; (4) climate-friendly buildings; (5) inter-municipal cooperation, environmentally friendly local procurement practices and waste avoidance; (6) public relations and advice.

Four different types of policy can be resorted to for these action fields (IEA and OECD, 2009): (1) governing by leadership – whereby cities or local authorities voluntarily set themselves climate protection targets and develop climate protection strategies; (2) self-governance – a local authority decides to supply public buildings with electricity from renewable energies, it forms voluntary agreements with private companies for low-carbon investment projects; (3) governance through enabling – promotion of low-carbon technologies through public procurement, e.g. in the transport sector, support of private sector actors, reviving local Agenda 21 processes; (4) governing by provision – this includes financial incentive systems at the local level, such as tax allowances to encourage low-carbon investments, or city centre parking charges to facilitate traffic management; (4) governing through authority – classical administrative command-and-control and regulations (Table 5.2-1).

Low-Carbon Urban Development and Global Discourse

The global urbanisation trend is also increasingly the subject of international debate, promoting awareness of the need for a sustainable global development. Important foundations and guidelines for concept and planning procedures are established on the one hand through the international debate in a United Nations context (UN Habitat, Human Settlement Conference Habitat II 1996), and in a relevant professional associations context (such as the International Society of City and Regional Planners) and on the other hand in the context of the Sustainable Buildings Network, which is supported by the G8 and newly industrialising countries to promote sustainable construction, and through the production of global assessment reports dealing with urbanisation (such as 'Cities and Climate Change'; OECD, 2010d). Overall, however, the issue of urbanisation has not yet reached a level of importance in the international climate and transformation debate that would be commensurate with its significance for climate protection. The urbanisation issue must therefore urgently be upgraded in the global governance system. Efforts should be made here to develop the UN Habitat programme further into a new organisation for sustainable urban development. Moreover, the founding of a 'World Commission on Low-Carbon Urban Planning' would lay the foundations for a sustainable global urbanisation process. At the same time, cities and local authorities should establish networks and partnerships to exchange information at an international level in order to learn from each other, and to develop specific solutions (Section 7.3.6).

5.4.5.3
Transformative Land-Use Governance

The transformation towards a low-carbon society also demands a radical change in land use and land-use systems, as almost a quarter of worldwide greenhouse gas emissions are a direct result of agriculture and land-use changes, particularly deforestation in the tropics (Section 4.1.7). However, land-use systems can never become completely zero-carbon, neither technologically nor through changes in behaviour. Moreover, in this transformation field, the ultimate goal of becoming a low-carbon society is superseded by other political goals – such as, in particular, guaranteeing food security, rural development, conservation of biodiversity and ecosystem services. A policy which addresses climate protection only would therefore fall short of these goals (WBGU, 2010a).

Land use has so far been internationally driven by the various sectoral markets (forestry, agriculture, energy and commodity markets) and national policies (WBGU, 2010a; UNEP, 2011). Competition exists – from a national and a global perspective – between the various uses, such as forests, agriculture, urbanisation, mining, infrastructures (e.g. energy, transport) and nature conservation (EEA, 2010b). In forested areas, competing land uses are deforestation of primary forests for agricultural production or forest plantations, as well as mining, or exploration of abiotic resources, timber exploitation and the conservation of ecosystem services. In the agricultural sector, competition exists between the cultivation of foodstuffs and feeds, energy and industrial plants, and pasture land. Land-use competition within this sector is also increasingly affected by a rising global population, growing wealth and the changes in eating habits and lifestyles associated with it, and changes in the energy basis. The land-use competition outlined here will intensify as a result of the effects of climate change once the local and global usable land diminishes, and the productivity of the land farmed declines (Section 1.2.5).

The transformation towards a low-carbon society could also intensify this land-use competition in future. The current technologies for generating bioenergy, or for energy generation by means of photovoltaics or wind power, and their associated infrastructures such as networks and storage facilities, for example, require additional land if selected fossil fuels are to be replaced with renewable energies. Even if deforestation were also stopped, and reforestation were promoted in certain locations, and agricultural production methods did become more climate-friendly, land-use conflicts could still continue (WBGU, 2010a; UNEP, 2011).

Current Trends

This transformation field and its multi-faceted conflicting aims have so far not been adequately addressed in all their complexity at either national or European, or indeed global level. This is a consequence of both the fragmentation of the different policy areas such as climate, agriculture and forestry, development, energy or environment at national and European level, and the institutional fragmentation at international level, where those tasked with addressing land-use issues include the FAO, UNEP, the World Bank, the UNFCCC, CBD and the UNCCD (UNEP, 2011). Moreover, the growing global challenge of sustainable land use has so far not been addressed in the international governance processes organised by these institutions. For this reason alone, cooperation on global land-use issues at the points where the respective organisations overlap must be increased, especially in the three Rio Conventions (Chapter 1, Section 7.3).

In the two major land uses forest and agriculture, the issues of climate protection and the transformation of land-use systems are accorded different levels of importance on the international agenda. Where climate protection is concerned, there are instruments and mechanisms to initiate and support the transformation in forest management at both national and international level. The greatest problem often lies in the lack of political and institutional capacities, and the inadequate enforcement of a sustainable forest policy (IUFRO, 2010). The transformation towards climate-friendlyness is only gradually gaining focus in the agricultural sector (UNEP, 2011; GO Science, 2011).

In principle, both the technologies and the techniques, as well as the political instruments, needed for the transformation towards climate-friendly land use are known with respect to all of the various land uses. However, they are not applied to their full extent because, quite apart from different governance structures, the political priorities in industrialised and developing countries also differ considerably. The agriculture and forestry sectors contribute 25% and more to the gross domestic product in the developing countries, and a mere 1% in the industrial countries (UNEP, 2011).

Governance for Land-Use Competition

In most industrialised countries, the instrument of spatial and land-use planning has been developed in order to balance land-use competition and take conflicting political objectives into account (Section 5.2). Spatial planning aims to coordinate political measures and economic activities related to land use in a specific region affecting its spatial development or function (i. e. measures relevant to spatial planning). For this purpose, a comprehensive plan is developed, taking into account the various different land uses and coordinating them with each other, balancing potential conflicts and ensuring that future uses allow, for example, the consideration of alternative locations and uses (Koch and Hendler, 2009).

The advantage of spatial planning over the approval of individual projects is that an amount of space is examined as a whole, with all its functions and uses, which also allows a long-term perspective with regard to regional development objectives, establishing these firmly and aiding the preparation of their implementation. Spatial planning can therefore guarantee the development and securing of an entire region even before specific projects are planned and realised, thereby ensuring sustainable land use at an early stage. The climate protection targets stipulated by a climate protection act, for example, can also simultaneously serve as regional planning objectives, thereby becoming an issue to be taken into account at administrative planning level (draft for a climate protection act, German state government of North Rhine-Westphalia, 22/02/2011, and draft of a first act for implementation of the climate protection act, German state government of North Rhine-Westphalia, 22/02/2011). For measures relevant to spatial planning, such as coal-fuelled power stations, approval would not be given due to the objective of climate protection.

Moreover, where there is an increased focus on climate protection issues and its associated risks, regional planning has proved itself to be a suitable instrument for dealing with the impacts of climate change, avoiding and mitigating climate change, and establishing cost-effective adaptation measures (EU COM, 2008d; Haber et al., 2010). Spatial planning could therefore also include measures to secure carbon storage and sinks, as well as low-carbon settlement development and adaptation measures for disaster prevention (Haber et al., 2010). An obligation to consider administrative plans at different levels prevents one-sided regional planning from one perspective only, as the different administrative levels have to be coordinated. In Germany, this obligation to consider results from the so-called principle of countervailing influence (§1 Section 3 Regional Planning Act), which, as an established element of regional planning law, regulates the mutually interdependent relationship between spatial planning for an entire area, and local planning for parts of this area (Spannowsky et al., 2010).

The instrument of spatial planning to allow the management of sustainable land use is increasingly also being discussed at an international level, as it allows the systemic and targeted linking of measures from various sectors (forestry, agriculture, energy, etc.). The aim is more efficient and sustainable land-use management through harmonisation of the various usage entitlements, but also through multi-faceted use to maintain multiple spatial services (Green et al., 2005). The WBGU therefore reaffirms its previous recommendation of establishing a new 'Global Commission for Sustainable Land Use' in order to identify the most important challenges of the range of issues related to global land use. It should determine the current state of scientific knowledge regarding global land use, and develop the foundations, mechanisms and guidelines needed for global land-use management. It should also examine how the instrument of spatial planning could be developed further for developing countries, and how it could be used at a European and global level for land-use management (WBGU, 2010a; Section 7.3.7).

Transformative Forest Governance

In the forest management sector, there is a consensus on the necessity of stopping emissions from deforestation and destructive forest use. The focus is here on the strategic expansion and maintenance of forests as carbon stores and sinks. However, the action fields for the transformative governance process go beyond the narrow focus of climate-friendly forest use. They include: (1) protecting the last primeval forests; (2) stopping deforestation and destructive forest use; (3) promoting sustainable forest management; (4) reforestation in certain locations; (5) protecting peatlands and wetlands; (6) agroforestry; (7) a certification scheme for forest management and forest products; (8) intelligent timber use.

The governance capacities, investment resources and technologies for the implementation of the relevant political measures are often lacking in these action fields, particularly in countries with rain forests. Existing national incentive structures need to be reviewed to create incentives for forest protection and sustainable, multifunctional forest management. These include the removal of distorting subsidies and export supporting strategies for timber and other agricultural products as well as payment for ecosystem services, forestry standards and a certification scheme, and land reforms to give incentives for sustainable management through property rights. The expansion and monitoring of conservation areas and the labelling of timber products also play an important role. Such a policy must be embedded in other land-use policies, particularly those pertaining to agriculture (UNEP, 2011).

The concept of payments for ecosystem services compensates the providers of certain ecosystem services, such as carbon sequestration, water cycle regulation, soil formation or primary production and creates economic incentives for ensuring their long-term provision (Section 5.2.3; Wunder, 2005). One such programme, for example, is Pagos por Servicios Ambientales, established in Costa Rica in 1997, whereby landowners receive payments for the provision of forest ecosystem services. The remarkable aspect of this system is that private beneficiaries of these services also make direct, voluntary payments. Beneficiaries are, for example, hydroelectric power stations, which are dependent on the regulation of the water cycle in their catchment areas. The system therefore goes beyond pure public subsidies for the provision of ecosystem services. Both the Millennium Ecosystem Assessment and the TEEB study use the concept of payments for environmental services to assess the value people attach to ecosystems, in order to develop price signals which will, in the long term, give incentives for sustainable development (MA, 2005a, b, c; TEBB, 2010).

In the forestry sector, the development and introduction of an instrument for forest protection in developing countries (REDD-plus) is being advanced at an international level as an element of UNFCCC negotiations. Specific aim is the establishment of policies and incentives to reduce emissions from deforestation and destructive forest use. This also includes the action fields of forest conservation, sustainable forest management, and the strategic expansion of carbon stocks in forests, as well as reforestation in certain locations.

In addition, various other sustainability and development dimensions must be taken into account, such as the conservation of natural forests and biodiversity, involving local and indigenous peoples, and respecting their rights. Vital is the development of a long-term international financing mechanism under the UNFCCC for the various political measures (Section 7.3.7). In the meantime, all signatory states are being encouraged to step up their current CO_2 emission reduction efforts, and to take or co-finance preparatory measures for a future REDD-plus regime, for example the collection of data, the establishment of monitoring systems, carrying out pilot projects, and the development of minimum social and ecological standards.

Transformative Agriculture Governance

The issue of climate protection in agriculture is becoming increasingly important around the world, a fact confirmed by its discussion both under UNFCCC, FAO and UNEP and within the EU, and through processes such as the IAASTD (EU COM, 2007c; IAASTD, 2009; UNEP, 2011). Global agriculture must meet the expected rapid growth in demand for food, bioenergy and biomass for industrial use in a sustainable manner, and at the same time significantly reduce greenhouse gas emissions, without making new land available through deforestation. As yet, there is no broad scientific or political consensus on which strategies are best suited to solving this global challenge (Section 7.3.7).

Around half of global greenhouse gas emissions from agriculture can be avoided by improved carbon sequestration in the soil, and a reduction of CH_4 and N_2O emissions from agriculture. The techniques and technologies required on the production side, and the necessary changes in behaviour on the consumer side, are known, but as yet they do not represent a political consensus.

The existing incentive structures with regard to the international trade in agricultural products and the subsidising of export products or agriculture in the industrialised countries must be reformed as soon as possible to create incentive structures for sustainable, climate-friendly agriculture (SRU, 2008). This also includes land reforms in developing countries in order to create incentives for both sustainable land management and investments in new agricultural techniques and technologies through property rights (UNEP, 2011). A rural, agrarian infrastructure must be established, particularly in developing countries, including the promotion of market access (UNEP, 2011; GO Science, 2011). Investments such as these can be supported by official development assistance through the organisations FAO, IFAD and the World Bank, but also bilaterally; Germany and the EU should take the initiative here.

However, particularly the increased use of bioenergy in the course of the transformation is also accompanied by significant risks with regard to various sustainability dimensions (WBGU, 2010a; Box 4.1-4). The establishment of an international regulatory framework for sustainable bioenergy use is an urgent requirement in order to have some control over the direct and indirect impacts of bioenergy on land-use competition. This regulatory framework should encompass minimum standards for sustainable bioenergy production and an international bioenergy strategy.

As in the forestry sector, it would make sense to pay for ecosystem services and climate protection measures in the agricultural sector (Section 5.2.3). The present EU subsidies in the agricultural sector should therefore be carried over into a system of payments for ecosystem services (SRU, 2008; Section 7.3.7). Concurrently, the conclusion of the Doha Round in the context of WTO negotiations on the liberalisation of the global agricultural trade needs to be accelerated. The industrialised countries would then need to reduce their import barriers for agricultural products, and phase out their own export subsidies (SRU, 2008; WBGU, 2010a).

To encourage changes on the demand side, it is important to promote climate-friendly eating habits. Increasing global wealth is accompanied by a rising demand for animal products. This is counterproductive in two respects: firstly, the expansion of livestock keeping exacerbates land-use competition in the agricultural sector and secondly, it leads to increasing greenhouse gas emissions. At the same time, eating a low-meat diet is sensible under the primacy of healthy nutrition (Section 7.3.7). Product labelling, information campaigns and government procurement policies can generate important impulses for changes in behaviour in this respect (Section 5.2.3). Taxation of foodstuffs according to emissions intensity may also provide an additional incentive to change behaviours (Section 7.3.7).

International Cooperation

The challenges in the transformation field land use must be met primarily with the aid of local, regional and national policy-making. As this transformation field is closed linked to economic development, above all in developing and newly industrialising countries, international coordination and cooperation is required to develop and finance the necessary governance structures (Sections 7.3.7, 7.3.10). A ,Global Commission for Sustainable Land Use' should be established, but the present relevant international organisations, such as particularly the FAO, should also be mandated accordingly. The FAO, for example, should develop a suitable range of instruments to ensure the climate-friendliness of national and global land-use paths. At the same time, land-use relevant decision processes, specifically those contained in the three Rio conventions UNFCCC, CBD and UNCCD, should be better linked. In addition, UNEP should be strengthened in order to systematically advance a sustainable and integrated land-use approach under the United Nations (Section 7.3.10).

5.4.5.4 Global Governance for Infrastructure Development

Low-carbon development processes must be accelerated globally in numerous economic sectors. Three fundamental infrastructures are central here (Section 7.1.1): energy systems, urbanisation and land-use systems. Compliance with the 2 °C guard rail is only possible if the course is changed towards low-carbon in all three of these fundamental structures of the global economy by 2020 (Section 7.3.10).

This is a completely new challenge for the international community. So far, the development of infrastructure systems in the three transformation fields of energy, urbanisation and land use has been viewed almost exclusively as a national political task, supported by international development policy only in the case of developing countries. Accordingly, the global governance mechanisms that do exist are not adequate enough to adjust these infrastructures at a global level, and accelerate the transformation towards low-carbon. As compliance with the 2 °C guard rail allows only a limited time window for the transformation, i. e. the crux of the matter is accelerated change, and a transformation which must take place at the same time all over the world in order to make it at all possible to achieve the required reduction in the volume of greenhouse gas emissions (WBGU, 2009). Global agreement processes and coordination mechanisms are essential.

The 2010 euro crisis showed that a common currency also requires the close coordination of the EU member states' economic policies, i.e. mechanisms for reciprocal adjustment, control and binding rules ('economic government') in order to avoid any freeriding behaviour on the part of individual nation states. Similarly, a rapid decarbonisation of the global economy's key infrastructures is also not likely to succeed without international coordination processes. There is nothing to indicate that the sum of the uncoordinated transformation efforts in the nation states in the three fields requiring action will, more or less by default, result in the decarbonisation level that is needed to avoid dangerous climate change. This is not a plea for global infrastructure planning. On the contrary, concrete future infrastructure development will continue to take place in the nation states (or regionally, for instance within the EU), but it must happen within a guard rail system that is compatible with the 2 °C guard rail. In all three transformation fields, the focus should now be on:

- The establishment of global transformation goals;
- The development of verifiable national and international transformation roadmaps;
- The definition of indicators to serve as a basis for monitoring development progress;

- The establishment of reporting and monitoring processes;
- And the creation of positive incentives for goal achievement (for example technology transfer).

These kind of global governance mechanisms can only be implemented by effective international organisations. The WTO, for instance, is a strong international organisation for the protection and further development of the global trade system. Based on the experiences made during the global financial crisis (2007–2009), the International Monetary Fund should be expanded into a risk management centre for the global financial market. All three transformation fields lack such strong organisations.

In the transformation field energy, there is no legitimised and internationally effective global energy organisation that could become a driver of the transformation towards low-carbon. The IEA is an organisation by OECD countries. It needs to focus more intensively on the goal of a sustainable energy system, and it must be opened up to developing and newly industrialising countries. IRENA is an organisation which will hopefully contribute to the diffusion of renewable energies, but it is still under development, and its role would need to be strengthened if it is to make an effective contribution to the transformation. Within the United Nations architecture, UN-Energy has only limited capacity for action. The global governance capacities in the area of energy are therefore fragmented, and as yet not in a position to become the drivers of the transformation of the worldwide energy systems (Section 7.3.9).

A similar picture emerges with regard to land use. In the coming years, foodstuffs and feed production and the production of biomass for the energy and industrial sectors will need to be significantly increased, whilst the emissions from land use (agriculture, deforestation) must be reduced. Again, the global governance structures required to achieve this are non-existent. Although the FAO does carry out important fundamental work on possible options for increasing global agricultural production, and the data it provides represents an indispensable contribution to the analysis of global land-use trends, the organisation's activities and spectrum of activities are not sufficient to significantly advance the global transformation towards climate-friendly, sustainable land use. The situation is similar in international forest protection: forest protection efforts by the CBD and the UNFCCC exist, but again, there are no recognisable sweeping successes. The WBGU has therefore also identified an urgent need for institutional improvement in this global policy field, for example – as already recommended by the WBGU (2009a) – the establishment of a 'Global Commission for Sustainable Land Use' (Section 7.3.7.1). It should develop new strategies for climate-friendly, sustainable land use. On the strength of this assessment by such a 'Global Commission for Sustainable Land Use', the FAO should ultimately develop a suitable range of instruments to ensure that national and global land-use paths are climate-friendly.

The institutional capacities in the transformation field urbanisation are even fewer, by comparison. The UN Habitat programme enjoys very limited visibility and importance in international politics. Moreover, UN Habitat views urbanisation from the (still relevant) perspective of how to deal with the slums that are the result of rural flight. The huge challenge a low-carbon development of the coming decades' urbanisation wave represents, on the other hand, is hardly addressed. The urbanisation issue must therefore urgently be upgraded in the global governance system. Efforts should be made here to incorporate the UN Habitat programme, which is not adequately equipped to deal with this acute problem, in a new specialised agency (Section 7.3.6). The WBGU therefore recommends the foundation of an ambitiously mandated specialised agency for sustainable urbanisation. If this is not possible in the short term, an attempt should initially be made to strengthen UN Habitat's standard setting role, and to increase the programme's focus on sustainability and climate protection. In the transformation field urbanisation, the establishment of a 'World Commission on Climate-Friendly Urban Planning' would again lay the foundations for guiding global urbanisation processes towards sustainability (Section 7.3.6).

Both commissions (Land use and Urbanisation) could, for example, be set up and mandated on the occasion of the Rio+20 conference. They should then proceed to present comprehensive reports by 2015, taking the corresponding complexity of their respective transformation fields into account (Section 7.3.10).

5.5 Conclusion

This chapter has made it clear that the required transformation process towards a low-carbon society represents a huge political challenge, even though the individual political instruments for the systematic transformation of economy and society are known, and some have been tried and tested. In this respect, the WBGU mainly views CO_2 pricing, the phasing out of subsidies for fossil fuels, and the worldwide diffusion of feed-in tariffs as central elements of a transformation policy. However, the analysis has also shown that political, institutional and economic path dependencies, interest structures and veto players impede the transition towards sustainability-focused policy-making. The issue is therefore not primarily a lack of instruments, concepts and ideas; the transformation is held back through the political process itself. The central question is therefore: how can these difficult reforms be initiated, in view of interest-driven blockades, in part also self-imposed by democratic procedure?

The WBGU concludes that the key to the transformation lies in a new form of statehood. Central element is a proactive and enabling state which actively sets priorities whilst also offering its citizens increased opportunities for participation, and affords the economy choices with regard to acting with sustainability in mind. New problematic situations call for a different kind of policy-making which takes on the challenge of the transformation through greater political self-commitment in the form of strict rules. It must create a new regulation framework, which society and the economy could and should adhere to. This set of rules encompasses a national climate protection objective, a stringent climate protection law that takes a long-term perspective, and climate policy mainstreaming of government institutions; it underlines the credibility of political agendas, establishes the scope for action (or for interpretation), reduces the influence of particular interests, and creates long-term planning horizons, thereby accelerating the transformation process.

This increased action capacity on part of the state must be inextricably linked to active citizenship. The civil society must help to shape the transformation process, as it sets the transformation in motion and gives it the requisite legitimacy (Chapter 6). By means of improved opportunities for information, participation and legal protection, such as the labelling of products, reformed approval procedures, extended collective legal action, the use of ombudspersons, the extension of deliberative processes into a 'future chamber' to complement the legislative, an open and participative transformation process should be achieved (for citizens and citizen consumers). The WBGU therefore concludes that the transformation needs more, rather than less, democracy.

National – and in part also sub-national – statehood continues to play a central role in the development of a transformation policy, in the reorganisation of the (energy) markets, the support of new technologies, and the restructuring of cities. However, this chapter also illustrates that global problems require a global policy, and therefore supra- and transnational solutions. As a bridge between national and global solutions, the EU is a model for this which should be developed further. The EU and similar regional alliances of states can, however, not replace the degree of global cooperation and coordination that is needed for a global transformation. In this respect, the analysis shows that there are still great deficits, particularly on the level of global policy-making, which need to be addressed as a matter of urgency. This applies in particular to the key transformation fields energy, urbanisation and land use. The issue here is that these policy areas need to be accorded far more weight at a global level; new institutions for global infrastructure development need to be developed, and a multilateralism that takes into account the new, multipolar world in order to develop and enforce transformative policies, from the level of subglobal change agent alliances to the entire international community of states.

Agents of Transformation: How Innovations Can Spread (Faster)

6

6.1 From Awareness to Action? – From Action to Awareness!

A consensus that 'something must be done' to prevent dangerous climate change, the loss of biodiversity, or the collapse of the global financial markets, is reached quickly, both at world climate conferences and during dinner table conversations. 'We' have a fairly good idea of what should be done; at least some of 'us' would also be prepared to give up 'our' habitual lifestyles. 'We' do have efficient technologies available to us, and 'we' have issued global declarations on preventing dangerous climate change and conserving biological diversity in international framework agreements, and passed policies at supranational, national and regional level. And still 'we' will fail, if this is as far as it goes. The difficulties lie in turning awareness into action, as path dependencies, barriers to innovation, and institutional routines (Section 2.4) stand in the way of the insights already gained, and paralyse the impulse to act.

At first glance, the transformation into a low-carbon society is one of those Herculean tasks which seem unsolvable at the outset: targets which are too ambitious, too few actors to achieve them, in too short a timescale. Perceptions such as these, and problematic global framework conditions, frequently lead to resignation and apathy. So the crux of the matter is defining concrete targets and interim targets for solving these global problems, to implement the realisation of these targets sensibly and to share the workload fairly, and to set priorities and draw up realistic timetables. The tight window for the avoidance of dangerous climate change (Chapter 1) must be met with prioritisation and acceleration. To succeed, the currently existing mental 'willingness' (Chapter 2) must be stimulated, thematically charged, and turned into action through the establishment of a network of actors – by a proactive state (Section 5.4.1). A historical review of great upheavals (Chapter 3) shows that time and again, there have been historical situations in which individuals or small groups have rebelled against the 'terrible fatalism of history' (Georg Büchner), to achieve that which seemed almost impossible, thus becoming change agents. The history of civil enlightenment and revolutions is as much proof of this as the colonies' fight for independence, symbolised by the peaceful resistance practised by Mahatma Gandhi and Nelson Mandela, and the Velvet Revolution in the Eastern European countries and the GDR, brought about by people like Lech Walesa and Bärbel Bohley, not forgetting Willy Brandt and Mikhail Gorbachev.

The above mentioned, diffuse 'we' must therefore be concretised, and shaped into local and supra-local task forces with the ability to communicate recommendations for action efficiently, and to secure them in effective identity structures ('we-feelings'). What is lacking both at a global and a national level is an awareness of the self-efficacy, and the realisation of the power that actors such as these have; people who are already, whether consciously or unconsciously, participators in the transformation. Governmental and non-governmental organisations must not only extend their scope for action (Chapter 5); they must above all create structures and networks that allow the swift and permanent mobilisation of actors who are committed to transformative objectives.

The structural preconditions for the conversion of such dispositions into action were elaborated in Chapter 3 on the basis of historical examples. The following chapter deals with how, and by which actors, a process such as this – difficult to predict and difficult to plan – can be initiated, shaped and supported. In the WBGU's view, turning awareness into requisite action cannot succeed through knowledge transfer, but also includes participative dimensions and feedback. Knowledge is nothing without those who know, and knowledge is disseminated only through actors: a transformation process is bound to fail if the 'experts' rely on the self-evidence of the reasonableness of their suggestions, arrived at after much theoretical debate, and then (hope to) motivate 'laymen' with information campaigns and incentive systems to accept the relevant measures after the event. As far as climate protection and adaptation, and 'even', ultimately, the creation of acceptance are concerned, it is probable that, according to participation and innovation research findings, policies and social movements that rely on early consultation (deliberation) of those concerned, and their active participation, to legitimise political-administrative measures (Walk, 2007; Schaal and Ritzi, 2009; Kristof, 2010) would be more successful than any attempts by political-administrative institutions. Technological innovations and political-legal steering must find a mobilised citizenship to fully develop their problem solving potential; this applies in 'normal' times, but even more so in escalating crisis situations, and in view of the time pressure due to the crisis of Earth system. This is the challenge for 21st century democratic policies (Leggewie, 2010).

There are plenty of examples of rapid cultural and social innovations, including changes to lifestyles, value systems and knowledge preferences. This includes the proliferation of Cistercian monasteries in the 12th century (Grübler, 1997), as well as the remarkable extent and qualities of the civil rights movements at the end of the 20th century (Evers and Zimmer, 2010). This will be examined in more detail later. These and other examples show that frequently, individual and collective innovation processes are triggered less by existing cognitive knowledge, and more by a need for reforms and change motivated by the immediate environment, communicated and/or implemented exploratively and experimentally (Epstein, 1994). A prime example to demonstrate this shift from experimental-explorative action to cognitive realisation is the worldwide women's movement post-1945. Its agenda (unlike that of the previous women's movements in the 19th and early 20th century) was initially 'tried and tested' by small, manageable groups in social niches whose words and actions defied convention. Political organisation on a grander scale took place only afterwards. The result of these explorations and experiments has been a change of collective practices within modern societies, reaching from equal opportunity laws and gender-neutral language to the integration of women in traditionally male domains like the military, major corporations, and political leadership.

The same applies to the environmental conservation movement. Through decentralised citizen's initiatives and demonstrations, it has defined and changed the face of the Federal Republic of Germany, Western Europe as a whole, and other OECD countries for good in terms of environmental consciousness and policies. Apart from the sudden, shocking realisation that the 'blue planet' is in danger, the impulse to change has gained momentum through personal experience of environmental damage locally (such as the pollution of rivers), although more abstract accounts, such as The Limits to Growth (Meadows et al., 1972), that deal with 'the bigger picture' have also managed to trigger impulses to change, albeit indirectly. Knowledge regimes such as these have been able to make a major contribution to the concretisation of ecological 'discomfort' (Hünenmörder, 2004).

For the implementation of a complex and modular measure bundle which adequately meets the challenges of the (re)stabilisation of our earth system, existing regulations, routines and role models i.e. the 'mind maps in our heads' (Wilke, 1998) must be questioned. Organisation theory teaches us that usually, actors initially respond to new challenges and uncertainty defensively through reinforcing the established action orientations, or with selective perception, i.e. by taking new exigencies on board only if they can be linked to established knowledge, interpretive and regulatory systems. For the most part, complex learning processes and comprehensive innovations are not initiated based on the quality of the various crisis diagnoses and cause analyses, but only through the establishment of convincing new orientation offers and action concepts (Wiesenthal, 1995), and the opening up of experimental platforms which allow the familiar to be rearranged into something new (Johnson, 2010).

6.2 The Concept of Change Agents: Definition, Typology and Roles

Transition research results (Grin et al., 2010) suggest that individual actors can play a far larger role in the transformation of social (sub-)systems than the one that has been accorded to them for quite some time, during which academic interest has usually focused on boundaries for action and the effects of systemic emergence. Thus the analysis of historical examples (Chapter 3) shows that social change is characterised not only by the emergence of new technologies and new major economic industries, but above all also by changes in mentalities and institutions driven by aspiring social classes. Identifiable actor constellations with sufficient power, resources and creativity, prepared to welcome innovations and reforms in order to overcome the established obstructive powers, emerge as the drivers of change. The speed of a transformation (or whether it can succeed at all) depends largely on the involved actors availing themselves of the existing opportunity structures.

However, examining contemporary and historical transition or transformation processes also clearly shows that actors cannot only profit from the windows

Table 6.2-1
Innovation dynamics and diffusion on three levels.
Source: WBGU

Social Level	Business as Usual	Innovation	Analysis Level
Micro	Veto Players	Change Agents	Interests
Meso	Loss Aversion	Pioneer Spirit	Emotions, Dispositions
Macro	Cultural Barriers	Innovation Cultures	Symbolic Level, Framework

of opportunity that open, but that frequently, they are also actively involved in the opening (Grin et al., 2010). Strategic groups and alliances function as role models and trendsetters during this process; in this way, they provide isolated innovation impulses with a 'cultural hegemony'. We know from diffusion and transition research that change agents – a term used to define strategic actors who are (sometimes unconscious) pioneers of social change, spreading an awareness of the chances it offers – play a key role when new technologies and ideas are introduced (Rogers, 2003; Grin et al., 2010; Kristof, 2010). The role of these change agents in the initiation and shaping of change processes has been examined in various disciplines dealing with diffusion and innovation processes (including business studies, sociology and psychology). The concept this approach is based on can be summarised as follows: 'Change agents have a convincing idea for change, and an initial concept for its realisation. They network and gain important fellow campaigners, in this way managing to win the critical mass over for change. Subsequently, they gradually develop the idea further together. The changing of routines and framework conditions, the establishment of new institutions, and a paradigm shift, conclude the process' (Kristof, 2010).

Change agents support certain changes, actively driving them ahead. Initially, change agents are, for the most part, single individuals and small groups (Kristof, 2010). They propagate innovations by questioning 'business as usual' policies and creating alternative practices, thereby challenging the established world views and paths, attitudinal and behavioural patterns, as well as providing others who think as they do (followers, early adopters) with a constant motivation for a self-sustaining change. This process typically includes long-term orientation and the overcoming of loss and risk aversions. Change agents therefore not only effect changes selectively, i.e. within their own sphere of experience, but also nudge comparably widespread transformation processes at local level and 'from below'. They find emulators and animate others to change their behavioural practices.

Schematically, a blockade situation that is governed by 'business as usual' policies can therefore be countered with an innovation scenario (Table 6.2.1). Change agents would replace veto players at the individual interest level, acting as previously elaborated. At the level of attitudes and dispositions, a pioneering spirit would be prevalent, rather than one of loss aversion. At a higher symbolic or framing level, the tone would be set by a culture of innovation, rather than cultural barriers.

The following identifies those change agents, not just individuals, but also organisations and groups who could support and transport the transformation outlined in this report. Based on precedents and syntheses, the focus will particularly be on change agents who accelerate conversion processes, substantiating and shaping ongoing socio-technological changes, legislative processes and market development as consumers, entrepreneurs and investors, as citizens, administrators and politicians. The conclusions that can be reached are necessarily interim and tentative. These can refer to findings from diffusion and transition research. On the basis of change management and organisation development studies (Reiß, 1997; Hauschildt, 1997; Bach, 2000), Kristof developed a 'promoter model' (2010) that summarises change agents' roles, competencies and main tasks (Table 6.2-2).

With reference to diffusion research, which has defined cycles of innovation and cycles of production, various functions can be differentiated here, and an analytical distinction can be made between types of change agents (Figure 6.2-1). In a cycle of innovation, change agents act by defining open questions and challenges and putting them on the agenda, by facilitating problem solutions as catalysts, by mediating between conflicting groups, or by freeing blocked decision-making processes within groups, by integrating disparate innovation requirements, or by nudging the institutional innovations which are required to solve a problem from 'below', or in the role of decision-making elite from 'above'. In the production cycle, change agents are active as the inventors, investors, entrepreneurs, developers or distributors of new concepts, products and services, but also as 'enlightened consumers' through demanding new products, and letting them circulate. Initially, this is an analytical distinction. Naturally,

Table 6.2-2
The promoter model: change agent roles promoting success.
Source: based on Kristof, 2010

Promoter role	Skills	Main task
Expert promoters	Professional expertise and object-specific expert knowledge	Initiation, identification of alternatives, problem solving, implementation
Process promoters	Combination of professional expertise and leadership skills	Problem definition, process design, communication
Power promoters	Leadership skills, hierarchic potential, (finanical) resources at their disposal	Initiation of change processes and promotion of their success
Relationship promoters	Relationship skills, network knowledge, interaction potential, conflict management	Supporting the process promoters in interaction processes

change agents can also fulfil several of these functions simultaneously.

In the face of the challenges to be overcome (Chapter 1), the significance of actors and actor constellations must be highlighted as a political core of 'ability awareness' (Meier, 1978) in a republican community: 'What makes man a political being is his faculty of action; it enables him to get together with his peers, to act in concert, and to reach out for goals and enterprises that would never enter his mind, let alone the desires of his heart had he not been given this gift – to embark on something new' (Arendt, 1970).

The analysis of various examples shows that, as far as the genesis and efficacy of change agents is concerned, there are usually four decisive elements: a certain social outsider position, the linking of several knowledge areas, the integration into a supportive network, and the respective era's favourable opportunity structures. Exemplary here is the history of Leonardo da Vinci (1452–1519), who managed to have a great impact on Renaissance Europe as painter and sculptor, inventor, architect and engineer, natural philosopher and author. Neither Leonardo da Vinci's genius, nor the claim that as a Renaissance man, he was 'a child of his times', offers sufficient explanation. All of the four elements typical for change agents come together in him: a personality developed from social marginality, a Zeitgeist focusing on change and innovation, an interdisciplinary knowledge organisation, and favourable political opportunity structures. As an illegitimate child and a homosexual, Leonardo da Vinci had to fight for recognition, and was predestined to grow up a heretic who distanced himself from the Church. Leonardo da Vinci found patrons, initially the city states of Milan and Florence, later the Vatican and the French court, without giving up his intellectual autonomy. In the second half of the 15th century, when letterpress printing accelerated the absorption and diffusion of the discoveries made by scientists and explorers, weakening the Church's authority, a receptiveness for actively steered change emerged. These opportunity structures (Leonardo da Vinci frequently emphasised the role of the seminal, transitory moment) were reflected and turned into processes in Leonardo da Vinci's generalist yet equally associative mindset, and as an 'apparatore', he was also well-received in his contemporary courtly society. Leonardo da Vinci understood painting as a 'mirror of the universe'; he was interested in the laws of godly nature, which he attempted to understand in associative links and various literary forms. Artistic, scientific and technical works fell together to create a universal programme, liberating numerous inventions.

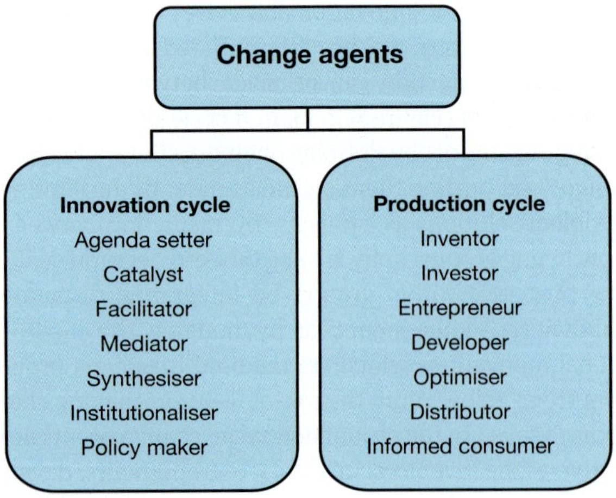

Figure 6.2-1
Typology of change agents.
Source: WBGU

In the Italian city states, innovation came about not so much through individual geniuses and a speedy orientation in terms of (market) application, as through the associative and experimental linking of 'good ideas' in the compact, yet also flexible, sounding board of the region, at that time the most urbanised in Europe (and the world), allowing a dramatic increase in the rate of innovation (Johnson, 2010). A similar speed of innovation was achieved in the course of the Industrial Revolution; as it progressed, one of the key issues became the improvement of the food situation as people were moving from agriculture to industrial manufacture, and from the country into the cities.

One prominent example of a change agent from that era is the chemist Justus Liebig, born in 1803 in Darmstadt. He is the recognised founder of organic chemistry, agricultural chemistry and nutrition physiology, and therefore one of the great scientific personalities of the 19th century (Leggewie, 2003). Playing different roles, he contributed to the transition into the industrial society by linking theory, pure research, applied research and product development. Liebig mainly worked on the improvement of agricultural productivity, not least because he had actually experienced a terrible famine himself in 1816, the 'year without a summer'. The practical result of his research was 'superphosphate', which is still the world's most used phosphate fertiliser. This fertiliser allowed significant increases in yield and food supply during the second half of the 19th century. It would not have been possible to feed the population of contemporary industrial societies without the knowledge of Liebig's principles of agricultural chemistry. Liebig summarised his scientific research in two works, 'Organic Chemistry in its Application to Agriculture and Physiology' (in short: 'Agricultural Chemistry'), and 'Animal Chemistry or Organic Chemistry in its Application to Physiology and Pathology'. His books attracted a great deal of attention both inside and outside scientific circles, and were translated into numerous languages (Liebig, 1840, 1842). Liebig was also an active entrepreneur, and co-founder of the Bayerische Aktiengesellschaft für chemische und landwirtschaftlich-chemische Fabrikate (BAG), a joint stock company for chemical and agricultural chemical products which still exists today under another name.

Social science research suggests that profound social and cultural changes often go hand in hand with generational changes (Mannheim, 1964; Bude, 1987; Leggewie, 1995; Jureit, 2006; Inglehart, 2008). Effectively, when major changes such as these occur, something happens at the social macro-level: younger groups show more openness towards innovations, and are in many cases early adopters of new technologies. This has been extensively documented in market and diffusion research. At the same time, historical research shows that cognitive and emotional discrepancies between peer groups, in part expressed as generational conflict, can mobilise social movements (Elias, 1994).

One important question is whether actors have sufficient strategic competence, or whether they can join forces with other change agents, in order to initiate or accelerate transformation processes (Grin et al., 2010). This means that not only the roles of technical experts, political-administrative decision-making elites, managers, entrepreneurs and so on must be examined, but also the roles of other key groups such as consumers, smaller communal initiatives and informal networks. Change agents can therefore be individuals who gain trust and repute at micro-level as leaders and role models, and who then work together at meso-level in manageable groups (for example in study and working groups, as members of a society, in interest groups, professional associations, in voluntary teams). And finally, they can also be major organisations like corporations, political-administrative units from local to supra- and transnational level, and other cooperatives (including certain professional groups or patrons). Besides a capacity for innovation and public spiritedness, the decisive criterion is the ability to communicate 'newness', and to engender feelings of identity and power awareness in their respective spheres of communication. These spheres of communication stretch from direct interpersonal communication to the cross-border virtual communication platforms of social and scientific networks. Change management and organisation development teach us that so-called 'soft factors', like social behaviour and the qualification to manage processes well are key to the success of change processes (Kristof, 2010).

The significance of 'niche markets' for economic development has already been noted in evolutionary economics (Saviotti, 1996; Levinthal, 1998; Frenken et al., 1999). Transition research (Grin et al., 2010) also assumes that, for the most part, transformation processes commence in niches, where they are initially confined and almost invisible. This marginality (Park, 1928) may have led to a significant (self-)underestimation of their impact; however, the decisive question is how isolated innovative impulses, often initiated by minorities and alleged outsiders viewed as 'mad' by the majority, manage to be accorded cultural hegemony and succeed. One aspect is that contemporary change agents in local and supra-regional initiatives, non-governmental organisations and so on typically create role models, turn attitude and behaviour patterns into action patterns, and are capable of motivating others.

Examples of this are the 'contagious' proliferation of the concept of Perestroika, and the 'Velvet Revolution' in Eastern Central Europe which started in the mid-1980s. They have led to the biggest political and cultural revolution in recent history, and to the opening up of the apparently unliftable Iron Curtain. They were always reliant on the social action of individual groups of change agents and charismatic individual personalities.

Considering the growing significance of strategic and/or sustainable consumerism, the influence of smaller communal movements (so-called grass roots initiatives) is also under discussion. Initiatives such as these exist in various forms of loose associations, from charitable associations to 'social enterprises'. Local actors have the advantage of being able to refer to context-bound knowledge, and can appreciate what will work under specific local conditions, and what will not. This corresponds with the often documented cognisance that change processes initiated top-down frequently fail precisely because they do not take local knowledge into account. However, taking local knowledge on board is a precondition for success in a specific cultural and social environment (Scott, 1998).

6.3 Where and how Change Agents are already Shaping the Transformation Today

6.3.1 Change Agents at Different Levels and in Various Fields

The change agents described so far must now be augmented by actors from the relevant climate and sustainability policy fields. The focus should stay on the paradigms, as there are also change agent careers that go through several transformation areas, moving, for example, from peace building, integration or development cooperation into ecological fields. One example of this is the Islamische Forum Penzberg, an Islamic forum in Upper Bavaria, initially viewed as exemplary in terms of integration into a multicultural community. By installing solar collectors on the minaret, however, it also took on a second role as an ecological pioneer in religious architecture (Merkur-Online, 08.07.2009). Also referred to are examples of change agents who are active in 'meta-fields' of (global) living environments for a higher level of conviviality (Illich, 1975), i.e. for a higher level of equality in terms of technological progress, and, from this perspective, are open for sustainability aspects and could be mobilisable. Exemplary here are movements which call for a 'decelerated' time management (Slow Food: deceleration through slow and pleasurable eating; Section 6.3.2.4) and propagate 'voluntary simplicity' (Küstenmacher and Seiwert, 2004). Impulses for the preservation and promotion of cultural diversity (for example religions and generations) and social entrepreneurship in the areas of education, development and poverty reduction, and the protection of human rights also number among these.

Change agents can be found at all social levels and in various fields of activity: for example in thematically focused environmental and citizen's initiatives and social protest movements, in governmental and non-governmental organisations (including churches and foundations), or they can be scientists, engineers, town planners and architects. Change agents can also be found in professional associations who make their members swear a 'Hippocratic Oath' (metaphorically speaking), from development cooperation to care for the elderly and other aspects of voluntary and private sector entrepreneurial activities. In accordance with the above described classifications, the exemplary change agents highlighted by the WBGU in the following are individuals, groups, organisations and both public and private networks who have developed sustainable initiatives in the needs categories described in Chapter 4. The following is therefore a monothematic channelling on the part of the WBGU, restricted to initiatives which are active in the areas of energy supply, mobility, urban development and land use (food production and forest protection). These are just some national and international sample initiatives; their inclusion neither signifies any special kind of seal of approval, nor, particularly in the case of private sector enterprises, is it intended as an express recommendation. Some sample change agents are introduced in the following sections in the form of brief portraits. So-called bifurcations have been incorporated in the fields of energy supply and mobility. They represent forked paths in dynamic systems: one fork continuing on the current growth path based on energy efficient and renewable technologies, i.e., for example, private transport, currently reliant on combustion engines, should principally be continued on the basis of electric mobility; the other fork leading to alternative mobility paths including, for example, the avoidance of private transport. This illustration serves only heuristic purposes; in reality, the likelihood will be mixed individual strategies and hybrid collective solutions. In individual cases, recourse might also be taken to historical change agents which have already made a major contribution to the desired transformation in the past.

In the areas of urbanisation and land use, these brief portraits are incorporated into a narrative relating to the above mentioned innovation or production cycle (Section 6.2). They serve to illustrate the history (Nünning and Nünning, 2002; Fuchs, 2009; Thier, 2010), from an early, at first usually marginal, innovative idea to initial realisation and collectivisation (Weber, 1984), to general habitualisation (Bourdieu, 1987; Elias, 1987; Veblen, 2007). Not all of the 'roles' in the innovation and production cycle have been cast in the narratives pertaining to the areas 'urban development' and 'land use', respectively; however, the concrete examples are consolidated, and the synopsis is shown in Figure 6.3-1.

6.3.2 Sample Successful Local Climate and Sustainability Initiatives (Supply Side)

6.3.2.1 Energy Supply

The Black Forest 'electricity rebels' from Schönau (Germany) represent the, at first glance unlikely seeming, case of an originally private sector, local initiative of electric power producers starting to produce energy themselves, using wind and solar energy, and later cogeneration and biomass, before the liberalisation of the German energy market in 1998. Over the past few years, the number of customers has multiplied, and by now, the Elektrizitätswerke Schönau (EWS) supply electric power to more than 100,000 private households, companies and industrial enterprises all over Germany, making them one of Germany's leading green energy suppliers. The EWS invest their profits into the development of a sustainable energy supply. They also subsidise small-scale electric power generating plants – i.e. combined heat & power heating systems or biogas plants, on application. The required funds are raised by being included in the price they charge for their electricity as an extra, the so-called 'sun cent'. This has made it possible to install more than 3,000 small-scale eco-power stations to date. Through these directly subsidised power stations alone, more than 10,000 t CO_2 are saved annually. Within a short period of time, a small, local initiative numbering just a few people grew into a successful business with impressive social and energy-political dynamics. Joined by a growing number of actors, it provided an incentive to change and soon grew in scope in terms of effect (Leggewie and Welzer, 2009).

Solarcomplex AG in Singen (Germany), whose ambition is the conversion of the Lake Constance region's energy supply to rely exclusively on renewable energies by 2030, operates in a similar fashion. Founded as recently as 2000 by around 20 local citizens, Solarcomplex AG started with the installation of a few individual solar energy plants in 2001. The AG has over 1,000 shareholders by now, and a prominent advisory council which includes climate and energy researchers; it also operates a range of power stations.

The Staudinger Gesamtschule school in Freiburg im Breisgau (Germany) commenced the energy-efficient refurbishment of its school building in 1999. The requisite funds were raised by means of a contracting system: external investors invest with a view to the future cost savings achieved through increased energy efficiency, and these savings then, in subsequent years, earn interest on the invested capital, which is paid back to the investors in this way. This practice has not only found many followers, leading to a diffusion of the socio-technological innovation of 'energy contracting'; it has also resulted in alternative role models and changed educational concepts in everyday school life (Leggewie and Welzer, 2009).

Such initiatives for change have the effect that (a) the actors, following the success of their measures, do not stay at entry level, but that they immediately start to look for further fields to which they can apply the experiences which they have gathered. The tangible experience that the immediate life-world is changeable provides a motive, or reinforces the motivation, to continue to change this life-world. Simultaneously (b), the experiencing of 'self-efficacy' (Bandura, 1977) has a paradigm-forming effect, and provides examples to be followed, therefore serving the diffusion of transformation impulses. This is achieved through (c) utilisation of the communication density of existing work, learning, and leisure time communities; ordinary communication (about work, learning or leisure activities) is episodically 'charged' for the common good. This leads to (d) a development of loose networks with a collective identity, with the establishment of internal shared habits ('this is the way we do it'), and creates additional, extrovert distinctions ('we don't do things like that (anymore)').

The initiatives by change agents for the establishment and development of a low-carbon energy supply described here were usually only made possible, or only gained pace, through changes in the regulatory framework. This exemplifies the role of the proactive state (Chapter 5) in the transformation process. The German Feed-in Law, or Stromeinspeisegesetz (StrEG), came into force in 1991, opening the electric power market for private generators of renewable power. Under the StrEG, the energy suppliers are legally obliged to buy the power generated from renewable energy sources in their supply region, and to pay at least 90% of the average profits from the sale of this electricity for it. Power from renewable energy sources, previously viewed as not financially viable (such as power generated by wind parks) was thereby made profitable. The monetary effects of this law were not financed by the public purse, but were met by the electricity suppliers and their customers (Ohlhorst, 2009). One peculiarity of the StrEG is that it had been initiated by a coalition consisting of members of all parliamentary parties, i.e. it was initiated directly by the parliament. A small group of Bundestag members, many of whom belonged to the Committee for Research and Technology, succeeded in putting the advantages of renewable energies on the political agenda – actively supported by the recently established German Renewable Energy Federation. The group included the speaker of the 'green party', the Bündnis 90/Die Grünen, on research policy, Wolfgang Daniels, who hoped that this initiative would accelerate the nuclear phase-out; the Bundestag member Matthias Engelsberger (CDU/CSU), who also operates a hydropower plant, and two members from northern Germany, Erich Maaß and Harry Peter Carstensen (also CDU/CSU), in whose constituencies wind turbines were being tested (Ohlhorst, 2009). Various applications by the group were supported by around 80 members from all of the parties represented in the Bundestag. The law was passed by the Bundestag on 7 December 1990 with a large majority (Ohlhorst, 2009).

In 2000, the law on renewable energies, Erneuerbare-Energien-Gesetz (EEG), developed the StrEG further. Instead of being linked to the average electricity price, long-term fixed prices for feed-in electricity from renewable energies were set, and remuneration was differentiated according to sector. Now, the fixed remuneration amount not only applies for as long as the law is valid, but is guaranteed for 20 years. The law has thus introduced strong incentives to invest in renewable energies. The energy supply companies had to commit themselves to buying the regeneratively generated power. For wind and photovoltaic energy plant operators, this means a high level of investment and planning security.

Examples of a locally initiated energy turnaround can also be found outside of Germany, of course: in 1997, the Danish Ministry of Climate and Energy ran a competition for choosing a test region to assess the potential of renewable energies. The aim was to make the test region completely carbon-neutral within 10 years with available technologies, and without any additional state subsidies. The island of Samsoe won the competition. An engineer from the mainland had submitted an application, suggesting the island. He had analysed the island's electric power and oil consumption, assessed how much biomass is grown on the island each year, how strongly the wind blows, and how long the sun shines for. The project's success was in no way predictable, as the island is a poor, rural region whose inhabitants had relatively little interest in climate protection. An organisation was established to realise the project; its speaker Sören Hermansen was voted as Time Magazine's 2008 'Hero of the Environment'. He convinced 450 of the island's 4,000 inhabitants to participate in the project. The climate project works on the basis of island inhabitants financing wind turbines and straw-powered heating systems through (significant) own investments. Ten offshore and eleven onshore wind parks were built, three central straw-powered district heating systems (operated only with straw from the island), and one solar/wood powered district heating system. As these systems are not owned by major corporations, but by the islanders themselves, creating new employment and investment opportunities, the income and profits generated remain on Samsoe. Hermansen said the secret of the project's success was that 'you mustn't do anything from the top down. Everything must belong to the people, it has to become their project'. Before the climate project, ships brought heating oil to the island, and electricity came via cable. CO_2 emissions were eleven tonnes per capita every year. After only eight years, energy production exceeded local consumption, so the island even turned into an energy exporter. The island's car traffic is the only CO_2 emitter these days, and the ferry to the mainland, which consumes 9,000 litres of diesel every day. However, arithmetically, Samsoe's energy production is zero-carbon, as electricity exports exceed oil imports. There are plans to link electric cars with the wind turbine electricity generation, so that the car batteries can charge when the wind blows, and discharge electricity in a lull.

The co-founder of Indian photovoltaic power company Selco India, Harish Hande, is an example of an entrepreneurially active change agent. Selco India sells small-scale photovoltaic units to households in India's rural regions. The company is outstanding because it sells its products without any subsidies from the Indian government's photovoltaic programme, and because it also provides a maintenance service. Independence from Indian government subsidies is possible because Hande links the sale of solar power units with the option of financing the purchase through a microloan. To date, Selco has supplied over 85,000 households in India with photovoltaic-based lighting. Hande was the first person to introduce and successfully establish this business model in India. By now, his concept receives financial support from various multilateral organisations (UNEP, GEF), and has also found a host of imitators in India, although these were less successful than he has been. The Selco company has shown that the electrification of rural regions does not necessarily have to happen through direct government subsidies and programmes. This initiative has set the global dis-

Box 6.3-1

Private Sector Change Agents: Companies and Investors

Stakeholders from the private sector – particularly manufacturers of climate-friendly technologies – have a key role to play in the transformation towards a low-carbon society. Change agents from the private sector promote and develop commercial innovations to increase market shares with better and new products for profit. In doing so, this type of change agent fulfils various functions:

- research and development and knowledge generation;
- provision of financial and human resources;
- initiation of self-reliant market processes;
- hinge function between research and application (diffusion);
- taking on Corporate Social Responsibility, CSR.

Stakeholders from different areas of the private sector can act as change agents: engineers and technicians in different companies across a wide range of industries (particularly in the renewable energies, energy efficiency and electromobility sectors) play a pivotal role in the development of new technologies. The insurance industry has also become involved in the area of climate change mitigation quite early on – not least because it expects global warming to lead to increasing financial pressure (Brunnengräber, 2009). Reinsurance companies such as Swiss Re communicate knowledge about climate change and its consequences, and the climate change mitigation that is required, and become active as investors in the establishment of a renewable energy system: the Munich Re reinsurance company, for instance, is one of the driving forces behind Desertec. Banks, insurance, and investment companies have joint the UNEP Finance Initiative. Consultancy firms such as McKinsey also actively raise awareness in the private sector, and develop solutions for the adaptation of individual corporations and companies to embrace climate protection (McKinsey, 2010). However, meta-studies (Rogers, 2003) have also shown that private sector change agents, due to their profit-oriented nature, do not enjoy the same level of credibility as other stakeholders. A mixing of private economic and common welfare interests can result in cognitive discrepancies and dissonances. Nevertheless, private sector stakeholders can still be included as change agents if the pursuit of their interests clearly shows awareness of common welfare responsibilities, and results in sufficient material impact for a sustainable way of operating.

cussion on various approaches for rural development in motion. Hande has won several awards for his activities, including the Indian Nand & Jeet Khemka Foundation's 'social Entrepreneur of the Year 2007'.

The project 'Desertec' (solar energy from the Sahara) is an international project which could become a central element in converting Europe's energy supply to renewable energy carriers. Desertec intends to build solar thermal power plants with minimal resource consumption and a high efficiency factor in sparsely inhabited desert regions with particularly high insolation. The electricity thus generated is to be used locally for development and modernisation, and the surplus is to be exported. High voltage direct current transmission is to ensure minimal transmission losses. The concept will be developed further by a cooperative of countries bordering the Mediterranean, both north and south; the solar power will be fed into the European supersmartgrid, and combined with electricity from other renewable energy sources. This project could create employment opportunities and generate income, and, in the long term, allow zero-carbon sea water desalination and improve industrial, traffic and transport infrastructures in the mostly little developed North African producer countries, but also in countries south of the Sahara. The concept was conceived by approximately 60 private individuals, some from the Club of Rome circle. In 2003, they founded the Trans-Mediterranean Renewable Energy Cooperation. This turned into the Desertec Foundation in 2008; in 2009, the Desertec Industrial Initiative (DII GmbH) was founded, a consortium of industrial and service provider companies now running feasibility studies. The DII GmbH's founding members include, besides the Münchener Rück, the Deutsche Bank, Siemens, ABB, E.ON, RWE, Abengoa Solar, Cevital, HSH Nordbank, M+W Zander Holding, MAN Solar Millennium and Schott Solar. Functioning pilot plants are in operation in Spain, with additional plants planned for Morocco, Algeria and Egypt. Although the project has also attracted some heavy criticism, for example with regard to the risk of supply insecurity in the case of a potential cartelisation, or the dangers of changing political constellations in the Maghreb states, and although private sector change agents might well play an ambivalent role in transformation processes (Box 6.3-1), the realisation would without a doubt be a key stepping stone on the way to fully supplying Europe (and possibly also parts of Africa) with renewable energies.

6.3.2.2
Mobility

In the view of the WBGU, establishing a sustainable and low-carbon transport and mobility system can be accomplished in various ways, in which individual elements – such as the promotion of electromobility or the further development of public transport systems – can be significant to varying degrees (Section 6.3.1). In addition, concepts for sustainable mobility must take existing infrastructures and local habits into account, as these can also vary greatly from country to country, and region to region. However, change agents aiming for a more climate-friendly, sustainable development are already at work in the different mobility areas, or on the various means of transport or vehicle types.

The foundations for developing electromobility further were laid as early as the 19th century. The English physicist Michael Faraday (1791–1867) discovered electromagnetic rotation in 1821, i.e. a process for transforming electric energy into mechanical energy. French engineer Gustave Trouvé presented the first drivable electric car at the International Exposition of Electricity in 1881 in Paris. Over the next few years, electric cars had their heyday, as they were superior to vehicles with combustion engines in terms of efficiency. In 1900, Ferdinand Porsche presented an electric vehicle on the Exposition Universelle world fair in Paris; at that time, 38% of the 'automobiles' in the USA were electric powered vehicles (compared to 40% steam powered, and 22% fuelled by gasoline). In New York, the share of electric vehicles among 'automobiles' was even as high as 50%. In 1912, twenty manufacturers built 33,842 electric cars worldwide (Möser, 2002).

However, with the invention of electric starter motors for combustion engines, and due to the cheap availability of oil, combustion engine powered vehicles gradually overtook their electric rivals. The key advantage they had over the electric vehicles, with their heavy batteries and long charging times, was that they were also suitable for long distances. Since the 1940s, electric cars had therefore been used only in certain transport sector niches. Golf buggies were the first mass-produced electric vehicles for consumers. Since the 1990s, electric vehicles are undergoing a renaissance, triggered by the oil crisis and the great fluctuations in oil prices due to tensions and conflicts in the Middle East, and by the general public's growing environmental awareness. This development has been supported by the progress in power accumulation technology. Since then, we have again seen an upsurge in research efforts in the area of electromobility. Apart from scientists, a great number of car manufacturers have shown particular commitment. In 2009 and 2010 alone, more than ten different models by different manufacturers have been launched on the market in various countries. The series produced roadster manufactured by the Californian company 'Tesla Motors' is currently one of the most advanced models in technical terms: the roadster has a range of around 320 km, and the batteries only need the comparatively short time of 3.5 hours to recharge.

Despite these successes, and the extensive media attention paid to this issue, the current market for electric cars still remains quite small. Only 162 of the 3.8 million new cars registered in Germany in 2009 were electric. In Germany, a total of 1,588 of these vehicles are licensed for road use (KBA, 2010). It is therefore important that policy-making actively promotes a conversion, and supports it financially. The German federal government's budget for this purpose between 2005 and 2013 totals € 700 million. The federal government's 'Nationaler Entwicklungsplan Elektromobilität', a national development plan for electromobility, plans to get 1 million electric vehicles on the national roads by 2020. Research and development will receive funding (energy storage, vehicle technology and grid integration), framework conditions will be improved (relevant qualification of human resources), and support will be given during market launches in order to achieve this goal.

Besides electromobility, one of the key elements of future mobility concepts is car sharing. The German national railway Deutsche Bahn is currently working on a concept which includes both elements. According to this concept, 10% of their hire cars will be electric by 2011. The comparatively low range of electromobiles is not an issue in the Deutsche Bahn concept, as the vehicles are intended to be used only for extended journeys into metropolitan areas. Customers should take the train to travel longer distances. This trend is supported by a decline in car ownership among young people living in the major cities, and the growing willingness to restrict car use for climate protection reasons (Albert et al., 2010). Short-term car hire is currently still a niche market in Germany, with less than 170,000 users (Financial Times Deutschland, 17.08.2010). According to analyses by consultancy firm Frost & Sullivan, however, the number of car sharing users will probably rise sevenfold to almost 1.1 million users by 2016. The consultancy firm has calculated that, with greater political support, the number of users might even grow to 2.1 million within the next five years. Europe-wide, the management consultancy assumes that by 2016, 5.5 million users will share around 77,000 vehicles (Frost & Sullivan, 2010). In Europe, outstanding commitment is shown by France; there, the government supports the extension of car sharing schemes, with reference to the success of the Parisian car sharing initiative Autolib. Particular attention is paid to the inclusion of electric cars. Currently, over 270 German cities also offer car sharing schemes. The Daimler corporation, for example, is currently testing a car sharing model named Car2Go in Ulm: in handy locations all over the city, vehicles of the Smart make are available for use by registered users. Just under 20,000 of Ulm's 170,000 inhabitants have already joined the scheme (Financial Times Deutschland, 17.08.2010). Deutsche Bahn is also active as a major provider of car sharing schemes in other countries (Switzerland, the Netherlands). Under the

Call a Bike scheme, they also hire out a total of 6,000 bicycles Germany-wide. In 2010, the Deutsche Bahn's car and bike sharing offer won the Bavarian state prize for electromobility in the category 'sustainable mobility concepts'.

Apart from the development of integrated traffic concepts with the inclusion of electromobility, the public transport system is central for the development of sustainable mobility concepts, particularly in the area of metropolitan mobility. According to German Federal Environment Agency calculations, 2.5 million t of CO_2 emissions per year could be avoided if public transport use in Germany were to double by 2020, and the use of cars were reduced in its favour (UBA, 2010). This is achievable only if the public transport system becomes more attractive for large parts of the population. Journey frequencies would have to be increased, fares decreased, and a safe and clean infrastructure would have to be provided. The efforts of the Belgian city of Hasselt can be considered as particularly successful. As early as 1996, Hasselt introduced a free public transport system on the initiative of town mayor Steve Stevaert (van Goeverden et al., 2006). To realise this concept, the local bus network was extended, traffic was banned from shopping areas, parking spaces were abolished, and car parking charges were introduced or increased. Since then, the number of public transport users in Hasselt has risen tenfold (from slightly more than 300,000 in 1996 to more than 4 million in 2006). There are also reports that this has had a positive effect on other aspects of city life (local business has picked up, for example). Traffic management professionals and urban planners are familiar with the Hasselt project, which has been copied by an as yet still small number of cities providing zero-tariff public transport services, although their numbers are growing worldwide (for example Aubagne/France, Hawaii/USA, Lübben and Templin/Germany, Manises/Spain, Vero Beach/USA).

In Germany, half of all journeys made by car are shorter than five kilometres, leading to CO_2 emissions of more than 14 million t in 2005. According to German Federal Environment Agency calculations, 5.8 million t of CO_2 emissions per year could be avoided if half of these journeys were made on foot or by bicycle by 2020 (UBA, 2010). In the past few years, cities, universities and non-governmental organisations have started to offer or fund free-of-charge bicycle maintenance services to motivate people to use their bicycles, and to increase road safety for cyclists. The German Cyclists' Federation Allgemeiner Deutscher Fahrrad-Club (ADFC), for example, provides a so-called 'autumn check' at several locations in Berlin. Major faults are listed, and cyclists are told how to repair them, or given the details of local bike repair shops. This campaign was supported by Berlin's Department for Urban Development and Traffic Management, the Senatsverwaltung für Stadtentwicklung und Verkehrslenkung Berlin (ADFC, 2010). Besides this practical measure to promote cycling, the ADFC's main function is the championing of cyclists' interests in politics and administration, and lobbying for the improvement of framework conditions for 'mobility by bicycle' in Germany. In cities like San Francisco and Vienna, cyclists can repair their bikes in so-called 'Bike Kitchens' at no charge. These are self-help maintenance shops that provide tools and materials, and a helping hand during repairs. In addition, Vienna's 'Bike Kitchen' is outstanding because it specifically targets immigrants and socially disadvantaged groups with what it has to offer, and links political lobbying (such as the promotion of cycling culture) with the provision of services.

Whilst it is relatively easy to find low-carbon alternatives for short journeys, there is currently no technical replacement for air traffic. The international air transport association IATA, which represents 230 airlines and 93% of international air traffic, has nevertheless set itself the ambitious target of zero-carbon growth as from 2020, and to reduce emissions to half of the 2005 values by 2050, despite its tremendous growth (Tagesspiegel, 30.11.2010). Biofuels play a key role in the realisation of this plan. The German airline Lufthansa is the first airline in the world to test the use of low-carbon biofuels in a long-term experiment on their regular Hamburg to Frankfurt route. The test begins in April 2011, and is scheduled to last six months in order to examine the potential impact on the engine. The Hamburg-Harburg and Munich technical universities are supporting the project. The German Aerospace Centre believes that significantly lower volumes of soot particles will be generated during combustion. Biofuel is also lighter than kerosene. This project could save up to 1,500 t CO_2.

In terms of renewable fuels fully replacing fossil fuels, the main problem is still the sourcing of sufficient amounts. Even if the fuel is won from non-edible plants, the risk of competition in terms of land use for cultivation areas remains (WBGU, 2010a). One potential alternative that is being considered for intercontinental air traffic is the use of magnetic levitation in a vacuum tunnel. If air were pumped out, the aerodynamic resistance would be reduced, and a vehicle moving along in such a tunnel could reach higher speeds with the same energy input. Rand Cooperation engineer Robert F. Salter already developed a transport concept for high speed trains in vacuum tunnels, so-called Vactrains, in the 1970s. One current project, named 'swissmetro', is hoping to use magnetic levitation trains in a vacuum tunnel for intercity traffic in Switzerland.

The journey time from Berne to Zurich, approximately 100 kilometres, could be reduced to 12 minutes. Since 2004, several testing phases related to this project have been carried out at the École Polytechnique Fédérale de Lausanne and the Numexia foundation. The search is also on for industry partners for a syndicate that will devise the Swissmetro transport system, and realise a first test route.

The mobility sector case studies included here intentionally cover a wide range of change agents: from internationally operating, profit-oriented corporations like the Deutsche Bahn to communities like Hasselt, or local, action-oriented associations like Bike Kitchen. We could have chosen differently, and the list could easily go on, as particularly in the area of mobility, a number of very diverse actors are working on establishing low-carbon and sustainable methods of mobility. Offers like those provided by the EMBARQ network, which provides information on sustainable transport systems on behalf of the World Resources Institute (WRI), are key in terms of orientation here.

6.3.2.3 Urban Development: Change Agents for Sustainable Urbanisation

As per the typology described above (Section 6.2), change agents can fulfil various functions in the transformation process. This is illustrated by examples from the fields of urbanisation, or sustainable building and habitation. Again it should be noted that individual agents can occupy several analytically diverse roles simultaneously.

The vision of a sustainable city was significantly influenced in the 20th century by the architect, designer, engineer, developer and author Buckminster Fuller (1895–1983). He came from a well-to-do merchant family, began his studies at Harvard in 1912, was thrown out of university, became a marine soldier, and then a 'failed existence'. 1927 brought a biographical turnaround: Fuller wanted to experiment to find out what an individual person can contribute to change the world for the greater good, and documented this self-awareness process over 50 years in a diary. Fuller was interested in global and cosmic perspectives ('Operating Manual for Spaceship Earth') and the 'integral function of humans in the universe'. Fuller was not only pioneering in the formulation of the concept of sustainable urbanisation, he was also active as an inventor and developer: in order to avert 'cosmic bankruptcy', he wanted to provide tools and techniques for sustainable development. As an architect, he found fame for his new types of building concepts, which were patented and marketed under the name of Dymaxion (Dymaxion Globe). Fuller's trademarks were the geodesic domes; the best-known is the 'Biosphere', the United States' exhibition pavilion at the 1967 Montreal World's Fair. The construction of the domes is based on a further development of simple basic geometric shapes (tetrahedrons as 3-simplex, octahedrons, and very densely packed spheres); these are extremely robust and can be manufactured using small amounts of materials. Fuller's works inspire architects, urban planners and artists to this day.

A number of engineers and architects all over the world are currently working on the development of technologies and materials for sustainable building, or sustainable urban development. One example is the Plus Energy House, developed by students in collaboration with engineer Manfred Hegger, Technical University of Darmstadt, as part of the German Federal Ministry of Transport, Building and Urban Development's research initiative 'Zukunft Bau' ('Future Building') in cooperation with the US-based Solar Decathlon programme. A Plus Energy House generates more energy than it needs for cooling and heating. The excess is used, for example, to operate household appliances or an electric car, or it is fed into the power grid. The house combines the fundamental pillars of sustainable building and living, like energy and material efficiency (through the use of renewable building materials, recycling, etc.) with comfort and aesthetic design. Between 2009 and 2011, a prototype Energy Plus House is part of a travelling exhibition through Germany's major cities, on show to the German public as a practical and informative example of the various aspects of energy saving and sustainable building. This house was developed as a consequence of the research initiative 'Zukunft Bau'.

Transformative changes triggered by those with a vision, like Buckminster Fuller, or pioneering engineers like Manfred Hegger and his team, can reach a wider audience through initiatives like the climate manifesto 'Common Sense for the World'. This 'Manifesto for sustainable architecture and civil engineering issues by architects, engineers and town planners in Germany' was drawn up in 2009 (DAI, 2009). The manifesto's preamble states: 'The contribution we can make in the form of sustainable architecture and civil engineering is essential to bring about the changes needed in the use of our natural resources.' There are to be regular public reports on the implementation of this climate manifesto. It is one of the most comprehensive self-imposed voluntary undertakings by a professional group ever to be presented to political decision-makers. Architects, town planners and civil engineers make clear that they do not just design and create individual buildings, but that the energy-related design of each house, each office building and each factory hall decides the level of greenhouse gases that are emitted. The location of buildings also determines how mobile people and goods have to be, or whether the need for mobility can be reduced. Moreover, construction waste represents around two-thirds of all waste. Therefore, if a major part of the climate problem is caused by architecture and urban construction work, the manifesto argues, this field also offers a considerable potential for avoidance. This paradigm shift is followed by practical improvements in the provision of lighting and shade, cooling, heating and insulating, in building materials, room allocation and much more. Construction sustainability is taken into account in training and further education, star architects are turned into global green building role models. The manifesto hopes that laws and certifications will encourage energy efficient and low-carbon architecture to move out of the eco-niche and into the mainstream.

To realise the principles and projects suggested in the climate manifesto needs companies like the long-established Bavarian company Baufritz, which constructs zero-carbon houses using bio-based construction materials. In doing so, the construction company proves that sustainable building is already possible, and contributes to changing social practices. In 2009, Baufritz built around 200 blocks of flats and detached homes which, according to their own data, bind more than 10,000 t CO_2, as well as whole estates, nursery schools, schools, hotel complexes, holiday villages and commercial buildings. As a pioneer, the company helps to implement the transformation in practical terms, and proves its achievability. Baufritz was awarded the German sustainability prize in 2009.

The first zero-carbon supermarket was built by the Tengelmann group. It is generally viewed as a lighthouse project in the German food retailing industry, as it demonstrates quite clearly that a modern supermarket concept can be zero-carbon, and operate with 50% less energy. For this pilot project, an energy efficiency concept was conceived that combines a great number of separate individual measures; in part, completely new solutions had to be specially developed. Some of these have already been on the market for years, but others were innovations, or had to be improved for this project.

A pilot project of completely different dimensions is the construction (from scratch) of zero-carbon cities, planned wholly on the drawing board, such as Masdar City or the Chinese cities Dongtan and Linglang. The realisation of such initiatives requires powerful investors. The realisation allows development, testing and diffusion of sustainability solutions for urban development, civil engineering, residential construction and mobility. Masdar City is being built by the Emirate of Abu Dhabi in anticipation of the time when local crude oil and natural gas reserves will be exhausted. Construction of Masdar City, which will also house the offices of the new International Renewable Energy Agency (IRENA), started in 2008, with completion planned for 2020. The Arabic word 'Masdar' means 'starting point', 'source', and is also used for 'energy source'. Around 40,000 inhabitants and almost 1,500 companies and ecological and sustainability industry organisations are to settle in an area covering six square kilometres. The 'zero-carbon Science City' Masdar's energy supply is to be 100% regenerative: besides the planned solar-thermal power plants, wind farms will be used to drive pumps which will pump the cooler air found below the ground into the houses. The water supply is to be secured through solar-powered desalination plants. In terms of transport, only electric vehicles are planned for Masdar City, and, by following a strict recycling regime, the city hopes to be almost entirely waste-free.

In Germany's Ruhr region, over 60 leading, mainly long-established and energy intensive major companies have joined up to found the initiative 'InnovationCity Ruhr' (ICR), to turn the formerly highly industrialised Ruhr region into a future ecological model region by investing in renewable energy and energy saving technologies. Under the motto 'Blue Skies, Green City', an entire city district with more than 50,000 inhabitants is to be converted into an exemplary low-carbon city. By 2020, CO_2 emissions in the pilot area are to be reduced to half of those in 2010. To achieve this, all of the existing buildings will have to be almost completely refurbished. New buildings to passive and plus energy standard have to be built. Innovative technologies such as heat pumps and solar plants will have to be used, and new kinds of transport systems like electric cars and buses for environmentally-friendly mobility to improve the quality of urban life must be ready to use. In 2010, a competition was held for 'climate city of the future'. Of the 16 applicants, five of which (Bochum, Bottrop, Essen, Mülheim an der Ruhr and Gelsenkirchen/Herten) reached the final round, the city of Bottrop won, convincing with a concept for energy-conscious urban reconstruction and a high level of citizen-mobilisation. As other cities developed similar concepts for the competition, and are planning to drive ahead with these under their own steam, despite their limited funds, the Ruhr region could become a model for climate change mitigation and energy turnaround for the whole of Germany and Europe. InnovationCity Ruhr views itself as a 'lighthouse project, yet also as a trigger for innovation', hoping to inspire the founding of yet more energy efficient companies in the other communities in the Ruhr region. So far, the project is underfinanced, and has won hardly any public attention, it is therefore more of a pledge than a master plan; nevertheless, its significance is not to be underestimated, for it makes a huge difference whether a national and European energy transition concept also includes regions like the Ruhrgebiet, which both factually and symbolically represents a typical, heavily industrialised area, or whether it is applied only to pioneering, pleasant 'green' cities like Tübingen or Freiburg. What makes this project so outstanding, compared to other climate and sustainability initiatives, is the fact of its realisation in one of Europe's oldest coal mining regions, an area which has lived for centuries from coal extraction with continued industry substance, and a transport system that is heavily reliant on automobility. A transformation towards sustainability in a medium-sized university town with a large number of cyclists, or on the drawing board with plenty of investment capital (see Masdar City) is not just comparatively easy, but also, it can hardly serve as a model for other industrial regions. InnovationCity Ruhr also represents a true reindustrialisation concept, as it accepts a quite radical transformation with huge consequences for lifestyles, working environments and production processes, towards a sustainable metropolitan economy and society (Engel et al., 2011).

It needs more than pilot projects and individual successful examples for the transformation into a low-carbon society to succeed. In the medium term, it will be necessary to institutionally anchor sustainable social practices. In this respect, the university town of Marburg has set an example: in 2008, the town passed a 'solar by-law', obliging anyone building new homes, or extending or converting buildings that require heating, to install and operate solar-thermal units for this purpose. The objective of this by-law was the protection of natural life-support systems, particularly climate and resources, for the common good, through locally implemented and locally impacting measures for the efficient use of energy, particularly that provided by insolation. This is what made Marburg's by-law unique in Germany. Nevertheless, in 2010, the Gießen administrative court decided this by-law was illegal, as, on the one hand, the German federal legal standards for new buildings as stated in the law on renewable energies and heating had not been accorded precedence, so the town in fact had no authority to impose the use of solar power. On the other hand, the terms of some of the individual regulations contained in the by-law were criticised, such as the lack of interim periods to allow adjustments, and the non-consideration of the fundamental constitutional trust and relativity law with regard to the inclusion of some buildings. In principle, however, the administrative court appreciated the town of Marburg's endeavours to make a contribution to climate change mitigation. As the administrative court also emphasised the fact that in principle, under Hessian regional building law, communities do have the authority to pass such 'solar by-laws', one can safely assume that a by-law that considered the above mentioned criticised points would indeed be legal.

Mayors and administrative leaders of cities from all global regions have come together in different networks to jointly lobby for the mitigation of greenhouse gases and sustainable urbanisation. The World Mayors Council on Climate Change, founded by the mayor of the Japanese city of Kyoto, Yorikane Masumoto, in 2005 shortly after the Kyoto Protocol came into force, currently has over 50 members. The aim of the network is to improve the international cooperation of cities in their climate change mitigation endeavours, and to lobby for ambitious climate protection targets at different political levels. Apart from political advocacy activities, for example at international climate conferences, members also introduce climate and sustainability initiatives to the public on a broader level. The C40 Cities Climate Leadership Group was also established in 2005, and since 2006, the foundation has enjoyed the financial support of former US president Bill Clinton's Clinton Climate Initiative (CCI) foundation. The CCI offers the C40 cities financial support for projects aimed at reducing energy consumption and greenhouse gas emissions. In urban planning, issues like buildings, lighting, waste, transport, etc., examples for 'best practice' are extensively documented and exchanged. Much broader in terms of issues addressed, and also in terms of numbers, is the ICLEI – Local Governments for Sustainability network, which represents over 1,200 city and community administrations globally in more than 70 countries, and therefore more than half a billion people. ICLEI's general aim is supporting cities and communities in the implementation of sustainability measures. In this respect, the network offers technical advice and practical training, and acts as an information service provider. Based on these three networks – the World Mayors Council on Climate Change, the C40 cities and ICLEI – the 'World Mayors and Local Governments Climate Protection Agreement' was agreed at the Conference of the Parties to the UN Framework Convention on Climate Change in 2007. This agreement has so far been signed by over 100 cities, to prove their commitment to, amongst other things, the immediate and significant reduction of their greenhouse gas emissions, to measuring and reporting this annual greenhouse gas mitigation, and to continuing their efforts to reduce their greenhouse gas emissions. The aim is the achievement of 60% or 80% mitigation of global greenhouse gas emissions by 2050, compared with 1990 levels.

6.3.2.4
Land Use: Change Agents in the Areas of Food Production and Forest Protection

Food production

One of the major actors who contributed to the success of the 'Green Revolution', i.e. the exceptional increase in agricultural productivity in the developing countries during the second half of the 20th century (Section 3.5.2), was the Consultative Group on International Agricultural Research (CGIAR). The International Rice Research Institute (IRRI) in Manila was the first of 15 'Future Harvest Centers' which together constitute the CGIAR network, established in 1971. It is included here to represent all of the CGIAR's 15 pioneering institutes, which also deal with maize or wheat (International Maize and Wheat Improvement Center, CIMMYT, Mexico), potatoes (International Potato Center, CIP, Peru) or tropical agriculture (International Center for Tropical Agriculture, CIAT, Colombia). The IRRI has made vital contributions to the breeding of new rice varieties. The development of a particularly resistant, short-stemmed variety of rice (IR-8) in the early 1960s is today viewed as the beginning of the 'Green Revolution' (Section 3.5.2) in rice cultivation, and the foundation for the Asian economic boom. The new, more resistant rice varieties led to increased yields, allowing prices to fall. However, this development also had negative impacts, such as causing major environmental problems (WBGU, 1999: 'Green-Revolution Syndrome'). Although the IRRI is the acknowledged inventor and developer, and a public face in the Green Revolution, it could not have started its work without the support of other change agents, in the role of investors: the IRRI was founded in 1960 by the Ford and Rockefeller Foundation in cooperation with the Philippine government. Today, the institute works on better education and training for rice farmers, and develops new sustainable cultivation methods, intended to bring maximum yields using as few pesticides or fertilisers, and as little water as possible.

Despite the undisputed successes, 20th century industrial agriculture and food production has attracted much criticism; there have also been counter-movements by those who felt that the new production methods did not adequately consider aspects of conservation, quality and health. However, whilst in the 20th century these were for a long time restricted to social groups in the margins of society – such as the Life Reform Movement in the 1920s, or the ecologically conscious alternative subcultures of the 1960s and '70s – sustainable forms of food production and ecological agriculture have rapidly expanded in almost all regions of the world since the 1990s (Willer et al., 2008). The international Slow Food movement is exemplary of the general social trend to attach more value to organic and traditional cultivation methods; however, it also wants to put the enjoyment factor back into eating. Slow Food's objective is the preservation of regional specialities and traditional production methods. Founder and international chairman Carlo Petrini defined the benchmark and basic principles of this 'new gastronomy': buono, pulito e giusto – good, clean and fair (Petrini, 2007). Slow Food's forerunner organisation, Arcigola, was founded by Carlo Petrini in Italy in 1986. Petrini was born in 1949 in Bra, still Slow Food's headquarters today. After studying sociology in Trient, Petrini became politically active; at one point, he was Bra's appointed town councillor. He also wrote articles about food and drink for Italian magazines, and was involved in the founding of the magazine 'Gambero Rosso', initially a monthly supplement of the daily newspaper 'Il Manifesto'. He later became a columnist for Italy's third-largest daily newspaper, 'La Stampa'. Petrini says that the key experience which motivated him to found Arcigola was a day trip to Montalcino in Tuscany with friends, where the group of travellers was served a disgusting soup, and, instead of the Brunello di Montalcino for which the region is famed, a watered down table wine. On the return journey, Petrini drafted his manifesto on the 'human right to the pleasures of good food', to the applause of his fellow travellers (Slow Food International, 1989). Contemporary events also leading to the foundation of Slow Food were the 1985/1986 methanol scandal (several people died after drinking Italian wine that had been adulterated with methanol), and the rising number of fast food restaurants and food chains in the mid-1980s. Since 1991/1992, Slow Food also has a branch in Germany. Today, the Slow Food movement has more than 100,000 members in over 132 countries. It aims to support regional food trade, lobbies for organic agriculture, and promotes awareness for good quality food. Moreover, the organisation is building up seed banks, hoping to contribute to biodiversity preservation, under the project name 'Ark of Taste'. Each member pays € 5 per year to a foundation for biodiversity. Slow Food holds a biennial international trade fair for regional and organic food, the 'salone del Gusto', in Lingotto, the former Fiat works in Turin. Since 2004, the 'Terra Madre', a gathering of farmers, producers, cooks and scientists from all over the world is held at the same time.

Apart from the fact that the Slow Food movement spread very quickly across many countries, the longing for ecologically compatible and better quality food has also directly led to social innovations. In almost all major cities in Germany, for example, so-called Green Box services have become established since the mid-

1990s, whereby a box of organically grown food is delivered directly to homes or workplaces. So-called 'urban gardening' has also gaining in popularity over the past few years in the metropolitan areas of many western industrialised states. The movement originated in 1970s New York: herbs and other useful plants were grown in 'community gardens', often formerly fallow areas, which were then harvested by those who established the garden, and/or those in need.

However, change agents have already impacted social practices not only by raising awareness of, and focusing on, an ecologically more compatible and healthier diet, moving the issue into the mainstream. There is also the remarkable success story of Bionade, a soft drink invented in 1995 by the privately-owned Peter brewery in Ostheim vor der Rhön (Germany). Bionade is a lemonade that is made from controlled, organically-grown raw materials. Inclusion in the range of a Hamburg drinks wholesaler in 1997 initially turned Bionade into a drink consumed in trendy restaurants and pubs. From there, the lemonade went increasingly further afield: by now, Bionade is not only stocked in most organic food shops, but also in most mainstream supermarkets, it is available in the dining cars of the Deutsche Bahn, and on the drinks menu in the restaurants of the McDonalds subsidiary company McCafé. Since 2007, Bionade has also been available in various other European countries; it has even conquered the USA recently. The success of this organic soft drink has led to the introduction of a number of copycat products by various producers.

Alongside the development of organic food, technical innovations also play a major role in the establishment of sustainable eating habits. One striking example of this is the invention of the CFC-free refrigerator. CFCs (chlorofluorocarbons) were long used as refrigerants in refrigerators, even though they impact strongly on ozone depletion. Moreover, CFC was also the blowing agent for the polyurethane foam used for insulation. The world's first modern CFC-free refrigerator was manufactured in 1992 by the Saxony-based company 'dkk Scharfenstein' (later 'Foron'). The development was suggested by Greenpeace and the Hygiene-Institut Dortmund, led by Harry Rosin. The first CFC-free refrigerator of this type was converted by Lare GmbH to be used as laboratory equipment at the Hygiene-Institut Dortmund. At that time, refrigerator manufacturers showed no interest whatsoever in introducing this technology. Since 2000, the number of household and commercial refrigerators with alternative refrigerants which neither damage the ozone layer further, nor increase the greenhouse gas effect, on the market has greatly increased. The electric refrigerator is also an example of how technical innovations themselves can evoke social change. Prior to the invention of refrigerators and freezers, food could only be stored for a very limited amount of time, and over longer periods only with relatively elaborate preservation methods. With the invention and mass diffusion of electric refrigerators and freezers, this has radically changed, leading to the development of frozen food – industrially produced, deep-frozen foodstuffs which, because of their packaging, cooling and transport requirements, carry a much higher negative environmental balance than fresh foods. The use of refrigeration technology creates a particularly high energy demand. In 1998, Europe introduced the energy label, showing the energy consumption of electric appliances to help consumers with their purchase decision. In 2003, the classes A+ and A++ were introduced for particularly energy-saving refrigerators and freezers, i.e. those that exceed even energy efficiency class A, indicating a very low energy consumption. Most of the household appliances available today are already class A according to the originally defined efficiency classes, or even better. In May 2010, the European parliament therefore redefined the household appliance energy classes. Directive 2010/30/EU, featuring the new additional class A+++, is in force as of 2011. This example shows how important it is that change agents accompany social change institutionally to support it. Over the past few years, projects calculating the carbon footprint of various products (i.e. the CO_2 equivalents created over the entire life cycle of a product, from resource extraction to disposal) have started in various European countries. Outstanding commitment in this area has been shown by the British supermarket chain Tesco, the Swiss store chain Migros, or the Casino chain in France; various Swedish food product suppliers have also become change agents by starting to label food according to its carbon footprint in 2009, to inform consumers about the impact their consumption has on climate.

Forest Protection

Forests cover around a third of the Earth's surface, and ensure the survival of human societies through a variety of ecosystem services. Forests are also one of the Earth's largest carbon stores, storing up to 650 Gt of CO_2, 286 GT CO_2 of this in the form of biomass alone. For the past 10 years, global forested areas are being reduced by approx. 13 million hectares per year, an area roughly four times the size of Belgium. The deforestation rate is primarily determined by the conversion of tropical forests into agriculturally used land, and destructive forest use. The reduction rate of carbon storage in forests is currently estimated to have amounted to 0.5 Gt C (1.8 Gt CO_2) per year between 2000 and 2010, totalling 5 Gt C (18 Gt CO_2) for the decade (FAO, 2010a). It is therefore vital to stop deforestation, and manage forests sustainably, in order to bind and store more CO_2 to avoid dangerous climate change.

Hans Carl von Carlowitz (1645–1714) is generally acknowledged as the father of sustainable forestry. The son of a master forester in the Electorate of Saxony, he studied law and public administration. His interest in natural science and mining led to his rise to head mining administrator at the Electorate of Saxony's court in Freiberg. His responsibilities there also included forest management, particularly with regard to supplies for mining. Confronted by heavily overused forests, he wrote the first comprehensive work on forest management, the 'sylvicultura oeconomica' (1713). In it, he summarised the forestry management knowledge which had for the most part been lost during the Thirty Years' War (Europe, 1618–1648), and added his own experiences. Although the focus is still clearly on securing a reliable supply of timber, i.e. on the economic aspect, Carlowitz also already recognised the ethical and aesthetical values of forests. His work also reflects the ecology of forests, and the responsibility for sustaining an ecosystem whose lifecycles often go past the horizon of individual human lifespans. Carlowitz is therefore generally viewed as one of the pioneers of the principle of sustainability in forest management.

The concept of sustainable forest management has since been developed further, and is now realised by many change agents in numerous initiatives all over the world. An example is the promotion of environmentally friendly, socially beneficial, and economically viable forest management that forms the focus of the work of the Forest Stewardship Council (FSC). The FSC was founded in 1993 as an independent, charitable non-governmental organisation as the result of the UN Conference on Environment and Development in Rio de Janeiro. The FSC certifies timber or paper products from responsible forestry. It also ensures that the products are not mixed with non-certified timber or paper along the processing and supply chain to the consumer. Products carrying the FSC label contribute towards safeguarding the use of forests in accordance with the social, economic and ecological needs of current and future generations, and towards providing consumer information. The Kenyan Wangari Maathai is active as a pioneer of change not just in one, but in several concurrent functions. In 1977, she founded the grass roots organisation Green Belt Movement, which has the aim of stopping deforestation and soil erosion. With her unique reforestation project, the professional biologist managed to unite and motivate many different people. By now, over 40 million trees have been planted all over Africa. The project also lobbies for women's rights, promotes democracy, and the self-confidence of whole communities. The organisation is now active in 13 African countries, and is planning to plant one billion trees worldwide. Wangari Maathai received the 'alternative Nobel prize', the Right Livelihood Award, in 1984 for her work with the Green Belt Movement. Exactly 20 years later, she was the first African woman to be awarded the Nobel Peace Prize for her commitment to 'sustainable development, peace and democracy'.

Figure 6.3-1 shows a summary of the change agents mentioned above, categorised according to the areas of 'urban development' and 'land use' (food production and forest protection) in the order of their respective roles in the innovation and production cycle.

6.3.3
The Consumers' Role (Demand Side)

Climate and environmental protection require resolute action at nation-state and supranational level, yet successful climate policy will only be possible once the populations of the main polluting countries come to see that they themselves are responsible, both actually and historically, and participate in changes, or even initiate them. Roughly speaking, research on sustainable consumerism or the role of consumers currently pursues three different directions: (1) Socio-ecological research (Sozial-ökologische Forschung, SÖF) and recently especially behavioural economics (Thaler and Sunstein, 2008; Reisch and Oehler, 2009) have revealed psychological as well as structural barriers to sustainable consumption, alongside situational influences on purchase decisions, and discuss various regulatory or market-based measures, and the 'smart' influencing of choice options ('nudging', Chapters 3, 5), in order to promote sustainable purchasing behaviour. (2) Representatives of a so-called post-growth economy assume that consumption, at least at the current level in industrialised countries, as such cannot be sustainable, as the absolute delinkage of economic performance and resource consumption from CO_2 emissions is not feasible. The actual sustainability achievement must therefore lie in a reduction or a mitigation of consumption (Jackson, 2009; Paech, 2009a, b). (3) Another category of relevant literature (Lamla and Neckel, 2006; Baringhorst et al., 2007) focuses on the potential of politicising consumption, integrating the consumer associations. In this context, the growing group of so-called 'strategic consumers' is seen as particularly important. These are people who not only seek to purchase organically grown or climate-friendly products, and consider ecological aspects when it comes to mobility, building and heating, but also question consumption patterns as such through their behaviour, and change them in line

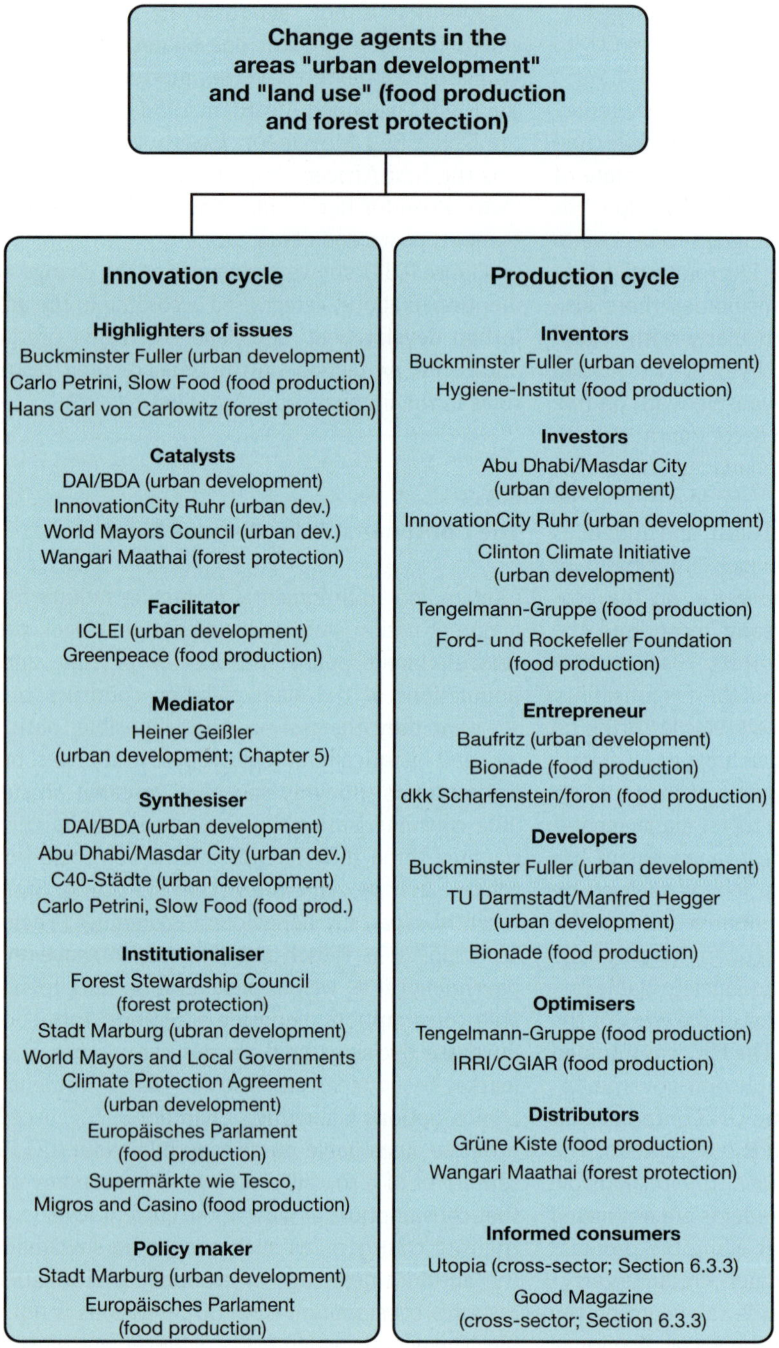

Figure 6.3-1
Change Agents: synopsis of case studies from the areas of 'urban development' and 'land use' (food production and forest protection). The illustration's categories are elaborated in Sections 6.3.2.3 and 6.3.2.4.
Source: WBGU

with sustainability considerations (Lamla and Neckel, 2006).

It has indeed been observed that in recent years, a growing number of consumers have become interested in the social and ecological conditions surrounding the production of the products they consume. Ecologically sound or fair trade products are showing significant growth rates. Particularly among social trendsetters, there appears to be a growing willingness to buy environmentally friendly products, even if they are more expensive. In terms of environmentally friendly shopping behaviour, such as a preference for energy efficient appliances with a long lifecycle, for purchasing regional products, and taking the environmental label 'Blue Angel' into account, the upper and upper middle social grades of the so-called 'sinus-Milieus' (the name refers to the originator of this grading concept, Sinus-Sociovision GmbH) show significantly higher ratings than the average population (Wipperman et al., 2009).

Data supplied by the manufacturers also shows that in the past few years, the European market for organic products has frequently shown two-digit growth figures, with 2009 turnover figures amounting to almost € 18 billion (BÖLW, 2010). Around € 5.8 billion of this annual turnover is generated in Germany; in 2000, the German market was worth only € 2.1 billion. The market for fair trade products reveals similarly dynamic growth figures in recent years (Krier, 2008). In 2004, the potential market of so-called LOHAS, the consumer group which pursues a 'lifestyle of health and sustainability', was estimated to be worth more than US$ 200 billion in Germany alone (Kreeb et al., 2008).

This change in consumer behaviour is primarily based on changing cultural norms (Chapter 2), according to which sustainability is increasingly becoming the new general orientation of a viable society. The consumption of goods is no longer led only by pure benefit considerations, but has also gained an 'ethical added value', which in the sum of individual consumer decisions can nudge sustainable long-term change. However, the process of participation in this community project, in a broader sense, also has an additional benefit beyond this result: the (self-)awareness of doing something useful and good for the environment and future generations, and of being appreciated by others for this (Frey and Stutzer, 2002). In this case, an individual's 'rational choice' gains aspects of collective identity and intervention. Such ethics-based meta-preferences can be powerful enough to supersede cost aspects: 'Anyone buying fair trade coffee or biodegradable T-shirts also buys a piece of ethical quality that has nothing to do with the useful function of the products, but contributes to questioning goods and services in terms of their social value.' (Heidbrink and Schmidt, 2009). The result of this development is growing pressure on companies and producers: in recent years, protest actions and high-profile campaigns like the Clean Clothes Campaign, which highlights the deplorable conditions in subcontracted Latin American and Asian manufacturing companies, have led to growing numbers of corporations confronting the issue of social and ecological standards at their suppliers' locations. Changing values on the part of the consumers have resulted in producers also having to deal with the social consequences of their business strategies. Goods and services which offer 'ethical added value' (Heidbrink and Schmidt, 2009) therefore represent an important market factor, and over the past few years, a growing number of companies has started to modify production and ranges accordingly (Centre for Corporate Citizenship, 2007). The internet platform 'Utopia' can be seen as the 'virtual home' of sustainable and strategic consumerism in Germany. According to data supplied by Utopia, the website currently counts more than two million visitors annually, and has 70,000 registered members (Langer, 2011). Utopia.de features information on low-carbon consumerism, products are introduced and rated, there are contributions and blogs where climate-political issues are discussed. Users also have the opportunity to network and exchange information. Every year, the Utopia Award is given to role models, ideas, products, companies and organisations, but 'preventers' are also highlighted. The Good Magazine fulfils a similar function on an international level. The magazine, founded in 2006 in the USA, has a circulation of around 25,000 issues. It reports quarterly on stakeholders and companies which lobby for improvements in the areas of environment, urban planning, food or health.

Nonetheless, the growing willingness on the part of consumers to consume sustainably is held back by obstacles and barriers: apart from certain consumers' lack of material resources, these are above all cognitive and motivational reasons. Many consumers feel overtaxed by the flood of offers and labels. They therefore tend to choose the ordinary, familiar products, even though sustainable alternatives would be available. Moreover, paradoxically, despite this flood of labels, the most important data consumers need to enable them to make a more conscious choice is missing: is it, for example, better to buy locally grown apples which have been stored over the winter, or fresh apples from distant regions? Also, corporate marketing and advertising can sometimes be distinctly misleading: products whose production conditions, or consumption, or usage is everything but sustainable are sometimes given a green image to make them attractive to ecologically-oriented consumer groups (so-called 'greenwashing'). Consumers' uncertainty as a consequence of confusing, missing or misleading information can represent an additional barrier for sustainable consumption.

However, this serves to highlight areas where law makers and official bodies have the chance to contribute to supporting consumers, thereby further promoting this willingness for sustainable consumption, or rather, to ensure that existing dispositions, apparent in surveys on the environmental attitudes of the population (Chapter 2; Kuckartz et al., 2008), are actually translated into an environmentally and socially compatible style of consumerism. Although decisions by consumers – which, these days, can even become so-called 'prosumers', i.e. consumers and producers rolled into one (for example through the feed-in of privately generated energy into the public power grid) – can certainly exert some influence over the market, this on its own is not enough to realise ambitious climate protection programmes. The abstract contrasting of markets, state or 'third sector' (service provider sector) as the respective main or monopoly actors for social and political change is outdated. Rather, room for opportunities to develop must be created, whereby market incentives and state control by way of imperative and prohibition can be combined with the social capital generated in the 'third sector'. Citizens are not just citizens who can change majorities through their voting decisions, and consumers are not just consumers who influence purchase decisions. On the contrary, the 'citizen consumer' is a case-by-case amalgamation of the two actor identities 'voice' (Hirschman) and 'choice' (LeGrand). In many hitherto public spheres, private consumers have long since started to be addressed as co-producers (for example where health is concerned, by prevention or choosing the right medical services, but also in terms of safety through increased public awareness) and impact indirectly on political decisions both as clients (for example for care services) and as private individuals from home (for example through internet use). Similar hybrid constellations are conceivable where the consumption of energy services is concerned, if their supply were to be designed so as to be even more transparent and market-based through legal measures. In recent years, the opportunities offered by consumer protection and the participation of consumers and citizens in the supply of public services (for example the electric energy supply, water management and rail traffic) has therefore also been increasingly discussed (Lell, 2010).

Not least, sociological research shows that conferring responsibility impacts upon action structuring (Gerhards et al., 2007). For the current problem field, this means that consumers also consider sustainability aspects less in their purchasing decisions if their responsibility is played down by 'public opinion leaders'. Vice versa, the emphasising of consumer responsibility can promote sustainable consumption.

6.3.4
Non-Governmental Organisations as International Policy Pioneers

For over three decades, civil society organisations and initiatives, and non-governmental organisations (NGOs), have been actively involved in the shaping of national and international political processes, particularly in the areas of environmental protection and human rights. As far as the areas of environmental protection and conservation are concerned, this can be explained not least by the fact that a great number of environmental problems require international measures, which lie beyond the direct political sphere of influence of states (Najam, 2005). The particular significance and legitimacy of civil society organisations rests less on their representativeness – to which specialised interest groups, inherently, can only lay a limited claim – but also on the expertise they generate, and their ability to develop new (solution) concepts in an experimental political arena. In this way, numerous non-governmental organisations act as policy entrepreneurs, at least partially filling on a global level the political vacuum created by the lack of global governance (Banuri and Najam, 2002). In recent years, civil society organisations have played a central role as agenda setters, as knowledge providers for international negotiations, in the mobilisation of public opinion, and in the implementation and monitoring of agreed measures. In the area of multilateral environmental agreements, they have not least been closely involved in the drawing up of a number of conventions (such as the UNECE Convention on Access to Information, Public Participation in Decision-making and Access to Justice in Environmental Matters (Aarhus Convention), the Convention on International Trade in Endangered Species of Wild Fauna and Flora (CITES), the Convention on Biological Diversity, or the UN Convention to Combat Desertification). Civil society organisations and initiatives can fulfil the following key functions (Muñoz and Najam, 2010):

1. Organisations like the World Resources Institute or the International Union on the Conservation of Nature function as recognised knowledge providers, and contribute through the supply of up-to-date data to dealing with global environmental problems. The Global Environmental Outlook published by the United Nations Environment Programme is an example of the formalised cooperation between international and civil society organisations in this area.
2. In the past, NGOs have repeatedly effected the creation of international agreements through campaigns, education, training and public relations work. The International Campaign to Ban Landmines, for example, awarded the Nobel Peace Prize in 1997, had a major influence on the creation of the Ottawa Treaty 'Anti-Personnel Mine Ban Convention', and the signing and ratification of the convention by numerous states.
3. Non-governmental organisations play a central role in the implementation of environmental and development measures, particularly in developing and newly industrialising countries, where the relevant state capacities are absent or insufficient. For example, in Chennai (India), non-governmental 'Civic Exnora' groups manage waste disposal for more than half a million people. Civil society stakeholders have also gained a reputation for implementing and monitoring the measures decided on under Agenda 21.

They can play various roles in the influencing of political processes (Muñoz and Najam, 2010): interceding where certain issues are concerned, NGOs and other civil society stakeholders actively lobby against opposed interest groups (for instance taking on the arms industry in the case of the landmine campaign), through extensive media campaigns, or the targeted diffusion of information (for example negotiator briefing). As 'watchdog', they monitor the extent of actual implementation of government measures pledged or decided on. Civil society organisations also have a long history of pursuing innovative policy approaches. By way of the United Nations, women's equal opportunity measures (such as the anchoring of demands for equality in all political areas) are now included in the regulations and legal practices of more than 100 states, thanks to feminist initiatives and networks (True and Mintrom, 2001). Not least, NGOs function as service providers for governments, administrations and companies. They offer expertise as much as material resources in the various stages of political processes (agenda setting, policy development, implementation). Particularly the role civil society and non-governmental organisations play in the implementation of agreed measures should be highlighted here, because ultimately, even international agreements – such as a global climate treaty – must also be implemented at a national and a local level. Civil society organisations play a vital role here: even in the stage of initial consultations, they can ensure that the voices of local groups are heard, to prevent agreements being decided on that might fundamentally hurt their interests. In turn, in the implementation phase, they significantly contribute to spreading relevant knowledge locally, in this way creating the ideal premises for successful implementation (Muñoz and Najam, 2010). One great strength of civil society organisations lies in the fact that they contribute a number of regional and cultural perspectives, as well as local experience, to negotiations and policy making processes, thereby helping to create early awareness of the complexity and extent of the respective challenges. Within the scope of the UN Convention to Combat Desertification (UNCCD), NGOs already have been accorded institutionalised participation rights, being permitted, for example, to hold plenary meetings with state representatives within the scope of the Conference of the Parties. Some UNCCD delegations, particularly those from the industrialised countries, admit NGOs officially to their governmental delegations in an advisory capacity. Other conventions – such as the CBD or the UNFCCC – provide similar participation opportunities. However, in recent years, there has also been a tendency towards isolating civil society groups, which has become apparent in the course of the stronger anti-globalisation movements within the scope of international summits (Najam, 2005). The diversity of civil society stakeholders, some of whose positions and solution suggestions are frequently perceived as rather extreme, should not, however, be viewed as a source of irritation by policymakers and negotiators, but, for the above mentioned reasons, explicitly recognised as a resource. Therefore, additional paths and opportunities for formally involving civil society organisations more in negotiation processes should be considered, rather than just allowing them to participate in important international negotiations on issue of climate protection and sustainable development in the form of side events. The interplay of the proponents of a global 'Green New Deal', or a global transformation towards a low-carbon society, from various spheres of society can lead to the creation of a new, positive culture of participation, articulated at all levels of political commitment: be it through voting, through membership in clubs, associations and parties, through participation in non-governmental organisations, or through involvement in extra-parliamentary campaigns and activities for climate change mitigation, energy system transformation and sustainability. Not least, civil society initiatives, political movements and NGOs – as exemplified particularly by the environmental movement – can provide useful feedback for state and supranational institutions, in this way initiating additional transformation processes.

6.4
Conclusion: Promote and Multiply Change Agents to Achieve a Rapid Transformation

This chapter has introduced different change agents from selected fields of sustainability politics, who voice their doubts regarding the status quo of the high-carbon regime in practical terms in important positions, thereby nudging considerable sectoral and cross-sectoral changes. How can these insular individual actors become the 'critical mass' required, pushing important levers for the transformation with the emphasis required to set the course? And how can individual actors achieve a shared feeling of collective self-efficacy, and come together in a widespread social movement? Or, to put it another way: how can the self-powering co-evolution in various social sub-systems (Grin et al., 2010), or the important 'concurrences of multiple change' (Osterhammel, 2009; Chapter 3) which are required to cause the imminent and already occurring change processes to densify into the 'great transformation' that is needed to stabilise the Earth system, and in particular the climate system, be brought about?

Figure 6.4-1 illustrates the paths change agents tend to follow, frequently from the margins of society where

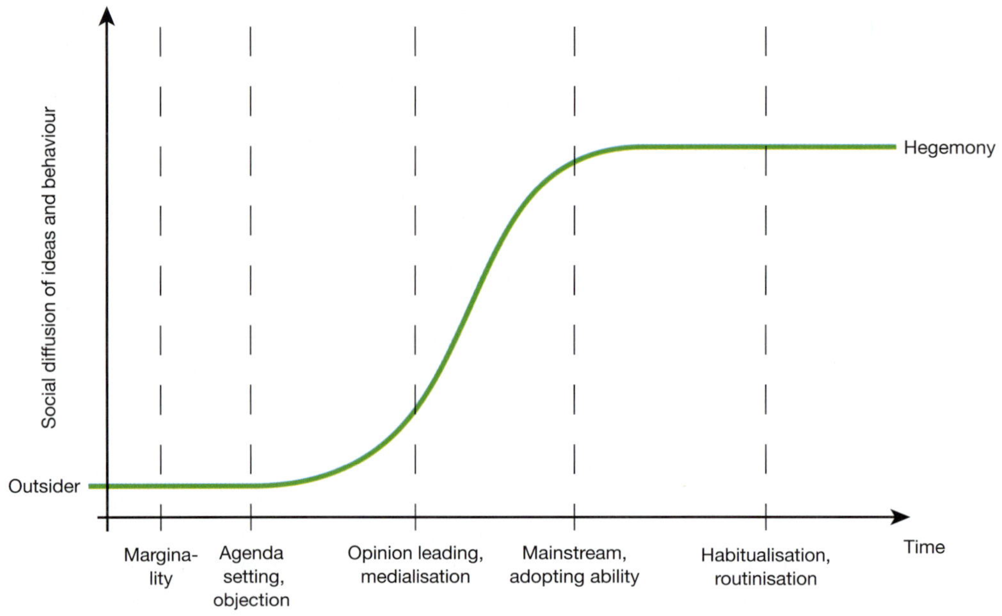

Figure 6.4-1
Phases of social diffusion of ideas and behaviours, and the roles of change agents in the transformation process.
Source: WBGU

unorthodox thinkers and outsiders are at home, out of the so-called niches, the birth place of visions of alternative development, through the stages of social communication (agenda setting, objection, opinion leader echo, mass medialisation) into wider innovation networks, then into the social and political mainstream, up to and including the habitualisation of initially marginal attitude patterns and behaviours.

A bottom-up transformation has far more chance of succeeding if change agents in their respective promoter roles (Table 6.2-2) manage to convince the broad majority of the plausibility of low-carbon life practices in everyday life, of their self-evidence, in fact, and to anchor them as the standard option. The synopsis of surveys and studies on changing values (Chapter 2), on the level of political awareness, on participative citizenship, and on the appeal of non-profit intermediary organisations (associations, or even parties) revealed roughly three (differently sized) segments of the population in wealthy industrial countries (such as Germany) who might be appropriate for an inclusive transformation strategy as pioneers, advocates and partners:

- a broad potential of people who, according to representative surveys, would in principle be willing to embrace low-carbon changes with regard to their own lifestyles, but who have not (as yet) taken any, or few, practical steps to do so (latency);
- a narrow band of dedicated and active citizens who more or less consistently follow this aim systematically in their daily practices (activism);
- a medium segment of people who are more or less actively involved at a civil and voluntary level in other areas of life (sports and leisure activities, humanitarian and technical aid organisations, culture and art, education and care of the elderly, corporate activities, voluntary services, etc.), as well as more informally by way of self-help groups or local neighbourhood schemes, in this way – mostly during critical biographical passages (starting a family, school enrolment and self-reliance of children, parents going into retirement, care, etc.) – addressing the aim of a 'good life' in taking on responsibility for others (or feel the lack of this aim).

The hypothetical path (and, if necessary, the concrete task at hand) for achieving a broad civil commitment to 'climate protection and sustainability' is therefore (a) to stimulate the latent willingness to act through pragmatic (if at all possible not moralising) input, (b) to communicate the actions of activists in the form of action patterns and standard options on a wider basis, and, in doing so, (c) to make sustainability aims plausible to a larger part of the citizenship. This can succeed even better if the familiar core arenas of civil commitment (such as social security, education, nature conservation and consumer protection, cultural life, sports, religious life, etc.) absorb aspects of sustainability, so that no 'additional (time consuming) aims', apart from the respectively preferred activities, are introduced; touching instead on central issues relating to services of general interest (and subjective life satisfaction), to enable the various levels of civil commitment to meet synergistically to create a collective identity (community building). This is vital to broaden the transformation agenda, and for the actors' self-efficacy (Bandura, 1977).

Sustainability commitment is expandable, thereby becoming 'habitual', through real and virtual communication communities which, initially, may very well have little or no relation at all to climate and sustainability policies, but where their requirements and modalities can be tangibly communicated and ingrained in social life-worlds. As already indicated, this includes sports clubs and voluntary groups, school classes and teaching staff, self-employed and pensioners, as well as social media online communities, working groups and professional associations. Such apparently apolitical actors are effective at grass roots level, and help to advance incremental reforms in many areas. The majority of their activities are not related to ecological issues in the narrower sense, but rather on the improvement of working lives, educational practices, care of the elderly and so on. They are about neighbours helping each other in everyday and emergency situations which highlight possible aims of a good life (or which serve to emphasise their lack).

The change agents' articulation and organisation skills are decisive. By and large, they are not organised in larger associations, and do not have long-term horizons; however, they do have political interests beyond the 'policy-making by politicians, for politicians' that is usually the subject of the media, which constantly makes an issue out of something, and makes demands, but in actual fact does and achieves too little, in the public perception. Any ecological policy-making hoping to achieve more than media presence and agreement in opinion polls must find these change agents within the spontaneous social networks, meet them at eye level, and win them over as respected network partners.

The exemplary outlined sustainable policy action fields can also become issues for these networks, generally through occasions which may well seem trivial:

- The refurbishment of a school building thanks to an economic programme, and the considerations with regard to energy in this respect, can turn into something more than ordinary (inconvenient) building works if teachers, school classes and parents take the occasion as an opportunity for pedagogical considerations that go beyond the mundane.
- Day nurseries and all-day schools introduce menus which are not just affordable and tasty, but which systematically integrate aspects of healthy eating, fair trade and a low-carbon diet, and ensure that 'incidentally', these also become the subject of lessons and school communication.
- Local working groups which hold regular meetings and have to travel long distances by train or car to do so change to suitable telecommunications media for these exchanges; this could in turn nudge profound changes in corporate policies and logistics, government administrative bodies, research and cultural institutions.

Not least, this affords the possibility of linking ecological commitment with usually employment-related forms of participation, for example in the form of voluntary activities on the part of companies and government bodies beyond their usual profit-generating or paid activities, or through a closer involvement of the unemployed in ecological activities in the form of appropriate voluntary social work. Generally, the task of mobilising voluntary, but also remunerated commitment to sustainability is to bring it in line with changed situations (Evers and Zimmer, 2010):

- with a working world that has been destandardised in many respects (working hours, temporary contracts, projects, career changes);
- with the various forms of a voluntary social year (already undergoing a review);
- with the integration of 'suitable' commitment phases in curricula vitae and life histories.

There are, however, numerous companies which have consolidated sustainable production, volunteering and social-progressive activities, and turned this into their business model. One such pioneering company is Patagonia Inc., based in Ventura (California), mentioned here just briefly by way of example as it bundles so many aspects of this chapter.

Patagonia manufactures leisure (sports) wear, and was founded in 1972 by the mountaineer Yvon Chouinard. The company mainly produces recyclable materials, including organically grown cotton. It regularly donates 1% of its turnover, or 10% of its profit, to environmental organisations, and is a co-founder of 'Alliance 1% for the Planet', where a number of companies have joined forces to do exactly what the name says. Some outlets and service centres have been awarded silver or gold LEED certificates (the United States Green Building Council's Leadership in Energy and Environmental Design certification) for ecological building. Staff and customers can actively participate in this environmental orientation. Since 1993, staff can take a paid holiday to engage in voluntary work for an environmental organisation. Customers can follow the entire lifecycle of a Patagonia product on the Footprint Chronicles website, from production to recycling, and are invited to suggest improvements. Here, a producer-consumer network is in the process of being created that allows a company to react directly to its customers' sustainability orientation.

The outlined self-organisation of change agents relies desperately on the consolidation and representation of their ideas and suggestions at a political-parliamentary level, in order to encourage feelings of self-efficacy at this level, too. Law makers should utilise these dynamics, and should integrate the various 'bottom-up' approaches in a comprehensive innovation scenario where well-founded imperative and prohibition, sensible market incentives and alternative technologies support citizens' expectations and hopes (Sections 5.4, 7.3.1). If transformative technologies are available, and they appear to be financeable, and if concurrently, there is a broad social consensus that many things will have to change, then one cannot help but wonder at the political elites' deficits in dealing with the growing willingness to protest and the urgent need for reform.

The will forming and interest aggregation of parties and organisations usually rests on their paying membership, private and/or state party financing, and mass-media communication. Local policy is usually also structured in this way, and guided by the local clientele. So far, professional politicians have shown little sense for, and grasp of, empowering the civil society. Examples of this are the mass demonstrations against 'Stuttgart 21' (the extension of a main railway station and its consequences), and the 2010 referendum on educational policy in Hamburg. The potential objections to wind farms and power cables are also examples of the integration tasks that lie before parties and organisations in order to create the room to develop and to experiment needed by the nuclei and clusters of sustainable everyday life, particularly prevalent, for example, in traffic and education projects. A formalisation of these informal networks, which very rarely tend to end in permanent, paying memberships, thereby mirroring the selective and episodic participation behaviour seen in contemporary democracies, would ensure the creation of a political space for the proactive state to motivate (Sections 5.4, 7.3.1), where the various operating modes and timespans with regard to the gaining of political power, the scientific search for solutions, technical innovation and application cycles, and economic and internal corporate cycles become easier to synchronise and, with a view to superior norms, to coordinate.

Recommendations for Action 7

7.1
Challenge Low-Carbon Transformation

In the WBGU's opinion, the transformation towards a low-carbon economy and society in order to overcome the worsening environmental and development crisis and secure humankind's natural life-support systems and future prospects is an urgent requirement. Over the past few years, avoiding anthropogenic climate change has become a topic at the centre of social discourse. A global political consensus has been reached; global warming must be limited to no more than 2 °C above pre-industrial levels in order to avoid dangerous, irreversible and hardly manageable risks for nature and society (Section 1.1.1; WBGU, 2009). This cannot be achieved without drastically reducing greenhouse gas emissions. Between 2011 and 2050, cumulative CO_2 emissions from fossil sources must not exceed 750 Gt CO_2 (Box 1.1-1). This global carbon budget would already be exhausted in around 25 years' time if emissions were frozen at current levels. Fast, transformative counteraction is therefore urgently required. Central to the transformation is the decarbonisation of energy systems (Section 4.6; Box 7.3-1). The transformation cannot succeed if the rapid urbanisation is not redirected to follow low-carbon development paths (Section 7.3.6). It is also essential to mitigate greenhouse gas emissions from land use, and to stop deforestation (Section 7.3.7).

All over the world, the fossil-fuel based economic system has been in a process of radical change for some time. The WBGU views this structural transition as the start of a 'Great Transformation' into a sustainable society (Chapter 3). The extent of the imminent transition can hardly be overestimated. Justifiably, it is identified as a great challenge for humankind. In terms of profound impact, it is comparable to the two fundamental transformations in world history: the Neolithic Revolution, i.e. the invention and diffusion of agriculture and animal husbandry, and the Industrial Revolution, i.e. the transition from agricultural to industrialised society. Contrary to these two historic transitions, the transformation into a low-carbon society must proceed within the planetary guard rails of sustainability (Box 1-1); it also has to happen significantly faster. It is also by no means a given, but must be driven by understanding, caution and providence if it is to succeed within the remaining, tight timeframe. This is unique in history, as the world's past great transformations were the result of gradual evolutionary change. Long-term studies show that an ever-increasing number of people worldwide desire this move towards sustainability (Chapter 2). Moreover, the nuclear disaster in Fukushima makes it clear that we should choose the fast lane towards a low-carbon future without nuclear energy.

The objective is clear, and the time pressure immense, yet because of inadequate national and international political efforts, the huge challenge of this transformation remains unsolved. This drastic change in direction must be accomplished before the end of the current decade in order to reduce global greenhouse gas emissions to a minimum by 2050 to maintain the possibility of avoiding dangerous climate change. Time is therefore of the essence: the later we act, and the bigger the volume of cumulative greenhouse gas emissions, the more difficult it will become to avoid dangerous climate change.

The urgent political task now is putting a stop to the barriers preventing such a transformation, and accelerating the change. In the WBGU's view, this requires the development of a long-term oriented regulatory framework which ensures that prosperity, democracy and security are achieved with the natural boundaries of the Earth system in mind. In particular, development paths must be chosen that are compatible with the 2 °C climate protection guard rail agreed by the global community at Cancún in 2010.

The imminent changes go well beyond technological and technocratic reforms: societies must switch to a new 'basis for doing business'. In fact, it is all about a new social contract for a low-carbon and sustainable global economic system (Section 7.2), based on the key concept that individuals and the civil society, states and the international community of states, as well as business and academia, carry the joint responsibility for the avoidance of dangerous climate change, and the aversion of other threats to humankind in its role as part of Earth system. The social contract consolidates a culture of attentiveness (born of a sense of ecological responsibility), a culture of participation (as a democratic responsibility), and a culture of obligation towards future generations (future responsibility). One central element of such a social contract is the proactive state (Chapter 5), which actively sets priorities for the transformation, and at the same time increases the number of ways in which its citizens can participate, whilst offering the companies choices in favour of sustainability (Section 7.3.1).

By highlighting the technical and economic feasibility of the transformation, by identifying change agents, and barriers - and developing political and institutional approaches to overcome these - the WBGU illustrates the 'conditions of possibility' (Immanuel Kant) for the transition to a low-carbon and sustainable society. In doing so, the WBGU wants to encourage policy-makers, but also business and social actors, to dare to go ahead with this change.

7.1.1 The WBGU's Transformation Strategy

The quest for suitable strategies for the transition to a low-carbon economy has gained hugely in importance for companies, in politics, in science, and in society as a whole. A niche issue has very quickly evolved into a key future issue in Germany and Europe, but also in many other countries around the globe. There are low-carbon development change agents in all areas of society. Many companies acknowledge the fact that in a prosperous world with soon-to-be 9 billion people, the next global innovation cycle simply has to be resource and climate friendly. Long-term investments, particularly in renewable energy as well as in energy and resource efficiency, not only serve atmosphere protection, but also reduce the numerous dependencies on the import of fossil fuels whilst at the same time determining future innovation centres and the reordering of global economic hierarchies. The conversion also opens up new perspectives in Europe for societies that are strong on innovation.

Those pioneers who argued in favour of sustainable development at the Earth Summit in 1992 in Rio de Janeiro are viewed as outsiders no more. In many countries, the positions held by low-carbon development or 'green growth' change agents can claim acceptance by the majority nowadays. The German federal government, Europe, South Korea, China, Indonesia, India, and some US states are actively attempting to delink prosperity increase and greenhouse gas emissions. They have presented strategies, green growth concepts, or conversion plans for their energy sectors.

Furthermore, many different low-emission technologies have seen dynamic global development over the past few years. Renewable energies have become an important economic and employment factor. Many cities all over the world are already implementing climate-friendly future concepts, in some major companies, formerly small departments for corporate social responsibility have grown into 'innovation centres for sustainable markets', and in science, research alliances for the transformation into a low-carbon society have been formed. So the transformation into a low-carbon society is already well under way, and things are changing in the right direction. Maybe, in twenty years' time, due to the 'concurrence of multiple changes' (Osterhammel, 2009) in terms of climate-friendly innovations, the first decade of the 21st century will be known as the decisive transitory stage towards a low-carbon economy – assuming the right course is now set in order to channel this process (Chapter 3).

However, not least the disappointing results of the 2009 Copenhagen Climate Conference prove that so far, few governments, despite local level searching processes for low-carbon solutions, are actually prepared to commit to course changes towards a sustainable global economy that would be binding under international law. And until that is the case, the change agents in economy, politics and society must, in the face of national and international path dependencies evolved during the course of 250 years of fossil-based industrial history, expend enormous efforts on their reform endeavours – just like the famous Sisyphus, who had to push his rock up a steep slope. Ultimately – despite the almost universal triumph of low-carbon reform approaches – the greenhouse gas intensity of global electric power production has nevertheless been on the increase again since the beginning of this decade. A transformation strategy must take these positive reform dynamics on board and multiply them, and also break down the key barriers (Figure 7.1-1). The steep slope of reform must be levelled off to allow the transformation to gain the momentum needed to avoid dangerous climate change.

Nevertheless, there is a very real danger that the dynamics between change and dogged insistence on the status quo will lead into a lock-in (Figure 7.1-2); the transformation into a low-carbon society could also fail. For example, the increasing energy efficiency of vehicles could be overcompensated by a more rapid growth in their number (rebound effect; Box 4.3-2).

Or states could, in principle, agree on mitigating their greenhouse gas emissions, yet only to a level well below the required ambition level. Renewable energies could gain in significance, but they might only be an addition to the still dominating fossil energy carriers, rather than a replacement for them. If the transformation were to be implemented in this kind of half-hearted and slow manner, it could lead to a '3–4 °C world' with almost uncontrollable consequences for nature and society. The important thing now is to set the course in such a way that this becomes improbable.

7.1.1.1
Facilitating and Impeding Factors

One positive aspect is that many important alternative courses of action to facilitate sustainable progress already exist (Figure 7.1-1). The respective technologies are already being used, or under development (Chapter 4). Thanks to modern communication technologies and global knowledge networks, low-carbon innovations and learning processes can spread quickly, even in countries where this is politically suppressed. The respective political and economic steering instruments are also well-known and could, assuming a corresponding public willingness to create favourable framework conditions, soon be adapted to decarbonisation (Section 5.2).

The financial challenges of the transformation are significant, but manageable (Section 4.5). Globally, the additional investments required by the transformation into a low-carbon society, compared to the cost of 'business as usual', probably lie somewhere in the region of at least 200 to up to 1,000 billion US dollars per year by 2030, significantly exceeding this amount between 2030 and 2050. These investments will be offset by later financial savings of similar dimensions, and the avoidance of the immense costs of dangerous climate change. Through innovative business models and financing concepts, it is indeed possible to resolve these issues.

Not least, one positive fact, in the WBGU's view, is that an ever-growing part of the global population is developing value systems which incorporate focusing on the protection of the natural environment (Chapter 2). There is a relatively broad, cross-cultural consensus to transform the predominant economic strategy so that it becomes embedded in sustainable environmental management. Political options that pick up on post-materialist values and sustainability-oriented attitudes are therefore not antitheses to the majority view in industrialised societies. They are also popular amongst opinion leaders in the industrialising countries counting on catch-up development. This makes it easier for policy-makers to make the intended transition agreeable to the vast majority (acceptance), to obtain their consent (legitimation), and to invite cooperation (participation). They should clearly show significantly more courage when it comes to making pro-climate protection decisions: the public is already far more willing to tackle this issue than generally thought.

However, this positive development is hindered by factors which impede a transformation. Political, institutional and economic path dependencies, structures of interests and veto players make the transition into a sustainable society more difficult. The worldwide subsidies for fossil energy carriers are one example of this. Over the past few years, according to various estimates, annual consumption subsidies for fossil-based energies range between 300 to over 500 billion US$ worldwide (Section 4.5). However, this is not just about a lot of money and the corresponding interests of the established high-carbon sectors of the economy. The economic model of the past 250 years, with its rules and regulations, research environments, training and qualification systems and social role models, and its foreign, security, development, transport, economic and innovation policies, has almost without exception been geared towards the use of fossil energy carriers. This complex system must now be fundamentally modified, with a view to a decarbonisation of the energy systems, and radical increases in energy efficiency. John Maynard Keynes put it in a nutshell when describing one of the key challenges of these kinds of profound system changes: 'The difficulty lies not so much in developing new ideas as in escaping from old ones.'

Moreover, the transformation must also be achieved within a very tight timeframe, which, for complex societies, particularly in the context of international negotiation systems, poses a significant challenge. At the same time, our societies must be willing to act in an anticipatory manner, on the basis of scientific findings. To facilitate this, politics, economy and society must wholeheartedly embrace a long-term orientation.

The urbanisation waves in the developing regions, a significant proportion of which are due to high-carbon based economic growth, are a further huge challenge for the transformation process, but also a great opportunity. Particularly in the rapidly growing newly industrialising countries, the transformation into low-carbon cities must be effected within a very short period of time. On the one hand, this means asking a lot of those countries in terms of their transformation and learning capacities. On the other hand, the prevailing tenet there tends to be that climate change has primarily been caused, and continues to be caused, by the OECD countries, and that therefore, the presumably costly investments into climate protection measures must, for the most part, be made in the established industrialised

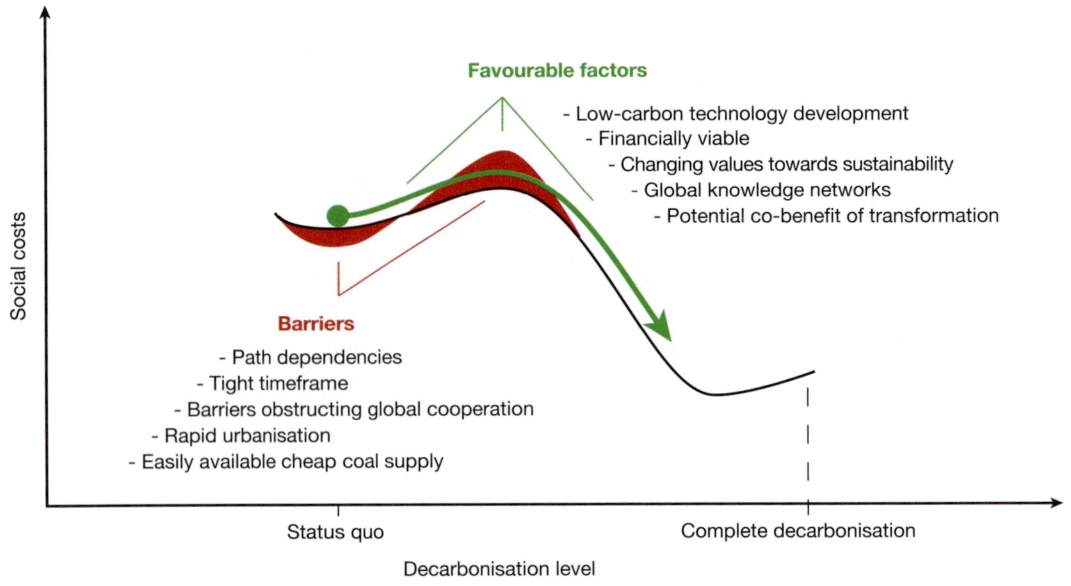

Figure 7.1-1
Topography of the transformation: the first step towards turning the global society's status quo into low-carbon (complete decarbonisation) is the overcoming of obstacles, shown here as an increase in social costs. This increase is currently intensified through barriers (red): the social costs of the status quo appear to be lower than appropriate, due to, for example, misguided incentives such as subsidies for fossil energy carriers, or environmental costs that are not internalised. At the same time, the barriers to be overcome appear to be higher than they actually are: although overcoming various barriers requires a high degree of effort, for example, the costly overcoming of path dependencies, this is compensated by favourable factors: many low-carbon technologies are already available, and their deployment is financially viable. Aided by the favourable factors, barriers can be diminished to pave the way for the transformation. Once the decisive barriers have been overcome, the move towards low-carbon can be expected to develop its own dynamics.
Source: WBGU

countries. This issue has so far not been resolved by a global burden sharing agreement. The situation is made more difficult by the ready availability of cheap coal in many of the newly industrialising countries.

The WBGU analysis also shows that current global governance institutions are not very well equipped to deal with the transformation. This applies in particular to the three key transformation fields energy, urbanisation and land use. Furthermore, currently, no truly assertive climate pioneer alliances exist to accelerate the establishment of post-fossil, transnational system structures.

Overall, though, the WBGU's central message is that the transformation into a low-carbon global society is necessary, and achievable. In some sectors, regions and countries, it has already begun. First and foremost, we must stop impeding the transformation, and instead forge ahead with initiatives that serve its acceleration.

7.1.1.2 Climate Protection in Three Key Transformation Fields

The transition policies towards a low-carbon, sustainable society should primarily address the following three main pillars of contemporary world society (Section 5.4.5): *firstly*, the energy systems, including the transport sector, which the whole economy depends on and which currently, due to the rapid development dynamics in the newly industrialising countries, are facing yet another wave of growth. The energy sector causes around two-thirds of today's long-lived greenhouse gas emissions. *Secondly*, the urban areas, currently responsible for three-quarters of global final energy demand, and whose population will double to 6 billion by 2050. *Thirdly*, the land-use systems (agriculture and forestry, including deforestation), which are currently responsible for almost a quarter of global greenhouse gas emissions. Agriculture does not just have to provide enough food for a world population that continues to grow, and to become ever more demanding; it also has to cover the growth in demand due to the increasing use of bioenergy and bio-based raw materials.

In all three fields, the world is still a long way from setting a clear course towards sustainability. The pledges for mitigation actions announced by the majority of governments within the scope of the international climate negotiations so far will certainly not be enough to comply with the 2 °C guard rail. Nevertheless, the incipient dynamics of the transformation

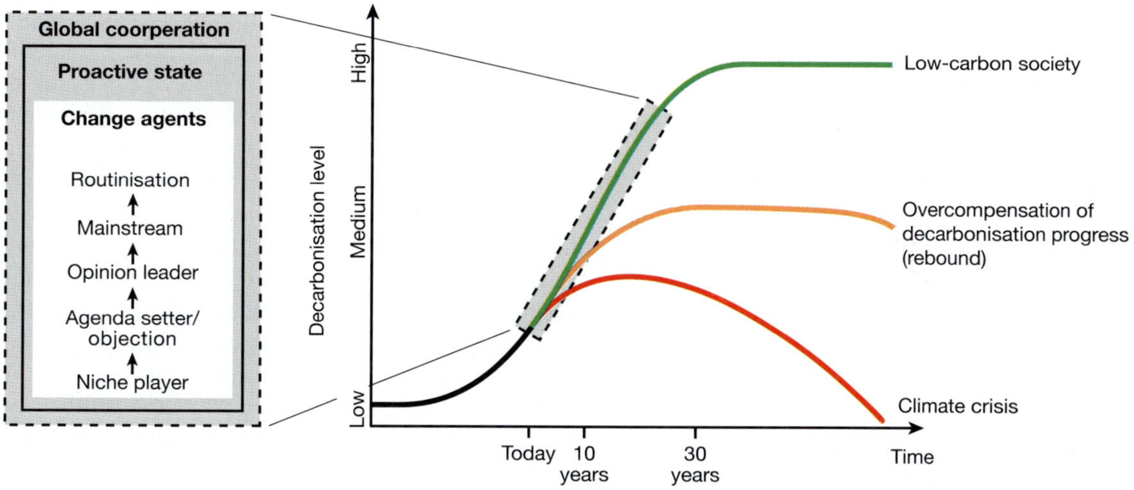

Figure 7.1-2
The transformation's temporal dynamics and action levels. The goal of the transformation is a low-carbon society. Central to the transformation is the decarbonisation of energy systems. Left: The proactive state and the change agents are the key players. As far as the change agents are concerned, they must move away from a marginalised existence and increase their impact through widespread inclusion in social routines. Right: Decisive action for a change of course towards transformation must be taken within the next decade if the conversion is to succeed within the next 30 years. The sustainable path (green) manages the transition from high-carbon to low-carbon society in time. Overcompensation for decarbonisation advances (for example through rebound effects) could lead to rendering climate protection measures ineffective, so that the transformation fails (yellow). Moderate endeavours only carry the risk of path dependencies that will lead to a global climate crisis (red).
Source: WBGU, modified acc. to Grin et al., 2010

should not be underestimated. The debate on the limits to growth, ongoing since the 1970s, and the quest for low-carbon development paths are now taking central stage in our societies. This opens up opportunities for extending the low-carbon experiments, industries, niches and efficiency islands that already exist in many countries, and gives us the chance to speed up the transition from dependence on the use of fossil energy carriers to a low-carbon way of doing business. Measures which, each taken on their own, do not appear to be particularly ambitious can, in such a dynamic transition period, develop significant impact as a whole, and trigger tipping points of development. The transition to a low-carbon society in all three fields is nevertheless a great challenge.

Transformation Field Energy

The transformation field 'energy' is so significant because the world is still continuing down a 'high-carbon growth path' with rapidly increasing CO_2 emissions. If the 2 °C guard rail is to be observed, though, the global emissions trend must be reversed by 2020 at the latest, as the drastic emissions reduction rates which would otherwise be necessary later would overtax societies. A global transformation towards sustainable energy systems that also takes global development dynamics into account is needed. More than 80% of the worldwide energy supply is still based on environment and climate damaging fossil energy carriers, whilst around 3 billion people still have no access to the essential basic supplies provided by modern energy services. The challenge lies in giving these people access to modern energy services as soon as possible, whilst at the same time significantly reducing global CO_2 emissions from the use of fossil energy carriers. This can only succeed if energy efficiency is drastically increased and lifestyle changes are triggered, leading to a limitation of the overall energy demand. The requisite decarbonisation of energy systems means that the pressure is on to act, not just in the industrialised countries, but also in the dynamically growing newly industrialising and developing countries. Even the poorer developing countries must veer towards a low-emission development path in the medium term. The era of fossil energy carrier reliant economic growth must be brought to an end. At the centre of any decarbonisation strategy must be the substantial extension of renewable energies, and the infrastructure they need.

In the WBGU's view, ambitious global climate protection without the use of nuclear energy is possible. A number of countries are currently planning to increase their use of nuclear energy. The WBGU urgently advises against this, above all because of the risks accompanying cases of serious damage, the still unresolved issues concerning final storage, and the danger of uncontrolled proliferation. Existing plants should be replaced by sustainable energy technologies as soon as possible, and, in the case of evident safety deficiencies, be closed down immediately. However, in the advisory council's view, the phase-out of nuclear energy must not be compensated by renewed or intensified brown or black coal based energy generation.

Transformation Field Urbanisation

The transformation field 'urbanisation' is so significant because the urbanisation process is a major driving force behind energy demand. Urban expansion creates new, long-lived infrastructures that are going to impact on the energy demand for a long time to come. Currently, already around half of the world's population lives in cities. In Asia, the urban population will double to almost 3 billion people within the next couple of decades. It is likely that by 2050, as many people will be living in cities as there are on Earth today. The current urbanisation wave must therefore be redirected towards low-carbon urban development very quickly indeed – and that in a situation where we do not have one single, functioning, low-carbon model city that we might learn from. The modification of existing urban structures is also very important; it is time-consuming and therefore requires a determined approach.

Transformation Field Land Use

In the transformation field 'land use', the conversion of natural ecosystems (forests, grasslands, wetlands) into agriculturally used land is one of the major sources of greenhouse gas emissions. Deforestation and forest degradation must therefore be stopped as quickly as possible. Worldwide, forest areas are currently being reduced at a rate of about 13 million hectares per year. According to projections by the Food and Agriculture Organisation of the United Nations (FAO), global food output must increase by up to 70% by 2050 in order to secure the food supply for a growing world population. Agriculture's challenge is covering the strong growth in demand for agricultural produce in a sustainable way that also incorporates the protection of biodiversity, whilst at the same time mitigating emissions along the whole of the supply chain, from field to consumer. One particular challenge here is presented by the changing eating habits in favour of animal products in many regions of the world.

7.1.1.3
Strategic Perspectives

The challenges in the three transformation fields energy, urbanisation and land use demonstrate that the transformation into a low-carbon society means a paradigm shift from fossil to post-fossil society. However, historical experiences and theoretical analysis from a management point of view both show that the transformation that is to be effected will be extremely difficult to realise, as widespread institutional and economic opposition against structural changes of this extent is to be expected. The biggest challenge is the overcoming of political, institutional and economic path dependencies, currently still the hallmark of high-carbon development paths. This may well lead to reasonable doubts as to whether such a global process is achievable, in terms of politics. As far as the transformation is concerned, Bill Clinton's rather well-known bon mot could easily be made to fit: 'It's politics, stupid!'. Still, the uncomfortable fact remains: in view of the impending effects of unabated climate change, there simply is no alternative. Considering the situation, the WBGU sees two very different, both promising, political strategies to move the transformation along:

1. *Polycentric strategy:* The current climate protection endeavours in the different sectors and at different levels are bundled and considerably stepped up. The WBGU is convinced that this strategy can be implemented soon, and with the existing means, and is reasonably realistic. Measures which, taken on their own, have little transformative impact can, through clever mixing and skilful combination, have a far greater impact and generate unexpected movement, far more than a simple addition might lead us to believe. Taken in total, a societal tipping point can be reached, beyond which resistance to the transformation significantly decreases, the requisite political willingness grows, and the acceleration gains considerable momentum.
2. *Focused strategy*: Here, the focus is on concentrating on just a few major course changes that can have high transformative impact – but which a great number of the protagonists currently view as unrealistic, because they would need to be pushed through in the face of powerful forces insistent on preserving the status quo. Some of these major course changes are however necessary to achieve the scale and speed the transformation into a low-carbon society needs to reach.

Both the polycentric and focused transformation strategies are aiming for a 'Great Transformation', and therefore differ from the incremental policies of short-term crisis management and the ever-procrastinating negotiation of compromises.

In this report, the WBGU advocates an intelligent combination of both strategies. There are concrete recommendations for the intensification of current climate protection endeavours with regards to the three transformation fields of energy, urbanisation and land use. The more small-scale measures show results, and the more change agents become actively involved, start networking, and start to initiate changes on different levels, all working towards a transformation, the sooner decision-makers will be encouraged to tackle the major, supposedly unpopular course changes. In a societal environment as dynamic as this, measures which are still viewed as unrealistic today could certainly become realisable tomorrow. The WBGU has therefore ranked its recommendations according to ambition level, i.e. according to their transformative impact and political achievability. This provides for explicitly including major course changes in our recommendations which may still seem unrealistic from today's point of view, but which may well turn out to be inevitable in the long term.

In this way, the transformation towards a low-carbon society has already progressed in some countries or regions. The new narrative or guiding principle is already deeply embedded; in many sectors of the economy and society, change agents are increasingly evolving into opinion leaders and accelerating the redesign of the dominant economic strategy, which is reliant on the use of fossil energy carriers.

Historical analyses show that a 'concurrence of multiple change' (Osterhammel, 2009) can trigger historic waves and comprehensive transformations (Chapter 3). The social dynamics for a change in the direction of climate protection must therefore be created through a combination of measures at different levels:

- It is knowledge-based, based on a shared vision, and guided by the precautionary principle.
- It relies heavily on the change agents, who can test and advance the options for leaving behind an economy reliant on the use of fossil resources, thus helping to develop new leitmotifs, or new visions, to serve as guiding principles for social transition. Initially, the change agents are involved as marginalised protagonists; they could, however, develop into an effective force, greatly advancing the transformation (Figure 7.1-2).
- It needs a proactive state to allow the transformation process to develop into a certain direction by providing the relevant framework, by setting the course for structural change, and by guaranteeing the implementation of climate-friendly innovations. The proactive state provides change agents leeway, and supports them actively (Section 5.4).
- It also counts on the cooperation of the international community, and the establishment of global governance structures as the indispensable driving force for the intended transformation momentum.

7.1.2 WBGU Guiding Principle for the Global Transformation into a Low-Carbon Society

A transformation as profound as this one, requiring significant changes in economic strategy, social structures, political action parameters, and lifestyles, needs a normative and methodical orientation framework: what should such a society look like, and how can that be achieved? The WBGU has developed a guiding principle for the transformation, intended as the basis for social debate. Its function is twofold: on the one hand, it serves to illustrate the aim of a low-carbon society, and to elaborate the characteristics of such a society. On the other hand, it serves to outline the direction that the transformation should take in order to comply with this intended aim. It includes the following points:

Sustainability Context

In the Anthropocene Age (Crutzen and Stoermer, 2000; Chapter 1), humankind must not only take on the responsibility for social development, but also for the conservation of humanity's natural life-support systems. The identification of planetary boundaries or guard rails makes it clear that the current economic strategy, accompanied as it is by increasing resource consumption and rising greenhouse gas emissions, is not sustainable. The Anthropocene requires new, long-term growth strategies which are accompanied by an awareness of the global consequences of local decisions and actions. This new narrative demands a renunciation of the current guiding principles for social and economic development.

In this context, the guiding principles for the transformation into a low-carbon society outlined by the WBGU cover the transition into a sustainable world only partially, as it also involves, beyond the avoidance of greenhouse gas emissions, fundamental ecological, social and economic development goals or guard rails (Box 1-1). However, climate protection plays a particularly important role, as it is a conditio sine qua non for sustainable development. Climate protection alone cannot guarantee the conservation of humankind's natural life-support systems, though. Yet without effective climate protection, essential development opportunities humankind needs will soon be erased.

Aim of the Transformation

The aim of the transformation analysed in this report is a low-carbon society and global economy. The global temperature increase must be limited to less than 2 °C above pre-industrial levels (Section 1.1.1). The amount of cumulative carbon emissions by 2050 will play a major role in determining whether this 2 °C guard rail can be adhered to. This requires emissions of no more than 750 billion t of CO_2 from fossil sources between now and 2050, and only very low amounts after that (Box 1.1-1; WBGU, 2009). To ensure that this global CO_2 budget is not exceeded, the energy systems must be decarbonised, i.e. for the most part more or less emissions-free, by the middle of the century (Box 7.3-1). At the same time, deforestation must be stopped, and the emission of other greenhouse gases caused by land use (Section 7.3.7) and other sources must be mitigated as far as possible.

It is not really possible to define a desired 'final status' beyond general preferences and the concrete climate aim. However, objectives and direction of global economic development can take their lead from globally established and, for the most part, universally accepted standards (Human Rights, UN Conventions). Widely accepted above all is the imperative that current actions should not result in irreparable damages for coming generations to deal with, i.e. that we should not offer them worse conditions, but, if at all possible, better conditions. The global perspective also dictates that despite all our differences and unique cultural characteristics, the global societies' development opportunities should not diverge too much. The principle of 'common but differentiated responsibilities' set down in the UN Framework Convention on Climate Change (UNFCCC) means that the developing and newly industrialising countries are given more leeway in terms of climate policy than the industrialised countries. The respective scope for action can be shaped in various ways, though; each society should – depending on the individual country's specific conditions – develop and follow its own transformation path.

Immediate Action Required

In order to avoid dangerous climate change, the course for the transformation into a low-carbon society must be set within the next decade. By the middle of the century, the global economy must by and large have been decarbonised. Already, in the current decade, the reversal of the global greenhouse gas emissions trend must be achieved.

Extend International Cooperation

Climate change is a global problem, climate protection will therefore always, inevitably, feature intergovernmental components. To achieve the long-term orientation in terms of politics, economy and society that is required for climate protection, the framework conditions must be set accordingly. This essentially needs much closer international cooperation (Section 7.3.9). This applies to the UNFCCC, for a start; all of the country groups will have to make major concessions. Beyond that, the development of a low-carbon global economy is only possible if other international political fields also keep this aim in mind, for example energy, agricultural, research and development policy making (Section 7.3.10).

Give Low-Carbon Development the Room to Grow

To promote a low-carbon transformation, the state must create the required regulatory preconditions, and provide the search for low-carbon solutions with room to grow (Section 5.4). The fossil-fuel based economic system is already changing, and the global finance and economic system is at a critical stage. This improves the chances for a fast transition to a low-carbon economy. Whilst the industrialised countries will go through a structural change, the developing and newly industrialising countries will need targeted support to leapfrog past stages of technological growth in order to be able to follow a different development path right from the outset. Lifestyle changes, particularly in industrialised and newly industrialising countries, are part of this reorientation process.

Mobilise Change Agents at all Levels

The aim of the transformation requires the participation of all social actors in government and administration, politics, companies, the civil society, and consumers (Chapter 6). This should occur across all levels, locally, nationally, and internationally. Change agents play a very important role here. They should be supported politically to allow social movements to leave their niches and impact more broadly.

7.1.3 Criteria for the Efficacy of Transformative Measures

Measures with great transformative effect are characterised by meeting many of the following criteria:

1. *Scale:* The extent of the structural changes is crucial. Low-carbon change processes are required in almost all sectors of the economy. The point here is for the changes to reach the requisite large scale in different areas.
2. *Acceleration:* The window of opportunity for setting the course to avoid dangerous climate change is very narrow. The course towards a low-carbon world must be set within the current decade if we are yet to avoid dangerous climate change. Therefore, measure bundles must be identified in order to significantly accelerate the current reform dynamics.

3. *Initiate Long-Term Directional Changes to Avoid Path Dependencies:* The large-scale and extensive conversion of energy, mobility and land-use system infrastructures needs long-term oriented visions, target systems and 'road maps' until 2050 and beyond in order to generate reliability in terms of expectations, for climate-compatible system changes to overcome existing path dependencies, and for the avoidance of new path dependencies.
4. *Initiate System Reforms:* The measure bundles must take into account that the central areas of the low-carbon transformation require synchronous reforms between networked systems. Low-carbon strategies to manage the global urbanisation wave depend on, amongst other things, interlocked measures in the areas of architecture, urban planning, energy and mobility. Sustainable land use is not just about forest protection, but also about climate-friendly agriculture, and about parallel investments in rural development, food security and the improvement of local governance structures.
5. *Global Extent of the Transformation Process:* Even if the emissions in the OECD countries were radically reduced, dangerous climate change could not be avoided. As the transformation process towards a low-carbon global economy is possible only through accelerated and closer international cooperation, the 'major reform leverages' must not only be designed and used in the field of climate policy, but also in the areas of for example, foreign, energy, research, innovation and development policies.
6. *Convince People, Activate them, Carry them along (Legitimation and Political Feasibility):* The climate-friendly conversion of the industrialised societies impacts the lifestyles and consumption habits of many people. Legitimation and moral support for the transformation can therefore only be created if people are convinced of the sensibility of these reform processes. At the same time, civil society organisations in particular are important drivers of low-carbon change. Low-carbon transition measure bundles must therefore not only be implemented in order to achieve technological breakthroughs and to mobilise substantial investment volumes, but also in order to bring about the winds of change within society, the economy, and politics.
7. *Potential for the Overcoming of Barriers and Path Dependencies:* Some decisions have the power to determine certain developments over decades. The refurbishment of large parts of a country's power generation network, for example, or its extension, determines the energy mix for decades to come. The same applies to the building of cities, as urban structures are highly persistent and can be changed only very slowly. It is therefore vital to influence the strategic direction in certain political areas, for example with regard to energy or infrastructure policies, in such a way that path dependencies are avoided, and potential barriers are overcome.

7.1.4
Ten Measure Bundles with Major Strategic Leverage: Overview

The scale and speed of the current transformation endeavours are by far not enough to avoid a dangerous climate change. We are still a long way away from reaching the tipping point towards a global low-carbon economy. In the following, the WBGU therefore outlines ten 'measure bundles with major transformative leverage' to accelerate and diffuse the transformation. The WBGU defines these bundles as measures requiring relatively little effort to achieve great transformative impact.

In part, the outlined recommendations which promise particularly effective strategic leverage show marked differences in terms of scope, time range of impact, and actors' involvement levels. The analysis in Chapter 3 has indicated that in the past, both the dissemination of steering activities, shared between distinctly different levels and actors, and the simultaneousness and synergetic amplifying effect of individual developments (multilevel, multi-action, co-evolution; Chapter 3) have been important preconditions for transformation processes. From the WBGU's point of view, the following ten measure bundles are of decisive importance to accomplish a global transformation towards sustainability within an acceptable time span (Section 7.3):

1. Improve the Proactive State with Extended Participation Opportunities,
2. Advance Carbon Pricing Globally,
3. Action Field Energy: Promote a common European Energy Policy,
4. Action Field Energy: Accelerate Promotion of Renewable Energies on a Global Level through Feed-In Tariffs,
5. Action Field Energy: Promote Sustainable Energy Supply Services in Developing and Newly Industrialising Countries,
6. Action Field Urbanisation: Steering the World's Rapid Urbanisation Towards Sustainability,
7. Action Field Land Use: Advance Climate-Friendly Land Use,
8. Encourage and Accelerate Investments into a Low-Carbon Future,
9. Support International Climate and Energy Policy,
10. Pursue a Revolution in International Cooperation.

The Transformation Rhombus

The key to a successful transformation into a low-carbon society lies in the interlocking of invention, innovation and diffusion processes, and their acceleration in order to adequately meet the pressure to transform. This is not exclusively about new technical solutions, but particularly also about social and political innovations.

Analysis of Germany's Wilhelminian era ('Gründerzeit', the years around 1870), around the turn of the last century before the first World War, show three closely linked key factors which, taken together, resulted in a 'golden triangle' for innovation processes (Box 3.6-1; Figure 3.6-1): (1) the bolstering of scientific-technological capacities in universities and research institutes, supported by professional training, (2) the emergence of future branches of the economy and (3) high net investment quotas facilitating the fast diffusion of innovations. Policies played a central role as they supported the establishment of research institutions and created favourable framework conditions for economic growth.

These three elements are also crucial for today's low-carbon transformation. However, the image must be extended to serve the illustration of the transformation: the 'golden triangle' is turned into a rhombus (Figure 7.1-3). The WBGU views the *new social contract* (Section 7.2) as pivotal for the transformation; it is therefore also to be found at the centre of the rhombus. It covers the social appreciation of the urgent necessity, and therefore represents legitimacy and acceptance of the transformation. The creation of extended participation opportunities for change agents (Chapters 5, 6) is a precondition that is particularly beneficial in terms of promoting the diffusion of new technologies, social innovations and political reforms within democratic societies.

Beyond this, the image is completed by an additional pillar: the *proactive state with extended opportunities for participation* (Section 5.4.1). One precondition for a successful transformation policy is the simultaneous empowerment of the state (through active prioritisation) and its citizens (through increased participation) with regard to the common goal of sustainable policy objectives.

The state should ensure that the framework conditions for the promotion of the transformation are given. As yet, regulatory policies shaped by the use of fossil energy carriers are prevalent in Germany, Europe, and also on a global level. Although there has been some pressure to adapt these, they have, as yet, not been fundamentally replaced by a climate-friendly regulatory framework and the corresponding incentive systems (Chapter 5). However, this does not mean that the state should be the sole and dominant actor in the transformation process. On the contrary, the WBGU very much feels that change agents exist at all social levels, and that these should be activated and given adequate room to grow and to manoeuvre. For the transformation, the state should in future extend its moderating role. Without a state which plays a proactive and empowering role, change agents' impact will also be limited. This applies to all levels of state action: communal, national, at the level of state federations like the EU and, not least, to international cooperation, for example within the scope of the United Nations.

What is also new is the global aspect of 'statehood'. A limited, national state perspective in terms of views and actions can deliver only less than adequate solutions to global environmental issues and the low-carbon transformation; international cooperation is more important than ever before in order to address these issues. As essential precondition for the transformation, international cooperation must be extended to a historically incomparable degree. It should not only incorporate climate policies within the scope of the UNFCCC and energy policies, but the entire spectrum of sustainability policies. As global governance extends across all three transformation areas, the respective recommendations for international cooperation are dealt with at the end of the Chapter (Sections 7.3.9, 7.3.10).

To redirect investments, the most important issue to be regulated at state level is adequate carbon pricing (Section 7.3.2). This is a key course-setting state action in favour of the transformation, which in this way can be realised, and 'globalised', relatively quickly. As long as greenhouse gas emissions do not carry a price tag in numerous industries and countries, and subsidies in the region of three-digit billions continue to be spent on high-carbon sectors of the economy at a global level, all of the outlined innovations are basically taking place with the handbrake engaged. A low-carbon transformation reliant on market forces must get rid of the price distortions that favour fossil-fuelled industries, because this then directly links competitiveness with climate protection. The introduction of carbon pricing can therefore make a significant contribution to the decarbonisation of the economy, and accelerate it.

In accordance with the rhombus' logic, the sequence of the other measure bundles with major strategic leverage can also be explained. What follows are the *future branches of the economy*, which are not least determined by the fact that some of the decisive economic and social sectors must undergo fundamental changes during the course of the transformation. The WBGU views the energy system, urbanisation and land use as key fields for the transformation into a low-carbon society (Section 7.1.1.2). New framework conditions

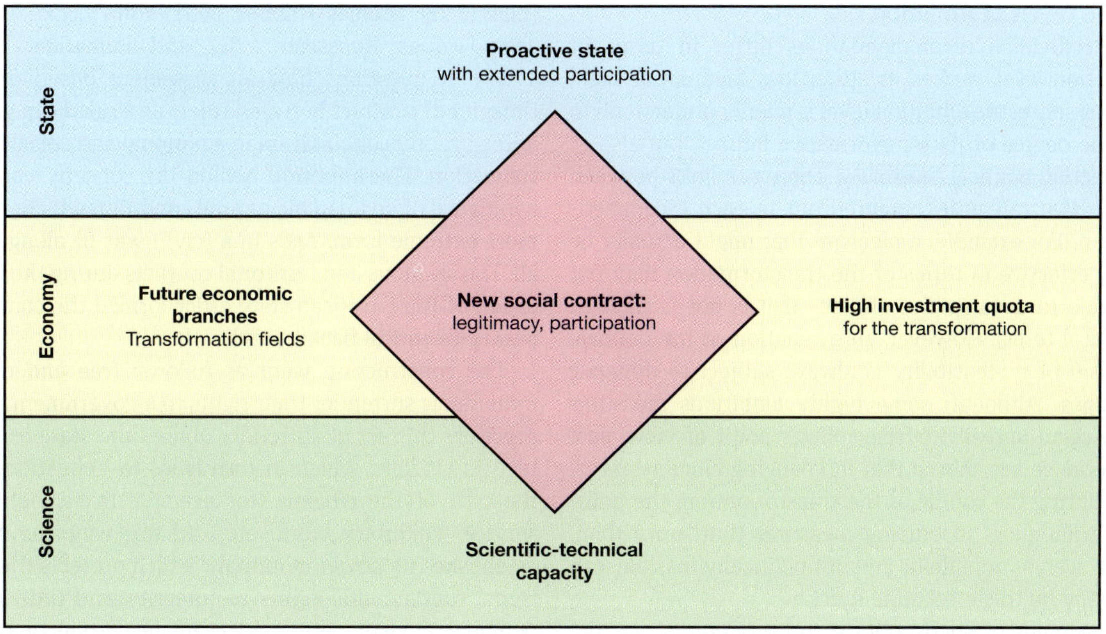

Figure 7.1-3
The Transformation Rhombus. This figure is an expansion of the 'golden triangle' (Figure 3.2-3) which serves to illustrate the innovative wave Germany experienced during the Wilhelminian era. Two elements are added for the transformation: the proactive state and the new social contract (Section 7.2) balancing the proactive state through extended citizen participation.
Source: WBGU

and the price of CO_2 serve as a guiding signal, making the reorientation required in the three decisive transformation fields easier. Here, the WBGU shows how innovative measures with a pilot character can develop systemic impact.

In the transformation field energy (Box 7.3-1), the WBGU advocates accelerating the harmonisation of energy policies across the EU states, not least in order to demonstrate that the transformation is feasible (Section 7.3.3). An EU-wide, standardised, ambitious feed-in tariff would accelerate the expansion of climate-friendly energy generation in Europe, and would be the most affordable way to establish a decarbonised energy system, preferably with a high proportion of renewable energies. This would, however, make sense at the earliest at some point within the coming decade, as the necessary infrastructure would have to be created at first. Beyond that, the WBGU is explicitly in favour of a global political initiative to subsidise feed-in tariffs in developing countries (Section 7.3.4). With a view to countries where future dynamic growth is to be expected, securing of access to sustainable energy services in the rural areas of developing and newly industrialising countries is one measure with great transformative leverage (Section 7.3.5).

The rapid growth of urban areas in Asia's newly industrialising countries is a megatrend of particular relevance for the transformation. In the transformation field urbanisation, the WBGU therefore recommends a whole measure bundle to promote sustainable urbanisation (Section 7.3.6). Inherently, this action field is characterised by pronounced temporal inertia, as urban structures are frequently of a persistent nature and slow to change.

In the transformation field land use, for example, as far as forest protection is concerned, rapid successes can be achieved if the REDD-plus agreements are rigorously implemented. Other changes are achievable only by adopting a long-term perspective, this particularly applies to the promotion of climate-friendly eating habits, but also to the mitigation of emissions globally caused by agriculture (Section 7.3.7).

On the right-hand side of the rhombus, the *high investment quota* can be found as the decisive nudge factor for low-carbon transformation. There is enough capital available globally to finance the investments required for the transformation in the direction of a low-carbon society; however, the challenge here is to utilise this capital for long-term investments in sustainability by introducing suitable incentives. New business models will make it considerably easier to mobilise the available capital for the transformation (Section 7.3.8).

And finally, the development of the scientific and technological capacities forms the basis of the rhombus, dealt with in Chapter 8.

Three Levels of Ambition

The individual recommendations differ in terms of ambition level, ranked as either low, medium or high. In this sense, the ambition level is mainly understood to be the degree of its transformative impact, but also as the actual political feasibility. There are links between these two categories, pointed out in each recommendation. For example, a measure that might actually be very effective in terms of the transformation may not be able to develop this efficacy if it is not feasible in political terms. However, an evaluation of the political realism of its feasibility is always subject to dynamic changes. Although some highly ambitious measures may seem unrealistic from today's point of view, past experience has shown that in changing circumstances, say during the course of the transformation, the political willingness to employ measures that, until then, were seen as unrealistic and not politically feasible, can actually be triggered quite quickly.

Examples of such political 'tipping points' are the three months' moratorium on Germany's oldest nuclear power stations, and the acceleration of the nuclear phase-out by the German federal government (2011), or Germany's all-party debate on the introduction of a financial transaction tax (2009/10). So, taking these facts into account, the WBGU advocates the inclusion of (apparently, from today's point of view) unrealistic, highest ambition level recommendations in all political considerations, rather than discounting them from the start.

Even the evaluation of the transformative impact is not static. Initially, low transformative impact recommendations may not seem particularly appealing, as these measures have little effect; however, some of these measures might prove significant in terms of paving the way, and through this have a surprisingly wide-reaching effect.

7.2 A New Global Social Contract

The constellation referred to as the Industrial Revolution's 'business basis' in Chapter 3 could also be described as the interaction between entrepreneurs, engineers and bankers with an open minded and progressive administration and a confident citizenship. Together, they divested themselves of feudal bonds and religious dogmas and, in an unwritten social contract and for mutual benefit, fastened the 'loose links' between the part systems of state/politics, economy/technology and civil society that had become autonomous as a result. The concept of a social contract developed from natural law of early modern philosophy (mainly by Thomas Hobbes 1651, John Locke 1690, Jean-Jacques Rousseau 1762 and Immanuel Kant 1797). It questions how an agreement based on an (imagined) contract between rulers and ruled can guarantee orderly cohabitation in a national and social confederation. The intention behind the concept was the avoidance of an anarchic natural condition which, in its most extreme form, ends in a (civil) war of all against all. The religious and territorial conflicts during the evolution of the European state order formed the contemporary historical background.

The construction went as follows: free and equal individuals surrender their rights to a government, and precisely this act of surrender obliges the state to protect its citizens, which in turn leads to obligations on the part of the citizens (for example taxes, national service, voluntary work, etc.). In this way, the state establishes its power monopoly, which protects the citizens' fundamental rights to integrity and individual personal development, and regulates property ownership. In turn, the citizenship must provide the state with the requisite resources for this, with the use of these resources being monitored by citizens' representatives elected in the course of developing parliamentary monitoring rights.

In analogy to legal acts, this multilayered agreement for mutual benefit lends legitimacy to the ruling organisation, in as far as it, ideally, enjoys the approval of all those concerned. The objective of the contract concept is not the description or definition of actual processes; however, it is an effective norm for the explanation of the modern state that is no longer the creation of God (or nature), but of sovereign people who – and this is only seemingly paradoxical – have voluntarily surrendered naturally existing liberties, and relinquished the fulfilment of egoistic needs.

In the classical natural-law doctrines, there are marked differences regarding the precise form of the social contract – the determination of the necessary citizens' rights and obligations and the state structure – depending on the author. Whilst Hobbes saw the state as a 'leviathan' equipped with absolute power, Locke argues that the states' power should be limited. This is based on differing anthropological assumptions of the respective contract theoreticians regarding the human condition in the so-called natural condition. Hobbes assumed that humankind is characterised by competitiveness, mistrust and a longing for glory. In the natural condition, this potentially means a war of 'all against all' and that 'man is naturally a wolf to man'. Locke, on the other hand, saw humankind as led by reason and, based on cognisance, fundamentally able to live in peace and harmony. Similarly, the considerations put forward here with regard to a rephrasing of the social contract are also led by a concrete image of humankind, and the question of whether we should have every confidence that Homo sapiens, being capable of reason, will be capable of dealing responsibly with the consequences of this crisis of the Earth system.

Society, politics and the economy have developed significantly, and differences are becoming more pronounced. A revised social contract must therefore address four major challenges:

1. Because of progressive economic and cultural globalisation, the nation state can no longer be considered the sole basis for the contractual relationship. Its inhabitants must responsibly take transnational risks and natural dangers, and the legitimate interests of 'third parties', i.e. other members of the world community, into account.
2. Traditional contract philosophy presupposed the fictitious belief that all members of a society are equal. Considering the disproportionate distribution of resources and capabilities in today's international community of states, we must have effective, fair global compensation mechanisms in place.
3. The natural environment should be given increased consideration when revising the social contract.
4. The contract has to bring two important new protagonists into the equation: the self-organised civil society and the community of scientific experts.

The Great Transformation, which requires huge innovations and investments, will face considerable, powerful forces in the societies, insistent on preserving the status quo. It therefore initially appears unrealistic to expect that the citizens of individual states – not least in view of the globally required solidarities – will voluntarily accept the innovations expected of them, and share their burden. Two examples from recent history, however, show the conditions needed to undermine this kind of dogged persistence to cling to the familiar and to finally do away with it:

1. The accelerated globalisation since the 1970s has placed great demands on societies in terms of flexibility and mobility. In part, these have been met voluntarily with a view to concrete expected benefits, and in part, as a result of 'alternative-less' inherent necessity, accompanied by the acceptance of a reduction in life satisfaction.
2. Welfare state arrangements are based on a (fictitious and in part self-referential) intergenerational contract that defers or desists the immediate consumption of resources in consideration of the welfare of senior citizens – who are either others (those who are old today) or the self (i.e. as the future older generation).

A new social contract (in the sense of a cosmopolitanism inspired by Kant and developed further) is based on different assumptions: on the approval of innovation expectations that are normatively linked with the sustainability postulate, and on the surrendering of the spontaneous desire to insist on the status quo in expectation of the resultant benefits and corresponding participatory rights. As elaborated in Chapter 5, the guarantor in this (again fictitious) contract is a strong, proactive and empowering state that involves its citizens in future decisions requisite to the agreement of sustainability targets, rather than merely permitting them to furnish their approval after the event. This links a culture of attentiveness (born of a sense of ecological responsibility) with a culture of participation (as democratic responsibility) and a culture of obligation towards future generations (future responsibility). This is no demand for a merely superficial or even resigned acceptance on the part of civil society; rather, it is acknowledged as an actively involved partner with shared responsibility for the success of the transformation process, and mobilised, thereby entering into the contract voluntarily – as assumed by the republican-liberal variant of the original social contract. The idea of a powerful state is therefore indelibly linked with the recognition of civil society and the way it has evolved since the 19th century, the innovative powers inherent in the economy, and the proactive and pro-innovation forces active in political and administrative elites. Today, all of this always applies in the global arena as well.

The Aarhus Convention as an Example for Participative Democracy

A good example for the operationalisation and implementation of the procedural side of this concept is the Aarhus Convention, the Economic Commission for Europe's treaty on the access to information, public participation in decision-making and access to justice in environmental matters (Section 5.4.2.2), with its model and pioneering character. The Convention also reflects a new take on the concept of participative democracy: raising the awareness of citizens and the public with regard to environmental protection in order to enable them to pressurise national administrations into stricter application of environmental laws. Through access to information, public participation in decision-making processes, and access to justice, citizens are expected to contribute to the application and enforcement of environmental laws, and also to democratisation – particularly in the former Eastern bloc countries. There is room for improvement in terms of implementation in Germany, especially as far as access to justice for environmental associations is concerned (Section 7.3.1.2).

Beyond that, the Aarhus Convention in its entirety is an expression of the communication process of an empowering state, as it aims 'to mobilise citizens to lobby for law enforcement' (Masing, 1997), and, through this, 'strengthen the public's role in the practical enforcement of environmental law' (von Danwitz, 2004).

Improve the Dialogue between Scientists and Policy-Makers

The community of scientific experts is part of the self-organised civil society. Government action led by scientific insights is essential in contemporary governance, even more so as the world is growing increasingly complex. This particularly applies to the low-carbon transformation as it is distinguished by acting under uncertainty. Scientific advice can make a particularly valuable contribution to policy-making if it reviews and presents complex facts in a comprehensive way, features integrated illustrations of solution options, and communicates conclusions effectively. Both sides are responsible for a functioning communication between politics and science. Science has an obligation to inform society, and scientific findings should therefore be made accessible by being presented in a way that can be understood by many, as it is then most useful. Policy-makers should seriously consider the scientific advice in the course of the decisions that must be made. Against this background, the structure of the dialogue between scientists and politicians should be improved. Generally speaking, transformative policy-making must be accompanied by systematic scientific advice. This requires a stronger accountability in the reception of scientific advice on the part of the politicians, as well as improved structured relations between science, politics and administration (Section 5.4.2.1).

7.3 Ten Measure Bundles with Major Strategic Leverage

7.3.1 Bundle 1: Improve the Proactive State with Extended Participation Opportunities

A central element in a social contract for transformation is the proactive state with extended participation in a multilevel system of global cooperation. This combines two aspects frequently thought of as separate or contradicting: on the one hand empowering the state, which actively determines priorities and underlines and implements them with clear signals (for example using a bonus malus system), and on the other hand, providing citizens with more extensive opportunities to have a voice, to get involved in decision-making, and to take a more active role in politics. A powerful (eco-)state is often thought of as restricting the autonomy of the 'man in the street', whilst at the same time, any meddling on the part of the citizen is viewed with misgivings as a disturbance factor to political-administrative rationality and routines. A precondition for a successful transformation policy, though, is the simultaneous empowerment of state and citizens with regard to the common goal of sustainable policy objectives.

The proactive state is firmly anchored in the tradition of a liberal and constitutional democracy, but it develops this democracy further with a view towards the future sustainability of democratic communities and liberal civil societies, and takes into account the boundaries imposed on economic and social development by a finite planet. Whereas climate protection is often regarded as a restriction and unreasonable deprivation, a proactive and enabling form of government has the explicit task of preserving available choices and the current room to manoeuvre for future generations and even, if possible, to extend these.

The WBGU recommends the approach of these goals on four interconnected levels: *constitutionally*, through the setting of a respective national objective regarding climate protection, *substantive*, through provision of climate protection targets in climate protection legislation, *procedurally*, through extending the opportunities for citizens and non-governmental organisations for public participation in decision-making, access to information and legal protection, and *institutionally* through mainstreaming the climate policies of government institutions. The measures elaborated in the following express and concretise the national objective regarding climate protection, which forces legislators, executives and the judiciary to act. The level of ambition and therefore the transformative impact of these elements, increases through combination and a corresponding definition of content.

7.3.1.1 Increase the Climate Political Responsibility of the State

The general climate political responsibility of the state and its proactive and empowering role in the transformation should be regulated by law. The WBGU recommends that the state's comprehensive self-commitment should be made absolutely clear in both constitutional and administrative law.

Introduction of a National Climate Protection Objective

In constitutional law, the state's climate political responsibility should be emphasised and increased by explicit reference. The WBGU recommends incorporating 'climate protection' as a national objective in the Federal Republic of Germany's Basic Law, possibly as an amendment to Article 20a. A national 'climate protection' objective such as this would emphasise the character of climate as a global common good, i.e. take into account the fact that it is a supra-individual protected property. The state and its agencies would be obliged to take climate protection into account when making climate-relevant decisions with the potential to widen the room to manoeuvre and consider. As an implied benchmark, such a national objective would also serve the judiciary's monitoring duties.

Introduction of Climate Protection Legislation

At the administrative level, this national objective should be concretised through climate protection legislation which stipulates guide values or maximum permissible values, or mandatory reductions of emissions. The WBGU suggests climate protection legislation with ambitious mitigation targets by 2050 as a key measure. Additionally, targets should also be set for the share of renewable energies in primary energy consumption, for the reduction of energy consumption, and for increasing energy efficiency rates. The WBGU's budget approach (WBGU, 2009) could serve as an orientation for the quantitative aspects of the mandatory targets to be set in this climate protection law. Subsequently, Germany should commit to the complete decarbonisation of its energy systems by 2050. This equals a 100% reduction of the CO_2 emitted from fossil energy sources in Germany by 2050. Although flexibility in terms of achieving interim targets within the scope of emissions trading schemes with stringent caps should be retained, the WBGU advises against the offsetting of reductions achieved in countries without emissions restrictions (CDM). Assuming the stated reduction (100% by 2050), Germany would exceed its CO_2 budget, as per the WBGU budget approach. Germany should therefore make additional payments within the scope of international climate financing (Section 7.3.10.1), and also stipulate these by law. Since a law such as this only contains the general commitment to climate protection measures, further-reaching legal regulations are necessary to specify concrete measures for achieving the respective interim targets, and mechanisms in the event of target shortfall. A climate protection committee along the lines of the British Committee on Climate Change could be tasked with a scientific advisory and monitoring function.

7.3.1.2 Extend Opportunities for Information, Participation and Legal Protection

Enhancing the state's proactive role can only claim legitimacy if the citizens participate in the decisions to be made. Extended opportunities for information, participation and legal protection for citizens and non-governmental organisations are the proactive state's counterpart. The public should be informed about projects that have a major impact on climate protection and the transition to sustainable energy systems at a point in time at which all the available options are still open, and become actively involved in the planning and approval process. Further avenues for legal remedy in the form of supra-individual collective actions should be opened up in favour of officially recognised non-governmental organisations, in addition to the existing legal remedies, to allow judicial examination of planning and approval decisions. The use of ombudspersons with a 'right to remonstrance' and a 'right to monitor', as well as prompt, iterative deliberation proceedings with the corresponding inclusion of scientific expert knowledge and non-professional expertise would, in the WBGU's view, complete the procedural system for climate protection relevant decisions by administrative and legislative authorities.

Planning and Approval Procedure Review

In the WBGU's view, one key task for a proactive and empowering state is the establishment of structures that allow effective participation, and to organise a 'constructive communication process', just as required by the Aarhus Convention. It obliges its member states to advise their citizens of environment-relevant projects, and provides them with ways in which to participate, obtain information, and have access to justice. The preconditions allowing the successful participation of citizens and those concerned in decision-making processes, particularly where major projects are concerned, are:

1. extensive and continuous public and local participation at the earliest opportunity, including the unbiased examination of alternative designs,
2. maximise process transparency, for example through increased use of radio and television broadcasting, new media or additional information platforms, or staging dedicated information events, as well as
3. asking independent third parties to intervene in conflict situations. Government agencies must be given more scope for mediation, although arbitration should remain an exception.

Extend the Scope of Collective Legal Action

Collective legal action means the right to appeal to the courts as a group, for example in the form of an officially recognised association, i.e. legal remedy can be sought without the infringement of any subjective rights (supra-individual collective legal action). Due to the legal system in Germany, which requires an impairment of subjective rights collective legal action would require new legislation. Collective European legal action is found above all in environmental and nature conservation law, but also in civil law. In nature conservation law, the concept of collective European legal action makes it possible to enforce legal rules that prove to bear relation to nature protection. The Environmental Appeals Act 2006 provided environmental associations with more scope to file collective European legal action in cases of infringements. The Environmental Appeals Act is the implementation of the EU directive 2003/35/EC, which in its part implements the Aarhus Convention. However, the revised environmental law does not allow associations to file legal action because of infringements of climate protection regulations, even in the case of major projects such as the construction of a coal-fuelled power station. Nevertheless, the exclusion to file the impairment of climate protection rules by the Environmental Appeals Act impairs EU law. It is to be expected that the European Court of Justice will soon decide that this implementation is against European law in proceedings which are currently pending. If climate protection provision infringements were enforceable by means of collective action, this could help to ensure that national climate protection objectives are actually taken seriously by the authorities responsible.

Appoint Ombudspersons

In a broader sense, legal protection also includes – apart from the judicial right to launch legal action – extra-judicial, alternative monitoring methods, which can also serve the assertion of supra-individual interests, such as climate protection, whilst also providing a means of monitoring the climate protection relevant activities of government agencies. Apart from arbitration and the right of petition (Article 24, subsection 2 in conjunction with Article 227 of the Treaty on the functioning of the European Union) this includes the institution of ombudspersons, originally a Scandinavian concept. Ever since the Treaty of Maastricht, the European Union also employs ombudspersons: the European Ombudsman (Article 24, subsection 3 in conjunction with Article 228 of the Treaty on the functioning of the European Union). The initial purpose of instituting ombudspersons is extra-judicial arbitration under administrative law conditions, and monitoring of the national or EU government bodies. The ombudspersons' monitoring rights serve as an extension to jurisdiction, and the protection of the legal order. In this way, the use of ombudspersons with monitoring rights, and the right to lodge judicial complaint, complements and improves the existing information, participation and monitoring rights of associations and the public.

Initiate Deliberative Discourse and Proceedings under Inclusion of Public and Science

Awareness of the necessity and achievability of a profound transformation should permeate all areas of society. A fundamental societal mood of taking issues of sustainable living and economic activities seriously should be strived for, and a 'business as usual' attitude must increasingly be seen as not socially acceptable. The requisite course changes can only be made through deliberative policy-making which takes the arguments and perspectives of all citizens, including scientists, on board and accepts them as advice. Politics should be tasked with initiating such a wide-reaching social dialogue. The issues of climate change, decarbonisation of energy systems, lifestyles and the transformation should be publicly debated, and elaborated with concrete transformation scenarios. To avoid addressing sustainability issues merely symbolically, or the danger of missing the point through inter-party squabbling, a carefully moderated debate under the patronage (and with active participation) of the German Federal President and the above mentioned ombudspersons, and with involvement of the future chambers elaborated in the following, should be instigated, using mainly digital information and communication media.

7.3.1.3
Institutionalise Climate Policy Mainstreaming

The German government, as a state actor, has the opportunity of improving the framework conditions through institutional reforms in such a way that transformation issues are accorded high priority, and are firmly anchored in government and parliament. The German federal administrative bodies should undergo a climate policy mainstreaming at federal, state and local level. In the WBGU's view, this should include the following elements:

Introduce Obligatory Climate Impact Assessment Scheme

In Germany, a comprehensive, obligatory climate impact assessment scheme for any legislative proposal should be institutionalised. It should determine whether individual planned regulations are relevant to the achieving of climate protection objectives. In any case, the respectively more climate-friendly alternative to meet the regulation objective would have to be chosen. Assessing the impacts of laws in such a way is generally not a new concept in Germany. For example, for the past few years, an ex-ante administrative burden assessment has been mandatory. Since May 2009, a so-called sustainability impact assessment must be carried out additionally. Regarding the areas of its application, it should be considered here that a climate impact assessment must be distinctly separate from a project's sustainability and the environmental impact assessments, and also from the strategic environmental assessment for plans and projects, in order to avoid repetition. This can be achieved through a tiered system, i.e. aspects which have been adequately analysed during the previous stage of the assessment do not need reassessing in the next stage.

Recommendations for the Executive Authority

To ensure that all political departments address the transformation towards a low-carbon society, and to improve harmonisation of interdepartmental policies, the issues of energy system decarbonisation, land-use related greenhouse gas emissions reduction and climate-friendly urbanisation should become priority themes for the Federal Committee of State Secretaries for Sustainable Development. Its role as an independent panel should also be strengthened.

To emphasise the transformation issue in German foreign policy, the WBGU recommends the creation of the post of a Minister of State for global sustainability issues, energy system decarbonisation and raw materials strategy in the Federal Foreign Office.

Nowadays, climate protection, nature conservation and sustainable regional planning tend to be addressed and taken into consideration by administrative bodies far more than they were in the early stages of environmental policy-making. However, what has so far not changed is the institutional marginalisation of the responsible departments in relation to political areas that are dedicated to the historical core problems of industrial and welfare societies, namely the finance, infrastructure and social departments. In the WBGU's view, the current departmental architecture prevents climate protection, nature conservation and regional planning from reaching the status they should have in the shaping of a post-fossil future, and the building of a sustainable economy. Therefore, in the long term, a partial modification of the current departmental architecture should be considered, for example by establishing a ministry for the environment, climate and energy.

One means of achieving the purpose of 'global education', and a very real recommendation for the federal government to consider, is an internationalisation of the ministerial departments, for example by staffing them with 10–15% of staff hailing from other OECD nations, developing and newly industrialising countries. In turn, German personnel could in exchange help to build up the required capacities, particularly in the developing and newly industrialising countries. In this way, national interests and perspectives could be brought into line with international perspectives and discourses right from the start, learning processes would be accelerated on both sides, and multilateral trust would be generated. A concrete step in this direction would be, for example, the setting up of exchange programmes for departmental staff, comparable to the German Academic Exchange Service (DAAD) for scientists.

Recommendations for the Legislative Authority

In addition to the climate impact assessment, the WBGU suggests a look at the various options of how parliament could take on a more effective role. If, for instance, the Parliamentary Advisory Council on Sustainable Development were to be turned into a permanent committee within the German Bundestag, it would be in a far better position to act and assert its objectives.

National policies have reached their limits, both in terms of time and scope. We must therefore discuss how the (supposed) interests of future generations can be taken into account in contemporary elections and polls, and how people beyond national borders can be included, in accordance with transnational democracy. The indirect 'children's right to vote' (by proxy, the parents' casting the vote) being discussed throws up major constitutional and practical problems. In order to provide an institutional anchor for future-oriented interests, the WBGU therefore proposes an extension to parliamentary legislative procedure in the form of a deliberative 'future chamber', to be referred to by the relevant political agendas, and with a right to put up a deferring veto if necessary. To avoid interest and party political interference, chamber membership should be decided by drawing lots.

7.3.1.4
Strengthen the Proactive State in a Multilevel System of Global Cooperation

Statehood transcends national borders and sovereignties, particularly as far as climate, energy and the environment are concerned; this aspect also requires new supra- and transnational institutions. One prime example for such improvement, in the opinion of the WBGU, is the European Union's network of institutions, as the EU, after all, will also benefit from impulses for a deepening of its integration through joint, citizen-friendly climate, environment and energy policies (Section 7.3.3). On an international level, central arenas for global governance of energy, urbanisation and land use would have to be established for the transformation (Section 7.3.10). The Aarhus Convention, so far limited to Europe, is exemplary for activating the global society.

Empower Newly Industrialising Countries to become Proactive States

For the global transformation to succeed, particularly the newly industrialising countries must become active agents in the low-carbon reorganisation. If Germany and Europe intend to nudge newly industrialising countries towards the low-carbon transformation, or build on any existing reform tendencies, they must take into account the differing initial conditions (Section 5.3.3).

China, for example, could become a driving force for climate-friendly development. This is supported by the fact that the challenges of climate change have undergone a recoding, from environmental to economic and innovation issue, in China over the past few years. Certain approaches in the Chinese government's new five-year-plan, published in 2011, also offer proof of this. Today, China already possesses the largest capacities worldwide for the manufacture of solar modules, and has some ambitious extension targets for renewable energies. Parts of the Chinese elite view 'green' development as a chance to improve China's national welfare as well as its reputation with regard to foreign affairs. In view of this, starting points for transformation alliances with China would be broadly impacting innovation and technology partnerships, particularly in the transformation fields energy and urbanisation, where, from a Chinese perspective, Germany and Europe are outstanding in terms of technological competence.

Brazil also has the potential to develop into a low-carbon pioneer economy, particularly because its natural environment and the initial political conditions (democracy, institutional capacities, high government legitimation) are favourable for the use of renewable energies, and there is a global willingness to protect the rain forests. Contrasting this is a social majority rooted in a traditional modernisation agenda. Brazil should be won as an important strategic partner for sustainable development, because the country, apart from its forests and agricultural resources, also has a significant amount of technical experience with regards to renewable energies to offer. Climate partnerships with Brazil should therefore focus primarily on cooperation in the energy and transport sector, as well as forest protection.

Alliances for climate-friendly growth should also be forged with India. Contrary to China, the country still has a chance of designing its modernisation process without taking the 'fossil detour', and to rely from an early stage on a low-carbon development path. In India, the public debate on low-carbon development is overshadowed by the discussion on economic capability and poverty reduction, even though the government has put the issues of energy efficiency and emissions control on the agenda. Here, it is above all important to demonstrate, through showcase alliances, for example in the area of renewable energies and infrastructure expansion, how the fight against poverty can go hand in hand with economic growth.

Overall, it can generally be said that only proving that climate protection, competitiveness and growth can be successfully combined will make you interesting as a partner for cooperation, thus establishing a credible basis for it. Above all, transformation towards a low-carbon economy must therefore be resolutely advanced by the highly developed economies.

7.3.2 Bundle 2: Advance Carbon Pricing Globally

The WBGU believes that carbon pricing is the most important political measure for energy system decarbonisation, and a necessary element of any regulatory framework for the transformation into a climate-friendly society. A CO_2 price signal can in principle be given through the introduction of a CO_2 tax (price control), or an emissions trading system (quantity control; Section 5.2.2). Provided that the institutional conditions for this are given, in the WBGU's opinion emissions trading systems are generally the more promising concept for carbon pricing in order to achieve a targeted emissions restriction. However, emissions trading can only guarantee an adequately high carbon price and long-term reliability of expectations through very strict capping in order to develop transformative impact. Where the requisite institutional opportunities are not given, a CO_2 tax at a corresponding level represents an alternative instrument for effective, transformative governance. As a guide value, from today's point of view, the 2020 carbon price in the OECD countries would have to be at least around 40–50 US$ per t CO_2 in order to have the transformative effect required by the 2°C guard rail (estimates based on IEA model calculations and the scenarios elaborated in Chapters 4.2.4 and 5.2.2). For carbon pricing to achieve maximum impact, the subsidies for fossil fuels which still exist in many countries should also be phased out at the earliest opportunity.

The aim of German and European efforts should be the establishment of a global emissions trade at corporate level in order to fully tap this instrument's potential in terms of environmental and efficiency benefits.

It must be said, though, that a comprehensive and binding climate protection treaty, which could include a global emissions trade at corporate level, does not appear to be realisable in the short or the medium term, even after the UN Conference at Cancún. Short-term national interests still block prompt and effective global climate protection agreements.

The WBGU suggests several paths with differing levels of transformative impact as interim solutions to aid the creation of a global carbon market. A first step is the further development and strengthening of the European emissions trading system, accompanied by endeavours to convince the most significant emitters to commit to CO_2 pricing. In addition, sub-global emissions trading systems, assuming a suitable design, could increase the willingness of countries to contribute to global emissions restriction. Ultimately, joint emissions restrictions complied with by all high-carbon countries could pave the way for a global carbon market. To be kept in mind: the higher the transformative impact of the paths described here, and the more countries subscribe to a carbon pricing system, the higher the demands for the state to act.

7.3.2.1 Low Ambition Level: Develop the European Emissions Trading System further, and Reach a G20 Agreement on Carbon Pricing

Supranational emissions trading systems such as the European Union Emissions Trading System (EU ETS) are important steps on the way to extensive CO_2 restrictions. The EU ETS should be continued and developed further. In particular, its administration should be made less complex in order to facilitate a future linking with a sustainable global emissions trading system at corporate level. Also important are more ambitious caps on emissions. The rather moderate emissions caps of past trading periods led to a relatively weak and volatile carbon price signal which did not adequately support many of the investments and changes on the demand side required for the transformation. The EU-wide goal for emissions reduction should be increased to at least 30% below 1990 levels by 2020 (WBGU, 2010b), and EU ETS emissions cap should be adjusted accordingly. In addition, a readjustment of the amount of allowances during auctioning, or, respectively, the trading period, should be considered. For example, the amount of allowances available during auctions could also be reduced to avoid a too low price on the carbon market. Apart from that, CO_2 pricing should be extended within the EU to include all fossil CO_2 sources. This could be effected by shifting the emissions trade to the first commercial level of the supply chain (upstream), i.e. on production or import of fossil energy carriers, or through the introduction of carbon taxation for so far not included, diffuse emission sources (transportation, for example), which are difficult to integrate into the current emissions trading system.

In the form described here, the EU ETS could develop significant transformation impulses within the European Union, and accelerate the reorganisation process towards a climate-friendly, resource efficient economic system. At the same time, the EU would serve as a showcase, and therefore role model, for other countries or country groups to move towards a low-carbon society. As the individual member states are responsible for the implementation of the above mentioned measures, this would require no further cooperation demands at international level, a favourable aspect for effective realisation.

Increasing its own reduction targets within a further developed emissions trading system is, in the WBGU's opinion, the minimum requirement to ensure that the EU regains its credibility with regard to international climate policy, and becomes a driving force in the global transformation towards a low-carbon society. This, however, can only be one element of its commitment, and must be complemented by further bi- and multilateral agreements and contributions on the part of the EU. Germany and the EU should, for instance, lobby for the introduction of policies leading to an adequately high carbon price in as many countries as possible. A joint commitment of all G20 states to the necessity of the introduction of carbon pricing in their countries could be an initial step. Such a commitment would be important in order to increase the states' credibility concerning the implementation of the unilateral pledges made within the scope of UNFCCC. For companies and investors, this would signalise that the G20 states are willing to create binding framework conditions for a decarbonisation of their energy systems.

7.3.2.2 Medium Ambition Level: Pursue Linking Emissions Trading Systems

Parallel to developing the EU ETS further within Europe, and all high-carbon countries subscribing to the introduction of carbon pricing, precise links for international cooperation during carbon pricing introduction and design should be sought.

One possibility is the linking of existing emissions trading schemes, which could be effected in several stages up to the definition of a joint, cross-national emissions cap. The linking of national emissions trading schemes can contribute to increased efficiency in terms of reaching the pledged mitigation targets, as more cost-efficient mitigation options can be fully tapped. Apart from that, this is also a further step towards the overall objective of a global carbon market. Probably even more important, though, is the political signal that linking existing emissions trading schemes would give with regard to international climate policy. The more countries participate, the higher the chances that other countries will follow their example, not least because they have more faith in a cooperative solution. The EU should therefore emphatically explore possibilities for cooperation with the linking of existing emissions trading schemes in mind. Moderate border adjustment measures could help to reduce distortions of competition for companies in pioneering countries, and to lower the incentives for free-rider.

However, the USA's failure to adopt a national climate protection law represents a serious setback for endeavours to establish a linked transatlantic carbon market. China, on the other hand, has announced that it intends to test carbon pricing and emissions trading within the scope of the 12th five-year-plan, initially regionally limited. An active partnership of Germany and the EU with China for the design of an appropriate system, particularly also with regard to the experiences made during the introductory phase of European emissions trading and its further structural development could possibly make a later linking to the EU ETS less difficult. Potentially, these steps could smooth the way for a geographically even more extensive system and the inclusion of further partners.

Sectoral approaches in emissions trading aim in a similar direction. Countries which so far have not introduced any national emissions restrictions could, initially with a sectoral or tiered approach, participate in extended European emissions trading (WBGU, 2010b). Initially, apart from binding caps, relative targets (i.e. efficiency targets) are also an option in order to achieve at least a minimum steering effect, and to create the structures for later, more demanding reductions with absolute capping. In light of the global emission reductions demanded by the 2°C guard rail, sectoral approaches should take into account the inclusion of potential, gradually increasing future reduction pledges right from the start.

Complementary to geographically extended emissions trading, the introduction of a CO_2 tax would be a reasonable measure in countries that are currently unable to introduce emissions trading systems due to a lack of institutional capacity. In the interim, these countries' decarbonisation efforts should be accompanied by financial transfers, for example within the scope of other measures of international climate policy (Sections 7.3.8, 7.3.9). The financial transfers should be linked to the generation of strategies for low-carbon development, or roadmaps, elaborated by the newly industrialising and developing countries themselves. Germany should lobby for the inclusion of the issue of carbon pricing as a framework condition in the low-carbon development strategies and roadmaps of these countries. The UN should offer advice and capacities for the implementation of these strategies, for example within the scope of the UN Conference on Sustainable Development 2012 (UNCSD, or Rio+20 Conference). Beyond this, financial transfers within the scope of the UNFCCC for mitigation in newly industrialising countries that have as yet not introduced carbon pricing should be linked to the condition of presentation of a draft strategy for ambitious carbon pricing.

7.3.2.3
High Ambition Level: Establish an Emissions Trading Scheme that is as global as possible, with joint Emissions Restrictions

The rapid and extensive integration of all high-carbon countries should be addressed, preferably parallel to the above described activities. This integration would ensure that significant global emissions reduction is achieved. Within the scope of common ambitious emission restrictions for the economies concerned, this would generate a strong, price signal with a broad impact. In this way, the requisite acceleration of the transformation could be achieved, and it would be an important step towards a global carbon market. This politically ambitious strategy seems called for if global emissions are to reach their peak in the current decade in order to retain an acceptably high probability of complying with the 2 °C guard rail. However, this would require a huge political effort significantly beyond current cooperation attempts in emissions trading.

The EU should therefore strive for extensive cross-national emissions restrictions as soon as possible. Considering the particularly heavy emission increases in the larger developing and newly industrialising countries, these nations should be included in cross-national capping at the earliest opportunity, as well as the major emitters in the industrialised countries. To facilitate this, actors from the industrialised countries willing to cooperate and BASIC countries could, for instance, negotiate the allocation of emissions rights whilst concurrently introducing efficient trading mechanisms within this coalition. However, the expansion of emissions restrictions to also include developing and newly industrialising countries can only succeed if the allocation is effected on a fair basis, and the respective agreements go hand in hand with the relevant technology transfers. The WBGU budget approach (2009b) provides an international compass for the determination of the emissions volumes still acceptable from an environmental point of view, and assumes the equal distribution of emissions rights on a per capita basis. These principles are also relevant for an implementation strategy within the scope of a sub-global emissions trading scheme at corporate level: a pioneer coalition's joint cap should be determined by taking the still admissible global emissions volume into account, and the resultant transformation pressure. A fair sharing of the burden of decarbonisation efforts can be ensured if the involved nations benefit from the auction revenues of a joint emissions trading scheme at corporate level on a per capita basis. To implement such an integrated system, structures should be established within the coalition that could serve as the prototype for a future world climate bank (WBGU, 2009).

This procedure is recommended to involve larger newly industrialising countries more closely in international negotiations, despite the current veto position of some major actors, notably the USA. In these rapidly growing economies, path dependencies should categorically be avoided, as continuing on a high-carbon growth path would lead to decades of excessively high global emissions, making the prospects of significant emission reductions utterly remote. Furthermore, if action were taken at a later date, the cost of global energy system decarbonisation would be far more substantial (Section 4.5.1).

Additional emissions reductions, which could be achieved through establishing a pioneer coalition, depend on the number of partners, and determining the joint emissions caps. A partnership between the EU and, for example, Japan, China, India and Brazil, would relate to currently around half of all global CO_2 emissions (estimated on the basis of WRI-CAIT, 2011, excluding land-use changes). If, however, the USA, Russia, Canada and Australia were to be included in a cross-national capping, this would cover around three-quarters of global emissions in 2007. An absolute emissions restriction leading to an effective reduction in the coalition's emissions, or at least to a peaking within the current decade, would also have the desired global signal effect, as the most densely populated and fastest growing newly industrialising countries would be tied into the system.

Major transformative impact can only be achieved with a very high level of international cooperation. To bring about global carbon pricing ultimately requires a kind of 'cooperation revolution', making strategic acting far beyond Europe's borders a necessity. Without global carbon pricing, however, significant emissions reductions and the requisite structural changes cannot be achieved in the long term.

7.3.3 Bundle 3: Promote a Common European Energy Policy

7.3.3.1 A Common Energy Policy as a Chance for Europe

In the face of the challenges of climate change, increasing dependency on imported fossil energy carriers, and increasing energy prices, a turnaround is absolutely vital for the EU. Goal of a common European energy policy should be the decarbonisation of the energy systems by the middle of the century. To achieve this, the WBGU recommends consistent and strong support for renewable energies, a coordinated, speedy extension of grid infrastructure, grid access, as well as storage facilities and strong foreign and development EU policies on energy to promote the integration of neighbouring states in North Africa and (primarily) constitutional and institutional changes to ensure that all EU policies take climate protection and transformation issues into account.

A common European energy policy would have a great symbolic effect, and would underscore Europe's commitment to joint action in key future-oriented fields, strengthen the Union's competitiveness, and serve as an inspiration to the global economy. Currently, the EU is lacking a new project that convinces and motivates its citizens and fills them with enthusiasm. Nowadays, energy and industrial policy initiatives in the area of renewable energies can kick-start a deepening of the European Union, similar to the political identity created by the European Coal and Steel Community on the basis of fossil-fuelled energies. A common European energy policy could lead the way into a new energy era, and prove to the world the achievability of a continent-wide, sustainable energy supply. Important directional changes are currently taking place regarding the further development of the European energy market and, in particular, the regulation of grid access (draft of the fourth internal energy market package). These developments towards decarbonisation of the energy supply on the basis of renewable energies must be advanced.

7.3.3.2 Low Ambition Level: Strengthening of the Objective 'Climate Protection' and elaborating Existing Energy Policy Measures

The EU has already laid the foundation for the decarbonisation of the European energy system with its existing energy policy approaches. The climate protection targets defined in the EU climate and energy package are an important guideline for the dynamics of renewable energy expansion and energy efficiency increase. Particularly the 2009 renewable energy directive, with targets set for 2020 regarding the share of renewable energies in final energy consumption and in the transport sector, attempts to step up the use of renewable energy carriers to make it possible to gradually phase out fossil energy carriers. However, the existing, moderate approaches for the promotion of renewable energy within the EU, and the member states' individual support programmes, are not enough. The EU should therefore, by continuing to update already existing energy policy measures, providing further incentives, and setting targets: beyond the (overall) targets set for 2020 defined in the renewable energies directive, ambitious targets by 2050 are necessary. Climate protection objectives must be developed further, and binding energy efficiency targets must be agreed. Medium-term targets allow the monitoring of the planned expansion targets and, if applicable, their adaptation based on the latest scientific and technological findings. These material provisions should be procedurally accompanied by extending monitoring scope, such as, for example, the introduction of collective European legal action.

The existing financial support enjoyed by renewable energy carriers in many countries also has an accelerating effect in terms of their expansion. However, currently, there is no standardised, Europe-wide subsidy system. Although according to the renewable energies directive, cross-national cooperation within the European Union with regard to renewable energy subsidies would be possible to ensure target flexibility, it is, however, not obligatory. The cooperation could therefore occur in the form of mutual statistical apportionment, joint projects (also with non-EU countries), as well as cross-national subsidy mechanisms. The latter would lead to a standardisation of subsidy amounts. So far, these options have not been explored, due to the high transaction costs, and uncertainty as far as the determination of national targets is concerned. A standardisation of subsidy systems and amounts, however, would reduce support costs Europe-wide, and would be an important step towards the full support harmonisation under EU law, which in the WBGU's view should be strived for in the medium term (Section 7.3.4). Therefore, the support measures suggested in the renewable energies directive should be implemented.

Constitutional and institutional changes at EU level could promote the update of energy policy measures. Climate protection already is one of several EU environmental policy objectives, and must be taken into account in all political departments as part of environmental protection. To increase the measure of consideration enjoyed by climate protection in all political EU measures, however, explicit referencing of climate protection in the list of objectives in Article 3 of the Treaty on the European Union (TEU), and in the horizontal clause of Article 11 of the Treaty on the functioning of the European Union, is required. Symbolic-constitutional anchoring demands and ensures continued support for energy policy measures. Simultaneously, the extensive consideration of climate protection issues must also be institutionally anchored. The introduction of climate policy mainstreaming can ensure that climate protection and transformation issues enjoy a high priority across all departments, and are duly considered when drafting potential legislation. Climate policy mainstreaming along these lines, focusing on a transformative energy policy, appears to have already begun in the Energy Directorate-General. Its energy policy, developed on the basis of the 'Europe 2020' strategy and the 'Energy 2020' communication, is aimed at ensuring the availability of technological innovations in the energy sector, as well as compliance with the energy and climate targets. Successful implementation of the climate protection objective at Union level nevertheless needs a stronger commitment to transformative policies across all organisation units, i.e. a mainstreaming of climate policies.

7.3.3.3
Medium Ambition Level: Realisation of a Single European Energy Market

One important step towards decarbonisation of the European energy systems, although by no means the last one, is the realisation of a single European energy market. Only a functioning, single European energy market can ensure a continent-wide sustainable energy supply: unrestricted grid access and cross-border networks are indispensable for the efficient integration of renewable energies into existing grids, and to guarantee a reliable supply. The EU's third internal energy market package from 2009 forms the basis for cross-border organisation of grid operation and market integration, so the foundations for a functioning internal energy market have already been laid. However, these measures have as yet not been completely implemented by all of the member states. Particularly unrestricted grid access should be ensured through the establishment of independent network operators, the only way that allows the development of a single European market for electricity with uniform prices. Hence the WBGU suggests that the federal government fully support the realisation of a climate-friendly single energy market by the EU, as the EU can, on the basis of its competency, ensure the implementation of the measures planned within the scope of the internal energy market package, and thus accelerate the realisation of a single energy market.

Box 7.3-1

Energy Use Transformation I: Decarbonisation of the Energy Systems

The most important starting point for the transformation towards a low-carbon society is the reduction of CO_2 emissions from the use of fossil energy carriers. Various analyses show that the decarbonisation of energy systems on a global level is feasible, both from a technical and an economic point of view (Chapter 4). Over the long-term, the economic costs of such a transformation are just a few percent of global GDP. If the transformation is to succeed, a vastly accelerated reduction of the CO_2 intensity of the economic output is vital. To follow an emissions path leading to emissions of no more than 750 billion t CO_2 from fossil sources by 2050, at an economic growth rate of 2–3%, the CO_2 intensity of the global economic output over the next few years would have to be decreased at least twice as fast as it has done in the past.

There are marked differences between the analyses in terms of the technology portfolio available for the energy system decarbonisation. i.e. there is more than one climate-compatible way to transform the energy systems. The actual energy path followed will differ between states and regions, depending on political, technological and cultural circumstances and preferences, and individual geographical features. Particularly the use of nuclear power and the relevance of carbon dioxide capture and storage (CCS) could develop in very different directions, both regionally and nationally – primarily through policy decisions. The WBGU advises against the use of nuclear energy, above all because of the risk of serious damages, the still unresolved issues concerning final storage, and the danger of uncontrolled proliferation. CCS, on the other hand, is a necessary mitigation option for countries which continue to use fossil energies if the 2°C climate protection guard rail is to be complied with. In combination with the use of bioenergy, CCS could also turn out to play a role in the active withdrawal of CO_2 from the atmosphere later on. In its recommendations, however, the WBGU focuses on development paths that accord these two technologies only a marginal role. Rather, the WBGU recommends a strategy that relies primarily on an accelerated use of renewable energies, with the prospective aim of covering 100% of the demand with renewable energies.

In the WBGU's opinion, a look at the various transformative scenarios (Section 4) suggests that the global final energy demand should not rise to more than 400–500 EJ per year by 2050 if the transformation is to succeed. Global final energy demand currently runs at approx. 350 EJ per year. Without a political change of course, the final energy demand could more than double. Limiting final energy demand is therefore a major challenge, particularly in the industrialised countries, as well as the rapidly growing newly industrialising countries, and corresponding strategies are extremely important.

Apart from decarbonisation, the second major goal of a remodelling of the energy systems is overcoming energy poverty (Box 7.3-2).

7.3.3.4
High Ambition Level: Europe-wide Energy Strategy on Union Basis

The most effective way to achieve the decarbonisation of the European energy systems would be if the EU were granted the authority to define a European energy strategy. This would accord the EU the right to establish a Europe-wide energy policy on union basis, which would include choosing the respective energy carriers, and the extension and modification of cross-border infrastructure. The EU could bundle the continent-wide renewable energy potential, not least owing to the competency to define the legal framework for the European energy mix, which in turn guides the member states' decisions on the choice of energy carriers. Considering the various geographical and economical potentials for the production and storage of renewable energies, it could drive ahead their cost efficient extension: wind energy from the Baltic and the North Seas, biomass from Eastern Europe, solar power generated in southern Europe, and expert knowledge regarding the extension of trans-European grids from Germany and other countries strong on technology. As the EU currently does not have the authority to decide the legal framework for the European energy mix (environmental and energy policy, Articles 191 and 194 of the Treaty on the functioning of the European Union), it should be accorded the corresponding legislative competence.

In order to function, such a common energy policy requires continent-wide networking of energy production, consumption and storage. A prerequisite is that a common, barrier-free single energy market exists, and that energy grids will be extended to cover the whole of Europe. The EU should therefore coordinate grid extension efforts: a transcontinental electricity supergrid should be created in Europe to facilitate the exchange of electric power within Europe. The grid should also be linked to neighbouring countries that produce power or store it, for example to Norway's storage power plants, to offshore wind farms, or, taking this concept one step further, to solar thermal plants in Africa. Apart from the balancing of regional fluctuations in terms of the energy offer, the grid contributes to the efficiency and improvement of the strategic security of energy supply. The grid expansion requires joint planning in order to be implemented, including the securing of the requisite investments. Although the third internal energy market package creates a new legal framework for the cross-border management of grid operation, there is no obligation for the expansion of the distribution networks; the EU should therefore pass new legal acts regarding grid expansion and construction. This particularly requires a Union-wide plan of needs which, somewhat like the German transport infrastructure plans, determines the expansion need and the extension of power grids and storage facilities.

Procedurally, the WBGU recommends a division of labour between the EU and its member states: the EU provides the legal framework for a Europe-wide energy strategy by stipulating the legal framework for the energy mix and the extension and rebuilding of infrastructural projects. The actual legal form and the implementation of planning and application procedures for infrastructure-related projects should be the member states' tasks. They must ensure early involvement and participation of the Union's citizens in EU-wide planning processes. These new measures for grid expansion require an extension of EU competencies within the scope of the Treaty on the functioning of the European Union.

Beyond that, expanding the networks also requires substantial investments, particularly in regions which are unable to attract private investors. These regions therefore require public support. The relevant funds should also be made available at European level. In addition, government incentives are called for (for example attractive loan offers) and, possibly, the introduction of a legal obligation to expand the grids, insofar as this is economically feasible.

And finally, the WBGU suggests extending international cooperation beyond the borders of the European Union, in the medium term. As far as this is concerned, it follows that the EU should be furnished with the respective authority to enter into agreements under international law. The decarbonisation of the EU-wide energy system by 2050 can be achieved more cost-effectively if Europe cooperates with its neighbouring nations. A core element would be the initiation of broadly impacting energy partnerships between the EU and North Africa (comparable to the EU partnerships with major newly industrialising countries), in order to utilise the favourable local conditions for renewable energies (wind and solar power). European-African energy partnerships should, on the one hand, contribute to the European energy supply and, on the other hand, help to establish sustainable energy supply infrastructures in Africa, and to effectively fight energy poverty. A future project such as this could, at the same time, establish a new sound basis for cooperation between Europe and Africa, based on common interests. Development, energy and stability policies would be bundled.

7.3.4 Bundle 4: Accelerate Expansion of Renewable Energies on a Global Level through Feed-In Tariffs

Until the implementation of global carbon pricing (Section 7.3.2), or the realisation of national and regional carbon pricing approaches, or until these have reached the required price level and reliability, and until we are some way further along the renewable energies learning curve, there is too little incentive for investors in most countries to accelerate the expansion of renewable energies (Box 5.2-4). However, only the installation of new energy generation plants from renewable sources can lead to lower costs due to learning effects, so that the further expansion of renewable energies can be achieved faster and more cheaply than it has been up to now. The targeted promotion of renewable energies is therefore an important complementary component in any list of transformative measures. The transformation speed needed for the necessary emissions reductions can only be achieved on the basis of the fast and increased utilisation of renewable energies. In this way, the threatening path dependencies of fossil energy technologies could also be limited.

So far, feed-in tariffs have proved to be the most effective, and at the same time – particularly in the early stages of technology diffusion – the most efficient tool for the promotion of renewable energies. They provide investors with long-term planning security, thereby helping to overcome investment barriers (Section 7.3.8). In addition, technology-specific feed-in tariffs allow the parallel promotion of different forms of renewable energy, thus opening up various ways of securing the future energy supply. In the WBGU's view, the increased investment security and the option of technology-specific promotion are the main arguments for feed-in tariffs, compared to quota-based promotion, or tradable certificates for renewable energies (Box 5.2-4).

The WBGU therefore advises the German federal government to strongly support, both at European Union and global level, the widespread use of feed-in tariffs. The most important accompanying measure, as it creates the one vital pre-condition an accelerated expansion of renewable energies depends on, is extension of the infrastructure, above all the construction of high-capacity transmission grids and storage facilities. This should go hand in hand with a political process to phase out subsidies for fossil energy carriers, as currently, on a global level, governments' expenditure related to fossil energy carrier subsidies is more than five times higher than the corresponding expenditure for the promotion of renewable energy carriers. This ratio should now be reversed as soon as possible.

7.3.4.1
Feed-In Tariffs in Europe: Use Efficiency Gains through Step by Step Harmonisation

Low Ambition Level: Improved Harmonisation of European Feed-In Tariffs

So far, feed-in tariffs or rewards exist in 21 EU member states. The German federal government should advocate the use of the instrument of feed-in tariffs in further EU member states, and for a better harmonisation of the existing support systems. To facilitate this, the EU should strive for a binding EU-internal agreement for the introduction of feed-in tariffs in all member states, and for gradual harmonisation of the various national feed-in tariffs. It should further aim for the coordinated, speedy expansion of the grid infrastructure, and the expansion of storage capacities. An improved harmonisation would reduce the risk of over-subsidising certain technologies at less favourably situated locations, and could instead accelerate the promotion in regions in other countries that are the most suitable for energy generation.

Currently, there is no standardised, Europe-wide support system for renewable energies. Although cross-national cooperation within the European Union with regard to renewable energies would be possible under the 2009 renewable energies directive to ensure target flexibility, this option has so far not been utilised (Section 7.3.3). Increased harmonisation of support systems and amounts, however, would reduce support costs Europe-wide, and would be an important step towards the full harmonisation of feed-in tariffs under EU law, which in the WBGU's view should be strived for in the medium term. This implementation, however, can not be realised immediately as the power grid transport capacities throughout the European member states are as yet far from sufficient (Section 7.3.3). Subsequent to the installation of these grids, however, the harmonisation of feed-in tariffs should be strived for.

Medium Ambition Level: Advance a Uniform European Support System

An EU-wide, uniform feed-in tariff would, in principle, increase the efficiency of promoting renewable energies. Power generation from renewable sources could then be effected at the most favourable locations for the least cost. The WBGU assumes that an EU-wide feed-in tariff would significantly accelerate the transformation towards low-carbon energy generation, as well as being overall the most efficient option for achieving the goal of covering European energy demand almost completely with renewable energies by 2050 (Section 4.4).

The WBGU therefore suggests a conscious striving towards the goal of one Europe-wide feed-in tariff by 2020. European energy policy should be structured accordingly (Sections 5.4.3, 7.3.3). An essential precondition for a uniform feed-in tariff is a stepped-up grid expansion and increased transmission capacities between the EU member states, as well as the availability of new infrastructures to manage fluctuations (Section 7.3.3). An immediate, pan-European, uniform feed-in tariff would conceivably slow down the expansion of renewable energies in some regions, particularly in Germany, without the ability to import sufficient electric power from renewable sources. Without the respective infrastructure, falling back on less sustainable forms of energy seems probable.

A speedy, cross-border infrastructure expansion requires the harmonisation of planning provisions in the EU member states, and the coordination of energy sector planning procedures, for example through a Union-wide assessment of needs. This calls for a transferral of the respective law-giving authorities from the member states to the EU. Furthermore, unrestricted grid access should be ensured through the establishment of independent network operators. The legal preconditions for EU-wide power distribution must also be fulfilled (Section 7.3.3).

In the WBGU's view, these preconditions can be created within a decade. During this time, national feed-in tariffs should gradually, taking the progressive grid expansion into account, be harmonised to the degree that the transition to the EU feed-in tariff system does not result in disproportionate fractions for certain technologies. To avoid a period of investment uncertainty, an interim phase which takes the safeguarding of already existing plants into account is needed – this is currently the case in Germany: plants built before a certain set date must still comply with the national regulations, which might continue to apply simultaneously during an interim phase. Nevertheless, the goal of a harmonised feed-in tariff must, in the WBGU's view, not be misappropriated and used as an argument to cut national feed-in tariffs before the preconditions for an effective and efficient Union-wide solution are given.

Another important component in any EU-wide system is that renewable energies should be given preference in terms of network feed-in. In addition, it would have to be examined how to support the most cost-effective options whilst also ensuring grid stability. In the view of the WBGU, careful selection of Europe-wide harmonised feed-in tariffs, and their dynamic alignment to the progress made in the cost degression of individual technologies can minimise the risk of over-subsidising favourable regions. In case of a dynamic alignment of the subsidy amount for new plants, favourable locations would initially be preferred, whilst less suitable regions would only follow once their use was economically viable due to the progress made in cost degression. The remuneration level should be subject to a gradual degression which takes into account changing market conditions (including initial production costs, CO_2 price) along the line of the German Renewable Energy Law (EEG). However, on the basis of the experiences regarding the various market dynamics gained there, the degression of feed-in tariffs should not be linked to a certain date, but rather to the cumulative installed output of the respective technology. This would provide additional cost reduction incentives, and renewable energies would be financially viable sooner.

A Europe-wide feed-in tariff should have the goal of optimising the increase of renewable energies, and reducing their costs even further. These primary objectives must, in the WBGU's view, take precedence over national infrastructure expansion strategies and the corresponding industrial policy-related interests. The WBGU assumes that the various technologies (solar thermal power, photovoltaics, wind power, bioenergy) will generally become competitive, and no longer in need of subsidies, once they have reached a global capacity of 5,000 TWh per year, so that the EU feed-in tariff scheme for wind power could be phased out as early as 2025, and for solar energy by around the middle of the century.

High Ambition Level: Examine the Inclusion of North Africa into a European Support Scheme

To increase the transformative impact of a uniform European energy market with harmonised feed-in tariffs even more, it should be examined at the earliest opportunity whether North Africa could be integrated into a European feed-in tariff system. The requisite (foreign) authority the EU would need for a binding integration of North Africa into a European feed-in tariff system, from a legal perspective, has already been granted (Section 5.4.3). Due to North Africa's geographical situation, further potentials could be tapped, particularly in the wind and solar energy sectors. At the same time, this would be a way of supporting the energy U-turn in the Maghreb states, and could be the first step on the way to improving the power supply for the entire African continent (Section 7.3.3). A precondition for this, however, would be a transcontinental supergrid, something probably not realisable before 2030. In addition, a trans-African grid would have to be constructed in order to also provide the 500 million people in the Sub-Saharan region who currently do not have access to it with electric power.

7.3.4.2 Global Diffusion of Feed-In Tariffs: Initiate Knowledge Exchange, Financial Transfers and Country Partnerships

Low Ambition Level: Knowledge Exchange and Capacity Building for efficient Support Schemes through the International Feed-In Cooperation

As a pioneer in feed-in tariffs (FiT), Germany should share its experiences and increase knowledge transfer to optimise the structure of FiT systems. As early as 2005, the German federal government founded the 'International Feed-in Cooperation' (IFIC), together with Spain and Slovenia, to facilitate knowledge exchange between countries with, and countries without, feed-in tariff schemes to encourage the global diffusion of best practices regarding the use of feed-in tariffs. Experiences and suggestions for improvement are discussed in workshops, held on a regular basis. The IFIC also contributes its expertise to policy-making discussions regarding the promotion of renewable energies, particularly at EU level.

Within the scope of this cooperation, the German government should continue to underline its commitment in terms of both financing and human resources, thus helping to build up the knowledge and capacities needed for the introduction of efficient feed-in tariffs by interested countries, including those beyond Europe's borders. Within the scope of the IFIC, the regular exchange of experiences between countries with feed-in tariffs should also be continued and extended in order to increase the efficacy and efficiency of existing national systems. In this way, the IFIC could become a knowledge centre for efficient feed-in tariffs, whose expertise would also be in demand on an international level.

Medium Ambition Level: Initiate Feed-In Tariffs in Developing Countries

The increased use of renewable energies on a global level could be accelerated further if as many countries as possible were to adopt or expand the use of feed-in tariffs, particularly the heavily populated and climate politically important BASIC states and the OECD countries which are not members of the EU. The OECD countries and India and China will probably cover around 70% of global electric power demand by the middle of the century, and it is therefore necessary that these countries switch to renewable energies as quickly as possible. Many countries are already using feed-in tariffs for individual regions or technologies; however, these would have to be developed further in order to accelerate the global expansion of renewable energies.

The German federal government should therefore go beyond knowledge transfer by suggesting the founding of an initiative to encourage global adoption of the feed-in tariff system. This could be done within the scope of the Rio+20 Conference. It could take the form of a declaration of intent by the participating countries to introduce feed-in tariffs in their countries, or to improve their current feed-in tariff systems. This should be accompanied by a commitment to the phasing out of fossil energy carrier subsidies.

To prove the seriousness of their declaration of intent, it should include concrete initiatives as the next step towards implementing the planned introduction of feed-in tariffs. These would have to address the various preconditions for the introduction of feed-in tariffs in different countries. Through use of the appropriate technologies, feed-in tariffs can also be introduced in small, local island networks, and are therefore also particularly important for overcoming energy poverty in developing countries.

Whilst in industrialised countries, it is ultimately the final consumers who finance feed-in tariffs through the electricity price, many of the consumers in developing countries are not in a position to do so. State or other subsidies for the feed-in of renewable energies must therefore be ensured, as much as the means for capacity building (knowledge transfer, training).

On the one hand, bilateral partnerships between industrialised and developing countries which cover support in terms of capacity building and financing should be suggested within the scope of the proposed initiative. Such partnerships would reduce the financial burden on the state and consumers in the least developed countries, and offer the chance of fully unlocking the potential of the individual geographical situations, thereby increasing the investment's cost efficiency.

On the other hand, an international financing mechanism modelled on the Global Energy Transfer Feed-in Tariffs (GET Fit) programme should be established (Section 5.2.3). This could (co)finance FiT systems in developing countries. The funding required for the extension of the necessary infrastructure, like grids and storage facilities, should also be taken into consideration here. A financing mechanism such as this would be closely linked to the initiatives for the reduction of energy poverty (Section 7.3.5). One option would be to position this financing mechanism within the scope of the UNFCCC's Green Climate Fund (Section 7.3.8). In as far as possible, the financial support for the extension of the infrastructures for renewable energies should be tied to market economic reforms of the energy markets (demerging energy generators and grid operating companies and the use of independent network supervisors) in order to stimulate competitiveness and market efficiency. Tenders for potential commissions to extend transmission grids should be invited globally, and orders awarded to suppliers who can guarantee the successful extension with the least volume of international financial aid.

High Ambition Level: Establish IRENA as a Coordination Platform, and for the Diffusion of Feed-In Tariffs

The promotion of the sustainable extension of the global use of renewable energies requires a coordinated and accelerated procedure. The International Renewable Energy Agency (IRENA), founded in 2009, has the task of advising and supporting both industrialised and developing countries during the introduction of renewable energies. IRENA intends to offer practical and concrete policy advice, to make capacity building, technology transfer, and financing easier, and to promote the exchange of knowledge. What counts now is the conclusion of the establishment stage in order to commence the actual task. Above all, IRENA's financing must be guaranteed, and a concrete long- and medium-term strategy must be decided on. The global diffusion of feed-in tariffs should be one of the objectives on the organisation's agenda.

IRENA could function as secretariat and coordination platform for the Rio+20 initiative for the diffusion of feed-in tariffs suggested by the WBGU. In particular, IRENA could be responsible for collating data on potential analyses, support policies and the financing of renewable energies, and arrange for capacity building in developing countries in close cooperation with the IFIC. The agency could also pave the way for partnerships between countries with joint targets for the expansion of renewable energies, which they hope to meet through mutual accreditation of new capacities and with jointly financed projects – somewhat similar to the European-African energy partnership. To allow IRENA to serve as the coordination platform for the introduction of feed-in tariffs, the German federal government should do all it can to ensure that the agency is accorded the highest level of international attention and importance regarding energy issues, so IRENA can advance the expansion of renewable energies on an equal footing and together with existing organisations (Section 7.3.9).

7.3.5 Bundle 5: Promote Sustainable Energy Supply Services in Developing and Newly Industrialising Countries

Low-carbon global growth can only succeed if the increasing energy demand in the developing and newly industrialising countries is steered towards the path of sustainability in time. There simply is no more room to manoeuvre left, as far as the pursuit of high-carbon growth paths is concerned (WBGU, 2009b). According to the UN Secretary-General's Advisory Group on Energy and Climate Change (AGECC), the first step must be to ensure that around 3 billion people have access to the basic modern energy supply by 2030, particularly for cooking, heating and lighting (AGECC, 2010). The modernisation of energy supplies used for production (for example for operating machinery) should also be considered. Above all, developing and newly industrialising countries need support in overcoming energy poverty, and in the leap-frogging of technological development stages (Box 7.3-2). Without credible commitment on the part of the industrialised countries in this area, there is no legitimation for implementing climate protection targets in cooperation with developing countries.

7.3.5.1
Low Ambition Level: Adapt Concepts and Strategies

Link Low-Carbon Growth with the Fight against Poverty

The overcoming of energy poverty is considered a fundamental requirement of successful poverty reduction strategies. At a national level, an important instrument in poverty reduction strategies for the least developed countries (LDC) are the 'Poverty Reduction Strategy Papers' (PRSP), drafted by the LDC with the support of aid organisations and with the participation of the local civil society, and updated regularly. They serve the steering of medium-term country development policies, and as a fundraising basis for the financial support required from the international community.

Use Development Banks for the Establishment of Low-Carbon Infrastructures

The WBGU reasserts its recommendation that the World Bank should increase its support of a low-carbon energy infrastructure in developing and newly industrialising countries. It should also understand itself to be a development bank for the promotion of sustainable energy in order to make it easier to leap-frog non-sustainable development stages (WBGU, 2004). Although the World Bank has developed a number of activities with regard to the promotion of renewable energies, to increasing energy efficiency and overcoming energy poverty over the past few years, the required transformation calls for a substantial upscaling of the extent and speed of World Bank programmes – with the aid of ambitious financial subsidies on the part of the donor countries. The WBGU recommends that the World Bank should develop a challenging strategy for low-carbon transformation, with the requirements of the 2 °C guard rail as the benchmark. Development cooperation should set concrete targets in terms of energy policy on this basis. Within the scope of its seat on the World Bank Board of Directors, the German federal government should lobby for this. A move in the right direction is the call by the Bundesministerium für wirtschaftliche Zusammenarbeit und Entwicklung (the Ministry for Economic Cooperation and Development, BMZ) for the World Bank to set a quota of 40% each with regard to energy investments, or renewable energies, within the scope of its new energy strategy.

The role of the regional development banks should also be strengthened during the implementation of a global energy system decarbonisation strategy. These tend to be firmly established in their respective region, and usually much more aware of the problematic issues encountered locally than the global institutions are. On the basis of earlier recommendations (WBGU, 2003), the WBGU advocates that Germany, in its role as contributor to regional development banks, and within the scope of its EU membership, should call for the large-scale promotion of a low-carbon energy supply in the least developed countries, for instance through the establishment and extension of access to sustainable energy service supplies, and energy efficiency improvements.

7.3.5.2
Medium Ambition Level: Extend the Use of Modern Energy in Rural Areas

Stepping up the use of existing technologies is one way to significantly improve the quality of life for many hundreds of millions of people, quickly and relatively inexpensively. Above all, the challenge lies in the widespread diffusion of modern forms of energy use in the rural regions of developing countries.

According to UN Advisory Group on Energy and Climate Change estimates, additional funding averaging around US$ 35–40 billion per year is required in order to secure access to the basic essentials of a modern energy supply for all people by 2030, i.e. approx. 5% of the expected total global investment in the energy sector for this period (Chapter 4; AGECC, 2010). The required funds are made up of grants for investments and capacity building in the least developed countries amounting to US$ 15 billion, as well as government and private sector loans amounting to around US$ 20–25 billion. In light of this, the WBGU suggests that the German federal government should lend its support in particular to the following measures.

Modernise Traditional Bioenergy Use and Mobilise Bioenergy Potentials

Efficiency improvements in the area of existing bioenergy use and the switch to modern forms of energy such as electric power and gas are an important precondition for overcoming energy poverty and covering the basic essential need in developing countries. Initially, the issue is the modernisation of the traditional forms of use through improving the existing bioenergy use by simple and affordable means (WBGU, 2010a), or its replacement through other, low-carbon energies. This can simultaneously lead to poverty reduction, prevent damage to health, and mitigate the utilisation pressure on natural ecosystems. Apart from the promotion of renewable energies, development cooperation should support the formulation and implementation of country-specific sustainable bioenergy strategies in order to mobilise the sustainable bioenergy potential in developing and newly industrialising countries.

To suitably prioritise access to energy and the transformation towards low-carbon development as an important element of successful poverty reduction, the WBGU suggests that climate-friendly development strategies should become a systematic constituent of PRSPs. Germany and the EU should emphatically support this. Along with this, matching small-scale and off-grid energy solutions should also be developed and supported.

Direct EU Energy Policy increasingly towards Low-Carbon Development

60% of the global investments in international development cooperation come from the EU region. The WBGU repeats its assessment that EU development policy is not suitably coordinated, and the funds are not adequately employed for raising the global profile of the new paradigm of low-carbon development (WBGU, 2003).

Beyond the Millennium Development Goals (MDG), which primarily focus on poverty reduction, European development cooperation should also be guided systematically by the goal of low-carbon growth. The Rio+20 Conference should be used as an opportunity to incorporate the themes of low-carbon energy generation and the overcoming of energy poverty into the MDG catalogue (WBGU, 2004, 2010a). European development cooperation can, particularly in the Sub-Saharan least developed countries and in Southern Asia, contribute to the establishment of low-carbon infrastructures, thereby also supporting 'green growth' in these countries. This would deliver concrete examples to demonstrate that poverty reduction and low-carbon development can go hand in hand. An intensified redirection of development cooperation in this way would increase the trust between industrialised and developing countries, something that is very much needed during the course of further climate negotiations.

7.3.5.3 High Ambition Level: Start and Accelerate Large-Scale Implementation Soon

Enter into Strategic Decarbonisation Partnerships with Developing and Newly Industrialising Countries

Strategic partnerships, particularly with developing and newly industrialising countries, are ideally suited for the extension and modernisation of low-carbon infrastructures, especially as far as climate-friendly energy systems are concerned. The EU should offer the establishment of partnerships for sustainable energy use that go far beyond the existing EU climate cooperations (WBGU, 2010). Cooperations such as these are important in order to enable individual countries to install a low-carbon infrastructure, to make true progress in the decarbonisation of the global energy systems, and in order to demonstrate that climate protection strategies can successfully combine competitiveness with social and ecological development. These kinds of partnerships can accelerate the global economy's U-turn towards climate-compatibility. Once a certain dimension, appeal, economic performance and collective innovative power are reached, high-carbon societies would increasingly be subjected to adaptation pressure.

Initiate Lighthouse Model Projects and Strengthen Existing Ones

The WBGU recommends the rapid, large-scale further development of existing model projects to promote the transformation. Such large-scale model projects would illustrate how technology leaps and the development of focused solutions in the energy supply sector can be realised and accelerated. Current model projects are lacking the speed and dimensions requisite to the transformation. For instance, at 40 TWh, Africa's total residential electric power consumption (excluding South Africa; IEA, 2010c) equals that of New York. A delay in expansion would lead to a substantial rise in the required investments, as currently, a switch would be relatively easy because there are no significant path dependencies as yet. According to World Bank estimates, Africa will grow into the leading market for solar powered mobile lighting units by 2015 (World Bank, 2010b).

In light of this, the WBGU suggests the following to the German federal government:

- to improve the preconditions needed for the upscaling, acceleration and multiplication of such model

projects for building up a sustainable energy supply within the scope of development cooperation,
- to actively support and considerably develop the objectives agreed in 2010 by the African Union and the EU for the realisation of the African-European energy partnership, particularly the objective of supplying 100 million Africans with sustainable energy,
- the potential southward expansion of Desertec,
- to significantly increase the dimensions of programmes for sustainable energy supply in developing countries along the lines of the German-Dutch programme 'Energising Development', which has so far provided 6.4 million people with access to electricity and modern cooking fuels.

The G20's Signal for the Rio+20 Conference

Accelerating and upscaling lighthouse projects should be supported by putting the transformation into a low-carbon society at the top of the agenda at the next G20 meetings. The G20 should make the required funds of US$ 35–40 billion, according to AGECC estimates, available to provide the developing countries with access to the basic essentials of a modern energy supply (AGECC, 2010). In the WBGU's view, the G20 should act as if the overcoming of energy poverty were already anchored in the MDG; on no account should they wait until 2015. Such an initiative by the world's wealthiest states even before the Rio+20 Conference would send out a major signal. In addition, mechanisms which contribute to the accelerated expansion of a low-carbon energy infrastructure should be approved. For example, financial support in the form of loans for development of the energy sector could be tied in with the anchoring of sustainability criteria in the countries' industry sector strategies.

Through the phasing out of fossil fuel subsidies, the competitiveness of sustainable energy supply structures could be increased to release the urgently required funds for the fight against energy poverty in the developing and newly industrialising countries. Already, endeavours towards this are being made within the G20. Germany should lobby emphatically for the speedy phase-out of such damaging subsidies for fossil-fuelled energies.

7.3.6
Bundle 6: Steering the World's Rapid Urbanisation towards Sustainability

Urban areas play a key role in the transformation process (Section 1.2.4). They consume around three-quarters of global final energy, and are the cause for an even higher share of energy-related greenhouse gas emissions (GEA, 2011). As far as rapidly growing urban structures are concerned, high-carbon path dependencies must be prevented, as they would hinder low-carbon development for many decades to come (Chapters 1, 4). The WBGU therefore views steering the current wave of urbanisation towards low-carbon development as an extremely effective lever that should be as high up as possible on the international political agenda. The global transformation can only succeed if the rapidly progressing urbanisation is used as an opportunity for climate stabilisation (Chapter 5.)

Against this background, the issue of sustainable urban development should move to the forefront of international consciousness. Due to the enormous time pressure, for example, a United Nations global emergency plan for the compliance with certain efficiency standards in cities would have to come into force within the one or two years. In view of this, the measures described in the following are important, yet hardly sufficient, steps towards solving the outlined problems.

7.3.6.1
Low Ambition Level: Improve Global Communication and Information

Initiate Global Progress Report on Urban Energy Use

The compilation of regularly published progress reports on global urbanisation trends ('Global Assessment of Urban Energy Use') should provide a scientifically substantiated and methodically harmonised overview over long-term global urbanisation trends. This would improve the scientific and technical foundations for decision-makers with regard to urban and regional planning, and stimulate international debate of this issue. Although the UN Habitat programme's 'State of the World Cities Reports', published every two years, provide a good basis for understanding current development deficit trends and, at least partially, the vulnerabilities caused by to climate change and how to adapt to it. They do however neglect the emissions reduction aspect, especially with regard to interactions between long-term urbanisation trends and other development dynamics (for example global environmental change).

Remodel UN-Habitat

On the basis of this, UN Habitat should be remodelled to allow the programme to lend the urgently required dynamics to the international debate on sustainable urban development. At a low ambition level, the norm-setting role of the UN Habitat programme could be strengthened to achieve this, additional human resources could be made available, and it could be developed further into a centre of expertise regarding sustainable urban development. The climate-compatibility of urban development should correspondingly become the key focus of the World Urban Campaign initiated by UN Habitat. Another opportunity is offered by the fact that this campaign could intentionally be linked with the international Green Economy debate being held in the context of the Rio+20 Conference. This could lend the requisite additional weight to the central transformation field urbanisation at a global level. At a medium ambition level, on the other hand, a more profound reform of UN Habitat is conceivable, which would ultimately lead to the establishment of a new organisation (Section 7.3.10.2).

Harmonise Data Collection

As urban and regional planning can make major contributions to climate protection, and there are some considerable variations in consumption patterns, the progress in these areas should be measurable and comparable. Recently, a range of initiatives in this direction have already been instigated; however, these are often distinguished by limited transparency and comparability in terms of the methods used (for example WRI, 2008; ICLEI, 2009; World Bank, 2010b; EU Covenant of Mayors, 2010). Frequently, the published data refers only to restricted relevant partial areas of the city (e.g. only those processes, buildings or vehicles that are under the municipality's direct control). The WBGU therefore recommends the development of verifyable methods and harmonised reporting of cities' greenhouse gas intensity and their carbon footprint which cover all the relevant actors and sectors (for example energy and transport sector, industry and service sector, private households and public administration), and take into account both direct and indirect emissions. Existing data availability deficits must be identified and addressed. Moreover, the possibility for coherent aggregation with regional and national data should be given. This initiative for the harmonisation of regional energy statistics and emissions inventories should be jointly developed by statistics agency experts, environmental ministries, and representatives from natural and social sciences, and from technical disciplines (Chapter 8). Reservations by data protection experts and industry advocates regarding the protection of local energy consumption data as a trade secret, should be weighed up against the common good. To achieve this objective, public purse subsidies (for example for energy infrastructure on the generator or the consumer side) could, for instance, be linked to data transparency provisions.

Examples of high-resolution sub-national statistics for direct energy consumption are the British or the Swedish communal energy and emissions register. Leading by example, the energy consumption data for public buildings should be made transparent (Carbon Culture, 2011). Examples how to measure indirect emissions (on the side of consumption), that are methodically more difficult to record, have been provided by non-government organisations and scientists in many countries (Dawkins et al., 2010).

7.3.6.2
Medium Ambition Level: Develop and Implement Technologies for Low-Carbon Cities

Establish a World Commission for Low-Carbon Urban Planning

The Rio+20 Conference could be used for the founding of a 'World Commission on Low-Carbon Urban Planning', modelled on the World Commission on Dams. One task would be the independent assessment and evaluation of climate-compatible urban planning activities currently being implemented all over the world. Further tasks would be 'best practice' development, and the development of strategies for their transferability. Similar to the World Commission on Dams, the World Commission for Urban Planning would include members of different interest groups. Contrary to UN Habitat, though, it would be more specialised, and would function as an independent institution outside of the UN system. The new World Commission could, for example, identify critical infrastructures (new grids, transport infrastructure, communication). To put the World Commission for Low-Carbon Urban Planning's findings into operation, the WBGU further recommends the establishment of a broadly mandated UN Specialised Agency for Sustainable Urbanisation at this ambition level. The UN Habitat programme is not adequately equipped to deal with this acute problem, and should be incorporated into this new structure (Section 7.3.10.2).

Timely Integration of High-Capacity Public Transport Axes

One of the great dangers of rapidly growing urban agglomerations is the delayed planning of integrated high-capacity public transport arteries. Once a city features a high-income middle class, and with it extensive car ownership, public and non-motorised mobility is frequently marginalised and at risk. The subsequent integration of high-capacity public transport systems (underground railway systems, tramway systems with their own track beds, metropolitan railway trains, bus lanes, monorails, etc.) at this point in time is fraught with difficulties as it can be carried out only very slowly, and, because of the high cost and other barriers, only in capitals or selected major cities (for

Box 7.3-2

Energy Use Transformation II: Overcoming Energy Poverty

Other than decarbonisation, the second objective of a conversion of the energy systems is the overcoming of energy poverty to provide all people with access to modern, clean and safe energy in the form of electricity or gaseous energy carriers by 2030 (WBGU, 2004). To meet this target, the developing and newly industrialising countries primarily need targeted support to leap-frog past stages of technological development, both for the overcoming of energy poverty and for the establishment of a sustainable energy infrastructure. If this does not succeed, there is a risk of path dependencies on high-carbon, fossil-based energy systems that would be very difficult and costly to overcome for the next decades. Access to energy services is also a precondition for achieving the Millennium Development Goals. In the WBGU's view, the global limiting of the final energy demand is compatible with the aim of overcoming energy poverty.

example Bangkok, Shanghai, New Delhi). Cheaper systems with a similar capacity and service quality such as, for instance, bus rapid transit systems with dedicated lanes (Curitiba, Sao Paulo, Bogota), however, require so much space that they have to be planned well in advance, and the space required for their routes must be reserved. The co-benefits of express bus systems are well-documented. They facilitate effective networking with commuter lines and non-motorised forms of transport (cycling and walking), and long-distance transport terminals, and integrate the city functionally, thereby upgrading areas of the city.

This kind of architecture can also be an important nucleus for the conversion of urban energy infrastructures, and can later be used as a basis for distribution networks. A wide range of renewable energy fuels that meet ambitious pollution standards are suitable for operating bus systems. Various energy gases, hybrid systems and electricity-based technologies have been in use for a number of years now.

Small and medium-sized towns in particular can potentially profit from this development as their structures are not yet 'blocked', and they still have some room for urban planners to act accordingly. Often, however, they are lacking representation, or negotiation skills, in their dealings with central governments or the regional development banks. Traffic issues usually also cross the lines between administrative authorities within a city.

So far, only two CDM projects have been successful in this area: the extension of New Delhi's underground railway system, and Bogota's Transmillenio BRT system. Both were built in capitals. Particularly for smaller cities, it is often not possible to meet the elaborate administrative demands of CDM (proof of an indisputable baseline, proof of the additionality of the emissions reductions, verifiability and so on).

A prioritised and simplified recognition of public transport systems, for example within the scope of Nationally Appropriate Mitigation Actions (NAMAs), should therefore be strived for. Consequently, capacity building and active support of small and medium-sized cities through development banks should be stepped up.

Subsidise the Development and Extension of Particularly Suitable Technologies

Some technologies and forms of renewable energy are particularly suitable for utilisation in urban areas, and special support programmes should therefore be decided within the scope of an 'emergency plan for sustainable urbanisation'. Contrary to most other renewable energy sources, geothermal energy is neither subject to temporal fluctuation, nor does it require much space. It makes the reliable provision of very high energy densities possible. In electric power generation, geothermal energy can easily provide sufficient base load. This affordable heat source can be used for a range of purposes (heating networks, greenhouses, industrial use, etc.). Electric power generation can be an option in particularly suitable locations. Solar refrigeration systems are particularly suitable for use in subtropical and tropical cities, as the timing of the resource supply runs parallel with the demand, thereby reducing peak time load. In many of the world's regions, the desalination of sea and brackish water for metropolitan water use already makes an important contribution.

Overall, the development efforts regarding technologies such as these must be stepped up. They should also take into account the resilience of these systems against the risks of climate change (droughts, flooding, heat waves, etc.). For example, disaster prevention measures should include a stock of refrigerated (mobile) protection rooms in case of a heat wave.

Within the scope of international cooperation, Germany should increase its promotion of technology development and technology cooperations (for example PPP, joint ventures). This should also include allowing access to patents and knowledge. To mitigate investment risks, the government should offer collateral securities.

Take Action at the Level of Cities and City Partnerships

Climate-friendly urban planning (Chapter 5) requires extended, independent financing and design options, particularly on a community level, where the potential for synergies and learning effects is very high. Change agents who are especially familiar with the local situation could, for example, make major contributions to the building of low-carbon cities. City partnerships and creating room to manoeuvre for change agents and movements towards urban low-carbon development are increasingly gaining in importance, as already existing community climate partnerships or the activities of individual stakeholders or social groups show (Chapter 6). Existing initiatives (climate federation), urban stakeholders (Covenant of Mayors, C40), city partnerships and stakeholder alliances (ICLEI, Local Agenda 21, World Urban Forum) should therefore build improved networks at various levels, both internationally and bilaterally, in order to advance sustainable urbanisation.

Adapt Urban and Regional Planning to Cope with Unavoidable Climate Change

Urban and regional planning must not only contribute to the avoidance of dangerous climate change, but must also take into account the potential problems to be expected as a result of the already unavoidable climate change. This applies especially to coastal towns and riverside cities. Amongst other things, the increased occurrence of urban heat islands must enter into the equation. However, such measures also bear the risk of 'mis-adaptation', for example the increased use of high-energy air conditioning units or the construction of dykes, which in turn promotes settlements in areas prone to flooding. The application of ecological risk management criteria (greening of roof spaces, shading of concrete areas, protection against high tides that takes temporary flooding into account, etc.) is therefore preferable. Adaptation funding should be allocated according to these priorities.

7.3.6.3
Medium Ambition Level: Direct Urban and Regional Planning Development Cooperation towards Climate-Protection

As far as urban development in developing countries is concerned, the first step is establishing the preconditions for future low-carbon growth. The WBGU believes that over the past few years, as a result of the focus of developmental policy debate on the MDG, several key development cooperation (DC) action fields have been neglected. These include urban and regional planning within the scope of DC. In the course of city or country partnerships, Germany could pass on its experiences with new business models and urban energy efficiency improvement institutions to developing regions. The development banks' programmes should also increasingly focus on sustainable urban development. Fundamental deficits in urban planning and administration should be compensated for by capacity building in order to improve the situation for people living in slums, and to build up a functioning basic infrastructure.

Start a Global Education Initiative for Urban and Regional Planners and Architects

The global lack of urban and regional planners and architects with the relevant qualifications hinders the speedy construction of climate-friendly cities. Therefore, to be able to meet the imminent challenges, well qualified, professional experts are needed. The WBGU recommends starting a global training initiative for sustainable urban planning and architecture, and the extremely speedy establishment and promotion of the respective specialised faculties all over the world.

In addition, the lack of qualified training and education centres for urban and regional planners and architects in developing countries should be overcome within the scope of development cooperation through the introduction of university study courses. To ensure that their content is always up to date, and that they are in line with the respective national standards, the courses should be based at, and cooperate with, research institutions.

Support the Institution and Reform of existing Urban Planning Schemes

Many developing countries lack the capacities for low-carbon urban and regional development, as existing regional planning authorities do not have the skilled human resources required to deal with aspects of climate protection, or their resources are already stretched to the limits of their capabilities with other tasks (provision of housing, drinking water, waste management, etc.). In both cases, development cooperation can alleviate the problem through capacity building.

Extend Financing Adequately

Measures for the promotion of sustainable urbanisation should receive financing at a level that is substantially higher than the current one in order to reach the required dimensions and acceleration. Germany's activities in terms of supporting low-carbon urbanisation in Asia within the scope of the Cities Development Initiative for Asia (CDIA), for example, amount to a mere € 20 million over 5 years. In light of the huge challenges, the WBGU considers an amount 100 times that as far more adequate. It is self-evident that high demands should be made in terms of good governance when it comes to the use of these funds, and the implementation of urban development guidelines in general.

7.3.6.4 High Ambition Level: Large-Scale Launch of Beacon Projects

Beacon Project: Low-Carbon Metropolis

To complement the above mentioned measures aimed at smaller and medium-sized cities, the symbolic power of megacities should also be utilised. The World Bank should therefore support the implementation of particularly ambitious climate protection strategies in megacities (for example the five best among the currently 21 megacities). The WBGU recommends investments in the region of two-digit billions.

Start EU Initiative for Asia's Low-Carbon Urbanisation

Asia's current rapid urbanisation is one of the focal areas of the global urbanisation trend, as it harbours an enormous potential for path dependencies that would hinder a low-carbon development for many decades to come. Recent endeavours to put this topic on the agenda of Asia-Europe Meetings (ASEM) have failed. The WBGU therefore recommends that Germany should call for a joint European initiative, which would develop actions to promote low-carbon urbanisation in Asia to send out a signal, and mobilise financing instruments. Amongst others, the Asian Development Bank and the World Bank should play a role in the financing.

Experiment: Priority for Sustainable Mobility in the Inner City Area of Berlin's Metropolitan Railway System's Circle Line

Germany can gain significant influence on the international stage if it also leads by example. More model regions (see also the BMBF competition for an 'energy efficient city') should be developed as testing grounds for new concepts. In general, change agents should be given room to manoeuvre and to experiment, and communities should embrace the chance to serve as precisely such spaces. The German architects' and town planners' climate manifesto 'Common Sense for the World' (2009) represents an important frame of reference for this.

Communities should generally show more courage when it comes to ambitious experiments that send out a signal, for instance to demonstrate new forms of inner city mobility. Instead of funding further road building schemes almost by default as soon as an increase in traffic volume is predicted, future urban lifestyles, outlined, for example, in the scenario 'Morgenstadt' ('tomorrow's city'; BMBF, 2010f) should be taken on board, and visionary alternative proposals for future-oriented and modern, sustainable mobility should be made. One measure at a high ambition level, for instance, would be the creation of a traffic zone that lies within the circular line of Berlin's metropolitan railway system, the S-Bahn, where sustainable mobility is given undisputed precedence. The aim should be to keep external traffic at bay as far as possible by providing attractive, alternative mobility options in the inner city area defined by the S-Bahn's circular line. Car owners living in this inner city area defined by the circular line should be legally obliged to purchase an annual season ticket for the public transport system, in this way contributing to its financing.

The funds released through the sinking costs for road traffic infrastructure should be used in favour of substantial investments into a public transport system that works reliably the whole year round and is affordable, comfortable and safe. This would increase the quality of life in the city, decrease the health hazard posed by traffic and its emissions, and make an important contribution to the transformation towards a low-carbon society. In part, smaller cities have already set an example: through the introduction of a free-of-charge public transport system in the Belgian town of Hasselt in 1996, around ten times more people use public transport (Chapter 6).

International Building Exhibition 2020: Demonstrate the Climate Political Potential of an Industrial Nation

The government of the city of Berlin is preparing an International Building Exhibition (IBA) for 2020. One of the themes of this third IBA (the first took place in 1957, the second in 1987) hosted by the city will be climate change and resource efficiency. International building exhibitions serve as an architecture and urban design showcase, temporarily providing exceptional environments. The IBA in Berlin in 2020 should be taken both as invitation and opportunity to show this modern industrial nation's skills and potentials when it comes to climate protection and adaptation to the effects of climate change, in one place in the form of a concrete, actually built and actually lived-in model city. European consortiums are planning climate-friendly cities in China or in the Persian Gulf, but due to Europe's large share of established buildings, there are hardly any regions or spaces suitable for the construction of a model project. With its generous open spaces, above all the already decommissioned, or soon to be decommissioned, airports at Tempelhof and Tegel, the conditions for building a German version of a city that is low-carbon, both in terms of living and commercial environments, are exceptionally good in Berlin. Berlin's reliable public transport system also offers an excellent opportunity of integrating low-carbon mobility concepts into this IBA. No other German city features such a wide cross-section of the different types of buildings usually found in Germany as Berlin does. An IBA under the topic of climate change should therefore also include exemplary refurbishment, convincing both in energetic and aesthetic terms, but also socially, of some of the city's existing buildings (fractal IBA). The WBGU recommends that the IBA concept should focus on the issues of climate protection and climate change in the sense of extending Berlin's capital as a city. Ambitious project criteria should be defined to ensure that the IBA is turned into a beacon project for low-carbon development with international appeal. The WBGU further recommends that the federal government should offer its fullest support to this third IBA hosted by the capital, both in material as well as idealistic terms, as an international showcase and proof of the seriousness of Germany's climate policy objectives.

7.3.7
Bundle 7: Advance Climate-Friendly Land Use

A priority of any globally sustainable land-use policy must be securing the food supply for just under a billion mal- and undernourished people. Furthermore, there will also be a significant rise in the demand for agricultural goods, as the population increase of an additional 2.6 billion people by 2050 will also mean an increase in the number of people with emissions-intensive eating habits, i.e. a large volume of animal-derived products. The increasing use of bioenergy and bio-based materials will also mean additional huge waves in terms of demand. At the same time, competition for arable land, by now a rare commodity, will become even fiercer due to soil degradation, water shortages and increasing climate impacts. Moreover, there is an international consensus to set aside larger, better connected protected areas for the conservation of biodiversity. Turning more natural ecosystems into arable land is not a sustainable option, for reasons of climate and nature conservation. Not least, the necessary mitigation of greenhouse gas emissions from land use is an additional challenge (Section 1.2.2).

For these reasons, the transformation of global land use is one of the central tasks for the future. In the view of the WBGU, the intensification of agricultural production must not only occur in a sustainable way, but new strategies for efficiency increase on the demand side, and particularly for the substitution of area-intensive or emissions-intensive products must be implemented (Section 7.3.7.1). Just under a quarter of global greenhouse gas emissions can be allocated to the transformation field land use, both from direct agricultural emissions and from land-use changes, the latter mainly from deforestation in the tropics (Section 4.1.7.1). These emissions can be mitigated, but land-use systems cannot become completely emissions-free, not least because of the nitrous oxide resulting from the use of nitrogen fertilisers. Without a significant contribution from the land-use sector, climate stabilisation cannot succeed. Mitigation of greenhouse gas emissions should therefore become another core element of new strategies for global, integrated land-use management. The following defines the most important starting points in the transformation field land use. This includes above all forest protection (Section 7.3.7.2), mitigating emissions attributed to agricultural production (Section 7.3.7.3), and the promotion of climate-friendly eating habits (Section 7.3.7.4).

7.3.7.1
Establish a Global Commission for Sustainable Land Use

Transforming global land use should be given a significantly higher priority on the political agenda. It should be addressed much more at an international level, and more firmly institutionalised. The WBGU emphasises its recommendation that a 'Global Commission for Sustainable Land Use' should be established in order to organise this international searching process (WBGU, 2010a). The commission's tasks should include the identification of particularly outstanding challenges in global land use, and the collation of the relevant current expert knowledge. On the basis of this, it should develop a vision, and the foundation, mechanisms and guidelines for global land-use management. The new commission, with extensive responsibility for integrated land use which would have to go far beyond agricultural or food security issues in the narrower sense, could be affiliated with UNEP, and cooperate with other UN organisations such as the FAO. Its findings should regularly feature on the international agenda within the framework of the agenda of the UNEP Global Ministerial Environment Forum, or the strategically important G20. The establishment of such a commission would rank as a medium-level ambition. In concrete terms, it should be tasked, amongst other things, with the following:

1. *Identification of the scientific status quo of global land use:* The International Assessment of Agricultural Knowledge, Science and Technology for Development (IAASTD, 2009), initiated by the World Bank, was an important step on the way to the joint

development, together with the various actors and their extremely diverging interests, towards a consensus, at least where agriculture is concerned. As this first step did not reach an overall consensus including all major multinational agricultural companies and important key states, this work should continue. In the forest management sector, there is widespread agreement on the necessity of stopping emissions due to deforestation; however, the appropriate international efforts required for the relevant consensus formation are lacking. Modelled on the IPCC (Intergovernmental Panel on Climate Change) and the IPBES (Intergovernmental Science-Policy Platform on Biodiversity and Ecosystem Services), the commission should initiate an integrated assessment of the scientific status quo on global land use which takes a cross-sector look at land use and the whole chain from land management right up until the finished product and its use.

2. *Set goals and start initiatives for climate-friendly eating habits:* As an international target, the WBGU recommends the reduction of the global average per capita consumption of emissions-intensive foodstuffs in order to mitigate the increasing land competition. In the industrialised countries, this requires less consumption of animal products. Simultaneously, the rapid increase occurring in developing and newly industrialising countries must be curbed (Chapter 4). To achieve this, the commission should stimulate initiatives, for example within the sphere of the UN organisations, to encourage international cooperation regarding the setting of targets for how much land should produce how much of the per capita food consumption. The WBGU further recommends the goal of halving agricultural post-harvest losses by 2050.
3. *Developing a minimum standard for all biomass products:* In the medium-term, the commission should develop a global biomass standard to regulate the production of all kinds of biomass for the various uses (food and feed, energetic and material) across countries and sectors (WBGU, 2010a).
4. *Evaluate options for global land management:* The elaborated challenges regarding global land use (Section 1.2.5) lead to the question of whether global land-use patterns will have to undergo a fundamental change in the medium-term. The 'ideal' form of land use would be forestry or agriculture optimally suited to the respective regional or edaphic situation (Schellnhuber and Huber, 2010). The production of foodstuffs, for example, would concentrate on the comparably rare favourable soils. One of the preconditions for such a system, however, would be a global agricultural trade without distortions, and a global remuneration of significant ecosystem services, for example for the biodiversity of natural ecosystems. The commission should evaluate ideas for such a global land-use management, and the framework conditions and instruments this would require.

7.3.7.2
Sustainable Forest Management and the Mitigation of Emissions from Deforestation and Forest Degradation

The largest emissions factor in the transformation field of land use is land conversion, particularly the conversion of forests and other natural ecosystems into agricultural land. Stopping deforestation is therefore an urgent objective. The global deforestation rate remains high, and forest carbon storage continues to decrease (Section 1.2.5). Important leverage for the transformation is therefore provided by (national and international) financial incentives for the enlargement of forest land, the cessation of deforestation and forest degradation, and the conservation and sustainable management of forests and peatlands.

Low Ambition Level: Extend Sustainable Forest Management

Forest protection and sustainable forest management play an important role in CO_2 binding and storage and the establishment of sinks. However, a purely climate protection driven transformation does not make sense in forest management. The WBGU recommends increasing the overall focus on ecosystem services, as the availability of safe water and soil quality are also decisive for the transformation. To achieve this, incentives and remuneration schemes for ecosystem services should be developed further, and implemented. The WBGU suggests that the respective individual countries' national and international forestry strategies and programmes should increasingly take CO_2 binding and storage, as well as other important ecosystem services, into account. This also applies to, for instance, the German federal government's Forestry Strategy 2020, currently under development. The national obligations resulting from the Convention on Biological Diversity (CBD) should be integrated. In addition, publicly owned forest land should lead by example through being managed and certified according to sustainability criteria such as those of the Forest Stewardship Council (FSC).

Medium Ambition Level: Promote Multiple-Use of Forest Product Resources

National raw material strategies for timber, such as, for example, the German federal government's 'Timber Charter' (Charta für Holz), are particularly important for the transformation. The rising demand for wood-fuelled energy and an increase in the use of timber products with a long lifecycle to substitute fossil and mineral raw materials have led to rising timber prices. Raw material strategies often focus on increasing the market volume of the raw material wood. Instead, they should rather consider the climate-friendliness and the conservation of ecosystem services. Forests should be managed so that they can continue to function as significant carbon sinks in order to promote the transformation. The focus should be on the multiple use of the raw material wood, accompanied by steering measures such as, for example, the phasing out of indirect subsidies for high-energy building materials. Public procurement, particularly also in terms of import, should rely on wood from forests which are sustainably managed and certified (e.g. in accordance with FSC standards).

Medium Ambition Level: Lend Political Support to Agro-Forestry

Agro-forestry schemes contribute to food security, and play an increasing role in the adaptation to climate change, in terms of carbon sequestration and indirect reduction of emissions (ICRAF, 2010). The WBGU therefore feels that it would make sense to improve cross-sector communication in the ministries (rural development, agriculture, forest, water and soil management) in order to use agro-forestry's potential to the utmost. The required information and incentive schemes must also be created, and the legal barriers preventing the establishment of agro-forestry that exist in a number of countries (including Germany) must be reduced. A review of EU agricultural policy should increasingly consider and promote agro-forestry through payments for ecosystem services.

Medium Ambition Level: Protect Peatlands

Peatlands are seen as extremely effective ecosystems for carbon storage. They therefore have a very important role to play in climate protection. The protection of peatlands, stopping their drainage, and renaturalising them is therefore extremely important, and should be supported through support programmes and regulatory policies. Redirecting EU agricultural policy towards direct payments for the conservation of ecosystem services, and funds gained on a national level through emissions trading, could finance the protection of peatlands.

Medium Ambition Level: Increase Strategic Alliances with the Relevant 'Forest Countries'

Germany has been committed to cooperation with the major 'forest countries', for example Indonesia, China, Brazil, the Philippines, Papua New Guinea and the Democratic Republic of Congo, for many years. By extending these sub-global alliances, the technological and administrative framework conditions that are a precondition for the rapid and successful realisation of REDD-plus projects could be developed and tested in collaboration (WBGU, 2010b). This applies equally to the development of monitoring and reporting systems for emissions measurement in forest areas, and to the question of how to take other important sustainability and development dimensions into account. This includes the conservation of the natural forests and biodiversity as much as the comprehensive participation of all interest groups, and the improvement of the land rights and use rights of indigenous peoples and local communities. These long-term oriented alliances allow the integration of the numerous experiences gained in individual projects into bi- or multilateral strategies, regional networking, and larger-scale acceleration. To further the partner countries' trust in the international processes, the release of the already pledged additional fast-start funds, and their additionality, must be secured, and an adequate share must be reserved for forestry. This is an important precondition for advancing strategic alliances with the major forest countries.

Medium Ambition Level: Support REDD-plus Interim Partnership

With the REDD-plus Interim Partnership, a process for international dialogue that deserves serious consideration has been created. Germany can utilise this important platform for REDD-plus in order to introduce the necessary ecological and social minimum standards and financing instruments into the globally rapidly developing projects and initiatives to complement the current negotiations under the UNFCCC.

High Ambition Level: Accelerate Multilateral REDD-plus Negotiations

A REDD-plus regime within the scope of the UNFCCC is urgently required to create the global framework for a legally binding mechanism, and to provide the necessary long-term planning security. To allow the anchoring of a schedule, and the global target of reducing global deforestation by half by 2020, and completely by 2030, in the next Conference of the Parties' set of decisions, the corresponding financial contributions on the part of industrialised countries must be made. This is required to allow the developing countries to develop national strategies in answer to REDD-plus. The forest countries need support in establishing baseline, monitoring and reporting systems, so that the reduced emissions can be evaluated, and performance-related payments guaranteed. In addition, a national information system, reporting on compliance with the social and ecological standards, should be established. Taking biodiversity and the rights of indigenous peoples and local communities into account is a decisive precondition for a successful REDD-plus regime. The WBGU views it as necessary to include incentives for forest conservation and sustainable forest management in any future treaty. Utilisation of the synergies with the Convention on Biodiversity (CBD) could be improved, for example by referring to the strategic plan laid down by the CBD in Nagoya in UNFCCC decisions. It is also important to consider a forest definition, or to call for a joint UNFCCC, CBD and FAO forest definition, as so far no distinction is made between natural forests, managed forests and plantations.

7.3.7.3 Promote Climate-Friendly Agriculture

Global agriculture must cover the expected rapid growth in demand for food, bioenergy and biomass as an industrial feedstock in a sustainable manner, and at the same time significantly reduce greenhouse gas emissions, without the option of making new arable land available through deforestation, since deforestation is irreconcilable with climate protection and nature conservation. This combination of demands is a significant challenge, in particular as the productive areas are becoming ever rarer through advanced soil degradation, water scarcity and climate change (Sections 1.2.5, 4.3.4, 7.3.7.1).

Around half of global agricultural greenhouse gas emissions could be avoided without economic loss, above all through improved carbon sequestration in the soil, and the mitigation of CH_4 emissions from livestock production, and N_2O emissions from nitrogen fertilisation. However, despite this major potential, only little progress has been made in this area over the last few decades. Although there is still a need for extensive research into low-carbon technologies to avoid emissions (Chapter 8), a great number of these have already been developed, and are ready to be used. One big step forward would be optimising the financing instruments to allow a rapid introduction of these technologies, and significantly improving the transfer of this knowledge and the technology to developing countries.

Low Ambition Level: Redirect Investments towards Climate-Friendly Agriculture

As in the energy sector (Section 7.3.8), there is not only a lack of access to information and technology transfer, but also not enough investment in sustainable agriculture and the rural agrarian infrastructure. In the face of the substantial investments required by the developing countries in any case, it is particularly important to increase the investments to be expected, and to steer them in such a way that synergetic measures for climate-friendly management and increased production enjoy exceptional promotion. Germany should demonstrate its commitment to this aim both within the EU, as well as to international institutions such as the FAO, IFAD or the World Bank, and focus its own development policy accordingly (Chapter 5).

Low Ambition Level: Create Incentives for Climate-Friendly Agriculture

Climate-friendly land management must also benefit agricultural enterprises in the long run. Due to the fact that monitoring greenhouse gas emissions at farm level is somewhat difficult, the incentives should be measure-related, rather than emissions-based. The WBGU would, for instance, advise against the direct tying-in of agricultural emissions into an emissions trading scheme at corporate level, such as the EU ETS. Agricultural climate protection measures should preferably enjoy direct funding, for example within the scope of the EU.

Low Ambition Level: Minimise Losses

The implementation of the available measures for reducing agricultural post-harvest losses and losses at consumer or household level should be emphatically advanced. The WBGU recommends the target of halving agricultural post-harvest losses all along the supply chain from farm to consumer by 2050.

Medium Ambition Level: Use Climate-Friendly Agrarian Technologies in Developing Countries

The developing regions offer a substantial potential for intensifying agricultural production through the use of sustainable agrarian practices. As the standard agrarian practices are reasonably well known, this is not so much a matter of technology transfer, but rather of strategic advice and large-scale capacity building (Chapter 5).

German federal government and EU bi- and multilateral development cooperation should here be led by IAASTD recommendations, and promote a systematic intensification of agricultural production in developing countries through the application of current agricultural expertise. Agro-forestry is particularly beneficial for the transformation: not only can it help poor farmers to increase their productivity, but it also contributes to carbon storage and improves soil carbon sequestration.

Using more land agriculturally, on the other hand, is accompanied by substantial emissions and, not least, the loss of biodiversity. As a matter of principle, the WBGU therefore recommends arguing against any extension of agriculturally used land in bi- and multilateral development cooperation and the relevant international forums.

Medium Ambition Level: Create International Framework Conditions for Sustainable Bioenergy

The WBGU confirms that particularly an expanding use of bioenergy bears significant risks for various sustainability dimensions (Box 4.1-4; WBGU, 2008). Since international agricultural trade renders impact chains and impact interactions extremely intransparent, only a global regulation framework can therefore guarantee sustainability regarding the use of bioenergy. An international consensus on the minimum standard for sustainable bioenergy production and a comprehensive international bioenergy strategy should be developed as soon as possible. One important element is the development of a global, GIS-supported land-use register with information on the respective production area of every single imported bioenergy carrier. The development of such a land-use register is not least also a research task (Chapter 8). Unless the suggested global regulation framework is established, bioenergy should be expanded only moderately (WBGU, 2010a).

High Ambition Level: Liberalise Global Agricultural Trade and Reform EU Agricultural Subsidies

The WBGU again emphasises the major significance of a rapid and more extensive liberalisation of global agricultural trade within the scope of the World Trade Organisation (WBGU, 2010a). Securing the food supply must be the highest priority in the liberalisation of agricultural trade. To achieve this, the global agricultural markets should instigate long-term investment and productivity increases, particularly in the poorer developing countries. The removal of import barriers for agricultural produce should be stepped up, particularly in the industrialised countries, along with the phasing out of export subsidies. Accordingly, the EU should continue to reduce agrarian subsidies for industrial agricultural production and the export of agricultural produce soon, and improve market access for developing countries. To promote an ecological performance that is on par with what society wants, direct performance-related remuneration is preferable to more general premiums per acreage or company (SRU, 2008). In view of the transformation, particularly subsidies favouring livestock production, either directly or indirectly (for example feed cultivation or stabling), or the use of fossil energy carriers in agriculture (agrarian diesel), should be reduced drastically, speedily and EU-wide.

The liberalisation could result in price increases that could have a particularly negative impact on the low-income food-deficit countries (LIFDC), as net importers of agricultural produce. These should be offset by international financial support, compensation and protection mechanisms (high ambition level; Chapter 4; WBGU, 2010a).

7.3.7.4
Promote Climate-Friendly Eating Habits

The key focus of the agricultural debate is above all how to meet the expected rise in demand with corresponding productivity increases. The transformative effect of influencing the demand side, however, should not be underestimated. Apart from population growth, the most dynamic factor affecting land use, due to the huge differences in the emissions intensity of different foods, are changing eating habits. In industrialised countries, and increasingly, also in the high-income social classes of the newly industrialising and developing countries, the consumption of animal products, whose production involves significantly higher greenhouse gas emissions than purely plant-based agricultural commodities, is on the increase. Livestock farming is already the most influential factor with regard to anthropogenic land use worldwide. Overall, i.e. directly and indirectly, this sector currently claims around three-quarters of farmland and is responsible for just under a fifth of anthropogenic greenhouse gas emissions (including land used for the cultivation of feed; Section 4.1.7.2); however, it also generates income for 1.3 billion people.

Low Ambition Level: Increase the Pioneering Role played by Public Institutions

Education and information campaigns to raise consumers' awareness of their behaviour can contribute to voluntary changes in consumption patterns. The message should be: a low-meat diet that includes a high proportion of preferably organically produced, fresh regional and seasonal produce is worth promoting, not just for climate protection, but also for health reasons. At the same time, awareness of the avoidable emissions and costs that are the result of food spoiling and wasting in households should be raised. The WBGU advises the federal government to step up education, together with food labelling identifying the environmental impact, as speedily implemented supportive measures to initiate this change.

The WBGU attaches particular importance to the pioneering role of state-run and public institutions (government agencies, hospitals, etc.). Canteens run by public authorities should schedule one or two meat-free days a week by way of setting an example. The educating effect is particularly promising if suitable attention is paid to this when catering for schools and kindergartens.

High Ambition Level: Increase Taxation on Emissions-Intensive Agricultural Goods

As it is difficult to change consumers' preferences solely by providing better information and role models, additional price signals, for example through the taxation of consumption, ought to be considered. The option of including the emissions intensity of foodstuffs as a criterion in the taxation of agricultural products within the scope of a tax reform should be examined.

7.3.8
Bundle 8: Encourage and Accelerate Investments into a Low-Carbon Future

The transformation into a low-carbon society needs substantial additional investments in sustainable energy and land-use systems. The initial additional global investments required for the transformation of the energy systems alone are in the region of several US$ hundred billion per year: estimates for the additional global investments required in 2030 range from at least US$ 200 to up to 1,000 billion per year, and assume steadily growing annual investment needs. Around half of the estimated annual investments, i.e. around US$ 100–563 billion, has to be invested in developing countries. Additional financial transfers with regard to the REDD-plus mechanism for the avoidance of deforestation in developing countries are also required. It needs approx. US$ 20–33 billion per year (Section 4.5.1) to halve global deforestation.

Although these additional investments are partially, or even wholly, offset by savings on fossil fuels, significant savings will not occur until a much later point in time. The core problem of many transformative investments, such as in efficiency technologies or renewable energies, is therefore that the upfront investment is extremely high, and is offset only by returns over a very long period of time, and rather small annual amounts. The amortisation period of such investments is therefore often longer, and they yield less than alternative investments. For this reason, there is a great danger of path dependencies on existing high-carbon technologies.

The central challenge for any government transformation policy is therefore the speedy redirection of the investment flow towards low-carbon technologies by making transformative investments more appealing, and by phasing out current misguided incentives and investment barriers. This challenge can only be met through the interaction of public and private investors or capital lenders, in close cooperation with the international finance organisations (World Bank, IMF) and the development banks.

Gradually Remove Investment Barriers: Increase the Yield and Reduce the Risks

In contrast to the established technologies, many of the climate-friendly technologies are as yet not competitive without state support. One of the reasons for this is that the negative external effects of fossil energy carriers are not taken into account when comparing profitability, i.e. these technologies are simply 'too cheap'. Also, currently, there is a lot of regulatory uncertainty for political reasons, leading to relatively high market risks for investments in (new) low-carbon technologies and products. This in turn has the effect that commercial financial institutions do not allocate enough capital to projects with new, as yet not very well established technologies, and these projects therefore are not realised, despite the fact that the required funds would actually be available in principle. The aim of any government policy must therefore be to make transformational investments more profitable, compared with alternative investment projects, and allowing investors access to enough capital. The risks of such investments would therefore have to be reduced with the help through government support.

Four Pillars for Promoting Investment for a Global Transformation into a Low-Carbon Society

To achieve a reduction of the above described investment risks, four areas would have to be changed, in the following referred to as the 'four pillars' of promoting investment for a transformation towards a low-carbon society: *Firstly,* the state and the international community would have to create stable framework conditions for low-carbon investments. *Secondly,* the states would have to tap new financing sources to make public investments and financial transfers to poorer countries possible. *Thirdly,* new financing mechanisms to encourage private investors would have to be established, and existing mechanisms would have to be strengthened. *Fourthly,* new business models which reduce the strain of high upfront investments should be promoted. The interaction of activities regarding these four 'pillars' should promote investment with the decisive impetus, so that changing track towards a low-carbon society can succeed. The ambition levels of the recommendations in the following four areas depend on the level of development of the respective countries (industrialised, newly industrialising, or developing), and on the stringency of their political implementation, so ambition levels are not explicitly identified.

7.3.8.1
Pillar 1: Provide Stable Framework Conditions for Climate-Friendly Investments

One important precondition for investments into low-carbon technologies is that the climate and energy political framework conditions offer long-term investment security, and guarantee attractive yields. The most important component of such a regulatory framework, from the WBGU's point of view, is carbon pricing, as this makes the use of fossil energy carriers more expensive whilst bringing forward low-carbon technologies (Sections 5.2.2, 7.3.2). Investment security and the revenue for transformative investments could be increased even more if additional technology-specific subsidies were granted. Binding efficiency standards for buildings, vehicles and energy-consuming products would also contribute to redirecting the investment flows.

Create Framework Conditions with Increasing Transformative Impact

Stable climate and energy political framework conditions with ambitious targets, for example within the scope of a climate protection law or a decarbonisation strategy, are preconditions for the relevant investments (Section 7.3.1).

Important components when creating such framework conditions are the further development of the European emissions trading scheme (EU ETS), and the further diffusion of feed-in tariffs in Europe. However, from a global perspective, these instruments alone, as they are, have only a very moderate transformative impact, due to their geographically restricted scope. They are nevertheless important, as they represent a model for other countries to follow. With this in mind, the German federal government should actively support the global diffusion of both carbon pricing instruments and technology-specific feed-in tariffs for renewable energies (Sections 7.3.2, 7.3.4). Gradually, a very high transformative impact could be achieved in this way.

Simultaneously, for carbon pricing to develop its full impact, the subsidies enjoyed by fossil energy carriers should be phased out worldwide to eliminate the subsidy-based cost advantage of fossil fuels. As a supportive measure, demanding and dynamically evolving efficiency standards for buildings, vehicles and energy-consuming products should also be defined. Existing approaches in Germany and Europe, such as, for example, the EU Directive on Eco-Design of Energy-Using Products, should be strengthened. If these framework conditions were binding at a national, supranational and international level, they could develop their guiding effect with regard to the investment flow even better.

These measures should be completed at national level through tax incentives and also, on the part of the capital lenders, for example through explicitly including sustainability in the lending decision criteria. Sustainable financial investments should enjoy preferential taxation for an interim period. To support grid extension, a grid regulation should be introduced which, in addition to aspects of economic efficiency, also takes long-term objectives into account which serve the establishment of a sustainable infrastructure.

Aim for the Credible and Long-Term Oriented Setting of Framework Conditions through International Treaties

Transformative changes of the necessary dimension are particularly to be expected if credible, long-term oriented framework conditions are set at a global level in the form of international treaties, i.e. if CO_2 emissions were suitably priced worldwide, if all subsidies for fossil energy carriers were phased out, and if renewable energies were systematically supported (Sections 7.3.2, 7.3.4.). Stable worldwide framework conditions for the decarbonisation would direct additional capital towards sustainable investments. The strongest transformative impact could, from the WBGU's point of view, be achieved by establishing a global scheme to limit CO_2 emissions, i.e. implemented through integrating newly industrialising and developing countries into a binding mitigation regime at UN level (Section 7.3.10). This could be realised, for example, through cross-national emissions trading schemes at corporate level with common caps (Section 7.3.2). In a system such as this, transformative investments would be favoured in two ways: on the one hand, the cap results in a powerful steering effect for investments in low-carbon technologies and products. On the other hand, a fair sharing of the burden between industrialised, newly industrialising and developing countries would also trigger significant financial transfers to developing regions, which could be used to finance transformative investments, or to support public financing mechanisms (pillar 2).

7.3.8.2
Pillar 2: Open Up New Financing Sources at State Level

Particularly investments in infrastructure, such as transmission grids and storage facilities, have a public good character, and must therefore be carried by the state to a large extent. To guarantee the financing of investments in infrastructure on the part of the state, thereby releasing the funds required to support the decarbonisation of the energy systems in developing countries and private investment projects, all states must consider various new opportunities for the generation of additional funds. Whilst in the industrialised countries, new funds could be generated through carbon pricing on the one hand, and further taxation on the other, developing countries largely depend, at least in the interim, on financial transfers from bi- and multilateral funds, for example under the UNFCCC. The transformative impact in each case depends on the earnings, and how they are spend.

A low transformative impact can be expected from moderate carbon pricing schemes in industrialised countries, such as, currently, the EU ETS, and from a marginal increase of the existing bi- and multilateral funds for the developing countries. If, however, the profits from adequate CO_2 taxation in as many countries as possible – including international aviation and shipping – or the revenues from the auctioning of emissions allowances in an ambitious emissions trading system were to be combined with further income sources (for example a moderate financial transaction tax) whilst simultaneously reducing the subsidies for fossil energy carriers and agriculture, the available funds could reach the level required for the transformation (Section 4.5.2).

Use Carbon Pricing as a Source for Financing the Transformation

Carbon pricing, whether in the form of CO_2 taxation or an emissions trading scheme, can lead to the generation of substantial revenues at national level. From the WBGU's point of view, it is therefore one of the most important new financing sources. The UN Secretary-General's High-Level Advisory Group on Climate Change Financing (AGF) estimates that the introduction of carbon pricing mechanisms in the industrialised countries from 2020 onwards, at a price of US$ 20–25 per t CO_2eq, could generate a total annual revenue of US$ 300 billion. Assuming that carbon prices will rise in future, and emissions caps will become stricter, the WBGU estimates that by around 2030/2040, the revenue generated could be substantially higher. However, the revenue can be expected to decrease towards the middle of the century, as by then, emissions would have gone down drastically, leading to a much lower taxation basis, or a greatly reduced volume of permits. Part of the revenues from carbon pricing should be used to finance national investments into the transformation; however, some of these should also be reserved for financial transfers to developing countries. National carbon pricing systems should be introduced globally. In newly industrialising and developing countries, the initial move towards carbon pricing and the parallel phasing out of fossil fuel subsidies could become part of low-carbon development strategies, and be supported by financial transfers from industrialised countries under the UNFCCC (Section 7.3.2).

Open Up Additional Financing Sources

Further sources, apart from the income generated by carbon pricing, should be used to secure the financing needed for the transformation. The phasing out of the misguiding energy and agricultural subsidies (Section 4.5), already announced by the G20 countries, could release substantial public revenues. Potential contributions released through the phasing out of fossil fuel subsidies in the G20 industrialised countries could amount to anything between US$ 8 and 10 billion per year, according to AGF estimates (AGF, 2010). The abolishment of these subsidies would also lead to significant savings in many developing and newly industrialising countries (Section 4.5). The financial resources thus released could be used in developing and newly industrialising countries for the expansion of an electric power infrastructure and the provision of access to energy on the basis of renewable energies, particularly in rural areas. In the area of land use, agricultural subsidies, particularly within the European Union, should gradually be phased out and replaced by a system for financing the conservation of ecosystem services (Sections 5.2, 7.3.7).

In addition, the endeavours regarding the taxation of international aviation and shipping – or, alternatively, the introduction of an international emissions trading scheme for these sectors – should also be advanced. According to AGF estimates, if 50 % of the revenue generated globally through the taxation were to be made available for the transformation, this would lead to an annual financial input of around US$ 10 billion (AGF, 2010). The AGF estimates further that an equally substantial amount could be achieved if an international financial transaction tax of a maximum of 0.01 % were introduced (AGF, 2010; Section 4.5). However, as the impact a financial market transaction tax would have on the international financial markets remains unclear, the rate of taxation should be kept very low if it were introduced, somewhere along the lines of the AGF's sample calculation.

A bundling of income from the various different financing sources, and the earmarking of a fixed ratio of the income generated in industrialised countries for financial transfers to developing countries, would be an important step on the way to a low-carbon global economy.

Secure Continued Financial Support for the Green Climate Fund, and Increase other Bi- and Multilateral Funds

Whilst the new financing sources elaborated above should above all be used by the industrialised countries, at least initially, the transformation in developing and newly industrialising countries must be financed by means of financial transfers. To facilitate these, the Green Climate Fund was established during the UNFCCC COPs in Copenhagen and Cancún. The Annex I Countries pledged to mobilise US$ 100 billion per year (Box 4.5-1). However, it is not clear yet how exactly these US$ 100 billion are to be generated, and to what extent they will pass through the as yet to be established fund.

The as yet non-binding pledges by the industrialised countries regarding payments into the Green Climate Fund should therefore immediately be turned into a legally-binding mechanism. Considering the amounts required for mitigation and adaptation in the developing countries, which are estimated to lie somewhere in the region of three-digit billions (approx. US$ 300–500 billion from 2020) for mitigation, and in the region of two-digit billions for adaptation (approx. US$ 10–100 billion), the funds should be allocated adequately weighted with regard to the different areas to be financed (adaptation, mitigation, technology transfer, capacity building). From the WBGU's point of view, around 60–70% of the Green Climate Fund monies should be allocated to mitigation projects or measures, and to technology transfer. The remaining 30–40% should be reserved for the areas of adaptation and capacity building.

To promote mitigation measures in newly industrialising and developing countries, ways of offering systematic support through the Green Climate Fund to Nationally Appropriate Mitigation Actions (NAMAs) planned by developing countries should be found. In the WBGU's opinion, the NAMAs supported by the Fund should be concrete measures that are embedded in extensive low-carbon development strategies; for example, the introduction of carbon pricing, the financing of feed-in tariffs for renewable energies (Sections 5.2, 7.3.2, 7.3.4), the expansion of grid and storage infrastructure (Section 7.3.3), or the introduction of climate-friendly transport systems in major cities (Section 7.3.5). NAMAs which bear all the hallmarks of isolated projects, on the other hand, should be supported only in the LDCs, if at all.

Unlike other multilateral funds, means from the Green Climate Fund should not be assigned in the form of loans, but as non-repayable grants. Green Climate Fund payments would thereby take on the character of true financial transfers, taking into account the industrialised countries' committment to support the developing countries' climate protection endeavours, a fair burden sharing, and the industrial countries' historical responsibility with regard to causing climate change (Section 7.3.10).

However, the Green Climate Fund will not be sufficient to cover all of the financing needed for the transformation in the world's developing regions. It is to be expected that the required investments will increase even more as of 2020. That is why financial means for mitigation projects in developing countries funded by existing multilateral funds should also be increased. Particularly suitable for this would be the World Bank's Carbon Partnership Facility, the GEF Trust Fund, the Clean Technology Fund, and the Strategic Climate Fund. Contrary to the Green Climate Fund, monies from the bi- and multilateral funds should be released in the form of loans and loan guarantees.

To ensure that the overall balance of direct transfers is not reduced through the inclusion of additional loans and loan guarantees, the funds pledged by the industrialised countries from 2020 for mitigation (grants and loans), adaptation, technology transfer and capacity building should in any case exceed the US$ 100 billion. Furthermore, it has to be guaranteed that the funds are additional with respect to general development aid (Box 4.5-2).

Strive for a Global Carbon Market with Fair Burden Sharing

As already recommended by the WBGU in Section 7.3.2, initial moves at national level towards carbon pricing should be transformed into a global carbon market at business level as soon as possible. In the interests of fair burden sharing, the revenues from the auctioning of emissions allowances could be redistributed to the participating countries, or the emissions rights themselves could be shared out amongst the countries in accordance with a fair burden concept. The scarcity of emissions allowances and the allocation of emissions rights according to a fair burden sharing principle would lead to significant financial transfers between the participating countries. Comparable financial transfers would be the consequence of the introduction of a global emissions cap, i.e. a binding mitigation regime, at UN level, with tradable emissions rights, as elaborated in the WBGU budget approach (Section 7.3.10; WBGU, 2009).

A political allocation of emissions rights can, in the WBGU's view, lead to the creation of a predictable long-term financing instrument for the transformation, whose volume is expected to lie significantly above that of the currently planned structures, such as the envisaged Green Climate Fund and the existing bi- and multilateral funds.

7.3.8.3
Pillar 3: Strengthen Mechanisms to Encourage Private Investments

Public funding is not the only important aspect. On the contrary, the majority of the investments must be financed by private actors. The state can create a favourable environment for such investments by reducing the risks for private investors through the creation of favourable framework conditions (pillar 1) and new financing mechanisms, i.e. by making government funds – sourced as elaborated above (pillar 2) – available in the form of soft loans and credit guarantees. Experience has shown that government financing mechanisms can develop a leverage effect, attracting private means at a ratio of approx. 3:1, in some cases up to 15:1. The leverage effect increases at the same rate as the government funds reduce the risk for private investors. The transformative effect of government financing mechanisms depends on how targeted the government funding is being used, i.e. how much the grants are tied to certain criteria which guide the investment towards a low-carbon economy.

Bundle Public Funding in National Green Investment Banks and Involving Institutional Investors

Individual countries can, through cheap loans from revolving funds or by taking over credit risk guarantees, make the initial financing of transformative investments easier. Following the UK's example, current funding sources should be consolidated and bundled through forming national Green Investment Banks. This would help to achieve the necessary dimension, and the awarding criteria could be made sustainable and transparent. The Green Investment Banks should provide a corresponding portfolio, including low-interest long-term loans, credit guarantees and risk capital for investors in renewable energies and other low-carbon technologies. Institutionally, these Green Investment Banks should emerge from existing national development banks (such as the KfW, in Germany, or the European Investment Bank, at EU level), or be established as a major segment of the national development banks' scope of activity. A share of the loans granted by Green Investment Banks in industrialised countries should be reserved for financing projects in developing countries, as is currently the case in the KfW's global climate protection fund.

Government financing of Green Investment Banks could primarily be topped up with funds from institutional investors, such as pension schemes and insurance companies, to finance the transformation, as these tend to have both the requisite capital and a long-term investment horizon. Their capital contributions to Green Investment Banks could attract a fixed rate of interest, along the lines of EU or World Bank climate bonds. Such funds, fed by both private and government means, would provide institutional investors with the chance of making low-risk investments with a steady interest rate whilst also providing a way of investing into a low-carbon future. This would also serve to extend the financing available through national Green Investment Banks.

Strengthen Equity and Venture Capital Markets

Another important element which would make it easier for private investors to invest preferably in new and not yet proven low-carbon technologies is the strengthening of equity and venture capital markets, as these can be crucial for the availability of important start-up financing for smaller companies with innovative products and technologies. This could be effected, for example, by improving the fiscal conditions for private equity and venture capital lenders. A further option would be the consolidation of public and private risk capital in venture capital funds; examples of these are the UK Carbon Trust Venture Capital Fund, or California Clean Energy Fund. A venture capital fund could also be established under the umbrella of a national Green Investment Bank.

Make Use of the Catalyst Function of Development Banks and Microfinancing

The development banks play a particularly important role when it comes to financing the transformation in the developing countries. They should extend their regular granting of loans in the area of renewable energies and energy efficiency, not least through the jointly financed Climate Investment Funds (CIF). The development banks' credit programmes should focus on the areas of energy infrastructure, access to sustainable energy, expansion of renewable energies, energy efficiency and low-carbon urban infrastructures, as well as sustainable land use. Development bank financing mechanisms can enable private financing intermediaries in developing countries to grant loans themselves. If this were to serve the acquisition of additional funds from private investors, it would have a catalyst effect. The technical expertise of energy service companies (ESCO) and development banks should be firmly integrated into financing solutions, in the form of accompanying consultancy services.

Microfinancing also plays an important role when it comes to decentralised renewable energy generation to transform the energy systems of developing countries, particularly in the rural regions. It also makes a significant contribution to overcoming energy poverty with the help of renewable energies. Current German development cooperation initiatives should be extended.

Tap the Potential of a Reformed Global Carbon Market

The role the international carbon market will play in developing countries remains uncertain, due to the lack of clarity regarding the future of the Kyoto Protocol. The WBGU advises against continuing the CDM mechanism in its current form, as this can lead to a weakening of the industrialised countries' mitigation targets. In its current design, it has also not fulfilled its original intention of promoting low-carbon development (Section 4.5). From the WBGU's point of view, the CDM should be limited to the least developed countries in future. In parallel, the CDM's development aspect should be emphasised, and the mechanism extended to cover sectoral measures – similarly to the programme-based CDM. This reform would, for instance, allow the consolidated financing of many smaller and diffuse efficiency potentials in microenterprises and private households, for example through financing biomass-fuelled stoves, or solar-powered water heaters. A programme-based or sectoral CDM could therefore also make a significant contribution to the reduction of energy poverty.

The continuance of the CDM, restricted to LDC, however, would have to be accompanied by considerably more ambitious reduction targets in the Annex I Countries, and reforms with regards to the attribution of emissions credits, for example from HFC-23 projects. To promote the transformation in the less poor developing countries and the newly industrialising countries, no mechanism should be relied on that rests on the attribution of industrialised countries' reduction target mitigations achieved there. As long as these states do not have binding emissions caps, which would make it possible to integrate them into emissions trading, the WBGU recommends restricting them to financial transfers. Financial transfers for the implementation of NAMAs in the above outlined sense should replace the CDM, particularly in newly industrialising countries.

7.3.8.4
Pillar 4: Encourage New Business Models

The burden that the high upfront investments represent for individual investors can be reduced by spreading them 'across several shoulders'. This can be achieved if traditional buyer-seller business models were turned into business models with new ownership and financing structures that reduce investment barriers, and change the incentive structure. The more market penetration such business models achieve, and in the more countries, the bigger their transformative impact.

Tap Efficiency Gains whilst Reducing Upfront Investments

These kinds of models are characterised by the fact that, for example, they offer their customers combined packages in different areas (for example mobility, housing, production, and consumption) that include combined goods and services, instead of just (tangible) consumer goods. The property rights to the goods remain with the provider, who is committed to efficient resource utilisation and goods recycling. Already established are concepts like car sharing, in the mobility sector, and energy contracting through Energy Service Companies (ESCO), in the energy supply and energy efficiency sector (Section 4.3). The tangible goods (i.e. car, heating system, energy raw material) again remain the property of the provider, whilst the goods required to meet user needs are only rented, hired, leased, or used communally together with other customers. Customers pay primarily for the (mobility or energy) services they have actually used, rather than the provision of a larger 'package' of potentially usable services.

These kinds of services, or integrated product-service systems, should be increasingly advertised and supported during the course of the transformation, for example through tax rebates. In order for the use of such business models, which are oriented to services rather than consumer goods, to become widespread amongst potential users, a fundamental value change is required on the part of both private customers and businesses (for example with regard to the status value attached to consumer goods).

Increase the Use of Cooperative Financing

Another business and financing model that is important for the transformation is cooperative financing, which can be particularly useful when it comes to the installation of plants for renewable energy generation. There are already some examples for this kind of business model to be found in Germany. The financing of such jointly purchased plants is provided by own as well as third party capital, to which a cooperative society is more likely to be given access than individuals. In many cases, cooperative banks also take on a part of the investments. These kinds of energy cooperatives can find refinancing through feed-in tariffs. Energy cooperatives could also serve as a model for developing countries, for the electrification of the rural areas using renewable energies. In principle, the cooperative society financing model can also be applied to other investments in low-carbon technologies.

To achieve a high transformative impact, business models such as these would have to leave their niche existence, and find acceptance on a broad basis. To facilitate this, the framework conditions (for example the infrastructure necessary for car sharing) should be optimised, so that what is on offer, in terms of flexibility, cost and ease of access to information, appeals to a great number of potential users. In addition, a public dialogue on ways towards a low-carbon society, for instance complemented by concept competitions and themed forums, should be actively encouraged. This would serve to give both companies and individuals ideas for the development of new business models that will pave the way towards a low-carbon future.

7.3.9 Bundle 9: Reinforce International Climate and Energy Policy

As infrastructures for energy generation, transport and production have a long lifetime, current global conversion and extension projects must already be geared towards climate protection, i.e. climate and energy policy should be systematically linked. Most of the additional energy infrastructures are expected to be built in developing and newly industrialising countries. Therefore, climate protection that is geographically limited to the more prosperous countries cannot solve the problem. Global cooperation to make the required investments in low-carbon development possible for poorer countries, and to ensure that climate protection technologies and the corresponding expert knowledge are available to all countries, is therefore indispensable.

International climate and energy policy is the forum for achieving a global consensus on transformation targets and ambitions. The UN level is also without compare when it comes to negotiations on balancing global equity. Although operative goals like the sharing of climate protection related knowledge and technologies can be advanced on a sub-global level, the strengthening and institutionalisation of the fragmented international energy policy, and its linking to climate policies, should nevertheless be systematically pursued to accelerate the technological shift.

7.3.9.1 International Climate Policy Post-Copenhagen and Post-Cancún

International climate policy, and particularly the way it has developed since the 1992 Earth Summit at Rio de Janeiro under the UN umbrella, nowadays represents the main normative framework for the transformation into a global low-carbon society.

However, the gap between the claims and the reality of international climate policy is widening. The decisions agreed at the 16th Conference of the Parties to the UNFCCC in Cancún include the long-term goal of holding the increase in global average temperature below 2 °C above preindustrial levels. The urgent need to act was identified, and a review process initiated to consider whether the temperature limit should even be reduced, down to 1.5 °C (UNFCCC, 2010). An effective regime with internationally binding commitments on limiting emissions seems to have been shelved for the time being. Even the survival of the Kyoto Protocol, which currently still regulates just under 30 % of global greenhouse gas emissions (excluding land-use change), is anything but certain. Climate protection currently depends on voluntary pledges by states to restrict their emissions – the only aspect that is obligatory is the international verification of the reported emissions (pledge-and-review procedure). The emissions limitations by 2020 which have currently been pledged are not enough, however, to steer global emissions onto a path that would allow compliance with the 2 °C guard rail (UNEP, 2010a).

Low Ambition Level: Ambitious Unilateral Targets within a Pledge-and-Review System

The absolute minimum in terms of what international climate policy should achieve is a tightening of the emissions limitations proffered by the states within the scope of a pledge-and-review system by 2020 to a level which allows compliance with the 2 °C guard rail. According to UNEP (2010a), global emissions would have to be limited to a maximum of 39–44 Gt CO_2eq in 2020 for a 'likely' (i.e. a probability of more than two-thirds) compliance with the 2 °C guard rail. The current pledges, however, would result in emissions of 49–53 Gt CO_2eq.

The WBGU recommends that the German federal government should ensure that the unilaterally pledged mitigations offered by Germany and the EU under a pledge-and-review system, and concessions in terms of finance and technology transfers, are guided by principles of fairness. If the WBGU's budget approach were used for orientation (WBGU, 2009), it could be argued that in 2020, each state would deserve a share of permitted emissions that equals its share of the 2010 world population. For example, as 1.2% of the 2010 world population lived in Germany, it would be entitled to 0.53 Gt CO_2eq of an overall total of 44 Gt CO_2eq. In theory, therefore, Germany would have to reduce its emissions by 56%, compared with 1990 (back then, its emissions were running at 1.2 Gt CO_2eq), to contribute its fair share of mitigation, if this scheme were applied. This could, for instance, consist of domestic emissions reductions of 40% (including offsets, or CDM), and complementary pledges in terms of finance and technology transfers, which would permit 0.2 Gt CO_2eq of additional emissions reductions in other countries.

Assuming mitigation costs of € 20–40 per t CO_2eq, Germany would have to make annual finance and technology transfers for mitigation worth at least € 4–8 billion in 2020, for example via the Green Climate Fund.

For the EU, with 7.2% of the global population, the fair share of the 44 Gt CO_2eq emissions in 2020 would be 3.2 Gt CO_2eq, which would mean reducing emissions by around 40% in comparison with 1990 (when emissions were running at 5.37 Gt CO_2eq). This could also be interpreted as a 30% emissions reduction within the EU, plus annual finance and technology transfers for mitigation of € 11–22 billion. The amounts mentioned refer to mitigation only. In the view of the WBGU, however, this would not suffice to free Germany and the EU from its obligations to contribute further by way of finance and technology transfers to aid adaptation (and possibly compensation for climate damages).

In return, if the global goal is not to be endangered, countries whose emission levels are still low, but which are on a growth path, i.e. countries which are currently required to invest hugely into energy infrastructure expansion, must avoid high-carbon expansion paths. Above all, this means that these countries must already, by 2020, strive for development paths with significantly lower emissions than the 2020 per capita share of the above mentioned 44 Gt CO_2eq would equal. This should be supported through the finance and technology transfers from high emission countries.

In general, the physical emission reductions achieved in the individual countries should be guided by the reduction potentials: in order still to reach the requisite global reductions in a fragmented mitigation regime that is the result of any pledge-and-review process, without pushing up the aggregate global mitigation costs too much, it is necessary for all states to create framework conditions which allow the unlocking of their mitigation potentials. The development of decarbonisation road maps is particularly suitable for this: plans such as this should be a condition for access to mitigation funds from the Green Climate Fund.

Of overriding importance is that double counting is avoided: for example, emissions reductions paid for by an industrialised country, but actually achieved in a developing country, must obviously be claimed for only once as it would otherwise not be possible to compare the emissions limitations pledged by the individual countries with the globally required mitigation. Another problematic issue could be that states that had reduction commitments under the Kyoto Protocol which they have more than fulfilled add these surplus emissions allowances to their pledged emissions limitations. The volume of these surplus emissions allowances countries plan to offset against their mitigation pledges must be taken into account when balancing the global ambitions level; the same applies to the crediting of emissions reductions achieved in the land-use sector (UNEP, 2010a).

It is also essential to develop a long-term global emissions target. The development of such a target for 2050 was decided upon at Cancún. Germany and the EU should become actively involved here, and strive to ensure that this target is developed under consideration of the latest scientific findings.

As it would not be internationally binding, a regime such as this would be fragile as far as compliance with the 2°C target is concerned; it is questionable whether the USA, for example, would compensate for their inadequate ambition level with regard to national emissions reduction with sufficiently high pledges in terms of finance and technology transfers. Germany and the EU should nevertheless lead the way and pledge emissions reductions, as well as finance and technology transfers, that correspond with the above elaborated ambition level.

Medium Ambition Level: Form Pioneer Coalitions for Mandatory Climate Protection

Not least the Cartagena Dialogue for Progressive Action, which is a group of progressive states discoursing on the options for global, ambitious and binding climate protection, is proof of the willingness of a great number of states to go beyond a pledge-and-review process when it comes to international climate protection. This impetus should be utilised to conclude ambitious partial treaties for climate protection. The EU should play an active role here, and advance coalitions both within the framework of the UN negotiation process as well as outside it. Bi- and plurilateral pioneer alliances could play a major role, for example in terms of forest protection (Section 7.3.7; WBGU, 2010b), the establishment of low-carbon infrastructures (Section 7.3.4), and the introduction of emissions trading schemes (Section 7.3.2). The WBGU believes that pioneer alliances such as these would develop transformative dynamics that would also have a positive effect on the UN process. They could also heighten the states' willingness for binding multilateral commitments, as they demonstrate the achievability of emissions reductions, and make them more calculable. Exchanging experiences, and cooperation on the development of national decarbonisation strategies, can also lead to a catalyst effect.

Beyond these alliances, however, the EU should also increasingly seek coalitions for a binding treaty within the scope of the UNFCCC. Apart from unconditionally tightening its own reduction targets, the EU should also show a clear commitment to continuation and further development of the Kyoto Protocol; not, however, without the condition of loophole closing and further development. The WBGU believes that a continuation of the CDM for newly industrialising countries is not appropriate. Instead, an agreement should be sought which links finance and technology transfers to an obligatory development of extensive low-carbon development strategies. The EU should emphatically continue to seek a dialogue with the progressive newly industrialising countries to achieve a commitment that is as binding as possible on this point. As the host of the next climate summit in December 2011, South Africa could play a special role here, as could Brazil, which will host the Rio+20 Conference in May 2012.

High Ambition Level: Strive for a Comprehensive Global Climate Protection Regime

A comprehensive, binding global climate protection agreement regarding global emissions restriction should be the ultimate goal of international climate policy. A maximum global emissions budget compatible with the 2 °C guard rail should be agreed for carbon dioxide from fossil sources, as these emissions, in the long run, are decisive when it comes to climate protection; milestones on a global emissions path that allows compliance with this budget should also be agreed (WBGU, 2009). The WBGU has suggested a burden sharing based on an equal per capita allocation of the emissions still permitted. The states should agree to present internationally verifiable decarbonisation road maps that clearly state the planned national emissions path up to 2050. Ideally, these should be implemented with flexible mechanisms to make use of cost optimisation opportunities (Section 7.3.2). However, as the global energy systems should already have undergone extensive decarbonisation by 2050 (Chapter 4), opportunities for offsetting, or for substituting own mitigation efforts by purchased emissions allowances, will decrease as time goes on. A global decarbonised energy system demands that the energy system of each and every individual country has been decarbonised. As the conversion of energy systems takes time (UNEP, 2010a), national decarbonisation roadmaps which take path dependencies in infrastructure decisions into account are extremely important. Particularly the expansion of renewable energies also relies on government planning, for example when it comes to expanding transcontinental grids and systems for balancing fluctuations (Chapter 4).

For the mitigation of CO_2 from non-fossil sources and other greenhouse gases, separate regulations could achieve a more direct impact. The CO_2 dynamics associated with the terrestrial biosphere differ substantially in many fundamental aspects – such as measurability, reversibility, long-term controllability, inter-annual fluctuations – from the CO_2 fluxes associated with the industrial use of coal, mineral oil or natural gas (WBGU, 2010a). That is why the WBGU has repeatedly suggested the creation of a separate intergovernmental agreement for the protection of terrestrial carbon stocks (WBGU, 2004). Priority should be given to swift and effective measures aiming to stop deforestation in developing countries. The fluorinated greenhouse gases currently covered by the Kyoto Protocol could be dealt with in a special agreement modelled on the Montreal Protocol, which could lead to accelerated and simplified mitigation (WBGU, 2009). For short-lived radiative forcing substances as yet unregulated by the Kyoto Protocol, for example soot particles and ozone-forming gases, there should be separate agreements directly related to national air pollution control.

This kind of globally binding mitigation regime, however, will only be enforceable if it is based on the UNFCCC's fundamental principles of equity, and if adaptation to unavoidable climate change is also given priority.

7.3.9.2
International Energy and Technology Policy

The most important pillars of the transformation of global energy use towards climate-friendliness are *firstly,* limiting the energy demand whilst at the same time guaranteeing all people access to energy, *secondly* the decarbonisation of the energy supply, particularly electric power generation, and *thirdly* the introduction of new, low-carbon technologies in the transport sector, in buildings technology, and in industry. International cooperation should ensure decisive advances in all three of these areas. One important starting point for international energy and technology policies is the agreement of norms and standards. International cooperation can further accelerate technology development: a number of key technologies are still in the development and test stages, for example in the electromobility or CCS sector. Ultimately, cooperation also plays an important role when it comes to removing barriers preventing the global diffusion of technologies for low-carbon development. Collaborations such as these not only serve the transfer of purely technological knowledge, but also the transfer of a much wider knowledge with respect to establishing the requisite framework conditions, without which a diffusion of low-carbon technologies is not possible.

Currently, there is a lack of legal and institutional foundations for an effective international energy policy for the transformation. The WBGU recommends utilising existing organisations to gradually institutionalise a global sustainable energy governance.

Low Ambition Level: Open-up IEA, Consolidate and Strengthen IRENA

The International Energy Agency (IEA) is an influential global institution. However, its membership, role and energy political objectives regarding a sustainable energy policy have so far been restricted. The German federal government should therefore emphasise its support for redirecting IEA content towards sustainable forms of energy and energy systems, for increasing transparency regarding its methods, and for continuing and intensifying the opening process to include non-OECD countries. The foundation of the International Renewable Energy Agency (IRENA) in 2009 equalled the establishment of a new organisation to advance the use of renewable energies in both industrialised and developing countries. In future, IRENA can play an important role in the promotion and diffusion of renewable energies and the respective industries. The WBGU recommends that the German federal government should continue giving its emphatic support to the organisation's development, and to campaign intensively for IRENA being accorded a major role with regard to global energy issues in order to accelerate the expansion of renewable energies, at eye level and in cooperation with existing organisations and the civil society.

Medium Ambition Level: Upgrade UN Energy

The link between energy policies and development assistance policies on a global level has long been neglected. Existing programmes and UN organisations have so far had only moderate effects in terms of sustainable energy policy. The WBGU suggests that the German federal government should lobby for the further promotion of UN Energy as a coordinating platform (inter-agency mechanism) within the UN system, and upgrading the organisation to programme level. The UN general assembly has declared 2012 the 'International Year for Sustainable Energy for All'. This should be utilised by the international community to agree the establishment of an additional Millennium Development Goal granting access to modern energy services by 2030 for all people (Section 7.3.5).

High Ambition Level: Make IRENA the Central Organisation for Global Sustainable Energy Policies

A strong, international energy agency is needed to accelerate the global transformation of energy systems. IRENA's mandate should be extended to cover all energy systems and climate-friendly energy options, including system integration issues, and energy efficiency on the demand side. Gradually, IRENA could then be developed into an International Sustainable Energy Agency, as previously suggested by the WBGU (2003). The WBGU advises the German federal government to show its fullest commitment to making IRENA one of the key organisations for a global sustainable energy policy in the long term.

High Ambition Level: Use G20 as the Driving Force for a Sustainable Energy and Climate Policy

Considering the urgency of the global energy transformation, far greater political will and leadership is required. As an alliance of economically and politically leading industrialised and newly industrialising countries, and with respect to their relevance for global climate protection, the G20 must play an exceptional role here (the G20 are responsible for approx. 80% of global greenhouse gas emissions). As an important member of this forum, the German federal government should encourage the G20 in their determined pursuit of a sustainable energy politicy agenda, and the creation of the institutional foundations required for effective global cooperation.

7.3.10
Bundle 10: Pursue a Revolution in International Cooperation

The theoretical and normative requirements for global governance are already known (Chapter 5). On the basis of the insights underpinned by this report, and with a clear commitment to increasing international cooperation, the WBGU recommends the following points:

1. The UN Conference on Sustainable Development (UNCSD, Rio+20 Conference) should be used as a chance for setting the course of international environmental and developmental policy towards improved cooperation and climate-friendliness (Section 7.3.10.1).
2. The way should be paved for a comprehensive cooperative global governance architecture, without which a worldwide transformation to sustainability cannot succeed (Section 7.3.10.2).

7.3.10.1
International Environmental and Developmental Policy in the Context of the Rio+20 Conference

Presently, the Rio+20 Conference scheduled for 2012 provides a unique opportunity for elaborating international environmental and developmental policies. In view of the two key issues defined for the conference by the UN member states, 'Green Economy in the Context of Sustainable Development and Poverty Eradication', and 'Institutional Framework for Sustainable Development', the WBGU recommends the following steps, in ascending order of ambition level:

1. The creation of a comprehensive 'Green Economy Roadmap', and profound institutional reforms within the scope of the United Nations,
2. a fundamental redirecting of multilateral environmental and developmental policies towards the transformation,
3. a fundamental restructuring of the United Nations ('United Nations 2.0').

Low Ambition Level: Agree a Green Economy Roadmap and Institutional Reforms

In reaction to the global financial and economic crisis, the United Nations Environmental Programme (UNEP) suggested a 'Global Green New Deal', introducing a 'Green Economy Initiative' within the scope of the United Nations. With the 'Green Economy Report' (2011), UNEP has now presented the Rio+20 Conference with comprehensive recommendations for a 'green' reorientation of the world economy, for an environmentally friendly and climate compatible way of doing business, and particularly for the worldwide decarbonisation of energy systems. This means that the international community at Rio now has a suitable and current basis for consultation and decisionmaking.

In this context, the WBGU cautions against repeating the mistakes made at the 1992 Rio Summit, and the ensuing debates on the interpretation of 'sustainable development': international discussion of the concept and definition of 'Green Economy' must not be allowed to turn into political escapism, being obscured by the three-dimensional understanding of sustainable development anchored in Agenda 21. On the contrary, the summit should translate the political objectives of a 'Green Economy' immediately into binding agreements on concrete targets, in this way reaffirming and emphasising the commitment to sustainable development already voiced back in 1992.

A binding 'UN Green Economy Roadmap' with specific targets in terms of both content and timing should be decided in Rio, to be implemented by 2030 within the framework of national Green Economy Strategies that include verifiable indicators. Apart from a transformation-friendly policy mix, these should especially include carbon pricing strategies (Sections 5.2, 7.3.2). The individual national strategies should be guided by the principle of 'common but differentiated responsibilities', taking existing resources and capacities adequately into account. Concrete, quantifiable targets and sub-targets, which have proven successful in the Millennium Development Goals, should primarily be defined for the conversion of energy systems, urban development issues, and sustainable land use.

Many states will fail to achieve the framework conditions required at national level without the provision of substantial financial funds and technical expertise. This should be given adequate consideration when agreeing such a roadmap. States which ultimately commit to the implementation of the roadmap and its respective national strategies and action plans should be offered country-specific, tailor-made advice and support by the United Nations, in cooperation with the World Bank, the regional development banks, and those involved in bilateral development cooperation.

Concurrently, international poverty eradication strategies, and especially the further implementation of the MDG, should be integrated into the higher-ranking Green Economy Roadmap in a way that explicitly allows its individual targets and sub-targets to directly focus on the demands of reaching the set goals in terms of environmental and climate protection. Fighting energy poverty with renewable energies and improving food security through productivity increases by means of sustainable agriculture are key starting points for this. A permanent coexistence of a conventional agenda for growth and a serious Green Economy Roadmap, on the other hand, would necessarily have to be considered as contradictory, even at a low ambition level.

The implementation of the UN Green Economy Roadmap and the regular monitoring of its progress should also be accompanied by long over-due institutional reforms. In the long run, the Rio+20 Conference offers a unique opportunity of overcoming the unsatisfactory ambition level of the currently fragmented endeavours for reform. With regard to these, the WBGU repeats its recommendation that UNEP should be replaced with a newly established UN specialised agency on the environment with far reaching authority, or that UNEP itself should be extended and upgraded to a world organisation capable of acting.

Particular attention must be paid to the development dimension of international environmental policy. The implementation of the Bali Strategic Plan, agreed back in 2005, offers a benchmark for the credibility of the industrialised nations, as well as a lever for increasing the developing countries' willingness to face reforms, and their capability to act (Section 5.4.4.4). Accordingly, the Rio+20 Conference also offers a unique chance, in view of the Green Economy discussion, for the elaboration of a more fundamental reform of the developmental policy architecture of the United Nations, and to pave the way for corresponding decisions. If the states were to miss the chance to bring about concrete reform decisions offered by this summit, the explicit and unanimous focusing on institutional framework conditions would be rendered absurd in front of the global public eye.

The organisational linking of environmental and development political institutions also offers the chance of countering the one-dimensional view of the United Nations, as a service provider for multilateral development cooperation, with a broader perspective that emphasises the potential transformative leverage of multilateral organisation. The WBGU advises the German federal government to work towards a coherent focusing of the operative strategies of the multilateral stakeholders in developmental policy on the demands of environmentally and climate friendly growth, to bundle their resources particularly in the transformation fields energy, urban development and land use, and to efficiently implement targets accordingly (Section 5.4.5).

The respective multilateral organisations should be given adequate political and financial support, whilst the promotion of conventional development programmes encouraging high levels of energy and land consumption should be reduced and gradually stopped. The rapid and consistent focusing of the developmental policies of all EU member states and the EU Commission on this system of objectives would significantly strengthen Europe's role as a pioneer in climate policy.

Medium Ambition Level: Fundamentally Reform Multilateral Environmental and Development Policy

An objective that goes further would be an extensive reshuffling of the United Nations' environmental and developmental architecture and that of other multilateral development organisations, with a view to transformation-friendly reorganisation. The Rio+20 Conference would provide the German federal government and the EU with the opportunity of immediately initiating a process in pursuit of a reorganisation and refocusing of the major operative development agencies (World Bank, Regional Banks, UNDP, UNIDO, etc.) in accordance with the objectives of the transformation.

The WBGU generally agrees with the reform recommendations made by the High Level Group established under UN Secretary-General Kofi Annan in 2006, with regard to system-wide coherence of development, humanitarian aid and the environment ('One UNO'), which have so far been insufficiently implemented. They should be pursued more consistently than they have been so far, whilst focusing explicitly on the demands of the Green Economy Roadmap, and an environmentally and climate friendly development policy. The Rio+20 Conference offers the best opportunity in the foreseeable future of overcoming the particular interests of individual special organisations and programmes whose structure features the same, or at least very similar, members, through authoritative decisions by the summit at the highest international level.

System-wide coherence, focussing on the transformation towards a low-carbon and sustainable society also demands the closure of obvious governance gaps in the key transformation fields of energy, urbanisation and land use on an international level for effective multilevel policy-making, and the simultaneous abolition of transformation-impeding and expensive parallel structures (Section 5.4.5). Accordingly, the states meeting at Rio should task the administrative organs of the responsible multilateral organisations with the drafting of concrete restructuring plans for their respective administrative apparatus, to be presented to the member states for decision-making within the next two years. An approach based on global systemic risks, as proposed by the Palais-Royal Initiative to reform the global monetary system in the context of the worldwide financial crisis, appears a suitable way forward (Section 5.4.4.2).

Parallel to the proposed climate legislation at a national level, the benchmark for any restructuring should always be the international climate policy's 2 °C guard rail. In accordance with this reform logic, multilateral development organisations not able or willing to comply with this would therefore lose their right to exist. Conversely, completely new organisations would have to be created if the global need for cooperation and regulation dictated by compliance with the 2 °C guard rail cannot foreseeably be met within the scope of the suggested reorganisation of already existing international organisations.

The outlined roadmap would allow the systematic interlinking of poverty-orientation and climate-compatibility in international development, energy and environmental policies by 2015. To support intergovernmental reform roadmaps such as these, the member states of the international organisations concerned, in particular those who are major contributors, should change their national policies and regional processes, and commit to the relevant reform plans for the reorganisation of their bi- and multilateral development cooperation, their energy cooperation, and their foreign economic policy.

High Ambition Level: Strive for a United Nations 2.0

Considering the scale of the described challenges of the global environmental and development crisis, the WBGU believes that there are plenty of arguments for an even more radical approach that would go beyond the existing UN architecture, a fundamental restructuring of the organisation. Currently, this hardly seems politically feasible, as it assumes a political leadership motivated by the realisation of global necessities, especially on the part of the permanent members of the World Security Council, and other western, industrialised nations and ambitious newly industrialising countries. If this were the case, a reform should start with a review of the UN Charter, and aim for a completely restructured United Nations organisation. Its purpose would be to take the planetary guard rails into account as a guiding principle that governs all UN actions, the pursuit of which would guarantee the protection of climate and environment in order to stabilise the Earth system as much as peace, security and development.

If the Rio+20 Conference were at least to commit to a vision along these lines, it could serve to initiate a intergovernmental consultancy process that would end in substantial amendments to the 1945 UN Charter, which would equal an appendix to the constitution to encompass climate protection at national level.

This would be the codified equivalent of a global social contract under international law, on the basis of which contemporary a reform of the United Nations' main bodies could be carried out – for example, a UN Council for Sustainable Development could be established, on par with the Security Council, to bring the United Nations up to date and reflect the 21st century – and which would serve as a formal expression of the normative need for a global 'We' identity. The co-evolution of the international protection of human rights and the Universal Declaration of Human Rights shows that these kinds of global visions can certainly lead to concrete changes in the real world.

7.3.10.2
Comprehensive Global Governance as the Transformation's Driving Force

The global transformation into an environmentally and climate friendly global community cannot succeed if it is limited to the narrowly defined political fields of environment and development. On the contrary, a generally high level of international cooperation, global coordination and political steering are key conditions for the success of the transformation towards a low-carbon society. The trend reversal that is needed for the transformation will therefore not be achievable without comprehensive, long-term oriented international regulatory policies with an equitable world order as their goal. In the following, the WBGU outlines three steps with progressive ambition levels on the path towards the necessary revolution in global cooperation.

Low Ambition Level: Revitalise Multilateralism

A lack of cooperation as far as the key questions of global environmental and climate change are concerned will almost inevitably lead to an escalation of conflicting interests and the related distribution issues, which in turn will cause additional difficulties in dealing constructively with any cross-border issues. The key actors in world politics, particularly the USA, the EU and China, as well as an extended group of states, notably the G20, should therefore soon find a mode of international diplomacy that will at least allow them to prevent the escalation of obvious conflicts of interest.

The WBGU believes that the G20 are a fundamentally suitable constellation of actors with the ability to overcome the established, ingrained structures of international cooperation in favour of a constructive multilateralism, and to become active beyond a global economic and financial policy. As a powerful microcosm of world regions they can make timely proposals regarding appropriate targets to the more inclusive United Nations in the transformation-relevant areas of policy-making, such as, in particular, energy policy, global land use and global urbanisation, and provide impulses to guide actions. In addition, the G20 not only carry a high level of climate political responsibility, but also have correspondingly high potentials for transformation.

The WBGU therefore recommends that the G20, or a comparable sub-global constellation, develop a roadmap with directions towards a global transformation towards a low-carbon society. To demonstrate credibility and output legitimacy, such a roadmap would have to be drawn up and implemented within the current decade. It should, at the earliest opportunity, guide the G20 towards making concrete decisions which reflect a decidedly global perspective of this problem, and which have as their benchmark, at the very least, the G20 crisis management in view of the global financial crisis. To be capable of ultimately guiding, motivating and mobilising the entire international community of states in the spirit of the transformation, the leading states would also inevitably have to credibly consider the interests of smaller and poorer developing countries without patronising them. At the same time, with regard to this, the German federal government and the European Union should aim for a high level of ambition, and meet the 'rest of the world' with a committed and mediating attitude. If they succeed, the G20 could then even become the driving force behind bringing the entire UN system up to date.

Medium Ambition Level: Improve Global Governance for Transformative Global Infrastructure Development

Low-carbon development processes must be accelerated globally, and in numerous economic sectors. As this study shows, three fundamental 'infrastructures' are central to achieving this: energy systems, urban areas and land-use systems. Compliance with the 2 °C guard rail is only possible if we have changed the course towards low-carbon in all three of these pillars of the global economy by 2020. On the one hand, energy policy, land-use management and urban development are primarily national issues; on the other hand, a global low-carbon conversion of these three core sectors of the global economy in such short time is not conceivable without international harmonisation processes.

This is a completely new challenge for the international community, as so far, global governance mechanisms for a global redirection of the infrastructures in the three transformation fields do not exist. All of the three fields therefore require the setting of global and national transformation targets, or the development of national and global transformation corridors, and the definition of indicators on whose basis development progress can be monitored, the relevant monitoring processes can be established, and positive incentives for reaching the targets can be introduced (for example development cooperation, technology transfer).

These kinds of global governance mechanisms can only be realised by capable international organisations. Accordingly, in the transformation field of energy, the German federal government should actively support a shift in IEA objectives towards sustainable energy policies and call for improved organisation accessibility for developing countries, and furthermore promote the strengthening of IRENA as the driving force behind the international diffusion of renewable energies, and the upgrading of the status of UN Energy (Section 5.4.5.1). In order to emphasise the issue of sustainable urban development, the WBGU suggests working directly towards a more profound institutional reform as an alternative to the proposed upgrading of UN Habitat (low ambition level; Section 7.3.6.1). At a medium ambition level, the WBGU recommends the establishment of a 'World Commission on Low-Carbon Urban Planning' and a Global Commission for Sustainable Land Use'.

Both commissions could be initiated and mandated through the Rio+20 Conference, and should then proceed to present comprehensive reports by 2015, taking the corresponding complexity of their respective transformation field into account. Based on the report produced by the Global Commission for Sustainable Land Use, the FAO should ultimately develop a suitable range of instruments for redirecting national and global land-use pathways towards climate-friendliness. To put the World Commission on Low-Carbon Urban Planning's findings into operation, the WBGU further recommends the establishment of a broadly mandated UN Specialised Agency for Sustainable Urbanisation. The UN Habitat programme, not adequately equipped to deal with this acute problem, could be incorporated into this.

High Ambition Level: Global Governance for a New, Equitable Global System

The ultimate aim of any future global governance must be the creation of a new, equitable global system whose institutions put the international community of states in a position, as early as within the first half of the 21st century, that leaves them capable of appreciating the complex interdependencies of the global society within the scope determined by the planetary guard rails, and responding in a timely and adequate manner. To be successful in the long run, a global system like this must not be restricted to action-capable 'islands' inhabited by those parts of humankind which are currently the wealthier ones; it must also include those who are currently excluded, and will be in the near future: the 'bottom billion'.

This, however, means that decision-makers in politics, business and society are facing fundamental political and intellectual challenges: politically, it requires a historically unprecedented transcending of established sovereignty concepts and purely power-driven global politics in favour of ensuring the long-term availability of global commons. Intellectually, it requires solid strategies and concepts that anchor sustainable global development in cross-border democratic structures, attempt to find answers to 21st century issues of global equity and fair distribution, and, not least, can claim global legitimacy for themselves.

Both do not equal a utopian demand for a global government or a global state. Instead, the parallel quests of global governance theoreticians, cosmopolitans, transnationalists, philosophers of justice and so on must focus on legitimately operable norms, rules and procedures, and base themselves on the fundamental principle of a virtual global social contract. Such a process would represent a quantum leap for civilisation, on par with the transition from feudalism to democracy and the rule of law in the 17th and 18th centuries, and the 19th century embedding of markets through the institutions of the welfare state.

In the WBGU's view, this is achievable at a global level only through the agreement on universal goals. The Universal Declaration of Human Rights immediately comes to mind here as an example that is not faultless, but nevertheless encouraging: even though the protection of human rights leaves much to be desired empirically, the concept of human dignity, and the special protection it deserves, is universally recognised. It should therefore also be fundamentally possible to reach a comparable consensus with regard to humanity's capability for survival within Earth's planetary guard rails.

A global transformation towards this necessarily presupposes extensive 'Global Enlightenment', which must be aimed at promoting cooperative behaviour, and accelerating the formation of the requisite global social standards and debate. Apart from the political responsibility to advance transformative policies in the basic architecture of economies and infrastructures carried by states and governments, the global civil society is also called upon to transport awareness of the trends and driving factors of global change in the quest for a new 'Global Enlightenment' (Chapters 2, 6).

The upcoming Rio+20 Conference offers an imminent and concrete historical chance to serve such an education process as a reference frame and anchoring point, thereby initiating a paradigm change with long-term impact. Exactly how this opportunity should be taken, and which concrete strategies and actions must follow to allow the creation of a new, equitable global system, are questions which so far neither scientists nor politicians have been able to fathom clearly, or to answer satisfactorily. However, what is evolving is an organic search process whose most urgent, decidedly action-oriented research issues are outlined by the WBGU in the following (Chapter 8).

7.4 Synthesis: The Composition of Measure Bundles

Transformation Strategy Dimensions

The success of the transformation requires a clever composition of measures which include elements of the ten strategic bundles whilst being embedded in a new global social contract. This contract is based on a growing cosmopolitan understanding of humankind as 'Earth citizens', which allows the taking on of responsibilities at a global level – in fact, demands it – and paves the way for a new dimension to international cooperation in terms of content and institutions. The new global social contract is guided by the real challenges of stabilising the climate and the earth system, which the WBGU analyses in this study. To follow this path, the global community must overcome existing barriers, correct path dependencies, and advance initiatives for the rapid establishment of low-carbon economic and social structures.

In the face of the imminent challenges, it is vital that politicians do not subscribe to escapism; instead, they should, through course setting, acceleration and an upscaling of the transformation process, use the next decade to pave the way for steps which currently still seem visionary, and which have therefore been accorded a high ambition level. However, measures of this extent will ultimately be required in order to stay within the planetary guard rails and facilitate the transformation to sustainability in time.

There is no one and only transformation path, there are many. To prioritise the numerous combination possibilities of strategic measures in order to draft and evaluate political strategies for the respective transformations required in particular countries and regions, political decision-makers have four dimensions to consider:

1. *Temporal impact:* In the short and medium term, this is primarily about accelerating the transformation to retain the chance of compliance with the planetary guard rails (Section 1.1). For a rapid decarbonisation of energy systems, clear carbon price signals are vital as a basis for investment and consumption decisions. Sustainability research and education initiatives, on the other hand, tend to impact cumulatively, and serve to secure the success of the transformation in the medium and long-term.
2. *Geographical scope:* Transformation policies cannot be successful if they are implemented only in some parts of the world. Ultimately, this is about reform coalitions, which enable a global economy trend reversal towards sustainability.
3. *Overcoming barriers:* Current path dependencies in a global economic system which continues to be fossil-fuel based act as transformation barriers. They are threatening to cement the status quo, or to increase the cost of the transformation, and must be overcome.
4. *Support change agents:* There are change agents at all levels of society and the economy, whose promotion and networking can create the 'critical mass' needed to shape transformation policies.

Whilst the first two dimensions relate to the urgency of rapid, preferably global action for the transformation, the latter criteria refer to veto players and actor constellations. Above all, the main concern is to refrain from preventing the transformation any longer.

Composition Options

The composition options of different measures with varying levels of ambition are arranged along a continuum between bottom-up approaches, with initially limited impact, and the creation of comprehensive global structures for the transformation into a low-carbon society that are also based on a new understanding of the value and limits of national sovereignty. Joint global action would be mirrored by a comprehensive and binding climate agreement to establish a global cap for emissions and instruments for a global emissions trading scheme, and initiate global governance mechanisms for the low-carbon transformation of energy systems, urbanisation and land use.

Along this continuum, however, there are many different starting points which, below the global level and when combined, can certainly initiate the dynamics needed for steps that go further. In order to be able to credibly launch these kind of polycentric transformation strategies, the European Union should, as far as emissions reductions are concerned, agree to raise its own reduction target to at least 30% for the year 2020, complemented by substantial, legally binding international climate protection financing commitments.

On the basis of this, ambitious, polycentric transformation policies can endeavour to trigger climate compatible dynamics on different paths.

Geopolitics: Establish Sub-global Pioneer Alliances

One important path for the acceleration of the transformation is the development of a geopolitical strategy for the forging of climate pioneer alliances to aid progress in the various transformation fields. For Germany and the EU, the major newly industrialising countries China, India and Brazil are particularly important in this respect. On the one hand, these countries will gain in geostrategic significance; on the other hand, these are also the countries where the highest emissions increases are to be expected, carrying the risk of new and far reaching fossil path dependencies like the ones which already exist in the industrialised countries. An ambitious and targeted transformation strategy could, for example, address the promotion of renewable energies, or emissions trading, where pioneer alliances set common standards and create structures which could then be successively globalised. Such an initiative would hardly be able to effect timely course corrections by the most important actors and of the required scale without a concurrent debate on fair burden sharing and decarbonisation efforts.

Create Incentive Structures for Dynamic Actors in the Transformation Fields

In the transformation fields, positive incentive systems for dynamic actors could speed up the transformation into a low-carbon society. Thus, generously funded programmes for low-carbon investment projects by the World Bank and the regional development banks, for instance in the sustainable energy services sector and urbanisation, could provide considerable incentives for leaving the established fossil development path. Substantial loan programmes for a competition to identify and support the 10 or 20 most ambitious models for the building of low-carbon cities in developing or newly industrialising countries could initiate or accelerate search processes in that direction. Such strategies would also still be effective if there were undue delays in the forging of geopolitical alliances.

Political Focus on Transformation Barriers

To break down transformation barriers, a politically supported alliance of change agents in the economy, civil society and science could develop transformative impact with regard to the phasing out of direct and indirect fossil energy carrier subsidies. This could at least partially correct the current blatant market distortions, which are sustained by global annual subsidies in the three-digit billion region. This outline of polycentric transformation strategies clearly shows the extensive scope of options for innovative paths towards climate friendliness. The ten bundles of measures developed by the WBGU are representative of the wide spectrum available for the composition of the requisite strategies. The 2 °C guard rail defines the level of the standard these measures have to meet.

The Knowledge Society's Role in the Transformation Process: Recommendations for Research and Education

8

Research and education will play a central role during the requisite transformation process into a low-carbon, sustainable society, as the realisation of the necessity for restructuring the global economy is mainly based on scientific knowledge. Despite its clear objectives and the already available low-carbon technologies, the transformation is a societal search process. In cooperation with politics and society, science is tasked with developing visions for a low-carbon society, exploring different development paths, and developing climate-friendly and affordable technological and social innovations. Technological innovations are of major importance to develop low-carbon alternatives to existing production and everyday technologies. Social innovations are necessary to allow the diffusion of low-carbon technologies, and to promote individual climate-friendly behaviour.

Research should generate both systemic, reflexive and anticipative knowledge. This must be additionally complemented by extensive participative elements, both in terms of social implementation and the research process as such, as participation in the transformation process itself creates the basis for its legitimation and acceptance. Only broadly legitimised politics and policies can lead to sustainable solutions, and a democratic transformation process.

There are still many open questions regarding the long-term transformation - these must be answered in order to be able to determine how to proceed. On the one hand, research helps to clearly define the transformation's guiding principles, on the other hand, it provides technical and social innovations, thereby enabling the transformation process. Ideally, it also leads to groundbreaking innovations which impact at the appropriate speed, and in various social sub-systems, inspiring further innovations.

Education should put people in a position to develop an awareness of the problems, and to act responsibly and appropriately. To enable education to support the transformation, scientific findings must be made comprehensible and accessible. Relevant knowledge should be communicated through education in all areas and to all age groups, from kindergarten to school, vocational training, or university, and extend to lifelong 'on-the-job' learning. Educational institutes should increasingly convey and teach orientation knowledge for sustainability and the skills necessary for lifelong learning and systemic thinking. Besides new curricula and degree courses and modules, completely new professions might become necessary. Active participation in research processes also has an educative effect; furthermore, it also contributes to knowledge generation and research legitimation.

Research and education are therefore necessary conditions for fulfilling the new social contract for the transformation towards a low-carbon society proposed by the WBGU. It is research and science's social responsibility to contribute actively to the success of the transformation towards a low-carbon society. The promotion of transformation-relevant research and education are therefore key tasks for any proactive state (Section 5.4.1).

A research and education reform unlocks future opportunities for those who participate in it. In view of this, educational institutes should increasingly teach and enable sustainability-oriented knowledge, and the skills necessary for lifelong learning and systemic thinking. This also includes a better understanding of how research gains insights and creates knowledge as well as the scope and the limits of the research process. In the medium and long term, this will benefit all members of society, allowing them to participate more specifically in the transformation process, thereby advancing it.

Young scientists could participate in the transformation process in the role of 'research pioneers' by innovatively focusing their individual endeavours on its requirements, thereby accelerating the transformation. This calls for a systemic, inter- and transdisciplinary approach.

German science and research policy could emerge as an international role model if it continues to develop further in the direction already pursued in part, towards systemic, transformation-relevant research, thereby actively paving the way for a knowledge-based, transformation-supportive society.

A New Contract Between Society and Science

Against the background of a rapidly changing Earth system (Chapter 1), and the resultant necessity for transformation, research should also increasingly focus on transformation-relevant issues.

This requires a review and a targeted consolidation of research structures as well as contents in terms of their present and possible contributions to the transformation. A new contract between science, society and the economy could result in the productive, comprehensive transformation-relevant orientation of research and science for the demands of the Great Transformation.

This restructuring of sustainability research as part of a 'Global Contract between Science and Society' was already proposed in the 2007 Potsdam Nobel Laureates Symposium's 'Potsdam Memorandum' (PIK, 2007). Such a contract would result in closer links between research and development activities and the socially expressed need for knowledge relevant to the transformation towards a low-carbon society.

By means of such a contract society would commit itself to identify relevant problems, to prioritise them, and to communicate them to scientists and researchers. Society would also agree to supply appropriate funding for the exploration of the identified problems.

In return, a steadily growing part of the scientific community and the economy would commit to increasing its focus on the social objectives within the Great Transformation. Scientific research would not only be assessed within its own expert community, it would be additionally tasked with developing relevant and credible solutions for the identified problems. In terms of policy-making, this would not only mean enhanced research funding, but also the task of initiating social dialogue on the goals of research and development activities.

8.1 Research for the Transformation

Social transformations are brought about by interrelated changes of technologies, social institutions and individual behaviours in a range of social sub-systems. Technological and social innovations are associated with changes in social context which are frequently a precondition for the further diffusion of these innovations, and they are therefore mutually dependent.

However, ex ante, no obvious turning or tipping points can be identified for clearly indicating the before and after of a transformation. Rather, transformations are characterised through a concurrence of multiple changes, some of which are directly or indirectly interrelated. So far, these were identifiable only after they have taken place (Chapter 3).

Past transformations have been co-evolutionary processes that led to profound and lasting changes. The transformation towards a low-carbon society is comprehensive, a process encompassing all social areas, in which specific actors and actor constellations play an important role. In contrast to earlier transformations, this one has a declared aim: a climate-friendly, sustainable society (Chapter 1). This transition requires changes in almost all sectors of industry and areas of society. Transformation-relevant research should therefore have a broad spectrum to include as many technological, economic and social aspects as possible.

Research should face the – at first glance apparently paradoxical – challenge of increasing the probability of non-determinable processes, namely the shaping and acceleration of the transformation, by finding potentially contributive alternatives. There is already an awareness of some options, such as the creation of spaces for experiments (Box 5.4-1) or the integration of social stakeholders' practical experience-based knowledge in cross-disciplinary research. These should be expanded. In addition, a systemic-oriented exploration of other options is needed to find new solutions. Conceptually, this means the differentiation between transformation research and transformative research. Transformation research is aimed at understanding transformation processes better, its subject are therefore transformation processes as such. Transformative research supports transformation processes in practical terms through the development of solutions and technical as well as social innovations, including economic and social diffusion processes and the possibility of their acceleration, and demands, at least in part, a systemic perspective and inter- and cross-disciplinary methods, including stakeholder participation (Section 8.1.4.9). The division in transformation research and transformative research serves the purpose of better illustration and systematisation; however, the boundaries between these disciplines are also blurred, and there are areas where they may overlap; in practice, this division is therefore not easy to maintain.

8.1.1 Goals, Requirements and Starting Points

8.1.1.1 Goals

The intended result of the transformation described by the WBGU is a low-carbon, sustainable society. To become practicable for individual research strategies and programmes, the overall objective of climate-friendlyness should be concretised for the transformation's various social elements and action fields. These goals could then be integrated in research strategies and programmes, and be operationalised. This operationalisation should provide a reflexive process for the identification of partial goals, and for the development of suggested measures from research results. It should also be open to subsequent adjustment.

8.1.1.2
Structural Requirements

As the challenges and problems during the transition into a low-carbon society are not purely technical or purely social issues, transformation supportive research should take this socio-technical 'mixed character' into account through interdisciplinarity.

Interdisciplinarity describes the cooperation of several independent individual sciences attempting to find an answer to a shared research issue with their own methods. Methods are communicated between the disciplines, and various research aspects are linked, ideally leading to new solution strategies; experts from different disciplines progressing along parallel lines without knowledge exchange is insufficient. Issues on the transformation of systems can only be sensibly addressed if ecological, technological and socio-economic aspects are linked to do justice to the various different dimensions of the system to be transformed. Natural and engineering sciences should therefore cooperate closely with social sciences and the humanities.

The issue places particularly great demands on social sciences and the humanities; these areas should therefore receive strong support as the organisation of the development, assessment, use and diffusion of low-carbon technologies and behaviours relies on social conditions as much as it does on respective technology. This also applies to the substitution of climate damaging technologies and behaviours, and the requirement of profound changes in production, consumption and lifestyles.

Transdisciplinarity also plays a major role by the involvement of relevant stakeholders in the research process. Transdisciplinarity encompasses a range of different aspects. Firstly, it means increasing the social relevance of research questions through the involvement of stakeholders in setting research goals. Secondly, it also applies to the involvement of stakeholders in the actual research process, i.e. the combination of scientific and practical knowledge (for example local, traditional or indigenous knowledge). To achieve and maintain acceptance throughout society as a whole and legitimation as indispensable factors for the transformation, research should be carried out with the participation of the appropriate stakeholders. It is particularly important that research and development cooperate with the business community, most importantly with regard to investments. Businesses play a major role in the development of prototypes and demonstration projects, for example, as their financing frequently exceeds the budgets of government-funded research institutions. However, the involvement of commercial enterprises in government-funded research does not diminish the need for government funding, as investments into research and development on a private basis are often only inadequately made, due to a lack of markets, a lack of infrastructure, or a lack of convergence between social and economic interests.

Transformation research should combine and further develop existing knowledge with future knowledge by means of searching and networking processes. It should be a knowledge exchange involving different disciplines, but also between basic and applied research. This could, for example, be realised by broadly examining basic research results with regard to their transformation-relevant innovation potential, subsequently to be combined with applied research with regard to technological realisation or the social implementation of transformative actions.

The Great Transformation requires acceleration and globality. The decarbonisation of the global economy must largely be concluded in 40 years' time, and, above all, it must take place on a global scale. Research (funding) should address these aspects when considering its priorities in terms of content, budget allocation and architecture, for example by also funding international research projects, also in cooperation with non-OECD countries.

Transformation-relevant research funding programmes should run over an extended term, as many innovations are still in the initial stages; their development, optimisation and adaptation will take considerable time. This long-term perspective should be applied to research funding policy, project and programme contents, and also be evident in the long-term maintenance of research capacities and the relevant qualification of young academics (Arrow et al., 2009).

8.1.1.3
Requirements in Terms of Content

If research is to support the transformation effectively, the results will ideally include three requisite components: (1) the development and assessment of low-carbon alternatives in the form of technological and social innovations, (2) the definition of the social preconditions for the diffusion of these innovations and (3), the development of political strategies and instruments to govern the transformation. The three dimensions are correlated, leading to interaction. The further development of a technology, for example, impacts on the preconditions for its diffusion. Simultaneously, any change in the social framework conditions impacts on the development of alternatives.

Developing and Assessing Low-Carbon Alternatives

Alternatives are low-carbon technical and social innovations, such as low-emission production processes and technologies, new forms of organisation, and suggestions for low-carbon consumption patterns and lifestyles. Low-carbon production technologies and climate-friendly products must be developed, and they must be used.

Alternatives should be examined with regard to their systemic interaction; both in terms of climate-friendlyness, the use of natural resources and other environmental impacts, and in terms of global economic and social impacts. If presently no sustainable alternatives exist in some transformation fields, these should be developed. And finally, research should – apart from the results useful for the transformation process as such – contribute to creating a systemic understanding of how fundamental services can be provided with the least negative impact on climate, or other sustainability aspects, through the combination of technological and social solutions.

The private sector does not invest sufficiently into research for radical alternatives, due to the lack of markets and social anchorage points (such as the required infrastructure) (Watson, 2009). In consequence, the main responsibility rests with the state, government funding is therefore particularly important to allow the speedy exploration of alternatives. Research budgets should reflect this.

Determining Conditions for the Diffusion of Innovations

The development of low-carbon innovations must be closely linked with their diffusion – from national to global level.

Chapters 3 and 6 both note the fact that the diffusion of low-carbon innovations may sometimes require considerable changes to existing social orders and framework conditions, or that these may be its consequence. The potential bandwidth here ranges from the expansion of physical infrastructures to the respective legal provisions and standards required for the market launch of a product, to the changing of existing social norms and individual consumption preferences. Research should therefore involve not only the development of technical alternatives, but also address the requirements of their (global) diffusion.

Moreover, diffusion depends very much on national and regional contexts. These are the result of, for example, the various development stages of different countries and their differing socio-cultural values, political systems, power constellations and consumption preferences. Research should also take these dimensions into account, and systemically consider regional variances, or adapt already existing alternatives to local contexts.

Developing Political Strategies and Instruments

Historical transformations took place largely without any steering, even though some individual elements may have been politically engineered, and without a uniform, clearly defined goal. The transformation towards a low-carbon society must be policy-driven (Chapters 5, 7). Low-carbon transformation relevant research should therefore take political shaping and political relevance into account, and suggest appropriate ways of policy-making. Research should include the exploration of political strategies and instruments for the diffusion of technological and social innovations, to be presented to policy-makers as possible courses of action.

8.1.1.4 Overall Requirements in Terms of Research for the Transformation

The aims elaborated above, and the demands on research with regard to structure and content for the transformation, result in a range of criteria (Table 8.1-1), allowing the evaluation of current research, and the shaping of future work. Central aspects are, on the one hand, the integration of the goal of achieving a global low-carbon transformation by 2050 within the scope of sustainability and, on the other hand, a systemic research approach. The integration of this goal stipulates the direction research must take, and clearly shows the urgent need for acceleration as a consequence of the immense time pressure. A systemic perspective aims at the change of a system, for example the energy system, and not merely on the development of a new technology or a new business model. Besides the development of an innovation, a systemic perspective must inevitably also explore the issue of how the respective system (including innovation use, legal framework conditions, competitive technologies and so on) must be adjusted to achieve its diffusion. This leads to questions which, ultimately, can only be answered by inter- and transdisciplinary research.

The expansion of transformation-relevant research does not mean that traditional sectoral research loses in importance, or that every research project must meet all of the named criteria in order to contribute to the transformation. Specific disciplinary research without

Table 8.1-1
Requirements for research for the transformation.
Source: WBGU

Goal	Structure	Result components
Global transformation towards a low-carbon society by 2050	Systemic Interdisciplinary Cross-disciplinary	Low-carbon innovations Conditions for diffusion
Global sustainability context	International cooperation Reflexive Long-term	Political strategies

transformation-relevance must, of course, continue to enjoy the funding it currently does. However, all inherently transformation-relevant, sectoral and disciplinary projects should meet these criteria by default to allow systemic research. An electromobility research programme should, for instance, include an integral research element which examines the implications of different electromobility structures, and the transformation of the transport sector under consideration of these technologies.

The WBGU emphasises that freedom of research is a major and important element of the science system, and central to scientific and social progress. Basic research will, and must, also contribute significantly to the transformation. However, in view of the fact that the current problem is so pressing, the WBGU believes that funding and promotion, both for problem-oriented basic and applied research – assuming they deal with the solving of one of the numerous problematic aspects on the path towards a low-carbon society – should increasingly also consider the requirements shown in Table 8.1-1. This would allow research to give full consideration to the complexity of the issue, and generate scientific results which can serve as the basis for adequate social response.

8.1.2 Research for the Social Contract

In Chapter 7, the WBGU noted the challenging role the state has to play in achieving the transformation towards a low-carbon society, and developed a range of demands on governmental action, including the relevant measure bundles. Nevertheless, as yet, it is not perfectly clear how this path might be shaped in practical terms. The WBGU has therefore outlined research issues relating to the basic requirements for a new social contract below, and developed a prototype of the new scientific discipline this problem seems to call for.

8.1.2.1 Research Issues for the Social Contract

To achieve a global social transformation within the planetary boundaries by 2050 requires suitable social framework conditions as well as a clear definition of fundamental challenges and potential barriers. The following identifies a range of central issues to be clarified.

Key Factors of the Transformation

The analysis of historical transformation processes (Chapter 3) clearly showed that, although there is already some knowledge regarding the key factors of a transformation (Box 8.1-1), it is only fragmentary with regard to their interaction. To develop transformation strategies, the interaction between these key factors should be examined more closely. This also applies to the opposition and barriers to the implementation of sustainable development. Issues which must be addressed include: Which actors oppose the low-carbon/sustainability transformation with the aid of which strategies? Which strategies and measures can be identified to overcome this opposition, these barriers, and these counteracting forces?

Global Cooperation

Unresolved issues with regard to the international willingness to cooperate, and the possibilities and limits of global governance, must be explored to implement the transformation at a globally networked level. Present incremental research into further development of the international institutional system does not go far enough. Global governance research is (currently) predominately shaped by political science and therefore thematically not broad enough to deal with the fundamental questions of global cooperation unaided. On the contrary, at macrolevel. The context of the planetary boundaries requires close cooperation with natural and engineering sciences when exploring a form of global governance that can potentially support sustainable development.

This is even more important when it comes to cooperative multilevel politics in the three action fields

Box 8.1-1

Complex causal relationships, illustrated using the example of the Industrial Revolution

The 'causal network' of groundbreaking innovations

One of the goals of transformation research, among others, should be to identify the parameters and key factors for self-propelled and self-proliferating innovation processes by means of historical analysis in order to utilise these for future developments.

These kinds of acceleration processes can be illustrated using the example of the Industrial Revolution (Box 3.2-1). Suitable framework conditions, as described in Box 3.2-1, allowed innovations which can be identified as the most important drivers of the Industrial Revolution. Figure 8.1-1 illustrates, in a very simplified way, the key technologies which led to the Industrial Revolution, embedded in a network of the major factors impacting its acceleration.

The visual outline should be interpreted as follows, starting with 'mechanical looms': the mechanisation of looms, which occurred in several stages of innovation, one improving on the other, in part inspired by offers of prize monies, led to the replacement of both manpower and animal power with hydropower for the first time in history in 1772, through the development of a water-driven spinning machine ('waterframe'). The resultant higher productivity in the textile sector contributed to meeting the increased demand in the clothing sector. At the same time, it triggered an increase in the demand for cotton. Thanks to a strong naval tradition, overseas trade and slavery, this increased demand could be met by the colonies.

However, expansion of the fleet, i.e. shipbuilding, had led to wood becoming a scare resource – besides the fact that it was also needed as firewood. Coal was already being used as an alternative. Its extraction proved difficult, though, not least because the mines inevitably flooded at regular intervals once the groundwater line was reached. At first, the shafts were kept dry by manpower and animal power. With the construction of the first large-scale, usable steam engine by Thomas Newcomen in 1712, this limited physical power could be replaced, for the first time ever, through steam power. Steam engines were constructed in the close vicinity of the pits, and powered with coal, the locally available resource. This created a positive feedback loop, and coal extraction became more lucrative (Sieferle et al., 2006). However, at 0.5%, the efficiency factor of Newcomen's steam engine was extremely limited, and it was subsequently substantially improved by James Watt. His partner, Matthew Boulton, recognised the potential of an alternative drive power, considering the, by then, already wide-spread, man- or hydropower driven mechanical looms, and he invested substantially into developing the steam engine further.

Around 1785, the Englishman Edmond Cartwright finally managed to construct the first automated power loom driven by steam. This change of energy basis, from hydropower to coal, allowed the production of clothing in unprecedented, industrial dimensions, leading to a rapid acceleration of already existing processes. The growing demand for steam engines also led to a growing demand for iron ore and coal, and the demand for the latter increased even more because it now also replaced wood in iron smelting. The invention of the railway in the early 19th century was the final breakthrough: the demand for resources rose in line with the distribution opportunities both for textile products and coal, thereby closing the continuously self-reinforcing loop between individual key factors.

The above sketch is neither exhaustive, nor does it do justice to the complexity of the overall picture. Each development had social implications, and rested on certain social and political conditions. These cannot be elaborated in all their complexity in this brief abstract. Nevertheless, this excursus is intended to provide a cursory insight into the necessity of employing a systemic perspective to identify and analyse conditions, key factors, and their constellations.

For the transformation towards a low-carbon society, it is vital to not only rely on historical analyses, but to draw on the real scope of possibilities in the present, and those of the future, with the help of research.

This requires a huge effort from science. Potential key factors and framework conditions favouring positive feedback loops should be systematically identified, thereby significantly increasing the probability of an accelerated transformation.

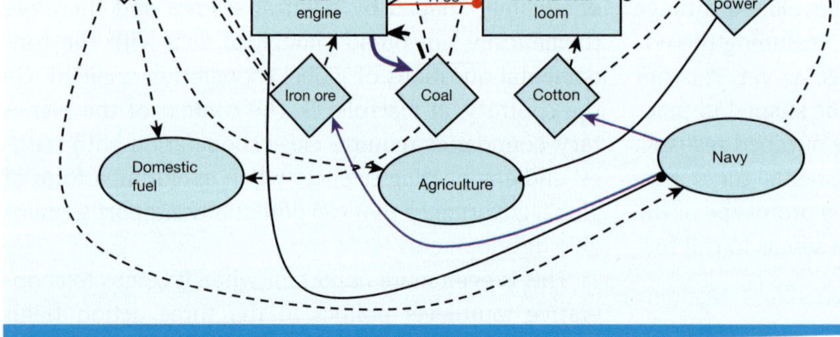

Figure 8.1-1
Illustration on the driving, interdependent factors of the acceleration of the Industrial Revolution.
Source: WBGU

especially relevant to the Great Transformation – energy, urbanisation and land use – (Section 5.4.5), where technical potential feasibility studies carried out in the disciplines of engineering and economics are particularly at odds with the socio-scientific knowledge regarding the impediments and barriers to realisation and action, respectively.

At microlevel, the issue of the human capability for cooperation as such is another central factor that has so far been largely ignored by global governance research. It still remains unclear, for example, whether there are natural limits to human intra- and intersocial capability to cooperate, or vice versa, whether humans, as 'cooperative animals' (Tomasello, 2009), are fundamentally capable of developing a global 'We' identity, as assumed, for instance, by democratisation theory as one of the key preconditions for legitimising governance and decision-making processes (Scharpf, 1999; Beisheim and Nuscheler, 2003). To date, the hypothesis is that cooperation requires the building up of trust and reputation. However, this has been proven to become more difficult in line with increases in distance, complexity, and scale of the reference group (Dunbar, 1993; Ostrom, 2003).

It must therefore be explored whether and how humans and human societies deal with the huge complexity of a globalised world economy, and how they can organise stability, security, wealth and fairness in a closely linked global community within the planetary boundaries. A respective global governance research should also focus on the development of political, economic and social strategies, and identify the limits of human cooperation capabilities, thereby helping to overcome them. Fundamental cultural differences in the action-guiding theories of democracy and justice applicable in individual cultural spheres must necessarily be taken into account.

In the same context, it must generally be determined whether there are cognitive boundaries which fundamentally overtax humans and human societies, and how these can be overcome, if applicable. Respectively, the present relevant knowledge of cognitive science, psychology, anthropology, cultural sciences and sociology should be assessed within the scope of global governance research, to ascertain what bearing, if any, this might have on the exploration of international cooperation.

With regard to the global transformation process, research must maintain its implementation orientation. In the contrary, a respective global governance research should also focus on the development of political, economic and social strategies, and identify the limits of human cooperation capabilities, thereby helping to overcome them. Fundamental cultural differences in action-guiding theories of democracy and justice of individual cultural spheres must necessarily be taken into account.

Political Organisation and Legitimacy

The nation state plays a key role during the transformation into a low-carbon society. It is the transformation's engine, and should generally set the central course at national, supranational and international level. Therefore, interdisciplinary research into a new concept of statehood, doing justice to the legitimacy requisite for any successful transformation needs, is vital. Both OECD and non-OECD countries should be included in this analysis. Issues contained in following range of topics require closer examination:

- *Long-term perspectives in policy-making:* How can a long-term orientation, which takes into account the different time scales of the impact – culture dependent – human activities have on the Earth system, thereby also affecting future generations, be embedded in national and international policy-making institutions? Accordingly, it should be clarified how governmental organisations, for example ministries and state departments, must be designed in order to realise the Great Transformation.
- *Legitimation and participation:* Realisation of the Great Transformation requires both differentiated and comparative research, at both national and international level, into how democratic participation – again at local, national, supranational or international level – can promote and accelerate acceptance and legitimation of political measures required for the transformation. Case studies of particularly committed social environments and change agents lend themselves to analysis. During the course of this research, the possibilities of actively integrating the participation needs of different actors in governmental transformation efforts should be identified and developed. Generally, a fundamental lack of analyses regarding democracy performance, and democracy audits can be noted.
- *Inclusion of knowledge:* Studies should identify how (global) knowledge regimes (for example IPCC), local expertise (for example climate adaptation in coastal regions) and the advisory institutions of parliamentary democracy can be effectively and efficiently linked. The required transformation of economy, society, policy-making and the legal system depends on the integration of knowledge that is constantly being updated. It should therefore be examined how the present state of (global) scientific knowledge is generated, and how it can be integrated in the politico-legal process of decision-making to achieve the appropriate results.

Mobilisation of Financial Capital

The acceleration of the transformation – and therefore its chances of success in terms of compliance with the planetary guard rails – is closely linked to the volume of investments in research, innovation and the diffusion of technological, social and organisational alternatives (Chapters 4 and 5). Apart from the recommendations for action with regard to financing the transformation made in Chapter 7, there are again some open questions here that research needs to address. In this context, it should be clarified which actors (state, banks, businesses, private households, foundations, international organisations) can make the requisite financial funds available in which way. The focus should above all be on actively developing new investment models. This would allow political decision-makers a more targeted selection of appropriate transformation shaping and financing measures, and their prompt implementation.

Legal Framework Conditions

In the area of legal sciences, there has been no adequate research to date into how transformative laws should be designed to appropriately meet the transformation's challenges.

Research on the law of technology assessment and risk law carried out since the 1970s, examine technological change from one perspective only, as their starting point is precautionary governmental action to protect individuals and/or supra-individual interests. The law of scientific technology assessment examines the extent to which law-making can take the obvious consequences of technological advances systematically and comprehensively into account, particularly with regard to legislative enactment procedure. Legal risk research analyses the legal aspects of the unknown risks to human health and the environment typically associated with the introduction of new technologies or procedures (genetic engineering, nanotechnology). Subjects include finding the right balance between the conflicting interests of those affected by any risks, and issues of public welfare (for example environmental protection) and the technology users (for example companies). However, the only recently established legal science discipline of innovation research goes beyond this by examining the role of the law in relation to innovative developments; it identifies which laws impede, and which promote innovation, and analyses whether a law contributes to the realisation of public welfare aims in innovative processes and avoiding adverse effects whilst reaching the declared aim – also during the transformation.

In terms of the technological, political, economic and social challenges elaborated in Chapters 4, 5 and 6, this rudimentary approach to research is not adequate. It must be examined how laws should be structured to achieve the proven aims of the transformation at various legal levels, or at least to promote it, and which laws are suitable for this, how the various legal levels should be interlinked, and the role of national, European and international law, particularly in terms of legitimising effect. In other words, the legal sciences must not just play a supporting role, accompanying the introduction of technological innovations; they must investigate the precise structure of the legal framework required for the transformation of social, political and economic systems. The proposed definition of this field of law shall be 'transformative law'.

Its first task is the development of a theory of transformative law at a so-called metalevel. It should examine aspects such as the plausibility of transformative innovations, the shaping of transformative processes under simultaneous consideration of individual and supra-individual interests (for example also those of future generations), and law revisability and openness to revision. Moreover, a transformative law theory should identify and further develop the characteristics of this field of jurisprudence.

There are three fundamental questions to be answered:

1. Can transformation into a climate-friendly and sustainable economic world order act as a guiding principle at all levels of the law?
2. What legitimatory role can such a legal principle play?
3. Could the basic principles of transformative law, in view of the international challenges of a transformation towards a global sustainable society, provide the forms, procedures and instruments needed to shape a global low-carbon social, economic and political order?

With regard to the latter, it should above all be taken into account that some key global level legal mechanisms – such as international law – are currently called into question, be it through the failure of the international law treaty system or through new technological developments threatening state sovereignty (virtual worlds).

Secondly, it must determine, through analysis of specific sectors (energy law, spatial planning law, urban planning legislation), the level of existing transformation-relevant legislation, and to what extent these fields – under consideration of constitutional, EU and international law parameters – require revision pursuant to the transformation towards a sustainable society.

Thirdly, analysis and evaluation of the transformative effect of the three divisions of legal governance, i.e. legislation, jurisprudence and the executive administrative bodies is needed. The role of the respective national and supra-national powers (international courts, etc.) has to date not been examined with regard to their transformative impact, this should be carried out both theoretically and empirically.

The legal sciences are therefore tasked

- with the development of a transformative law theory (legal principle, legitimatory function, forms, procedures, instruments),
- the analysis and assessment of transformative sectors of the law (energy law, spatial planning law, urban planning legislation), and the development of sector-specific transformation-relevant aims, instruments and procedures,
- the analysis and assessment of the transformative effects of the three powers, i.e. legislation, jurisprudence and executive administrative bodies.

To address the issues elaborated above requires intradisciplinary (public law, civil and criminal law) and interdisciplinary approach (for example social, political and economic sciences), and increased international legal research networking.

8.1.2.2
Sustainability Science and Global Change Research

The transformation outlined in this flagship report should be regarded as part of a very profound social transition towards a low-carbon society (Chapter 1). The issues elaborated above (Section 8.1.2.1) represent profound societal changes. Their aim is the establishment of the preconditions for the transition into a society capable of maintaining its natural life-support systems through compliance with the planetary boundaries. Taking this perspective, research must address the possibilities of profound social changes, and propose modification paths, yet it must also exchange knowledge with the sciences investigating changes in the natural life-support systems. An attempt to understand and structure social change within the scope of planetary boundaries has already been made with the introduction of the sustainability sciences concept, and its operationalisation in the form of global change research.

Sustainability Science

The term sustainability science (also sustainable development research) refers to the consolidation of the various efforts to support science and technology during the transformation process. Sustainability science is tasked with understanding the consequences of anthropogenic activities on nature, and the associated repercussive impact on societies, and the exploration of options for the avoidance and mitigation of negative effects from the perspective of sustainable development (ICSU et al., 2002). Apart from interdisciplinarity, this also includes aspects of a systemic perspective, of political relevance, and of normative focusing. In Germany, socio-ecological research is one of the terms under which sustainability science has established itself (Section 8.1.4.7). It primarily addresses the exploration of options for the avoidance of harmful impacts.

The general term sustainability science also covers global change research activities. Global change research has evolved since the 1980s, and focuses on either natural or anthropogenic physical and biogeochemical environmental changes. The Earth is viewed as a system, divided into physical, chemical, biological and social subsystems whose respective processes and interactions determine the earth system's status quo and its development dynamics.

International Global Transformation Research

Global change research has been institutionalised at a global level since 2001, in form of the Earth System Science Partnership (ESSP). The ESSP encompasses four programmes: Diversitas (an international scientific programme on biodiversity), the International Geosphere-Biosphere Programme, the World Climate Research Programme, and the International Human Dimensions Programme on Environmental Change. Under the umbrella of sustainability research, the first three programmes primarily investigate Earth system changes, the role of human behaviour on the observed changes, and the impact these changes have on societies.

The International Human Dimensions Programme on Global Environmental Change also focused on the analysis of the interfaces between natural subsystems and the Earth system's social subsystems: what is the anthropogenic impact on the biosphere, biodiversity, or the atmosphere, and how do the subsequent changes in their turn impact humankind or societies (Clark et al., 2005; Leemans et al., 2009). Exceptions are the almost concluded Industrial Transformation Project, and the Earth System Governance Project. Aim of the Industrial Transformation Project was to gain a better understanding of the options for combining economic and social development with a reduction of harmful environmental impacts. Individual sub-projects explore a range of transformation-relevant aspects.

The Earth System Governance Project is not a research project with a dedicated aim, but a network which links existing international research activities investigating governance systems for the avoidance and minimisation of anthropogenic negative impacts on the Earth system.

Various ESSP reviews have concluded that the programme has delivered key contributions in terms of comprehension of the complexity and vulnerability of the Earth system, and should be continued in the future. However, the reviews also emphasise that in future, global change research must also increase its focus on the development of social strategies to achieve a sustainable society. Even at the beginning of the global debate on global change research, scientists emphasised the importance of interdisciplinarity in terms of a tighter interlinking of natural and social sciences. However, to date, this interlinkage has not been adequately realised. Future exploration should therefore also focus on how social institutions and economies should be structured to induce behaviour changes in order to achieve global sustainability. This also includes technological and social innovations, including social acceptance of these innovations, to achieve global sustainability (Reid et al., 2010; ICSU, 2010).

German Global Change Research

In Germany, the Federal Ministry of Education and Research (BMBF) funds various global change research projects. Again, as with the ESSP, the focus has so far been on understanding the Earth system, and the effects human behaviour (for example anthropogenic emissions) has had on it. However, future global change research in Germany should also increasingly focus on issues relevant to the transition towards a low-carbon society (NKGCF, 2008).

8.1.2.3
A New Research Field: Transformation Research

The necessity of accelerated diffusion of innovations, and the integration of systemic perspectives in applied research presume knowledge and understanding of transformation processes. First steps have already been taken, for example within the scope of global change research, or the research approaches discussed in Chapter 3; these should however be modified to meet the challenge of the Great Transformation. In the view of the WBGU, this also requires the establishment of a new research field that goes beyond current global change research to accompany, support and accelerate the search process and the transformation's global diffusion.

Better Understanding of Global Transformation Processes

Subject of the new, reflexive research field 'transformation research' should be the global transformation towards a low-carbon society under consideration of the sustainability guard rails and the tight timeframe (decarbonisation by 2050). Whilst output-wise, global change research is based on a systemic understanding of requirements for behavioural change and modification, this output also doubles as input for transformation research. Aim of these research activities is therefore a better understanding of global transformation processes, their dynamics, the exploration of whether it can be shaped, and their acceleration. The WBGU recommends that the new research field focuses on the following key research themes:

Key Research Theme 1: Social Transformation Processes and Transformation Ability

The focus of the first key theme is on analysing past and present transformation processes and upheavals, with the aim of identifying central drivers and framework conditions. Already existing research approaches such as the transition management approach (Chapter 3), or historical transformation or innovation research, can be developed further for this purpose.

Apart from an understanding of transformation processes, however, an understanding of the preconditions required for their political shaping, and to what extent societies already meet these requirements, must also be gained.

Key Research Theme 2: Transformation Paths

The new research field should also be tasked with the exploration and vivid illustration of what future societies which respect the planetary boundaries might look like. Possible social development paths and their respective implications on other elements of the bio- and sociosphere require cross-disciplinary elaboration under consideration of future limits, as shown by way of example in Box 8.1-2

This research particularly calls for the integration, expansion and redirection of future research, and its close cooperation with various disciplinary research institutions, and model-based scenario development, to determine the modification or further development of existing models for possible new paths towards a sustainable global society. Potentially, this could also take the form of a further development of the BMBF's 'Foresight' processes. Vice versa, this new research field should also assess the impact of different social development paths on natural life-support systems and societies as a whole.

Further subjects for the new research field deal with the monitoring, evaluation and the reflexive adjustment of transformation processes depending on subsequent progress. This aspect also focuses on the development of a (transformation) indicator, or a respective set of indicators.

Key Research Theme 3: Scope for Acceleration

Apart from defining the social preconditions for a successfully structuring, or the influenceability of transformation processes, this theme should also examine what the options for accelerating such a process are.

Box 8.1-2

Analysis of possible development paths with regard to the energy productivity of land area

Future paths of the energy productivity of land area

The development of the energy productivity of land area (the land area needed for supplying the required per capita energy amount), and the analysis of its possible future paths can be seen as an example for the research content of research theme2 of the transformation research. Figure 8.1-2 illustrates the facts: it shows the relationship between per capita energy land area requirement and per capita annual energy turnover, in the past and up to date, and for two alternative future scenarios. From the hunter and gatherer cultures to the time of the Industrial Revolution, energy productivity has significantly increased, particularly due to the increasing use of fossil energy sources.

Society is now at a crossroads (industrial society); research should now identify options for future developments, and show the respective implications. The red path to 'high energy society' could, for instance, be followed via nuclear fusion. This would require no further physical space; it would, however, have significant other implications. As fusion technologies cannot make any significant contribution to the global energy supply by 2050, enormous amount of fossil energy would have to be used by then if the red path were followed, making climate stabilisation impossible. At the same time, the pursuit of this path rests on the illusion that the current development model can simply be continued. But even if sufficient zero-carbon energy were available, other planetary boundaries would be transgressed in the medium-term, if 9 billion people were to lead a western lifestyle with similarly high material flows.

A development along the green path towards a 'sustainability culture' via the use of renewable energies and the tapping of efficiency potentials, on the other hand, leads to decentralisation, resulting again in increased land area use. The subsequent implications, such as, for example, land-use conflicts or conflicts with the local population, or in terms of development and implementation of technologies (Section 5.4.5.3), should be taken into account and minimised (for example through shared use).

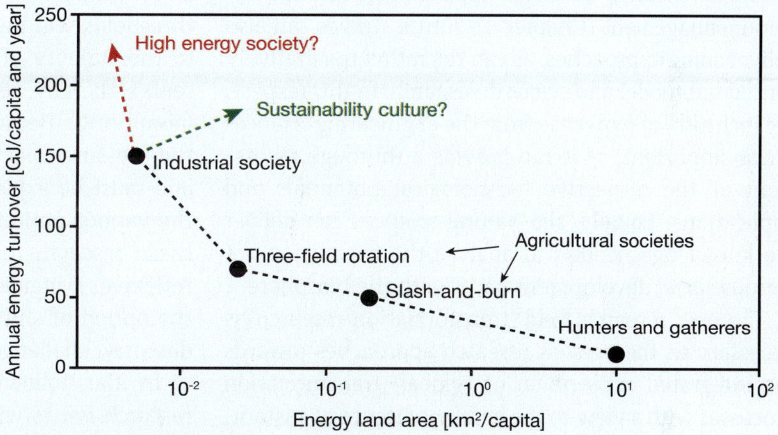

Figure 8.1-2
Development of land area productivity. Shown is the per capita energy land area requirement compared to per capita annual energy turnover, in the past and up to date (black), and for two alternative future scenarios (red and green).
Source: WBGU, own illustration based on the data sources in Table 2.2 from Sieferle et al., 2006

Particular focus should be on the examination of social tipping points and central starting points, as identified in the first key research theme. Beyond a historical understanding, technical expertise is as relevant here as it is in insights into intercultural processes, not least in terms of the global dimensions and legitimacy.

Key research theme 4: Global Cooperation and Global Transformations

The transformation towards a low-carbon society is inevitably also a global process which must be supported by the appropriate institutions and global governance mechanisms. In this context, the as yet to be developed field of transformation research must examine whether and how global governance can support the processes investigated in the three key research themes elaborated above. This means that transformation research should examine the role of global governance and global cooperation in historical transformation processes and times of major upheaval to learn from the past in order to shape the future. Moreover, it should investigate whether and in which form global governance can support the structuring of future development paths towards climate-friendliness and sustainability. Transformation research would also have to explore how global governance processes, which are extremely time-consuming due to the great number of actors and the complexity of interest structures, can be accelerated.

Problem Analysis, Problem Solving, and Problem Communication

In addition to the focus points in terms of content elaborated above, the new research field should be defined by a range of specific characteristics. In terms of the preconditions and possibilities for a global transformation towards a low-carbon society, this research can refer to the extensive knowledge stock of contributions by the established research traditions with regard to some aspects of the transformation process. This knowledge should be examined for transformation-relevant issues, and be made available.

To date, socio-scientific transformation research delivers important details and analyses regarding the influenceability and social embeddedness of transformation processes (Chapter 3). The new research field can therefore consolidate and combine methods and various different theories from a multitude of already existing research directions. This includes the socio-scientific research on the transformation of political systems, the systemically oriented innovation research, historical research, and fresh approaches, such as transition management (Chapter 3), future studies can also deliver some approaches, as can the rather qualitatively carried out model and scenario research. In this respect, the inclusion of expertise from the engineering sciences is also important, as it can provide a thorough assessment of the respective technological potentials and implications. Equally, the natural sciences can deliver the knowledge needed to analyse the interactions of various social development paths with the biosphere.

The new research field 'transformation research' is necessary as the present research approaches towards the integrated exploration of (global) transformation processes with a view to the imminent issues of sustainability and limited natural resources must be expanded. Inter- and transdisciplinary research approaches which have set themselves the task of overcoming social problems are just the beginning. However, they must also be developed further, in particular with regard to the proposed comprehensive perspective. Although there is some rudimentary knowledge about decisive transformation factors, little is known about the interaction of the influencing factors, especially in a globalised world. The new research field should also pursue a global, culture comparing perspective whilst accommodating local characteristics. A central issue here, as in all research for the transformation, is the communication and relaying of research results to policy-makers, as they have to make the decisions required to shape the transformation, and to society as a whole, as, ultimately, society will have to assist implementing these transformation process relevant decisions.

8.1.3 Research Issues for the Transformation Fields

This section describes particularly relevant, transformative (i.e. transformation promoting) research issues in the key transformation fields which must be answered to achieve the transformation towards a low-carbon society. This report has already shown some first steps and measures for shaping the transformation (Chapters 5 and 7). The political imperative to act is here based on the current knowledge of future environmental changes as a consequence of anthropogenic activities, and the resultant threat to the natural life-support systems. In the WBGU's view, this knowledge provides sufficient reasons for political intervention to accelerate the transformation.

Naturally, the further development and expansion of this knowledge regarding environmental changes will continue to be relevant, not least for the transformation. Earth system science examines, apart from other aspects, how rapidly potentially negative impacts affect the system, and at what point potentially critical thresholds will be exceeded (for example with regard to the stability of ice shields, or the survival of coral reefs), thereby also providing transformation process monitoring. Because these developments determine the pressure to act with respect to the transformation, and must be explored to allow detailed assessment of the various options for action (Chapter 1). In addition, these research results are an essential element of a reflexive, systemic research approach, which includes the option of shifting the research focus to accommodate new challenges.

In the following, the WBGU mainly addresses research issues which are priorities in terms of determining the next steps towards the transformation, with the objective of its acceleration (transformative research). The issue at hand is therefore to identify technological, social and organisational options for the avoidance and mitigation of climate damaging impacts on the Earth system, and to develop strategies for their global diffusion.

It should be noted here the following list of issues is by no means exhaustive, nor is it static. Research which, as part of the transformation, represents an active searching process, should address the newly emerging issues and partial aspects that will evolve from the interlinking of individual areas, and from the progression of the transformation. The following research issues were actually chosen because it can be expected that they will contribute significantly to acceleration, and to a reflexive understanding of the transformation. Because it is assumed that a science which addresses the listed subjects under consideration of the requirements identified in Section 8.1.1 will make major contributions to the success of the global transformation. However, it is vital that the individual issues are addressed systemically, and embedded in the context of sustainability at all times.

To conform with the analyses in Chapters 4 to 6, the following research issues have been allocated to the three transformation fields, energy, urbanisation and land use.

8.1.3.1
Transformation of the Energy System

If energy research is to support the transformation effectively, it is vital that the systemic perspective described in Section 8.1.1 again plays a key role. The three German Academies of Science Leopoldina, acatech and the Berlin-Brandenburg Academy of Sciences and Humanities fully support this notion (Leopoldina, 2009). It follows that technology development, which has so far been the focus, should only be one field of research, embedded within systemic research on the energy supply needs of human societies and the climate-friendly and sustainable provision of energy.

The analysis in Chapter 4 has revealed the following priorities for further technology development:

- *Provision of renewable and other zero-carbon energies:* In the long term, to achieve the complete shift to an energy system based fully on zero-carbon energies as quickly and cost-effectively as possible, the various technologies for converting the renewable energy generated by sun, wind, biomass, water, ground heat and the sea must urgently be explored further. In all of these areas, research has the potential to unlock both short-term, incremental, and medium- and long-term, groundbreaking improvements in efficiency and costs (FVEE, 2010).
- *Efficient energy use in all sectors:* This is a precondition for the transformation, presently not adequately taken into account by any of the political measures under discussion, or in the presently used energy models: technologies for the efficient use of electricity, fuels or direct heat from renewable energies must be developed (further) in all consumption sectors. A sustainable energy supply can only be achieved by containing the (final) energy demand. The exploration of end-use efficiency improvements must also include new business models for energy services.
- *Low-carbon mobility solutions:* Endeavours should especially focus on the transport sector, as it continues to rely on fossil-based liquid fuels due to a lack of modern technologies. Apart from (further research into) the use of alternative energy carriers such as, for example, renewable gases, which are also needed for freight transport, magnetic levitation technology (maglev) should be explored further for long distance passenger transport. Particularly for short and medium distance mobility it is clear that sustainable transport systems not only require technological developments, but also interlinked research efforts under consideration of health, environmental protection and urban aspects.
- *Urban energy consumption:* The specific role of urban areas as demand centres for energy, goods and services, buildings and mobility is frequently ignored, and often features in energy models only indirectly. Particularly because of the long lifespan of these infrastructure elements, extensive path dependencies exist in these areas. At the same time, options for climate protection are unlocked if urban planning is determinedly guided by greenhouse gas efficiency primacy, especially if energy efficiency potentials are also realised.

Chapter 4 made it clear that the conversion to renewable energies is only achievable if the energy distribution system undergoes some fundamental changes. In consequence, the following technical, economic and socio-scientific energy system research issues must be explored for the energy system:

- *Future European power grid:* The rapid expansion of transcontinental power grids (supergrids) in regions, where the energy demand is already high, is extremely transformation-relevant, as the shift towards a low-carbon energy supply can be achieved most cost-efficiently within a single energy market. The stability and supply security of a continental supergrid should therefore be explored on the basis of models at the earliest possible point in time. Furthermore, the cost of the various different expansion variants must be determined, and alternative financing concepts for the expansion must be explored. Europe already has a high density of transmission lines, however, these must be modernised and cross-border linked. Moreover, expansion must be pursued especially in locations with a high resource potential (North Sea/Atlantic coasts: wind; southern Europe: solar, etc.). For all of these steps, the required legal framework conditions must be clarified, and solid participative procedures for planning and line installation must be developed.
- *Storage technologies:* Both continental supergrids, as planned for Europe, and decentralised minigrids, currently being considered for regions where there is no access to electricity as yet to overcome energy poverty, will require short- and long-term storage facilities due to the high proportion of fluctuations in renewable energy supply. The exploration of different storage technologies and their optimised inte-

gration into the energy grids should therefore be stepped up in future. Energy gases generated through the temporary power surplus of renewable energies, such as hydrogen or methane, represent a sustainable energy resource for fuels which, apart from their potential for electromobility use, can also lead to an extensively interlinked, integrated energy system beyond the electricity-heating-fuel boundaries.

› *Electricity market of the future:* Currently under discussion is whether, assuming a rising share of fluctuating renewable wind and solar energy, the currently marginal costs based electricity market continues to provide sufficient incentives for investments in generation capacities to guarantee supply security on the electricity market. The present debate therefore includes the discussion of proposals such as the introduction of capacity markets for conventional peak power stations, in line with discussions on payments in the balancing power market. The energy generated (and therefore the profit achieved on the current market) by conventional power stations decreases as the share of energy generated through wind and photovoltaic technology rises. However, their back-up supply is still needed until other options such as storage, or balancing with the aid of a European supergrid, are available. With regard to the fluctuating renewable energies, it must be explored which market regulation is the most appropriate for financing these plants once they are competitive, and after the German Renewable Energy Source Act (Erneuerbare-Energien-Gesetz, EEG) has expired. Incentives for an efficient regional and temporal distribution of generation capacities should be given.
› *Impediments and barriers for a supranational energy policy:* Suitable legal framework conditions are the basis for a transformation process that is based on scientific insights, as the contemporary situation, in contrast to past transformations (Chapter 3), the incentives for sustainable production and lifestyles must not least be provided by government intervention (Chapter 5). There are still considerable gaps in the relevant research: the redirection of the global and supra-national energy supply proposed in Chapter 4, for example, assumes a legal framework which, to date, does not exist. So far, even the European Union does not enjoy the legal authority to comprehensively steer the energy supply for its citizens. The installation of a trans-European supergrid would already require a law-making authority which the EU (to date) does not have. Such an extension of EU authority would have to be compatible with existing regulations, particularly EU constitutional law. To what extent restrictions apply, and whether the existing authority base might possibly suffice, needs to be examined by legal scientists.

In addition, more general energy use issues must also be addressed, particularly illustrating the call for interdisciplinarity and a systemic approach:

› *Zero-carbon city:* Both existing and currently emerging urban regions require specific research approaches to determine cost-effective paths to climate neutrality. Present low-carbon urban development projects should be accompanied by socio-scientific research. One aspect is the development of 'business concepts' for both new, prototype cities such as Masdar City, and redevelopment projects like the one in Bottrop, which also examine the economic viability and possible comparative advantages of such settlements.
› *Technology portfolio:* It should be examined to what extent a sustainable global energy system needs to be a broad range of technologies, or whether a few selected technologies suffice. New modelling approaches pursue evolutionary strategies of alternative technology trees, and agent-based models of evolutionary developments.
› *Exploitation of energy efficiency potentials:* The analysis of barriers impeding the full exploitation of energy efficiency potentials, and the development of strategies to overcome these, is an important research issue which is key to the mobilisation of the required investments. It still remains largely unfathomable why certain economically viable efficiency potentials are not fully exploited, even without carbon pricing. Further research is needed here, for example on the basis of the principal-agent theory, to discover precisely which barriers are responsible for this fact, both at individual and commercial level, and the role of asymmetric information, incomplete contracts and the discounting of future return on investment in this respect.
› *Enforcement of existing laws:* Both Germany and the EU have instigated numerous legal measures to increase energy efficiency, for example the Act to Promote Energy Savings in Buildings (Energieeinsparungsgesetz – EnEG), stipulating energy saving measures in buildings, and the German Energy Savings Ordinance (Energieeinsparungsverordnung – EnEV). In Germany, recent studies have revealed that energy efficiency targets are not even remotely realised, due to the lack of implementation at German state level (Länder), and a lack of enforcement by the responsible state authorities (Ziehm, 2010). Intensive empirical research is therefore needed in the area of enforcement of efficiency-relevant cli-

mate protection laws to allow the timely revelation of existing deficits and their rectification.

- *Effective energy efficiency financing models:* Further in-depth examination is needed with regard to the basic question of financing energy efficiency investments both in an industrial and a private household context. The potential role of energy efficiency bonds as a financing instrument should, for instance, be analysed, as this would redirect the capital of private individuals or institutional investors towards efficiency investments at an attractive rate of interest. The preconditions and framework conditions needed for the diffusion and effectiveness of relatively new linked business and financing models, such as, for example, Energy Service Companies (ESCO) or Power Purchasing Agreements (PPA) should also be investigated more intensively in this context.
- *Impact of consumer behaviour:* Apart from the uncertainties regarding technical innovations on the supplier side, the lifestyle-guided consumer behaviour on the demand side is the biggest source of uncertainties in the development of energy scenarios. Socio-scientific research should therefore clarify what changes are actually possible on the demand side, and what can realistically be expected. The so-called rebound effect, describing increased consumption as an unwanted consequence of efficiency improvements, should also be better understood. These findings should be integrated in integrated assessment models, and taken into account in the development of energy scenarios. They also provide a basis for further research to identify the scope for effectively influencing consumer behaviour. In this context, the best way of raising consumer awareness of the impact of their behaviour should also be identified, to enable consumers to carry out the most effective emissions reductions themselves. Not yet completely understood is, for example, the significance of indirect greenhouse gas emissions (Hertwich, 2005; Peters and Hertwich, 2008a, b; Hertwich and Peters, 2009), a concept which examines broader regional disaggregation levels (for example the urban level), and is increasingly gaining in importance.
- *New technologies like CCS or geoengineering* require society-wide risk assessment and control. Decisions are needed on 'whether at all', on 'under what circumstances', on 'the level of risk deemed acceptable', and on 'how' with regard to the use of these technologies. The legal framework regarding the exploration and utilisation of these kind of technologies is currently only rudimentary. It is therefore an open question whether specific laws are needed with regard to research and testing, possibly extending over a finite period, and subsequently subject to review (and evaluation). Social acceptance based on participation in the law-making procedures for this area is the premise for any effective large-scale testing and development of new technologies if they are to find subsequent acceptance in the population. It should therefore also be scientifically investigated what role early citizen participation could play in the development of new statutory foundations and transparent communication strategies in law-making processes (Section 7.4.3).

As elaborated in Section 8.1.1, it is important that these issues are not addressed independently, but inter- and transdisciplinary, and that particularly technology-oriented research refers back to, and is coupled with, the general, broader research described above.

8.1.3.2
Transformation in the Field of Urbanisation

Urban infrastructures are characterised by their long lifespan. They set the course for decades and centuries to come, and are the fundamental basis for consumption patterns and scope of action (for example with regard to transport needs, and in the buildings sector). In view of the urgency with which the emissions trend must be reverted to be able to restrict global warming to a maximum of 2 °C, and the currently accelerated urbanisation process, this sector is of major importance for the transformation (Chapter 1). Science should investigate ways in which the globally progressing urbanisation can be steered towards climate-friendliness without transgression of the planetary boundaries. Major aspects are:

- design issues and incentive structures for low-carbon urban transformation processes;
- requirements for international cooperation;
- essential research issues and joint research on urbanisation dynamics and their various sustainability implications;
- development of curricula on sustainable urbanisation.

Additionally, related paths should be identified to show what low-carbon cities might look like in 2030 in different contexts (rampant urban sprawls in Africa; shrinking cities in Europe; cities designed on the drawing board and growing metropolises in Asia, coalescent urban regions in Europe, Asia, America, etc.). Cities are characterised by the huge complexity and heterogeneity of actors and interest groups, turning them into hotspots of potential social conflict, as well as climate change impact. Research should here investigate how the different aspects can be effectively interlinked to reveal sustainable development paths that include all components of sustainable development (ecological, economic, social).

Data on Urbanisation Trends

Global basic data on the phenomenon of urbanisation itself is needed. The UN data so often used is based on the respective country-specific definitions of urbanisation, which vary greatly. Also, only settlements with more than 500,000 inhabitants are listed, which together accommodate less than 50% of the global urban population. Methodically uniform global data, such as, for example the remote satellite-imagery derived data used for the Global Rural-Urban Mapping Project (CIESIN, 2005), is only available for a few individual past points in time, and has been collated using differing methods. Projections regarding the future regional distribution of the global population and its socio-economic activities are limited to just a few academic studies (Grübler et al., 2007).

What would be needed would be complementary data that goes beyond these projections, on urban level infrastructure equipment and resource consumption. Current studies on this subject are largely limited to collected individual case studies. Again, these are dominated by capital cities in OECD countries, which represent the global urban system only to a certain extent (GEA, 2011).

In most cases, urban land use and energy consumption currently grow significantly faster than the city's population. Identifying this development's decisive factors is a precondition for developing regulating measures. Additional and methodically comparable data on new forms of urban living, working and mobility is required to allow simulations of integrated technical and social structures.

Urban Culture and Lifestyle

It must be clarified what low-carbon city cultures and lifestyles might look like. Current trends should be analysed for this. The advent of cheap airlines, for example, has brought a rapid increase in weekend trips to major European cities, increasing air traffic and the respective emissions. On the other hand, cars are losing importance as a status symbol for younger people in western cities, but the new communication media are becoming more important as a status symbol. The question is what impact these developments will have on mobility behaviour, and whether this can be actively influenced. It must also be clarified how large-scale renovation, refurbishment and modernisation processes, particularly those undertaken for energy saving reasons, in established and new residential districts impact on urban development and culture, to allow early identification of potential undesirable developments and conflicting aims in order to be able to avoid them in future.

Participation in Regional and Urban Planning

To work as efficiently as possible at community level, residents and the wider public must be systematically involved. Qualitative research into neighbourhood relations, residential properties and social environments – i.e. into social relationships, networks and living conditions – is required. Particularly important research issues concern the forms of mediation, expertise and local knowledge which might be effective in terms of conflict prevention and mediation, to aid the mitigation of any social resistance against major infrastructural projects. Deliberative forms of planning and consultation should therefore be developed, and it should be investigated how citizen participation in local political processes, and participative accompaniment and shaping of the above named change processes, can be organised in the form of citizen assemblies, community parliaments, interest groups and societies. The generation of transferable data is again an important aspect.

Low-Carbon Regional and Urban Planning

Managing the energy system transformation described in Chapter 4, and the transformation of urban areas, requires cross-border regional and infrastructure planning (Section 5.4.5.3). To date, the existing relevant legal framework is limited. Its development therefore also calls for legal scientific research to take spatial planning experiences and conclusions on board, to analyse the available range of instruments, and to draw conclusions from this for its further development.

8.1.3.3 Transformation of Land Use

Transdisciplinary research can develop options for substantial emissions reductions through sustainable land use, and reveal paths, such as, for example, achieving the requisite increased food production in a climate-friendly manner. Research efforts with regard to the efficient and fair inclusion of diverging interests, and the mitigation of land-use conflicts are hugely important for a permanent transformation. Moreover, the eating habits of consumers are decisive. The following elaborates the research priorities in the subject area of land use.

Global Land Use: Monitoring, Models and Scenarios

Model and scenario development are important tools for the development of political strategies for the transformation process, as these instruments help to evaluate the potentials of global land use in total, and in their various sectors. Key to a findings-driven transformation is therefore the continuous improvement of the amount of land-use data. Apart from more extended and detailed land-use monitoring, methods for a reliable quantification of emissions from land-use changes (deforestation, land degradation, desertification, soil erosion) and agricultural and forestry use, must be developed further with the aid of satellite imagery and observations at ground level. In addition, models on future land-use development and the resultant greenhouse gas emissions should be improved to allow a more accurate determination of this sector's contribution to total emissions, and to precisely record the effectiveness of various mitigation strategies, such as, for example, biomass use. Currently, there are only a few instruments which allow the simulation of global land-use strategies and scenarios. Overall, these works are important building blocks for a scientific basis for a global vision of future land use (Section 7.3.7).

Sustainability and Indirect Land-Use Changes

Land-use decisions in Germany or Europe can have considerable remote impacts on sustainability, and in particular greenhouse gas emissions of other regions. Risks to the natural environment are caused by the additional cultivation of plants for biomass energy or material use, triggering or exacerbating direct or indirect land-use competition. This shift is given an international dimension via the world market for agricultural produce. So far, their interrelatedness has been difficult to quantify, however, they do play a decisive role in greenhouse gas balances. These interrelations must be investigated for the transformation of land use, as biomass use, in all its many varieties, will continue to grow in future, also in international trade. In recent years, research into the relevant methods or factors has increased, however, the results should be analysed in more detail to make them less difficult to apply for the various stakeholders. One of the aspects that should be improved is the regional differentiation with regard to the risks caused by emissions from land-use change.

In the course of the transformation towards a low-carbon society, the clear distinction between biomass use for food, feed, energy and industry could become blurred, as these markets increasingly overlap. Natural scientific-technical and implementation-oriented research on the general sustainability certification of biomass should therefore be stepped up.

Emissions from Deforestation and Forest Degradation

On the subject of forests, it must be clarified how a forestry sector transformation can be achieved in the tropical forest countries. Analyses on the drivers of forest loss, and of the reasons for the failure of present forest policies and pioneering efforts, form the basis for this. Moreover, concepts for sustainable tropical forest management must be developed, particularly with reference to the potential role of payments for ecosystem services (Section 5.4.5.3). Furthermore, in view of the rapidly growing and uncontrolled huge number of REDD-plus initiatives and projects under the guidance of various international and national organisations, and their various ideas for financing REDD-plus, the best way to take the required social and ecological standards into account should also be examined. Various different research questions, regarding, for example, the national and international legal framework conditions, must be answered to, for instance, ensure that indigenous population groups and local communities are given the chance to participate, and to guarantee that their rights are respected, or to avoid the planting of extensive plantation forests in former peatlands. Also decisive is the analysis of the best way to formulate, or set, different models and incentives to achieve general participation in REDD-plus, and the achievement of a high investment level. Moreover, it is important to understand how the fair and transparent distribution of the financial remunerations for REDD-plus can be organised, from national down to project level, and to what extent aspects of good governance and biodiversity protection can be integrated as co-benefits.

Agriculture and a Climate-Friendly Diet

Basic knowledge must be improved to develop and implement the global transformation aim of a climate-friendly agriculture and eating habits. It must be clarified how emissions can be reduced over the entire lifecycle of agricultural produce. With regard to cultivation, the main task will be improving the proportions of organic carbon in the soils (soil recarbonisation) through improved soil management. However, this only partially concerns natural scientific-technical research; it should also be examined why current agricultural methods are not changed to tap the existing and well-known potential for emissions reductions. In this context, the effect of price incentives, subsidies and other political instruments must also be investigated. Agriculture requires a number of innovations and their rapid diffusion to reduce its negative impacts on soils, climate and biodiversity, whilst also providing sufficient food for 9 billion people. To achieve this, science should clarify, on the one hand, which forms really are sustainable and climate-friendly. It is also just as important to review to what extent a catalogue of 'best practice' criteria for sustainable and climate-friendly agriculture in the various regions can be developed, and what funds and instruments would be required at international, national and sub-national level for their practical implementation. The transformation towards a climate-friendly agricultural sector calls for substantial investments. In this respect, it must be clarified how existing and additional funds may be mobilised, and how farmers could gain access to the necessary capital.

Transdisciplinary research is also needed to develop strategies for the avoidance of post-harvest indirect emissions, for example through rotting or wastage. Extremely important is the issue of eating habits: which trends are apparent in different parts of the world? How can instruments be developed to influence these? What is the best way to communicate information on sustainability and emissions to farmers and consumers? It should be clarified to what extent consumer decisions can contribute to increased climate-friendlyness, and which price incentives, education and information strategies are appropriate for influencing eating habits positively towards this end.

Bioenergy Use

The imperative need for a systemic research approach becomes most apparent with regard to the subject of bioenergy. The WBGU has already stated its position on this subject in a previous report (WBGU, 2010a). The complex, reciprocal dependence of the technical, social, economic and ecological factors of bioenergy was exemplarily highlighted by the effects of increased bioenergy use on food production; this proves that the results of isolated research analyses do not suffice to assess the effectiveness of individual mitigation strategies. On the technical side, next generation bioenergy use should therefore be explored, which should have less impact on food production. From the legal and economic perspective, it should be clarified which proportion of agricultural activities for food and bioenergy production is economically sensible, and which legal framework conditions can be established to ensure that particularly the poorest benefit from this economically ideal use.

8.1.4 Analysis of Selected Research Strategies and Programmes

The following sub-chapter analyses to what extent the selected research strategies and programmes meet transformation research demands, and to what extent they already address the research issues highlighted by the WBGU. The focus is on general, as well as subject specific, European Union and German federal government strategies and programmes that are both politically prominent and thematically relevant. This elaboration is by no means a comprehensive evaluation. Rather, it intends to highlight the status quo, and starting points for changes, and provides suggestions for the further development and direction of German and international research policies.

Strategy and Programme Analysis Guidelines

Analysis and elaboration of the research strategies and programmes is based, on the one hand, on the criteria shown in Table 8.1-1; these in turn are based on the transformation research demands discussed in Section 8.1.1. On the other hand, they were matched with the transformation field research issues identified in Section 8.1.3.

As already elaborated above, a reflexive and systemic approach is key to this research. However, it is not included here as a separate criterion, but operationalised by the requirements of interdisciplinarity, transdisciplinarity, international scope, and the consideration of diffusion conditions.

The translation of the individual requirements into different criteria shown in Table 8.1-2 adds transparency to the analysis and facilitates their discussion. The results of the analysis are divided into the analysis areas 'research aims', 'research structure' and 'research results'. They are also presented aggregated across several programmes. This allows a highlighting of the current research funding environment and reveals general transformation-relevant leanings and trends. Overall, the analysis rests on documents of a strategic and programmatic nature, i.e. the following conclusions may not necessarily apply to each individual project funded within the scope of these particular funding measures.

8.1.4.1 European Research Policy

The dedicated aim of current EU research policy is the establishment of a single European Research Area by 2020, to allow the seamless movement of researchers, knowledge, and technologies among EU member states. The European Research Area as such is intended to contribute to the sustainable development and competitiveness of the European Union.

The basis for its further development is the 2007 Green Paper on the European Research Area (EU COM, 2007b). Important EU research policy elements which are constitutive to the European Research Area were also analysed: the Seventh Framework Research Programme's Cooperation programme (EU COM, 2006a), the Joint Programming of Research Planning instrument (Joint Programming; EU COM, 2008a), the European Institute of Innovation and Technology (EIT; EU COM, 2008b), and the Joint Technology Initiatives (EU COM, 2005, 2007a).

The thematically relevant strategies Strategic Energy Technology Plan (SET Plan; EU COM, 2009a), the Public-Private-Partnership (PPP) roadmap for (more)

Table 8.1-2
Criteria for the analysis of research funding strategies and programmes.
Source: WBGU

Analysis field	Requirements	Criteria
Goals	Climate-compatibility	Sole aim, partial goal, subordinate; conflicting aims
	Embedding in the context of sustainability	Reflection of the interactive impact of own research subject with other environmental problems, effects on sustainable growth and global equity in distribution
Structure	Interdisciplinarity	Cooperation between engineering and natural sciences, or social sciences
	Social relevance	Diffusion of research results to policy-makers and society
	Transdisciplinarity	Co-operation with stakeholders
	Acceleration	Political priority, adequate funding
	International scope	Integration of scientists from non-OECD countries
Results	Technological and social innovations	Generation of low-carbon alternatives to existing technologies and social practices; solution-orientation
	Conditions for diffusion of innovations	Consideration of global diffusion, acceptance and national or international framework conditions
	Political strategies	Development and discussion of political measures for the improvement of diffusion conditions, or transformation realisation

energy-efficient buildings (EU COM, 2010a), and the Knowledge and Innovation Centers (Climate KIC, 2011) within the scope of the European Institute of Technology (EIT) were also considered.

Goals

Most of these programmes feature climate-friendlyness as a direct or indirect partial goal – either in the form of integration in broader environmental protection targets, or as part of the more general objective of responding to social challenges. Even if climate-friendlyness is a directly stated goal, as is the case, for example, in the PPP roadmap for (more) energy-efficient buildings or the SET Plan, its level of importance is almost always equal to economic development and/or competitiveness goals. Climate-friendlyness is not a goal of the Joint Technology Initiative. One of the stated objectives of Joint Programming is the financing of research to find solutions to social challenges.

Of the three major aspects of sustainable development – ecology, economy, society – most of the strategies and programmes analysed directly and prominently address the aspects of economic development and environmental protection. Social development aspects are only taken into account in the Green Paper on the development of the European Research Area.

Structure

All programmes and strategies analysed include interdisciplinary cooperation as a potential form of cooperation. The strategy for the creation of a single European Research Area also envisages the promotion of measures to support interdisciplinary research. However, none of the strategies analysed explicitly demand a commitment to interdisciplinarity, nor are the necessarily participating disciplines precisely qualified. Only the PPP roadmap for (more) energy-efficient buildings formulates a few open research issues, thereby suggesting that engineering and social sciences must cooperate to address these. The individual components of the Strategic Energy Technology Plan envisage purely technical research projects without any input from the social sciences.

Stakeholder cooperation is an option within the scope of all of the EU policies analysed, and, in most cases, an explicitly named goal. The process of creating an European Research Area names public-private cooperation as an explicit goal. However, cooperation is not described in detail as the documents analysed are broader strategies or frameworks. With a few exceptions, if there is any elaboration at all on the form stakeholder cooperation is to take, this usually involves only corporations. They are also the only stakeholders considered for direct involvement in the research process. Society and policy-makers are usually named as recipients of research results only. Exceptions are the EIT, the EIT-funded Climate Knowledge and Innovation Community (KIC) and the Joint Programming Initiative.

The EIT envisages that funded research should seek the dialogue with the civil society. The Climate KIC also involves representatives from the civil society, as it funds this research, politicians, and representatives from universities to aid the development of curricula. Stakeholder research participation is an explicitly stated goal of the Joint Programming initiative. Corporate involvement is also an option, however, premise for the realisation of projects is the cooperation of various different governments (Public-Public, rather than Private-Public). The PPP roadmap for (more) energy-efficient buildings does not contain any direct references on the integration of stakeholders.

Grants under the Seventh EU Research Programme's section 'Cooperation' amount to a total of € 32.4 billion. € 2.4 billion of this budget is intended for energy research, and € 1.9 billion is allocated to environmental issues, including climate change (EU COM, 2011c). The most substantial grants are € 9.1 billion for information and communication technologies, and € 6.1 billion for health-related issues. For the period 2008 to 2013, the European Energy Institute has a budget of € 309 million, whilst fund for the PPP roadmap for (more) energy-efficient buildings amount to € 1 billion (2009 to 2013). Within the scope of European research funding, the issues of energy and environment/climate change are therefore, considering their major relevance for the transformation, clearly substantially underfunded.

The SET Plan does not fund any research at all as such; however, it suggests the amounts which should be invested in the various individual technology areas under the scope of the European Industrial Initiatives (EII) in order to develop affordable low-carbon technologies. The EU Commission has estimated the total investments required by industry, member states and EU over ten years to amount to around € 58.5–71.5 billion, with the funds allocated as shown in Table 8.1-3 (EU COM, 2009b).

The SET Plan fund allocation clearly shows the EU Commission's priorities; fossil and nuclear energy continue to enjoy major importance. The WBGU believes that wind and power grid technologies should be given far greater consideration. It should also be deliberated whether the SET Plan should be expanded to include not only the supply-side of energy technologies, but also the consumer-side, as energy efficiency also plays a major strategic role. Scientific research funding studies have also concluded that research funding priorities must shift (Grübler and Riahi, 2010; IEA, 2010b).

Table 8.1-3
Estimated Total Cost of European Industry Initiatives.
Source: EU COM, 2009b

European Industry Initiatives	Estimated Total Cost over 10 Years [€ billions]
Wind	6
Solar (PV & CSP)	16
Bioenergy	9
CCS	10.5–16.5
Power Grids	2
Nuclear	5–10
Smart Cities	10–12

Compared to the Seventh EU Research Framework Programme and the SET Plan, initiatives which promote innovative research concepts, or at least do so rudimentarily, such as the European Energy Institute, are relatively small. The PPP energy-efficient buildings roadmap shows that the EU is certainly in a position to put on medium-scale, thematically accomplished research programmes in a relatively short time. This should also happen for transformation-relevant research programmes, such as, for example, magnetic levitation technology (maglev).

Although the majority of these strategies and programmes envisages international cooperation as an option, it is however a declared aim in only a few exceptional cases. International cooperation, if it is mentioned at all, is also not embedded in the sustainable development context. In the case of the European Innovation and Technology Institute, for example, international cooperation is merely intended to ensure the European economy's competitiveness. The Strategic Energy Technology Plan recommends international cooperation with industrialised countries in the areas of safety and social acceptance, and at basic research level. The international cooperation with newly industrialising and developing countries is intended to serve the unlocking of new markets for EU-manufactured energy technologies. Only the PPP roadmap for (more) energy-efficient buildings states overcoming climate change as the objective of cooperation with developing countries.

Results

Almost all of the strategies and programmes analysed support exclusively technological, rather than social, innovations. However, the support of technological innovations does not unequivocally mean that climate-friendlyness is their only goal. The Seventh EU Research Framework Programme, for example, supports innovations in general, in principle, this also includes climate-damaging innovations. One positive example is the EIT, which explicitly states the development of new products and services as goals. This also applies to the Joint Programming Initiative, on the basis of its stated goal of overcoming social challenges, i.e. social innovations could also be a goal. The SET Plan, on the other hand, explicitly states that only low-carbon technical innovations are its goal.

Across the board, the reflection of diffusion conditions is taken into account through corporate participation. Their cooperation in research projects is intended to ensure that research leads to marketable products, and that these products are then distributed via the markets. The fact that further diffusion mechanisms besides markets will be required for the envisaged technological innovations is made clear only in the Strategic Energy Technology Plan and the PPP roadmap for more energy-efficient buildings. However, it remains open whether the identification of the required diffusion conditions should also be a part of each individual research project.

The strategies and programmes analysed provide no evidence of any intention of developing political strategies for achieving these diffusion conditions. This is certainly due to the fact that the diffusion conditions are not explicitly reflected, or compared to existing markets.

8.1.4.2 German Research Policy

The next sections examine some German federal government cross-thematic research strategies and programmes: the High-Tech Strategy (BMBF, 2010a), the National Research Strategy BioEconomy 2030 (BMBF, 2010b), the framework programme Research for Sustainable Development (FONA; BMBF, 2009), Social-ecological Research (SÖF; Pt-DLR, 2007) and the Joint Initiative for Research and Innovation (BMBF, 2010g). This is followed by an analysis of subject-specific research funding programmes.

Goals

Almost all of the programmes and strategies analysed have stated climate protection alongside other environmental goals, and the competitiveness objective. Climate protection is one of the key action fields in the High-Tech Strategy, and in the FONA framework programme. BioEconomy and SÖF mention climate-friendlyness, and it is one of their priority goals. Only the Joint Initiative for Research and Innovation does not mention climate protection as a goal, as its main objective is the creation of dynamic networks within the science system and the establishment of partnerships between science and industry.

An explicit reference to sustainability, and to the equal importance of all of the three sustainability aspects, can be found in both the FONA framework programme and the Social-ecological Research Programme. The other strategies, and the BioEconomy strategy, mention sustainability as a goal, however, exactly how much importance is ascribed to each of its three dimensions remains unclear. The Joint Initiative for Research and Innovation makes no reference at all to sustainability.

Structure

All programmes facilitate interdisciplinarity. It is a declared goal in the FONA framework programme, in the Social-ecological Research, and in the Joint Initiative for Research and Innovation. However, only the FONA framework programme, the Social-ecological Research, and the BioEconomy Research Strategy explicitly promote cooperation of natural, engineering and social sciences. Within the High-Tech Strategy's Climate Protection Programme, socio-economic research is still a separate part and not, at least at programmatic level, embedded or at all connected to the other programme parts, which tend to focus on the natural and engineering sciences.

All programmes include the goal of stakeholder participation. However, with the exception of FONA and SÖF, these envisaged research programme participants are exclusively of a corporate nature. There is no integration of other social stakeholders. The BioEconomy Strategy considers society merely as the recipient of research results, it is, however, not involved in setting goals or carrying out research.

International cooperation features in all programmes. Declared goals of the FONA framework programme and the BioEconomy Strategy are academic capacity building in developing countries, and cooperation with world-class research institutions. Cooperation with China and India is also explicitly mentioned within the scope of the High-Tech Strategy. Only the Joint Initiative for Research and Innovation does not state global cooperation to be one of its goals.

Results

Low-carbon innovations are the goal of most of the programmes analysed. Their focus, however, is on technological innovations. Only the FONA framework programme and Social-ecological Research Programme also address social innovations. Particularly the BioEconomy Research Strategy should focus more on the search for social innovations. In view of the expected demand increases in the area of land use (Section 1.2), the focus should not merely be on increasing productivity on the supply-side. Research should also concentrate to a far greater extent on demand-side efficiency strategies and the substitution of particularly land- or emissions-intensive products. Demand drivers should be analysed in more detail, and political strategies should be developed. An important driver are eating habits featuring a high proportion of land-intensive animal products, which are hardly likely to be globalisable in a sustainable way. Research questions concerning lifestyle changes in conjunction with eating habits should be linked to health research issues. Another driver is the development of bioenergy, which can trigger huge waves of increased demand. Uncontrolled bioenergy expansion bears significant risks in terms of sustainability and food security, and exacerbates land-use conflicts. In its bioenergy report, the WBGU therefore included not only recommendations for technology research, but also some bioenergy policy-making suggestions, for example with regard to standard setting (WBGU, 2010a).

Both the FONA framework programme and the High-Tech Strategy address the issue of innovation diffusion conditions. However, the High-Tech Strategy narrows diffusion conditions down to the aspects of favourable investment climate and corporate planning security.

Only the FONA framework programme explicitly states the development of political strategies as one element of research. As many social innovations appear to have been neglected as such, research into the political strategies for the diffusion of these is only rudimentary. Particularly the influence of demand for material services, for example through prices, should be addressed by the BioEconomy Research Strategy.

8.1.4.3
Energy Research Funding

In the field of energy research, funding in Germany largely continues to use the federal government's superordinated 5th Energy Research Programme for guidance, which is to be reviewed in the spring of 2011. To allow an informed in-depth assessment of the strategic level of energy research funding in Germany, the 5th Energy Research Programme (5. EFP; BMWA, 2005), now almost six years old, was analysed along with the more current programme texts of relevant programme elements in the areas of energy efficiency (BMWi 2008a, 2010a), smartgrids (BMWi, 2008b, 2010b), electromobility (Federal Government, 2010), as well as basic energy and environmental research (BMBF, 2008; BMU, 2009, 2010b, 2011). The somewhat succinct information regarding energy research contained in the German Federal Government's Energy Concept (BMWi and BMU, 2010), which alluded preliminarily to some of the details later featured in the 6th Energy Research Programme, were also taken into account.

Goals

As an element of environmental protection, climate protection is firmly anchored in the German energy policy goals. All of the programme texts reflect this aspect. However, whilst the 5th EFP still includes a balanced 'energy mix including hard coal and lignite' (BMWA, 2005) as the ultimate energy system to be pursued, the 6th Energy Research Programme, according to the Energy Concept, is to facilitate 'the transition into the era of renewable energies'. The German federal government has therefore taken a step towards the consistent concretisation of climate protection by way of a fully decarbonised energy system. The unambiguous formulation of this guiding principle as a goal in the 6th EFP text would be desirable.

The importance of a secure and generally affordable energy supply to the German economy and society is emphasised in each case, however without addressing national and international distributional effects or the international sustainability impacts of different energy systems. Environmental compatibility is stated as one of the three cornerstones of energy policy. The environmental impact of various different energy technologies, other than their impact on climate, are addressed explicitly only in the BMU's ecological accompanying research within the scope of the 5th EFP.

Structure

Energy research funding programmes continue to show a deficit with regard to the structural requirements. Although interdisciplinarity is sometimes mentioned, it is not understood as a central element in targeted energy research, except in the sub-programme 'Basic Energy Research 2020+' (BMBF, 2008). Social sciences are referred to only in the BMU's research on 'general research issues in the field of renewable energies' (BMWA, 2005), and in some energy-relevant environmental research concept projects. Their involvement is not a central aspect in any of the research funding programmes.

The direct participation of business actors in the research process is actively pursued, whilst cooperation with policy-makers and the civil society in research is not mentioned at all. The funding programme 'Climate Protection and Energy Efficiency' (BMWi, 2008a) at least includes a project to support the diffusion of the research results, the BINE information service, although here again, the primary target group is the medium-sized businesses, apart from decision-makers, investors, and multipliers in the education sector.

The amount of energy research funding has sharply increased over the past five years, from € 450 million in 2005 to € 691 million in 2010 (BMBF, 2010c). However, with 5.4% in 2010 (€ 691 of 12.707 million;

BMBF, 2010c), energy research continues to attract a relatively insubstantial share of German federal government research and development funding. In 1991, at 7.1%, this share was still considerably higher than in 2010; even the absolute value of grants, at slightly more than € 700 million, exceeded the 2010 values (BMWi, 2011). In 2010, 25.6% (€ 177 million) were spent on nuclear energy research, decommissioning of nuclear plants and nuclear fusion research. The remaining funds, totalling € 514 million, were allocated to coal and other fossil energy carrier related research and development, and research into renewable energies and efficient energy use (BMBF, 2010c).

Whilst the 5th ERP originally enjoyed a budget of € 1.7 billion over 4 years (BMWA, 2005), the 6th ERP is to be more substantially funded through grants from the Energy and Climate Fund (BMWi and BMU, 2010).

The International Energy Agency (IEA) estimates that current public funding for research on renewable energy, energy efficiency and smartgrids, presently US$ 5.5 billion annually, would have to be extended by a factor of between 6 and 13 to implement ambitious climate protection (IEA, 2010b). The European Commission estimates that by 2020, € 31 billion will have to be invested in wind, solar and bioenergy research and development in the European Union to meet the challenge of climate change, provide energy security, and ensure economic competitiveness (EU COM, 2009b). In view of this, German federal government energy research funding should be extended considerably faster than in recent years, with a clear focus on renewable energies and efficient energy-use.

The grants extended in the area of nuclear fusion research – this field enjoyed grants of € 143 million in 2010, or 21% of total energy research funding (BMBF, 2010c) – are still extremely substantial, and should be adjusted to take the current situation into account. By 2050, i.e. over the period in which the transformation towards a low-carbon society must be concluded, power plants generating energy from nuclear fusion will not be available, The potentially possible long-term contributions to the energy supply from this source should, however, not be discounted completely; this could be achieved through extending research efforts over a longer period of time in order to release funds for work with a higher priority.

International research cooperation is an element of every large-scale programme. However, this cooperation explicitly focuses on EU and OECD countries, and direct EU and IEA cooperation. As noted by the BMWi, although only OECD countries are IEA members, the IEA at least pursues closer cooperation with the important countries: Russia, China, and India (BMWi, 2008a).

Results

In the WBGU's view, research generally continues to focus excessively on technical applications. Identification of the requisite diffusion conditions, and of the political measures potentially suitable to lend the appropriate support, continues to enjoy little attention, although this appears to be changing. The majority of research is carried out in the engineering and natural science disciplines, i.e. the main focus is the development of technological innovations aimed at more efficient, cheaper and more environmentally friendly energy use. However, there are also other projects pursuing the development of new behavioural patterns and business models in the area of energy use, particularly the E-Energy development scheme (BMWi, 2008b). In future, this focus should also be extended in other programmes, especially those relating to energy demand and efficiency improvement.

In most cases, energy technology research is viewed as a contribution to improving export opportunities for German companies; global diffusion is therefore taken into account. National framework conditions for the blanket implementation of these innovations are sometimes taken into consideration, for example in the concept 'The Energy Efficient City' (BMWi, 2008a). Even though a changed energy base has been a decisive element in every Great Transformation to date (Chapter 3), and despite the realisation that a systemic change to modern, renewable energies is imminent, there is not a single research programme for the systematic analysis of energy system transformation processes. However, within the scope of several programmes, energy system and integrated assessment models (Section 4.2) are used to develop scenarios to illustrate energy use over the next decades (BMWi, 2008a, 2010a; BMU, 2010b). It is not clear to what extent these research results are used to determine research priorities for individual technologies.

The development of political strategies for innovation diffusion does not feature prominently in any of the research programmes; at most, these kind of issues are addressed in the course of accompanying research.

Content Comparison

In terms of content, the focus of German federal government research funding in the area of energy has clearly shifted in recent years, towards the issues identified by the WBGU as vital for the realisation of a decarbonised energy system.

In 2005's 5th EFP, the key aspect of 'Modern Power Plant Technologies on the Basis of Coal and Gas' is still top priority, followed by other various renewable energy and energy efficiency related aspects. The 6th EFP energy concept elaborations, on the other hand, focus exclusively on renewable energies, energy efficiency and questions related to the integration of a functioning energy system, thereby matching the research areas identified by the WBGU as priorities with regard to the energy system (Section 8.1.3.1). Decisive in this context is that this acknowledgment of the priority of renewable energies with regard to the future energy system during the course of developing the 6th EFP is then followed by a further increase in research funding focussing on these issues.

To be commended are the content key aspects of the 'E-Energy' funding programme (BMWi, 2008b), and those of the 'future energy supply grids' funding concept (BMWi, 2010c). Many of these agree with the WBGU recommendations regarding smartgrid development (Chapters 4, 7). The WBGU suggests a thematic expansion from power to energy grids to allow for the consideration of systemic energy solutions from the outset.

Overall, both systemic and global issues should play an even bigger role in energy research, as this research is tasked with discovering stable paths towards achieving the goals identified in the German federal government's energy concept. Research should step up the systemic investigation of the preconditions requisite to accelerating the change process, such as, for example, social acceptance, the mobilisation of high investments, and how to interlink the various elements of the transformation (Section 8.1.3.1).

8.1.4.4
Urbanisation Research Funding

Several German urbanisation research programmes are currently running in the form of bilateral cooperation between German and international research institutions. This also includes the Federal Ministry's of Education and Research 'Future Megacities' programme analysed in the following (BMBF, 2010d). The following also elaborates on the Federal Ministry's of Transport, Building and Urban Development research programme 'Experimental Housing and Urban Development' (ExWoST), as this includes an explicit reference to climate with the research field 'Urban Strategies and Potentials to Combat Climate Change' (BMVBS, 2010b).

A look at EU research shows that urbanisation research is also promoted at this level. According to the European Commission, there are over 20 current projects dealing with this subject (EU COM, 2010g).

Goals

Explicit objective of the BMBF programme 'Future Megacities' is the development of 'a toolbox, equipped with applied, tried and tested and transferable solutions for dealing with the challenges energy efficiency, resource consumption and climate change' (ad hoc translation by the WBGU, based on BMBF, 2010d). Climate-friendlyness is therefore included as a goal. Programmatically, the necessity of a course change towards initiation of the transformation process has also been acknowledged. The ExWoSt programme focuses more on adaptation to climate change, particularly in the property sector. Urbanisation related programmes frequently tend to focus more on adaptation than on mitigation potentials. Nevertheless, there is a connection to climate protection here in the form of potential energy savings, as the programme objective is 'to plan, develop and realise in an exemplary way technical and non-technical innovations for the establishment of energy- and climate-efficient structures' (BMVBS, 2010b). Projects with a sustainability context running within the scope of the Seventh EU Research Framework Programme's Socio-Economic Sciences and Humanities (SSH) funding are aiming for 'post-carbon cities', thereby addressing transformation-relevant issues.

In general, international programmes also consider the sustainability context. This is done explicitly in the BMBF 'Future Megacities' programme. At German national level, the BMBVS ExWoSt programme is narrower, due to its (more) specific focus on properties and communities, using model plans and pilot projects; it does not explicitly take interaction with other sustainability aspects into account.

Structure

In principle, all of the named programmes feature interdisciplinarity. The 'Future Megacities' programme is broadly structured on account of its ten bilateral projects' thematic key aspects, ranging from hydrology (LIWA) to future research (EnerKey), from cooperative sciences (Sustainable Hyderabad) to political sciences (Metrasys). Nevertheless, more weight is obviously accorded to urban and regional planning, and the engineering sciences. Under the BMVBS programme, each project is supported by accompanying research. On site, this is based on areas such as urban construction and traffic (Aachen), urban planning and construction (Essen), geography (Nuremberg), but also ecology and communication (Syke; BBSR, 2009a). At EU level, the various disciplines are also linked, for example 'Science of Citizenship' and metallurgical engineering (PACT), or political sciences and sociology (GILDED).

All of the named programmes promote stakeholder involvement. Cooperation is pursued at different levels: local authorities and civil society are involved to the same degree as representatives of the economy.

Goals should also be consolidated in order to reach a certain dimension in terms of funding. 'Future Megacities' receives a total of € 50 million in funding over a period of 9 years (2005–2013) from the framework programme 'Research for Sustainable Development' (FONA), whilst nine cities received grants of up to € 80,000 in connection with the ExWoSt research field 'Urban Strategies and Potentials to Combat Climate Change' (BBSR, 2009a). German federal government spending on research and development in the funding area of spatial and urban development is going down again after it had increased for a while. € 16.4 million were spent in 2005. The 2009 budget amounted to € 25.8 million, which was reduced to € 20.5 million in 2010 (BMBF, 2010d). Government spending on construction research shows a similar trend. In 2005, the German federal government spent € 26.9 million, in 2009, the budget was € 38 million, and in 2010 € 26.4 million.

As all programmes lack the concrete target of low-carbon urbanisation by 2050, funding is not of a scale commensurate with the tight timeframe and the pressure to act. To be welcomed is the fact that particularly the BMBF programme, thanks to numerous cooperation-based projects, aims at internationality. It would generally be advisable if development cooperation and research were to work together at an international level. The Cities Development Initiative for Asia (CDIA), for example, promises to generate relevant data whilst enjoying funding from the German Federal Ministry for Economic Cooperation and Development (BMZ). Research, however, does not appear to be an integral part of the programme here.

Results

Social relevance through the integration of relevant stakeholders is called for in all cases, as the programmes pursue applied solutions. It is the focus on transferable solutions that makes the development of technological and social innovations the implicit goal of these programmes, as problematic urbanisation issues can only be solved through these. None of the programmes directly addresses innovation diffusion conditions. However, the BMVBS ExWoSt programme aims to identify 'framework conditions which favour integrated concepts and cooperation to achieve climate protection targets' (ad hoc translation by the WBGU, based on BBSR, 2009b). As there is however no focus on technical aspects, it is not clear whether the diffusion conditions for technical innovations are taken into account here.

Content Comparison

The issues addressed in the application-oriented programmes considered are generally to be welcomed, as they represent important systemic transformation research aspects.

As they feature international cooperation and a focus on solution-oriented research, the programmes at least partially match the content recommended by the WBGU (Section 8.1.3.2). Accordingly, solution-oriented approaches reflected in the initiatives should enjoy substantially increased funding, and therefore considerable expansion, assuming the transformation as a concrete, set target. The consolidation of measures, and ensuring that the research results and data generated are transferable are also vital.

Particularly the cultural aspects, which – as they determine innovation acceptance and diffusion and consumption behaviour – are central to the transformation success, are not sufficiently taken into account in the programmes, or not explicitly mentioned. It is therefore to be expected that although cultural aspects will impact somewhat as a consequence of international cooperation, the targeted generation of relevant data and their comparability is being neglected. This also applies to legal framework conditions, even though ExWoSt is an exception here at national level.

If rapid transformation is the set normative target, as recommended by the WBGU, and in accordance with sustainable urbanisation, the present research fields contain valuable elements which should be integrated into a low-carbon urbanisation research approach at global level.

8.1.4.5
Land-Use Research Funding

In the area of land use, the German federal government research strategies and programmes elaborated above, such as the National BioEconomy Research Strategy 2030 (BMBF, 2010b), Research for Sustainable Development (FONA), and Social-ecological research (SÖF) represent an important overall context (Section 8.1.3.2).

In the following, research funding for 'Sustainable Land Management' (NLM) (BMBF, 2010e), which started in 2010, and the Global Research Alliance on Agricultural Greenhouse Gases (GRAAG, 2010), in which Germany is actively involved, are examined with regard to their transformative aspects. In addition, the Seventh EU Research Framework Programme's (FRP7) relevant subjects are also considered, i.e. Theme 2: 'Food, agriculture, fisheries and biotechnology', and Theme 6: 'Environment' (including climate change) (EU COM, 2010b, c).

Goals

Climate protection is stated as a goal, or partial goal, in all of the programmes and strategies analysed. The mitigation of greenhouse gas emissions is anchored in the NLM as a partial goal; the contribution of land-use changes and land management strategies to greenhouse gas emission reduction targets is to be researched systemically. Beyond this, any goal-related conflicts between best-possible low-carbon land management and other social demands, such as food production, biodiversity conservation or ecosystem functions are also to be investigated. The GRAAG focuses mainly on making agriculture more climate-friendly by mitigating the emissions intensity in general, and increasing the soil's capability for carbon sequestration. The relevant FP 7 themes, however, focus on supporting climate change adaptation as a research goal; climate-friendlyness as such is not directly addressed.

The analysed programmes are generally embedded in a sustainability context. Particularly the NLM, as a Research for Sustainable Development (FONA) funding priority, but also GRAAG are intended to contribute directly to sustainable development, in accordance with the national sustainability strategy goals and the German federal government's climate protection targets. They take the interrelatedness of their own research with other problematic sustainability issues into account, and consider global sustainable development challenges such as food security, for example. The analysed FRP7 themes are intended to contribute to the European Sustainability Strategy.

Structure

All of the analysed programmes pursue and promote some kind of interdisciplinary approach. The NLM particularly pursues an interdisciplinary research approach, and the interlinking of sectoral expert knowledge by way of acknowledging the complexity of a sustainable land management.

Stakeholder cooperation is addressed in all of the measures analysed as a structural element, it does, however, play a secondary role in the FRP7's themed subjects. The NLM pursues a transdisciplinary approach in order to promote involvement of regional actors and recipients and a better understanding of the problems so as to be in a position to develop corresponding, practicable solutions. Beyond this, external communication and the development of points of interface with political processes play an important role so that the results can be made available to potential user groups, and transferred to international political processes. GRAAG also features stakeholder work as an inherent element in order to, on the one hand, be able to integrate practical experience into the research process and, at the same time, be able to communicate research results, technologies and best practices right to the target groups' core (research institutes, farmers (associations), NGO, private sector).

With € 100 million by 2015, the extent of research funding for the NLM is not adequate to meet the huge challenge of sustainable land use in a progressive climate change and food security context. The WBGU therefore recommends that NLM research funding should be increased to cope with the imminent transformation in the area of land use, and to accelerate it, as it must be largely completed by 2050.

The NLM funding measures should concretise the German federal government's strategy for the internationalisation of science and research. International networking is therefore an important aspect in NLM research, hence global regions with extremely dynamic growth (for example southern Africa, Brazil, China) are involved. Germany's active participation in GRAAG is an important step to promote international agriclimate research networking, particularly with non-OECD countries, and to bring together researchers, as well as their research results, from different regions all over the world. The FRP7's themed subjects also state international cooperation as an important precondition for successful research.

Results

The programmes and strategies generally all mention the goal of developing technological and social innovations. The NLM is explicitly tasked with the development of innovative technologies and services (for instance with regard to the areas of information, advice and financing) for sustainable land management. In addition, this also includes the important aspect of technology impact assessment. Moreover, NLM and GRAAG directly refer to innovations intended to lead to greenhouse gas emission reductions.

The NLM funding priority emphasises communication, networking and public relations work. Solutions are to be developed and diffused which can help society progress towards sustainable development. These are to have a role model character, i.e. they are to be transferable to other regions, and actor cooperation and communication is to be increased. This also covers innovative governance and participation models. Particular consideration, also in terms of implementation, is here given to the socio-economic framework conditions for, and the consequences from, the integration of climate protection targets in land-use decisions. The GRAAG aims to internationally improve the low-carbon agricultural research network, to expand platforms and make knowledge more accessible, and to communicate research results more widely. The regional and national exchange between different target groups (research institutes, farmers (associations), NGO, private sector) on new findings is to be improved.

Communication of the research results to policymakers is generally acknowledged as important in all of the programmes and strategies. Within the scope of the NLM, the research results are to be communicated to policy-makers and practical applicants, and political measures are to be discussed (science policy interface). The research results are also to be taken on board in important policy-making processes under CBD and UNFCCC. The FRP7 theme subjects analysed state the goal of at least supporting policy development.

Content Comparison

The NLM funding priority has been reviewed and updated in its research approaches. The WBGU welcomes the international perspective taken with regard to research issues on the interrelated impact and mutual dependencies between land management, climate change and ecosystem services. The systemic investigation of future land management under consideration of climatic, but also structurally-demographic changes in rural and urban areas also promises important impulses and innovative solutions for the transformation in the subject area of land use.

The GRAAG focuses specifically on innovation solutions for agricultural sector emissions reductions at an international level, which the WBGU also views as decisive (Chapter 4).

The analysed FP 7 theme subjects 2 and 6 view climate change under the aspect of adaptation to climate change and supply security for the population. The research issues highlighted by the WBGU are not reflected in the analysed theme subjects in terms of content; the 'Greenhouse Gas Management in European Land Use Systems' project is the only one that has any bearing on these in the widest sense (Section 8.1.3.3).

8.1.4.6
Funding of Research in the Humanities and Social, Economic and Legal Sciences

Considering the priority research issues named above (Section 8.1.2), there are also a range of other issues and initiatives deserving priority funding besides the large-scale strategies and programmes which – if correspondingly structured – could provide valuable insights and contributions to the transformation. The following were examined: Economics for Sustainability ('WiN'; ecological economy 2007; BMBF, 2005, 2009), 'Knowledge-based decision making – research on the relationship between science, politics and society' (BMBF, 2011a, b), 'Economics of climate change' (BMBF, 2011c), 'Käte Hamburger Collegia' (BMBF, 2011d) and 'Interaction between Natural Sciences and the Humanities' (BMBF, 2011e).

Goals

With the exception of WiN, no direct reference to climate protection, or to any of the three sustainability aspects, is made, as the goals are mostly formulated to describe the goals in a specific funding context. The goals mentioned, such as the investigation of the interaction between politics, science and society, long-term capacity building in the economic sciences, or a mutual augmentation of humanities and natural sciences can also have a transformation-supportive effect, although feedback with regard to a superordinated common goal would also be useful.

Structure

All funding measures mention interdisciplinarity, albeit differently designed. Some only demand consideration of interdisciplinary aspects within the scope of a primarily disciplinary research (for example 'Economics of climate change').

Stakeholder participation in the sense of transdisciplinary research is prominently anchored only in WiN, which attempts to integrate relevant actors from different areas and levels of practical application. Although reception of research is given some attention, particularly in politics, there is no plan to involve actors from society in the actual research process. The demand for 'research with', rather than 'research on', voiced when the Käte Hamburger Collegia were announced, should therefore be expanded, from the aspect of internationality to this kind of networking between academics and stakeholders.

Concerning the promotion of internationality, it should be noted that despite mentioning this aspect, none of the programmes explicitly refer to a cooperation with research institutions in non-OECD countries.

Results

To what extent any of the funded research projects actually have concrete technical and social innovations as their goal is not evident from the programmes. Social innovations may potentially be what is meant when the development of strategies, for example in the case of WiN and 'Knowledge-based decision making', or corporate measures, as is the case in 'Economics for climate change', is called for. A clearer definition of the research output to include suggestions for (potential) direct application, for example in the form of new business models, would be advisable in all cases.

There are also no concrete statements from which it could be inferred that the formulation of innovation diffusion conditions is in any way a research priority. At least, during the first WiN funding phase (2005–2008), international diffusion processes and their macroeconomic effects were empirically analysed; 'Economics for climate change' also highlighted the fact that there is a knowledge gap with regard to the diffusion of technologies and services. A broader examination of diffusion conditions might be introduced as one element of the 'Interaction between Natural Sciences and the Humanities' funding priority.

The research output focus of the first three initiatives named – WiN, 'Knowledge-based decision making', and 'Economics of climate change' – is on formulation and analysis of political instruments. Whilst the first and the third tend to concentrate more on the development and evaluation of environmental and climate protection measures, the second initiative hopes to build up socio-scientific advisory capacities for research policy.

With regard to the research results, the structuring of the various programmes therefore shows a job-sharing character. This leads to the question of whether a kind of synergy might result from a superordinate coordination and an institutionalised exchange between the programmes.

Content Comparison

The contents of the initiatives discussed here are clearly defined by the respective specific goal formulation. In the case of the collegia, which tend to envisage more structural goals, as does 'Economics of climate change', the research contents can even be chosen quite freely by the applicants. The systematic comparison with the research issues identified by the WBGU is therefore not possible. However, it should be noted that some of the issues highlighted by the WBGU are certainly already anchored in current projects, such as, for example, global fairness issues, or the acceleration and global extension of diffusion and transformation processes.

8.1.4.7 Conclusions

The analysis shows that research policy and science are addressing the low-carbon transformation, both thematically and organisationally. A number of the analysed research strategies and programmes already take subjects, contents and methods on board which ensure that the research is led by the demands of the transformation, and therefore produce transformation-relevant knowledge.

The goal of climate protection is directly or indirectly anchored in most of the analysed programmes. Climate-friendlyness is frequently put on an equal footing with the goals of economic growth or competitiveness. The interlinking of both goals at strategical level, and the operationalisation of this close link through research on innovative, low-carbon technologies is reasonable. However, the programmatic equality of the goals of climate protection and economic growth must not lead to the illusion that in practice, achieving both goals is extremely challenging, and may not always happen at the same time. The more general goal of climate protection should be amended and made more precise through the goal of almost complete decarbonisation by 2050. It is the precondition for compliance with the 2 °C guard rail, and requires the vast acceleration of all climate protection activities, a fact that research should also address.

With regard to embedding research in the sustainability context, it can be noted that the references to the social dimension must continue to be expanded. The cross-disciplinary research programmes FONA and SÖF's promising approaches on social dimension integration, and those contained in funding priorities such as 'Sustainable Land Management' or 'Future Megacities' should be extended to all research, for example also in the energy area.

With regard to research structure, the conclusions are ambiguous. Although interdisciplinarity is an option in all cases, it is never a declared, or even obligatory, funding criterion, except under SÖF and Sustainable Land Management. In many cases, it can be expected that turning strategies into actual research projects will lead to interdisciplinary research. However, as long as interdisciplinarity is not a set goal and funding criterion, it remains to be seen how often, and in what form, it will actually be realised at project level. Particularly questionable is whether the all-important cooperation between natural and engineering sciences and social sciences and humanities will actually take place.

Ultimately, this rather unusual, but for the transformation extremely important cooperation depends on the research issues identified in each of the funding opportunity announcements, and the scientists' reaction. At programme level it transpires that SÖF in particular, but also NLM and some elements of urbanisation research, have a very strong interdisciplinary focus. The BioEconomy Research Strategy also emphasises the importance of interdisciplinary research. Whether the funded programmes will ultimately contain the requisite interdisciplinarity between natural, engineering and social sciences remains to be seen during the course of future funding opportunity announcements. In the WBGU's view, other programmes, such as BMWi Technology Promotion or the National Mobility Development Plan (NEP), do not consider this aspect adequately.

Likewise, stakeholder participation is also only partially integrated. Although policy-makers and relevant social stakeholders are sometimes named as important recipients of research results, it is mostly only corporations that are involved in the actual research process. Corporate involvement is important with regard to technological capacities, its capital and market closeness. However, the participation of a wider spectrum of stakeholders in sustainability research is vital. Positive exceptions here are SÖF, NLM and EIT. Due to the major importance of interdisciplinarity and stakeholder participation for transformation research effectiveness, the WBGU elaborates these demands in the following in more detail (Section 8.1.4.8).

The global scope of the research, as expressed in cooperation with scientists from non-OECD countries, is also usually not integrated, apart from in a few exceptional cases such as GRAAG. Against the background of increasing research and development spending in the newly industrialising countries, however, closer international cooperation seems advisable. In 2007, 1.7% of global GDP, or US$ 1,146 billion, were spent on research and development. Scientific capacity building has dramatically accelerated in the newly industrialising countries, particularly in China, India and South Korea, due to the 1996 to 2007 phase of global economic growth. Accordingly, the newly industrialising countries' overall share of global research and development spending has increased, whilst decreasing in the USA, the EU and Japan. The USA are still leading globally, although their share of global R&D spending has decreased from 35.1% in 2002 to 32.5% in 2007. The same applies to the European Union and Japan, whose shares reduced over the same period from 26.1% to 23.3%, and from 13.7% to 12.9%, respectively. The share of global spending on R&D has increased in China (from 5% to 8.9%), South Korea (from 2.8% to 3.6%), India (from 1.6% to 2.2%), Brazil (from 1.6% to 1.8%) and South Africa (from 0.3% to 0.4%; UNESCO, 2010).

Research goals are frequently technical innovations. Even though technical developments give important transformation-relevant impulses, the transition towards a low-carbon society also needs a wide range of social innovations. This applies in particular to analysis of the demand-side, the area of mobility and, equally, the fields of nutrition/dietary habits and consumption in general. NEP and the BioEconomy Strategy revealed particular deficits in this respect. Positive exceptions are, for instance, the multi-faceted foci of the 'Future Megacities' programme, or the goals of EIT and SÖF.

With regard to reflections on diffusion conditions, it was noted that these are often made only via corporate participation in the research process. In the course of their cooperation, companies are expected to support the application of research results in product development, and their diffusion across markets. In this respect, corporate participation is to be pursued. For the diffusion of low-carbon social innovations, or those technological innovations that will probably not be market-ready in the near future, however, corporate participation is not an adequate substitute for research into diffusion conditions. The development of strategic options for promoting the diffusion of low-carbon innovations, realised in the form of appropriate policies, or serving as inspiration for political measures, should therefore become more firmly established. The communication of research results alone is an important step, however, it cannot replace analysis of innovation diffusion conditions. The research issues identified by the WBGU for progressing with, and accelerating, the transformation (Section. 8.1.2) have, in many cases, been addressed by research funding. Many funding programmes already – more or less –take transformation-relevant subjects into account. Their budgets, however, are still insufficient. Promising funding priorities enjoy comparatively little financial support, such as, for instance, the NLM with € 100 million, or 'Future Megacities' with € 50 million. In particular the FP7's funding distribution does not focus adequately on the highly transformation-relevant area of environment, including climate protection and energy.

The distribution of funds in energy research does not reflect the requirements of the transformation, both at European and German level. Whilst EURATOM makes € 2.75 billion available for nuclear research (nuclear fusion and fission) between 2007 and 2011, the other energy technologies share the around € 2.3 billion from the FP7 Cooperation programme's energy research budget from 2007 to 2013 (EU COM, 2006a, b). Although the predominance of nuclear energy research has decreased somewhat over the past decade in Germany, it continues to enjoy the largest technological share of federal government energy research funding, albeit including nuclear plant decommissioning work. The still substantial funding of nuclear fusion research (in 2010, € 143 million, or 21% of the total energy research funding budget, were allocated to this area; BMBF, 2010c) should also be adapted to the current situation, as nuclear fusion power plant generated energy will not be available by the time the low-carbon transformation should be concluded. Rather than discounting the potentially possible long-term contributions to the energy supply from this source completely, research efforts should be extended over a longer period of time in order to release funds for higher priority projects.

To summarise: research funding must also focus on breaking path dependencies faster, and on optimising conditions for innovations, both of a structural nature and in terms of content. The goal should be the coordinated alignment of individual research programmes with regard to their contribution to climate-friendliness by 2050.

National Starting Points

At a national level, particularly suitable starting points for a research that meets the requirements formulated for research in Section 8.1.1.4 are provided under the German framework programme Research for Sustainable Development (FONA), including the funding priority Social-ecological Research (SÖF).

FONA conceptually addresses a range of global challenges such as climate change, water shortages, or the threat of biodiversity loss. The promotion measures encompass research for a better understanding of the Earth system, on innovations development, and on their social diffusion.

The funding priority SÖF refers directly to the research approach of the same name, developed by German non-university research institutes. The approach consolidates cross-disciplinary knowledge to solve concrete social sustainability problems. On the one hand, this calls for interdisciplinary cooperation between academics from both natural and social sciences; on the other hand, local expert knowledge must be taken into account when developing concrete solutions for life-world problems. Social actors have therefore been integrated into the research process in different ways. SÖF is particularly outstanding in terms of its specific accompanying research. It collects and synthesises research results to communicate them purposefully to the relevant research communities and social groups, and observes their impact. This research is (also) normative, as it pursues an ecological social conversion that takes both social equity and economic demands into account. The FONA framework programme and the SÖF funding priority therefore meet almost all points of the transformation-relevant research demands. More emphasis should be placed on the requirement of a global transition towards sustainability and its necessary acceleration; the latter in consequence of the almost complete reduction of greenhouse gas emissions by 2050, necessary for climate protection.

8.1.4.8 Interdisciplinarity

Section 8.1.1 called attention to the importance of interdisciplinarity in transformation-relevant research. The analysis in Section 8.1.4.7 led to the conclusion that interdisciplinarity is currently not adequately anchored at a strategic and programmatic level. However, integrating interdisciplinarity more firmly as a goal in research strategies and programmes will not suffice to actually guarantee it at project level - because the German science system contains a range of structural barriers that must be overcome.

Some promising starts with regard to interdisciplinarity have been made in Germany. These include interdisciplinary research institutes such as the Potsdam Institute for Climate Impact Research (PIK), or the Centre for Environmental Research (UFZ) in Leipzig, but also real or virtual centres and platforms, new types of schools such as the Berlin School of Mind and Brain, excellence cluster Topoi, Berlin ('The Formation of Space and Knowledge in Ancient Civilisations'), the Rachel Carson Center for Environment and Society in Munich, funded by the BMBF, the Geocycles research centre at Johannes Gutenberg University Mainz, or interdisciplinary science collegia, such as, for example, the Institute for Advanced Sustainability Studies (IASS) in Potsdam.

However, scale, structures and, in particular, their incentive, accreditation and evaluation mechanisms are not enough to lend sufficient weight to interdisciplinary transformation-relevant research and education. The scientific community often objects to interdisciplinarity; this applies particularly, but not exclusively, to universities.

University management, faculties, scientists and students frequently protest against the establishment of new kinds of inter- or transdisciplinary schools and colleges, as, for example, recently proposed by the science council (WR; 2010a), and are very reluctant to permit the extended interdisciplinary combination of Bachelor and Masters degree courses. Interdisciplinary degree courses are often circumvented with the argument of a lack of recognised professions for interdisciplinarily qualified graduates. Fact is that these days, an academic researcher can usually only afford a second, interdisciplinary career subsequent to a successful first disciplinary career; only few therefore choose this path.

Following the comprehensive statistical bibliographical evaluation of six research domains between 1975 and 2005, a quantitative analysis on interdisciplinarity has reached the conclusion that the often-cited increase in interdisciplinarity is actually perfunctory, or applies only to a small percentage (Porter and Rafols, 2009). In fact, the number of named research areas and citations within the 30-year period analysed actually increased by around 50%, the number of co-authored works even by 75%. Nevertheless, the number of actual interdisciplinary publications seemingly only rose by 5% (based on application of a numerical 'Disciplinary Diversity Index').

Inappropriate incentive systems

The reasons for the inadequate implementation of interdisciplinary approaches seem to lie in the science system's gratification and reputation mechanisms: these days, scientists must prove their expertise above all with the support of disciplinary third-party funding and publications in high-ranking disciplinary scientific journals. Particularly in the natural sciences, the only publications relevant are those listed in the Citation Index (ISI Web of Knowledge), this also applies to Germany. Under the German system, the *habilitation* or *venia legendi* being accorded for certain part-disciplines can also prevent individual lecturers from taking an interdisciplinary and transdisciplinary approach to academic research and teaching.

At universities, a major share of institutional grants is now awarded performance-based. Works published extra-disciplinarily – i.e. in a journal outside an academic's originally chosen discipline – are usually not accredited to scientist working interdisciplinarily. More or less the same applies to inter- or transdisciplinary third-party funding procurement or teaching outside of their own faculty.

As a scientist, remaining as monodisciplinary as possible whilst also participating in interdisciplinary projects both bear their pitfalls. The present assessment structure does not necessarily favour the awarding of grants to academics from different professional disciplines aiming to establish an interdisciplinary research project or curriculum. Reviewers for specific disciplines are usually referred to, who frequently do not believe in a systemic approach and often – perfectly logically, from their point of view – assess the disciplinary segment to be assessed as underrepresented or as lying below a critical mass. The evaluation report on the priority funding for the BMBF's 'Social-ecological Research' even criticised the fact that, despite the conscious, intentional interdisciplinarity, no structural effects with regard to interdisciplinary research were evident, as the 'universities, in view of the growing competitiveness, tended to stick to their core research areas and showed little willingness to open themselves up to interdisciplinary research beyond their area' (ad hoc translation by the WBGU). Junior research groups subscribing to the interdisciplinarity of SÖF research, however, enjoyed no representation in the structure-giving decision committees (EvaConsult, 2006).

Instruments for interdisciplinary research

Suitable existing structures for inter- and transdisciplinary projects are cross-disciplinary and cross-institutional platforms, centres, colleges, schools, explicitly interdisciplinary institutions and the German universities' Excellence Initiatives. As German universities do not tend to support inter-departmental cooperation, and their faculties tend to be structured mono- or oligo-disciplinarily, implementation appears inadequate at present.

Above all there are few or no existing structures that would serve the promotion or fecundity of integrative transformative research. To date, hardly any of the Excellence Initiative clusters and graduate schools are explicitly transformation-relevant. The excellence cluster 'Topoi', which investigates the formation and transformation of space and knowledge in ancient civilisations, is hosted by the Freie Universität Berlin and the Humboldt-Universität Berlin, together with several other non-university partners. It is somewhat of an exception to the above rule. Also to be viewed positively are the efforts towards more integrative research rating criteria, as recommended, and still under discussion, by the German Council of Science and Humanities, both for the humanities (WR, 2010b) and technical sciences (WR, 2009). Particularly to be welcomed is the fact that the 'transfer to non-scientific recipients' rating criterion is proposed alongside the criteria of 'research quality' and 'research facilitation'. It is here that transdisciplinary aspects such as stakeholder participation or paths for knowledge transfer into society should also be integrated. However, apart from briefly mentioning the importance of the humanities' lesser-sized disciplines in interdisciplinary projects (WR, 2010b), or inclusion in the list as 'background information' (WR, 2009), these rating proposals also pay scant further attention to interdisciplinarity, let alone in the context of a potential evaluation criterion.

8.1.4.9
The Four Transformative Pillars of the Knowledge Society

The elaborations so far show that science relates to the transformation in two ways. On the one hand, in the form of the transformation research (Tr) proposed by the WBGU, it focuses on the forthcoming task of shaping the transformation (Section. 8.1.2). Here, transitory processes are explored in order to come to conclusions on the factors and causal relations of transformation processes. Examples from history can serve as a basis for analysing observed transformative moments. The subjects of transformation research are therefore the basic principles, conditions and progression of transformation processes.

In contrast, research that meets the requirements identified by the WBGU (Section 8.1.1), is defined by the WBGU as *transformative research (tR)*. Transformative research is therefore only indirectly related to the transformation through the promotion of conversion processes by way of specific innovations in the relevant sectors. It supports transformation processes in practical terms through the development of solutions and technical and social innovations, including diffusion processes in economy and society, and opportunities for their acceleration, and demands, at least in part, systemic perspectives and inter- as well as transdisciplinary procedure methods, including stakeholder participation.

As previously explained, this division in transformation research and transformative research serves the purpose of better illustration and systematisation; however, the boundaries between these disciplines are also blurred and these areas may sometimes overlap; in practice, this division can therefore not be stringently maintained (Figure 8.1-3; Section 8.1). Both types of research should be mutually inspirational, and support the transformation through exchange with society, economy and policy-makers. This requires an improved, differentiated and participative form of science communication. The new media should also be used for this, as they provide numerous options for interactive social dialogues.

Education encompasses two dimensions: *transformation education (Te)* makes the findings of transformation research available to society. As 'education for participation', it critically reflects on the requisite basic requirements, such as a thorough understanding of the pressure to act and a global sense of responsibility, promotes systemic thinking, and generates a systemic understanding of different options for action (Colucci-Gray et al., 2006). It also communicates information on the environmental problems that necessitate the transformation, and their scientific exploration. At the same time, it generates goals, values and visions to guide the actions of individuals towards the necessary direction. Transformation education should also have the goal of inspiring social participation and political action, as both are preconditions for a democratically legitimised transformation.

Transformative education (tE) generates an understanding of different options for action and solution approaches. This includes, for example, encouraging informed low-carbon mobility behaviour, sustainability-conscious eating habits, or an awareness of cross-generational responsibilities. Related educational content would, for example, be innovations that are likely to have transformative impact, or which have already had one.

Both educational aspects should communicate the basic principle of responsible behaviour to as many members of the global community as possible. This would also prepare future researchers for their tasks. Education for the transformation should not be understood as a mere extension of current educational offerings. Rather, a paradigm change must be brought about, towards a well-informed society in which all understand themselves to be transformation agents who contribute to the legitimation of the transformation process through participating in knowledge generation (Section 8.2.2).

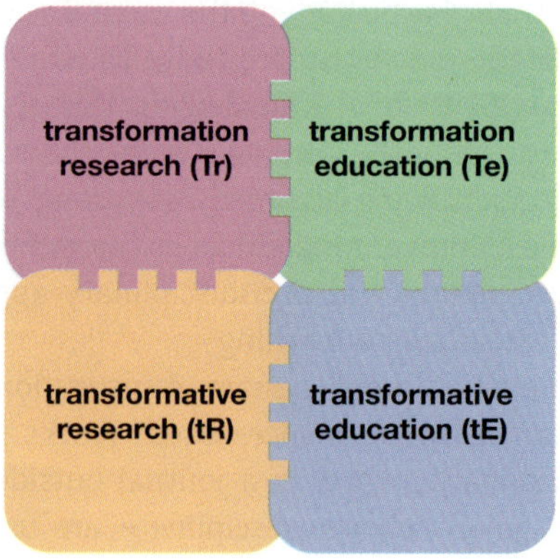

Figure 8.1-3
Typification of transformation research and education.
Source: WBGU

8.2 Education for the Transformation

In the WBGU's opinion, the transformation towards a sustainable, low-carbon society has considerably better chances of succeeding if – accompanied by a great number of other measures (Chapter 7) – the population's transformation-relevant awareness can be raised or sharpened through education. In this context, the education sector must also take on more responsibility. As an important channel of knowledge communication, this sector provides the foundations for each individual's knowledge-based self-concept, thereby contributing to the establishment of the social preconditions needed for the transformation. Transformation research should therefore be closely linked to education for the transformation.

Contents to be communicated cover a wide spectrum, encompassing both an understanding of individual innovations and the comprehensive realisation of the necessity for, and also the interdependence of, certain individual factors of the transition. The corresponding educational content would therefore, for example, relate to innovations that are likely to have transformative impact, or which have already had a transformative impact. The current status quo of scientific knowledge should be presented in an understandable, yet also differentiated, way, and should be actively, and especially participatively, shared with society. To facilitate this, education offers should, if possible, attempt to establish a relation to the key factors of the transformation. For example, renewable energies could be a topic in physics lessons, whilst concurrently, international energy partnerships are being discussed in the social science subjects; or geography lessons might, for instance, focus on low-carbon cities.

Beyond such focused contents, however, knowledge transfer at the points where engineering, Earth system and social sciences meet, should also enjoy stronger support. Appropriate narratives of change could be developed here to illustrate the interrelation of individual key factors, thereby integrating systemic thinking in education. These could enter the everyday discourse through creative forms of knowledge communication, and be developed further interactively. Through an exemplary focus on the role of change agents, an awareness of the preconditions for the transformation can be firmly ensconced in education. Only a dynamic picture of the world allows the contemplation of change and communicates the chance to participate positively in the shaping of ongoing processes.

8.2.1
Challenges of Knowledge Communication

As outlined above, the education sector must be involved in creating the requisite foundations for a participative culture. It is faced with a range of challenges or difficulties which have already been described quite often in the discussion on sustainability education (Rost, 2002). Enabling individuals to view themselves as part of the transformation process requires far-reaching insights and a certain level of identification with the knowledge contents. Both the specifics of scientific methods, so far removed from everyday life, and the continuously deteriorating trust in science create a new point of departure for knowledge communication to which research and education policies should react.

Facilitating the absorption of knowledge becomes even more important in the dialogue between science and politics when it comes to taking scientific insights into account during the policy-making process. Referring to scientific expert knowledge has become a vital element in contemporary governing and international, European and national law-making; this specific expertise is particularly indispensable when it comes to environmental and technological legislation. This applies especially to the low-carbon transformation process, as it is distinguished by actions under uncertainty.

Knowledge Growth and Knowledge Weighting
Comprehension of the Earth system and the interrelationships between its individual elements (climate, water cycle, soils, biodiversity, etc.) is steadily growing. The knowledge regarding natural and social systems is extremely complex. Although it mainly rests on empirical data, even their interrelationships alone are usually incomprehensible to laypersons. The probability-based models resultant from this data are also not always easy to communicate. Against this background, it becomes obvious that understanding the transformation towards a low-carbon, sustainable society requires a high degree of comprehension of complex systems and scientific methods. Transformation education should take this as its starting point in order to make systemic thinking as experienceable in the context of everyday life as possible, and therefore easier to understand. Historical abstracts and abstracts focusing on transformations could serve to make impact interrelatedness comprehensible as the illumination of the economic and social consequences of global environmental changes has only just begun. Therefore, education policies should increase their respective efforts to afford a better understanding of precaution-oriented, risk-calculating political action.

In this context, the question of which knowledge aspects are particularly relevant to transformation education arises, and what level of pure process and system knowledge is required. Again, as in the research area, a search process should emerge, during the course of which successes and newly emerging barriers are reflected in education concepts and educative content. It is also unclear exactly how much weight should be accorded to transformation education and transformative education, respectively, in knowledge communication, and how they are to be structured. However, what is fundamentally clear is that education should lead to a critical understanding of a mixture of problems and processes, goals and values, and instructional knowledge. To be able to review and develop these curricula (further), certain questions must be answered, such as: what is the best way to structure cross-generational thinking and action in education? Could new values also be possibly generated via education?

Dealing with Complexity and Statistical Probabilities
Science and research play a central role in the assessment of the dimensions of (long-term) potential threat that global environmental changes pose to humankind's natural life-support systems. This applies particularly to climate change, as, so far, climate change is (hardly) directly experienceable, and must be made visible or illustrated with the aid of scientific findings or via proxies, i.e. its impact on the biosphere, and communicated by political and social actors (Beck, 2007). Structurally, this analysis can be extended to the wider issue of the transformation towards sustainability, as a basic comprehension of complex systems is also required of the broad public; it is the precondition for understanding global environmental problems and transformation processes in industrialised, developing and newly industrialising countries. Interdisciplinary education

offers are key towards orientation in a complex world. They can ensure comprehension of individual key factors (for example social or technical innovations) and promote systemic thinking. However, at present, education offers and relevantly skilled knowledge communicators, such as the teaching staff in primary and secondary schools, are rare, despite first reformative steps in Germany at federal and state level (Programm Transfer-21, 2007).

Science and Climate Scepticism

Science scepticism tends to spread in leaps and bounds, in part, and understandably, for reasons of self-protection; this should be considered in the deliberations regarding education formats and programmes. Science scepticism is particularly rife when scientific findings impact on own interests, own behaviour, or on how each individual perceives humankind as a whole (Leinfelder, 2010b).

Knowledge particularisation represents a particularly serious problem as the causality context is lost. People can therefore feel alienated in a knowledge community. To relativise knowledge, or to presume intrumentalisation purposes, can then serve as self-justification in order to avoid having to confront complex facts, or facts whose consequences are felt to impact negatively on personal lives (Weingart, 2001; Rauchhaupt, 2005). This process can be exacerbated through knowledge falsification and ideological reservations (Mojon-Azzi et al., 2002; Fanelli, 2009; Zia und Todd, 2010).

The loss of trust in science resultant from this is particularly critical, and therefore in the knowledge society (for example Rauchhaupt, 2005), science scepticism in education (and research) therefore must be addressed as it is vital for the transformation process.

Climate scepticism is a perfect example to illustrate some of the challenges knowledge communication should address with regard to the problem of science scepticism. A first analysis here could help to identify starting points for building up trust in science. In many respects, the climate sceptics' argumentation is quite similar to the approach taken by evolution, and other science, sceptics. Proven knowledge, for example, is often emphatically relativised ('we don't know enough yet'), or simply disputed ('climate change is not happening'). Scientific proof to the contrary is well-known and available in an easy-to-understand, consolidated form (for example Cook, 2010; Archer and Rahmstorf, 2010). However, it is above all the argumentation techniques employed that can breed uncertainty. Again there are distinct similarities to the techniques used by evolution sceptics, particularly fallacies, ambiguousness, false causal relations, appeal to emotion, misuse of technical terminology, or discreditation (Neukamm, 2009).

From Awareness to Action

Empirically supported knowledge is a premise, but no guarantee for the social solving of complex (environmental) problems. The mixed results of current global climate policy illustrate particularly well that proven expert knowledge, as contained in the IPCC's assessment reports, alone is not enough to convert insights directly, or through mobilisation of the adequately large public, into globally effective actions.

Knowledge appropriation is therefore the first precondition for transformation-supporting actions, it is, however, certainly not enough. For this reason, a quite justifiably recurring theme in the debate on sustainable development education is that education must not just be the communication of purely cognitive knowledge, but must also encompass, on the one hand, practical aspects which can be applied to actions and, on the other hand, competence building to enable those learning to reflect on their actions, and empowering them to shape their future (de Haan, 2003; Rauchhaupt, 2005).

Life-Long Learning

Life-long learning is both an urgent necessity and a challenge facing science and education (Thielen, 2009). The transformation is a process spanning many decades, and needs the active participation and support of a great range of different social actors. Also, the process should be continuously reviewed and adapted. The content of transformation-relevant education therefore changes in the course of a lifespan. In this context, there are open questions, such as: how can the motivation for life-long learning be inspired, taught, and achieve a steady level of permanence? Is this (only) a matter of generating and updating orientation-knowledge, or will the re-education of a broader spectrum of the working population, for example toward transformation management, become more important?

Curricula which support an ongoing trust in science should make it possible to thoroughly understand the scientific process as such. The actual integration of this aspect in curricula – for instance by way of example-based methodology and science history teaching – is as necessary as continuous transparency and active communication on the part of the scientific community. Therefore, the issue is not merely the creation of a public understanding of science based on scientific findings, but the actual promotion of a public understanding of research.

8.2.2
Solutions

Knowledge acquisition is a requisite, but by no means the only precondition for transformation-supporting actions. Participation is a step towards action. The WBGU expects that latent or immanent acceptance barriers – particularly in relation to climate research results, biodiversity and agricultural technology research – can be reduced through education, in particular by direct social participation in the research process (Rauchhaupt, 2005; Mejlgaard and Stares, 2010). Integration of participative elements would promote the diffusion and acquisition of knowledge on natural and environmental events. The inadequate translation of knowledge into precautionary action to date can be addressed particularly with involvement, transparency, participation and ongoing participative success or status monitoring in a range of different environment or transformation related fields. Civil society participation in education is therefore inextricably bound to participation in research, they are mutually dependent and reinforcing. Respective education and participative research offerings and structures are therefore an important premise for enabling individuals to develop both a systemic understanding with regard to the need for action, and for making certain solution and action options experienceable to promote their acceptance.

Participative Knowledge Society

This report cannot place enough emphasis on the importance of civil participation, acceptance and legitimacy as a vital element for the transformation towards a low-carbon, sustainable society. The research process therefore also requires a broad level of social participation. In addition to the stakeholder participation in research goals and pursuit alluded to in Section 8.1, science can contribute to a higher level of acceptance of transformation-relevant political actions by involving non-scientists into the research itself. However, to date, research tends to feature few participative elements.

The evolutionary-biologically anchored curiosity of children concerning our environment must be reawakened and permanently appealed to for the sake of sustainability. You can only appreciate the things you know to want to protect them. Anyone directly involved in research processes and the gaining of scientific insights will relate differently to science, and will judge its capabilities, and its limits, differently (Irwin, 1995; Trumbull et al., 2000). And vice versa, science benefits when the practical knowledge and life-world perceptions of 'laypersons' complement the various scientific perspectives (Funtowitz and Ravetz, 1993; Young and Matthews, 2007).

The participative knowledge society needs intensive cooperation between science and civil society, during the course of which the civil society is participatively involved in the sourcing and acquisition of knowledge. Ultimately, the responsibility for shaping the transformation will fall to this 'middle' social level whose knowledge-based state depends on the close cooperation between civil society and scientific findings, i.e. research. Civil society participation in knowledge generation therefore has two interlinked aspects: 1) the specific and existing stakeholder knowledge or support on the part of the civil society regarding the generation of new research data discussed in Section 8.1.1.2, and 2) the active knowledge acquisition as a foundation for the transformation, and therefore the legitimation and active support of transformation research and of the entire transformation process as a genuine, direct or indirect transformation actor.

In the area of knowledge generation and acquisition with regard to natural and environmental events, museums, botanical gardens and zoos increasingly offer a multitude of options for intelligent independent exploration as 'environment stations', where scientists and citizens learn together (Daim, 2009; Leinfelder, 2009, 2010a). Transformation education will be anchored even more firmly and permanently when the well-informed citizen becomes active as a co-researcher, rather than reconstructively, and is involved in the research process itself at the earliest possible stage. These days, it is not unusual for non-professional researchers to gather important data and time series for scientific data bases and research programmes. Examples are the International Day for Biological Diversity activities, or the established bird and insect monitoring and other projects, such as the European 'Evolution MegaLab', started in the Darwin Year 2009 to study the variability and diffusion of banded snails all over Europe (Evolution MegaLab, 2011). The results were the basis for important new scientific findings (Silvertown et al., 2011).

In a participative knowledge society, even the sum total of seemingly insignificant individual actions can trigger the requisite self-energisation, proliferation and acceptance processes which can make a considerable contribution towards achieving the transformation towards a low-carbon society. The many small-scale scientific research participation projects which are hardly interlinked should therefore be strengthened and consolidated (for example the biodiversity and environmental monitoring stations). It is important to turn purely exemplary, frequently event-related participative projects into continuous long-term programmes. If time series are generated over many years, the involvement of the participating civil society is not only temporary, but permanent; the citizens are thereby turned into permanent research participants.

An outstanding example for a successful and permanent cooperation between science and civil society is Reef Check, a globally active NGO for the monitoring and conservation of coral reefs (Box 8.2-1). Without Reef Check, the global time series comparative data on the condition of coral reefs would never have reached the extent it has. Reef Check's activities have also provided divers with a new self-understanding, as they have started to organise further qualification courses of their own accord, and are now also actively involved in other areas (lake research). Through their participation, the divers can now fully relate to the coral reef knowledge generation process; they no longer view coral reefs merely as a venue for an exciting sport or relaxation, but as precious research objects worth protecting due to the ecosystem goods and services they provide.

The German federal government has also recognised the importance of social participation in the research process, as not least suggested by the BMBF citizen dialogue on future technologies ('Bürgerdialog Zukunftstechnologien') which started in March 2011 (BMBF, 2011f). It would be desirable to embed future-relevant issues in the context of the Great Transformation as early as possible in the course of such dialogues. However, citizens must be motivated to identify with the transformation process through their own actions – beyond the staging of dialogue events. The same applies to education at school. Initiatives such as 'science exchange', also initiated by the BMBF (Forschungsbörse, BMBF, 2011a), which arranges visits by academics to school classes, are fundamentally to be encouraged. However, as far as participation is concerned, scientists are not the only people who should 'put out their feelers' towards society. Rather, society should participate actively in the research process, not least within the scope of school education.

New education and research programmes prepared by the German federal government and the EU should be structured accordingly. Their motto should be 'knowledge and education by everyone', rather than 'knowledge and education for everyone'. Increasingly, the focus should be on Public Understanding of Research (PUR) as an element of Public Understanding of Science and Humanities (PUSH) (Field and Powell, 2001; Feinstein, 2011). A key element for adequate PUR is direct and preferably permanent participation in the research process. The successful 'Science in Dialogue' initiative, which has been running for approximately ten years now by the Stifterverband, the business community's innovation agency for German science, with substantial support by the BMBF, for example, could be complemented by a particularly dedicated participative element (education through active research participation), and its operation funded by a special BMBF programme.

Establishing Voluntary Social Year 'Education and Research'

Intensified and intensive participation of education and research with civil society input could also be created in the form of a voluntary social year. A joint 'umbrella structure' would be advisable, covering not only existing modules, such as the voluntary social or ecological year or the development volunteers service 'weltwärts', but also complementing these by the option of a voluntary science and technology year. A voluntary social year with different elective modules could here link a range of existing options synergetically and structurally to offer new choices.

Appropriate incentives should be introduced to allow a voluntary social year to take the form of a science and technology year. This is not about replacing functioning concepts. It is rather about the consolidation, organisation and extension of many small-scale and hardly interlinked participation projects, particularly in the area of participative research, for example the implementation of biodiversity or environmental monitoring stations or practical development political activities suggested above with the aid of those volunteering in these areas.

The contributions made during a voluntary social year should have a permanent impact, i.e. the data gathered should be documented and fed into networks as experiences to draw on, thereby becoming available to everyone. The range and interactive character of the new media could be utilised to this end, as own activities only obtain a special meaning when others can benefit from them. Thus, they become motivating. Politically supported motivation for a voluntary 'civilian service 2.0' could thereby become another key to establishing a participative knowledge society.

Science and Research Communication

Scientific processes and insights are complex and often communicable to the general public only in a very simplified way. Good science rarely automatically answers for successful communication of the insights gained and the actions required. A further important dimension of the participative knowledge society is therefore also a well-founded and differentiated science and research communication. It is distinguished by science presenting, for example, the deductions and reasoning behind scenario development and action recommendations in a way that is also transparent, logical and generally understandable for laypersons. Authentification of the research data, for instance through the illustra-

Box 8.2-1

Reef Check

Under the aegis of the globally active NGO Reef Check, divers, fishermen and scientists have been recording the 'state of health' of coral reefs since 1996, based on biological and sedimentological proxies for the purpose of a participative assessment and long-term monitoring project. Numerous factors (current situation, temperature situation, epidemics, fishery, over-fertilisation, acidification, sludge accumulation, pesticide input, storms, tourism, etc.) indicate the condition of a reef; nevertheless, the long-term monitoring and the comparison of global and regional data allows evaluation of individual factors (for instance different damage patterns, such as the bleaching caused by El Niño, algae increase due to over-fertilisation, over-fishing, storm damage), to create a differentiated illustration of the impact of global and regional environmental changes that the broad public can also understand and relate to.

The Reef Check Monitoring project gathers biophysical indicators with the aid of standardised protocols to obtain information on anthropogenic impact on the reefs. The data is entered into Excel tables and sent by e-mail to a central data input centre. The data is available soon after being collected, and serves, together with other scientific data, as the foundation for scientific work and the management of protected areas. It flows into global data bases, and via these, into the status reports published on a regular basis by the Global Reef Coral Monitoring Programs, GCRMN (1998). GCRMN is part of the Global Ocean Observing System, jointly supported by the Intergovernmental Oceanographic Commission (IOC/UNESCO) and UNEP, IUCN, the World Bank and the Convention on Biological Diversity. Hodgson and Liebeler have provided a comprehensive report on the methods and results of the first five years of Reef Check's activities (2002).

tion of source materials, illustrating how research processes are based on historical examples, or the additional, vivid illustration of well-known scientists can aid knowledge identification and absorption. In recent years, natural science and technical museums have increasingly relied on personalisation (Einstein, Darwin, Humboldt, Zuse, etc.) as a fresh approach for conveying the contents of various scientific fields.

Exploiting and Stabilising the UN Decade 'Education for Sustainable Development' Fully and Adding Permanence

The low-carbon transformation into a sustainable society is only achievable together in dialogue with the civil society; the civil society must, ultimately, carry out this process. In essence, this thought was one of the reasons behind the establishment of the currently running UN Decade 'Education for Sustainable Development' (2005–2014). Education for sustainable development means raising sustainable thinking and action awareness among children, young people and adults. It intends to enable people to make decisions for the future with an awareness of how their own actions impact on future generations or life in other regions of the world. This requires a far more systemically oriented education (Colluci-Gray et al., 2006). The Bonn Declaration, drawn up at the UNESCO World Conference on Education for Sustainable Development in Bonn, Germany (2009), concludes that education for sustainable development is still progressing at an extremely varied pace in different countries. The coming years will require major efforts by industrial and developing countries, the civil society and international organisations to achieve the desired progress in this area.

8.3 Recommendations

A comprehensive transformation towards a low-carbon, sustainable society places great demands on the development, diffusion, legitimation and application of knowledge, and thereby also on the goals and form of research and research policies. Both must bear a high level of responsibility for the whole of society.

From the WBGU's perspective, transformation-oriented research demands substantial additional funding, in order to be able to become commensurate with the dimensions of this challenge. At the same time, research policy-makers should also be guided to a far greater extent by transformation-relevant research demands than has so far been the case when it comes to deciding content and structure of research strategies and programmes. However, the WBGU is by no means advocating a blanket reallocation of funds within the German scientific community, and emphasises clearly that independent research should continue to enjoy a high status. Simultaneously, new social visions and paradigms should be developed; this can be advanced by skilful policy-making on behalf of the government, but succeed only if actively supported by science.

In view of the fact that the transformation is a societal search process involving all social actors, education is also a vital requirement for a successful transformation. Society can only acquire the requisite capacities for active participation in the transformation process in all its complexity through a broad spectrum of different and diverse education structures and a review of education content. The WBGU believes it has neither the qualifications nor the competency to carry out an elaborate all-encompassing evaluation of present transformation-relevant education contents and structures. Rather, it would just like to point out some of the demands that transformation and transformative education, which should be based on a common basic principle of participation, should meet – as befits a culture of democratic participation.

Because, in the WBGU's view, it is an indisputable fact that the participation of a wide range of social environments and different actors, both in education and in research, is indispensable in order to, on the one hand, generate understanding, acceptance and the ability to participate in the transformation process and, on the other hand, make research results more implementation-oriented, and therefore relevant, by bringing in local, traditional, everyday, and cultural knowledge. Science should particularly involve social actors more intensively and as early as possible in the research process, also through participation in the formulating of problematic or research issues, and visions. Not least this will (also) help to increase acceptance of research results.

Against this background, the WBGU has developed the following key recommendations in terms of research and education for the transformation.

8.3.1
Research

- Science and research should address the challenges of the low-carbon transformation (even more). Research should concentrate more on transformation-relevant issues and subjects, and the new field of transformation research. At the same time, it should meet various structural requirements, such as, for instance, systemic, long-term and inter- and transdisciplinary orientation. It should develop technological and social low-carbon innovations, evaluate them, and assess the conditions required for their global diffusion. This also includes the development, evaluation, and public discussion of political strategies and options for action to guide policy-makers. Research programmes should therefore reflect these demands correspondingly.
- The WBGU calls for the creation of a new research field, 'transformation research', to examine transformation processes and the social preconditions within the scope of planetary boundaries. To develop this new field of scientific research, the WBGU proposes a socially embedded search and discussion process. This process could be overseen by The Alliance of Science Organisations in Germany.
- Overall, in order to face the current challenges successfully and accelerate the transformation, substantial additional research and development funding is required. Research should also be coordinated and consolidated at EU and international level, as no country can develop all of the required solutions on its own.
- Funding for the central transformation field of energy should be increased substantially. The WBGU had already recommended in 2003 to increase direct public spending on energy research and development in the industrialised countries tenfold, largely through reallocation. The WBGU maintains this recommendation, as, according to International Energy Agency estimates, the need for further additional funding continues (IEA, 2010b). Grants for energy generation through nuclear fusion could be stretched across a longer term to release funds for higher priority tasks.
- The WBGU urges the German federal government to raise budgets in the areas spatial and urban development and construction technology by a tenfold. At the same time, research should focus more on climate-compatibility, and become internationalised to facilitate comprehensive and long-term research on low-carbon urbanisation, acknowledging the central importance of this transformation field for the successful transformation into a climate-friendly society.
- Current German Federal Ministry of Education and Research (BMBF) sustainability research funding, particularly the framework programme 'Research for Sustainable Development' (FONA), and 'Social-ecological Research' (SÖF) should be significantly increased, and SÖF´s global perspective should be considerably extended.
- Interdisciplinary research should be supported by concrete measures. Existing incentive systems need to be changed, and new ones introduced. This includes, for instance, additional funds for interdisciplinary research project applications, start-up financing for interdisciplinary transformation research, a prominent scientific award for interdisciplinary research, transformation funds, and the consideration of interdisciplinary research for additional incentive payments. The WBGU proposes that the German Conference of University Presidents the Joint Science Conference, the German Research Foundation and the Academy of Sciences consult on recommendations and directives for the implementation and rating of interdisciplinary transformation research. Interdisciplinary transformation research could also be supported through 'innovation' or 'high-risk-research' prioritisation, not unlike the Leibniz Association's Senatsausschuss Wettbewerb (SAW) competitive procedure categories for

allocating Joint Initiative for Research and Innovation funding.

- The German federal government should call for increased consideration of research for the transformation in the course of the development of the Eighth EU Research Framework Programme, in particular for extended environmental and energy research.
- Internationally, Germany and the EU should forge stronger transformation-relevant research alliances with new, innovative research centres in the newly industrialising countries.
- In the scope of its development cooperation, Germany should step up the promotion and support of education, science and research capacities dealing with climate-friendly problem solving in the less developed countries.
- The WBGU suggests priority consideration of transformation-contributive clusters, schools and future concepts during the coming round of the Excellence Initiative, and the announcement of one Excellence Initiative round dedicated completely to the subject of research in a transformation context for a ressource-efficient and sustainable society worth living in.
- The current review of the Consultative Group on International Agricultural Research (CGIAR) is an opportunity to direct its activities more consistently towards climate-friendlyness and sustainability.
- Research communication with society and policymakers should continue to be improved. Research results should increasingly be integrated into the political process.

8.3.2 Education

- Transformation education should be given a higher priority in the German sustainability strategy, and in all departmental strategies. It should also be integrated into school and university curricula, vocational qualification, and further studies. This encompasses exchange programmes, new combinations of bachelor and masters courses, teacher training modules for transformation-relevant systemic education, and transformation science degree courses.
- Through coherent policies, subject-relevant education and vocational qualification systems should be redesigned in such a way that they can dedicate themselves to the requirements of sustainable development. At the same time, opportunities for lifelong on-the-job learning should be extended through publicly funded further education courses and post-graduate qualifications, for example in the form of a transformation-relevant 'sabbatical' for employees. Besides new curricula and degree courses and modules, completely new professions might be needed.
- The WBGU also suggests the establishment of low-carbon business schools and interdisciplinary faculties for low-carbon land use, energy science, urbanisation and transformation-specific management in order to lend important support to the transformation process.
- During the UN 'Decade of Education for Sustainable Development', institutional mechanisms should be developed to ensure that sustainable development education continues once the decade has passed. A – UNESCO initiated – process is conceivable here, run not unlike the International Decade for Natural Disaster Reduction (IDNDR). The UN named the 1990s as the decade for natural disaster reduction to raise public awareness and support the strategy development for combating natural disasters. Once the decade was over, various states continued their activities in the form of national committees. Successful UN Decade of Education for Sustainable Development activities could continue in a similar way in the form of local and national institutions.

8.3.3 Interactive Field Education – Research

- The WBGU recommends the establishment of a German federal university with a research and education profile that focuses on accelerating the transformation towards sustainability. Research and teaching should be inter- and transdisciplinary.
- The WBGU suggests an extensive education and research programme, 'Participation in Transformation Research', with the objective of education and knowledge generation for the benefit of the environment and sustainability, achieved through participation of non-scientists.
- Research policy and science should initiate various cross-science and cross-social dialogues to be able to promote research for the transformation. Dialogues and citizens' forums with topics such as 'visions for a decarbonised society', 'requirements for transformation research', 'stepping up inter- and transdisciplinary research', or 'priority research issues' are conceivable. This could also include dialogue in a cultural and artistic format, for example in museums, at future exhibitions or music and short film festivals.
- Increased involvement of social actors, including so-called laypersons, in research should be encouraged. Establishing participative, networked biodiversity,

environment and climate stations, running citizen surveys on transformation processes including participation in the analysis of results, or self-reflexive model participation projects in the areas of, for example, electromobility, agriculture or new types of housing are appropriate options to achieve this. Already existing, successful examples are the annual bird counts in Germany and the UK, or the monitoring under the aegis of Reef Check.
- The community of citizens should be directly involved in the formulation of future paths and visions, for instance through dialogues processes or citizens' conferences, but also exemplarily through participation in the practical realisation of this vision.
- The WBGU proposes the introduction of a voluntary social year in 'education and research'.

8.3.4 Concrete Research Priorities in the Three Transformation Fields

Energy

The key aspects of the 'E-Energy' funding programme (BMWi, 2008b), and those of the future energy supply grids funding concept ('Netze für die Stromversorgung der Zukunft', BMWi, 2010c) are to be commended. Many of these comply with the WBGU recommendations on smartgrid development. The WBGU suggests the thematic expansion from power to energy grids to allow for systemic energy system solutions from the outset.

Existing projects pursuing the development of new behavioural patterns and business models in the area of energy use, particularly the E-Energy development scheme (BMWi, 2008b), are a step in the right direction. In future, this focus should also be extended in other programmes, especially those relating to energy demand and efficiency improvements.

Land Use

The WBGU advocates the expansion, financial support and optimisation of sustainable land management, Global Research Alliance on Agricultural Greenhouse Gases, and socio-ecological research to create the linked research initiative that is needed in order to manage the huge global challenge of sustainable land use in the context of progressive climate change and securing the food supply whilst guaranteeing the continued functioning of ecosystem services.

Urbanisation

The numerous, already existing networks which are, above all, also dedicated to linking global urbanisation research efforts, and in which the German federal government is actually already involved (for example the 'European Urban Knowledge Network'), should be consolidated, not least also with regard to goals, to achieve the required funding dimensions.

The present urbanisation research programmes already partially correspond to WBGU recommendations in terms of content. Solution-oriented approaches with the transformation as a direct and concrete goal should be substantially extended and receive increased funding. However, the transferability of research results and generated data must be ensured. These programmes should form part of a low-carbon urbanisation research approach of global dimensions.

8.3.5 Conclusions

This analysis by the WBGU shows that research for the transformation has already commenced to a certain extent. For quite some time now, a number of research strategies and programmes have included subjects, contents and methods which ensure that research conforms to the requirements of the transformation identified by the WBGU, and produces knowledge that is relevant for this process. What matters now is to consolidate this knowledge, to significantly strengthen the already existing respective research processes, to globally diffuse its results and, where necessary, to start the new research processes described.

Overall, research funding must in future also focus on breaking path dependencies faster, and on optimising conditions for research innovations, both of a structural nature and in terms of content. The goal here should be the coordinated structuring of individual research programmes with regard to their contribution to climate-friendliness by 2050.

References

9

Abbate, J. (1999): Inventing the Internet. Cambridge, MA: MIT Press.

Adams, W. P. (2008): Die USA im 20. Jahrhundert. Oldenbourg Grundriss der Geschichte. Volume 29. Munich: Oldenbourg Wissenschaftsverlag.

Adams, W. P. (2009): Die USA vor 1900. Oldenbourg Grundriss der Geschichte. Volume 28. Munich: Oldenbourg.

ADB – Asian Development Bank (2009): The Economics of Climate Change in Southeast Asia. A Regional Review. Manila: ADB.

ADFC – Allgemeiner Deutscher Fahrradclub Berlin (2010): ADFC-Herbst-Check 2010. Website: http://www.adfc-berlin.de (viewed 14. March 2011). Berlin: ADFC.

Adler, A. B. (2009): Gross National Happiness in Bhutan: A Living Example of an Alternative Approach to Progress. Website: http://www.grossnationalhappiness.com/OtherArticles/GNHPaperbyAlejandro.pdf (viewed 17. November 2010). Bhutan: The Centre for Bhutan Studies.

Adler, F. and Schachtschneider, U. (2010): Green New Deal, Suffizienz oder Ökosozialismus? Konzepte für gesellschaftliche Wege aus der Ökokrise. Munich: Oekom.

AGECC – Advisory Group on Energy and Climate Change (2010): Energy for a Sustainable Future. The Secretary-General's Advisory Group on Energy and Climate Change Summary Report and Recommendations. New York: AGECC.

AGF – High Level Advisory Group on Climate Change Financing (2010): Report of the Secretary-General's High-level Advisory Group on Climate Change Financing. New York: AGF.

Akerlof, G. A. and Shiller, R. J. (2009): Animal Spirits: Wie Wirtschaft wirklich funktioniert. Frankfurt/M.: Campus.

Alber, G. and Kern, K. (2008): Governing Climate Change in Cities: Modes of Urban Climate Governance in Multi-level Systems. OECD Conference Proceedings 'Competitive Cities and Climate Change', Milan, Italy, 9–10 October 2008. Paris: Organization for Economic Co-operation and Development.

Albert, M., Hurrelmann, K., Quenzel, G., Schneekloth, U., Gensicke, T., Leven, I., Picot, S. and Willert, M. (2010): 16. Shell Jugendstudie: Jugend 2010. Frankfurt/M.: Fischer.

Allen, M. R., Frame, D. J., Huntingford, C., Jones, C. D., Lowe, J. A., Meinshausen, M. and Meinshausen, N. (2009): Warming caused by cumulative carbon emissions towards the trillionth tonne. Nature 458, 1163–1166.

Allison, I., Bindoff, N. L., Bindschadler, R. A., Cox, P. M., de Noblet, N., England, M. H., Francis, J. E., Gruber, N., Haywood, A. M., Karoly, D. J., Kaser, G., Le Quére, C., Lenton, T. M., Mann, M. E., McNeil, B. I., Pitman, A. J., Rahmstorf, S., Rignot, E., Schellnhuber, H. J., Schneider, S. H., Sherwood, S. C., Somerville, R. C. J., Steffen, K., Steig, E. J., Visbeck, M. and Weaver, A. J. (2009): The Copenhagen Diagnosis. Sidney: The University of New South Wales, Climate Research Centre.

Alter, K. J. (2001): Establishing the Supremacy of European Law: The Making of an International Rule of Law in Europe. Oxford, New York: Oxford University Press.

Alter, K. J. (2006): Delegation to International Courts and the Limits of Recontracting Political Power. Evanston, IL: Northwestern University, Department of Political Science.

Andersen, S. O. and Sarma, K. M. (2002): Protecting the Ozone Layer. The United Nations History. London: Earthscan.

Angerer, G., Erdmann, L., Marscheider-Weidemann, F., Scharp, M., Lüllmann, A., Handke, V. and Marwede, M. (2009a): Rohstoffe für Zukunftstechnologien. Einfluss des branchenspezifischen Rohstoffbedarfs in rohstoffintensiven Zukunftstechnologien auf die zukünftige Rohstoffnachfrage. Karlsruhe: Fraunhofer IRB.

Angerer, G., Marscheider-Weidemann, F., Wendl, M. and Wietschel, M. (2009b): Lithium für Zukunftstechnologien. Nachfrage und Angebot unter besonderer Berücksichtigung der Elektromobilität. Karlsruhe: Fraunhofer ISI.

Archer, D. and Rahmstorf, S. (2010): The Climate Crisis. Cambridge, New York: Cambridge University Press.

Arendt, H. and Uellenberg, G. (1970): Macht und Gewalt. Munich: Piper.

Arrow, K. J., Cohen, L., David, P. A., Hahn, R. W., Kolstad, C., Lee Lane, W., Montgomery, D., Nelson, R. R., Noll, R. and Smith, A. E. (2009): A Statement on the Appropriate Role for Research and Development in Climate Policy. Reg-Markets Center Working Paper No. 08-12. Washington, DC: Washington AEI Center for Regulatory and Market Studies.

Atomium Culture and Lund University (2009): Governance for a Low-Carbon Society. Combating Climate Change Requires a Major Transition Towards a Sustainable Energy Future. What Technologies and Approaches to Governance will make this Transition a Success? Website: www.atomiumculture.eu (viewed 5. July 2010). Brussels: Atomium Culture.

Ayres, R. U. and Simonis, U. E. (1994): Industrial Metabolism: Restructuring for Sustainable Development. Tokyo: United Nations University Press.

Babiker, M. H. and Rutherford, T. F. (2005): The economic effects of border measures in subglobal climate agreements. The Energy Journal 26 (4), 99–125.

Bach, N. (2000): Wandel individuellen und kollektiven Mitarbeiterverhaltens. In: Krüger, W. (ed): Excellence in Change: Wege zur strategischen Erneuerung. Wiesbaden: Gabler, 221–260.

Bai, Z. G., Dent, D. L., Olsson, L. and Schaepman, M. E. (2008): Global Assessment of Land Degradation and Improvement. 1. Identification by Remote Sensing. Report 2008/01. Website: http://www.isric.org/UK/About+ISRIC/Projects/Current+Projects/GLADA.htm (viewed 14. March 2010). Wageningen: World Soil Information Centre (ISRIC).

Bandura, A. (1977): Social Learning Theory. New York: General Learning Press.

Banuri, T. and Najam, A. (2002): Civic Entrepreneurship. Civil Society Perspectives on Sustainable Development. Islamabad: Gandhara Academy Press.

Baringhorst, S., Kneip, V., März, A. and Niesyto, J. (eds) (2007): Politik mit dem Einkaufswagen. Unternehmen und Konsumenten als Bürger in der globalen Mediengesellschaft. Bielefeld: Transcript.

Barnes, S. and Kaase, M. (1979): Political Action. Mass Participation in Five Western Democracies. Beverly Hills, London: Sage Publications.

Barnett, M. N. and Finnemore, M. (2004): Rules for the World: International Organizations in Global Politics. Ithaca, NY: Cornell University Press.

Barnett, M. N. and Finnmore, M. (2005): The power of liberal international organizations. In: Barnett, M. N. and Duvall, R. (eds): Power in Global Governance. Cambridge, NY: Cambridge University Press, 161–184.

Barnosky, A. D., Matzke, N., Tomiya, S., Wogan, G. O. U., Swartz, B., Quenta, I. B., Marshall, C., McGuire, J. L., Lindsey, E. L., Maguire, K. C., Mersey, B. and Ferrer, E. A. (2011): Has the Earth's sixth mass extinction already arrived? Nature 471, 51–57.

Bartsch, M., Becker, S., Bode, K., Friedmann, J., Hollersen, W., Kaiser, S., Kurbjuweit, D., Müller, P., Popp, M. and Schmid, B. (2010): Volk der Widerborste. Der Spiegel 35, 64–72.

BASE – Basel Agency for Sustainable Energy and SEFI – Sustainable Energy Finance Initiative (2006): Public Finance Mechanisms to Increase Investment in Energy Efficiency. A Report for Policy Makers and Public Finance Agencies. Basel, Paris: BASE, SEFI.

Bättig, M. B. and Bernauer, T. (2009): National institutions and global public goods: are democracies more cooperative in climate change policy? International Organization 63, 281–308.

Bauer, S. (2008): UN-Umweltprogramm: Reform der kleinen Schritte. Politische Ökologie 26 (112–113), 102–103.

Bauer, S. (2009): Weltpolitik in aufgeheizter Atmosphäre: Frieden und Sicherheit in Zeiten des Klimawandels und der Multipolarität. Die Friedens-Warte. Journal of International Peace and Organization 84 (2), 45–70.

Bauer, S. and Biermann, F. (2005): The Debate on a World Environment Organization: An Introduction. In: Biermann, F. and Bauer, S. (eds): A World Environment Organization: Solution or Threat for Effective International Environmental Governance? Aldershot: Ashgate, 1–23.

Bauer, S. and Richerzhagen, C. (2007): Nachholende Entwicklung und Klimawandel. Aus Politik und Zeitgeschichte 57 (47), 20–26.

Bauer, S. and Sommer, B. (2011): Wegbereiter eines Weltklimavertrags? Subglobale Allianzen in der internationalen Klimapolitik. Ökologisches Wirtschaften 2, 26–27.

Bauer, S., Fues, T., Messner, D. and Weinlich, S. (2011): Engagement für Entwicklung und Umwelt. Informationen zur politischen Bildung: Vereinte Nationen (310), 37–49.

BBC (2010): BBC Climate Change Poll – February 2010. Website: http://news.bbc.co.uk/nol/shared/bsp/hi/pdfs/05_02_10climatechange.pdf (viewed 17. November 2010). London: BBC.

BBSR – Federal Institute for Research on Building, Urban Affairs and Spatial Development (2009a): ExWoSt: Urbane Strategien zum Klimawandel: Kommunale Strategien und Potenziale. Aufruf für Modellvorhaben. Website: http://www.bbsr.bund.de/BBSR/DE/FP/ExWoSt/Studien/2009/KlimaStadtentwicklung/09__AufrufModellvorhaben.html (viewed 22. February 2011). Bonn: BBSR.

BBSR – Federal Institute for Research on Building, Urban Affairs and Spatial Development (2009b): ExWoSt: Urbane Strategien zum Klimawandel: Immobilien- und wohnungswirtschaftliche Strategien und Potenziale zum Klimawandel. Start (II). Website: http://www.bbsr.bund.de/nn_821220/BBSR/DE/FP/ExWoSt/Forschungsfelder/2010/UrbaneStrategienKlimawandel/Forschungsschwerpunkt2/01__Start.html (viewed 5. March 2011). Bonn: BBSR.

Beach, D. (2005): The Dynamics of European Integration – Why and When EU Institutions Matter. Houndmills: Palgrave MacMillan.

Beck, U. (2007): Weltrisikogesellschaft: Auf der Suche nach der verlorenen Sicherheit. Frankfurt/M.: Suhrkamp.

Beecher Stowe, H. (2001): Uncle Tom's Cabin or, Life Among the Lowly. London: Penguin.

Beisheim, M. and Nuscheler, F. (2003): Demokratie und Weltgesellschaft. In: Hauchler, I., Messner, D. and Nuscheler, F. (eds): Globale Trends 2004/2005. Fakten, Analysen, Prognosen. Frankfurt/M.: Fischer, 31–47.

Beisheim, M. and Simon, N. (2010): Neuer Schwung für die Reform der internationalen Umweltgovernance. SWP-Aktuell 37/2010. Berlin: Stiftung Wissenschaft und Politik (SWP).

Benedick, R. E. (1999): Contrasting Approaches: The Ozone Layer, Climate Change and Resolving the Kyoto Dilemma. Berlin: Wissenschaftszentrum Berlin für Sozialforschung (WZB).

Berensmann, K., Fues, T. and Volz, U. (2011): Die G20: informelles Machtzentrum mit wachsender entwicklungspolitischer Bedeutung E+Z Entwicklung und Zusammenarbeit 52 (1), 17–20.

Berg, J.-R. (2008): Schöpfer einer neuen Welt. Geo Epoche 30, 24–37.

Bertelsmann Foundation (2010): Bürger wollen kein Wachstum um jeden Preis. Website: http://www.bertelsmann-stiftung.de/cps/rde/xbcr/SID-76A90915-D95DE342/bst/xcms_bst_dms_32005_32006_2.pdf (viewed 5. January 2011). Gütersloh: Bertelsmann Foundation.

Besson, S., Marti, J. L. and Seiler, V. (2006): Deliberative Democracy and it's Discontents. London: Ashgate Publishing.

Biermann, F. (2005): Re-launching the UN Environment Programme: The Rationale for a World Environment Organization. In A World Environment Organization: Solution or Threat for Effective International Environmental Governance? Aldershot: Ashgate.

Biermann, F. (2007): 'Earth system governance' as a crosscutting theme of global change research. Global Environmental Change 17, 326–337.

Biermann, F. (2008): Earth System Governance. A Research Agenda. In: Young, O. R., King, L. A. and Schroeder, H. (eds): Institutions and Environmental Change. Principal Findings, Applications, and Research Frontiers. Cambridge, MA: MIT Press, 277–301.

Biermann, F. and Siebenhüner, B. (2009): Managers of Global Change. The Influence of International Environmental Bureaucracies. Cambridge, MA: MIT Press.

Biermann, F., Pattberg, P., van Asselt, H. and Zelli, F. (2009): The fragmentation of global governance architectures. A framework for analysis. Global Environmental Politics 9 (4), 14–40.

Binswanger, H. C. (2006): Die Wachstumsspirale – Geld, Energie und Imagination in der Dynamik des Marktprozesses. Marburg: Metropolis.

BIP – Biodiversity Indicators Partnership (2010): Headline Indicator: Converage of Protected Areas. Website: http://www.bipindicators.net/pacoverage (PDF). Cambridge, UK: UNEP World Conservation Monitoring Centre.

Bischoff, J. (2008): Vorwärts durch Raum und Zeit. Geo Epoche 30, 56–71.

Blanke, B., Lamping, W., Schridde, H. and Plaß, S. (2002): Der Aktivierende Staat. Positionen, Begriffe, Strategien. Bonn: Friedrich-Ebert-Stiftung.

BMBF – Federal Ministry of Education and Research (2005): Bekanntmachung von Förderrichtlinien des BMBF zum Förderschwerpunkt 'Wirtschaftswissenschaften für Nachhaltigkeit'. Zuwendungszweck und Rechtsgrundlage. Berlin: BMBF.

BMBF – Federal Ministry of Education and Research (2008): Grundlagenforschung Energie 2020+. Die Förderung der Energieforschung durch das BMBF. Berlin: BMBF.

BMBF – Federal Ministry of Education and Research (2009): Forschung für nachhaltige Entwicklungen FONA. Rahmenprogramm des BMBF. Berlin: BMBF.

BMBF – Federal Ministry of Education and Research (2010a): Hightech-Strategie 2020 für Deutschland. Website: http://www.hightech-strategie.de/de/350.php (viewed 22. February 2011). Berlin: BMBF.

BMBF – Federal Ministry of Education and Research (2010b): Nationale Forschungsstrategie BioÖkonomie 2030 – Unser Weg zu einer biobasierten Wirtschaft. Berlin: BMBF.

BMBF – Federal Ministry of Education and Research (2010c): Bundesbericht Forschung und Innovation 2010. Berlin: BMBF.

BMBF – Federal Ministry of Education and Research (2010d): Megastädte – Die Welt von morgen nachhaltig gestalten. Berlin: BMBF.

BMBF – Federal Ministry of Education and Research (2010e): Nachhaltiges Landmanagement. Website: http://nachhaltiges-landmanagement.de (viewed 8. March 2011). Berlin: BMBF.

BMBF – Federal Ministry of Education and Research (2010f): Morgenstadt – Eine Antwort auf den Klimawandel. Berlin: BMBF.

BMBF – Federal Ministry of Education and Research (2010g): Neue Dynamik in der Forschung. Beispiele aus dem Pakt für Forschung und Innovation. Berlin: BMBF.

BMBF – Federal Ministry of Education and Research (2011a): Bekanntmachung der Förderrichtlinien 'Wissen für Entscheidungsprozesse - Forschung zum Verhältnis von Wissenschaft, Politik und Gesellschaft'. Website: http://www.bmbf.de/foerderungen/677_5448.php (viewed 22. February 2011). Berlin: BMBF.

BMBF – Federal Ministry of Education and Research (2011b): Bekanntmachung der Förderrichtlinien 'Neue Governance der Wissenschaft - Forschung zum Verhältnis von Wissenschaft, Politik und Gesellschaft' des Bundesministeriums für Bildung und Forschung. Website: http://www.bmbf.de/foerderungen/12150.php (viewed 22. February 2011). Berlin: BMBF.

BMBF – Federal Ministry of Education and Research (2011c): Ökonomie des Klimawandels. Bekanntmachung des Bundesministeriums für Bildung und Forschung von Richtlinien zur Förderung von Forschungs- und Entwicklungsvorhaben im Förderschwerpunkt. Website: http://www.bmbf.de/foerderungen/14682.php (viewed 22. February 2011). Berlin: BMBF.

BMBF – Federal Ministry of Education and Research (2011d): 'Käte Hamburger Kollegs' (Internationale Kollegs für Geisteswissenschaftliche Forschung). Bekanntmachung des Bundesministeriums für Bildung und Forschung von Richtlinien zur Förderung Website: http://www.bmbf.de/foerderungen/14076.php (viewed 22. February 2011). Berlin: BMBF.

BMBF – Federal Ministry of Education and Research (2011e): Wechselwirkungen zwischen Natur- und Geisteswissenschaften. Bekanntmachung von Förderrichtlinien des Bundesministeriums für Bildung und Forschung (BMBF) Website: http://www.bmbf.de/foerderungen/7774.php (viewed 22. February 2011). Berlin: BMBF.

BMBF – Federal Ministry of Education and Research (2011f): BMBF Bürgerdialog Zukunftstechnologien: Bürger diskutieren über neue Technologien. Berlin: BMBF.

BMF – Federal Ministry of Finance (2008): Gesetz zur Umsetzung eines Maßnahmenpakets zur Stabilisierung des Finanzmarktes (Finanzmarktstabilisierungsgesetz – FMStG) vom 17. Oktober 2008. Berlin: BMF.

BMU – Federal Ministry for the Environment, Nature Conservation and Nuclear Safety (2009): UFOPLAN Forschungsrahmen des Bundesumweltministeriums und Umweltforschungsplan 2009. Berlin, Dessau: BMU, Umweltbundesamt (UBA).

BMU – Federal Ministry for the Environment, Nature Conservation and Nuclear Safety (2010a): Akzeptanz und Umweltverträglichkeit der Hinderniskennzeichnung von Windenergieanlagen. Website: http://www.erneuerbare-energien.de/files/pdfs/allgemein/application/pdf/bericht_akzeptanz_windraederkennzeichnung_bf.pdf (viewed 17. November 2010). Berlin: BMU.

BMU – Federal Ministry for the Environment, Nature Conservation and Nuclear Safety (2010b): UFOPLAN Forschungsrahmen des Bundesumweltministeriums und Umweltforschungsplan 2010. Berlin: BMU.

BMU – Federal Ministry for the Environment, Nature Conservation and Nuclear Safety (2010c): Leitstudie 2010. Langfristszenarien und Strategien für den Ausbau der erneuerbaren Energien in Deutschland bei Berücksichtigung der Entwicklung in Europa und global. Berlin: BMU.

BMU – Federal Ministry for the Environment, Nature Conservation and Nuclear Safety (2011): UFOPLAN Forschungsrahmen des Bundesumweltministeriums und Umweltforschungsplan 2011. Berlin: BMU.

BMVBS – Federal Ministry of Transport, Building and Urban Development (2009a): Integrierte Stadtentwicklung in Stadtregionen. Berlin: BMVBS.

BMVBS – Federal Ministry of Transport, Building and Urban Development (2009b): Der Beitrag des Bundes zur nachhaltigen Stadtentwicklung. Berlin: BMVBS.

BMVBS – Federal Ministry of Transport, Building and Urban Development (2010a): Urbane Strategien zum Klimawandel. Dokumentation der Auftaktkonferenz 2010 zum ExWoSt-Forschungsfeld. Berlin: BMVBS.

BMVBS – Federal Ministry of Transport, Building and Urban Development (2010b): ExWoSt-Informationen 39/1: StadtKlima. Kommunale Strategien und Potenziale zum Klimawandel. Ein ExWoSt-Forschungsfeld. Berlin: BMVBS.

BMVBS – Federal Ministry of Transport, Building and Urban Development and Difu – Deutsches Institut für Urbanistik (2010): Berliner Gespräche zum Städtebaurecht. Volume I: Bericht. Berlin: BMVBS.

BMWA – Bundesministerium für Wirtschaft und Arbeit (2005): Innovation und neue Energietechnologien. Das 5. Energieforschungsprogramm der Bundesregierung. Berlin: BMWA.

BMWi – Federal Ministry of Economics and Technology (2008a): Klimaschutz und Energieeffizienz. Forschung, Entwicklung und Demonstration moderner Energietechnologien. Berlin: BMWi.

BMWi – Federal Ministry of Economics and Technology (2008b): E-Energy. IKT-basiertes Energiesystem der Zukunft. Berlin: BMWi.

BMWi – Federal Ministry of Economics and Technology (2010a): Forschung für Energieeffizienz. Website: http://www.bmwi.de/BMWi/Navigation/Service/publikationen,did=361086.html (viewed 22. February 2011). Berlin: BMWi.

BMWi – Federal Ministry of Economics and Technology (2010b): Zukunftstechnologien. Website: http://www.bmwi.de/BMWi/Navigation/Energie/Energietraeger/netze,did=354342.html (viewed 22. February 2011). Berlin: BMWi.

BMWi – Federal Ministry of Economics and Technology (2010c): Förderkonzept 'Netze für die Stromversorgung der Zukunft'. Berlin: BMWi.

BMWi – Federal Ministry of Economics and Technology (2010d): Rohstoffstrategie der Bundesregierung. Berlin: BMWi.

BMWi – Federal Ministry of Economics and Technology (2011): Energie: Statistik und Prognosen. Website: http://www.bmwi.de/BMWi/Navigation/Energie/Statistik-und-Prognosen/Energiedaten/energieforschung.html (viewed 8. February 2011). Berlin: BMWi.

BMWi – Federal Ministry of Economics and Technology and BMU – Federal Ministry for the Environment, Nature Conservation and Nuclear Safety (2010): Energiekonzept für eine umweltschonende, zuverlässige und bezahlbare Energieversorgung. Berlin: BMWi, BMU.

BMZ – Federal Ministry for Economic Cooperation and Development (2010): Development Policy Stance on the Topic of Land Grabbing – the Purchase and Leasing of Large Areas of Land in Developing Countries. Berlin: BMZ.

BNEF – Bloomberg New Energy Finance (2010): Crossing the Valley of Death. Solutions to the Next Generation Clean Energy Project Financing Gap. New York, London: BNEF.

Boden, T. A., Marland, G. and Andres, R. J. (2010): Global, Regional, and National Fossil Fuel CO_2 Emissions. Oak Ridge: Carbon Dioxide Information Analysis Center.

Bohle, H.-G. (1989): 20 Jahre 'Grüne Revolution' in Indien. Geographische Rundschau 41 (2), 91–98.

Böhringer, C., Rosendahl, K. and Fischer, E. (2010): The Global Effects of Subglobal Climate Policies. Washington, DC: Resources for the Future.

BÖLW – Bund für Ökologische Lebensmittelwirtschaft (2010): Zahlen, Daten, Fakten. Die Bio-Branche 2010. Website: http://www.boelw.de/uploads/media/pdf/Dokumentation/Zahlen__Daten__Fakten/ZDF_gesamt2010.pdf (viewed 13. April 2010). Berlin: BÖLW.

Bosch (2010): eMobility Solution – Die Zukunft der Mobilität. Kundeninformation. Website: http://www.bosch-emobility.com/de/system.html (viewed 15. March 2011). Gerlingen-Schillerhöhe: Robert Bosch GmbH.

Bourdieu, P. (1977): Outline of a Theory of Practice. Cambridge, New York: Cambridge University Press.

Bourdieu, P. (1987): Die feinen Unterschiede. Kritik der gesellschaftlichen Urteilskraft. Frankfurt/M.: Suhrkamp.

Bouwman, A. F., Beusen, A. H. W. and Billen, G. (2009): Human alteration of the global nitrogen and phosphorus soil balances for the period 1970–2050. Global Biogeochemical Cycles 23, doi:10.1029/2009GB003576.

Braakmann, A. (2009): Wie lässt sich Wohlstand messen? Wirtschaftsdienst 12, 783–787.

Brand, K.-W., Nölting, B. and Schäfer, M. (2007): Sozial-ökologische Handlungsansätze im Feld. Landwirtschaft und Ernährung – Eine Zwischenbilanz. In: Nölting, B. and Schäfer, M. (eds): Vom Acker auf den Teller. Munich: Oekom, 177–193.

Braudel, F. (1958): Histoire et sciences sociales. La longue durée. Annales Economies Sociétés Civilisations XIII (4), 725–753

Braungart, M. and McDonough, W. (2002): Cradle to Cradle: Remaking the Way We Make Things. San Francisco: North Point Press.

Bread for the World, BUND and EED – Church Development Service (2008): Zukunftsfähiges Deutschland in einer globalisierten Welt. Ein Anstoß zur gesellschaftlichen Debatte. Frankfurt/M.: Wuppertal Institut für Klima, Umwelt, Energie.

Bredenkamp, H. and Pattillo, C. (2010): Financing the Response to Climate Change. IMF Staff Position Note 10/06. Washington, DC: International Monetary Fund.

Brock, L. (2003): Nord-Süd-Beziehungen: Handlungsfelder und Kontroversen. In: Knapp, M. and Krell, G. (eds): Einführung in die Internationale Politik. Munich: Oldenbourg, 616–650.

Broschek, J. and Schultze, R.-O. (2006): Wahlverhalten: Wer wählt wen? Theoretische Erklärungsmodelle und empirische Befunde. In: Hoecker, B. (eds): Politische Partizipation zwischen Konvention und Protest. Eine studienorientierte Einführung. Opladen: Budrich, 23–54.

Brown, J., Bird, N. and Schalatek, L. (2010): Climate Finance Additionality: Emerging Definitions and Their Implications. Climate Finance Policy Brief No. 2. Washington, DC, London: Heinrich Böll Stiftung North America, Overseas Development Institute.

Bruinsma, J. (2009): The Resource Outlook to 2050: By How Much Do Land, Water and Crop Yields Need to Increase by 2050? Rome: Food and Agricultural Organization.

Brunnengräber, A. (2009): Die politische Ökonomie des Klimawandels. Munich: oekom.

Brusis, M. (2008): Reformfähigkeit messen? Konzeptionelle Überlegungen zu einem Reformfähigkeitsindex für OECD-Staaten. Politische Vierteljahresschrift 49 (1), 92–113.

Brzezinski, Z. (2004): The Choice. Global Domination or Global Leadership. New York: Basic.

Buchstein, H. (2009): Demokratie und Lotterie. Das Losverfahren als politisches Instrument von der Antike bis zur EU. Frankfurt/M.: Campus.

Buchstein, H. (2010): Reviving randomness for political rationality: elements of a theory of aleatory democracy. Constellations 17 (3), 435–454.

Buchstein, H. and Hein, M. (2009): Randomizing Europe. The lottery as a decision-making procedure for policy creation in the EU. Critical Policy Studies 3 (1), 29–57.

Bude, H. (1987): Deutsche Karrieren. Lebenskonstruktionen sozialer Aufsteiger aus der Flakhelfer-Generation. Frankfurt/M.: Suhrkamp.

Bunse, M., Dienst, C. and Wallbaum, H. (2007): Micro-financing of renewable energy systems. In: ECEEE – European Council for an Energy Efficient Economy (eds): ECEEE 2007 Summer Study Saving Energy – Just Do it! Panel 3: Local and Regional Activities. Stockholm: ECEEE, 481–490.

Burkhalter, A., Kaenzig, J. and Wüstenhagen, R. (2009): Kundenpräferenzen für leistungsrelevante Attribute von Stromprodukten. Zeitschrift für Energiewirtschaft 2, 161–172.

Burniaux, J.-M., Chateau, J. and Duval, R. (2010): Is There a Case for Carbon-Based Border Tax Adjustment? An Applied General Equilibrium Analysis. OECD Economics Department Working Papers No. 749. Paris: Organization for Economic Co-operation and Development.

Busby, J. W. (2010): Moral Movements and Foreign Policy. Cambridge, UK: Cambridge University Press.

Caddedu, S. (2004): The proceedings of the European Ombudsman. Law and Contemporary Problems 68, 161.

Caldecott, B. (2010): Green Infrastructure Bonds: Accessing the Scale of Low Cost Capital Required to Tackle Climate Change. London: Climate Change Capital Head Office.

Caldeira, K., Granger Morgan, M., Baldocchi, D., Brewer, P. G., Chen, C.-T. A., Nabuurs, G.-J., Nakicenovic, N. and Robertson, G. P. (2004): A portfolio of carbon management options. In: Field, C. B. and Raupach, M. R. (eds): The Global Carbon Cycle: Integrating Humans, Climate, and the Natural World. Washington, DC: Island Press, 103–129.

Calliess, C. (2010): Die neue Europäische Union nach dem Vertrag von Lissabon – Ein Überblick über die Reformen unter Berücksichtigung ihrer Implikationen für das deutsche Recht. Tübingen: Mohr.

Calliess, C. and Ruffert, M. (2007): EUV/EGV, Das Verfassungsrecht der Europäischen Union mit Europäischer Grundrechtecharta – Kommentar. Munich: Beck.

Camdessus, M., Lamfalussy, A., Padoa-Schioppa, T., Aleksashenkp, S., Al Sayari, H., Boorman, J. T., Crockett, A., de la Dehesa, G., Fraga, A., Gyohten, T., Hu, X., Icard, A., Köhler, H., Ortiz, G., Ramos, M., Reddy, Y. V., Truman, E. M. and Volcker, P. A. (2011): Reform of the International Monetary System: A Cooperative Approach for the Twenty First Century. New York: Palais-Royal Initiative.

Campbell, J. Y. and Froot, K. A. (1993): International Experiences with Securities Transaction Taxes. NBER Working Paper No. 4587. Cambridge, MA: National Bureau of Economic Research.

Canadell, J., Le Quéré, C., Raupach, M. R., Field, C. B., Buitenhuis, E. T., Ciais, P., Conway, T. J., Gillett, N. P., Houghton, R. A. and Marland, G. (2007): Contributions to accelerating atmospheric CO_2 growth from economic activity, carbon intensity, and efficiency of natural sinks. Proceedings of the National Academy of Sciences 104 (47), 18866–18870.

Carbon Culture (2011): 3–8 Whitehall Place. Our Energy Use. Website: http://www.carbonculture.net/orgs/decc/whitehall-place/ (viewed 15. March 2011). London: Carbon Culture.

Carson, R. (1962): Silent Spring. Boston: Houghton Mifflin.

Casillas, C. E. and Kammen, D. M. (2010): The energy-poverty-climate nexus. Science 330, 1181–1182.

Cazenave, A., Dominh, K., Guinehut, S., Berthier, E., Llowel, W., Ramillien, G., Ablain, M. and Larnicol, G. (2008): Sea level budget over 2003–2008: A reevaluation from GRACE space gravimetry, satellite altimetry and Argo. Global and Planetary Change 65, 83–88.

CBD – Convention on Biological Diversity (2004): Protected Areas (Articles 8 (a) to (e)). Decision VII/28. Montreal: CBD.

CBD – Convention on Biological Diversity (2010a): Updating and Revision of the Strategic Plan for the Post-2010 Period. Decision X/2. Montreal: CBD.

CBD – Convention on Biological Diversity (2010b): Global Biodiversity Outlook 3. Montreal: CBD Secretariat.

CCICED – China Council for International Cooperation on Environment and Development (2009): China's Pathway Towards a Low Carbon Economy. Website: http://www.sfu.ca/international-development/cciced/pdf/2009_TFonLowCarbonEconomy.pdf (viewed 14. March 2011). Beijing: CCICED.

CDIAC – Carbon Dioxide Information Analysis Center (2011): Global Data 1751–2007. Website: http://cdiac.ornl.gov/ftp/ndp030/global.1751_2007.ems (viewed 7. January 2011). Oak Ridge, TN: CDIAC.

Centre for Corporate Citizenship (2007): Corporate Citizenship. Gesellschaftliches Engagement von Unternehmen in Deutschland und im transatlantischen Vergleich. Berlin: Centre for Corporate Citizenship.

Chalmers, D., Hadjiemmanuil, C., Monti, G. and Tomkins, A. (2006): European Union Law. Cambridge, New York: Cambridge University Press.

Chandler, T. (1987): Four Thousand Years of Urban Growth: An Historical Census. New York, Lewiston: St. David's University Press.

Chapin III, F. S., Zavaleta, E. S., Eviner, V. T., Naylor, R. L., Vitousek, P. M., Reynolds, H. L., Hooper, D. U., Lavorel, S., Sala, O. E., Hobbie, S. E., Mack, M. C. and Diaz, S. (2000): Consequences of changing biodiversity. Nature 405, 234–242.

Chapman, G. P. (2002): The Green Revolution. The Companion to Development Studies. London: Arnold.

Chen, S. and Ravallion, M. (2008): The Developing World is Poorer than Thought but No Less Successful in the Fight Against Poverty. World Bank Policy Research Working Paper 4703. Washington, DC: World Bank.

Chinese Government (2011): Environmental Protection. Special Report. Website: http://english.gov.cn/special/envir_index.htm (viewed 14. March 2011). Beijing: Chinese Government.

Chivian, E. and Bernstein, A. (eds) (2008): Sustaining Life. How Human Health Depends on Biodiversity. Oxford, New York: Oxford University Press.

Church, J. A. and White, N. J. (2006): A 20th century acceleration in global sea-level rise. Geophysical Research Letters 33, L01602.

CIESIN – Center for International Earth Science Information Network (2005): Global Rural-Urban Mapping Project (GRUMP). Urban Extends. Palisades, NY: CIESIN, Columbia University, International Food Policy Research Institute, World Bank, Centro Internacional de Agricultura Tropical.

Clark, A. and Oswald, A. J. (1994): Unhappiness and unemployment. Economic Journal 104 (5), 648–659.

Clark, W. C., Crutzen, P. J. and Schellnhuber, H. J. (2005): Science for global sustainability: toward a new paradigm. In: Schellnhuber, H. J., Crutzen, P. J., Clark, W. C., Claussen, M. and Held, H. (eds): Earth System Analysis for Sustainability. Cambridge, MA: MIT Press, 1–28.

Cleaver, H. (1972): The Contradictions of the Green Revolution. American Economic Review 62 (2), 177–186.

Cleveland, C. J., Costanza, R., Hall, C. A. S. and Kaufmann, R. (1984): Energy and the U.S. economy: a biophysical perspective. Science 225 (4665), 890–897.

Colucci-Gray, L., Camino, E., Barbiero, G. and Gray, D. (2006): From scientific literacy to sustainability literacy: An ecological framework for education. Science Education 90 (2), 227–252.

Conway, G. R. and Barbier, E. B. (1990): After the Green Revolution. Sustainable Agriculture for Development. London: Earthscan.

Conzelmann, T. and Faust, J. (2009): 'Nord' und 'Süd' im globalen Regieren. Politische Vierteljahresschrift 50 (2), 203–225.

Cook, J. (2010): Wissenschaftlicher Leitfaden zur Klimaskepsis. The Scientific Guide to Global Warming Skepticism. Website: http://www.skepticalscience.com/The-Scientific-Guide-to-Global-Warming-Skepticism.html (viewed 7. March 2011). Online Portal: Skepticalscience.

Cooper, A. F. and Antkiewicz, A. (2008): Emerging Powers in Global Governance. Lessons from the Heiligendamm Process. Waterloo, ON: Wilfrid Laurier University Press.

Cordell, D. (2010): The Story of Phosphorus. Sustainability Implications of Global Phosporus Scarcity for Food Security. Doctoral thesis. Linköping: Linköping University, Department of Water and Environmental Studies.

Cordell, D., Drangert, J.-O. and White, S. (2009): The story of phosphorus: global food security and food for thought. Global Environmental Change 19, 292–305.

Corfee-Morlot, J., Kamal-Chaoui, L., Donovan, M. G., Cochran, I., Robert, A. and Teasdale, P.-J. (2009): Cities, Climate Change and Multi-Level Governance. OECD Environmental Working Paper. Paris: Organization for Economic Co-operation and Development.

Craswell, E. T., Tiessen, H. and Vlek, P. L. G. (2010): Peak Phosphorus: Implications for Agricultural Production, the Environment and Development. Bonn: Zentrum für Entwicklungsforschung.

Crouch, C. (2004): Post-Democracy (Themes for the 21st Century). San Francisco: Wiley.

Crutzen, P. J. (2002): Geology of mankind. Nature 415, 23.

Crutzen, P. J. and Schwägerl, C. (2010): Living in the Anthropocene: Toward a New Global Ethos. Essay. Website: http://e360.yale.edu/feature/living_in_the_anthropocene_toward_a_new_global_ethos_/2363/ (viewed 4. March 2011). New Haven, CT: environment360.

Crutzen, P. J. and Stoermer, E. F. (2000): The 'Anthropocene'. IGBP Newsletter 41, 17–18.

Czech, B. and Daly, H. E. (2009): Die Steady-State-Ökonomie: Was sie ausmacht, was sie mit sich bringt und was sie genau bedeutet. Nachhaltiges Wachstum? Wissenschaft und Umwelt Interdisziplinär 13, 115–121.

Czisch, G. (2005): Szenarien zur zukünftigen Stromversorgung. Kostenoptimierte Variationen zur Versorgung Europas und seiner Nachbarn mit Strom aus erneuerbaren Energien. Dissertation. Kassel: University Kassel.

Dahl, R. A. (1970): After the Revolution. Authority in a Good Society. New Haven: Yale University Press.

Dahl, R. A. (1987): Sketches for a democratic Utopia. Scandinavian Political Studies 10, 195–206.

Dahl, R. A. (1989): Democracy and its Critics. New Haven: Yale University Press.

Dahl, R. A. (1992): The problem of civic competence. Journal of Democracy 3, 45–59.

Dahrendorf, R. (1957): Soziale Klassen und Klassenkonflikt in der industriellen Gesellschaft. Stuttgart: Ferdinand Enke.

DAI – Verband Deutscher Architekten und Ingenieurvereine (2009): Klimamanifest der Architekten, Ingenieure und Stadtplaner. Website: http://www.dai.org/oeffentlichkeitsarbeit/meldungen/304-klima-manifest-der-architekten-ingenieure-und-stadtplaner (viewed 13. December 2010). Berlin: DAI.

Daim, F. (2009): Linking the Public with Science and Research – Zusammenfassung der Ergebnisse. In: Hanft, A. and Knust, M. (eds): Weiterbildung im Elfenbeinturm!? Münster, New York, Munich, Berlin: Waxmann, 104–106.

Daly, H. E. (1974): The economics of the steady state. The American Economic Review 64 (2), 15–21.

Daly, H. E. (1996): Beyond Growth. The Economics of Sustainable Development. Boston, MA: Beacon Press.

Danish Board of Technology (2009): World Wide Views on Global Warming. From the World's Citizens to the Climate Policy Makers. Copenhagen: Danish Board of Technology.

Davis, S., J. and Caldeira, K. (2010): Consumption-based accounting of CO_2 emissions. Proceedings of the National Academy of Sciences (early edition), 1–6.

Dawkins, E., Roelich, K. and Owen, A. (2010): A Consumption Approach for Emissions Accounting – the REAP Tool and REAP Data for 2006. Stockholm: Stockholm Environment Institute.

DB – Mobility Networks Logistic (2010): Carsharing der Bahn – Die intelligente Art der Autonutzung. Kundeninformation. Website: http://www.dbcarsharing-buchung.de (viewed 15. March 2011). Frankfurt/M.: DB.

de Grazia, A. (1951): Public and Republic: Political Representation in America. New York: Knopf.

de Haan, G. (2003): Bildung als Voraussetzung für eine nachhaltige Entwicklung – Kriterien, Inhalte, Strukturen, Forschungsperspektiven. In: Kopfmüller, J. (ed): Den globalen Wandel gestalten. Forschung und Politik für einen nachhaltigen globalen Wandel. Berlin: edition sigma, 93–113.

Deaton, A. (2008): Income, Health, and Well-Being around the World: Evidence from the Gallup World Poll. Journal of Economic Perspectives 22 (2), 53–72.

Debiel, T., Roth, M. and Ulbert, C. (2010): Globale Trends im Schatten der Weltfinanzkrise: Herausforderungen, Kräfteverschiebungen und Optionen für Global Governance. In: Debiel, T., Messner, D., Nuscheler, F., Roth, M. and Ulbert, C. (eds): Globale Trends 2010. Frieden, Entwicklung, Umwelt. Frankfurt/M.: Fischer, 11–21.

Delbrück, J. (1998): 'Das Völkerrecht soll auf einen Föderalismus freier Staaten gegründet sein'. Kant und die Entwicklung internationaler Organisation. In: Dicke, K. and Kodalle, K.-M. (eds): Republik und Weltbürgerrecht. Weimar: Böhlau, 180–213.

Delta Committee (2008): Working Together with Water. A Living Land Builds for its Future. The Hague: Delta Committee.

DeMartino, S. and Le Blanc, E. (2010): Estimating the Amount of a Global Feed-in Tariff for Renewable Electricity. UN DESA Working Paper 95. New York: United Nations Department of Economic and Social Affairs.

DENA – German Energy Agency (2010): Integration erneuerbarer Energien in die deutsche Stromversorgung im Zeitraum 2015–2020 mit Ausblick auf 2025. Strategisches Konzept zur Weiterentwicklung des Stromnetzes in Deutschland. Berlin: DENA.

Déry, P. and Anderson, B. (2007): Peak phosphorus. Energy Bulletin (13.08.), 10.

Deutscher Familienverband (2003): Aktionsleitfaden zum Schwerpunktthema Familienwahlrecht Hintergrundinformationen – Argumente – Anregungen. Berlin: Deutscher Familienverband.

Diaz, R. J. (2001): Overview of hypoxia around the world. Journal of Environmental Quality 30 (2), 275–281.

Die Welt Online (2010): Geißler fordert Reform des deutschen Baurechts. Hamburg: Die Welt Online (12.11.2010).

Diekmann, A. and Preisendörfer, P. (1991): Umweltbewusstsein, ökonomische Anreize und Umweltverhalten. Schweizer Zeitschrift für Soziologie 17 (2), 207–231.

Dienel, P. (1978): Die Planungszelle. Eine Alternative zur Establishment-Demokratie. Opladen: Westdeutscher Verlag.

Dienel, P. C. (2002): Die Planungszelle. Der Bürger als Chance. Mit Statusreport 2002. Wiesbaden: VS.

Dingwerth, K. (2007): The New Transnationalism: Transnational Governance and Democratic Legitimacy. Hampshire: Palgrave.

Dingwerth, K. and Pattberg, P. (2006): Global Governance as a Perspective on World Politics. Global Governance: A Review of Multilateralism and International Organizations 12 (2), 185–203.

Dinner, I., Johnson, E. J., Goldstein, D. G. and Liu, K. (2009): Partitioning Default Effects. Why People Choose Not to Choose. Working Paper. Rochester, New York: Social Science Research Network.

DLR – German Aerospace Center (2006): Trans-Mediterranean Interconnection for Concentrating Solar Power. Final Report. Stuttgart: DLR.

Doney, S. C., Fabry, V. J., Feely, R. A. and Kleypas, J. A. (2009): Ocean acidification: the other CO_2 problem. Annual Review of Marine Sciences 1, 169–192.

Dowie, M. (2001): American Foundations: An Investigative History. Cambridge, MA: MIT Press.

Downie, D. L. (1995): UNEP and the Montreal Protocol: New roles for international organizations in regime creation and change. In: Bartlett, R. V., Kurian, P. A. and Malik, M. (eds): International Organizations and Environmental Policy. Westport, CT: Greenwood Press.

Downs, A. (1968): Ökonomische Theorie der Demokratie. Tübingen: Mohr Siebeck.

Drescher, S. (2009): Abolition. A History of Slavery and Antislavery. Cambridge, New York: Cambridge University Press.

Dröge, S., van Asselt, H., Brewer, T., Ismer, R., Mehling, M., Monjon, S., Quirion, P., Neuhoff, K., Schumacher, K., Mohr, L., Suwala, W., Takamura, Y., Voituriez, T., Wang, X. and Grubb, M. (2009): Tackling Leakage in a World of Unequal Carbon Prices. Cambridge, UK: Climate Strategies.

Dunbar, R. (1993): Coevolution of neocortex size, group size and language in humans. Behavioral and Brain Sciences 16 (4), 681–735.

Dunbar, R. (2010): How Many Friends Does One Person Need? Dunbar's Number and Other Evolutionary Quirks. London: Faber.

Easterlin, R. A. (1974): Does economic growth improve the human lot? In: David, P. A. and Reder, M. W. (eds): Nations and Households in Economic Growth: Essays in Honor of Moses Abramovitz. New York: Academic Press, 89–125.

Eckersley, R. (2009): Population Measures of Subjective Wellbeing: How Useful are They? Social Indicators Research 94 (1), 1–12.

Eckes, T. and Six, B. (1994): Fakten und Fiktionen in der Einstellungs-Verhaltens-Forschung. Eine Meta-Analyse. Zeitschrift für Sozialpsychologie 15 (4), 253–271.

Ecologic (2007): Akzeptanz und Strategien für den Ausbau Erneuerbarer Energien auf kommunaler und regionaler Ebene. Website: http://ecologic.eu/download/projekte/950-999/991/verbundprojekt_izt_endbericht-teilprojekt_zw_akzeptanz_ecologic.pdf (viewed 17. November 2010). Berlin: Ecologic.

Edenhofer, O. and Kalkuhl, M. (2009): Das grüne Paradoxon – Menetekel oder Prognose. In: Beckenbach, F., Weimann, J., Minsch, J., Nutzinger, H. G. and Witt, U. (eds): Jahrbuch Ökologische Ökonomik. Volume 6: Diskurs Klimapolitik. Marburg: Metropolis, 115–151.

Edenhofer, O. and Stern, N. (2009): Towards a Global Green Recovery – Recommendations for Immediate G20 Action. A Study Initiated by the Federal Foreign Office and Carried out by the Potsdam Institute for Climate Impact Research and the London School of Economics. Potdam: Potsdam Institute for Climate Impact Research.

Edenhofer, O., Carraro, C., Hourcade, J.-C., Neuhoff, K., Luderer, G., Flachsland, C., Jakob, M., Popp, A., Steckel, J., Strohschein, J., Bauer, N., Brunner, S., Leimbach, M., Lotze-Campen, H., Bosetti, V., de Cian, E., Tavoni, M., Sassi, O., Waisman, H., Crassous-Doerfler, R., Monjon, S., Dröge, S., van Essen, H., del Río, P. and Türk, A. (2009a): The Economics of Decarbonisation. Report of the RECIPE Project. Potsdam: Potsdam Institute for Climate Impact Research.

Edenhofer, O., Hulme, M., Neufeldt, H. and Ritchie, A. (2009b): Adaptation and Mitigation Strategies. Supporting European Climate Policy. Final Report. Norwich: Tyndall Centre for Climate Change Research, University of East Anglia.

Edenhofer, O., Knopf, B., Barker, T., Baumstark, L., Bellevrat, E., Chateau, B., Criqui, P., Isaac, M., Kitous, A., Kypreos, S., Leimbach, M., Lessmann, K., Magné, B., Scrieciu, S., Turton, H. and van Vuuren, D. P. (2010): The economics of low stabilization: model comparison of mitigation strategies and costs. The Energy Journal 31 (Special Issue 1), 11–48.

EEA – European Environment Agency (2010a): SOER 2010: The European Environment State and Outlook 2010. Material Resources and Waste. Copenhagen: EEA.

EEA – European Environment Agency (2010b): SOER 2010: The European Environment State and Outlook 2010. Land Use. Copenhagen: EEA.

EEAC – European Environment and Sustainable Development Advisory Councils (2009): Towards Sustainable European Infrastructures. Statement and Background Document. Brussels: EEAC.

Eger, H., Fleischhauer, E., Hebel, A. and Sombroek, W. G. (1996): Taking action for sustainable land-use: Results from 9th ISCO Conference in Bonn, Germany. Ambio 25 (8), 480–483.

Ehrlich, P. R. and Holdren, J. P. (1971): Impact of population growth. Science 171, 1212–1217.

EIB – European Investment Bank (2007): EPOS II – The 'Climate Awareness Bond'. EIB Promotes Climate Protection via Pan-EU Public Offering. Press Release 22.05.2007. Luxembourg: EIB.

EIB – European Investment Bank (2009): EIB Launches Debut Swedish Krona Climate Awareness Bonds. Press Release 03.11.2009. Luxembourg: EIB.

Eifert, M. (2009): Innovationsfördernde Regulierung. In: Eifert, M. and Hoffmann-Riem, W. (eds): Innovationsfördernde Regulierung. Berlin: Duncker & Humblot, 11–19.

Elias, N. (1987 [1996]): Wandlungen der Wir-Ich-Balance. In: Elias, N. (ed): Die Gesellschaft der Individuen. Frankfurt/M.: Suhrkamp, 207–315.

Elias, N. (1994): Studien über die Deutschen. Machtkämpfe und Habitusentwicklung im 19. und 20. Jahrhundert. Frankfurt/M.: Suhrkamp.

Ellis, E. C. and Ramankutty, N. (2008): Putting people in the map: anthropogenic biomes of the world. Frontiers in Ecology and the Environment 6, doi:10.1890/070062.

Engel, K., Großmann, J. and Hombach, B. (2011): Phönix flieg! Das Ruhrgebiet erfindet sich neu. Essen: Klartext.

Environics (2007): Energy Attitudes. Website: http://www.americanenvironics.com/PDF/EnergyAttitudesSummer2007.pdf (viewed 17. November 2010). Oakland, CA: American Environics.

Epiney, A. (2000): Welthandel und Umwelt. Deutsches Verwaltungsblatt 115, 77–86.

Epstein, S. (1994): Integration of cognitive and the psychodynamic unconscious. American Psychology 49, 709–724.

Erbguth, W. and Schlacke, S. (2009): Umweltrecht: Lehrbuch. Baden-Baden: Nomos.

EREC – European Renewable Energy Council and Greenpeace (2008): Energy [R]evolution. A Sustainable Global Energy Outlook 2008. Brussels, Amsterdam: EREC, Greenpeace International.

EREC – European Renewable Energy Council and Greenpeace (2009): Energy [R]evolution. A Sustainable Global Energy Outlook 2009. Brussels, Amsterdam: EREC, Greenpeace International.

EREC – European Renewable Energy Council and Greenpeace (2010): Energy [R]evolution. A Sustainable Global Energy Outlook. Advanced Scenario. Third Edition 2010. Brussels, Amsterdam: EREC, Greenpeace International.

Eswaran, H., Lal, R. and Reich, P. F. (2001): Land degradation: an overview. In: Bridges, E. M., Hannam, I. D., Oldeman, L. R., Pening de Vries, F. W. T., Scherr, S. J. and Sompatpanit, S. (eds): Responses to Land Degradation. Proceedings of the 2nd International Conference on Land Degradation and Desertification, Khon Kaen, Thailand. Delhi: Oxford Press.

EU – European Union (2009): Directive 2009/31/EC of the European Parliament and the Council of 23 April 2009 on the Geological Storage of Carbon Dioxide. Brussels: EU.

EU COM – European Commission (2005): Report on European Technology Platforms and Joint Technology Initiatives: Fostering Public-Private R&D Partnerships to Boost Europe's Industrial Competitiveness. Brussels: EU COM.

EU COM – European Commission (2006a): Council Decision of 19 December 2006 Concerning the Specific Programme 'Cooperation' Implementing the Seventh Framework Programme of the European Community for Research, Technological Development and Demonstration Activities (2007 to 2013) (2006/971/EC). Brussels: EU COM.

EU COM – European Commission (2006b): Council Decision of 18 December 2006 Concerning the Seventh Framework Programme of the European Atomic Energy Community (Euratom) for Nuclear Research and Training Activities (2007 to 2011) (2006/970/Euratom). Brussels: EU COM.

EU COM – European Commission (2007a): Joint Technology Initiatives: Background, State-of-Play and Main Features. Commission Staff Working Document. Brussels: EU COM.

EU COM – European Commission (2007b): Green Paper. The European Research Area: New Perspectives {SEC(2007) 412}. Brussels: EU COM.

EU COM – European Commission (2007c): Preparing for the 'Health Check' of the CAP reform. Communication from the Commission. COM(2007) 722 final. Brussels: EU COM.

EU COM – European Commission (2008a): Joint Programming of Research. Communication from the Commission to the European Parliament, the Council, the European Economic and Social Committee and the Committee of the Regions of 15 July 2008: 'Towards Joint Programming in Research: Working Together to Tackle Common Challenges more Effectively' [COM(2008) 468 final]. Brussels: EU COM.

EU COM – European Commission (2008b): Establishing the European Institute of Innovation and Technology. Regulation (EC) No 294/2008 of the European Parliament and of the Council of 11 March 2008 Brussels: EU COM.

EU COM – European Commission (2008c): The Raw Materials Initiative — Meeting our Critical Needs for Growth and Jobs in Europe. COM(2008) 699. Brussels: EU COM.

EU COM – European Commission (2008d): Green Paper: Adapting to Climate Change in Europe – Options for EU Action. SEK(2007) 849. Brussels: EU COM.

EU COM – European Commission (2009a): Investing in the Development of Low Carbon Technologies (SET-Plan). COM(2009) 519 final. Brussels: EU COM.

EU COM – European Commission (2009b): Accompanying Document to the Communication from the Commission on Investing in the Development of Low Carbon Technologies (SET-Plan): A Technology Roadmap SEC(2009) 1295. Brussels: EU COM.

EU COM – European Commission (2010a): Energy-Efficient Buildings PPP. Multi-Annual Roadmap and Longer Term Strategy. Brussels: EU COM.

EU COM – European Commission (2010b): Cooperation Theme 6 – Environment (Including Climate Change). Catalogue of Projects 2009. Brussels: EU COM.

EU COM – European Commission (2010c): Food, Agriculture and Fisheries, and Biotechnology. About Knowledge-Based Bio-Economy (KBBE). Website: http://cordis.europa.eu/fp7/kbbe/about-kbbe_en.html (viewed 7. March 2011). Brussels: EU COM Community Research and Development Information (CORDIS).

EU COM – European Commission (2010d): Commission Staff Working Document: Financing for Development – Annual Progress Report 2010. Getting Back on Track to Reach the EU 2015 Target on ODA Spending? (SEC(2010)420). Brussels: EU COM.

EU COM – European Commission (2010e): Energy Infrastructure Priorities for 2020 and Beyond – A Blueprint for an Integrated European Energy Network. Communication from the Commission. COM(2010) 677/4 final. Brussels: EU COM.

EU COM – European Commission (2010f): Energy 2020. A Strategy for Competitive, Sustainable and Secure Energy. Communication from the Commission. COM(2010) 639 final. Brussels: EU COM.

EU COM – European Commission (2010g): World and European Sustainable Cities. Insights from EU Research. Brussels: European Commission Directorate-General for Research, Socio-Economic Sciences and Humanities.

EU COM – European Commission (2010h): Critical Raw Materials for the EU. Brussels: EU COM.

EU COM – European Commission (2011a): A Roadmap for Moving to a Competitive Low Carbon Economy in 2050. Communication from the Commission. COM(2011) 112 final. Brussels: EU COM.

EU COM – European Commission (2011b): Energy Efficiency Plan 2011. Communication from the Commission. COM(2011) 109 final. Brussels: EU COM.

EU COM – European Commission (2011c): Budget Breakdown of the Seventh Framework Programme of the European Community (EC) (2007-2013) and Euratom (2007-2011) (in EUR million). Website: http://cordis.europa.eu/fp7/budget_en.html (viewed 22. February 2011). Brussels: EU COM Community Research and Development Information.

EU COM – European Commission (2011e): Mission Statement of DG Energy. Developing and Implementing a European Energy Policy. Website: http://ec.europa.eu/dgs/energy/mission_en.htm (viewed 5. March 2011). Brussels: EU COM.

EU Covenant of Mayors (2010): How to Develop a Sustainable Energy Action Plan (SEAP). Brussels: European Union.

Eurobarometer (2006): Attitudes Towards Energy. Website: http://ec.europa.eu/public_opinion/archives/ebs/ebs_247_en.pdf (viewed 17. November 2010). Brussels: Europäische Kommission.

Eurobarometer (2007): Energy Technologies: Knowledge, Perception, Measures. Website: http://ec.europa.eu/public_opinion/archives/ebs/ebs_262_en.pdf (viewed 17. November 2010). Brussels: Europäische Kommission.

Eurobarometer (2009): Europeans' Attitudes Towards Climate Change. Website: http://ec.europa.eu/public_opinion/archives/ebs/ebs_313_en.pdf (viewed 17. November 2010). Brussels: Europäische Kommission (EU COM).

Eurostat (2001): Economy-Wide Material Flow Accounts and Derived Indicators – A Methodological Guide. Luxemburg: Office for Official Publications of the European Communities.

EvaConsult (2006): Bewertungsbericht zum Förderschwerpunkt 'Sozial-ökologische Forschung'. Berlin: EvaConsult.

Evans, K. R. (2008): An Abundance of Lithium. Santiago: World Lithium.

Evenson, R. E. and Gollin, D. (2003): Assessing the impact of the Green Revolution, 1960 to 2000. Science, 758–762.

Evers, A. and Zimmer, A. (2010): Third Sector Organizations Facing Turbulent Environments: Sports, Culture and Social Services in Five European Countries. Baden-Baden: Nomos.

Evolution MegaLab (2011): Evolution MegaLab: Alle verfügbaren historischen Daten über Bänderschnecken. Website: http://www.evolutionmegalab.org/de/information/viewBackground (viewed 14. March 2011). Berlin: Evolution MegaLab.

EWI – Energiewirtschaftliches Institut an der Universität Köln, Prognos AG and GWS – Institute of Economic Structures Research (2010): Energieszenarien für ein Energiekonzept der Bundesregierung. Projekt Nr. 12/10. Cologne, Basel, Osnabrück: EWI, Prognos, GWS.

EWZ – Energiewerke Zurich (2007): Ökologisch! Oder konventionell? Die Wahl Ihres persönlichen Stromprodukts hat viel bewirkt. Zurich: EWZ.

Faiers, A. and Neame, C. (2006): Consumer attitudes towards domestic solar power systems. Energy Policy 13 (14), 1797–1806.

Fanelli, D. (2009): How many scientists fabricate and falsify research? A systematic review and meta-analysis of survey data. PLoS ONE 4 (5), doi:10.1371/journal.pone.0005738

FAO – Food and Agriculture Organization of the United Nations (ed) (2003): World Agriculture: Towards 2015/2030. London: Earthscan.

FAO – Food and Agriculture Organization of the United Nations (2006): World Agriculture: Towards 2030/2050. Prospects for Food, Nutrition, Agriculture and Major Commodity Groups. Interim Report. Rome: FAO.

FAO – Food and Agriculture Organization of the United Nations (2008): The State of Food Insecurity in the World 2008. Rome: FAO.

FAO – Food and Agriculture Organization of the United Nations (2009a): Global Agriculture Towards 2050. High-Level Expert Forum – How to Feed the World in 2050. Rome: FAO.

FAO – Food and Agriculture Organization of the United Nations (2009b): The State of World Fisheries and Aquaculture 2008. Rome: FAO.

FAO – Food and Agriculture Organization of the United Nations (2009c): Food Security and Agricultural Mitigation in Developing Countries: Options for Capturing Synergies. Rome: FAO.

FAO – Food and Agriculture Organization of the United Nations (2009d): Review of Evidence on Drylands Pastoral Systems and Climate Change. Implications and Opportunities for Mitigation and Adaptation. Rome: FAO.

FAO – Food and Agriculture Organization of the United Nations (2010a): The Global Forest Resources Assessment 2010 – Key Findings. Rome: FAO.

FAO – Food and Agriculture Organization of the United Nations (2010b): The State of Food and Agriculture 2009. Livestock in the Balance. Rome: FAO.

FAO – Food and Agriculture Organization of the United Nations (2010c): Greenhouse Gas Emissions from the Dairy Sector. A Life Cycle Assessment. Rome: FAO.

FAO – Food and Agriculture Oganization of the United Nations (2011): Food Price Index. Website: http://www.fao.org/worldfoodsituation/wfs-home/foodpricesindex/en/ (viewed 10. March 2011). Rome: FAO.

FAO – Food and Agriculture Organization of the United Nations and IFAD – International Fund For Agricultural Development (2008): Financing Climate Change Adaptation and Mitigation in the Agriculture and Forestry Sectors. 'Submission by the Food and Agriculture Organization (FAO) and the International Fund for Agricultural Development (IFAD) to the UNFCCC'. Website: http://unfccc.int/resource/docs/2008/smsn/igo/015.pdf. Rome: FAO.

FAO – Food and Agriculture Organization of the United Nations, IIED – International Institute for Environment and Development and IFAD – International Fund For Agricultural Development (2009): Land Grab or Development Opportunity? Agricultural Investment and International Land Deals in Africa. Rome, London: FAO, IIED, IFAD.

Faust, J. (2006): Die Dividende der Demokratie. Politische Herrschaft und gesamtwirtschaftliche Produktivität. Politische Vierteljahresschrift 47 (1), 62–83.

Federal Government (2010): Etablierung der Nationalen Plattform Elektromobilität am 3. Mai 2010. Gemeinsame Erklärung von Bundesregierung und deutscher Industrie. Berlin: Bundesregierung.

Feinstein, N. (2011): Salvaging science literacy. Science Education 95 (1), 168–185.

Field, H. and Powell, P. (2001): Public understanding of science versus public understanding of research. Public Understanding of Science 10, 421–426

Figueres, C. (2008): Programmatic CDM: Regulatory Hurdles That Can Be Overcome. PoA Paper for IETA. Website: http://figueresonline.com/publications/PoA%20paper%20for%20IETA.pdf (viewed 16. February 2011). New York: United Nations Framework Convention on Climate Change.

Financial Times Germany (17.08.2010): Deutsche Bahn düpiert Autobranche. Der Schienenkonzern baut zurzeit die größte Flotte von Elektroautos bundesweit auf und integriert sie in sein Carsharing-Angebot Website: http://www.ftd.de/unternehmen/handel-dienstleister/:e-mobilitaet-deutsche-bahn-duepiert-autobranche/50157592.html (viewed 14. March 2011). Frankfurt/M.: Financial Times Germany.

Finzsch, N., Horton, J. O. and Horton, L. E. (1999): Von Benin nach Baltimore. Die Geschichte der African Americans. Hamburg: Hamburger Edition.

Fisahn, A. (2004): Effektive Beteiligung solange noch alle Optionen offen sind – Öffentlichkeitsbeteiligung nach der Aarhus-Konvention. Zeitschrift für Umweltrecht, 136–141.

Fischer, G. (2009): World Food and Agriculture to 2030/50: How do Climate Change and Bioenergy Alter the Long-Term Outlook for Food, Agriculture and Resource Availability? Rome: Food and Agriculture Organization.

Fischer, D. (2010): Comparing transitions: insights from the economic transition processes in former socialist countries for sustainability transitions. Osteuropa-Wirtschaft 55 (4), 289–310.

Fischer, C. and Newell, R. G. (2008): Environmental and technology policies for climate mitigation. Journal of Environmental Economics and Management 55, 142–162.

Fischer, C. and Fox, A. K. (2009): Comparing Policies to Combat Emissions Leakage. Border Tax Adjustments versus Rebates. Washington, DC: Resources for the Future.

Fischer-Kowalski, M. and Haberl, H. (1997): Stoffwechsel und Kolonisierung: Konzepte zur Beschreibung des Verhältnisses von Gesellschaft und Natur. In: Fischer-Kowalski, M., Haberl, H., Hüttler, W., Payer, H., Schandl, H., Winiwarter, V. and Zangerl–Weisz, H. (eds): Gesellschaftlicher Stoffwechsel und Kolonisierung von Natur. Ein Versuch in Sozialer Ökologie. Amsterdam: Gordon & Breach Fakultas, 3–12.

Fisher, B., Nakicenovic, N., Alfsen, K., Corfee-Morlot, J., de la Chesnaye, F., Hourcade, J. C., Jiang, K., Kainuma, M., La Rovere, E., Matysek, A., Rana, A., Riahi, K., Richels, R., Rose, S. and van Vuuren, D. (2007): Issues related to mitigation in the long-term context. Chapter 3. In: IPCC – Intergovernmental Panel on Climate Change (ed): Climate Change 2007 – Mitigation of Climate Change, Contribution of Working Group III to the Fourth Assessment Report of the Intergovernmental Panel on Climate Change. Geneva: IPCC.

Fishkin, J. S. (1991): Democracy and Deliberation. New Haven: Yale University Press.

Fishkin, J. S. (1995): The Voice of the People: Public Opinion and Democracy. New Haven: Yale University Press.

Fishkin, J. S. (2009): When the People speak! Deliberative Democracy and Public Consultation. Oxford, New York: Oxford University Press.

Flemes, D. (2010): Regional Leadership in the Global System. Ideas, Interests and Strategies of Regional Powers. Aldershot, UK: Ashgate.

Frankfurt, H. (2001): Freiheit und Selbstbestimmung. Ausgewählte Texte. Berlin: Akademie-Verlag.

Freedom House (2010): Freedom in the World 2010. Erosion of Freedom Intensifies. Washington, DC: Freedom House.

Freeman, C. (1992): The Economics of Hope. Essays on Technical Change, Economic Growth and the Environment. New York, London: Pinter Publishers.

Freeman, C. (1996): Long Wave Theory. International Library of Critical Writings in Economy. Cheltenham: Edward Elgar.

Freeman, C. and Louçã, F. (2001): As Time Goes By. From the Industrial Revolution to the Information Revolution. Oxford, UK: Oxford University Press.

Frenken, K., Saviotti, P. P. and Trommetter, M. (1999): Variety and niche creation in aircraft, helicopters, motorcycles and minicomputers. Research Policy 28, 469–488.

Frey, B. S. and Stutzer, A. (2002): Prozessnutzen in der Demokratie. In: Rehbinder, M. and Usteri, M. (eds): Glück als Ziel der Rechtspolitik. Bern: Stämpfli, 193–209.

Frey, B. S. and Stutzer, A. (2009): Glück: Die ökonomische Analyse. IEW Working Paper No. 417. Zurich: University Zurich. Institute for Empirical Research in Economics.

Friedlingstein, P., Houghton, R. A., Marland, G., Hackler, J., Boden, T. A., Conway, T. J., Canadell, J. G., Raupach, M. R., Ciais, P. and Le Quéré, C. (2010): Update on CO_2 emissions. Letter to the Editor. Nature Geoscience (advance online publication), 1–2.

Friedman, T. (2009): Was zu tun ist. Eine Agenda für das 21. Jahrhundert. Frankfurt/M.: Suhrkamp.

Fritsche, U. R. and Eberle, U. (2007): Treibhausgasemissionen durch Erzeugung und Verarbeitung von Lebensmitteln. Arbeitspapier. Darmstadt: Öko-Institut.

Frost & Sullivan (2010): Car Sharing – Auf dem Weg in eine grünere Zukunft. Website: http://www.frost.com/prod/servlet/press-release.pag?docid=193332392 (viewed 13. December 2010). London, Oxford, Frankfurt/M.: Frost & Sullivan.

Fuchs, W. T. (2009): Warum das Gehirn Geschichten liebt. Munich: Haufe-Lexware.

Fulton, M., Kahn, B. M., Mellquist, N., Soong, E., Baker, J. and Cotter, L. (2009): Paying for Renewable Energy: TLC at the Right Price. Achieving Scale through Efficient Policy Design. Frankfurt/M.: Deutsche Bank Group DB Advisors.

Fulton, M., Kahn, B. M., Mellquist, N., Soong, E., Baker, J. and Cotter, L. (2010): GET FiT Program – Global Energy Transfer Feed-in Tariffs for Developing Countries. Frankfurt/M.: Deutsche Bank Group DB Advisors.

Funtowicz, S. and Ravetz, O. (1993): The emergence of post-normal science. In: von Schomberg, R. (ed): Science, Politics, and Morality: Scientific Uncertainty and Decision Making. Dordrecht, Boston, London: Kluwer Academic Publishers, 85–123.

FVEE – Forschungsverbund Erneuerbare Energien (2010): Beitrag des FVEE zum 6. Energieforschungsprogramm der Bundesregierung. Forschungsaufgaben in den Bereichen erneuerbare Energien, Energieeffizienz und Systemintegration. Berlin: FVEE.

Galloway, J. N., Dentener, F., Capone, D. G., Boyer, E. W., Howarth, R. W., Seitzinger, S. P., Asner, G. P., Cleveland, C. C., Green, P. A., Holland, E. A., Karl, D. M., Michaelis, A. F., Porter, J. H., Townsend, A. R. and Vörösmarty, C. J. (2004): Nitrogen cycles: past, present, and future. Biogeochemistry 70, 153–226.

Gallup (2010): Americans' Global Warming Concerns Continue to Drop. Website: http://www.gallup.com/poll/126560/americans-global-warming-concerns-continue-drop.aspx (viewed 17. November 2010). Berlin, Brussels, London: Gallup.

Garz, H., Ötzsch, R., Haas, A., Wirtz, P. and Zank, S. (2009): Deutsche Stromversorger – In der CO_2-Falle? Ein neues Spiel hat begonnen. Düsseldorf: West LB.

Gates Foundation (2010): Agricultural Development. Website: http://www.gatesfoundation.org/agriculturaldevelopment/Pages/default.aspx (viewed 5. March 2011). Seattle, WA: Bill & Melinda Gates Foundation.

GCP – Global Carbon Project (2010): Carbon Budget. Summary Highlights (brief). Website: http://www.globalcarbonproject.org/carbonbudget/09/hl-compact.htm (viewed 5. January 2011). Canberra: Global Carbon Project.

GCP – Global Carbon Project (2011): Carbon Budget. Highlights (full). Website: http://www.globalcarbonproject.org/carbonbudget/09/hl-full.htm#ffcement (viewed 7. January 2011). Canberra: GCP.

GCRMN – Global Coral Reef Monitoring Network (1998): Status of Coral Reefs in the World. Website: http://www.gcrmn.org/publications.aspx (viewed 22. February 2011). Townsville: GCRMN.

GEA – Global Energy Assessment (2011): Global Energy Assessment. Laxenburg: IIASA (forthcoming).

Geißler, H. (2010): Schlichterspruch zu Stuttgart 21 am 30.11.2010, direkt übertragen von Phoenix-TV. Bonn: Phoenix.

Genth, M. (2008): Ist das neue Umwelt-Rechtsbehelfsgesetz europarechtskonform? NuR, 28–32.

Georgescu-Roegen, N. (1971): The Entropy Law and Economic Process. Cambridge, MA: Harvard University Press.

Gerhards, J., Offerhaus, A. and Roose, J. (2007): Die öffentliche Zuschreibung von Verantwortung, Zur Entwicklung eines inhaltsanalytischen Instrumentariums. Kölner Zeitschrift für Soziologie und Sozialpsychologie 59 (1), 105–124.

German Parliament (2003): Mehr Demokratie wagen durch ein Wahlrecht von Geburt an. Drucksache 15/1544. Berlin: German Parliament.

German Parliament (2008): Der Zukunft eine Stimme geben – Für ein Wahlrecht von Geburt an. Drucksache 16/9868. Berlin: German Parliament.

Germanwatch and Climate Action Network Europe (2008): Der Klimaschutz-Index. Ergebnis 2009. Bonn, Berlin, Brussels: Germanwatch, Climate Action Network Europe.

Germanwatch and Climate Action Network Europe (2009): Der Klimaschutz-Index. Ergebnis 2010. Bonn, Berlin, Brussels: Germanwatch, Climate Action Network Europe.

Giannakopoulos, A. and Tänzler, D. (2009): Deutsche Ansichten zur Korruption. Aus Politik und Zeitgeschichte 3–4, 13–18.

Giddens, A. (1984): Die Konstitution der Gesellschaft. Grundzüge einer Theorie der Strukturierung. Frankfurt/M.: Campus.

Giddens, A. (2009): The Politics of Climate Change. Oxford, UK: Oxford University Press.

Gilbert, R. (2001): Sustainable transportation. In: Munn, R. E. (ed): Encyclopedia of Global Environmental Change. Volume 4. London: Wiley, 426–435.

Gleditsch, N. P. and Sverdrup, B. O. (2002): Democracy and the environment. In: Page, E. A. and Redclift, M. (eds): Human Security and the Environment. International Comparisons. Cheltenham: Edward Elgar, 45–70.

GMF – The German Marshall Fund of the United States Ecologic Institute and Ecologic (2010): Transforming Economies Through Green Investment. Neds, Progress, and Policies. Washington, DC, Berlin: GMF and Ecologic Institute.

GO Science – The Government Office for Science (2011): Foresight. The Future of Food and Farming. London: GO Science.

Godfrey, H. C. J., Crute, I. R., Haddad, L., Lawrence, D., Muir, J. F., Nisbett, N., Pretty, J., Robinson, S., Toulmin, C. and Whiteley, R. (2010): The future of global food system. Philosophical Transactions of the Royal Society B 365, 2769–2777.

Goerres, A. and Tiemann, G. (2009): Kinder an die Macht? Die politischen Konsequenzen des stellvertretenden Elternwahlrecht. Politische Vierteljahresschrift 50 (1), 50–74.

Goldblatt, M. (2010): Comparison of emissions trading and carbon taxation in South Africa. Climate Policy 10, 511–526.

GRAAG – Global Research Alliance on Agricultural Greenhouse Gases (2010): Homepage. Information on the Alliance. Website: http://www.globalresearchalliance.org/ (viewed 7. March 2011). Wellington: GRAAG.

Graham, C. (2010): Happiness Around the World. The Paradox of Happy Peasants and Miserable Millionaires. Oxford, New York: Oxford University Press.

Green Investment Bank Commission (2010): Unlocking Investment to Deliver Britain's Low Carbon Future. Report. London: Green Investment Bank Commission.

Green, R. E., Cornell, S. J., Scharlemann, J. and Balmford, A. (2005): Farming and the fate of wild nature. Science 307, 550–555.

Gregory, P. J., Ingram, J. S. I. and Brklacich, M. (2005): Climate change and food security. Philosophical Transactions of the Royal Society B 360, 2139–2148.

Grin, J., Rotmans, J. and Schot, J. (2010): Transitions to Sustainable Development. New Directions in the Study of Long Term Transformative Change. London: Routledge.

Gross, P. (2005): Die Multioptionsgesellschaft. Frankfurt/M.: Suhrkamp.

Groß, T. (2009): Welche Klimaschutzpflichten ergeben sich aus Art. 20a GG? Zeitschrift für Umweltrecht 7–8, 364–367.

Grözinger, G. (1993): Achtung, Kind wählt mit! Ein Beitrag zur allmählichen Aufhebung der Diktatur der Gegenwart über die Zukunft. Blätter für deutsche und internationale Politik 38, 1261–1267.

Grübler, A. (1997): Time for a change: on the patterns of diffusion of innovation. In: Ausubel, J. and Langford, H. D. (eds): Technological Trajectories and the Human Environment Washington, DC: National Academies Press, 14–32.

Grübler, A. (2008a): Technology and Global Change. Cambridge, New York: Cambridge University Press.

Grübler, A. (2008b): Energy Transitions. Website: http://www.eoearth.org/article/Energy_transitions (viewed 7. August 2011). Washington, DC: The Encyclopedia of Earth.

Grübler, A. (2010): The costs of the French nuclear scale-up: A case of negative learning by doing. Energy Policy 38 (9), 5174–5188.

Grübler, A. and Nakicenovic, N. (1996): Decarbonizing the global energy system. Technological Forecasting and Social Change 53 (1), 97–110.

Grübler, A. and Riahi, K. (2010): Do governments have the right mix in their energy R&D portfolios? Carbon Management 1 (1), 79-87.

Grübler, A., O'Neill, B., Riahi, K., Chirkov, V., Goujon, A., Kolp, P., Prommer, I., Scherbov, S. and Slentoe, E. (2007): Regional, national, and spatially explicit scenarios of demographic and economic change based on SRES. Technological Forecasting and Social Change 74 (7), 980–1029.

Grundmann, R. (1999): Transnationale Umweltpolitik zum Schutz der Ozonschicht. USA und Deutschland im Vergleich. Papers of the Max Planck Institute for the Study of Societies. Volume 37. Frankfurt/M., New York: Campus.

GSI – Global Subsidies Initiative (2009): Achieving the G-20 Call to Phase Out Subsidies to Fossil Fuels. Policy Brief. Geneva, London: GSI.

Gu, J., Humphrey, J. and Messner, D. (2008): Global governance and developing countries. The implications of the rise of China. World Development 36 (2), 274–292.

Günther, K. (2006): Politik des Kompromisses. Dissensmanagement in pluralistischen Demokratien. Wiesbaden: VS.

Gupta, A. (2010): Transparency in Global Environmental Governance: A Coming of Age? GEP 10 (3), 1–9.

Gupta, S. and Tirpak, D. A. (2007): Policies, Instruments and Co-operative Arrangements. In: IPCC – Intergovernmental Panel on Climate Change (ed): Climate Change 2007: Mitigation. Contribution of Working Group III to the Fourth Assessment Report of the Intergovernmental Panel on Climate Change. Cambridge, New York: Cambridge University Press, 745–809.

Gurr, T. R. and Eckstein, H. (1975): Patterns of Authority: A Structural Basis for Political Inquiry. New York: Wiley.

Haas, E. B. (1958): The Uniting of Europe. Stanford: Stanford University Press.

Haas, P. M. (1992): Obtaining international environmental protection through epistemic communities. In: Rowlands, I. H. and Greene, M. (eds): Global Environmental Change and International Relations. Basingstoke: Macmillan Palgrave.

Haber, W., Bückmann, W. and Endres, E. (2010): Anpassung des Landmanagements in Europa an den Klimawandel. Natur und Recht 32, 377–383.

Haberl, H. (2006): The global socioeconomic energetic metabolism as a sustainability problem. Energy – The International Journal 31, 87–99.

Haberl, H., Erb, K. H., Krausmann, F., Gaube, V., Bondeau, A., Plutzar, C., Gingrich, S., Lucht, W. and Fischer-Kowalski, M. (2007): Quantifiying and mapping the human appropriation of net primary production in Earth's terrestrial ecosystems. Proceedings of the National Academy of Sciences 104 (31), 12942-12947.

Häcker, H. and Stapf, K. H. (1994): Dorsch Psychologisches Wörterbuch. Bern, Göttingen, Toronto, Seattle: Hans Huber.

Hajer, M. (1995): The Politics of Environmental Discourse. Oxford: Oxford University Press.

Halweil, B. and Nierenberg, D. (2011): Charting an new path to eliminating hunger. Worldwatch Institute (ed): State of the World 2011. Innovations that Nourish the Planet. Washington, DC: Worldwatch Institute, 3–12.

Hamilton, C. and Turton, H. (2002): Determinants of emissions growth in OECD countries. Energy Policy 30, 63–71.

Handoh, I. C. and Lenton, T. M. (2003): Periodic mid-cretaceous oceanic anoxic events linked by oscillations of the phosphorus and oxygen biogeochemical cycles. Global Biogeochemical Cycles 17 (4), doi:10.1029/2003GB002039.

Hansen, J. C. (2000): Environmental contaminants and human health in the Arctic. Toxicology Letters 112–113, 119–125.

Harich, J. (2010): Change resistance as the crux of the environmental sustainability problem. System Dynamics Review 26 (1), 35–72.

Hastings, A. and Wysham, D. B. (2010): Regime shifts in ecological systems can occur with no warning. Ecology Letters doi: 10.111/j.1461-0248.2010.01439.x, 9.

Hauschildt, J. (1997): Innovationsmanagement. Munich: Vahlen.

Hawkins, D. G., Lake, D. A., Nielson, D. L. and Tierney, M. J. (2006): Delegation under anarchy: states, international organizations and principal-agent theory. In: Hawkins, D. G., Lake, D. A., Nielson, D. L. and Tierney, M. J. (eds): Delegation and Agency in International Organizations. Cambridge, MA: Cambridge University Press, 3–38.

Heberer, T. and Senz, A. (2007): Die Rolle Chinas in der internationalen Politik. Innen- und außenpolitische Entwicklungen und Handlungsspielräume. DIE Discussion Paper. Bonn: German Development Institute.

Heidbrink, L. and Schmidt, I. (2009): Die neue Verantwortung der Konsumenten. Aus Politik und Zeitgeschichte 32–33, 27–32.

Hein, M. and Buchstein, H. (2009): Zufall mit Absicht. Das Losverfahren als Instrument einer reformierten Europäischen

Union. In: Brunkhorst, H. (ed): Demokratie in der Weltgesellschaft (= Soziale Welt Special Volume 18). Baden-Baden: Nomos, 351–384.

Heinberg, R. and Fridley, D. (2010): The end of cheap coal. Nature 468, 367–369.

Held, D., McGrew, A., Goldblatt, D. and Perraton, J. (1999): Global Transformations. Politics, Economics and Culture. Stanford: Stanford University Press.

Hellriegel, M. (2002): Mediation im Umweltrecht. Berlin: Duncker und Humblot.

Hellriegel, M. (2008): CO_2-Abscheidung und -Ablagerung. Teil 1: Anwendbarkeit und Anforderungen des geltenden Rechts. Recht der Energiewirtschaft 4, 111–117.

Helm, D. (2009): Infrastructure investment, the cost of capital, and regulation. An assessment. Oxford Review of Economic Policy 25 (3), 307–326.

Helm, D. (2010): Infrastructure and infrastructure finance: the role of the government and the private sector in the current world. EIB Papers 15 (2), 8–27.

Herr, H. (2001): Finanzströme und Verschuldung. In: Hauchler, I., Messner, D. and Nuscheler, F. (eds): Globale Trends 2002. Fakten, Analysen, Prognosen. Frankfurt/M.: Fischer, 267–287.

Herring, H. (2008): Rebound effect. In: Cleveland, C. J. (ed): Encyclopedia of Earth. Website: http://www.eoearth.org/article/Rebound_effect (viewed 1. March 2011). Washington, DC: Environmental Information Coalition, National Council for Science and the Environment.

Hertwich, E. G. (2005): Life cycle approaches to sustainable consumption: a critical review. Environmental Science & Technology 39 (13), 4673–4684.

Hertwich, E. G. and Peters, G. P. (2009): Carbon footprint of nations: a global, trade-linked analysis. Environmental Science & Technology 43 (16), 6414–6420.

Herz, J. H. (1950): Idealist internationalism and the security dilemma. World Politics 2, 157–180.

Herzog, H. J. (2010): Scaling up carbon dioxide capture and storage: from megatons to gigatons. Energy Economics doi:10.1016/j.eneco.2010.11.004.

Herzog, T. (2009): World Greenhouse Gas Emissions in 2005. WRI Working Paper. Website: http://www.wri.org/publication/navigating-the-numbers (viewed 13. April 2010). Washington, DC: World Resources Institute.

Hinze, J. and Kirchesch, K. (1999): Zusammenhang zwischen Gewinnen und Investitionen gelockert. HWWA-Konjunkturforum. Wirtschaftsdienst XI, 677–682.

Hirsch, F. (1977): Social Limits to Growth. London: To Excel/Kaleidoscope.

Hodgson, G. and Liebeler, J. (2002): The Global Coral Reef Crisis: Trends and Solutions 1997–2001. A Review of the First Five Years of Reef Check. Pacific Palisades, CA: The Reef Check Foundation.

Hoegh-Guldberg, O., Hoegh-Guldberg, H., Veron, J. E. N., Green, A., Gomez, E. D., Lough, J., King, M., Ambariyanto, Hansen, L., Cinner, J., Dews, G., Russ, G., Schuttenberg, H. Z., Peñafl or, E. L., Eakin, C. M., Christensen, T. R. L., Abbey, M., Areki, F., Kosaka, R. A., Tewfik, A. and Oliver, J. (2009): The Coral Triangle and Climate Change: Ecosystems, People and Societies at Risk. Full Report. Brisbane: WWF Australia.

Hoffmann, M., Hilton-Taylor, C., Angulo, A., Böhm, M., Brooks, T. M., Butchart, S. H. M., Carpenter, K. E., Chanson, J., Collen, B., Cox, N. A., Darwall, W. R. T., Dulvy, N. K., Harrison, L. R., Katariya, V., Pollock, C. M., Quader, S., Richman, N. I., Rodrigues, A. S. L., Tognelli, M. F., Vié, J.-C., Aguiar, J. M., Allen, D. J., Allen, G. R., Amori, G., Ananjeva, N. B., Andreone, F., Andrew, P., Aquino Ortiz, A. L., Baillie, J. E. M., Baldi, R., Bell, B. D., Biju, S. D., Bird, J. P., Black-Decima, P., Blanc, J. J., Bolaños, F., Bolivar-G., W., Burfield, I. J., Burton, J. A., Capper, D. R., Castro, F., Catullo, G., Cavanagh, R. D., Channing, A., Chao, N. L., Chenery, A. M., Chiozza, F., Clausnitzer, V., Collar, N. J., Collett, L. C., Collette, B. B., Cortez Fernandez, C. F., Craig, M. T., Crosby, M. J., Cumberlidge, N., Cuttelod, A., Derocher, A. E., Diesmos, A. C., Donaldson, J. S., Duckworth, J. W., Dutson, G., Dutta, S. K., Emslie, R. H., Farjon, A., Fowler, S., Freyhof, J., Garshelis, D. L., Gerlach, J., Gower, D. J., Grant, T. D., Hammerson, G. A., Harris, R. B., Heaney, L. R., Hedges, S. B., Hero, J.-M., Hughes, B., Hussain, S. A., Icochea M., J., Inger, R. F., Ishii, N., Iskandar, D. T., Jenkins, R. K. B., Kaneko, Y., Kottelat, M., Kovacs, K. M., Kuzmin, S. L., La Marca, E., Lamoreux, J. F., Lau, M. W. N., Lavilla, E. O., Leus, K., Lewison, R. L., Lichtenstein, G., Livingstone, S. R., Lukoschek, V., Mallon, D. P., McGowan, P. J. K., McIvor, A., Moehlman, P. D., Molur, S., Alonso, A. M., Musick, J. A., Nowell, K., Nussbaum, R. A., Olech, W., Orlov, N. L., Papenfuss, T. J., Parra-Olea, G., Perrin, W. F., Polidoro, B. A., Pourkazemi, M., Racey, P. A., Ragle, J. S., Ram, M., Rathbun, G., Reynolds, R. P., Rhodin, A. G. J., Richards, S. J., Rodríguez, L. O., Ron, S. R., Rondinini, C., Rylands, A. B., Sadovy de Mitcheson, Y., Sanciangco, J. C., Sanders, K. L., Santos-Barrera, G., Schipper, J., Self-Sullivan, C., Shi, Y., Shoemaker, A., Short, F. T., Sillero-Zubiri, C., Silvano, D. L., Smith, K. G., Smith, A. T., Snoeks, J., Stattersfield, A. J., Symes, A. J., Taber, A. B., Talukdar, B. K., Temple, H. J., Timmins, R., Tobias, J. A., Tsytsulina, K., Tweddle, D., Ubeda, C., Valenti, S. V., van Dijk, P. P., Veiga, L. M., Veloso, A., Wege, D. C., Wilkinson, M., Williamson, E. A., Xie, F., Young, B. E., Akçakaya, H. R., Bennun, L., Blackburn, T. M., Boitani, L., Dublin, H. T., da Fonseca, G. A. B., Gascon, C., Lacher Jr., T. E., Mace, G. M., Mainka, S. A., McNeely, J. A., Mittermeier, R. A., McGregor Reid, G., Rodriguez, J. P., Rosenberg, A. A., Samways, M. J., Smart, J., Stein, B. A. and Stuart, S. N. (2010): The impact of conservation on the status of the world´s vertebrates. Science 330, 1503–1509.

Hoffmann, W. G. (1965): Das Wachstum der Deutschen Wirtschaft seit der Mitte des 19. Jahrhunderts. Berlin, Heidelberg, New York: Springer.

Hoffmann-Riem, W. (1999a): Finanzkontrolle als Steuerungsaufsicht im Gewährleistungsstaat. Die Öffentliche Verwaltung, 221–227.

Hoffmann-Riem, W. (1999b): Telekommunikationsrecht als europäisiertes Verwaltungsrecht. Deutsches Verwaltungsblatt, 125–134.

Hofmann, M. and Schellnhuber, H. J. (2009): Oceanic acidification affects marine carbon pump and triggers extended marine oxygen holes. Proceedings of the National Academy of Sciences 106 (9), 3017–3022.

Holmes, I. and Mabey, N. (2010): Accelerating the Transition to a Low Carbon Economy. The Case for a Green Infrastructure Bank. London, Berlin: E3G Change Agents for Sustainable Development.

Holst, I. and Fischer, H. (2008): Das Ende der alten Zeit. Geo Epoche 30, 22–23.

Holstenkamp, L. and Ulbrich, S. (2010): Bürgerbeteiligung mittels Fotovoltaikgenossenschaften. Marktüberblick und Analyse der Finanzierungsstruktur. Working Paper Series in Business and Law volume 8. Lüneburg: Leuphana University Lüneburg.

Homer-Dixon, T. (2009): Carbon Shift. How the Twin Crisis of Oil Depletion and Climate Change Will Define the Future. Toronto: Random House.

Honohan, P. and Yoder, S. (2010): Financial Transactions Tax – Panacea, Threat, or Damp Squib? Policy Research Working Paper 5230. Washington, DC: World Bank.

Hooijer, A., Silvius, M., Wösten, H. and Pape, S. (2006): PEAT-CO_2. Assessment of CO_2 Emissions From Dained Peatlands in SE Asia. Delft: WL Delft Hydraulics.

Houghton, R. A. (2008): Carbon Flux to the Atmosphere from Land-Use Changes: 1850–2005. Falmouth, MA: Carbon Dioxide Information Analysis Center.

Hovi, J., Sprinz, D. and Underdal, A. (2009): Implementing long-term climate policy: Time inconsistency, domestic politics, international anarchy. Global Environmental Politics 9 (3), 20–39.

Hünenmörder, K. F. (2004): Die Frühgeschichte der globalen Umweltkrise und die Formierung der deutschen Umweltpolitik (1950–1973). Stuttgart: Franz Steiner.

Huntington, S. P. (1991): The Third Wave: Democratization in the Late Twentieth Century. Norman, OK: University of Oklahoma Press.

Hurrelmann, K. (1997): Für eine Herabsetzung des Wahlalters. In: Palentien, C. and Hurrelmann, K. (eds): Jugend und Politik. Neuwied: Luchterhand, 285.

Hutchings, J. A. and Myers, R. A. (1994): What can be learned from the collapse of a renewable resource? Atlantic cod, Gadus morhua, of Newfoundland and Labrador. Canadian Journal of Fisheries and Aquatic Sciences 51 (9), 2126–2146.

Hutchinson, C. F. and Herrmann, S. M. (2008): The Future of Drylands – Revisited. 50 Years of Drylands Research. Berlin: Springer.

IAASTD – International Assessment of Agricultural Knowledge Science and Technology for Development (2009): Agriculture at Crossroads. Global Report. Washington, DC: Island Press.

IAEA – International Atomic Energy Agency (2000): World Energy Assessment 2000. Energy and the Challenge of Sustainability. Paris: IAEA.

IAEA – International Atomic Energy Agency (2011): Latest News Related to Pris and the Status fo Nuclear Power Plants. Website: http://www.iaea.org/programmes/a2/ (viewed 5. March 2011). Paris: IAEA.

ICLEI – Local Governments for Sustainability (2009): International Local Government GHG Emissions Analysis Protocol (IEAP). Version 1.0. Bonn: ICLEI.

ICRAF – World Agroforestry Centre (2010): Annual Report 2009–2010: Going Evergreen for a Climate-SMART Agriculture. Nairobi: ICRAF.

ICSU – International Council of Scientific Unions (2010): Earth System Science for Global Sustainability. The Grand Challenges. Paris: ICSU.

ICSU – International Council of Scientific Unions, TWAS – The Academy of Science for the Developing World and ISTS – International Initiative on Science and Technology for Sustainable Development (2002): Science and Technology for Sustainable Development. Series on Science for Sustainable Development. Volume 9. Paris: ICSU, TWAS, ISTS.

IEA – International Energy Agency (2002): World Energy Outlook 2002. Paris: IEA.

IEA – International Energy Agency (2007): Mind the Gap. Quantifying Principal-Agent Problems in Energy Efficiency. Paris: IEA.

IEA – International Energy Agency (2008a): Deploying Renewables. Paris: IEA.

IEA – International Energy Agency (2008b): Energy Technology Perspectives 2008. Paris: IEA.

IEA – International Energy Agency (2008c): 2008 Energy Balance for World in Thousand Tonnes of Oil Equivalent (ktoe) on a Net Calorific Value Basis. Website: http://www.iea.org/stats/balancetable.asp?COUNTRY_CODE=29 (viewed 14. March 2011). Paris: IEA.

IEA – International Energy Agency (2009a): Energy Balances of OECD Countries. Paris: IEA.

IEA – International Energy Agency (2009b): World Energy Outlook 2009. Paris: IEA.

IEA – International Energy Agency (2010a): Energy Technology Perspectives 2010. Scenarios & Strategies to 2050. Paris: IEA.

IEA – International Energy Agency (2010b): Global Gaps in Clean Energy RD&D. Paris: IEA.

IEA – International Energy Agency (2010c): World Energy Outlook 2010. Paris: IEA.

IEA – International Energy Agency (2010d): Energy Balances of IEA Countries. Online Datenbank. Website: http://www.oecd-ilibrary.org/energy/data/energy-projections-for-iea-countries_eneforec-data-en (viewed 5. March 2011). Paris: IEA.

IEA – International Energy Agency (2010e): CO_2 Emissions from Fuel Combustion. 2010 Edition. Paris: IEA.

IEA – International Energy Agency (2010f): Energy Balances of non-OECD Countries. Paris: IEA.

IEA – International Energy Agency and OECD – Organization for Economic Co-operation and Development (2009): Cities, Towns and Renewable Energy. Paris: IEA, OECD.

IEA – International Energy Agency, OECD – Organisation for Economic Co-operation and Development, OPEC – Organization of the Petroleum Exporting Countries and World Bank (2010a): Analysis of the Scope of Energy Subsidies and Suggestions for the G-20 Initiative. IEA/OPEC/OECD/World Bank Joint Report prepared for Submission to the G-20 Summit Meeting Toronto (Canada), 26–27 June 2010, 16 June 2010. Paris, Washington, DC: IEA, OECD, World Bank.

IEA – International Energy Agency, UNDP – United Nations Development Programme and UNIDO – United Nations Industrial Development Organization (2010b): Energy Poverty – How to Make Modern Energy Access Universal? Paris, New York: IEA, UNDP, UNIDO.

IEG – Consultative Group of Ministers or High-level Representatives on International Environmental Governance (2010): Elaboration of Ideas for Broader Reform of International Environmental Governance. Information Note from the Co-Chairs of the Consultative Group of 27 October 2010. Nairobi: United Nations Environment Programme.

IIASA – International Institute for Applied Systems Analysis (2009): Representative Concentration Pathway Database. Website: Laxenburg: IIASA.

IISD – International Institute for Sustainable Development (2010): Summary of the Simultaneous Extraordinary COPs to the Basel, Rotterdam and Stockholm Conventions and the 11th Special Session of the UNEP Governing Council/Global Ministerial Environment Forum: 22–26 February 2010. Earth Negotiations Bulletin 16 (84), 15.

Illich, I. (1975): Tools for Conviviality. New York: Harper and Row.

Inglehart, R. (1977): The Silent Revolution. Changing Values and Political Styles among Western Publics. Princeton, NJ: Princeton University Press.

Inglehart, R. (1998): Modernisierung und Postmodernisierung. Kultureller, wirtschaftlicher und politischer Wandel in 43 Gesellschaften. Frankfurt/M., New York: Campus.

Inglehart, R. (2003): Human Values and Social Change. Findings from the Value Surveys. Leiden, Boston: Brill.

Inglehart, R. (2008): Changing values among western publics from 1970 to 2006. West European Politics 31 (1–2), 130–146.

Inglehart, R., Welzel, C. and Klingemann, H.-D. (2003): The theory of human development: a cross-cultural analysis. European Journal of Political Research 42, 341–379.

Inglehart, R., Foa, R., Peterson, C. and Welzel, C. (2008): Development, freedom and rising happiness: a global perspective 1981–2007. Perspectives Psychological Science 3 (4), 264–285.

Iniyan, S., Suganthi, L. and Samuel, A. A. (2001): A survey of social acceptance in using renewable energy sources for the new millennium. Renewable Energy 24 (3–4), 657–661.

Internet World Stats (2010): Internet World Stats. Usage and Population Statistics. Website: http://www.internetworldstats.com (viewed 9. February 2011). Internet World Stats.

IPCC – Intergovernmental Panel on Climate Change (1996): Revised 1996 IPCC Guidelines for National Greenhouse Gas Inventories. Geneva: IPCC.

IPCC – Intergovernmental Panel on Climate Change (2001): Climate Change 2001: The Scientific Basis. Contribution of Working Group I. Cambridge, New York: Cambridge University Press.

IPCC – Intergovernmental Panel on Climate Change (2005): Carbon Dioxide Capture and Storage. A Special Report of Working Group III of the IPCC. Cambridge, New York: Cambridge University Press.

IPCC – Intergovernmental Panel on Climate Change (2006): IPCC Guidelines for National Greenhouse Gas Inventories 2006. Berlin: Institute for Global Environmental Strategies (IGES).

IPCC – Intergovernmental Panel on Climate Change (2007a): Climate Change 2007: The Physical Science Basis. Working Group I Contribution to the Fourth Assessment Report. Cambridge, New York: Cambridge University Press.

IPCC – Intergovernmental Panel on Climate Change (2007b): Climate Change 2007: Impacts, Adaptation and Vulnerability. Working Group II Contribution to the Fourth Assessment Report. Cambridge, New York: Cambridge University Press.

IPCC – Intergovernmental Panel on Climate Change (2007c): Climate Change 2007: Mitigation of Climate Change. Working Group III Contribution to the Fourth Assessment Report. Cambridge, New York: Cambridge University Press.

Irmen, A. (2011): Ist Wirtschaftswachstum systemimmanent? Discussion Paper Series No. 509. Heidelberg: University Heidelberg, Department of Economics.

Irwin, A. (1995): Citizen Science. A Study of People, Expertise and Sustainable Development. Oxford, New York: Routledge.

Ismer, R. and Neuhoff, K. (2007): Border tax adjustment: a feasible way to support stringent emission trading. European Journal of Law and Economics 24, 137–164.

Ison, N. (2010): From Command and Control to Local Democracy. The Governance of Community Energy Projects. Mimeo, Berlin Conference on the Human Dimensions of Global Environmental Change 2010. Berlin 8.–9. October 2010. Berlin: Mimeo.

IUFRO – The Global Network for Forest Science Cooperation (2010): Embracing Complexity: Meeting the Challenges of International Forest Governance. A Global Assessment Report. Prepared by the Global Forest Expert Panel on the International Forest Regime. IUFRO World Series Volume 28. Wien: IUFRO.

IWMI – International Water Management Institute (2007): Water for Food. Water for Life. A Comprehensive Assessment of Water Management in Agriculture. London, New York: Earthscan.

Jachtenfuchs, M. and Kohler-Koch, B. (2003): Europäische Integration. Opladen: Leske + Budrich.

Jackson, T. (2009): Prosperity Without Growth? The Transition to a Sustainable Economy. London: Sustainable Development Commission.

Jacobsen, N. B. (2006): Industrial symbiosis in Kalundborg, Denmark: a quantitative assessment of economic and environmental aspects. Journal of Industrial Ecology 10, 239–255.

Jaeger, C. C., Horn, G. and Lux, T. (2009): Wege aus der Wachstumskrise. Potsdam, Kiel, Düsseldorf: European Climate Forum, Potsdam Institute for Climate Impact Research, Kiel Institute for the World Economy, Institut für Makroökonomie und Konjunkturforschung.

Jaeger, C. C., Paroussos, L., Mangalagiu, D., Kupers, R., Mandel, A. and Tabara, J. D. (2011): A New Growth Path for Europe. Generating Prosperity and Jobs in the Low-Carbon Economy. Synthesis Report PIK, University of Oxford, ICCS, Université Paris 1, European Climate Forum. Potsdam: Potsdam Institute for Climate Impact Research.

Jakob, M., Bosetti, V., Waisman, H., de Cian, E., Steckel, J., Leimbach, M. and Baumstark, L. (2009): The RECIPE Reference Scenarios. RECIPE Working Paper. Website: http://www.pik-potsdam.de/RECIPE (viewed 4. March 2010). Potsdam: Potsdam Institute for Climate Impact Research.

Jänicke, M. and Lindemann, S. (2009): Innovationsfördernde Umweltpolitik. In: Eifert, M. and Hoffmann-Riem, W. (eds): Innovationsfördernde Regulierung. Berlin: Duncker & Humblot, 171–195.

Jann, W. (1983): Staatliche Programme und 'Verwaltungskultur': Bekämpfung des Drogenmissbrauchs und der Jugendarbeitslosigkeit in Schweden, Großbritannien und der Bundesrepublik Deutschland im Vergleich. Opladen: Westdeutscher Verlag.

Jepma, C. J. and Nakicenovic, N. (2006): Sustainable Development and the Role of Gas. Hoersholm: International Gas Union.

Jobert, A., Laborgne, P. and Mimler, S. (2007): Local acceptance of wind energy. Factors of success identified in French and German case studies. Energy Policy 35 (5), 2751–2760.

Jochem, E., Battaglini, A., Cremer, C., Förster, H., Henning, E., Kasper, B., Köwener, D., Lass, W., Mannsbart, W., Meißner, F., Radgen, P., Rauschen, M., Riffeser, L., Schade, W., Toro, F., Wietschel, M., Jaeger, C., Bradke, H., Eichhammer, W., Hass, A., Idrissova, F., Köhler, J., Krause, J., Lilliestam, J., Müller, M., Pflüger, B., Ragwitz, M., Reitze, F., Saure, K., Sensfuß, F. and Walz, R. (2008): Investitionen für ein klimafreundliches Deutschland. Studie im Auftrag des Bundesministeriums für Umwelt, Naturschutz und Reaktorsicherheit. Synthesebericht. Potsdam: Potsdam Institute for Climate Impact Research.

Joosten, H. (2010): The Global Peatland CO_2 Picture. Peatland Status and Drainage Related Emissions in all Countries of the World. Greifswald: University Greifswald, Wetlands International.

Jörke, D. (2010): Was kommt nach der Postdemokratie? Zeitschrift für Bürgerrechte und Gesellschaftspolitik 190, 17–25.

Johnson, S. (2010): Where Good Ideas come From. The Natural History of Innovation. New York: Riverhead

Jungclaus, J. H., Lorenz, S. J., Timmreck, C., Reick, C. H., Brovkin, V., Six, K., Segschneider, J., Girogetta, M. A., Crowley, T. J., Pongratz, J., Krivova, N. A., Vieira, L. E., Solanki, S. K., Klocke, D., Botzet, M., Esch, M., Gayler, V., Haak, H., Raddatz, T. J., Roeckner, E., Schnur, R., Widmann, H., Claussen, M., Stevens, B. and Marotzke, J. (2010): Climate and carbon-cycle variability over the last millennium. Climate of the Past 6, 723–737.

Jureit, U. (2006): Generationenforschung. Göttingen: Vandenhoeck & Ruprecht.

Kahl, W. (2009): Die Kompetenzen der EU in der Energiepolitik nach Lissabon. EuR Europarecht 5 (44), 601–621.

Kahneman, D. and Tversky, A. (1979): Prospect Theory: An Analysis of Decision under Risk. Econometrica 47 (2), 263–291.

Kamal, A. (2010): Grameen Shakti's Renewable Energy Role. Dhaka: The Daily Star.

Kaplinsky, R. and Messner, D. (2008): The impacts of Asian Drivers on the developing world. World Development 36 (2), 197–209.

Kappel, R. (2011): Der Abstieg Europas und der Vereinigten Staaten – Verschiebungen in der Weltwirtschaft und der Weltpolitik. GIGA Focus Global 1/2011. Hamburg: GIGA.

Karns, M. P. and Mingst, K. A. (2004): International Organizations. The Politics and Processes of Global Governance. Boulder, CO: Lynne Rienner Publishers.

Kastenhofer, K. and Rammel, C. (2005): Obstacles to and potentials of the societal implementation of sustainable development: a comparative analysis of two case studies. Sustainability: Science, Practice & Policy 1 (2), 5–13.

Kates, R. W. (1996): Population, technology, and the human environment: a thread through time. Daedalus 125 (3), 1–29.

KBA – Federal Motor Transport Authority (2010): Bestand am Personenkraftwagen am 1. Januar 2010 nach Bundesländern und Kraftstoffarten absolut. Website: http://www.kba.de/cln_015/nn_269000/DE/Statistik/Fahrzeuge/Bestand/EmissionenKraftstoffe/2010__b__emi__eckdaten__absolut.html (viewed 13. December 2010). Flensburg: KBA.

Kennedy, P. (1988): The Rise and Fall of the Great Powers: Economic Change and Military Conflict from 1500–2000. New York: Harper Collins.

Kennedy, P. (2006): The Parliament of Man. The Past, Present, and Future of the United Nations. London: Allen Lane.

Kenny, C. (2007): Construction, Corruption, and Developing Countries. World Bank Policy Research Working Paper 4271. Washington, DC: World Bank.

Keohane, R. O. (2006): The contingent legitimacy of multilateralism. In: Newman, E., Thakur, R. and Tirman, J. (eds): Multilateralism under Challenge? Power, International Order, and Structural Change. Tokio: United Nations University, 55–76.

Keohane, R. O. and Nye, J. S. (2000): Globalization: What's new? What's not? (And so what?). Foreign Policy 118, 104–119.

Keohane, R. O. and Nye, J. S. (2001): Power and Interdependence. New York: Longman.

Keohane, R. O. and Victor, D. G. (2010): The Regime Complex for Climate Change. The Harvard Project on International Climate Agreements. Cambridge, MA: Harvard University.

Keyzer, M. A., Merbis, M. D., Pavel, I. F. P. W. and van Wesenbeeck, C. F. A. (2005): Diet shifts towards meat and the effects on cereal use: can we feed the animals in 2030? Ecological Economics 55, 187–202.

KfW Entwicklungsbank (2010): Startschuss für globalen Klimaschutzfonds. Mitteilung. Website: http://www.kfw-entwicklungsbank.de/DE_Home/KfW_Entwicklungsbank/Aktuelles/Archiv_2008_bis_2009/Startschuss_fuer_globalen_Klimaschutzfonds.jsp (viewed 16. February 2011). Frankfurt/M.: KfW.

Khanna, P. (2008): Der Kampf um die Zweite Welt. Berlin: Berlin-Verlag.

Klages, H. (2001): Werte und Wertewandel. In: Schäfers, B. and Zapf, W. (eds): Handwörterbuch zur Gesellschaft Deutschlands. Opladen: Westdeutscher Verlag, 726–738.

Klaus, T., Vollmer, C., Werner, K., Lehmann, H. and Müschen, K. (2010): Energieziel 2050: 100% Strom aus erneuerbaren Quellen. Dessau: Umweltbundesamt.

Klein, A., Held, A., Ragwitz, M., Resch, G. and Faber, T. (2008): Evaluation of Different Feed-In Tariff Design Options – Best Practice Paper for the International Feed-In Cooperation. Karlsruhe: Fraunhofer ISI, Energy Economics Group.

Kleiner, K. (2008): Nuclear energy: assessing the emissions. Nature Reports Climate Change 2, 130–131.

Kleinhückelkotten, S. (2006): Soziale Milieus als Zielgruppe für Nachhaltigkeitskommunikation. Vortrag im Rahmen der Expertenwerkstatt 'Zielgruppen für die Nachhaltigkeitskommunikation' 30.11.2006, Hannover. Hannover: 21-kom Kommunikation für eine nachhaltige Entwicklung.

Klima-KIC – Knowledge and Innovation Centers (2011): Climate Innovations to Europe. Website: www.climate-kic.org (viewed 5. March 2011). Brussels: Klima-KIC.

Kluckhohn, C. (1951): Values and value-orientation in the theory of action: An exploration in definition and classification. In: Parsons, T. and Shils, E. (eds): Toward a General Theory of Action. Cambridge, MA: Harvard University Press, 388–433.

Knopf, B., Edenhofer, O., Flachsland, C., Kok, M. T. J., Lotze-Campen, H., Luderer, G., Popp, A. and van Vuuren, D. P. (2010): Managing the low-carbon transition – from model results to policies. The Energy Journal 31, 223–245.

Koch, H.-J. and Hendler, R. (2009): Baurecht, Raumordnungs- und Landesplanungsrecht. Stuttgart: Richard Boorberg.

Köhler, H. (2011): Die Reform des Internationalen Währungssystems: ein Projekt kooperativer Weltwährungspolitik. Speech at the Eberhard Karls University Tübingen on 24. January 2011. Tübingen: Eberhard Karls University.

Kohler-Koch, B. (1993): Die Welt regieren ohne Weltregierung. In: Böhret, C. and Wewer, G. (eds): Regieren im 21. Jahrhundert. Zwischen Globalisierung und Regionalisierung. Opladen: Leske + Budrich, 109–141.

Kondratieff, N. (1926): Die langen Wellen der Konjunktur. Archiv für Sozialwissenschaft und Sozialpolitik 56, 573–609.

Kosakova, A. (2005): Switched on to Switching? A Survey of Consumer Behaviour and Attitudes, 2000–2005. NCC Findings. London: National Consumer Council (NCC).

Koselleck, R. (1990): Staat und Souveränität. In: Brunner, O., Conze, W. and Koselleck, R. (eds): Geschichtliche Grundbegriffe: Historisches Lexikon zur politisch-sozialen Sprache in Deutschland. Volume 6. Stuttgart: Klett-Cotta, 1–154.

Krausmann, F., Gingrich, S., Eisenmenger, N., Erb, K.-H., Haberl, H. and Fischer-Kowalski, M. (2009): Growth in global materials use, GDP and population during the 20th century. Ecological Economics 68 (10), 2696–2705.

Kreeb, M., Motzer, M. and Schulz, W. F. (2008): LOHAS als Trendsetter für das Nachhaltigkeitsmarketing. In: Schwender, C., Schulz, W. F. and Kreeb, M. W. (eds): Medialisierung der Nachhaltigkeit – Das Forschungsprojekt balance[f]: Emotionen und Ecotainment in den Massenmedien. Marburg: Metropolis, 303–314

Krey, V., Canadell, J. G., Nakicenovic, N., Abe, Y., Andruleit, H., Archer, D., Grübler, A., Hamilton, N. T. M., Johnson, A., Kostov, V., Lamarque, J.-F., Langhome, N., Nisbet, E. G., O´Neill, B., Riahi, K., Riedel, M., Wang, W. and Yakushev, V. (2009): Gas hydrates: entrance to a methane age or climate threat? Environmental Research Letters 4 (3), 1–6.

Krier, J.-M. (2008): Fair Trade 2007: New Facts and Figures From an Ongoing Success Story. A Report on Fair Trade in 33 Consumer Countries. A Survey on behalf of DAWS – Dutch Association of Worldschops. Website: http://www.european-fair-trade-association.org/efta/Doc/FT-E-2007.pdf (viewed 13. April 2010). Schin op Geul: European Fair Trade Association Head Office.

Kristof, K. (2010): Wege zum Wandel. Wie wir gesellschaftliche Veränderungen erfolgreich gestalten können. Munich: oekom.

Kroll, G. (2006): Rachel Carson – Silent Spring: A Brief History of Ecology as a Subversive Subject. Website: http://www.onlineethics.org/CMS/profpractice/exempindex/carsonindex/kroll.aspx (viewed 8. March 2010). Washington, DC: National Academy of Engineering Online Ethics Center.

Krosnick, J. A. (2010): The Climate Majority. New York: New York Times.

Kuckartz, U. (2010): Nicht hier, nicht jetzt, nicht ich – Über die symbolische Bearbeitung eines ernsten Problems. In: Welzer, H. (ed): KlimaKulturen: soziale Wirklichkeiten im Klimawandel. Frankfurt/M., New York: Campus, 144–160.

Kuckartz, U., Rheingans-Heintze, A. and Rädiker, S. (2008): Vertiefungsstudien im Rahmen des Projektes 'Repräsentativumfrage zu Umweltbewusstsein und Umweltverhalten im Jahr 2006' im Auftrag des Umweltbundesamtes. Berlin, Dessau: Umweltbundesamt.

Kumar, A. and Messner, D. (eds) (2010): Power Shifts and Global Governance. Challenges from South and North. London, New York: Anthem Press.

Kupchan, C. A., Adler, E., Coicaud, J.-M. and Khong, Y. F. (2001): Power in Transition: The Peaceful Change of International Order. Tokyo: UNU Press.

Küstenmacher, W. T. and Seiwert, L. (2004): Simplify your life: Einfacher und glücklicher leben. Frankfurt/M.: Campus.

Lake, D. A. (1993): Leadership, hegemony, and the international economy: naked emperor or tattered monarch with potential? International Studies Quarterly 37 (4), 459–489.

Lal, R. (2004): Soil carbon sequestration impacts on global climate change and food security. Science 304, 1623-1627.

Lal, R., Griffin, M., Apt, J., Lave, L. and Morgan, M. G. (2004): Managing soil carbon. Science 304, 393.

Lamla, J. and Neckel, S. (eds) (2006): Politisierter Konsum – konsumierte Politik. Wiesbaden: VS.

Landes, D. S. (1969): The Unbound Prometheus: Technological Change and Industrial Development in Western Europe from 1750 to the Present. Cambridge, UK: Cambridge University Press.

Landfried, C. (2002): Das politische Europa. Differenz als Potenzial der Europäischen Union. Baden-Baden: Nomos.

Langer, C. (2011): Wir haben das Ohr der Wirtschaft. Im Interview mit Barbara Gruber. Schrot&Korn 1, 28–31.

Latouche, S. (2010): Inzwischen kennt die französische Öffentlichkeit den Begriff 'Décroissance'. In: Seidl, I. and Zahrnt, A. (eds): Postwachstumsgesellschaft. Konzepte für die Zukunft. Marburg: Metropolis, 201–204.

Layard, R. (2005): Happiness: Lessons from a New Science. London: Penguin.

Le Quére, C., Raupach, M. R., Canadell, J. G. and Marland, G. (2009): Trends in the sources and sinks of carbon dioxide. Nature Geoscience 2, 831–836.

Leakey, R. and Lewin, R. (1996): Die sechste Auslöschung. Lebensvielfalt und die Zukunft der Menschheit. Frankfurt/M.: Fischer.

Leemans, R., Asrar, G., Busalacchi, A., Canadell, J. G., Ingram, J., Larigauderie, A., Money, H., Norbre, C., Partwardhan, A., Rice, M., Schmidt, F., Seitzinger, S., Virji, H., Vörösmarty, C. and Young, O. R. (2009): Developing a common strategy for integrative global environmental change research and outreach: the Earth System Science Partnership. Environmental Sustainability 1, 1–10.

Leggewie, C. (1995): Die 89er. Porträt einer Generation. Hamburg: Hoffmann und Campe.

Leggewie, C. (2003): Justus Liebig trifft Georg Büchner: Sturm und Dung — eine fiktive Begegnung. Chemie in unserer Zeit 37 (6), 410–415.

Leggewie, C. (2010): Klimaschutz erfordert Demokratiewandel. vorgänge 2, 35–43.

Leggewie, C. (2011): Bewegte arabische Welt. Kommentar. Berlin: taz (21.01.2011).

Leggewie, C. and Welzer, H. (2009): Das Ende der Welt, wie wir sie kannten. Klima, Zukunft und die Chancen der Demokratie. Frankfurt/M.: Fischer.

Lehmann, P. (2009): Climate Policies with Pollution Externalities and Learning Spillovers. Leipzig: Helmholtz Centre for Environmental Research.

Lehmbruch, G. (2002): Der unitarische Bundesstaat in Deutschland: Pfadabhängigkeit und Wandel. MPIfG Discussion Paper 2002/2. Cologne: Max Planck Institute for the Study of Societies.

Lehmbruch, G. (2003): Verhandlungsdemokratie. Wiesbaden: Westdeutscher Verlag.

Leibfried, S., Nullmeier, F. and Winter, G. (2010): Möglichkeiten einer globalen Transformation hin zu einer klimaverträglichen Gesellschaft. Expertise for the WBGU Report 'World in Transition: A Social Contract for Sustainability'. Website: http://www.wbgu.de/wbgu_jg2011_Expertise_Winter.pdf. Berlin: WBGU.

Leimbach, M., Bauer, N., Baumstark, L., Lüken, M. and Edenhofer, O. (2010): Technological Change and International Trade – Insights from REMIND-R. The Energy Journal 31 (2), 109–136.

Leinfelder, R. (2009): Wie kann Wissenschaft für die Öffentlichkeit attraktiv gestaltet werden? Ein Vorgehen mit allen Sinnen am Beispiel des Museums für Naturkunde Berlin. In: Hanft, A. and Knust, M. (eds): Weiterbildung im Elfenbeinturm!? Münster, New York, Munich, Berlin: Waxmann, 113–121.

Leinfelder, R. (2010a): Vom Handeln zum Wissen – das Museum zum Mitmachen. In: Damaschun, F., Hackethal, S., Landsberg, H. and Leinfelder, R. (eds): Klasse, Ordnung, Art. 200 Jahre Museum für Naturkunde. Rangsdorf: Basilisken-Presse, 62–67.

Leinfelder, R. (2010b): Wir sind kein reiner Zufall! Evolution und Kreationismus. In: Gerhardt, V. and Schulte, D. (eds): Faszination Leben. Munich: Fink, 125–149.

Leiserowitz, A. A., Kates, R. W. and Parris, T. M. (2006): Sustainability values, attitudes, and behaviors: a review of multinational and global trends. Annual Review of Environment and Resources 31, 413–444.

Leiserowitz, A., Maibach, E., Roser-Renouf, C. and Smith, N. (2010): Climate Change in the American Mind: Public Support for Climate & Energy Policies in June 2010. Yale Project on Climate Change Communication. Website: http://environment.yale.edu/climate/files/PolicySupportJune2010.pdf (viewed 17. November 2010). New Haven, CT: Yale University and George Mason University.

Lell, O. (2010): Dienste für Bürger und Verbraucher. Politische Perspektiven für Stromversorgung, Wasserwirtschaft und Bahnverkehr. Gutachten im Auftrag des Gesprächkreises Verbraucherpolitik der Friedrich-Ebert-Stiftung. Bonn: Friedrich-Ebert-Stiftung.

Lenzen, M. (2008): Life cycle energy and greenhouse gas emissions of nuclear energy: a review. ScienceDirect 49, 2178–2199.

Leopoldina (2009): Konzept für ein integriertes Energieforschungsprogramm für Deutschland. Halle/Saale: Deutsche Akademie der Naturforscher Leopoldina.

Lepsius, M. R. (2000): Die Europäische Union als rechtlich konstituierte Verhaltensstrukturierung. In: Dreier, H. (ed): Rechtssoziologie am Ende des 20. Jahrhunderts. Tübingen: Mohr Siebeck, 289–305.

Lesage, D., van de Graaf, T. and Westphal, K. (2009): The G8's Role in Global Energy Governance Since the 2005 Gleneagles Summit. Global Governance: A Review of Multilateralism and International Organizations 15 (2), 259–277.

Lesage, D., van den Graaf, T. and Westphal, K. (2010): Global Energy Governance in a Multipolar World. Surrey: Ashgate.

Lesser, J. A. and Su, X. (2008): Design of an economically efficient feed-in tariff structure for renewable energy development. Energy Policy 36, 981–990.

Levinthal, D. A. (1998): The slow pace of rapid technological change: gradualism and punctuation in technological change. Industrial and Corporate Change 7 (2), 217–247.

Levy, D. L. and Egan, D. (2003): A neo-gramscian approach to corporate political strategy: conflict and accommodation in the climate change negotiations. Journal of Management Studies 40 (4), 803–829.

Li, Q. and Reuveny, R. (2006): Democracy and environmental degradation. International Studies Quarterly 50, 935–956.

Li, F., Stolarski, R. S. and Newman, P. A. (2009): Stratospheric ozone in the post-CFC era. Atmospheric Chemistry and Physics 9, 2207–2213.

Lichtblick (2010): Das ZuhauseKraftwerk. Kundeninformation. Website: http://www.lichtblick.de/h/Ueberblick_286.php (viewed 15. March 2011). Berlin: Lichtblick.

Liebig, J. (1840): Die organische Chemie in ihrer Anwendung auf Agricultur und Physiologie. Braunschweig: Viehweg.

Liebig, J. (1842): Die Thierchemie oder die organische Chemie in ihrer Anwendung auf Physiologie und Pathologie. Braunschweig: Viehweg.

Liebowitz, S. J. and Margolis, S. E. (1995): Path dependence, lock-in and history. Journal of Law, Economics, and Organization 11, 205–226.

Lindenthal, A. (2009): Leadership im Klimaschutz. Die Rolle der Europäischen Union in der internationalen Umweltpolitik. Frankfurt/M.: Campus.

Lindenthal, A. (2010): Die G20-Umweltreform als Element einer Dekarbonisierungsstrategie. Annex to Expertise for the WBGU Report 'World in Transition: A Social Contract for Sustainability'. Website: http://www.wbgu.de/wbgu_jg2011_Expertise_Winter.pdf. Berlin: WBGU.

Loorbach, D., van Bakel, J., Whiteman, G. and Rotmans, J. (2010): Business strategies for transitions towards sustainable systems. Business Strategy and the Environment 19, 133–146.

Lorenzoni, I., Nicholson-Cole, S. and Whitmarsh, L. (2007): Barriers perceived to engaging with climate change among public and their policy implications. Global Environmental Change 17, 445–459.

Lotze-Campen, H., Popp, A., Beringer, T., Müller, C., Bondeau, A., Rost, S. and Lucht, W. (2009): Scenarios of global bioenergy production: the trade-offs between agricultural expansion, intensification and trade. Ecological Modelling 221 (18), 2188–2196.

Lübbert, D. (2007): CO_2 Bilanzen verschiedener Energieträger in Vergleich – Zur Klimafreundlichkeit von fossilen Energien und erneuerbaren Energien. Berlin: Parliament of the Federal Republic of Germany.

MA – Millennium Ecosystem Assessment (2005a): Ecosystems and Human Well-Being. Summary for Decision Makers. Washington, DC: Island Press.

MA – Millennium Ecosystem Assessment (2005b): Ecosystems and Human Well-Being. Current State and Trends. Washington, DC: Island Press.

MA – Millennium Ecosystem Assessment (2005c): Ecosystems and Human Well–Being. Synthesis. Washington, DC: World Resources Institute.

MA – Millennium Ecosystem Assessment (2005d): Living Beyond Our Means. Natural Assets and Human Well–being. Statement from the Board. New York: MA Board.

MA – Millennium Ecosystem Assessment (2005e): Ecosystems and Human Well-Being: Desertification Synthesis. Washington, DC: World Resources Institute.

Mackenzie, F. T., Ver, L. M. and Lerman, A. (2002): Century-scale nitrogen and phosphorus controls of the carbon cycle. Chemical Geology 190, 13–32.

Macknick, J. (2009): Energy and Carbon Dioxide Emission Data Uncertainties. IIASA Interim Report IR-09-32. Laxenburg: International Institute for Applied Systems Analysis.

Maddisson, A. (2010): Historical Statistics of the World Economy: Statistics on World Population, GDP and Per Capita GDP 1–2008 AD. Groningen: Groningen Growth and Development Centre.

Magliveras, K. (1995): Best intentions but empty words: the European Ombudsman. European Law Review 4, 401–409.

Malloch-Brown, M. (2008): Can the UN be reformed? Global Governance: A Review of Multilateralism and International Organizations 14 (1), 1–12.

Malthus, T. R. (1798): Essay on the Principle of Population. London: Johnson.

Mann, M. E., Zhang, Z., Hughes, M. K., Bradley, R. S., Miller, S. K., Rutherford, S. and Ni, F. (2008): Proxy-based reconstructions of hemispheric and global surface temperature variations over the past two millennia. Proceedings of the National Academy of Sciences 105 (36), 13252–13257.

Mannheim, K. (1964): Das Problem der Generationen. In: Wolff, K. H. (ed): Wissenssoziologie. Auswahl aus dem Werk. Neuwied, Berlin: Luchterhand, 509–565.

Mansbridge, J. (2003): Rethinking representation. American Political Science Review 97 (4), 515–528.

Maras, K. (2009): Lobbyismus in Deutschland. Aus Politik und Zeitgeschichte 3–4, 33–38.

Marlow, H. J., Hayes, W. K., Soret, S., Carter, R. L., Schwab, E. R. and Sabatê, J. (2009): Diet and the environment: does what you eat matter? The American Journal of Clinical Nutrition 89 (supplement), 1699S–1703S.

Marshall, M. G. and Cole, B. R. (2009): Global Report 2009. Conflict, Governance, and State Fragility. Wien: Center for Systemic Peace and Center for Global Policy.

Marshall, T. H. (1992): Bürgerrechte und soziale Klassen. Zur Soziologie des Wohlfahrtsstaates. Frankfurt/M.: Campus.

Martinez-Alier, J., Pascual, U., Vivien, F.-D. and Zaccai, E. (2010): Sustainable de-growth: mapping the context, criticsms and future prospects of an emergent paradigm. Ecological Economics 69, 1741–1747.

Masing, J. (1997): Die Mobilisierung des Bürgers für die Durchsetzung des Rechts. Berlin: Duncker & Humblot.

Matthes, F. (2010): Der Instrumenten-Mix einer ambitionierten Klimapolitik im Spannungsfeld von Emissionshandel und anderen Instrumenten. Bericht für das Bundesministerium für Umwelt, Naturschutz und Reaktorsicherheit. Berlin: BMU.

Mattoo, A., Subramanian, A., van der Mensbrugghe, D. and He, J. (2009): Reconciling Climate Change and Trade Policy. Washington, DC: Peterson Institute for International Economics.

Maunz, T. and Dürig, G. (2010): Grundgesetz. Loseblatt-Kommentar. Munich: Beck.

Mayntz, R. (1997): Soziale Dynamik und politische Steuerung: theoretische und methodologische Überlegungen. Frankfurt/M.: Campus.

Mayntz, R. (2002): Kausale Rekonstruktion: Theoretische Aussagen im akteurzentrierten Institutionalismus. Mannheimer Vorträge Nr. 17. Mannheim: Mannheimer Zentrum für Europäische Sozialforschung.

Mayntz, R. (2009): Über Governance. Institutionen und Prozesse politischer Regelung. Schriften aus dem Max-Planck-Insitut für Gesellschaftsforschung. Volume 62. Frankfurt/M.: Campus.

McKinsey (2009): Pathways to a Low-Carbon Economy. Version 2 of the Global Greenhouse Gas Abatement Cost Curve. Report. New York: McKinsey & Company.

NorGer (2011): NorGer in Zahlen. Website: http://www.norger.biz/norger/deutsch/das_projekt/article45629.ece (viewed 13. January 2011). Kristiansand: NorGer.

Nullmeier, F. and Dietz, M. (2010): Möglichkeiten einer globalen Transformation hin zu einer klimaverträglichen Gesellschaft – institutionelle, instrumentelle und legitimatorische Anforderungen. Part 1 of the Expertise for the WBGU Report 'World in Transition: A Social Contract for Sustainability'. Website: http://www.wbgu.de/wbgu_jg2011_Expertise_Winter.pdf. Berlin: WBGU.

Nünning, V. and Nünning, A. (2002): Erzähltheorie transgenerisch, intermedial, interdisziplinär. Trier: WVT.

Nuscheler, F. and Messner, D. (2009): Wandel von weltpolitischen Kräftekonstellationen und Machtordnungen. In: Debiel, T., Messner, D., Nuscheler, F., Roth, M. and Ulbert, C. (eds): Globale Trends 2010. Frieden, Entwicklung, Umwelt. Frankfurt/M.: Fischer, 35–60.

Oasa, E. K. (1987): The political economy of international agricultural research in glass. In: Glaeser, B. (ed): The Green Revolution Revisited: Critique and Alternatives. Sydney: Allen & Unwin, 13–55.

Oberthür, S. and Gehring, T. (2005): Reforming international environmental governance: an institutional perspective on proposals for a World Environment Organization. In: Biermann, F. and Bauer, S. (eds): A World Environment Organization: Solution or Threat for Effective International Environmental Governance? Aldershot: Ashgate, 205–235.

ODI – Overseas Development Institute (2008): The Global Financial Crisis and Developing Countries. ODI Background Note. London: ODI.

Odum, H. T. (1971): Environment, Power and Society. New York: Wiley.

OECD – Organization for Economic Co-operation and Development (2001): Environmentally Related Taxes in OECD Countries – Issues and Strategies. Paris: OECD.

OECD – Organization for Economic Co-operation and Development (2008): OECD Umweltausblick bis 2030. Paris: OECD.

OECD – Organization for Economic Co-operation and Development (2009a): The Economics of Climate Change Mitigation. Policies and Options for Global Action Beyond 2012. Paris: OECD.

OECD – Organization for Economic Co-operation and Development (2009b): Eco-Innovation in Industry. Paris: OECD.

OECD – Organization for Economic Co-operation and Development (2010a): Interim Report of the Green Growth Strategy: Implementating our Commitment for a Sustainable Future. Meeting of the Council at Ministerial Level, 27–28 May 2010. C/MIN(2010)5. Paris: OECD.

OECD – Organisation for Economic Co-operation and Development (2010b): The OECD Innovation Strategy. Getting a Head Start on Tomorrow. Paris: OECD.

OECD – Organization for Economic Co-operation and Development (2010c): Perspectives on Global Development 2010: Shifting Wealth. Paris: OECD.

OECD – Organization for Economic Co-operation and Development (2010d): Cities and Climate Change. Paris: OECD.

Offe, C. (1972): Strukturprobleme des kapitalistischen Staates. Aufsätze zur politischen Soziologie. Frankfurt/M.: Campus.

Offe, C. and Guggenberger, B. (1984): An den Grenzen der Mehrheitsdemokratie. Politik und Soziologie der Mehrheitsregel. Opladen: Heun.

Ohlhorst, D. (2009): Windenergie in Deutschland. Konstellationen, Dynamiken und Regulierungspotenziale im Innovationsprozess. Wiesbaden: VS Research.

Ohndorf, M., Schubert, R. and Rohling, M. (2010): Mainstreaming Impact Over Time – Who Measures What For Whom? Prepared for the KfW Financial Sector Development Symposium 2008 'Greening the Financial Sector – How to Mainstream Environmental Finance in Developing Countries'. Zurich: ETH.

Ökologisches Wirtschaften (2007): Wirtschaftswissenschaften für Nachhaltigkeit. Sonderveröffentlichung des BMBF in der Zeitschrift Ökologisches Wirtschaften, Heft 4. Munich: oekom.

Oldeman, L. R., Hakkeling, R. T. A. and Sombroek, W. (1990): World Map of the Status of Human-Induced Soil Degradation. Explanatory Note. Wageningen: International Soil Reference and Information Centre.

Oldeman, L. R., Hakkeling, R. T. A. and Sombroek, W. G. (1991): World Map of the Status of Human-Induced Soil Degradation. Global Assessment of Soil Degradation GLASOD. Wagingen: International Soil Reference and Information Centre.

Osterhammel, J. (2009): Die Verwandlung der Welt. Eine Geschichte des 19. Jahrhunderts. Munich: Beck.

Ostrom, E. (2003): Toward a behavioral theory linking trust, reciprocity, and reputation. In: Ostrom, E. and Walker, J. (eds): Trust and Reciprocity. New York: Russels Sage Foundation, 19–79.

Ostrom, E. (2009): A Polycentric Approach for Coping with Climate Change. Background Paper to the 2010 World Development Report. Policy Research Paper 5095. Washington, DC: World Bank.

Ostrom, E. (2010): Polycentric systems for coping with collective action and global environmental change. Global Environmental Change 20, 550–557.

Ostrom, E. and Walker, J. (2003): Trust and Reciprocity: Interdisciplinary Lessons from Experimental Research. New York: Russell Sage Foundation.

Oswald, A. J. (1997): Happiness and economic performance. Economic Journal 107 (5), 1815–1831.

Otto, F. (2008): Der Prophet des Kapitalismus. Geo Epoche 30, 38–39.

Paech, N. (2005): Nachhaltiges Wirtschaften jenseits von Innovationsorientierung und Wachstum. Marburg: Metropolis.

Paech, N. (2009a): Die Postwachstumsökonomie – ein Vademecum. Zeitschrift für Sozialökonomie 46 (160–161), 28–31.

Paech, N. (2009b): Wachstum light? Qualitatives Wachstum ist eine Utopie. Wissenschaft & Umwelt Interdisziplinär 13 (84–93),

Park, R. E. (1928): Human migration and the marginal man. American Journal of Sociology 33, 881–893.

Parks, B. C. and Roberts, J. T. (2006): Environmental and ecological justice. In: Betsill, M. M., Hochstetler, K. and Stevis, D. (eds): International Environmental Politics. Houndmills, Basingstoke: Palgrave Macmillan.

Parson, E. A. (2003): Protecting the Ozone Layer: Science and Strategy. Oxford, New York: Oxford University Press.

Pattberg, P. H. (2007): Private Institutions and Global Governance. The New Politics of Environmental Sustainability. Cheltenham, UK: Edward Elgar.

Pauly, D. (1995): Anecdotes and the shifting baseline syndrome of fisheries. Trends in Ecology & Evolution 10, 430.

Payne, R. A. (1995): Freedom and the environment. Journal of Democracy 6 (3), 41–55.

PBL – Netherlands Environmental Assessment Agency (2009a): Growing within Limits. A Report to the Global Assembly 2009 of the Club of Rome. Bilthoven: PBL.

PBL – Netherlands Environmental Assessment Agency (2009b): Meeting the 2 °C Target. From Climate Objective to Emission Reduction Measures. Bilthoven: PBL.

PBL – Netherlands Environmental Assessment Agency (2010): Rethinking Global Biodiversity Strategies. Exploring Structural Changes in Production and Consumption to Reduce Biodiversity Loss. Bilthoven: PBL.

Pereira, H. M., Leadley, P. W., Proenca, V., Alkemade, R., Scharlemann, J. P. W., Fernandez-Manjarres, J. F., Araujo, M. B., Balvanera, P., Biggs, R., Cheung, W. W. L., Chini, L., Cooper, H. D., Gilman, E. L., Guenette, S., Hurtt, G. C., Huntington, H. P., Mace, G. M., Oberdorff, T., Revenga, C., Rodrigues, P., Scholes, R. J., Sumaila, U. R. and Walpole, M. (2010): Scenarios for global biodiversity in the 21st century. Science 330, 1496–1501.

Perez, C. (2002): Technological Revolutions and Financial Capital – The Dynamics of Bubbles and Golden Ages. Cheltenham, UK: Edward Elgar.

Perlmutter, D. D. (2008): Blogwars: The New Political Battleground. Oxford, New York: Oxford University Press.

Peters, G. and Hertwich, E. (2008a): Post-Kyoto greenhouse gas inventories: production versus consumption. Climatic Change 86 (1), 51–66.

Peters, G. P. and Hertwich, E. G. (2008b): CO_2 embodied in international trade with implications for global climate policy. Environmental Science & Technology 42 (5), 1401–1407.

Petrini, C. (2007): Gut, sauber und fair. Grundlagen einer neuen Gastronomie. Wiesbaden: TreTorri.

Pew Research Center (2009): Modest Support for 'Cap and Trade' Policy. Fewer Americans See Solid Evidence of Global Warming. Website: http://people-press.org/reports/pdf/556.pdf (viewed 17. November 2010). Washington, DC: Pew Research Center.

Piepenbrink, J. (2009): Editorial Korruption. Aus Politik und Zeitgeschichte 3–4, 2.

Pierson, P. (2000): Increasing return, path dependence, and the study of politics. American Political Science Review 94, 251–268.

Pierson, P. (2004): Politics in Time – History, Institutions and Social Analysis. Princeton, New York: Princeton University Press.

PIK – Potsdam Institute für Climate Impact Research (2007): Potsdam-Memorandum: Main Conclusions from the Symposium 'Global Sustainability: A Nobel Cause', Potsdam, Germany, 8-10 October 2007. The Need for a Great Transformation. Potsdam: PIK.

Polanyi, K. (1944): The Great Transformation: The Political and Economic Origins of our Time. Boston, MA: Beacon Press.

Pollack, M. A. (2003): The Engines of European Integration: Delegation, Agency and Agenda Setting in the EU. Oxford, NY: Oxford University Press.

Pollack, M. A. (2006): Delegation and discretion in the European Union. In: Hawkins, D. G., Lake, D. A., Nielson, D. L. and Tierney, M. J. (eds): Delegation and Agency in International Organizations. Cambridge, UK: Cambridge University Press, 165–196.

Popp, A., Lotze-Campen, H. and Bodirsky, B. (2010): Food consumption, diet shifts and associated non-CO_2 greenhouse gases from agricultural production. Global Environmental Change doi:10.1016/j.gloenvcha.2010.02.001, 451–462.

Porter, A. L. and Rafolds, I. (2009): Is science becoming more interdisciplinary? Measuring and mapping six research fields over time. Scientometrics 81, 719–745.

Pötter, B. (2010): Ausweg Öko-Diktatur? Wie unsere Demokratie an der Umweltkrise scheitert. Munich: oekom.

Priewe, J. and Rietzler, K. (2010): Deutschlands nachlassende Investitionsdynamik 1991–2010. Ansatzpunkte für ein neues Wachstumsmodell. Expertise im Auftrag der Abteilung Wirtschafts- und Sozialpolitik der Friedrich-Ebert-Stiftung. Bonn: Friedrich-Ebert-Stiftung.

Programm Transfer-21 (2007): Bildung für nachhaltige Entwicklung in der Lehrerbildung – Kompetenzerwerb für zukunftsorientiertes Lehren und Lernen. Berlin: Programme Transfer-21, Coordination Center University Berlin.

Project Catalyst (2010): From Climate Finance to Financing Green Growth. Brussels: Climate Works Foundation, European Climate Foundation (ECF).

Prugh, T., Flavin, C. and Sawin, J. L. (2005): Changing the oil economy. In: Worldwatch Institute (ed): State of the World 2005: Redefining Global Security. Washington, DC: Worldwatch Institute, 100–120.

PT DLR – Project Management Agency – Part of the German Aerospace Center (2007): Sozial-ökologische Forschung. Rahmenkonzept 2007–2010. Bonn: PT DLR.

PTRC – Petroleum Technology Research Centre (2011): IEA-GHG Weyburn-Midale CO_2 Monitoring & Storage Project. Response to the Petro-Find Geochem. LTD. Study. Regina, SK, Canada: PTRC.

Putterman, L. (2008): Agriculture, diffusion and development: ripple effects of the Neolithic Revolution. Economica 75, 729–748.

Raeithel, G. (1995): Geschichte der nordamerikanischen Kultur. Volume 1: Vom Puritanismus bis zum Bürgerkrieg 1600–1860. Frankfurt/M.: Zweitausendeins.

Ragwitz, M., Huber, C. and Resch, G. (2007): Promotion of renewable energy sources: effects of innovation. International Journal of Public Policy 2 (1/2), 32–56.

Rahmstorf, S. (2007): A semi-empirical approach to projecting future sea-level rise. Science 315, 368–370.

Ramankutty, N., Evan, A. T., Monfreda, C. and Foley, J. A. (2008): Farming the planet: 1. geographic distribution of global agricultural lands in the year 2000. Global Biogeochemical Cycles 22, 19.

Raskin, P., Banuri, T., Gallopín, G., Gutman, P., Hammond, A., Kates, R. and Swart, R. (2002): Great Transition – The Promise and Lure of the Times Ahead. Report of the Global Scenario Group. SEI PoleStar Series Report No. 10. Boston: Stockholm Environment Institute.

Raskin, P. D., Electris, C. and Rosen, R. A. (2010): The century ahead: searching for sustainability. Sustainability 2, 2626–2651.

Rauchhaupt, U. (2005): Wittgensteins Klarinette. Gegenwart und Zukunft des Wissens. Berlin: Berliner Taschenbuchverlag.

Raupach, M. R., Marland, G., Ciais, P., Le Quéré, C., Canadell, J. G., Klepper, G. and Field, C. B. (2007): Global and regional drivers of accelerating CO_2 emissions. Proceedings of the National Academy of Sciences 104 (24), 10288–10293.

Ravallion, M. and Chen, S. (2010): The Impact of the Global Financial Crisis on the World's Poorest. Website: www.voxeu.org/index.php?q=node/3520 (viewed 5. March 2011). London: VoxEU.org.

Reiche, D. (2005): Zur zentralen Bedeutung des Nationalstaates im Mehrebenensystem. Ein Beitrag zur gegenwärtigen Governance-Diskussion. FFU-Report 04-2005. Berlin: FU Berlin, Environmental Policy Research Centre.

Reid, W. V., Chen, D., Goldfarb, L., Hackmann, H., Lee, Y. T., Mokhele, K., Ostrom, E., Raivio, K., Rockström, J., Schellnhuber, H. J. and Whyte, A. (2010): Earth system science for global sustainability: grand challenges. Science Education 330, 916–917.

Reinalda, B. (2011): Non-State actors in the international system of states. In: Reinalda, B. (ed): The Ashgate Research Companion to Non-State Actors. Aldershot: Ashgate, 3–19.

Reinert, E. (2007): How Rich Countries Got Rich … and Poor Countries Stay Poor. London: Constable.

Reisch, L. A. and Oehler, A. (2009): Behavioural Economics: Eine neue Grundlage für die Verbraucherpolitik? DIW Vierteljahreshefte zur Wirtschaftsforschung, 'Verbraucherpolitik zwischen Markt und Staat' 78 (3), 30–43.

Reiß, M. (1997): Change Management als Herausforderung. In: Reiß, M., von Rosenstiel, L. and Lanz, A. (eds): Change Management: Programme, Projekte und Prozesse. USW-Schriften für Führungskräfte 31. Stuttgart: Schäffer-Poeschel, 5–29.

REN21 (2010): Renewables Global Status Report 2010. Paris: REN21.

Riahi, K., Dentener, F., Gielen, D., Grubler, A., Klimont, Z., Krey, V., McCollum, D., Nakicenovic, N., Pachauri, S., Rao, S., van Ruijven, B., van Vuuren, D. and Wilson, C. (2010): Knowledge Module 17: The GEA Scenario – Energy Transition Pathways for Sustainable Development. Laxenburg: International Institute for Applied Systems Analysis.

Rickerson, W. H., Sawin, J. L. and Grace, R. C. (2007): If the shoe FITs: using feed-in tariffs to meet U.S. renewable electricity targets. The Electricity Journal 20 (4), 73–86.

Roadmap 2050 (2011): Roadmap 2050. A Practical Guide to a Prosperous, Low Carbon Europe: Volume 1 – Technical and Economic Analysis. Website: http://www.roadmap2050.eu/downloads (viewed 14. March 2011). The Hague, Brussels: European Climate Foundation, Energy Strategy Center.

Roberts, J. T. and Parks, B. C. (2007): A Climate of Injustice. Global Inequality, North-South Politics, and Climate Policy. Cambridge, MA: MIT Press.

Roberts, T. J., Starr, K., Jones, T. and Abdel-Fattah, D. (2008): The Reality of Official Climate Aid. Oxford, UK: Oxford Institute for Energy Studies.

Robine, J.-M., Cheung, S. L. K., Roy, S. L., Oyen, H. V., Griffiths, C., Michel, J.-P. and Herrmann, F. R. (2008): Death toll exceeded 70,000 in Europe during the summer of 2003. Comptes Rendus Biologies 331 (2), 171–178.

Rochester, M. J. (1986): The rise and fall of international organizations as a field of study. International Organization 40 (4), 777–813.

Rockström, J. and Karlberg, L. (2010): The quadruple squeeze: defining the safe operation space for freshwater use to achieve a triply green revolution in the anthropocene. Ambio 39, 257–265.

Rockström, J., Steffen, W., Noone, K., Paersson, A., Chapin III, F. S., Lambin, E. F., Lenton, T. M., Scheffer, M., Folke, C., Schellnhuber, H. J., Nykvist, B., de Wit, C., A., Hughes, T., van der Leeuw, S., Rodhe, H., Sörlin, S., Snyder, P. K., Costanza, R., Svedin, U., Falkenmark, M., Karlberg, L., Corell, R. W., Fabry, V. J., Hansen, J., Walker, B., Liverman, D., Richardson, K., Crutzen, P. and Foley, J. A. (2009a): A safe operating space for humanity. Nature 46, 472–475.

Rockström, J., Steffen, W., Noone, K., Persson, A., Chapin, F. S., Lambin, E. F., Lenton, T. M., Scheffer, M., Folke, C., Schellnhuber, H. J., Nykvist, B., de Witt, C. A., Hughes, T. M. C., van der Leeuw, S., Rodhe, H., Sörlim, S., Snyder, P. K., Constanza, R., Svedin, U., Falkenmark, M., Karlberg, L., Corell, R. W., Fabry, V. J., Hansen, J., Walker, B., Livermann, D., Richardson, K., Crutzen, P. J. and Foley, J. A. (2009b): Planetary boundaries: exploring the safe operating space for humanity. Ecology and Society 14 (2), 32.

Rogers, E. M. (2003): Diffusion of Innovations. New York: Free Press.

Rokeach, M. (1968): Beliefs, Attitudes and Values: A Theory of Organization and Change. San Francisco: Jossey-Bass.

Rosen, R. A., Electris, C. and Raskin, P. D. (2010): Searching for Sustainability. Global Scenarios for the Century Ahead. Boston: Tellus Institute.

Rosenau, J. N. and Czempiel, E.-O. (1992): Governance Without Government: Order and Change in World Politics. Cambridge, UK: Cambridge University Press.

Rosenberg, R. (2010): Does Microcredit Really Help Poor People? Focus Note No. 59 Washington, DC: Consultative Group to Assist the Poor.

Ross, E. (1998): The Malthus Factor: Poverty, Politics and Population in Capitalist Development. London: Zed Books.

Rössel, J. (2006): Daten auf der Suche nach einer Theorie. Ronald Ingleharts Analysen des weltweiten Wertewandels. In: Möbius, S. and Quadflieg, D. (eds): Kultur. Theorien der Gegenwart. Wiesbaden: VS, 545–556.

Rost, J. (2002): Umweltbildung – Bildung für eine nachhaltige Entwicklung: Was macht den Unterschied? Zeitschrift für Internationale Bildungsforschung und Entwicklungspädagogik 1, 1–10.

Rotmans, J., Kemp, R. and van Asselt, M. (2001): More evolution than revolution: transition management in public policy. The Journal of Futures Studies, Strategic Thinking and Policy 3 (1), 15–31.

Ruddigkeit, D. (2009): Border Tax Adjustment an der Schnittstelle von Welthandelsrecht und Klimaschutz vor dem Hintergrund des Europäischen Emissionszertifikatehandels. Beiträge zum Transnationalen Wirtschaftsrecht Heft 89. Halle (Saale): University Halle-Wittenberg.

Ruttan, V. (1977): The green revolution: seven generalizations. International Development Review 19, 16–23.

Saretzki, T. (2007): Demokratie und Umweltpolitik: Konzeptionelle und methodologische Probleme der makroquantitativ ausgerichteten vergleichenden Umwelt- und Demokratieforschung. Politische Vierteljahresschrift 48 (Special Issue 39), 409–429.

Sartori, G. (1992): Demokratietheorie. Darmstadt: Wissenschaftliche Buchgesellschaft.

Saviotti, P. P. (1996): Technological Evolution, Variety and the Economy. Cheltenham: Edward Elgar.

Schaal, G. and Ritzi, C. (2008): Rationale Selbstbindung und die Qualität politischer Entscheidungen – liberale und deliberative Perspektiven. In: Schaal, G. S. (ed): Rationale Selbstbindungen. Berlin: Lit, 55–74.

Schaal, G. S. and Ritzi, C. (2009): Empirische Deliberationsforschung. Cologne: Max Planck Institute for the Study of Societies.

Scharpf, F. W. (1985): Die Politikverflechtungs-Falle: Europäische Integration und deutscher Föderalismus im Vergleich. Politische Vierteljahresschrift 26 (4), 323–356.

Scharpf, F. W. (1993): Positive und negative Koordination in Verhandlungssystemen. In: Héritier, A. (ed): Policy Analyse. Kritik und Neuorientierung. Politische Vierteljahresschrift. Sonderheft 24. Opladen: Westdeutscher Verlag, 57–83.

Scharpf, F. W. (1999): Regieren in Europa. Effektiv und demokratisch? Frankfurt/M.: Campus.

Scheffer, M. (2009): Critical Transitions in Nature and Society. Princeton: Princeton University Press.

Scheffer, M., Carpenter, S., Foley, J. A., Folkes, C. and Walker, B. H. (2001): Catastrophic shifts in ecosystems. Nature 413, 591–596.

Schellnhuber, H. J. and Huber, V. (2010): Towards a great land-use transformation? In: Richardson, A. D. (ed): Synthesis Report – Climate Change: Global Risks, Challenges & Decisions. Second Edition. Copenhagen: University of Copenhagen, 35.

Schimank, U. (2009): Die Moderne: eine funktional differenzierte kapitalistische Gesellschaft. Berliner Journal für Soziologie 19, 327–351.

Schirm, S. (2007): Die Rolle Brasiliens in der globalen Strukturpolitik. DIE Discussion Paper Nr. 16. Bonn: German Development Institute.

Schlacke, S. (2007): Das Umwelt-Rechtsbehelfsgesetz. Natur und Recht 8 (13), 8–16.

Schlacke, S. (2008): Information, Beteiligung und Rechtsschutz im Umweltgesetzbuch. In: Köck, W. (ed): Auf dem Weg zu einem Umweltgesetzbuch nach der Föderalismusreform. Baden-Baden: Nomos, 107–136.

Schlacke, S., Schrader, C. and Bunge, T. (2010): Informationsrechte, Öffentlichkeitsbeteiligung und Rechtsschutz im Umweltrecht: Aarhus-Handbuch. Berlin: Duncker & Humblot.

Schmalz-Bruns, R. (1995): Reflexive Demokratie. Baden-Baden: Nomos.

Schmidt, M. G. (2006): Demokratietheorien. Eine Einführung. Wiesbaden: VS.

Schneider, H. K. (1991): Abschied vom Wirtschaftswachstum und vom Stabilitätsgesetz? In: Stratmann-Mertens, E., Hickel, R. and Priewe, J. (eds): Wachstum – Abschied von einem Dogma. Kontroverse über eine ökologisch-soziale Wirtschaftspolitik. Frankfurt/M.: Fischer, 117–126.

Schneider, U. and Smith, P. (2009): Energy intensities and greenhouse gas emission mitigation in global agriculture. Energy Efficiency 2 (2), 195–206.

Schneider, M., Thomas, S., Froggatt, A., Koplow, D. and Hazemann, J. (2009): The World Nuclear Industry Status Report – with particular emphasis on economic Issues. Berlin: Federal Ministry for the Environment, Nature Conservation and Nuclear Safety.

Schoch, F. (2008): Gewährleistungsverwaltung: Stärkung der Privatrechtsgesellschaft? Neue Zeitschrift für Verwaltungsrecht 245, 241–247.

Schomerus, T. (1989): Ein Ombutsmann mit Klagebefugnis statt Verbandsklage im Naturschutzrecht? Natur und Recht, 171.

Schreiber, W. (2006): Wahlrecht von Geburt an – Ende der Diskussion? Deutsches Verwaltungsblatt, 1341ff.

Schüler, D., Buchert, M., Liu, R., Dittrich, S. and Merz, C. (2011): Study on Rare Earths and their Recycling. Freiburg: Öko-Institut.

Schultze, R.-O. (2003): Wahlforschung. In: Andersen, U. and Woyke, W. (eds): Handwörterbuch des politischen Systems der Bundesrepublik. Opladen: Leske+Budrich, 681–685.

Schultze, R.-O. (2010): Artikel Partei. In: Nohlen, D. and Schultze, R.-O. (eds): Lexikon der Politikwissenschaft. Munich: Beck, 616–618.

Schwägerl, C. (2010): Menschenzeit. Zerstören oder gestalten? Die entscheidende Epoche unseres Planeten. Munich: Riemann, Random House.

Schwarze, J. (2009): EU-Kommentar. Baden-Baden: Nomos.

Schweizer-Ries, P. (2010): Abschlussbericht. Umweltpschologische Untersuchung der Akzeptanz von Maßnahmen zur Netzintegration Erneuerbarer Energien in der Region Wahle – Mecklar (Niedersachsen Hessen). Website: http://www.forum-netzintegration.de/uploads/media/Abschlussbericht_Akzeptanz_Netzausbau_Juni2010.pdf (viewed 17. November 2010). Berlin: Forum Netzintegration.

Scott, J. (1998): Seeing Like a State. New Haven: Yale University Press.

Scrace, I. and MacKerron, G. (eds) (2009): Energy for the Future. A New Agenda. Basingstoke: Palgrave Macmillan.

Seidl, I. and Zahrnt, A. (2010): Postwachstumsgesellschaft. Konzepte für die Zukunft. Marburg: Metropolis.

Sen, A. (1999): Development as Freedom. New York: Anchor.

Service, R. F. (2010): Chinese policies could pinch U.A. efforts to make electric vehicles. Science 329, 377.

Seubert, S. (2009): Das Konzept des Sozialkapitals. Eine demokratietheoretische Analyse. Frankfurt/M.: Suhrkamp.

Shearman, D. and Smith, J. W. (2007): The Climate Change Challenge and the Failure of Democracy. Westport, London: Praeger.

Shiklomanov, I. A. (2000): Appraisal and Assessment of World Water Resources. Water International 25 (1), 11–32.

Shiklomanov, I. A. and Rodda, J. C. (2003): World Water Resources at the Beginning of the 21st Century. Cambridge, NY: Cambridge University Press.

Shiva, V. (1989): The Violence of the Green Revolution: Ecological Degradation and Political Conflict in Punjab. Dehra Dun: Research Foundation for Science and Ecology.

Shiva, V. (1991): The Violence of the Green Revolution: Third World's Agriculture, Ecology and Politics. Penang: Third World Network.

Sidiras, D. K. and Koukios, E. G. (2004): Solar systems diffusion in local markets. Energy Policy 31 (18), 2007–2018.

Siebold, T. (1995): Die sozialen Dimensionen der Strukturanpassung. Eine Zwischenbilanz. INEF-Report 13. Duisburg: INEF.

Sieferle, R. P. (2010): Lehren aus der Vergangenheit für die Transformation zu einer klimafreundlichen Gesellschaft. Expertise for the WBGU Report 'World in Transition: A Social Contract for Sustainability'. Website: http://www.wbgu.de/wbgu_jg2011_Expertise_Sieferle.pdf. Berlin: WBGU.

Sieferle, R. P., Krausmann, F., Schandl, H. and Winiwarter, V. (2006): Das Ende der Fläche. Zum gesellschaftlichen Stoffwechsel der Industrialisierung. Cologne: Böhlau.

Sijm, J. P. M. (2002): The Performance of Feed-in Tarrifs to Promote Renewable Electricity in European Countries. Petten: Energy Research Centre of the Netherlands.

Siller, P. (2010): Demokratie und Klimawandel: Ökologen als Vordenker einer Expertokratie? Website: http://www.boell.de/stiftung/akademie/akademie-postdemokratie-expertokratie-8729.html (viewed 2. December 2010). Berlin: Green Academy of the Heinrich Böll Foundation.

Silvertown, J., Cook, L., Cameron, R., Dodd, M. and McConway, K. (2011): Citizen science reveals unexpected continental-scale evolutionary change in a model organism. Public Library of Science ONE 6 (4), e18927. doi:18910.11371/journal.pone.0018927.

Simms, A., Johnson, V. and Chowla, P. (2010): Growth isn't Possible – Why we Need a new Economic Direction. London: New Economics Foundation.

Simon, N. (2010): Internationale Umweltgovernance für das 21. Jahrhundert: Herausforderungen, Reformprozesse und Handlungsoptionen vor der Rio-Konferenz 2012. Berlin: German Institute for International and Security Affairs.

Sinn, H.-W. (2008): Public policies against global warming: a supply side approach. International Tax and Public Finance 15, 360–394.

Sinn, H. W. (2010): Euro-Krise. Ifo-Schnelldienst 10 (Special Issue), 3–9.

Skopcol, T. (1982): Bringing the state back. Social Science Research Items 36, 1–8.

Slow Food International (1989): Bewegung zur Wahrung des Rechts auf Genuss. Manifest. Website: http://slowfood.de/wirueberuns/slow_food_manifest_paris/ (viewed 14. March 2011). Paris: Slow Food International.

Smil, V. (2000): Feeding the World. A Challenge for the Twenty-First Century. Cambridge, MA: MIT Press.

Smith, G. (2009): Democratic Innovations. Cambridge, NY: Cambridge University Press.

Smith, P., Martino, D., Cai, Z., Gwary, D., Janzen, H., Kumar, P., McCarl, B. A., Ogle, S., O´Mara, F., Rice, C., Scholes, B., Sirotenko, O., Howden, M., McAllister, D. E., Pan, G., Romanenkow, V., Schneider, U. A. and Towprayoon, S. (2007): Policy and technological constraints to implementation of greenhouse gas mitigation options in agriculture. Agriculture Ecosystems & Environment 118, 6–28.

Smith, P., Martino, D., Cai, Z., Gwary, D., Janzen, H., MKumar, P., McCarl, B., Ogle, S., O´Mara, F., Rice, C., Scholes, B., Sirotenko, O., Howden, M., McAllister, T., Pan, G., Romanekov, V., Schneider, U., Towprayoon, S., Wattenbach, M. and Smith, J. (2008): Greenhouse gas mitigation in agriculture. Philosophical Transactions of the Royal Society 363, 789–813.

Soares–Filho, B. S., Nepstad, D. C., Curran, L. M., Cerqueira, G. C., Garcia, R. A., Ramos, C. A., Voll, E., McDonald, A., Lefebvre, P. and Schlesinger, P. (2006): Modelling conservation in the Amazon basin. Nature 440, 520-523.

Sommer, B. (2011): Interdependenzen und Ungleichzeitigkeiten im Kontext des anthropogenen Klimawandels. Leviathan: Berliner Zeitschrift für Sozialwissenschaft 39, 55–72.

Son, S.-W., Tandon, N. F., Polvani, L. M. and Waugh, D. W. (2009): Ozone hole and southern hemisphere climate change. Geophysical Research Letters 36 (L15705), 5.

Sorrell, S. (2007): The Rebound Effect: An Assessment of the Evidence for Economy-wide Energy Savings from Improved Energy Efficiency. London: UK Energy Research Centre.

Sovacool, B. K. (2008): Valuing the greenhouse gas emissions from nuclear power: a critical survey. Energy Policy 36, 2950ff.

Spannowsky, W., Runkel, P. and Goppel, K. (2010): Raumordnungsgesetz – Kommentar. Munich: Beck.

Specht, M., Baumgart, F., Feigl, B., Frick, V., Stürmer, B., Zuberbühler, U., Sterner, M. and Waldstein, G. (2009): Speicherung von Bioenergie und erneuerbarem Strom im Erdgasnetz. Themenheft 'Forschen für globale Märkte erneuerbarer Energien'. FVEE Jahrestagung 2009. Berlin: Renewable Energy Research Association.

Sprinz, D. F. (2009): Long-term environmental policy: definition, knowledge, future research. Global Environmental Politics 9 (3), 1–8.

SRU – German Advisory Council on the Environment (2008): Umweltgutachten 2008: Umweltschutz im Zeichen des Klimawandels. Berlin: SRU.

SRU – German Advisory Council on the Environment (2010): 100% erneuerbare Stromversorgung bis 2050: klimaverträglich, sicher, bezahlbar. Berlin: SRU.

SRU – German Advisory Council on the Environment (2011): Wege zur 100% erneuerbaren Stromversorgung. Sondergutachten. Berlin: SRU.

SRzG – Foundation for the Rights of Future Generations (2009): Generationengerechtigkeit, das Wahlrecht durch Eintragung und weitere Beteiligungsrechte von Kindern und Jugendlichen. Website: http://www.generationengerechtigkeit.de/images/stories/Publikationen/positionspapiere/pp_kinderrechte.pdf (viewed 11. February 2011). Stuttgart: SRzG.

Stadler, I. (2006): Demand Response: Nichtelektrische Speicher für Elektrizitätsversorgungssysteme mit hohem Anteil erneuerbarer Energien. Habilitation. Berlin: dissertation.de.

Staffhorst, M. (2006): The Way to Competitiveness of PV – An Experience Curve and Break-even Analysis. Doctoral Thesis. Kassel: Kassel University Press.

Stanford University (2010): Global Warming Poll. Website: http://woods.stanford.edu/docs/surveys/Global-Warming-Survey-Selected-Results-June2010.pdf (viewed 17. November 2010). Stanford, CA: Stanford University.

Steffani, W. (1999): Wahlrecht von Geburt an als Demokratiegebot? Zeitschrift für Parlamentsfragen 30, 563–567.

Steffen, K., Crutzen, P. J. and McNeill, C. I. (2007): The anthropocene: are humans now overwhelming the great forces of nature. Ambio 36 (8), 614–621.

Stehfest, E., Bouwman, L., van Vuuren, D. P., den Elzen, M. J. G., Eickhout, B. and Kabat, P. (2009): Climate benefits of changing diet. Climatic Change 95, 83–102.

Steiner, A., Wilde, T., Bradbrook, A. J. and Schutyser, F. (2006): International institutional arrangements in support of renewable energy. In: Assmann, D. (ed): Renewable Energy. A Global Review of Technologies, Policies and Markets. London: 152–162.

Steinfeld, H., Gerber, P., Wassenaar, T., V., C., Rosales, M. and de Haan, C. (2006): Livestock's Long Shadow. Environmental Issues and Options. Rome: Food and Agriculture Organization of the United Nations, Livestock Environment and Development (LEAD) Initiative.

Stern, N. (2006): The Economics of Climate Change. Cambridge, NY: Cambridge University Press.

Stern, N. (2008): A Blueprint for a Safer Planet. London: Random House.

Sterner, M. (2009): Bioenergy and Renewable Power Methane in 100% Renewable Energy Systems. Limiting Global Warming by Transforming Energy Systems. Doctoral Thesis. Website: http://www.upress.uni-kassel.de/publi/abstract.php?978-3-89958-798-2 (viewed 18. November 2009). Kassel: Kassel University Press.

Sterner, M. (2010): Nachhaltige Weltenergiesysteme: Wege in eine kohlenstoffarme Energiezukunft. In: Debiel, T., Messner, D. and Nuscheler, F. (eds): Globale Trends 2010. Frieden, Entwicklung, Umwelt. Frankfurt/M.: Fischer, 299–317.

Sterner, M., Gerhardt, N., Saint-Drenan, Y. M., von Oehsen, A., Hochloff, P., Kocmajewski, M., Lindner, P., Jentsch, M., Pape, C., Bofinger, S. and Rohrig, K. (2010): Energiewirtschaftliche Bewertung von Pumpspeicherwerken und anderen Speichern im zukünftigen Stromversorgungssystem. Kassel: Fraunhofer IWES.

Stevenson, B. and Wolfers, J. (2008): Economic Growth and Subjective Well-Being: Reassessing the Easterlin Paradox. Brookings Papers on Economic Activity. Washington, DC: Brookings Institution.

Stiglitz, J. E., Sen, A. and Fitoussi, J.-P. (2009a): Survey of Existing Approaches to Measuring Socio-Economic Progress. Website: http://www.stiglitz-sen-fitoussi.fr (viewed 17. November 2009). London: Commission on the Measurement of Economic Performance and Social Progress.

Stiglitz, J. E., Sen, A. and Fitoussi, J.-P. (2009b): Report by the Commission on the Measurement of Economic Performance and Social Progress. Website: http://www.stiglitz-sen-fitoussi.fr (viewed 17. November 2009). London: Commission on the Measurement of Economic Performance and Social Progress.

Strassburg, B., Turner, K., Fisher, B., Schaeffer, R. and Lovett, A. (2008): An Empirically-Derived Mechanism of Combined Incentives to Reduce Emissions from Deforestation. CSERGE Working Paper ECM 08-01. Norwich: Centre for Social and Economic Research on the Global Environment.

Streek, W. (1994): Staat und Verbände. Politische Vierteljahresschrift Sonderheft, 7–36.

Streek, W. and Schmitter, P. C. (1985): Private Interest Government: Beyond Market and State. Beverly Hills, London: SAGE Publications.

Strengers, B., Leemans, R., Eickhout, B., de Vries, B. and Bouwman, L. (2004): The land-use projections and resulting emissions in the IPCC SRES scenarios as simulated by the IMAGE 2.2 model. Geo Journal 61, 381–393.

Stuenkel, O. (2010): Responding to Global Development Challenges. Views from Basil and India. DEI Discussion Paper Nr. 11. Website: http://www.die-gdi.de/CMS-Homepage/openwebcms3.nsf/(ynDK_contentByKey)/ANES-89YHBD?Open&nav=expand:Publikationen;active:Publikationen%5C

ANES-89YHBD (viewed 14. March 2011). Bonn: German Development Institute.

Subak, S. (1999): Global environmental costs of beef production. Ecological Economics 30, 79–91.

Suding, K. N., Lavorel, S., Chapin III, F. S., Cornelissen, J. H. C., Diaz, S., Garnier, E., Goldberg, D., Hooper, D. U., Jackson, S. T. and Navas, M.-L. (2008): Scaling environmental change through the community-level: a trait-based response-and-effect framework for plants. Global Change Biology 14, 1–16.

Sukhdev, P. (2008): The Economics of Ecosystems & Biodiversity. An Interim Report. Brussels: European Communities.

Sullivan, J. L., Clark, C. E., Han, J. and Wang, M. (2010): Life-Cycle Analysis Results of Geothermal Systems in Comparison to Other Power Systems. Argonne, IL: Center for Transportation Research Energy Systems Division, Argonne National Laboratory.

Sumner, A. (2010): Global Poverty and the New Bottom Billion: Three-quarters of the World's Poor Live in Middle-Income Countries. Brighton: Institute of Development Studies.

Sünderhauf, H. (1997): Mediation bei der außergerichtlichen Lösung von Umweltkonflikten in Deutschland. Schriften des Vereins für Umweltrecht Nr. 10. Berlin: Verein für Umweltrecht.

SVR – German Council of Economic Experts (2008): Das deutsche Finanzsystem – Effizienz steigern, Stabilität erhöhen. Expertise im Auftrag der Bundesregierung. Wiesbaden: SVR.

SVR – German Council of Economic Experts (2009): Die Zukunft nicht aufs Spiel setzen. Jahresgutachten 2009/10. Wiesbaden: SVR.

SVR – German Council of Economic Experts (2010): Chancen für einen stabilen Aufschwung. Jahresgutachten 2010/11. Wiesbaden: SVR.

Swartz, W., Sala, E., Tracey, S., Watson, R. and Pauly, D. (2010): The spatial expansion and ecological footprint of fisheries (1950 to present). Public Library of Science ONE 5 (12), doi:10.1371/journal.pone.0015143.

SZ – Süddeutsche Zeitung (2010): Geißler – Schlichterspruch enthält Nachbesserungen. Website: http://www.sueddeutsche.de/politik/stuttgart-geissler-schlichterspruch-enthaelt-nachbesserungen-1.1028582 (viewed 25. November 2010). Munich: SZ.

Szydlik, M. (2000): Lebenslange Solidarität? Generationenbeziehungen zwischen erwachsenen Kindern und Eltern. Opladen: Leske + Budrich.

Tagesspiegel (30.11.2010): Lufthansa fliegt mit Biosprit. Als weltweit erste Fluggesellschaft will die Deutsche Lufthansa den Einsatz von umweltfreundlichen Biokraftstoffen bei einem Langzeitversuch im regulären Liniendienst erproben. Website: http://www.tagesspiegel.de/wirtschaft/lufthansa-fliegt-mit-biosprit/3508950.html (viewed 14. March 2011). Berlin: Tagesspiegel.

Tahil, W. (2007): The Trouble With Lithium. Implications of Future PHEV Production for Lithium Demand. Martainville: Meridian International Research.

Tans, P. (2011): Trends in Atmospheric Carbon Dioxide – Recent Global CO_2. Globally Averaged Marine Surface Annual Mean Data. Website: http://www.esrl.noaa.gov/gmd/ccgg/trends/global.html (viewed 12. January 2011). Boulder, CO: National Oceanic and Atmospheric Administration.

Taylor, R. P., Govindarajalu, C., Levin, J., Meyer, A. S. and Ward, W. A. (2008): Energy Efficiency – Lessons from Brazil, China, India and Beyond. Washington, DC: World Bank.

TEEB – The Economics of Ecosystems and Biodiversity (2010): The Economics of Ecosystems and Biodiversity: Ecological and Economic Foundations. London: Earthscan.

Terberger, E. (2002): Mikrofinanzierung: Allheilmittel gegen Armut? Ruperto Carola Ausgabe 3/2002. Heidelberg: University Heidelberg.

Teske, S., Schäfer, O., Zervors, A., Beranek, J., Tunmore, S. and Krewiit, W. (2008): energy [r]evolution. A Sustainable Global Energy Outlook. Berlin: European Renewable Energy Council and Greenpeace.

Tetzlaff, R. (1996): Weltbank und Währungsfonds: Gestalter der Bretton-Woods-Ära. Opladen: Leske + Budrich.

Thaler, R. H. (1985): Mental accounting and consumer choice. Marketing Science 4 (3), 199–214.

Thaler, R. H. (1999): Mental accounting matters. Journal of Behavioral Decision Making 12, 183–206.

Thaler, R. H. and Sunstein, C. R. (2008): Nudge. Improving Decisions About Health, Wealth, and Happiness. New Haven: Yale University Press.

Thalmann, P. (2004): The public acceptance of green taxes: 2 million voters express their opinion. Public Choice 119, 179–217.

The Royal Society (2005): Ocean Acidification due to Increasing Atmospheric Carbon Dioxide. London: The Royal Society.

The St. James's Palace Memorandum (2009): St. James's Palace Memorandum. The St James's Palace Memorandum 'Action for a Low Carbon and Equitable Future' London, UK, 26–28 May 2009. Cambridge, UK: University of Cambridge, Potsdam Institute for Climate Impact Research.

Thiele, R. and Wiebelt, M. (2000): Sind die Anpassungsprogramme von IWF und Weltbank gescheitert? Eine Bilanz der Erfahrungen von zwei Jahrzehnten. Kiel Discussion Papers 357. Kiel: Kiel Institute for the World Economy.

Thielen, M. (2009): Zur Zukunft des lebenslangen Lernens in Hochschulen und in Wissenschaftseinrichtungen. In: Hanft, A. and Knust, M. (eds): Weiterbildung im Elfenbeinturm!? Münster, New York, Munich, Berlin: Waxmann, 13–16.

Thier, K. (2010): Storytelling. Eine narrative Managementmethode. Heidelberg: Springer Medizin.

Thorpe, A. (2009): Enteric fermentation and ruminant eructation: the role (and control?) of methane in the climate change debate. Climatic Change 93, 407–411.

Tichy, G. (2009): Nachhaltiges Wachstum? Zum Thema dieses Hefts. Forum Wissenschaft und Umwelt: Nachhaltiges Wachstum? Wissenschaft und Umwelt Interdisziplinär. Wien: Forum Wissenschaft und Umwelt.

Tomasello, M. (2009): Why we Cooperate. Cambridge, MA: MIT Press.

Toyota Motor Corporation (2010): Toyota startet Batterie-zu-Batterie-Recycling. Website: http://www.toyota.de/innovation/environment/news/details_2010_12.aspx (viewed 15. March 2011). Cologne: Toyota.

Tranaes, F. (2006): Danish Wind Energy. Website: http://www.dkvind.dk/eng/publications/danish_wind_energy.pdf (viewed 17. November 2010). Arhus: Danish Wind Turbine Owners Association.

Transparency International (2005): Global Corruption Report. Special Focus: Corruption in Construction and Post-Conflict Reconstruction. Berlin: Transparency International.

Transparency International (2008): Global Corruption Report 2008: Corruption in the Water Sector. Cambridge, UK: Cambridge University Press.

Transparency International (2011): Working Paper No 01/2011: Reducing Demand for Illegal Timber: Targeting Corruption in Customs and Procurement. Berlin: Transparency International.

True, J. and Mintrom, M. (2001): Transnational networks and policy diffusion: the case of gender mainstreaming. International Studies Quarterly 45 (1), 27–57.

Trumbull, D. J., Bonney, R., Bascom, D. and Cabral, A. (2000): Thinking scientifically during participation in a citizen-science project. Science Education 84 (2), 265–275.

Tsebelis, G. (2002): Veto Players. How Political Institutions Work. Princeton, New York: Princeton University Press.

Tukker, A., Bausch-Goldbohm, S., Verheijden, M., de Koning, A., Klejin, R., Wolf, O. and Pérez Dominguez, I. (2009): Environmental Impacts of Diet Changes in the EU. EUR 23783 EN. Brussels: European Commission Institute for Prospective Technological Studies.

Tully, J. (2009): The Crisis of Global Citizenship, Article Presented at a Lecture in the Goethe University Frankfurt/M. under the Auspices of the Cluster of Excellence on the Formation of Normative Orders. Frankfurt/M.: University Frankfurt.

Turner, W. R., Bradley, B. A., Estes, L. D., Hole, D. G., Oppenheimer, M. and Wilcove, D. S. (2010): Climate change: helping nature survive the human response. Conservation Letters 00, 1–9.

UBA – Federal Environment Agency (2008): Grenzsteuerausgleich für Mehrkosten infolge nationaler europäischer Umweltschutzinstrumente – Gestaltungsmöglichkeiten und WTO-rechtliche Zulässigkeit. Climate Change 05/08. Dessau: UBA.

UBA – Federal Environment Agency (2010): Leitfaden Klimaschutz im Stadtverkehr. Dessau: UBA.

UBA – Federal Environment Agency (2011): Statusbericht zur Umsetzung des Integrierten Energie- und Klimaschutzprogramms der Bundesregierung. Climate Change 6. Dessau: UBA.

UKERC – UK Energy Research Centre (2009): UKERC Energy 2050 Research Report 1: Pathways to a Low Carbon Economy: Energy SystemsModelling. London: King's College London.

Ulvila, M. and Pasanen, J. (eds) (2009): Sustainable Futures. Replacing Growth Imperative and Hierarchies with Sustainable Ways. Helsinki: Ministry for Foreign Affairs.

UN – United Nations (1992): Rio Declaration on Environment and Development. New York: UN.

UN – United Nations (2008a): Energy Statistics Yearbook. New York: UN Statistics Division.

UN – United Nations (2008b): World Urbanisation Prospects: The 2007 Revision. New York: UN Department of Economic and Social Affairs, Population Division.

UN – United Nations (2009a): Report of the Commission of Experts of the President of the United Nations General Assembly on Reforms of the International Monetary and Financial System. Website: http://www.un.org/ga/econcrisissummit/docs/FinalReport_CoE.pdf (viewed 13. December 2010). New York: UN.

UN – United Nations (2009b): Introduction – The Significance of Cooperatives to a World in Crisis. Background Paper on Cooperatives. Website: http:www.un.org/esa/socdev/social/kooperatives/documents/survey/background.pdf (viewed 21. February 2011). New York: UN.

UN – United Nations (2010): The Millennium Development Goals Report 2010. New York: UN.

UNCTAD – United Nations Conference on Trade and Development (2009): Review of Marine Transport. New York, Geneva: UNCTAD.

UNCTAD – United Nations Conference on Trade and Development (2010a): Promoting Poles of Clean Growth to Foster the Transition to a More Sustainable Economy. Geneva: UNCTAD.

UNCTAD – United Nations Conference on Trade and Development (2010b): World Investment Report 2010. Investing in a Low-Carbon Economy. Geneva: UNCTAD.

UN DESA – United Nations Department of Economics and Social Affairs (2009a): Promoting Development, Saving the Planet. World Economic and Social Survey 2009. E/2009/50/Rev.1ST/ESA/319. New York: UN DESA.

UN DESA – United Nations Department of Economic and Social Affairs/Population Division (2009b): World Population Prospects: The 2008 Revision. Website: http://esa.un.org/unpp (viewed 16. September 2010). New York: UN DESA.

UN DESA – United Nations Department of Economic and Social Affairs (2010): World Urbanization Prospects: The 2009 Revision. File 17a: Urban Population (Thousands), Number of Cities and Percentage of Urban Population by Size Class of Urban Settlement, Major Area, Region and Country, 1950–2025. POP/DB/WUP/Rev.2009/2/F17a. New York: UN DESA.

UNDP – United Nations Development Programme (2006): Human Development Report 2006. Beyond Scarcity: Power, Poverty and the Global Water Crisis. New York: UNDP.

UNDP – United Nations Development Programme (2007): Human Development Report 2007/2008. Fighting Climate Change: Human Solidarity in a Divided World. New York: UNEP.

UNDP – United Nations Development Programme (2010): Human Development Report 2010. The Real Wealth of Nations: Pathways to Human Development. New York: UNDP.

UNDP – United Nations Development Programmei and ESMAP – World Bank Energy Sector Management Assistance Program (2005): Energy Services for the Millennium Development Goals. The Millennium Project. Washington, DC: World Bank.

UNECE – United Nations Economic Commission for Europe (2010): Financing Global Climate Change Mitigation. ECE Energy Series No. 37. Geneva: UNECE.

UNEP – United Nations Environment Programme (2002): Global Environment Outlook GEO-3. Past, Present and Future Perspectives. Nairobi: UNEP.

UNEP – United Nations Environment Programme (2003): Regionally Based Assessment of Persistent Toxic Substances. New York: UNEP.

UNEP – United Nations Environment Programme (2007): Global Environment Outlook GEO-4. Environment for Development. Nairobi: UNEP.

UNEP – United Nations Environment Programme (2008): Reforming Energy Subsidies. New York: UNEP.

UNEP – United Nations Environment Programme (2009): A Global Green New Deal. Report Prepared for the Economics and Trade Branch, Division of Technology, Industry and Economics. Geneva: UNEP.

UNEP – United Nations Environment Programme (2010a): The Emissions Gap Report. Are the Copenhagen Accord Pledges Sufficient to Limit Global Warming to 2 °C or 1.5 °C? Nairobi: UNEP.

UNEP – United Nations Environment Programme (2010b): UNEP Emerging Issues: Environmental Consequences of Ocean Acidification: A Threat to Food Security. Nairobi: UNEP.

UNEP – United Nations Environment Programme (2010c): Assessing the Environmental Impacts of Consumption and Production. Nairobi: UNEP.

UNEP – United Nations Environment Programme (2010d): Priority Products and Materials Report. Website: http://www.unep.org/resourcepanel/ (viewed 17. February 2011). Nairobi: UNEP.

UNEP – United Nations Environment Programme (2011): Towards a Green Economy: Pathways to Sustainable Development and Poverty Eradication. Nairobi: UNEP.

UNEP Risoe – United Nations Environment Programme Centre on Energy Climate and Sustainable Development (2011): CDM Projects by Host Region. Website: http://cdmpipeline.org/cdm-projects-region.htm (viewed 15. February 2011). Roskilde: UNEP Risoe Centre.

UNEP SEFI – United Nations Environment Programme Sustainable Energy Finance Initiative (2008): Public Finance Mechanisms to Mobilise Investment in Climate Change Mitigation. An Overview of Mechanisms Being Used Today to Help Scale up the Climate Mitigation Markets, with a Particular Focus on the Clean Energy Sector. New York: UNEP SEFI.

UNEP SEFI – United Nations Environment Programme Sustainable Energy Finance Initiative (2009a): Private Financing of Renewable Energy. A Guide for Policymakers. New York: UNEP SEFI.

UNEP SEFI – United Nations Environment Programme Sustainable Energy Finance Initiative (2009b): Global Trends in Sustainable Energy Investment 2009. New York: UNEP SEFI.

UNEP-SEFI – United Nations Environment Programme Sustainable Energy Finance Initiative and BNEF – Bloomberg New Energy Finance (2010): Global Trends in Sustainable Energy Investment 2010. Analysis of Trends and Issues in the Financing of Renewable Energy and Energy Efficiency. Paris: BNEF.

UNESCO – United Nations Educational Scientific and Cultural Organization (2009): Water in a Changing World. The United Nations World Water Development Report 3. New York: UNESCO.

UNESCO – United Nations Educational Scientific and Cultural Organization (2010): UNESCO Science Report 2010. Zusammenfassung. Bonn: Deutsche UNESCO-Kommission.

UNFCCC – United Nations Framework Convention on Climate Change (2008): Investment and Financial Flows to Address Climate Change – An Update. Bonn: UNFCCC Sekretariat.

UNFCCC – United Nations Framework Convention on Climate Change (2009): Copenhagen Accord. Decision 2/CP.15. Bonn: UNFCCC Sekretariat.

UNFCCC – United Nations Framework Convention on Climate Change (2010): The Cancun Agreements: Outcome of the work of the Ad hoc Working Group on Long-term Cooperative Action under the Convention. Decision 1/CP.16. Bonn: UNFCCC Sekretariat.

UNGA – United Nations General Assembly (1948): Allgemeine Erklärung der Menschenrechte. UNGA Res. 217/A (III) vom 10. Dezember 1948. New York: UNGA.

UNICEF – United Nations Childrens Fund and WHO – World Health Organisation (2004): Meeting the MDG Drinking Water and Sanitation Target. A Mid-term Assessment of Progress. New York: UNICEF, WHO.

UN-Energy (2010): Looking to the Future. New York: UN.

UN-Habitat – United Nations Human Settlements Programme (2002): Global Campain on Urban Governance. Concept Paper. Nairobi: UN-Habitat.

UN-Habitat – United Nations Human Settlements Programme (2008): State of the World's Cities 2010/2011: Bridging the Urban Divide. London: Earthscan.

UN-Habitat – United Nations Human Settlements Programme (2009): Planning Sustainable Cities. Global Report on Human Settlements. Nairobi: UN Habitat.

UN-Habitat – United Nations Human Settlements Programme (2010a): State of African Cities Report. Nairobi: UN Habitat.

UN-Habitat – United Nations Human Settlements Programme (2010b): The State of China's Cities 2010/2011. London: Earthscan.

Underdal, A. (1998): Leadership in international environmental negotiations: designing feasible solutions. In: Underdal, A. (ed): The Politics of International Environmental Management. Dordrecht: Kluwer, 101–127.

Urry, J. (2010): Consuming the planet to excess. Theory, Culture & Society 27 (2–3), 191–212.

US-AID – US Agency for International Development (2009): Microfinance and Climate Change: Can MFIs Promote Environmental Sustainability? Speaker's Corner Summary Report. Washington, DC: US-AID.

US-DoE – US Department of Energy (2006): Practical Experience Gained During the Operation of the Great Plains Gasification Plant and Implications for Future Projects. Washington, DC: US-DoE.

US-DoE – US Department of Energy (2011): Clean Renewable Energy Bonds (CREBs). Website: http://www.dsireusa.org/incentives/incentive.cfm?Incentive_Code=US45F&State=federal&currentpageid=1&ee=0&re=1 (viewed 16. February 2011). Washington, DC: Database of State Incentives for Renewables & Efficiency.

US-EIA – US Energy Information Administration (2010): International Energy Outlook 2010. Washington, DC: US-EIA.

US-EPA – United States Environmental Protection Agency (2006): Global Anthropogenic Non-CO_2 Greenhouse Gas Emissions: 1990–2020. Washington, DC: US-EPA.

USGS – US Geological Survey (2010a): Lithium. 2008 Minerals Yearbook [Advanced Release]. Website: http://minerals.usgs.gov/minerals/pubs/commodity/lithium/myb1-2008-lithi.pdf (viewed 9. March 2010). Reston, VA: USGS.

USGS – US Geological Survey (2010b): Lithium. Mineral Commodity Summaries 2010. Website: http://minerals.usgs.gov/minerals/pubs/commodity/lithium/mcs-2010-lithi.pdf (viewed 9. March 2010). Reston, VA: USGS.

USGS – US Geological Survey (2010c): Phosphate Rock. Mineral Commodity Summaries 2010. Website: http://minerals.usgs.gov/minerals/pubs/commodity/phosphate_rock/mcs-2010-phosp.pdf (viewed 9. March 2010). Reston, VA: USGS.

Vaccari, D. A. (2009): Phosporus: a looming crisis. Scientific American 6, 54–59.

van den Bosch, S. and Rotmans, J. (2008): Deepening, Broadening and Scaling Up. A Framework for Steering Transition Experiments. Delft, Rotterdam: Knowledge Centre for Sustainable System Innovations and Transitions, TNO Strategy and Policy.

van Goeverden, C., Rietveld, P., Peeters, P. and Koelemeijer, J. (2006): Subsidies in public transport. European Transport 32, 5–25.

van Vuuren, D. (2009): Growing within Limits. A Report to the Global Assembly 2009 of the Club of Rome. Bilthoven: PBL Netherlands Environmental Assessment Agency.

van Vuuren, D. P., den Elzen, M. G. J., Lucas, P. L., Eickhout, B., Strengers, B. J., van Ruijven, B., Wonink, S. and van Houdt, R. (2007): Stabilizing greenhouse gas concentrations at low levels: an assessment of reduction strategies and costs. Climatic Change 81 (2), 119–159.

van Vuuren, D. P., Isaac, M., den Elzen, M. G. J., Stehfest, E. and van Vliet, J. (2010): Low stabilization scenarios and implications for major world regions from an integrated assessment perspective. The Energy Journal 31 (Special Issue 1), 165–192.

Vasa, A. and Neuhoff, K. (2011): The Role of CDM Post 2012. Carbon Pricing for Low-Carbon Investment Project. Berlin: Climate Policy Initiative, German Institute for Economic Research.

Vaubel, R. (2006): Principal-agent problems in international organizations. Review of International Organizations 1 (2), 125–138.

Veblen, T. (2007): Theorie der feinen Leute: Eine ökonomische Untersuchung der Institutionen. Frankfurt/M.: Fischer.

Velders, G. J. M., Andersen, S. O., Daniel, J. S., Fahey, D. W. and McFarland, M. (2007): The importance of the Montreal Protocol in protecting climate. Proceedings of the National Academy of Sciences 104 (12), 4814–4819.

Verba, S., Schlozman, K. L. and Brady, H. E. (1995): Voice and Equality: Civic Voluntarism in American Politics Cambridge, New York: Harvard University Press.

Vermeer, M. and Rahmstorf, S. (2009): Global sea level linked to global temperature. Proceedings of the National Academy of Sciences (early edition), doi/10.1073/pnas.0907765106.

Victor, P. A. (2008): Managing Without Growth: Slower by Design not Disaster. Cheltenham: Edward Elgar.

Vié, J.-C., Hilton-Taylor, C. and Stuart, S. N. (2008): Wildlife in a Changing World: An Analysis of the 2008 IUCN Red List of Threatened Species. Gland: IUCN.

Vitousek, P. M., Aber, J. D., Howarth, R. W., Likens, G. E., Matson, P. A., Schindler, D. W., Schlesinger, W. H. and Tilman, D. G. (1997a): Human alteration of the global nitrogen cycle: sources and consequences. Issues in Ecology 7 (3), 737–750.

Vitousek, P. M., Mooney, H. A., Lubchenco, J. and Melillo, J. M. (1997b): Human domination of Earth's ecosystems. Science 277, 494–499.

Vollmers, F. (2011): Die ungeliebte Artenvielfalt. Frankfurt/M.: Frankfurter Allgemeine Zeitung (22.01.2011), C4.

von Alemann, K. (1989): Organisierte Interessen in der Bundesrepublik. Opladen: Leske+Budrich.

von Alemann, U. (2005): Dimensionen politischer Korruption. Beiträge zum Stand der internationalen Forschung (Sonderheft 35 der Politischen Vierteljahresschrift). Wiesbaden: VS.

von Braun, J. (2010): Ursachen und Konsequenzen internationaler Landakquirierung in Entwicklungsländern. Zeitschrift für Außen- und Sicherheitspolitik 3 (3), 2.

von Braun, J. and Meinzen-Dick, R. (2009): Land Grabbing by Foreign Investors in Developing Countries: Risks and Opportunities. Washington, DC: International Food Policy Research Institute.

von Danwitz, T. (2004): Aarhus-Konvention: Umweltinformation, Öffentlichkeitsbeteiligung, Zugang zu den Gerichten. Neue Zeitschrift für Verwaltungsrecht, 272–282.

von Hirschhausen, C., Wand, R. and Beestermöller, C. (2010): Bewertung der dena-Netzstudie II und des europäischen Infrastrukturprogramms. Gutachten im Auftrag des WWF Deutschland. Berlin: TU-Berlin WIP.

von Koerber, K., Kretschmer, J. and Prinz, S. (2008): Globale Ernährungsgewohnheiten und -trends. Expertise for the WBGU Report 'World in Transition: A Social Contract for Sustainability'. Website: http://www.wbgu.de/wbgu_jg2008_ex10.pdf (PDF). Berlin: WBGU.

Wagner, H.-J., Koch, M. K., Burkhardt, J., Größe Böckmann, T., Feck, N. and Kruse, P. (2007): CO_2 Emissionen der Stromerzeugung. Brennstoff, Wärme, Kraft 59 (10), 44–52.

Walk, H. (2007): Partizipative Governance. Beiteiligungsformen und Beteiligungsrechte im Mehrebenensystem der Klimapolitik. Wiesbaden: VS.

Walk, H. (2008): Partizipative Governance. Beteiligungsformen und Beteiligungsrechte im Mehrebenensystem der Klimapolitik. Wiesbaden: Verlag für Sozialwissenschaften.

Walsh, J. E. and Chapman, W. L. (2001): Twentieth-century sea ice variations from observational data. Annals of Glaciology 33, 444–448.

Wang, Y. (2009): Chinese diplomacy since 1949. Beijing Review 52 (45), 10–13.

Wara, M. and Victor, D. G. (2008): A Realistic Policy on International Carbon Offsets. Stanford Law School Working Paper 74. Website: http://www.law.stanford.edu/publications/details/4032/ (viewed 16. February 2011). Stanford: Stanford Law School.

Watson, J. (2009): Technology assessment and innovation policy. In: Scrase, I. and MacKerron, G. (eds): Energy for the Future. A New Agenda. Basingstoke: Palgrave, 123–147.

WBCSD – World Business Council for Sustainable Development (2004): Mobility 2030: The Sustainable Mobility Project. Geneva, Washington, DC: WBCSD.

WBGU – German Advisory Council on Global Change (1995a): World in Transition: The Threat to Soils. Flagship Report 1994. Bonn: Economica.

WBGU – German Advisory Council on Global Change (1995b): Scenario for the Derivation of Global CO_2-Reduction Targets and Implementation Strategies. Special Report 1995. Berlin: WBGU.

WBGU – German Advisory Council on Global Change (1999): WaysTowards Sustainable Management of Freshwater Resources. Flagship Report 1997. Berlin, Heidelberg: Springer.

WBGU – German Advisory Council on Global Change (2001a): Conservation and Sustainable Use of the Biosphere. Flagship Report 1999. Berlin, Heidelberg, New York: Springer.

WBGU – German Advisory Council on Global Change (2001b): New Structures for Global Environmental Policy. Flagship Report 2000. Berlin, Heidelberg: Springer.

WBGU – German Advisory Council on Global Change (2004): Towards Sustainable Energy Systems. Flagship Report 2003. Berlin, Heidelberg, New York: Springer.

WBGU – German Advisory Council on Global Change (2005): Fighting Poverty through Environmental Policy. Flagship Report 2004. Berlin, Heidelberg, New York: Springer.

WBGU – German Advisory Council on Global Change (2006): The Future Oceans – Warming Up, Rising High, Turning Sour. Special Report 2006. Berlin: WBGU.

WBGU – German Advisory Council on Global Change (2007a): New Impetus for Climate Policy: Making the Most of Germany's Dual Presidency. Policy Paper 5. Berlin: WBGU.

WBGU – German Advisory Council on Global Change (2007b): Bali Climate Conference Closes: Last-minute Breakthrough for Global Climate Protection. WBGU Press Release of 17.12.2007. Berlin: WBGU.

WBGU – German Advisory Council on Global Change (2008): Climate Change as a Security Risk. Flagship Report 2007. Berlin, Heidelberg: Springer.

WBGU – German Advisory Council on Global Change (2009): Solving the Climate Dilemma: The Budget Approach. Special Report 2009. Berlin: WBGU.

WBGU – German Advisory Council on Global Change (2010a): Future Bioenergy and Sustainable Land Use. Flagship Report 2008. Berlin, Heidelberg, New York: Springer

WBGU – German Advisory Council on Global Change (2010b): Climate Policy Post-Copenhagen: Action at Three Levels offers Prospect of Success. Policy Paper 6. Berlin: WBGU.

Weber, M. (1984): Soziologische Grundbegriffe. Tübingen: Mohr.

Weber, M. (1992): Politik als Beruf (Vortragsmitschrift mit Nachwort von Ralf Dahrendorf). Frankfurt/M.: Reclam.

WEC – World Energy Council (2004): Comparison of Energy Systems Using Life Cycle Assessment. London: WEC.

Welzel, C. (2006): A Human Development View on Value Change Trends (1981–2006). Website: http://www.worldvaluessurvey.org (viewed 17. November 2009). Stockholm: World Values Survey.

Weiler, J. H. H. (1991): The transformation of Europe. The Yale Law Journal 100, 2403–2483.

Weingart, P. (2001): Die Stunde der Wahrheit? Zum Verhältnis der Wissenschaft zu Politik, Wirtschaft und Medien in der Wissensgesellschaft. Weilerswist: Velbrück.

Weinlich, S. (2011): Reform of the UN Development System: New Multilateralist Reform Coalition Needed. DIE-Briefing Paper Bonn: German Development Institute.

Weisdorf, J. L. (2005): From foraging to farming: explaining the Neolithic Revolution. Oxford Economic Papers 58 (2), 264–287.

Weiss, T. G. (2009): What happened to the idea of world government? International Studies Quarterly 53 (2), 253–271.

Weiss, T. G. and Daws, S. (2007): World politics: continuity and change since 1945. In: Weiss, T. G. and Daws, S. (eds): The Oxford Handbook on the United Nations. New York: Oxford University Press, 3–38.

Weitzman, M. L. (1974): Prices versus quantities. Review of Economic Studies 41 (4), 477–491.

Welzel, C. (2006): A Human Development View on Value Change Trends (1981–2006). Website: http://www.worldvaluessurvey.org (viewed 17. November 2009). Stockholm: World Values Survey.

Wende, P. (2001): Großbritannien 1500–2000. Oldenbourg Grundriss der Geschichte. Volume 32. Munich: Oldenbourg Wissenschaftsverlag.

Wende, P. (2008): Das Britische Empire: Geschichte eines Weltreichs. Munich: Beck.

Westle, B. (2006): Wahlrecht von Geburt an – Rettung der Demokratie oder Irrweg? Zeitschrift für Parlamentsfragen 37, 96–114.

White, T. (2000): Diet and the distribution of environmental impact. Ecological Economics 34 (1), 145–153.

WI – Wuppertal Institute for Climate, Environment and Energy (2006): Microfinance and Renewable Energy. Investing in a Sustainable Future, I. Issue 2006, WISONS of sustainablity, PREP 5. Wuppertal: WI.

Wiegmann, K., Eberle, U., Fritsche, U. R. and Hünecke, K. (2005): Ernährungswende. Umweltauswirkungen von Ernährung. Stoffstromanalysen und Szenarien. Darmstadt, Hamburg: Öko-Institut.

Wiesenthal, H. (1995): Konventionelles und unkonventionelles Organisationslernen. Zeitschrift für Soziologie 2, 137–155.

Willke, H. (1998): Systemisches Wissensmanagement. Stuttgart: UTB. Wilkinson, R. and Willett, K. (2009): The Spirit Level: Why More Equal Societies Almost Always Do Better. London: Penguin.

Willer, H., Yussefi-Menzler, M. and Sorensen, N. (2008): The World of Organic Agriculture – Statistics and Emerging Trends 2008. Website: http://orgprints.org/13123/4/world-of-organic-agriculture-2008.pdf (viewed 13. December 2010). Bonn: IFOAM, FiBL.

Willis, R., Webb, M. and Wilsdon, J. (2007): The Disrupters. Lessons for Low-carbon Innovation from the New Wave of Environmental Pioneers. London: NESTA.

Windolf, P. (2005): Finanzmarkt-Kapitalismus: Analyse zum Wandel von Produktionsregimen. Wiesbaden: VS.

Winkler, H. A. (2009): Geschichte des Westens. Von den Anfängen in der Antike bis zum 20. Jahrhundert. Munich: Beck.

Winter, G. (2010): Zur Architektur globaler Governance des Klimaschutzes. Part 2 of the Expertise for the WBGU Report 'World in Transition: A Social Contract for Sustainability'. Website: http://www.wbgu.de/wbgu_jg2011_Expertise_Winter.pdf. Berlin: WBGU.

Winters, A. and Shahid, Y. (2007): China and India: Competing With Giants. Washington, DC: World Bank.

Wippermann, C. (2009): Die soziokulturelle Karriere des Themas 'Ökologie': Eine kurze Historie vor dem Hintergrund der Sinus-Lebensweltforschung. Website: http://www.sociovision.de/uploads/tx_mpdownloadcenter/karriere_oekologie.pdf (viewed 17. November 2010). Heidelberg: Sinus-Institut.

Wippermann, C., Kleinhückelkotten, S., Flaig, B. B. and Calmbach, M. (2009): Umweltbewusstsein und Umweltverhalten der sozialen Milieus in Deutschland. Dessau: Federal Environment Agency.

Wittmann, V. (2006): Digital Divide – auf dem Weg zu einer Weltinformationsgesellschaft? In: Debiel, T., Messner, D. and Nuscheler, F. (eds): Globale Trends 2007. Frankfurt/M.: Fischer, 209–224.

Wolff, P. (2005): Entwicklungspolitik und Armutsbekämpfung. In: Messner, D. and Scholz, I. (eds): Zukunftsfragen der Entwicklungspolitik. Baden-Baden: Nomos, 54–69.

Woodcock, J., Edwards, P., Tonne, C., Armstrong, B. G., Ashiru, O., Banister, D., Beevers, S., Chalabi, Z., Chowdhury, Z., Cohen, A., Franco, O. H., Haines, A., Hickman, R., Lindsay, G., Mittal, I., Mohan, D., Tiwari, G., Woodward, A. and Roberts, I. (2009): Public health benefits of strategies to reduce greenhouse-gas emissions: urban land transport. The Lancet 374 (9705), 1930–1943.

Woods, M. (2003): Conflicting environmental visions of the rural: windfarm development in Mid Wales. Sociologia Ruralis 43 (3), 271–288.

World Bank (2009a): Swimming Against the Tide: How Developing Countries are Coping with the Global Crisis. Background Paper Prepared by World Bank Staff for the G20 Finance Ministers and Central Bank Governors Meeting, Horsham United Kindom on March 13–14, 2009. Washington, DC: World Bank.

World Bank (2009b): World Development Report 2009: Spatial Disparities and Development Policy. Washington, DC: World Bank.

World Bank (2010a): Global Monitoring Report 2010. The MDGs after the Crisis. Washington, DC: World Bank.

World Bank (2010b): World Development Report 2010: Development and Climate Change. Washington, DC: World Bank.

World Bank (2010c): Making the Most of Public Finance for Climate Action. Issues Brief #2. Washington, DC: World Bank.

World Bank (2011a): Data by Country. Website: http://data.worldbank.org/country (viewed 5. March 2011). Washington, DC: World Bank.

World Bank (2011b): World Development Indicators 2011. Washington, DC: World Bank.

Worldwatch Institute (2004): State of the World 2004: Special Focus – The Consumer Society. Washington, DC: Worldwatch Institute.

WR – German Council of Science and Humanities (2009): Bewertungsmatrix für das Forschungsrating in der Elektro- und Informationstechnik. Cologne: WR.

WR – German Council of Science and Humanities (2010a): Empfehlungen zur Differenzierung der Hochschulen. Drs. 10387-10. Cologne: WR.

WR – German Council of Science and Humanities (2010b): Empfehlungen zur vergleichenden Forschungsbewertung in den Geisteswissenschaften. Cologne: WR.

WRAP – Waste & Resources Action Programme (2009): Household Food and Drink Waste in the UK. Final Report. Banbury, UK: WRAP.

WRI – World Resources Institute (2008): The Greenhouse Gas Protocol. A Corporate Accounting and Reporting Standard. Revised Edition. Washington, DC: WRI.

WRI-CAIT – World Resources Institute - Climate Analysis Indicator Tool (2011): The CAIT Climate Analysis Indicator Tool. Washington, DC: WRI.

Wright, A. (1984): Innocence abroad: American agricultural research in Mexico. In: Colman, B., Jackson, W. and Wendell, B. (eds): Meeting the Expectations of the Land: Essays in Sustainable Agriculture and Stewardship. San Francisco: North Point Press, 124–138.

WTO – World Trade Organization and UNEP – United Nations Environment Programme (2009): Trade and Climate Change. Geneva: WTO and UNEP.

Wunder, S. (2005): Payments for Environmental Services: Some Nuts and Bolts. CIFOR Occasional Paper 42. Bogor Barat: Center for International Forestry Research.

Wüstenhagen, R., Wolsink, M. and Bürer, M. J. (2007): Social acceptance of renewable energy innovation: An introduction to the concept. Energy Policy 25 (5), 2683–2691.

WVS – World Values Survey (2009): World Values Survey 2005 Official Data File v. 20090901. Stockholm: World Values Survey Association

WVS – World Values Survey (2010): Values Change the World. World Values Survey. Stockholm: World Values Survey Association.

Yang, G. (2009): The Power of the Internet in China. Citizen Activism Online. New York: Columbia University Press.

Young, N. and Matthews, R. (2007): Experts' understanding of the public: knowledge control in a risk controversy. Public Understanding of Science 16 (2), 123–144.

Zahran, S., Kim, E., Chen Xi and Lubell, M. (2007): Ecological development and global climate change: a cross-national study of Kyoto Protocol ratification. Society & Natural Resources 20 (1), 37–55.

Zakaria, F. (2008): The Post-American World. New York: W.W. Norton.

Zangl, B. and Zürn, M. (2004): Make Law, Not War: Internationale und Transnationale Verrechtlichung als Bausteine für Global Governance. In: Zangl, B. and Zürn, M. (eds): Verrechtlichung: Bausteine für Global Governance? Bonn: Dietz, 12–45.

Zelli, F., Biermann, F., Pattberg, P. and von Asselt, H. (2010): The consequences of fragmented climate governance architecture: a policy appraisal. In: Biermann, F., Pattberg, P. and Zelli, F. (eds): Global Climate Governance Beyond 2010. Cambridge, UK: Cambridge University Press, 25–34.

Zhao, M. and Running, S. W. (2010): Drought-induced reduction in global terrestrial net primary production from 2000 through 2009. Science 329, 940–943.

Zia, A. and Todd, A. M. (2010): Evaluating the effects of ideology on public understanding of climate change science: How to improve communication across ideological divides? Public Understanding of Science 19 (6), 743–761.

Ziehm, C. (2010): Vollzugsdefizite im Bereich des Klimaschutzrechts. ZUR 2010, 411–418.

Ziesing, H.-J. (2009): Modell Deutschland – Klimaschutz bis 2050 – Vom Ziel her denken. Frankfurt/M.: WWF Deutschland.

Zschiesche, M. and Rosenbaum, M. (2005): Empirische Analysen zur Öffentlichkeitsbeteiligung in den neuen Ländern am Beispiel immissionsschutzrechtlicher Genehmigungsverfahren im Zeitraum 1991–2001. Berlin: Independent Institute for Environmental Issues.

Zürn, M., Ecker-Ehrhardt, M. and Binder, M. (2007): Politische Ordnungsbildung wider Willen. Zeitschrift für Internationale Beziehungen 14, 129–165.

Glossary

10

Aarhus Convention
The Aarhus Convention is the first international law treaty to regulate citizen access to information, public participation in decision-making and access to justice in environmental matters. The treaty was signed in 1998 in the Danish city of Aarhus under the aegis of the UN Economic Commission for Europe (UNECE), and came into force in 2001. To date, 40 European and Central Asian countries have ratified the Convention. It comprises three pillars: rights of access to information on environmental matters, public participation rights in environment-related procedures, and access to justice in environmental matters. This more prominent role of the public in the enforcement of environmental protection represents a new level in environmental law development.

Anthropocene
The term Anthropocene is used to refer to the Age of Humankind and was inspired by names of geological epochs (such as the Palaeocene or the Holocene). This neologism was first used by Nobel Laureate Paul Crutzen and Eugene Stoermer in 2000 to define the geological epoch in which the environmental impacts of anthropogenic activities have reached a global dimension. This has led to a range of ecosystem changes, some of which have been considerable, even resulting in complete destruction. Two of the most serious consequences of anthropogenic activities are climate change and the Antarctic ozone hole.

Carbon leakage
Carbon leakage refers to the (geographical) shifting of CO_2 emissions as a consequence of national or regional climate policy, undermining their effectiveness. Carbon leakage can be caused by (1) relocation of companies from one country (or region) with a climate policy to a country without a climate policy due to competitive pressure and operating efficiency considerations, (2) substitution of products from countries with climate policy by products from countries without climate policy due to price advantages or (3) increasing demand for high-carbon energy carriers or products in countries without climate policy due to lower global market prices for high-carbon energy carriers as a consequence of the decrease in demand in countries with climate policy.

Carbon Dioxide Capture and Storage (CCS)
CCS is the process of separating the CO_2 from combustion processes for energy generation or from industrial processes and transporting it to a storage facility for sequestration. Its objective is the long-term isolation of CO_2 from the atmosphere.

Carbon dioxide equivalents (CO_2eq)
Carbon dioxide equivalents are a measure of the degree to which a mixture of gases contributes to global warming. With the aid of a conversion factor, the Global Warming Potential, the climate impact of non-CO_2 greenhouse gases is expressed as the quantity of CO_2 that would cause the equivalent warming effect. This makes it possible to include all greenhouse gases in a unit and allows a comparison of their individual impact.

Change agents
Change agents is a term used in diffusion, innovation and transition research to describe actors who play a central role in the initiation and shaping of change processes. Initially, these are usually single individuals and small groups fulfilling various tasks or functions in transformation processes, including the identification of alternatives, development, communication and mediation, synthesis, investing, optimisation, diffusion, etc.

CO_2eq
→ Carbon dioxide equivalents

CO_2 pricing
CO_2 pricing refers to the internalisation of the social costs of CO_2 emissions by means of a price mechanism. CO_2 pricing can be introduced through a CO_2 tax or by restricting CO_2 emissions and introducing a tradable

permits scheme. In the latter case, the CO_2 price for the emission of one unit of CO_2 is determined on the market by supply and demand of emission permits. In theory, the CO_2 tax or the amount of CO_2 permits issued should be set at a level where the price for emitting one unit of CO_2 reflects the social cost of emissions, i.e. the future damage caused by one unit of CO_2 emitted in the present is discounted.

Combined Heat and Power (CHP)
CHP plants not only generate electricity from the fuel consumed, but also make use of the waste heat. This heat can be used in heating systems, for example district heating. In industry, it can be used for heat-dependent production processes. CHP is also used in the form of small-scale combined heat and power units.

Decarbonisation
The decarbonisation of energy systems describes the historically observable trend of the shift from high-carbon energy sources (biomass, coal) to less carbon-intensive fuels (oil and gas), and increasingly, zero-carbon energy carriers (solar, wind, hydropower). Modern energy carriers often also provide a higher energy density, they have a much broader range of applications (for example electricity) and are safer, cleaner, and more convenient for the final consumer.

Deliberative participation procedures
A deliberative participation procedure is a procedure for a discourse-oriented process to reach a democratic consensus and make decisions. Carrying out so-called 'Deliberative Opinion Polls', political scientist James S. Fishkin invited a representative group of citizens to jointly discuss a current political topic and develop decision-making recommendations. His intention was to determine the citizens' political preferences subsequent to having been given the chance to thoroughly acquaint themselves with the issue to be decided on and discuss it in detail. In practical terms, deliberative decision processes should be designed in such a way that they really do provide benefits in terms of information and reflexion.

Economic growth
An increase of an economy's performance, measured on the basis of actual gross domestic product, i.e. the added value of all goods and services produced within a certain period of time in comparison to a reference period, valued in market prices. Real economic growth can for instance be the result of better utilisation of existing production capacities, expansion of production capacities, or improvements in the quality of products produced.

Ecosystem services
Ecosystem services are benefits people gain from ecosystems. These include supply services such as food or water, regulatory services such as protection against flooding or against the spread of disease, cultural or recreational services, and support services such as nutrient cycles that maintain Earth's life-support systems.

Emissions trading
Emissions trading is a market-based instrument for limiting or reducing environmentally harmful emissions. The emissions volume is restricted and divided into tradable permits. Emissions allowances can be traded among participants in a trading scheme, ideally resulting in a cost-efficient allocation of the set overall reduction. The Kyoto Protocol to the UN Framework Convention on Climate Change introduced this instrument at state level for those countries which have undertaken commitments. Beyond this, some states or groups of states (such as the EU) have introduced emissions trading schemes in which companies can trade their emissions allowances among themselves.

Energy efficiency
Energy efficiency refers to the technical efficiency of end-user devices (for instance household appliances) or facilities (for example power plants), most often quantified through their efficiency during energy conversion.

Energy intensity
Energy intensity is the ratio of energy input to gross domestic product.

Energy poverty
Energy poverty refers to a lack of choices to meet basic energy needs, and insufficient access to energy services that are affordable, reliable, high-quality and safe, and cause no undue health or environmental impacts. Countries where energy poverty is widespread are generally characterised by low human development. Energy poverty affects around 38% of the world's population. They primarily depend on traditional biomass use. Pollutants from traditional hearths cause more than 1.5 million deaths each year.

Feed-in tariff
Feed-in tariffs are payments received for electricity fed into the public power grid, for instance from the use of renewable energy sources. The feed-in tariff has a considerable impact on the economic viability of electricity generating plants, and is usually structured degressively over a set period of time.

Final energy

Final energy is the energy that is available to the final user in a usable form subsequent to the conversion of primary energy into secondary energy and transport to the consumer (for example coal briquettes, electric power from sockets, petrol at the petrol station). Final energy is the third stage of the energy flow chain from primary through secondary to useful energy.

G8/G8+5

An informal forum of heads of state and government which took place in the form of a meeting of the G6 (Germany, France, United Kingdom, Italy, Japan and the USA) for the first time in 1975. Canada joined in 1976, and Russia in 1998, making up the G8. At G8 summits, the European Commission is also represented. Initially a purely economic summit of the world's leading economies, the G7/G8 has since evolved into one of the most important forums of global policy-making. Since 2005, in reaction to allegations of lacking global legitimacy, the five leading → newly industrialising countries Brazil, China, India, Mexico and South Africa have been invited to join in the dialogue as so-called 'outreach countries' to extend it (G8+5). With the establishment of the → G20 at heads of state and government level, the G8's dialogue invitation became obsolete.

G20

A global forum which formed in 1999 in response to economic globalisation and the Asian crisis to discuss global economic and financial governance issues. In the context of the 2008/2009 global financial crisis, the G20 gained significant political weight in other policy areas. Through the inclusion of heads of state and government it became established as an alternative forum to the →G8/G8+5. The G20 members are Argentina, Australia, Brazil, China, Germany, France, United Kingdom, India, Indonesia, Italy, Japan, Canada, Mexico, Russia, Saudi Arabia, South Africa, South Korea, Turkey, the USA and the European Union.

Global governance

There is no universally agreed definition of the concept of global governance; it is sometimes used normatively, and sometimes analytically. It generally denotes a deepening of international cooperation and the creation and reinforcement of multilateral regimes in order to master global challenges. In particular, global governance describes the cooperation between states and non-government actors from the global to the local level. The term 'global governance architecture' refers to the corresponding multilateral international structure.

Governance

Governance generally describes a political entity's governing and regulation systems. The concept evolved as a distinction from the term government, and is intended to convey the fact that political control is enacted not only hierarchically by the state, but also by private actors such as interest-based organisations. 'Governance capacities' refers to the ability to govern through functioning institutions and regulatory systems.

Great Transformation

The concept of a 'Great Transformation' was described by the Hungarian economist Karl Polanyi in his 1944 analysis of the Industrial Revolution, also entitled 'The Great Transformation'. It examines the comprehensive systemic change national economies undergo in interactive response to global economic structures. To reflect Polanyi's understanding of transformation, the WBGU defines a comprehensive transition to take the → planetary guard rails into account as a Great Transformation requiring the modification of both the national and the global economy within these guard rails in order to avoid irreversible damages to the Earth system and its ecosystems, and the impact of these damages on humankind.

Green Growth

Green Growth is compatible with the conservation of natural resources by increasingly redirecting the production factors of an economy (land, labour, capital) towards environmental-friendly production. The goal of Green Growth is a decoupling of economic growth from emissions and resource consumption in absolute terms, primarily through the promotion of technological innovations. It is hoped that increasing resource efficiency and closing material cycles will minimise resource extraction in the long term. Green Growth will have been achieved when positive economic growth does not cause further environmental burdens and resource extraction, or these even show a reverse trend.

Guard rails, planetary

Planetary guard rails are a concept introduced by the WBGU to describe quantitatively defined damage limits whose transgression would have intolerable or even catastrophic consequences. One example is the climate protection guard rail, which means that an increase in the global mean temperature by more than 2 °C above the pre-industrial level should be prevented. Sustainable development pathways do not transgress these guard rails. The approach is based on the realisation that it is hardly possible to define a desirable, sustainable future in terms of a state to be achieved. It is, however, possible to agree boundaries for a range that is recognised as unacceptable, and which society agrees to avoid. Compliance with the guard rails is a necessary, but not sufficient, criterion for sustainability.

International Renewable Energy Agency (IRENA)
The IRENA was founded in Bonn, Germany, in 2009 by 75 states as an international governmental organisation with the aim of promoting the use of renewable energies worldwide. Its foundation statute came into force in 2010 and was ratified by 148 countries and the EU. The organisation is based in Abu Dhabi in the United Arab Emirates.

Load management
Balancing of electricity demand and supply by means of demand management. Consumers whose demand is not tied to certain times can be steered towards demanding energy primarily at peak generation times. Generation and load management (for example with → smartgrids) helps to balance out fluctuations in the supply of electricity. Industrial production, trade and private households are all expected to have a sizeable potential for load management.

Learning curve
A learning curve describes changes in the ratio between expenditure/costs and earnings occurring in line with the multiple repetition of a production process, or the increasing output volume of a product. Reasons for an improved expenditure to earnings ratio are gains due to routinisation, technical progress, more cost-effective use of production factors and economies of scale, i.e. cost savings resulting from the production of a greater number of units.

Lock-in effect
The term lock-in effect describes being locked in a certain situation due to having decided on a certain technology. High investment costs (sunk costs) or other structural limitations prevent a change for reasons of economic viability or unmanageable organisation. Certain technologies can for example have a lock-in effect (→ path dependency) when a later change to alternative technologies entails substantial costs, or entire production chains and social structures would have to be adapted.

Multilaterism
Institutionalised cooperation between states in international organisations (such as the UN) or other regulatory mechanisms (for example conventions). Unilateralism, on the other hand, describes a one-sided policy approach guided by the national interests of a state. Unilateralism pursues multilateral solutions to problems only if they appear necessary in order to protect own interests.

Multipolar world order
Term referring to a world order shaped by the competition between several major powers in the international system. Its opposite is unipolarity, in which one single powerful actor (hegemon) determines global politics. The international system conflict between East and West during the Cold War represented a bipolar world order dominated by the USA and the Soviet Union.

Newly industrialising countries
Countries undergoing a successful fast-track process of industrialisation or economic development, i.e. they are in the process of becoming industrialised countries within a short time span. Social development indicators, such as the literacy rate, infant mortality or life expectancy may sometimes lag far behind a country's economic indicators. The acronym BRIC(S) countries (initially Brazil, Russia, India, China, since 2010 also South Africa) was first used by the Goldman Sachs Group in 2001 in the context of anticipatable global power shifts in respect of the global economy's future growth poles. In an international climate policy context, the acronym BASIC (Brazil, South Africa, India, China) is often used to refer to these countries.

Nudges
Nudges is a term first used in the context of 'libertarian paternalism' by Richard Thaler and Cass Sunstein. Nudges refer to the intentional influencing of decision-making situations to guide an individual's decisions into a certain direction (they will benefit from), for instance by providing the option to opt-out. This is based on the insight that individuals are not always in a position to make rational decisions under consideration of all the relevant information, as this is accompanied by high transaction costs and cognitive effort.

Path dependency
Path dependency describes a situation in which an ongoing development is determined by historical evolution or past decisions, thereby following a path with structures that become increasingly rigid as time goes by (→ lock-in effect). One technology becoming predominant on the market, for example, cannot necessarily be subscribed to the fact that it is the best, but can be the result of historical coincidences and of reinforcing feedback processes. Compared to the initial investments required for a new technology, the costs of the 'traditional' technology are low, as learning effects can be drawn on in its application and compatible tech-

niques and standards can be resorted to.

Primary energy

→ Box 4.1-2

Proactive state

The proactive state is a central element in a → social contract for the transformation towards a low-carbon society outlined by the WBGU. It conveys two aspects frequently thought of as separate or contradicting: on the one hand empowerment of a state which actively determines priorities in the political multilevel system and underlines these with clear signals (for example bonus/malus solutions) and, on the other hand, the provision of more extensive participation opportunities to citizens to make their voices heard, get more involved, and join in decision-making processes.

Rio+20 Conference

→ United Nations Conference on Sustainable Development 2012

Smartgrids

Intelligent networks make it possible to connect electric power generators, storage facilities and users with each other and manage the network by means of information technology. This facilitates optimisation of the individual network elements.

Social contract

A social contract is a hypothetical construct which substantiates governance systems in so-called contract theories. According to exponents of classical contract theory – including Thomas Hobbes, John Locke or Jean-Jacques Rousseau – individuals voluntarily come together in a political community and undertake to obey its rules and fulfil their duties to protect themselves against violence and other evils. The key concept of the new social contract developed by the WBGU is that individuals and civil societies, states and the international community, as well as economy and science, take on the collective responsibility for preventing dangerous climate change and the conservation of humankind's natural life-support systems. A central element of a social contract such as this is a → proactive state.

Supranationality

Characterises a specific type of union of countries that differs greatly from the usual cooperation between sovereign states; it can therefore be described as being 'above the nation state', or supranational. Supranationality is distinguished by the unusual fact that an intergovernmental institution is granted the authority to pass legal acts which impact directly on member countries' intrastate matters. It is possible only because the member states have ceded sovereign rights to the intergovernmental institution, thereby diminishing their own rights. The EU is one example of such a supranational organisation.

Supergrid

Energy infrastructure for transporting electricity over long distances (frequently transcontinental grids). This is made possible with moderate energy loss by High Voltage Direct Current (HVDC) transmission.

Sustainable development

In 1987, sustainable development was defined by the Brundtland Commission as development that 'meets the needs of the present without compromising the ability of future generations to meet their own needs'. Today, there are many different definitions of sustainability. Common to all is the requirement that economic, social and environmentally-friendly development must go hand in hand.

Transformation (transition)

These terms refer to the form and progression of a transition or a change; however, they are viewed and defined differently in different scientific disciplines (including genetics, mathematics, linguistics, technology). In this report, the WBGU uses these terms primarily in the sense they are used in socio-scientific transition research focusing on the analysis of political system changes. As transition research is a branch of comparative politics studies, it usually refers to the transition from authoritarian regimes to democracies. The term transition is here often used synonymously with the term transformation, amongst others. The far-reaching processes of social, economic, cultural and political change are always the research subject (see → Great Transformation).

UNCSD 2012

→ United Nations Conference on Sustainable Development 2012

United Nations Conference on Sustainable Development 2012 (UNCSD 2012)

The UNCSD 2012 (also referred to as the Rio+20 Conference) will be held in 2012, twenty years after the United Nations Conference and Development (UNCED, also known as the 1992 Earth Summit). 'Green Economy in the Context of Sustainable Development and Poverty Eradication' and 'Institutional Framework for Sustainable Development' are the two key issues defined for the UNCSD 2012, again held in Rio de Janeiro, also the venue for the UNCED 1992.

WBGU budget approach
The WBGU budget approach is a concept for a global burden sharing with regard to climate protection. The key element of the approach is an agreement among the international community of an upper limit or cap for the total amount of carbon dioxide that may be emitted from fossil sources by 2050 (global budget) in order to avoid dangerous climate change. The global budget is divided among all countries in proportion to their population. Through an international → emissions trading scheme, countries which are likely to exceed their budgets due to high per-capita emissions can buy additional emissions allowances whilst countries with low per-capita emissions can generate income through the sale of emissions allowances.